The WorldatWork Handbook of Compensation, Benefits & Total Rewards

A Comprehensive Guide for HR Professionals

WorldatWork®

John Wiley & Sons, Inc.

This book is printed on acid-free paper. ♾

Copyright © 2007 by WorldatWork. All rights reserved.

Published by John Wiley & Sons, Inc., Hoboken, New Jersey.
Published simultaneously in Canada.

Wiley Bicentennial Logo: Richard J. Pacifico

The WorldatWork group of registered marks includes: WorldatWork®, workspan®, Certified Compensation Professional or CCP®, Certified Benefits Professional® or CBP, Global Remuneration Professional or GRP®, Work-Life Certified Professional or WLCP®, WorldatWork Society of Certified Professionals®, and Alliance for Work-Life Progress or AWLP®.

For general information on our other products and services please contact our Customer Care Department within the United States at (800) 762–2974, outside the United States at (317) 572-3993 or fax (317) 572-4002.

Wiley also publishes its books in a variety of electronic formats. Some content that appears in print may not be available in electronic books. For more information about Wiley products, visit our web site at www.wiley.com.

Library of Congress Cataloging-in-Publication Data:

The WorldatWork handbook of compensation, benefits & total rewards: a
comprehensive guide for HR professionals/WorldatWork.
   p. cm.
ISBN 978-0-470-08580-6 (cloth : alk. paper)
1. Compensation management—Handbook, manuals, etc. I. WorldatWork
(Organization)
HF5549.5.C67W65 2007
658.3'2—dc22

                                                    2007002715

Printed in the United States of America.

10   9   8   7   6

Contents

Introduction: Redefining Employee Rewards

Anne C. Ruddy, CCP, CPCU
President, WorldatWork

Not long ago, human resources professionals seemed to have that "pay thing" down to a science. Reward employees with decent dollars for compensation, add top-notch health care and retirement benefits, and voila! People came, people stayed, and people worked. Employers had their pick from a seemingly endless talent pool. And, with any luck, employees matched their career aspirations and enjoyed life-long service with a company.

So much for yesterday.

The birth of new industries and emerging markets have sprouted mergers and acquisitions, downsizings, globalization, corporate restructurings, and technological advances. All of this has occurred in a rapidly changing economy with a tight labor market. With every dollar at stake, nothing remains sacred as employers increasingly look for ways to work smarter, faster, and more efficiently.

At the same time, the sea of faces in the workforce has changed. Today's labor pool is more diverse and mobile, with a rapidly growing group of older workers and retirees. More women, working parents, dual-income households, single parents, Gen X-ers, and Gen Y-ers crowd the market. And baby boomers—tired of toiling long hours—are questioning their prior commitment levels.

Indeed, job-related attitudes, expectations, and priorities are changing on both sides of the desk. As employers retool, HR professionals must rethink their directions and realign their focus. The question becomes: *Does your current structure of HR investments help ensure the success of your organization's business strategy?*

If not, it's time to abandon the tried-and-true ways of thinking and redefine employee rewards against the new employee deal.

Strangely enough, the new employee deal isn't about just pay increases or offering employees more money. That's not to say that the almighty dollar has lost its power or punch, but the way money talks requires an updated translation. It requires focusing on more than pay. It requires focusing on total rewards.

The process of addressing total rewards begins by balancing the organization's business strategy, capabilities, and values with employees' needs, abilities, and values. It ends with assembling and marketing a compelling rewards package that will attract, motivate, and retain the people you need for organizational success. With the right rewards strategy and programs in place, the organization can reasonably expect two interrelated outcomes: improved business results and a positive shift in employee behavior and contributions.

THE EVOLUTION OF REWARDS

Step back in time to the early 1900s. The owner or operator usually bore the responsibility for people's pay, and little was offered outside of cash compensation. Only a handful of companies offered pensions, profit sharing, and guaranteed wages to skilled workers. There was minimal government regulation, and, consequently, few safety nets such as medical insurance, unemployment compensation, overtime pay, or Social Security.

Early in the twentieth century, benefits were practically nonexistent for the common worker. Benefits became popular as an acceptable way to evade wage and price controls during World War II because benefits were not counted as wages. Labor unions likewise increased their focus on benefits in the mid-1900s.

After World War II, the industrial boom introduced increased competition, but many industries were still unregulated. The majority of companies competed only domestically. Manufacturing was the order of the day. Few staff functions existed. Salary structures were just that—rigid and highly controlled—and benefits programs were based largely on formulas that served the entire employee population, which was far more homogeneous than it is today.

By the 1970s and 1980s, organizations recognized that strategically designed compensation and benefits programs could give them the edge in a rapidly changing environment. Suddenly, the relatively simple compensation and benefits programs of the past were requiring consideration of their strategic impact and relationship to one another. Integration became key, and compensation and benefits professionals emerged as critical strategic partners in their organizations' leadership—a position still occupied by leaders in the field today.

In the 1990s, the profession continued to mature. Increasingly, it became clear that the battle for talent involved much more than highly effective, strategically designed compensation and benefits programs. While these programs remain critical, the most successful companies have realized that they must take a much broader look at the factors involved in attraction, motivation, and retention.

As a result of rewards that traditionally were slotted into single-silo solutions of pay, benefits, training, or labor—and having companies manage these solutions separately—the programs tended to be disconnected from one another and from the broader business strategy. When questions arose, problems were dealt with piecemeal. In some cases, they even undercut one another or sent conflicting messages.

Increasingly, organizations have demanded interdisciplinary solutions to complicated problems. Bundling HR disciplines to address these complexities is what has emerged as *total rewards.*

Total rewards can be defined as all of the employer's available tools that may be used to attract, motivate, and retain employees. This encompasses every single investment that a company makes in its people and everything its employees value in the employment relationship. Why do employees choose to remain with a particular employer? Why do they leave? What factors motivate performance and commitment? These questions are answered with a total rewards perspective.

The objective of a well-designed total rewards program is to drive desired behaviors in the workforce, reinforce overall business strategy, and ensure organizational success. The solution is to find the proper mix of rewards that satisfies the personal and financial needs of a current and potential workforce given existing business conditions and cost constraints.

Total rewards integrates several classic HR disciplines and innovative business strategies. Designing a total rewards program can't be done with a cookie cutter. What's right for one organization may be wrong for another. But while the optimum mix differs from company to company—and even within the same company over time—the goal is the same: to produce desired, measurable results that send the right signals to employees and deliver an excellent return on your organization's investment.

WorldatWork hopes you find this book helpful in performing your job requirements but, more importantly, we hope you find this book instrumental in taking your job to the next level and developing your skills as a future human resources leader and total rewards professional.

About the Author

This book is the collaborative effort of a team of WorldatWork faculty, staff, and consulting experts. WorldatWork (www.worldatwork.org) is the association for human resources professionals focused on attracting, motivating, and retaining employees. Founded in 1955, WorldatWork provides practitioners with knowledge leadership to effectively implement total rewards—compensation, benefits, work-life, performance and recognition, development and career opportunities—by connecting employee engagement to business performance. WorldatWork supports its 30,000 members and customers in 30 countries with thought leadership, education, publications, research, and certification.

For more information, see www.worldatwork.org.

Total Rewards: *Everything* That Employees Value in the Employment Relationship

1

Fifty years ago, when a group of visionary professionals formed what was to become WorldatWork, the world of work and the world of pay were much simpler than they are today. Compensation was the primary "reward" and benefits, still in their infancy, were a separate and seemingly low-cost supplement for employees. The concept of combining these things—let alone using them with still other "rewards" to influence employee behavior on the job—was decades away.

Today we are only partially through an evolution from a largely industrialized business environment to a far more virtual, knowledge- and service-based environment, at least in North America and Europe. Among some major shifts:

- Business increasingly operates as a global village, with work moving to different parts of the world to take advantage of lower-cost labor and address skill gaps.
- Technology continues to revolutionize work, not only in terms of automating more jobs, but also in enabling the virtual workplace as more professionals conduct business in home offices or remote locations.
- Women are equally represented in the overall workforce, if not yet fully in the ranks of senior management.
- Traditional hierarchical distinctions have eroded in the name of faster decision making and speed to market. Teamwork is one of the most common behaviors rated in performance reviews.
- More businesses and business units in the United States are owned by European or Asian parents, which expect their practices and norms to be followed and respected in the workplace.
- Job mobility is taken for granted, with workers averaging six employers over the course of a career.
- Gender, race, and religious differences are a common part of most work environments. Diversity has become a respected value, demonstrated through a range of specific programs.

- Business leaders increasingly regard employees as drivers of productivity, rather than as relatively interchangeable cogs in a larger wheel.

Along with these changes have come dramatically different views about the nature of rewards. In the shift toward a more knowledge- and service-based economy, the relationship, or deal, between employer and employee began to evolve as well. Viewing employees as performance drivers meant thinking differently about what it would take to attract, keep, and engage them in giving discretionary effort on the job. And so *total rewards* entered the lexicon to address these needs.

BROADENING THE DEFINITION OF TOTAL REWARDS

The definition of total rewards always sparks debate. For example, Figure 1.1 includes a comprehensive list of items that have shown up at one time or another in one company's definition of total rewards. From this, it is easy to see how people can use the term in conversation only to find that they are referring to very different notions.

Generally speaking, there are two prevailing camps of definitions:

- *Narrow definitions.* These virtually always comprise compensation and benefits, and sometimes include other tangible elements (e.g., development). This sometimes is referred to as *total compensation* or *total remuneration.*
- *Broad definitions.* These can expand to encompass everything that is "rewarding" about working for a particular employer or everything employees get as a result of their employment. Sometimes terms such as *value proposition* or *total value* are used interchangeably with *total rewards.*

While the narrower definitions have been around for a long time, it is the broader notion that is generating buzz. (See Sidebar 1.1.) Indeed, much of the current activity in total rewards involves companies moving to a broader definition. There are several reasons for this:

- *Erosion of the "core" elements of the package.* The traditional elements of rewards—pay, benefits, and stock awards—are no longer differentiating factors for organizations. The competitive position for pay is trending toward median or mean. Benefits costs continue to rise. Stock programs, such as the distribution of options, do not offer the appeal they once did. Given all of this, a logical response is to broaden what companies provide for the overall employment package.
- *Pressure for operational efficiency and effectiveness.* Total rewards can represent a major cost element. As companies seek to manage costs tightly, there is more emphasis on ensuring that all costs are counted and managed. By redefining rewards more broadly and focusing on those elements that achieve the biggest payoff, organizations can drive toward efficiency.
- *Catering to diverse needs.* Companies today are managing a much more heterogeneous population. For the diverse workforce, no single component becomes a value driver. Employees have choices to make and a need for greater flexibility. A broad definition of total rewards helps employers show how their slate of rewards responds to the broad needs of today's global workforce.
- *Need to more strongly reinforce business strategy.* Companies are concerned about sending clear business messages to employees. A properly structured total

FIGURE 1.1 Total rewards: different things to different employers.

Direct Financial
Base Salary
Bonus
Cash Profit Sharing
Employee Referral
    Program (Cash)
Stock Programs
Suggestion Program
    (Cash for Ideas)

Indirect Financial
Adoption Assistance
College Savings Plan
College Tuition and
    Fees
Commuter Reimburse-
    ment (Pre-tax)
Company Cafeteria
Company Store
Dependent Care
Dependent Scholarships
Discount Tickets
Educational Assistance
Fitness Facilities Dis-
    counts
Health and Welfare
    Benefits
Incremental Dependent
    Care (Travel)
Insurance (Auto/Home)
    via Payroll Deduction
Long-Term Care Insur-
    ance
Matching Gifts
Relocation Program
Retirement Plan(s)
Saving Bonds via Payroll
    Deductions
Scholarships
Stock Purchase Program
Student Loans
Tuition Reimbursement

Work
Autonomy
Casual Dress Policy
Challenging Work
Constructive Feedback
Covered Parking
Ergonomics/Comfortable
    Workstations
Flexible Work Schedules
Free Parking
Interesting Work
Job Skills Training
Modern, Well-Maintained
    Workspace
Open Communication
Performance Manage-
    ment
Promotion
    Opportunities
Safe Work Environment
Suggestion Program
    (No Cash)
Telecommuting
    Opportunities
Uniforms/Uniform
    Allowance
Workshops

Career
360° Skills Assessment
Career Advancement
Coaching
Lunch and Learn Series
Management
    Development
Mentoring Program
Open Job Posting
Preretirement
    Counseling
Service Awards
Training and
    Development

Affiliation
Athletic Leagues
Community
Involvement
Diversity Programs
Employee Celebrations
Employee Clubs
Professional Associations
Seminars
Spring and Holiday
Parties
Support Groups
Volunteer Connection

Other/Convenience
ATMs Onsite
Carpooling/Van
    Pooling/Shuttles
Car Seat Vouchers
    (for Newborns)
Child Care Resources
Credit Union
Employee Assistance
    Program
Employee Card and Gift
    Shop
Expectant Parent Pro
    gram
Legal Services
Medical Center
Military Deployment
    Support
Online Services
Onsite Dry Cleaning
    Pickup
Onsite Flu Shots
Onsite Food Services
Onsite Post Office
Personal Travel Agency
Wellness Program
Worldwide Travel
    Assistance

rewards package sends a key message—by aligning all the components of total rewards with the overall business vision, a company ensures its workforce is on the same page.

Given these factors, it is not surprising that a broader definition is gaining favor in the marketplace. Companies still need to decide how broadly they want to define total rewards, based on what they can adequately measure and manage.

Sidebar 1.1: How We Define It

For the purposes of this book, the term *total rewards* refers to *everything* that employees value in the employment relationship (i.e., everything an employee gets as a result of working for the company).

WorldatWork defines total rewards as the monetary and nonmonetary return provided to employees in exchange for their time, talents, efforts, and results. It involves the deliberate integration of five key elements that effectively attract, motivate, and retain the talent required to achieve desired business results. The five key rewards elements are:

- Compensation.
- Benefits.
- Work-Life.
- Performance and Recognition.
- Development and Career Opportunities.

Total rewards strategy is the art of combining these five elements into tailored packages designed to achieve optimal motivation. (See Figure 1.2: Components of total rewards.)

For a total rewards strategy to be successful, employees must perceive monetary and nonmonetary rewards as valuable.

FIGURE 1.2 Components of total rewards.

EVOLUTION OF THE WORLDATWORK TOTAL REWARDS MODEL

In 2000, when the American Compensation Association changed its name to WorldatWork, the association affirmed its commitment to the concept of total rewards as a more comprehensive model reflecting the value employees receive from their employment.

In the same year, after facilitating discussion with leading thinkers in the field, WorldatWork introduced a total rewards framework intended to advance the concept and help practitioners think and execute in new ways. The model focused on three elements:

- Compensation (e.g., pay, incentives).
- Benefits (e.g., health care, retirement funding).
- The Work Experience.
  - Acknowledgment.
  - Balance (of work and life).
  - Culture.
  - Development (career/professional).
  - Environment (workplace).

Up to this point, the association had focused solely on compensation and benefits. Yet, specialists and generalists alike agreed that compensation and benefits—while foundational and representing the lion's share of human capital costs—cannot be fully effective unless they are part of an integrated strategy of other programs and practices to attract, motivate, and retain top talent.

Thus, "the work experience" aspect of the first WorldatWork total rewards model included aspects of employment that may be programmatic or just part of the overall experience of working. For instance, acknowledgment may be part of a formal rewards program or may be as simple as a "thank you" from the boss or a coworker. Workplace flexibility (part of work-life) may manifest itself as a formal telework program or as having a culture or practice that embraces work-life flexibility.

From 2000 to 2005, the bodies of knowledge associated with total rewards became more robust as practitioners experienced the power of integrated strategies. Organizational and departmental structure changes allowed for better integration, and professional understanding improved, as well. Advanced literature, research, and case studies accelerated visibility for total rewards beyond the Human Resources (HR) profession, garnering notice from line managers, and, indeed, the C-suite.

Given this advanced thinking and the increased importance of total rewards as a core business strategy, WorldatWork convened teams of leading professionals in the field to create an enhanced view of total rewards. The result: a comprehensive model that demonstrates the context, components, and contributions of total rewards as part of an integrated business strategy. (See Figure 1.3.)

There are five elements of total rewards, each of which includes programs, practices, elements, and dimensions that collectively define an organization's strategy to attract, motivate, and retain employees. These elements are:

- Compensation.
- Benefits.
- Work-Life.
- Performance and Recognition.
- Development and Career Opportunities.

FIGURE 1.3 WorldatWork total rewards model.

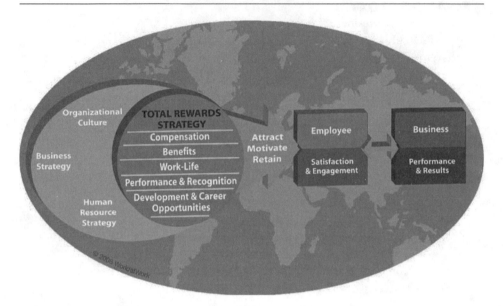

The elements represent the toolkit from which an organization chooses to offer and align a value proposition that creates value for both the organization and the employee. An effective total rewards strategy results in satisfied, engaged, and productive employees who, in turn, create desired business performance and results.

As defined here, the elements are neither mutually exclusive nor intended to represent the ways that companies organize or deploy programs and elements within them. For instance, performance management may be a compensation-function–driven activity, or decentralized in line organizations; it can be managed formally or informally. Likewise, recognition could be considered an element of compensation, benefits, and work-life.

The WorldatWork model recognizes that total rewards operates in the context of overall business strategy, organizational culture, and HR strategy. Indeed, a company's exceptional culture or external brand value may be considered a critical component of the total employment value proposition. The backdrop of the model is a globe, representing the external influences on business, such as legal/regulatory issues, cultural influences and practices, and competition.

Finally, an important dimension of the model is the "exchange relationship" between the employer and employee. Successful companies realize that productive employees create value for their organizations in return for tangible and intangible value that enriches their lives.

EXPLORING THE KEY AREAS

Following is a brief description of the five elements of the WorldatWork total rewards model. (See Figure 1.4 and Figure 1.5.)

FIGURE 1.4 Total rewards definitions.

Total Rewards Component	Definition
Compensation	Pay provided by an employer to an employee for services rendered (i.e., time, effort, and skill). Includes both fixed and variable pay tied to levels of performance.
Benefits	Programs an employer uses to supplement the cash compensation that employees receive. These health, income protection, savings, and retirement programs provide security for employees and their families.
Work-Life	A specific set of organizational practices, policies, and programs plus a philosophy that actively supports efforts to help employees achieve success at both work and home.
Performance and Recognition	*Performance:* The alignment of organizational, team, and individual efforts toward the achievement of business goals and organizational success. It includes establishing expectations, skill demonstration, assessment, feedback, and continuous improvement. *Recognition:* Acknowledges or gives special attention to employee actions, efforts, behavior, or performance. It meets an intrinsic psychological need for appreciation for one's efforts and can support business strategy by reinforcing certain behaviors (e.g., extraordinary accomplishments) that contribute to organizational success. Whether formal or informal, recognition programs acknowledge employee contributions immediately after the fact, usually without predetermined goals or performance levels that the employee is expected to achieve. Awards can be cash or noncash (e.g., verbal recognition, trophies, certificates, plaques, dinners, tickets, etc.).

(continued)

FIGURE 1.4 *(Continued)*

Development and Career Opportunities	*Development:* A set of learning experiences designed to enhance employees' applied skills and competencies. Development engages employees to perform better and engages leaders to advance their organizations' people strategies. *Career opportunities:* A plan for employees to advance their career goals. May include advancement into a more responsible position in an organization. The organization supports career opportunities internally so that talented employees are deployed in positions that enable them to deliver their greatest value to their organization.

FIGURE 1.5 Model definitions.

Total Rewards
Total rewards is the monetary and nonmonetary return provided to employees in exchange for their time, talents, efforts, and results. It involves the deliberate integration of five key elements that effectively attract, motivate, and retain the talent required to achieve desired business results. The five key rewards elements are:

- Compensation.
- Benefits.
- Work-Life.
- Performance and Recognition.
- Development and Career Opportunities.

Total rewards strategy is the art of combining these five elements into tailored packages designed to achieve optimal motivation. For a total rewards strategy to be successful, employees must perceive monetary and nonmonetary rewards as valuable.

Compensation
Pay provided by an employer to an employee for services rendered (i.e., time, effort, and skill). Compensation comprises four core elements:

- *Fixed pay:* Also known as "base pay," fixed pay is nondiscretionary compensation that does not vary according to performance or results achieved. It usually is determined by the organization's pay philosophy and structure.
- *Variable pay:* Also known as "pay at risk," variable pay changes directly with the level of performance or results achieved. It is a one-time payment that must be re-established and re-earned each performance period.

- **Short-term incentive pay:** A form of variable pay, short-term incentive pay is designed to focus and reward performance over a period of one year or less.
- **Long-term incentive pay:** A form of variable pay, long-term incentive pay is designed to focus and reward performance over a period longer than one year. Typical forms include stock options, restricted stock, performance shares, performance units, and cash.

Benefits

Programs an employer uses to supplement the cash compensation that employees receive. These programs are designed to protect the employee and his or her family from financial risks and can be categorized into the following three elements:

- **Social Insurance**
  - Unemployment.
  - Workers' compensation.
  - Social Security.
  - Disability (occupational).

- **Group Insurance**
  - Medical.
  - Dental.
  - Vision.
  - Prescription drug.
  - Mental health.
  - Life insurance.
  - AD&D insurance.
  - Disability.
  - Retirement.
  - Savings.

- **Pay for Time Not Worked:** These programs are designed to protect the employee's income flow when not actively engaged at work.
  - At work (breaks, clean-up time, uniform changing time).
  - Away from work (vacation, company holidays, personal days).

Work-Life

A specific set of organizational practices, policies, programs, plus a philosophy, which actively supports efforts to help employees achieve success at both work and home. There are seven major categories of organizational support for work-life effectiveness in the workplace. These categories encompass compensation, benefits, and other HR programs. In combination, they address the key intersections of the worker, his or her family, the community, and the workplace. The seven major categories are:

- Workplace flexibility.
- Paid and unpaid time off.
- Health and well-being.
- Caring for dependents.
- Financial support.
- Community involvement.
- Management involvement/culture change interventions.

(continued)

FIGURE 1.5 *(Continued)*

Performance and Recognition

Performance
A key component of organizational success, performance is assessed in order to understand what was accomplished, and how it was accomplished. Performance involves the alignment of organizational, team, and individual effort toward the achievement of business goals and organizational success.

- Performance planning is a process whereby expectations are established linking individual with team and organizational goals. Care is taken to ensure goals at all levels are aligned and there is a clear line of sight from performance expectations of individual employees all the way up to organizational objectives and strategies set at the highest levels of the organization.
- Performance is the manner of demonstrating a skill or capacity.
- Performance feedback communicates how well people do a job or task compared to expectations, performance standards, and goals. Performance feedback can motivate employees to improve performance.

Recognition
Acknowledges or gives special attention to employee actions, efforts, behavior, or performance. It meets an intrinsic psychological need for appreciation for one's efforts and can support business strategy by reinforcing certain behaviors (e.g., extraordinary accomplishments) that contribute to organizational success. Whether formal or informal, recognition programs acknowledge employee contributions immediately after the fact, usually without predetermined goals or performance levels that the employee is expected to achieve. Awards can be cash or noncash (e.g., verbal recognition, trophies, certificates, plaques, dinners, tickets, etc.).
The value of recognition plans is that they:

- Reinforce the value of performance improvement.
- Foster continued improvement, although it is not guaranteed.
- Formalize the process of showing appreciation.
- Provide positive and immediate feedback.
- Foster communication of valued behavior and activities.

Development and Career Opportunities

Development
A set of learning experiences designed to enhance employees' applied skills and competencies; development engages employees to perform better and leaders to advance their organizations' people strategies.

Career Opportunities
A plan for employees to advance their own career goals and may include advancement into a more responsible position in an organization. The organization supports career opportunities internally so that talented employees are deployed in positions that enable them to deliver their greatest value to their organization. Development and career opportunities include the following:

- **Learning Opportunities**
  - Tuition assistance.
  - Corporate universities.

- New technology training.
- Attendance at outside seminars, conferences, virtual education, etc.
- Self-development tools and techniques.
- On-the-job learning; rotational assignments at a progressively higher level.
- Sabbaticals with the express purpose of acquiring specific skills, knowledge, or experience.
- **Coaching/Mentoring**
  - Leadership training.
  - Access to experts/information networks—association memberships, attendance and/or presentation at conferences outside of one's area of expertise.
  - Exposure to resident experts.
  - Formal or informal mentoring programs; in or outside one's own organization.
- **Advancement Opportunities**
  - Internships.
  - Apprenticeships with experts.
  - Overseas assignments.
  - Internal job postings.
  - Job advancement/promotion.
  - Career ladders and pathways.
  - Succession planning.
  - Providing defined and respectable "on and off ramps" throughout the career life cycle.

An Integrated Total Rewards Strategy

Culture
Culture consists of the collective attitudes and behaviors that influence how individuals behave. Culture determines how and why a company operates in the way it does. Typically, it comprises a set of often unspoken expectations, behavioral norms, and performance standards to which the organization has become accustomed. Culture change is difficult to achieve because it involves changing attitudes and behaviors by altering their fundamental beliefs and values. Organizational culture is subject to internal and external influences; thus, culture is depicted as a contextual element of the total rewards model, overlapping within and outside the organization.
Source: Schein, E. "Organizational Culture." *American Psychologist* 43, no. 2 (February 1990): 109–19.

Environment
Environment is the total cluster of observable physical, psychological, and behavioral elements in the workplace. It is the tangible manifestation of organizational culture. Environment sets the tone, as everyone who enters the workplace reacts to it, either consciously or unconsciously. Because they are directly observable and often measurable, specific elements of the environment can be deliberately manipulated or changed. The external environment in which an organization operates can influence the internal environment; thus, environment is depicted as a contextual element of the total rewards model, overlapping within and outside the organization.

(continued)

FIGURE 1.5 *(Continued)*

Attraction

The ability an organization has to draw the right kind of talent necessary to achieve organizational success. Attraction of an adequate (and perpetual) supply of qualified talent is essential for the organization's survival. One way an organization can address this issue is to determine which "attractors" within the total rewards programs bring the kind of talent that will drive organizational success. A deliberate strategy to attract the quantity and quality of employees needed to drive organizational success is one of the key planks of business strategy.

Retention

An organization's ability to keep employees who are valued contributors to organizational success for as long as is mutually beneficial. Desired talent can be kept on-staff by using a dynamic blend of elements from the total rewards package as employees move through their career life cycles. However, not all retention is desirable, which is why a formal retention strategy with appropriate steps is essential.

Motivation

The ability to cause employees to behave in a way that achieves the highest performance levels. Motivation comprises two types:

- *Intrinsic Motivation:* Linked to factors that include an employee's sense of achievement, respect for the whole person, trust, appropriate advancement opportunities, and others, intrinsic motivation consistently results in higher performance levels.
- *Extrinsic Motivation:* Extrinsic motivation is most frequently associated with rewards that are tangible such as pay.

There also are defined levels of intensity with regard to motivation:

- *Satisfaction:* How much I like things here.
- *Commitment:* How much I want to be here.
- *Engagement:* How much I will actually do to improve business results.

Another key plank of the business strategy, motivation can drive organizational success.

Compensation

This includes fixed pay (base pay) and variable pay (pay at risk). It also includes several forms of variable pay including short-term incentive pay and long-term incentive pay. While one of the most traditional elements of total rewards, it remains a necessity for business success.

Benefits

While this area seems to be continuously challenged during this time of shrinking health care benefits and expanding health care premiums, businesses are trying to redefine the traditional benefits program. In basic form, benefits programs protect employees and their families from financial risks. This area includes traditional programs such as Social Security, medical and dental insurance, but also nontraditional programs such as identity theft insurance and pet insurance.

Work-Life

This area refers to any programs that help employees do their jobs effectively, such as flexible scheduling, telecommuting, child-care programs, etc. One of the most talked about areas of late, work-life has become the "secret sauce" in many organizations' recipes for business success.

In 2003, Alliance for Work-Life Progress (AWLP) joined the WorldatWork family of organizations, reflecting work-life as an integral component of total rewards.

Performance and Recognition

Perhaps one of the anchors in talent management, performance involves the alignment of organizational and individual goals toward business success.

Recognition is a way for employers to pay special attention to workers for their accomplishments, behaviors, and successes. Recognition is a necessity in order to reinforce the value of performance improvement and foster positive communication and feedback. It can be programmatic or simply cultural in execution.

Development and Career Opportunities

This key area focuses on the concept that motivating and engaging the workforce entails planning for the advancement and/or change in responsibilities to best suit individual skills, talents, and desires. In this way, both the business and the employee benefit from this symbiotic relationship. Tuition assistance, professional development, sabbaticals, coaching and mentoring opportunities, succession planning, and apprenticeships are all examples of career enhancement programs.

2 Why the Total Rewards Approach Works

Throughout the decades, there has been compelling evidence showing that the best way to attract, engage, and retain employees is to focus on total rewards, not just pay and benefits.

In the 1950s, Frederick Hertzberg conducted his famous study of factors affecting job attitudes. He identified 16 factors and categorized them into 10 "hygiene factors" and 6 motivators (growth, advancement, responsibility, work itself, recognition, and achievement). Note that the motivators do not include pay and benefits—these are hygiene factors. To motivate, a total rewards approach must be taken.

Since the 1960s, psychologists (including Abraham Maslow) stressed how less tangible needs, such as growth and self-actualization, were equally important to individuals' sense of worth. Figure 2.1 illustrates how total rewards maps to Maslow's famous hierarchy. This message has been reinforced over the years by other leading thinkers and management gurus, including Maslow, Ed Lawler, Peter Drucker, and Edward Demming.

Most data show that work and career opportunities, leadership, and recognition are leading drivers in employee engagement and retention—not pay.

What do you do when you get a job offer? Take a sheet of paper, draw a vertical line down the middle, label one column "stay" and the other "take the offer." Then fill in the columns with a list of the total rewards associated with each opportunity. If a total rewards mindset is used to make this individual decision, shouldn't the same mindset be applied when thinking about how to attract, retain, and motivate the broader workforce?

In today's environment, the case for a total rewards approach is stronger than ever:

- *Total rewards addresses today's business needs for managing costs and growth.* Research suggests that a more limited view of rewards can be more costly, because organizations tend to respond to every situation with cash. Total rewards supports moving away from ineffective programs toward those that help drive the business forward.

FIGURE 2.1 The link between total rewards and Maslow's hierarchy of needs.

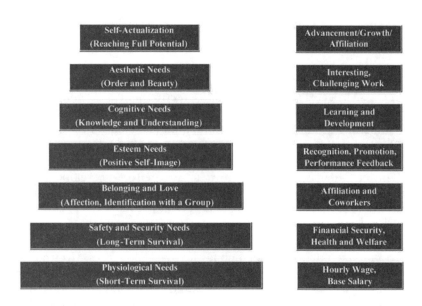

- *Total rewards meets the evolving needs of today's employees.* As the workforce continues to diversify, employees' expectations change. For example, there is stronger emphasis on job enrichment, flexible work schedules, and the overall work environment. A total rewards approach better addresses many of these varying employee needs.
- *Total rewards fits with a movement away from cash and stock.* As the role of stock becomes deemphasized in most companies, the hunt is on for other items that help redefine a compelling and differentiated offer in the market for talent. Total rewards can help do this.

THE TOP FIVE ADVANTAGES OF A TOTAL REWARDS APPROACH

1. Increased Flexibility

With the one-size-fits-all approach essentially gone, the twenty-first century may well become the "rewards your way" era. Just as companies create niche products and services to cater to small consumer segments (micromarketing), employers need to start creating different blends of rewards packages for different workforce segments. This is particularly true in a global labor market where workforce diversity is the rule, not the exception, and when specific skills are in short supply.

A total rewards approach—which combines transactional and relational awards—offers tremendous flexibility because it allows awards to be mixed and remixed to meet the different emotional and motivational needs of employees. Indeed, flexibility is a two-way street. Both employers and employees want more of it.

As the importance of flexibility has become more understood, more companies are allowing employees to determine when they work, where they work, and how they work. Total rewards recognizes that employees want, and in many instances demand, the ability to integrate their lifestyle and their work.

2. Improved Recruitment and Retention

Organizations are facing key shortages of best-in-class workers (top performers), Information Technology (IT) workers with hot skills, and workers for entry-level, unskilled jobs. The classic initial solution to a recruitment and retention dilemma is to throw money at the problem. But because this solution is so overused, it does not offer a competitive advantage. Furthermore, it immediately raises costs.

A total rewards strategy is critical to addressing the issues created by recruitment and retention. It can help create a work experience that meets the needs of employees and encourages them to contribute extra effort—developing a deal that addresses a broad range of issues and spending rewards dollars where they will be most effective in addressing workers' shifting values.

Indeed, today's workers are looking beyond the "big picture" in deciding where they want to work. Work and personal life should be seen as complementary priorities, not competing ones. When a company helps its employees effectively run both their personal and work lives, the employees feel a stronger commitment to the organization. In addition, numerous studies show that employees look at the total rewards package when deciding whether to join or stay with an organization.

An actual summary statement can be prepared for potential employees, enabling them to see the whole value of being employed by a company. As such, as highly desirable job candidates explore their options with various companies, companies with total rewards have a competitive advantage because they are able to show the "total value" of their employment packages.

3. Reduced Labor Costs/Cost of Turnover

The cost of turnover—often the driver of recruitment and retention—is sometimes invisible. In reality, it's far from cheap. Estimates of the total cost of losing a single position to turnover range from 30 percent of the yearly salary of the position for hourly employees (Cornell University) to 150 percent, as estimated by the Saratoga Institute, and independently by Hewitt Associates (Lermusiaux 2003). In addition, the cost of turnover includes indirect costs such as losses from customers and sales, as well as decreased efficiencies as productive employees leave and the remaining workers are distracted.

4. Heightened Visibility in a Tight Labor Market

Talent shortages have become a chronic condition of business life, and experts agree that the tight labor market is going to get tighter. As a result, employers can no longer afford to simply view their employees as interchangeable parts. Organizations quickly are realizing that every employee matters even more when there are not enough employees to fill the available jobs.

In addition, demographic shifts (e.g., the increasing number of women in the workforce) coupled with new economic forces (e.g., global competition) have changed the employment landscape, creating an unprecedented need for committed employees at a time when loyalty is low. If people can find an environment that's more in sync with their needs, they will make changes for that. Likewise, they will stay put when they feel their needs are being met.

By gaining a clear understanding of what employees value, and mixing and matching rewards within a comprehensive framework, companies can reallocate their investment dollars to match what employees say they value most, and can communicate the total package versus a patchwork of individual components.

5. Enhanced Profitability

Aside from the high costs of technology, HR professionals also are saddled with escalating benefits costs and changes in health care coverage and medical protocols. Employees want a "new deal" at the same time that companies—struggling to deliver their financial targets—are readily cutting programs to trim costs. How to balance these two realities? Change the mix.

A big misconception about total rewards packages is that they are more expensive. That's because a number of companies equate the notion of rewards with "more"—more pay, more benefits, and more combinations of rewards. What companies need to realize is that by remixing their rewards in a more cost-effective way, they can strengthen their programs and improve employees' perception of value without necessarily increasing their overall investment. It's largely a matter of reallocating dollars rather than finding more dollars.

Indeed, as companies discover the power of targeted reallocation of rewards and begin promoting the total value of their programs, they are abandoning the practice of setting pay, benefits, and other budgets in isolation, without reference to broad strategic and cost objectives. As they begin understanding their true aggregate costs—often for the first time—they are in a position to measure the extent to which their expenditures are in line with, over, or under competitive practice. And they can then measure whether they're getting a reasonable return on their overall investment.

In addition, today's workforce includes several distinct generations, each with a different perspective of the employer-employee relationship. Most employee research indicates that younger employees place a far higher priority on work environment and learning and development than on the traditional rewards components. In contrast, older workers put more emphasis on pay and benefits. All employees are concerned with health care, wealth accumulation, career development, and time off. It simply is no longer possible to create a set of rewards that is universally appealing to all employees or to address a series of complex business issues through a single set of solutions.

The challenge is to develop and implement a flexible program that capitalizes on this diverse workforce. Valuing each employee includes understanding that everyone does not want to work the same way or be rewarded the same way. To achieve excellence, employers need a portfolio of total rewards plans.

REFERENCE

Lermusiaux, Yves. *Calculating the High Cost of Employee Turnover.* Taleo Research, 2003. www.taleo.com.

3 Developing a Total Rewards Strategy

While many companies agree with the *idea* of total rewards, they often don't actually put a total rewards strategy into practice. The compensation department may design a sales force compensation program separately from the benefits department that revises the 401(k) program. This piecemeal approach is common, but it's akin to building a state-of-the-art skyscraper on top of the foundation of a 30-year-old, mid-rise office building. That skyscraper isn't going to be structurally sound using a base that wasn't designed to support it. The same thing can happen when new or revised benefits are built without regard to the overall compensation and benefits structure.

THE TOTAL REWARDS BLUEPRINT

Starting a total rewards program off on the right foot is a matter of taking a complete inventory of the programs already in place, ranking each program's effectiveness and finding the linkages between the rewards and the business strategy.

- *Inventory.* Find out what's already in the mix—every program, plan, and perk, even those not currently in use.
- *Rank.* Determine the effectiveness of each program and how close it is to being a best practice in the industry. Effectiveness can be defined several ways. For instance, low participation can mean low interest, or possibly low understanding of a particular program. Ask line managers to list the top five and bottom five programs in the current package.
- *Link.* This is a difficult step, but an important one. Take a look at the company business strategy and map where rewards complement or help to drive the specifics of the strategy.

For example, consider an organization that developed a business strategy that focused on providing an integrated customer service experience to its clients. If the company tried to blend 10 separate products and three different sales groups into one seamless offering, the structure of the company's sales force and the compensation programs likely would *not* support this collaborative approach. In fact, the pay structure for the sales force, customer service personnel, and sales support team could be inconsistent and actually motivate people *not* to work together. Good compensation programs are important, but linking total rewards to business strategy is essential.

FIVE COMMON WAYS A TOTAL REWARDS STRATEGY CAN GO ASTRAY

1. *Trying to re-engineer programs in pieces.* When moving to a total rewards approach, review and re-engineer the *entire* program. Don't re-engineer the short-term variable pay programs this year and take on base salary programs next year. This defeats the purpose of making sure all the programs are working together to deliver the business results necessary for success.

2. *Trying to implement changes all at once.* Yes, re-engineering the entire program is essential; however, implementing the changes all at once can have a detrimental effect. It's much better to phase in new rules and new programs over time. There's only so much change that employees can absorb and adapt to at once. In addition, it is necessary to build in time for managers and employees alike to move through the learning curve. When planning to implement radical changes to a total rewards program, it's advisable to allow a two- to five-year timeline.

3. *Limiting the number of people involved.* A broad coalition of people should be involved in a total rewards effort. All stakeholders need a place at the table—human resources, executives, finance, employees, board of directors, customers. While it may be easier to exclude some groups for the sake of simplicity, it's far too easy to overlook key elements without input of every group that will be impacted by the programs.

4. *Not doing a thorough impact analysis.* Before implementing any piece of the total rewards program, do a thorough analysis of the financial, organizational, employee, and customer impact of the plans. View these impacts both today and into the future. Don't forget to look at the full range of outcomes. What happens to the total rewards program if company profits drop by 50 percent, or sales and revenues increase threefold? It's a huge disservice not to know how the program elements will behave at different points in the company's life cycle.

5. *Not communicating effectively.* Many times when companies make these kinds of large-scale changes to their compensation and benefits programs, they communicate too much, too early, to employees, creating a workforce that gets full on hype and expectations. The flipside, communicating too little, too late, also is a problem because employees don't understand the business reasons for the changes or how these changes will impact their individual situations. Proper communication of total rewards changes is essential to success. (See Chapter 5.) Determine the right amount of information, the right time to deliver it, and the right format to use for delivery.

CRYSTALLIZING THE SPIRIT OF YOUR TOTAL REWARDS PLAN

When carefully evaluated, developed, and woven into a comprehensive total rewards strategy, the elements of the total rewards puzzle work together to produce an impact on employee attraction and retention that is greater than any of the elements considered individually. It is truly a strategy whose whole is greater than the sum of its parts.

In addition, a total rewards strategy maximizes the organization's return on compensation, benefits, and other rewards dollars invested; provides managers with multiple tools for encouraging employee development and rewarding performance; and creates a rewards package that meets or exceeds the value of a competitor's total rewards offerings. As with any effective, competitive HR program or initiative, a total rewards strategy should not be created in a vacuum. (See Figure 3.1.)

FIGURE 3.1 Embracing total rewards: 10 rules of the road.

Consider these 10 essential rules of the road that came out of the Hewitt Total Rewards Research Forum (April 2003). The forum was attended by senior HR leaders from 27 of the world's largest organizations, representing more than $1 trillion in revenues, more than $200 billion in total annual spending on people programs, and more than 10 million employees and their dependents.

1. Focus on the broad concept of total rewards, *however you define it, whatever you call it.* Push yourself to define total rewards broadly rather than narrowly. Conveying the total value of work experience is always more compelling to your employees.
2. *Clarify the business direction first.* A total rewards program and strategy needs to support a clearly defined business strategy. It is impossible to motivate and reward the right behaviors and results unless you know what they are.
3. *Articulate a clear, compelling, and specific strategy.* Generic reward strategies are a waste of time. They do not help leaders see how reward programs can help drive the business forward. They do not help HR professionals to focus the design or administration of reward programs. They do not help employees see what is expected of them and what they can expect in return. Well-conceived strategies force organizations to make choices. You can be broad in your definition of what total rewards is, and specific in your positions on what the strategy is and what each reward element represents.
4. *Communicate with quality, not quantity.* Employees who understand the true value of their total rewards package are more likely to appreciate the investment their employer is making in them, to stay with the company, and to deliver business results. Focus on delivering targeted rewards information to employees that is accessible, up-to-date, and meaningful.
5. *Seek to manage the whole value.* As pay becomes more competitive at the same time that we have fewer dollars to spend, and as equity becomes less of an option while the choices become more narrow, it is important to leverage the whole as opposed to one segment. The more you work the whole package, the more the perceived value of each element rises.

6. *Balance between flexibility and adherence to the core.* As you think about making choices in defining a total rewards strategy, recognize the need for core values and principles that are unifying and distinguishing. How is it that IBM is still IBM and GE is still GE, even as these organizations provide flexibility in their total rewards approaches across the globe? The answer lies in each company's ability to balance the two sides—offering enough flexibility so the needs of differing populations are met and defining common principles that anchor the company.

7. *Manage what you can measure.* The breadth of a total rewards strategy is its value to organizations. Yet companies need to make sure they are equipped to manage such an inclusive approach. This means an ability to measure and track the inputs into and results from a total rewards program. Including every reward element possible in a plan may sound appealing, but is ultimately useless if the value of such an approach cannot be demonstrated to the business.

8. *Recognize that the recipient defines value.* The value of any reward element will vary by population segment whether by geography, business unit, gender, age, or tenure. Only recipients can define the value of the rewards they receive. Think about individuals first, and then see if they can be clustered into groups.

9. *Beware of simple solutions.* We tend to put in place things that are easy to execute and the hard stuff is left for another day. Most of us focus on things that are important but somewhat incremental. In time, the harder, transformational things need to be tackled.

10. *Copy how great companies think, not what they do.* Think about how great companies become great and what are the things that make sense for them and why they do the things they do. Don't copy the practices that they put in place. Try to emulate their thinking.

Factors to consider when developing the strategy include:

- The desired level of external competitiveness (i.e., market leading, market competitive, or market following).
- The programs that will be offered to various employee groups to achieve organizational objectives while also maintaining appropriate internal equity.
- How the total rewards strategy will support the achievement of key organizational objectives.
- Ensuring that all elements developed or enhanced comply with state and federal regulations.

Also, effective communication is imperative for a total rewards strategy to be successful. Given that the message is more complex than the traditional focus on base pay only, a strong communication campaign that clearly identifies the value of the additional components of the total rewards package is essential.

Creating a total rewards program that is unique to an organization and based in competitive practices is not a simple task, but one that requires significant thought, analysis, and refinement. (See Figure 3.2.)

FIGURE 3.2 10 steps to a more effective total rewards program.

Following are 10 steps that employers can take to better design and implement their total rewards programs and maximize their effectiveness (conclusions drawn from *2005 Strategic Rewards Study*, Watson Wyatt and WorldatWork):

1. *Focus on Alignment.* High-performing companies are more successful at aligning employee behavior with company goals than low-performing companies are.

2. *Ask Employees What They Want.* Rewards only work if they are meaningful to employees and influence their affiliation with the organization. Study data show more companies need to ask employees about their rewards preferences and use their input to shape program offerings. Too many companies are missing the opportunity to understand whether their investments in different rewards plans are valued by employees and support the company's attraction, motivation, and retention goals.

3. *Measure and Manage Costs and Risks.* Successful rewards plans strike a balance between effectiveness and cost. However, too small a percentage of employers formally measure the cost-effectiveness of their total rewards program to a moderate or great extent. The lack of information means companies are missing opportunities to make changes to boost program performance.

    Companies also need to identify and manage total rewards–related risks. They should, for example, have a plan to manage financing risks related to defined benefit or stock plans. They need to understand time-based risks such as costs escalating over time for skill-based pay. And they have to be prepared if rewards don't influence employees' behaviors in intended ways.

4. *Strengthen Performance Management Systems.* While many companies have adopted designs that feature best practices, their managers are not faithfully or effectively carrying them out.

    Just as important are the perception gaps related to pay for performance and performance improvement. Most employers say they link pay decisions to the results of the review process, but not enough employees see the linkage for themselves. Even more troubling, most employers say they help poor performers improve, but few poor performers would agree.

    One way to strengthen the connection between performance management and rewards is by investing in formal training for managers. Managers are the linchpins of the system—if they don't understand and aren't comfortable with their organizations' total rewards strategies, they won't send the right message to employees. Organizations that formally train managers to manage employee performance rate more favorably on key performance management measures than organizations that do not formally train their supervisors.

5. *Sharply Differentiate between Top Performers and Everyone Else.* Employers need to identify their critical skills groups and their best-performing employees, let these employees know they are considered top performers, and reward them with significantly better salary increases, recognition and incentive awards, and opportunities for learning and development.

6. *Make Greater Use of Incentive-Based Pay.* One of the best ways to reward top performers and spur them to greater achievement is to make incentive-based pay a key element of the total rewards strategy. Companies that use incentive-based pay to motivate performance benefit financially.

7. *Review Incentive Funding Metrics and Targets.* Funding metrics for short-term incentives are important. Higher-performing firms fund short-term incentive plans at higher rates than low-performing firms. They also are slightly more focused on revenue growth, while low-performing firms focus more on operating income growth and cash flow. In addition, high-performing firms are slightly more likely to include nonfinancial measures that drive financial performance, such as customer satisfaction and quality outcomes.

   Finally, incentive targets should be updated regularly to reflect new company priorities and goals.

8. *Make Communication and Education a Priority.* Total rewards strategies only work if employees understand and support them. Unfortunately, employers and employees alike agree that such understanding is missing.

   Poor communication has real consequences. Most employees, for example, continue to value small annual pay increases over other compensation structures that could result in larger rewards.

9. *Use Long-Term Incentives throughout the Organization.* Long-term incentives continue to be important rewards vehicles for executives and nonexecutives alike. In fact, organizations with broad eligibility for stock-based programs significantly outperform organizations with limited eligibility. In light of decreased eligibility of other stock-based programs, companies should consider maintaining Employee Stock Purchase Plans (ESPP), despite the unfavorable accounting treatment.

10. *Manage Rewards in a Truly Integrated Way.* Many companies are not making a connection between compensation, benefits, finance, and other functions. This absence of integration means many companies are missing the opportunities true total rewards approaches offer, such as efficiencies in plan design and administration and a detailed understanding of current and projected costs and risk profiles across all components of their total rewards programs.

A total rewards strategy statement helps crystallize the spirit of a total rewards plan. It should provide specific, motivating direction when choosing what to focus on (and choosing what *not* to focus on). Rewards strategies should follow two primary aims:

- To articulate a distinctive value proposition for current and prospective employees that attracts and retains employees who have the capabilities and values the employer needs.
- To provide a framework from which the employer designs, administers, and communicates rewards programs with the maximum motivational impact to drive desired behaviors.

The total rewards strategy should ensure that the rewards framework matches the strategic needs of the business, and that the mechanics of the total rewards structure reinforce the desired corporate culture and management style. Also, it should help structure the components of the rewards system to influence and motivate employee behavior in the right direction.

ISSUES THAT A TOTAL REWARDS STRATEGY SHOULD ADDRESS

A well-conceived strategy should address several elements:

- *Strategic Perspective.* A total rewards strategy begins with an articulation of the company's values and business strategies. The link to business needs and aims should be spelled out right up front. The total rewards strategy is the place to be clear about where, when, and how the links between business goals and rewards should and should not be made.
- *Statement of Overall Objectives.* The strategy should include statements that describe how the rewards system will support the needs of the business and the company's customers, employees, shareholders, and other key stakeholders. This typically includes a delineation of the role of each reward element. If you cannot clearly define a role for any given element of total rewards, then you should question why it is being offered at all.
- *Prominence.* The strategy should describe the overall importance of rewards relative to other tools that can focus and affect actions and decisions (e.g., shared values, cool products, inspiring leadership, etc.). One way to think about prominence is to imagine an employee talking to a friend about working for the company. As the employee relates what is great about the company, prominence involves two key questions:
  - At what stage in the conversation would you like the employee to mention the rewards package (as opposed to things such as the culture, quality of leadership, focus on customers, etc.)? This helps define the importance of total rewards in the context of the total employee experience. Do you lead with total rewards, or is it a supporting component?
  - Which elements of the package would you like to hear mentioned first, and which should be mentioned last—or not at all? What does your company want to be famous for? What is the signature program? These questions are aimed at culling the handful of reward elements that deserve 80 percent or 90 percent of your attention in design, administration, and communication.
- *Performance Measures.* The strategy should clearly identify the performance criteria to be rewarded, the appropriate level of measurement for each (e.g., corporate, business unit, region, work group, individual, etc.) and which reward elements will be linked to which measures. Also, the strategy should describe the degree to which rewards are expected to drive employee actions and decisions through variability, influence over outcomes (controllability), and the explicitness of the pay-performance link.
- *Competitive Market Reference Points.* The total rewards strategy should describe the types of companies, industries, or other reference points that will be used as the basis for determining the competitiveness of the rewards package. What are the comparators? Do they differ among business units? Why?

A common response to the question about comparators is that they should be composed of companies against which we compete for talent. It's a sound approach, usually resulting in a list dominated by companies in the same industry or geography. Another angle to consider is what you want the company to be famous for. Perhaps benchmark the company's signature program against companies that already are famous in that area, even if it means looking beyond the industry or geography.

- *Competitive Positioning.* The strategy should clearly describe the desired competitive position relative to the competitive reference points in the labor market. Ideally, it should define how the competitive positioning is expected to vary with performance or other criteria.

It is worth noting that many companies define the median as the desired competitive benchmark for all components of rewards with increasing frequency. This raises a question: If you position all elements at the median, how will you differentiate? Defining a "signature" program is one way to avoid the creation of a plain set of rewards that looks like what every other company offers.

- *Degree of Internal Equity and Consistency.* The statement should address the extent to which the total rewards strategy will be applied uniformly throughout the company, both horizontally and vertically. To take the view that both internal and external relativities are important is fine, but defining a strategy is about making choices. A good strategy clearly defines which is more important when the two are in conflict.
- *Communication and Involvement.* The strategy should define how much information about the rewards programs will be disclosed and explained to employees. It also should outline the degree of participation that employees will have in the design and ongoing administration of the rewards programs. This includes a clear delineation of where HR's responsibility for designing and managing rewards ends and management's accountability begins. It also should include the company's policy toward employee unions, works councils, and other representative or collective bargaining units.
- *Governance.* While core principles governing the rewards program should remain fairly constant, the underlying programs need to be revised and refreshed periodically to ensure that they are competitive and compelling. The rewards strategy should delineate how frequently such reviews will occur, and who plays which roles in carrying out the review and redesign.
- *Data and Information Management.* The rewards strategy should specify guidelines for data management, information sources, collection and reporting methodologies, and processes for using data for decision support. The strategy also should include an overall process for measuring the efficacy of the total rewards program, and the supporting data.

What do the results of such an exercise normally look like? Typically, results are reflected in a written report that is anywhere from 8 to 20 pages in length. Though involving a lot of work, it's worth the effort for three reasons.

1. Clear, Compelling Strategies Help People Make Good Decisions Faster

Clear and compelling strategies define what is in bounds and what is out of bounds. They help employees and prospective employees make their own choices with regard to whether the company is the right place for them. Finally, clear strategies help the people who design and administer programs to operate with clarity and confidence. Consider these statements from companies that have developed clear and compelling strategies:

- "We will be market driven. Market competitiveness will be given priority over internal equity."
- "We will avoid reinforcing status distinctions via the provision of perquisites and other visible status symbols that are not based on business needs."
- "We do not seek to use benefits as a strong differentiator in our rewards package."
- "We aim to differentiate ourselves in recruiting and retaining talent by focusing on the opportunities we provide, particularly in the form of variable pay and developmental and career growth. We provide competitive pay and benefits, but we do not seek to differentiate ourselves through these elements of the total rewards package."
- "We actively develop our reputation as a desirable place to grow professionally. We provide employees with opportunities for personal growth, capability improvements, organizational advancement and employment security. Employees are responsible for driving their own professional growth with support from managers. They are encouraged to take a proactive approach to developing and planning their careers. Managers who develop people well are recognized and rewarded. Managers who do not develop people well are coached and, if needed, replaced."
- "To help employees manage the demands of their work and personal lives, we create an environment in which we are open to flexible work arrangements, exhibit leadership behaviors that support our employees in times of high demand on them, and continue to examine work content and job design to ensure appropriate work-life balance."

2. Clear, Compelling Strategies Help Identify Potential Friction Points

One company worked with a consulting firm to develop a global total rewards strategy that included roughly 130 statements similar to the preceding statements. The statements were placed in a matrix alongside the client's major geographic regions.

Representatives from the company's global HR function took 20 minutes to answer "yes" or "no" for each of the 130 strategy statements and how they relate to their particular region. By doing this, the consulting firm was able to determine the degree of alignment between current state and desired state. The exercise uncovered a potential friction point relating to the section of strategy dealing with recognition: Most Anglo-Saxon cultures answered "yes," while most of the rest of the world answered, "no." This forced a re-examination of the relevance and applicability of some of the statements, and whether the articulated strategy was "too Anglo-Saxon."

3. Clear, Compelling Strategies Help Provide Supporting Architecture

Some companies create a supporting framework or architecture to help audit and implement the strategy worldwide. Such architectures can provide enough clarity to be used to evaluate whether the current approach is in line with the articulated strategy, and, if not, where the work needs to be done to bring the rewards program in line.

The use of an architecture model goes beyond evaluation of total rewards. It provides broad specifications that can be used to design programs. In this sense, the rewards strategy provides the broad description of the type of house we are building, and the architecture provides a blueprint that the craftsmen can follow.

With the strategy clearly defined, attention can be turned to the other challenges: execution and communication.

THE BOTTOM LINE

Effectively executing an appropriate total rewards strategy can increase a company's market premium. Unfortunately, weak execution means many companies are leaving at least some of this money on the table.

Problems with execution are understandable. Many rewards and benefits programs evolved in a fragmented way, without consideration for how the parts fit together or whether they reinforce business goals. Even in organizations with truly integrated designs, effective delivery depends on successful implementation of performance management, change management, communication, and the use of technology.

Every organization has the ability to develop *and* execute a superior total rewards solution. By taking a step back and analyzing the design and delivery of each component of their total rewards strategy, companies can identify the steps they need to take to maximize its effectiveness.

4 Designing a Total Rewards Program

The following six processes have been identified to assist with formulating a total rewards program.

STEP 1: ANALYZE AND ASSESS

The first activity involved in developing a total rewards program is to get a clear understanding of the existing situation. This involves defining the current state, inventorying current rewards, assessing the current total rewards mix in terms of both people and dollars, and listening to what current and potential employees regard as important. Collectively, this data provides critical clues that will help identify the type of rewards that best suit an organization and how to use a total rewards program to full competitive advantage.

Why Conduct an Assessment?

While a natural reaction is to jump in and get started, it is important to systematically create a total rewards program that supports an organization's current and emerging business strategy. Why conduct an assessment?

- *Avoid incomplete information.* Moving too rapidly, forming assumptions too quickly, or shortchanging the process could be dangerous. Succumbing to temptations without sufficient time and effort could result in a total rewards program with limited or no long-term business strategy.
- *Substantiate your position.* An assessment provides the reasons why a total rewards program should be implemented and provides a framework for building a total rewards program.

- *Increase credibility with management.* Backup data provide the ammunition needed to sell the total rewards program. Assessments also are useful when making changes or introducing new programs because they provide a starting point for comparing the evaluation phase of the process. Improvements can be documented.
- *Assure compliance with the law.* Certain laws require recordkeeping and statistical analysis in defense of charges against the company. It is important to not lose sight of this as decisions are made about a total rewards program.

How to Conduct an Assessment

An assessment provides a reality check about an organization's current practices and values. It forces organizations to think about "what is" and "what should be." The gap defines the elements to be addressed in the actual design phase of the project. So how is an assessment conducted? Essentially, an assessment requires the effective collection, organization, and analysis of data. What exists needs to be documented.

- *Glean readily available internal and external data.*
  - *Internal Data.* Employee demographics (age, gender, ethnicity, geographic location, lifestyle), employee opinion surveys, performance objectives, salary structures, benefit options, employee contributions.
  - *External Data.* Government statistics (Bureau of Labor Statistics, Chamber of Commerce), salary survey data, cost-of-living data, employment data from competitors, industry surveys, vendor reports from outsourced functions, court case law, data from professional associations.
- *Benchmark the organization's strategies, policies, and practices against top-performing companies.* This will help gain a more in-depth understanding of how specific reward elements are used and integrated, and will provide a picture of how successful organizations use reward elements to support key values, changes, and results. For example, *Fortune* magazine conducts an annual survey identifying the "100 Best Companies to Work For" in America. Using benchmark information from these organizations may provide data to assist in attraction, motivation, and retention issues.
- *Collect additional data, both formal and informal.* Questions can be posed to senior management via individual interviews. Input from line managers can be gathered using focus groups or through conversations with various key leaders, depending on the organization's size and complexity. Information from employees can be obtained through focus groups, opinion surveys, or other questionnaires. It is helpful to ask what management most wants employees to know, do, and care about. That is what the rewards system should reinforce. It is helpful to ask employees what they value and how they perceive their current rewards package. Sample questions could include:
  - What is the level of employee satisfaction with pay and benefits?
  - What makes employees satisfied in their jobs?
  - Do employees plan to stay with the company? If not, when do they plan to leave?
  - What factors are influencing their decisions to stay or go?
- *Synthesize business data from various sources into an accurate and thematic summary.* Is the company perceived to be a high, moderate, or low paying employer? Are

employees generally satisfied with pay levels? Is there a strong nonmonetary recognition and rewards practice in place? To what extent is the current focus understood and valued by employees? Is there a statement of the desired culture regarding employee involvement?

- *Assess your current practice in light of the goal to create a total rewards program.* What are the critical aspects of culture that should be reinforced by the total rewards structure/strategy? What values should total rewards reinforce? Would employees be receptive to a total rewards approach? What factors could limit success?
- *Define improvement opportunities and goals.* The analysis should conclude with relevant implications and specific recommendations for change, including future intentions and needs wherever possible.

What to Consider in an Assessment

After learning the lay of the land, look at several other considerations that could significantly impact the total rewards program.

- *Organizational Culture.* Understand the challenges facing the organization. What are the company's internal and external strengths, weaknesses, opportunities, and threats? Does your organization have a bureaucratic or highly entrepreneurial leadership style? Is management directive or participative? Is the company viewed as a great place to work? Does the organization have the talent it needs to be successful in the future? Does it have the leadership strength to be successful? Does the company create an engaging environment for employees?
- *Role of Human Resources.* Look closely at how HR is viewed in the organization. Is it perceived as:
  - A business partner?
  - An enabler to attracting and retaining top talent?
  - Providing effective support systems to employees?
  - Efficient and effective with regard to processes and transactions?
  - Helping meet the needs of external customers?
  - Being supported by company leadership to create an environment that encourages integration and shared vision?
  - Improving efficiency through the use of technology?
  - A propagator of competitive plans and programs?
  - Cost-effective?
- *Employer Needs.* Know from the outset what the company wants to accomplish and how a total rewards program will get you there. For example, is the organization moving from a domestic to a global business? From manual to automated production? From a knowledge- to technology-based company? Process map the organization's way of doing business. Each company is in a different stage of development, and each has different needs and resources. Also, consider whether current employees' competencies and skills mesh with current and future organizational needs. HR professionals need to balance the current state with the desired state. Employer desires could include:
  - Improve recruitment.
  - Retain and motivate.

- Manage cost effectively.
- Increase competencies.
- Improve organizational performance.
- Support organizational change.
- Align behaviors with business strategy.
- *Employee Needs.* Determine why people join and remain with the organization. Retention plans fail when they are too complicated or the rewards are not meaningful to the intended group. Investigate what people value, what they enjoy, and what gets them excited. Explore employees' "motivational buttons" and learn how to push them. Employee wants and needs could include:
  - Stock options or opportunities.
  - More competitive salary.
  - Positive work environment.
  - Lower health care costs.
  - Rewards and recognition.
  - Increased flexibility.
  - Career opportunities.
- *Budgetary Concerns.* Conduct a cost analysis to examine the company's current investment in total rewards programs. Can costs be eliminated or combined? What did it cost other organizations to implement total rewards programs? Are benchmark data on total rewards available from other companies in the industry, or does a benchmark investigation need to be conducted?
- *Administrative Process.* Consider the current process for administering rewards programs. What kind of structure is in place to support a total rewards program? What changes might have to be made? A program that is too complex or labor-intensive may threaten success. Likewise, a program could be destined for failure if the proper resources are not available to successfully maintain the plan. Are the financial and human resources available to administer the program? If not, are they obtainable?
- *Readiness for Change.* Finally, assess the organization's readiness to implement a new total rewards program. Timing is everything. Does the capability or capacity for change exist? Would the proposed program align with organizational and cultural shifts? Is a paradigm shift required? Are managers, who may be asked to increase their involvement in a given process, willing and able to make the adjustment? Know the odds of creating a winning program before venturing out the starting gate. Can the organization afford not to consider a total rewards approach?

STEP 2: DESIGN

A design process starts with the corporate mission, vision, and business strategy. The HR philosophy flows from this and serves as a guiding light in the design of all HR programs. Total rewards philosophy and strategy are incorporated within the HR philosophy and strategy. From this, strategies and practices/programs are developed within the five facets of total rewards. Establishing a total rewards strategy helps ensure that rewards become a strategic driving force in the accomplishment of organizational goals. It also helps to align the rewards system with the organization's culture and change efforts.

Define the Corporate Mission and Vision

The corporate mission is an organization's reason for existence or purpose for being. Some conglomerates have more than one mission to reflect different missions for different industry sectors. Knowing "what business you are really in" is key to an organization's survival and growth. For example, railroads stopped growing because they defined themselves in the train business instead of in the transportation business. To create success, an organization needs to define itself in terms of the market and the customer, rather than the products or services it offers.

The corporate vision delineates the organization's aspirations and goals. While the mission concentrates on what the organization needs to do in the immediate future for growth and success, the vision provides a blueprint for the organization's long-term viability. It's how you see the organization 3, 5, even 10 years from now. The corporate vision keeps you on course as you make decisions and plans that affect the company's future.

Define the Business Strategy

Business strategy is a company's plan for competitively positioning its products or services with the intent to accomplish or support corporate mission and vision goals. Business strategy drives HR philosophy and total rewards design. Business strategy elements include:

- Pricing.
- Quality.
- Product innovation.
- Service excellence.
- Market responsiveness.
- Required rate of return.
- Cost structure.
- Target market.
- Marketing and sales.
- Production.
- Finance.
- Product design.
- Differentiation from competitors.
- Distribution.

Define the HR Philosophy and Strategy

The HR philosophy consists of management's values and beliefs about its approach to the employee relationship. Both HR philosophy and business strategy are key components to the development of an HR strategy. HR strategy consists of the organization's overall plan for recruitment, retention, and talent management of employees. The total rewards strategy follows from the HR strategy. It consists of the plans that will be used to support the organization's HR strategy.

Define the Total Rewards Philosophy Statement

The total rewards philosophy statement expresses management's values and beliefs about total rewards. The process of developing a statement unifies management's thoughts about total rewards programs. The total rewards philosophy statement serves many purposes:

- Communicate commitment and expectations to employees.
- Facilitate HR plan design.
- Serve as a reference point to measure the success of total rewards programs.
- Reinforce company culture and goals.

A starting point to develop a total rewards philosophy statement is to ask broad questions about current rewards programs, the organization, its culture, and its employees. Answering these questions thoroughly and systematically can generate the essential elements of the philosophy statement.

- What is the company culture and environment?
- What needs to be done to attract, motivate, retain, and engage employees?
- What are your objectives? (In employment? Retention?)
- What is the role of HR? (Attracting employees? Retaining employees? Increasing employee satisfaction? Achieving the organization's performance goals?)
- What are the company's performance goals?
- What cost constraints on the total rewards program can be defined in terms of profit or revenue and expense?

Once these questions are answered, it's time to begin putting together the total rewards philosophy statement. Components of that generally include:

- Program objectives.
- Desired competitive position in the labor market (often stated as a percentile of the market).
- Values regarding factors that should be considered in maintaining internal equity (identification of compensable job factors, the relationship of pay and performance and the relationship between pay and tenure).
- Values regarding total rewards communication (open versus secretive).
- Values regarding benefits cost sharing.
- Desired mix of total rewards elements.

The total rewards philosophy statement should be communicated widely and regularly. Employees should understand the statement. They should have the opportunity to discuss the philosophy, ask questions about it, and give management feedback.

Define Your Total Rewards Strategy

The total rewards strategy determines detail beyond that provided in the total rewards philosophy. It narrows the HR strategy to the specific plan with regard to the total rewards mix that supports the HR philosophy and strategy. The total rewards strategy identifies:

- The optimal mix of total rewards elements for each employee group. The mix may be high in some elements and low in others. For example, more organizations are moving toward placing a higher emphasis on work-life. In addition, the life cycle of the business can affect the mix. In a high-tech startup, there may be a cash shortage, so wages and benefits may be low, but stock options and work-life may be high.
- The manner in which each element will be earned and allocated (performance versus entitlement, individual versus group incentives, fixed versus flexible benefits).
- Appropriate labor market segments for each employee group in which the market is identified according to industry, size, geographic location, or performance.
- Desired competitive position in the marketplace for each employee group.

Many companies want to offer a rewards program targeted at the 50th percentile in the market. However, the average in one market may be considered high or low in another. Therefore, it is important to define the marketplace in which the organization operates. Without a sense of vision and overall strategic direction, people don't feel as invested in what they're doing. Therefore, as the total rewards strategy is defined, it is important to remember how it will be viewed and embraced by key players, both within and outside of your organization. (Chapter 3 elaborated on the critical formulation of a total rewards strategy.)

Key stakeholders include:

- Senior management/board of directors. This group needs to approve and be willing to support the philosophy and strategy. They also are important for buy-in and ownership.
- HR leadership. This group articulates the HR philosophy and strategy, while its staff facilitates the process.
- Employees. Internal, external, or exit surveys may provide guidance in identifying the relative importance of total rewards elements to various employee groups.
- Outside consultants. If outside consultants are used, they should work closely with HR to facilitate the process.

STEP 3: DEVELOP

Developing a total rewards program is both a science and an art. The steps shown constitute the general steps followed in the development process. Organizations may want to add steps. The key is to have a basic process and adjust it to the organization's culture, objectives, and specific needs. In general, program design involves the determination of:

- Purpose and objectives of the program.
- Eligibility of individual participants in specific aspects of the program.
- Baseline for measurement and goals.
- Funding of program initiatives.

- Plan selection and structure.
- Course of action and timeline.

Program Purpose/Objectives

Rewards systems represent both a major cost to the organization and a critical means of linking employees to business performance. As such, total rewards programs should be strategically designed for the purpose they are intended to plan and the results they are trying to drive.

Your *purpose statement* should communicate why the program is being developed and how the company plans to gain a competitive advantage. The purpose statement normally identifies critical organizational objectives and their link to the program. For example:

- To enhance recruitment and retention.
- To reduce the fixed compensation element of the total rewards opportunity.
- To help develop people so they can make greater contributions to the organization.
- To celebrate individual effort or group cooperation.
- To reward innovation and creativity.
- To reinforce performance improvements.

Guiding principles describe the program's key attributes. For example:

- Changes in the rewards system will support business objectives and the desired culture.
- Anticipated support from managers and participants will be considered and factored into the program design.

The *program objectives* give a clear description of what the company wants to achieve. It is recommended that the number of objectives be limited to three or less (no more than five). Characteristics of objectives include:

- Link to corporate mission, vision, business strategy, and total rewards philosophy.
- Identify specific performance areas and outcomes of program targets.
- Complementary to objectives of other plans.
- Clear and easily understood.
- Measurable.
- Acceptable to stakeholders.

Eligibility

A key advantage to a total rewards program is its flexibility. In designing the program's structure, decisions need to be made about which employees or organizational units will benefit from different elements of the program mix.

- *Determine program criteria.* Define who will be offered what and what the eligibility criteria will be.
- *Consider the implications of exclusionary programs.* For employees not included, will morale be affected ("haves" versus "have nots")?
- *Look at competitive practices.* Do competitors offer similar rewards to their employees? Does your rewards mix truly reflect a competitive advantage?

Baseline for Measurement

Two critical questions in program design involve how to define improvement and how to measure it.

- What is improvement? There is no one correct answer. The definition varies by organization and the baselines established.
- How can improvements be measured? Once defined, management must identify appropriate measures to collect improvement data.

Good measurement tools tend to have six characteristics in common:

- Reflect objectives. Send the appropriate message to employees reinforcing business unit objectives.
- Tangible, visible, complete measures that are clear and unambiguous.
- Credible to all parties, free of undue influence by outside factors.
- Verifiable and accurate.
- Understandable to eligible participants.
- Affected by participants (line of sight).

In designing the measurement process, consider the metrics and targets by which management will judge performance, the ease of administration in evaluating the program, and the credibility that the measures will carry with the organization and its employees. The three most common types of measurements are financial, business process, and customer. Also, decisions need to be made about what will be measured (retention, employee satisfaction, performance) and how that data will be reported.

Establishing a plan baseline for measurement varies significantly from organization to organization. There are several options available depending upon how performance history is defined. Baselines and targets generally are set using:

- Historical averages.
- Recent experience.
- Projected future performance.
- Internal reference points (e.g., equity in salary ranges and midpoints).
- External reference points (e.g., competitors).

Funding

Funding will come from a combination of costs incurred and savings derived from the five elements of total rewards. For example, productivity improvements can be converted to financial savings based on increased production and reduced labor per unit produced.

- *Develop an initial cost estimate.* Estimate a worst-case scenario.
- *Set realistic budget constraints.* Adequate funding of a new total rewards program should consider the allocation and reallocation of dollars among the components.
- *Assign a price tag to each initiative.* Keep an eye out for pesky hidden costs. For example, if you are considering a telework program, calculate what it would cost to purchase equipment supplies for a home office.

- *Determine appropriateness.* Assess whether improvement, no matter how technically proficient, is cost justified and value added. Sometimes a change may be needed, but could be too costly to make.
- *Evaluate legal and tax implications.* There may be a legal necessity to change something, even though costs may be excessive.
- *Determine available alternatives to meet program goals and budget constraints.*

The Concept of Present Value

When projecting the program's long-term cost, remember the concept of present value. A dollar is worth more today than it is in the future due to inflation and opportunity costs. Be sure to equate any capital expenses back to today's dollars.

Selection of Rewards Elements and Structure

Now, down to the nitty-gritty. Which elements will be offered in the total rewards program, and how will it be structured? Generally, the total rewards equation should:

- Embrace the full range of things that employees value in their work, so there's a sufficiently compelling proposition for people to join and stay with a company.
- Link with business objectives, so employees get the right signals about desired actions and behaviors and deliver the necessary return on investment for the organization.
- Track with projected shifts in demographics and labor market patterns so the company can position itself to become an employer of choice for the types of people who are critical to its future success.

Creating the Rewards Mix

Which rewards would most help to bring about the desired behaviors in your organization?

- *Identify the behaviors desired by the organization.* Link rewards to these behaviors.
- *Identify where overlaps and gaps exist in your current programs.* Do the programs conflict with one another? Do they all support the same philosophy and desired outcome?
- *Explore various mixes.* Map the interrelationships of the components.
- *Determine the appropriate mix to offer.* The final mix should be the one with the greatest cost-benefit ratio for the individual and the organization.
- *Involve employees in the design and administration.* Test progress along the way to ensure the program is understood and on the right track.

Global Considerations

Most employers can no longer view rewards programs solely through U.S. glasses. They need to offer rewards that are meaningful and valued across cultures. When developing a multinational total rewards program, remember:

- *Be sensitive to cultural issues.* Weigh rewards in the context of the employees' social, cultural, and geographic backgrounds. What motivates U.S. employees may not work for their counterparts in Latin America, Asia, or Europe. Worse, the same action might be inappropriate or produce negative reactions. For example, individual versus team incentives, communication methods, and recognition styles all vary greatly from culture to culture.
- *Know the laws.* Each country has its own set of regulations, policies, and customs.
- *Balance external competitiveness* (based on market standards for geographic locale; e.g., the same country or region) with internal equity, such as equal rewards for equal work regardless of geography.
- *Don't swerve too far off the map.* The design should have broad commonality around the company's global strategy and values.

Course of Action/Timeline

What is your planned course of action?

- *Consider what the company is capable of managing.* Some organizations move slowly, implementing changes over time. Others take a progressive approach and revamp their programs at one time.
- *Develop a reasonable timeline.* Include time for management approval, pretesting the program, and production of communication materials.
- *Decide which individuals and departments will be in charge of which areas and responsibilities.*
- *Plan to continue tracking, monitoring, and assessing the program periodically to ensure that its measures and structure are still relevant.*

STEP 4: IMPLEMENT

The implementation process is the "action" part of the plan. It's where the rubber meets the road.

Obtain Senior Management Approval

You've done your homework. Now it's time for the test. A convincing case for total rewards needs to be built, and it should be accepted and supported by management. Identify and communicate to management the following elements:

- The strategic need for total rewards.
- What the competition is doing.
- Total rewards philosophy.
- The new program's purpose/objectives.
- Proposed design (What are the changes to the current program? How much will the program cost?).
- Competitive market trends.
- Implementation schedule and timing of rollout.
- Key participants. (Who are the key players? Will you require a top management sponsor? Will you have a multifunctional team lead the effort? Who is the project coordinator?)

- Level of employee involvement (How much time will be required for program design and administration?).
- Communication plan to introduce the program.
- Evaluation plan.

When making a presentation to senior management, remember to talk their language. Executives have their own agenda and will support a proposal for their reasons, not yours. While a proposal may be great for the company, it won't go anywhere unless the key decision makers accept your reasons as valid. A few tips to ensure the presentation is successful include:

- *Do some prospecting.* Find out what the needs are, then provide the appropriate solutions.
  - Get to know the system and the "whys" behind company policies and practices.
  - Develop a rapport with key decision makers. These can include not only top executives, but well-respected middle managers or other "swing" people who are influential in the organization.
  - Understand the power structure and how decisions get made.
- *Sketch a framework for the decision-making process.*
  - Identify the ultimate decision maker (it may not be the chief executive officer [CEO]) and who influences that person.
  - Identify the reasons why various players would support or oppose the program.
  - Understand why the program may (or may not) be personally beneficial for each player.
  - Weigh your credibility. Players who view the HR professional as highly credible will tend to accept recommendations more quickly.
- *Assure management that there is a plan to follow up with periodic reports highlighting the new program's impact.*

Form an Implementation Team

To avoid having the program tagged as strictly another "HR program," involve other employees in the implementation process. Don't be a stage hog; share the spotlight. Convening a task team of employees to help with design and implementation of the new program sets you up for success. Anytime someone is asked to accept a new program or policy change—even if it is for the good—that person is really being asked to change. The possibility that the recommendation could be viewed as threatening always exists. But when key players are involved in the design and implementation, most employees will look forward to new programs. When forming a team:

- Choose members with broad-based representation (including key functional groups and top management sponsor[s]).
- Define the team's role and support mechanisms (expectations/deliverables, resources/budget, authority and nature of supervisors/degree of autonomy).
- Provide training on what to do and how to do it.
- Define the role of HR.

Finally, it is advisable to conduct a pilot test of the total rewards program with a small group of employees before going public.

- Are they receptive to the total rewards concept?
- What are their concerns?
- What do they like best about the program?
- Do they see the new program as a gain or a loss?
- What would they change?
- What suggestions do they have for communicating about total rewards?

It is critical to check the organization's pulse before proceeding. Remember: Employees hold the five components of total rewards near and dear. Know what the problematic issues are before introducing the program.

STEP 5: COMMUNICATE

Once a total rewards program is developed, it needs to be effectively communicated. Many aspects of HR are not well understood by employees—from how pay is determined to why a company conducts salary surveys or provides certain benefits. Educating management and employees on the plan, its objectives, link to the business strategy, its payout, and what each employee can do to affect the performance measures is critical to the plan's effectiveness. In essence, an effective communication program is important because it:

- Provides an opportunity for management to share information with employees.
- Helps set expectations of the total rewards program.
- Helps employees understand the total value of their compensation package.
- Conveys commitment to employees.
- Lets employees know the opportunities available in their organization.
- Is required by law (although most communication is voluntary, some is government mandated).

How organizations communicate with employees plays a key role in creating a high-performance organization, a status sought by most business leaders. To achieve this goal, they are focused on finding ways to instill employees with a high level of commitment—a business term for passion.

There's a strong belief that employees who have passion for their work—especially employees who do cerebral work—will outperform employees who lack it. A key element in creating passion in a business or personal relationship is trust. Where there is little trust, there will be little passion.

If the organization intends to have an honest, straightforward approach in communicating with employees, but sends out empty slogans that generate more questions than answers, it is saying one thing and doing another. Flunking the say/do test is a trustbuster. Without trust, there's no passion and no high-performance organization.

Communicating and selling total rewards programs require the utmost integrity. This responsibility is important to total rewards professionals, not only in established relationships with peers and management, but also with employees. Integrity is telling the truth, establishing trusting relationships, being honest and conveying written or verbal reports that contain no slanting or puffery.

Building a Trusting Relationship

Total rewards professionals can forge bonds, maintain ease in relationships, and increase trust through honest two-way communication. The following elements help establish integrity between management and employees:

- *Never answer a question if you do not know the correct answer.* Rather, respond with, "I will get back to you on that." Then, promptly follow up with an answer based on facts.
- *Do not use buzz, loaded, slanted, or puffed words.* (See Figure 4.1.)
- *Be pragmatic and positive.*
- *Establish good two-way communication by probing and thoroughly understanding the question or problem.*
- *Verbal and written reports should be clear, concise, and verifiable.* Reports and plans should exclude inferences, but should contain observable and verifiable facts. Many inferences are pure guesses, particularly when loaded with verbiage that can be easily misconstrued.

FIGURE 4.1 Words that fuel miscommunication.

"Buzz" Words	**Example**
Feedback	"Give me feedback on that."
Spin	"What's the spin on our salary structure?"
Slanted Words	**Example**
Thrifty	"Being thrifty is always the best approach in the design of a compensation and benefits program."
Neutralize	"Let's neutralize that situation."
Loaded Words	**Example**
Free	"This program is absolutely free."
Zero cost	"There is zero cost to the company."
Protection	"This new compensation program offers maximum protection against unionization."
Puffed Words	**Examples**
Greatest	"This is the greatest compensation structure I have seen."
Biggest	"This benefits plan will produce the biggest benefits to the company."
Unqualified	"Our compensation program is an unqualified success."

Know the Facts

It is important to never answer questions affirmatively without knowing the answer. This is one reason why total rewards professionals should continually read, understand, and educate themselves about:

- Current outside practices, such as competitors' compensation practices and salary and benefits trends.
- Current federal and state laws, including the Fair Labor Standards Act of 1938 (FLSA), the Employee Retirement Income Security Act of 1974 (ERISA), the Consolidated Omnibus Budget Reconciliation Act of 1985 (COBRA), and Internal Revenue Service case decisions.
- The organization's current situation.

Crystal Clear Communication

Total rewards professionals should communicate to management and employees in a candid manner. Also, by "walking the talk" through words, actions, policies, practices, and procedures, their communication efforts will be more effective and meaningful.

Employee benefits plans should be conveyed as legally required. By adopting a full disclosure policy, both good and not-so-good information is shared. This approach helps eliminate rumor and speculation.

From the communicator's perspective, total rewards professionals need to understand what they are communicating, learn from written and verbal communication, and, lastly, dispose of or decide the issue under consideration. The receiver needs to fully trust and expect all information to be accurate and verifiable.

Honesty: The Best Policy

Being honest pays huge dividends. Employees at all levels will understand and appreciate a straight shooter and modify or mend their own behavior, if necessary. Truthfulness also will increase employees' appreciation and loyalty to the organization.

Conversely, communicating inaccurate information to employees can lead to mistrust, diminishing loyalty, collective bargaining efforts, and increased employee turnover. Employees have a need for security and affiliation with the organization and are not prepared or willing to accept messages from management until a trusting relationship exists.

Audience

In developing a communication plan, it is important to consider specific employee audiences, the key messages to convey, how those messages will be disseminated, the amount of money available, the timeline for implementation, and how to gather employee feedback. Orientation and education are needed to ensure that participants understand the plan, know how they can affect measurements, and what advantages the new program provides. It's time to communicate, communicate, communicate!

Communications should be tailored to specific audiences. For example, one might start with an executive-level briefing, followed by a manager orientation and planning session, supervisor workshops, and finally a widespread employee education and orientation program. The key is that all employees at all levels are able to comprehend the new rewards system.

Management

Different communications may need to be planned for different levels of management. Plan to communicate details about the total rewards process and any anticipated obstacles. Provide exercises on how management can get their employees engaged and provide a list of messages to be communicated. Also, outline management's role in the implementation process. Good employee communication typically starts with clarification of the organization's mission and vision—and that must come from top executives.

Front-Line Supervisors

Front-line supervisors are perhaps the most critical element to success. When communication breaks down, it's usually at this level either because messages don't make it down from the top or they are misconstrued. Avoid this by holding separate group meetings with front-line managers and ensuring they are informed about the process from the beginning.

Employees

Who are they? What are their interests, needs, and concerns? Demographic information on age, sex, education, marital status, income, job type, length of service, and geographic location helps determine how messages should be delivered. Face-to-face communications usually are the best because this ensures that employees are receiving consistent messages, and it enhances credibility. But this simply may not be realistic, especially for multinational companies with numerous locations. Decide what would be most appropriate for each employee group.

External Audiences

How will you announce the new program to shareholders? Customers? Vendors? Are there other groups outside the organization who have a "need to know" about the program changes?

Key Messages

Effective communication starts with a clear vision of what you want to accomplish. Let employees know what's in it for them and what's in it for the company. Messages should help employees see the advantages of the new approach, instill a new mindset, and secure their tie-in and commitment. Tips to remember include:

- Keep messages simple, consistent, and timely.
- Begin communication at the time of concept approval.
- Don't let up; communicate frequently.
- Continue as long as the program is in effect (amount and intensity of communication should vary with need).
- Focus on the plan's main elements: how it works, the advantages to the employee and employer, and the timeline for implementation.

Media

In today's fast-paced, multichannel communications environment, it's not enough to convey a message one time through one medium. The audience and level of complexity in the message should determine the methods used. For example, some employees prefer to read information on a printed page; others prefer to access the information online; and still others prefer the message be delivered face-to-face in team meetings. In some companies, the message may need to be delivered in a language other than English, or communicated by using sign language or Braille.

The best communication campaign involves multiple messages delivered in a variety of ways over a long period of time. By reinforcing messages using multiple channels, you help to ensure that the program is understood. (See Figure 4.2.) The broken-record syndrome has to be the name of the game.

FIGURE 4.2 Types of communications media.

Audiovisual	• Flip charts • Overhead transparencies • Slides • Films/movies • Videotapes • Audiotapes • Teleconferences
Print	• Brochures • Booklets or handbooks • Articles in employee newsletters or other company publications • Letters • Memos • News bulletins • Summary plan descriptions • Compensation manuals • Paycheck stuffers • Personalized total rewards statements • Posters • Bulletin boards • Question-and-answer columns • Reply cards • Special interest bulletins
Personal	• Large meetings • Small gatherings • One-on-one counseling • Manager/employee sessions

Electronic	• Interactive personal computer programs
	• E-mail
	• Kiosks
	• Telephone voice-response systems (voicemail)
	• Conference calls
	• Personalized total rewards statements
	• Internet
	• Intranet
	• Multimedia

Budget

Start by looking at what is currently being spent. How are the dollars being allocated? Can existing communication dollars be used more effectively? Can additional dollars be obtained by working with other departments, such as employee communications? After finding out what is available, the challenge becomes how to get the most bang for your buck. Decide how to best reach the audiences involved with the least amount of money.

Timeline

Establish a timetable that outlines the campaign's important steps and sets dates for their completion. A realistic production schedule includes time for writing, editing, layout, design, and printing. Time to review and make revisions to drafts or scripts should be included in the timetable. Also, calculate the time and costs associated with duplication, mailing, and distribution.

Feedback

What are employees saying about the total rewards program? Are the right messages getting through to the right audiences? Look for ways to establish two-way communication, whether it is through question-and-answer sessions or focus groups. Hold follow-up meetings and issue follow-up reminders. Communicate progress on the goals. Most important, when employees ask questions, get back to them with answers. There's no better way to build credibility.

How to Communicate Bad News

No one enjoys being the deliverer of bad news, but someone has to do it. It's not unusual for people to become angry when hearing bad news; therefore, it's important to address negative feelings at the beginning of the change process to diffuse any anger. To be successful as the messenger, consider the following guidelines:

- *Keep the message short.* The goal is to convey facts with minimal embellishment.
- *Explain why the company decided to make the change.* The company's decision often is the best in a series of bad options. For example, a company facing a large deficit may be forced to cut benefits or freeze wages. No one wants to hear this.

But if the alternative is to lay off workers, then cutting benefits or wages may be a viable option.

- *Ensure that employees clearly understand how the change will affect them.*
- *Have face-to-face meetings with workers.* Don't just rely on written communication.

In the 1990s, a Fortune 500 company announced it was terminating an important benefits plan and replacing it with an alternative. The company used e-mail and an internal web site to announce the change. No employee meetings were held. The communication highlighted the benefits to employees of the alternative plan, including a sizeable savings for the company. Unfortunately, the company did not make it easy for employees to understand the impact of converting to the new plan.

Company workers took it upon themselves to "figure out" the impact. Many workers became outraged when they discovered they would lose considerable coverage compared to what they expected to receive under the original plan. In response, employees began communicating among themselves via a web site to plan next steps. Because of the employee "revolt," the company eventually decided to modify its position.

Fallout from the company's decision to change the benefits arrangement caused:

- Intervention from governmental regulators to determine the appropriateness of the change.
- A serious union drive among employees.
- Severe morale problems—many workers felt personally hurt by what they perceived as the company's insensitivity to them and lack of candor by not explaining how the change would adversely affect them.
- The company to not save the money it had expected.

Changes sometimes are initially perceived as takeaways or negatives. But direct interaction between HR professionals and workers should help employees understand the "why" for the change, positive and negative effects of the change, and how employees and the company can benefit from the change. This type of interaction takes time. However, the end result is greater employee acceptance.

STEP 6: EVALUATE AND REVISE

No program is complete until you find out if it works. A total rewards strategy should demonstrate that it has made a difference. It is important to recognize that straight lines are difficult to draw from changes in total rewards programs to organizational performance outcomes, and numerous variables exist. It is, nonetheless, necessary to identify expectations and assess results. The name of the game is measurement. How did the program perform against stated measures of success?

When measuring success, realize that no one program will fully satisfy the needs of every employee. Therefore, evaluate the program based on its ability to retain and reward top performers, recruit highly desirable talent, and motivate and satisfy the broader employee population.

The Review Process

Evaluating and revising the total rewards program is the final, ongoing step in the development process. This is an opportunity to see the plan in action, make adjustments, and maintain its currency and value in a changing world.

- *Who Should Conduct the Audit?* Usually, this is an HR function or a function of the design team. Depending on the organization, it also could fall on the shoulders of the operations committee, implementation team, or a dedicated reassessment team.
- *How Will the Program Be Assessed?* A general course of action is to collect baseline information, measure the qualitative and quantitative results, and review anecdotal and survey feedback from managers and employees.
- *When Should the Audit Be Conducted?* Review and audit are part of a continuous improvement process and should be conducted regularly and periodically. Usually, a good time to conduct an audit is after a program has been completed (e.g., annually).
- *What Should Be Audited?* Initially, you may choose to review the entire program. Going forward, perhaps only review selected pieces of the program.
- *What Should the Audit Include?* In general, the audit should provide:
  - Information about goal achievement.
  - A financial review.
  - A comparison of expected and actual results.
  - Perceptions of managers, employees, and plan designers regarding the plan.
- *How Should the Audit Be Conducted?* Audits need to be comprehensive, structured, detailed, and planned according to schedule. There should be a self-managed timetable. If a problem or issue is identified (e.g., absenteeism, turnover, productivity, profitability, job satisfaction, etc.), look for appropriate measures to evaluate the successful resolution of the problem.
- *On Which Output Data Should Focus Be Placed?* An audit only identifies issues. It doesn't solve anything. Develop recommendations and follow up with appropriate actions.

Measurements

So, the big question: Exactly how do you measure whether the total rewards program is supporting and reinforcing the company's mission, vision, values, strategies, and goals?

There is no one right answer. But most organizations would agree that there are two primary schools of thought, and both are important: *quantitative measurements* and *qualitative measurements*.

Quantitative Measurements

To prove to senior management that the amount of money spent on programs like total rewards is worthwhile, quantitative measures are essential. Knowledge of measurements, basic formulas, and ratios—even if they are homegrown statistics—provides increased credibility.

Exactly what should you be measuring? Outcomes can be grouped into three major categories:

- Direct performance outcomes can be largely attributed to the impact of an organization's total rewards strategy, such as reduced turnover and recruiting acceptance rates.

- Evaluative outcomes are objective conclusions that result from a total rewards design, such as the organization's competitive market position, its total rewards cost per employee, and its rewards mix.
- Indirect performance outcomes may be partially attributable to an organization's total rewards strategy, such as revenue per employee, profit per employee, productivity, customer retention, and various ratio measures.

There are four key categories of quantitative measures. The measures that should be included in an analysis depend on the specific objectives that have been set for the program. (See Figure 4.3.)

FIGURE 4.3 Quantitative measures to consider.

Results
- Employee attraction and retention
  - Number of openings
  - Duration of openings
  - Number of resignations
- Compliance with applicable laws and regulations
  - Lawsuits
  - Statistical analyses, such as EEO information, affirmative action, etc.
- Results of performance-based pay policies
  - Turnover by performance level
  - Percentage of payroll allocated in a performance-dependent manner
  - Correlation between pay and performance levels
- Cost of total rewards programs (protection of the organization's financial resources)
  - Benefits expense as a percentage of total payroll
  - Pay as a percentage of the operating budget (both historical and product competitors)
  - Organization rates and market rates
  - Mix of the total rewards program
- Nontraditional work arrangements
  - Productivity measures

Process Improvements
- Staff productivity
  - Ratio of HR employees to total employees
  - Absenteeism
- Cost of analytical/data collection activities
  - Job analysis
  - Job documentation
  - Job evaluation
  - Survey data
- Cost of data processing/consulting support
- Management's time
  - Amount of management time required for rewards program administration
  - Backlog of requests for evaluations and re-evaluations

- Timeliness of pay increase planning and processing
- Timeliness of performance appraisal data
- Claims processing turnaround time
  - Chart time for claims to be completed

Compliance and Alignment
- Pay relationships of employees relative to policy and market considerations
  - Actual rates and ranges versus market position specified by policy
  - Compa-ratios
  - Percent of employees outside of pay ranges
- Extent of compliance with pay policy
  - Salary increase policies
  - Starting rate policies
  - Promotional increase "size" (percentage)
- Consistency of pay grade and range assignments with job-evaluation results
- Compliance with applicable laws and regulations
  - Equal Employment Opportunity Act (Affirmative Action)
  - Family Medical and Leave Act of 1990 (FMLA)
  - Equal Pay Act of 1963
  - Employee Retirement Income Security Act of 1974 (ERISA)
  - Local wage and hour laws
  - Fair Labor Standards Act of 1938 (FLSA)
  - Americans with Disabilities Act of 1990 (ADA)
- Compliance of qualified retirement plans with nondiscrimination requirements
  - 401(k) limits on contributions
  - 401(a)(17) combined compensation limits
  - 403(b)

Documentation
- Percentage of employee files with current appraisals
- Compliance with FLSA requirements
- Existence of written policies
- Benefits plan documentation
- Retention of documents for required timeframe

- *Results.* Do programs add value and achieve results?
- *Process Improvements.* What is the general satisfaction level of customers? What is the timeliness and effectiveness of program administration?
- *Compliance/Alignment.* Is the program aligned with policy and program objectives?
- *Documentation.* How effective and efficient is the recordkeeping and approval practice?

Warning! Quantitative measurements are just one way to examine program effectiveness. Metrics may not tell the whole story. They get to the efficiency side of things, but this can be out of context without looking at the value-creation side. For example, hiring people who will never leave can lower turnover rates, but that's not necessarily good. The key is to assess strategic value and effectiveness, not just efficiency.

Qualitative Measurements

Another way to evaluate total rewards is to look at quality improvements that result from the program. While qualitative measurements may be more subjective, they are equally important in determining effectiveness. Many hard and fast quantitative measures have meaningful qualitative components.

For example, was productivity increased without adding staff? Were work-life improvements added without having an adverse effect on productivity? Do employees say they are more likely to stay with the company? Are they willing to go the extra mile to meet business needs? What is this worth?

One way to look at qualitative measures is to go back to the assessment and design phases. Look at where the organization started and what objectives were set for the total rewards program. Examine where the baseline measurements were and compare them against where the company wants to be. Did the program work? Did it do what it was intended to do? Qualitative measures help provide explanations on why the numbers look the way they do. Ask the tough questions. Did the program accomplish the following?

- Foster and reward the "right" behaviors that are consistent with the total rewards strategy?
- Offer the "right" incentives?
  - Adequate?
  - Equitable?
  - Competitive?
  - Appropriate (for employer and employees)?
  - Valued?
- Attract and retain the "right" people?
- Facilitate changes in the workforce?
- Help develop the skills needed to remain competitive?
- Move the organization closer to its desired culture?
- Receive a positive response from employees as well as middle to top management?
- Drop old measures? Add new measures? Offer a well-integrated approach?
- Provide communication that created a high level of awareness? Understanding?
- Align employees' interests with the organization's business objectives?
- Deliver a meaningful return on investment for the money spent?

Evaluative Outcomes

After collecting and assembling all of this information, what do you do with it? The program review and audit provide the validation step in the total rewards cycle. (See Figure 4.4.) Some major issues are going to identify themselves (i.e., those parties with issues will let you know). However, other venues for gathering data on the success and/or challenges of the program should be considered. These include employee surveys, focus groups, or questionnaires.

FIGURE 4.4 Principles for evaluating success.

- The program has a clear link to the organization's philosophy and core values.
- The program is supported and championed by senior management.
- Unit and front-line managers own the plan.
- The program is viewed as an investment, not an expense.
- The program is tailored to recognize cultural differences. Different forms of recognition motivate employees from different cultures. The program should be flexible enough to make adjustments for these differences.
- A high level of communication and education exist throughout the organization. Employees are engaged in making processes better.
- Any good program is continuously evaluated and renewed for improvement.

Some possible groups to poll in the postimplementation phase include recruiters and HR staff, management, supervisory personnel, a general sampling of employees. Some questions include:

- In general, what went well and what did not go well in the total rewards implementation?
- On a scale of 1 to 10 (1 being "inadequate" and 10 being "terrific"), how would you rate our implementation of total rewards?
- Overall, what do you think of the total rewards approach?
- What do you think are the advantages to the organization by doing this?
- What aspects of the program are problematic?
- What ideas or suggestions do you have for the future?
- In general, how satisfied are you with the total rewards program?

A total rewards program needs to be reviewed to ensure that it meets the organization's goals and is still aligned with mission, vision, and strategy. In the final analysis, the program should be able to be evaluated by comparing the value attributed to the program with the costs incurred by the program. The importance of this rationale is to justify the program to management and provide an overall measurement of its effectiveness. Factors to consider include:

- Plan costs.
- Value of performance improvements.
  - Financial value.
  - Operational value.
  - Nonfinancial value.
- Ratio of value to costs.

Based on the information collected and the program's results, it's time to make a decision on whether to:

- Continue the program as it stands and celebrate its success.
- Refine the program, building on progress made. (Examine what happened and what was learned. Introduce "new" plans or adjustments to measures, baselines, targets, etc.)
- Terminate the program (only as a last resort).

In most cases, modifications will be necessary. The evaluation should help develop a list of recommendations for improvement. As times change and issues arise (e.g., demographics, new/modified legislation, internal/external issues, premium increases, etc.), the program will need to be revised to keep current. The design, development, and implementation strategies should mirror those explained earlier.

5 Communicating Total Rewards

Ineffective communication is a deal breaker. A company can have some of the most well conceived, elegantly designed programs, but if the word doesn't get out to people—current and prospective employees alike—then it's all for nothing because, ultimately, the value of a total rewards program is defined by the recipient. If employees do not perceive value, then companies do not benefit in terms of engagement, productivity, or improved business results.

Unfortunately, very little excellent communication on total rewards exists. At best, companies tend to provide a list of what the elements are. An effective communication approach will not only clear away the confusion for employees, but will enhance the perceived value of the program.

So, what keeps employers from providing better communication?

- *Fears about Unintentionally Raising Expectations to Unattainable Levels.* For example, some employers have found that their efforts to be recognized as a "best employer" led to an increased entitlement mentality among employees. But the concern about raising expectations goes beyond fears about unintended consequences. Some employers are genuinely concerned about their ability to make any promise to employees that they will not break someday.
- *Cluttered Channels.* Getting attention is difficult. Getting information across is nearly impossible for many companies. Yet, major airlines let their customers choose the channels—monthly statements in the mail, special e-mail offers, upgrades through text messages to cell phones, cancellations and delays via voice mail. This type of customer-oriented thinking should be applied when reaching out to employees about total rewards.
- *Overreliance on Mass Communication.* Mass communication works well for some elements of total rewards, but for the most important elements and the most important employees, it's probably not the best choice. In this sense, the Internet has been both a blessing and a curse. On one hand, it offers tremendous

potential as a central information repository. On the other hand, the technology has led to list and database mania in the realm of total rewards.

- *Global Challenges.* Finally, sometimes companies forget they operate in a global world. Communications should be either universally appropriate or culturally specific—or both.

A COMMUNICATIONS APPROACH WITH OOMPH

Companies that are prepared to take action on the communication issue should think about approaches that are:

- *Comprehensive* to cover the totality of rewards and address all employees' needs and questions.
- *Personalized* to meet expectations of the day. Remember the airline story? Mass customization is the way to go.
- *Searchable* so employees can get what they need when they need it. Use technology to allow "event-driven" searches. Employees should be able to look under "birth of a child" in a search engine to find all the information regarding various reward programs that need reviewing or commencing when they are expecting a baby.
- *Accessible* 24 hours a day, seven days a week. To do anything less is out of step with the messages most companies are sending about work-life balance.
- *Human* because, while technology can solve many problems, rewards-related communication should not be overly dependent on technology. There is a time for high-tech and a time for high-touch.

THE POWER OF COMMUNICATION

The underlying objective of a total rewards program is to drive the workforce behaviors that ensure organizational success. But you cannot achieve that goal unless employees know what is expected of them and how their behavior affects the rewards they can earn. Studies show that the employee who understands his or her employer's total rewards program is more likely to be focused in the workplace. That is, the thorough communication of total rewards increases the likelihood of employee job satisfaction, which, in turn, enhances performance.

One problem with maintaining the alignment of total rewards with corporate goals is that all five components of total rewards can be influenced by both internal and external factors. The employer may not be able to control these factors. Fortunately, one influence under an employer's power is the way in which total rewards are communicated.

Communication is the creation of understanding and the transferal of meaning. It is a critical element in the success or failure of a total rewards program. Employees expect it to be honest, thorough, understandable, and relevant. Carefully designed communication:

- Links business goals with personal outcomes for employees (e.g., increased profitability can lead to bonuses, increased benefits, or additional work-life programs).

FIGURE 5.1 The power of communication.

From the Employee's Perspective
- Provides necessary education
- Provides timely information
- Clarifies expectations
- Increases awareness
- Reinforces the decision to join and remain with the company

From the Employer's Perspective
- Helps achieve program goals
- Streamlines administration
- Meets legal requirements
- Changes employee attitudes and behavior
- Improves utilization, leading to improved return on investment
- Increases ability to understand and respond to employees
- Reinforces corporate philosophy, culture, and values

- Defines the relationship between employees and the employer such that communication often is the reason that an employee makes or breaks that relationship.
- Motivates employee to increase productivity.

(See Figure 5.1.)

For example, after a merger, a large pharmaceutical company needed to communicate its new global compensation and benefits initiatives to its newly integrated workforce of about sixty thousand employees in more than 30 countries. The population ranged from line workers to research Ph.Ds.

The company developed a series of newsletters that were distributed to all benefits-eligible employees worldwide. Printed copies were mailed to homes in the United States, and a CD-ROM with a newsletter PDF was sent to local-country human resources representatives for translation, intranet posting, and distribution for international locations.

The premier edition of the newsletter featured a column by the CEO in which he reiterated the corporate mission and goals. The publication included the introduction of new human resources initiatives and an explanation of how these programs would support and facilitate the achievement of the company's goals.

The newsletters successfully gave the human resources department a medium to communicate big-picture issues and create the links between corporate goals, individual performance, and rewards. The newsletters also set the stage for specific benefits and compensation program communications that progressively conveyed the company's high-level messages to employees. Ultimately, the company's messages were individualized through each employee's performance development plan and review.

TOP MANAGEMENT BUY-IN

A communication campaign's success depends on management buy-in at all levels. Specifically, top management needs to understand that a well-designed communication campaign provides a good return on investment by enhancing loyalty, retention, and productivity. (See Figure 5.2.)

An ineffective communication campaign, on the other hand, can generate employee dissatisfaction that can be more costly to the company in the long run than a good communication campaign would have been initially. Thus, a key to attaining management buy-in is to demonstrate that skimping on communications may be penny-wise, but pound-foolish. The best way to do this is to ensure that the company can clearly evaluate the program's success.

THE BOTTOM LINE

Communication's impact on a company's bottom line results from showing employees the benefits of aligning their attitudes and behaviors with those of the company. (See Figures 5.3 and 5.4.)

COMMUNICATION FUNDAMENTALS

Communication often is thought of merely as the transmittal and receipt of information. But sending a memo is not communication if the receiver doesn't understand the message. Communication can better be defined as *creating understanding* and *transferring meaning*.

Communication is an interactive process requiring a sending and a receiving, each with the ability to influence communication. It is a two-way, reciprocal process of transferring meaning and creating understanding. Note that the *sender* determines whether information is sent, and the *receiver* determines whether

FIGURE 5.2 Requirements for attaining management buy-in.

- Policy and program approval and resource allocation
- An executive champion or change agent
- A supportive corporate culture
- Information supporting return on investment
- Identification of how success will be evaluated

FIGURE 5.3 Characteristics of effective communication.

- Begins with honest and direct feedback of information
- Is a reciprocal process that involves the listener and speaker
- Is never judgmental
- Produces timely responses to all parties involved
- Encourages additional communication
- Recognizes all input is valuable
- Is easily understood
- Clarifies and enlightens
- Produces results

FIGURE 5.4 Barriers to effective communication.

- Stereotyping
- Past frames of reference
- Selective listening
- Value judgments
- Source credibility
- Communication overload
- Semantic problems
- Filtering
- In-group language
- Different statuses
- Time pressures
- Noise

communication actually has taken place. Ultimately, the goal of communication is to obtain a shared understanding of the same information between the sender and receiver.

MODELS OF COMMUNICATION

Several theoretical models can be used to flesh out this definition of communication.

The *Shannon-Weaver Model* stresses that message senders should consider the effects of interference or "noise" on message receivers. Noise is anything that is not part of the original message that the sender intended to transmit. Noise may include job pressures, personal distractions, past experience, timing, or environmental setting, and it is can have a strong negative impact on communication.

The *Osgood and Dance Circular Model* suggests that communication is a constantly revolving spiral of sending a message and receiving feedback about that message. That is, the more often a sender and receiver complete this cycle, the closer they come to achieving understanding and the more their communication improves. Consequently, receiving feedback, and, if necessary, refining the message based on that feedback is an integral part of good communication.

Finally, *Schramm's Model* emphasizes that every message receiver has a frame of reference or an experience level that shapes the reception of that message. Because this "sphere of experience" directly influences the receiver's understanding of the message, total rewards professionals need to be sensitive to employees' prior experiences throughout the communication process.

For example, imagine an organization is communicating the introduction of a cash-balance pension plan. The receivers of the message may have prior experiences with traditional pensions or already-formed opinions about cash-balance plans. Considering the media's post-Enron focus on the funding and security of high-profile company pensions, employees are constantly exposed to information about retirement plans. These experiences would affect employees' interpretations of the message introducing changes in retirement benefits.

Because the purpose of total rewards communication is to influence employees to behave in ways that support the organization's goals and values, it also is important to keep this behavior pyramid in mind.

THE COMMUNICATION PROCESS

The following eight steps can be used as a framework to develop effective communications:

Step 1: Analyze the Situation

First, identify the specific changes or events in compensation, benefits, and the work experience programs to be communicated. Before moving to Step 2, it is important to analyze the situation from both a strategic and tactical perspective. Use the traditional questions: Who? What? Where? When? Why? How? (See Figure 5.5.)

Step 2: Define the Objectives

To be effective, establish objectives for your communication using the SMAART approach. Each objective should be:

Specific.
Measurable.
Attainable.
Audience-specific.
Relevant.
Tied to the business.

For example:

- *Compensation:* Increase "paid fairly" perceptions among managers from 56 percent to at least 70 percent.
- *Benefits:* Increase 401(k) plan participation by 5 percent among hourly employees.
- *Work-Life Effectiveness:* Promote new features for an on-site fitness center to all employees and achieve 50 new member sign-ups.

FIGURE 5.5 Strategic and tactical questions to ask.

Strategic Questions
- Who will support this change? Who will oppose it?
- Who needs to be involved in communicating this change?
- What is working in our favor?
- What are the potential barriers to success?
- Where are the major challenges in creating acceptance?

Tactical Questions
- What is this change being introduced?
- When will this change become effective?
- Who will be affected by this change?
- How will this change affect eligible employees?
- Where are the affected employees located?
- What other programs will this change affect?

Objectives are set to determine and direct both the style and content of the communication campaign. Stated objectives then become the criteria for measuring the effectiveness of the content, design, and impact of the communication.

Communication objectives should be succinct, clear, focused, and meet the SMAART criteria. Best practices can be used to provide company benchmarks for setting appropriate objectives.

Your objectives also will become the criteria by which you measure the effectiveness of the content, design, and impact of the communication. It is important to identify the measurements (e.g., retention rates, sick days, benefits claims, performance ratings, productivity, etc.) that will validate the success of your communication campaign.

Step 3: Conduct Audience Research

By understanding your audience, messages can be tailored to meet their diverse needs. Specifically, by defining your audience's sphere of experience early in the design of a communication campaign, you can avoid the noise that might distort the message or give it a negative impact. Often, plan or program design cannot be changed, but the communicator can adapt the materials' messages so employees understand what is changing, how the change(s) will affect them, and what actions they need to take. (See Figure 5.6.)

Audience research can be conducted before and after a communication campaign. Knowing your audience and their frames of reference can be pivotal in:

- Identifying the key appeals of a new plan or program to learn what features to emphasize in the communication process.
- Ascertaining what information employees think is important.

FIGURE 5.6 Questions to determine audience "sphere of experience."

- Who are your audiences (e.g., socioeconomic profiles, cultural makeup, native languages)?
- How well do employees understand current compensation, benefits, and work experience programs?
- How does this project fit in with corporate culture and philosophy?
- How does this project fit with recent or upcoming changes in your total rewards program?
- Do managers have the plan knowledge and presentation skills to effectively deliver the message?
- Do employees know what is expected of them and how to link their work activities to company goals?
- Do employees clearly see a performance-to-reward connection?
- How does top management view communication concerning total rewards?
- How does the company want to be perceived by the workforce?
- What is the employee relations climate?
- What other events or circumstances exist that must be considered?

- Previewing a possible approach to see if its style and tone are appropriate.
- Determining how well critical information is getting through to employees.
- Uncovering trouble spots, disconnects, or pitfalls before they become critical.
- Identifying special information needs on the part of particular audience segments.
- Establishing a benchmark for later analysis.

The best audience research results in both *qualitative feedback* and *quantitative feedback.*

- *Qualitative feedback.* Qualitative feedback helps determine why employee attitudes exist. With this knowledge, you can identify how to reinforce positive attitudes and how to correct negative attitudes.

    Qualitative data can be obtained from opinion leaders, cross-functional teams, individual interviews, and focus groups. Listening is the key to gathering qualitative data. Fight the temptation to give feedback during a data-gathering session. Listening, in itself, will build trust and foster confidentiality.
- *Quantitative feedback.* Quantitative feedback helps statistically determine how many employees hold certain opinions and whether various employee subgroups have similar or different points of view. The challenge in obtaining good quantitative feedback is to develop a set of questions that are both comprehensive and clear. These questions should address all relevant issues. More important, employees should be able to clearly understand what they are being asked and have the comfort to respond to the questions honestly. Quantitative data can be obtained from employee questionnaires, exit interviews, and electronic surveys.

    For example, a manufacturing company with some very long-term employees needed to modernize its retirement plans to integrate the employee populations of both old and newly acquired divisions. Because the plan changes already were approved, the company was skeptical about the value of conducting focus groups. Rather than conduct focus groups to gather opinions on the plans, however, the company sent communication consultants to test the pilot communication campaign. Conducting these focus groups allowed consultants to determine ways in which to better communicate the plan changes. The information garnered in these meetings led to modifications of the planned communications that significantly improved the clarity, emotional impact, and ultimate success of the plan.

Step 4: Determine Key Messages

After defining the communication objectives, it's time to determine key messages. (See Figure 5.7.) Key messages link the content of the communication to its objectives. Even for limited communication campaigns, it is important to determine a theme, as it can help the campaign achieve its objectives by grabbing employees' attention, creating interest, and establishing a recognizable association with the total rewards program.

The theme should:

- Fit the message being communicated.
- Tie to the strategy behind the program.

FIGURE 5.7 Key messages.

Key Messages to Increase Participation in a 401(k) Plan
- Saving for retirement is critical to your financial future.
- Contributing on a pre-tax basis allows more money to be put away than other retirement savings vehicles.
- 401(k) contributions could reduce the amount of personal income tax you owe at year-end.
- Not taking advantage of company matching contributions leaves money on the table.
- No other plan gives you a 25-percent to 100-percent match on contributions.

Key Messages to Increase "Paid Fairly" Perceptions
- Both the employer and employee benefit from everyone being paid fairly.
- The company devotes substantial resources to achieve fair pay.
- Fair pay is both subjective and objective. It is subjective on an individual basis; it is objective on a macro basis.
- What is fair depends on your point of view.

- Act as an identifier and unifier.
- Set the context and tone for the campaign.
- Frame key messages.
- Complement the human resources and corporate brand.

Effectively using a theme involves both written copy and graphic consistency (e.g., a logo, color palette, and design guidelines). For instance, several companies have used the phrase "Performance at Work" to brand either their total rewards program or one of its components.

"Performance at Work" is a particularly good theme because it can simultaneously convey several positive messages, including:

- What employee performance means to the company.
- What company performance means to employees.
- How rewards offered by the company perform for employees.

A theme such as "Performance at Work" can even send the message that the employer has put its program in place so employees will not have to worry about work experience issues, saving for retirement, or taking care of their families so that they can better focus on their work.

Step 5: Select Communication Channels

Media can be described as "vehicles of communication," and can include written, verbal, and electronic tools. To design a successful communication campaign, think creatively in terms of message, media, and theme. Take into account the needs of your audience and your organization, as well as the best media for the nature of your message. Choose various media and convey your message via a continuous theme consistently running through it. (See Figure 5.8.)

FIGURE 5.8 Media selection considerations.

Audience
- Culture
- Language
- Education level
- Preferred reception method
- Past media choices
- ADA/legal requirements

Organization
- Budget
- Time and resources

Message
- Urgency
- Privacy
- Complexity

Step 6: Develop the Communication Campaign

If not done already, it is now time to document all the data collected and decisions made up to this point in a project plan. The project plan is an important tool for effectively managing the communication campaign.

- Create a project plan:
  - Summarize/document findings up to this point—Document the situation analysis, communication objectives, target audience, key messages, and communication channels that will be used.
  - Detail action times—Identify tasks/action items including who is responsible for these items and timeframes for completing them.
  - Detail cost estimates—Estimate costs for creating and implementing the campaign, detail the budget, and outline the approach to be used if outsourcing, including details for accepting bids.
  - Detail evaluation plan—the evaluation plan should include the steps to take to measure whether the program has met its goals and objectives.

Once the project plan is developed, additional items to think through when developing the communication include:

- Preintroduction—Determine how to build interest and gain support for the campaign. Things to think about for the preintroduction include:
  - Creating a teaser—part of the campaign that builds excitement with any themes that may have been chosen.
    - Place teaser in the newsletter, memos, via e-mail, etc.
    - Mail postcard teasers.
    - Display posters.
  - Determining who needs to know about the details of the communication in advance.

- Obtain senior management approval.
- Conduct executive briefings and obtain buy-in.
- Prepare Q & A for supervisors.
- Conduct train-the-trainer sessions—Train HR and line management to be able to answer employee questions.
- Decide how to obtain feedback from employees on preintroduction.
- Release—Decide specifically how the message will be communicated and the objective achieved. Think about the following issues:
  - The types of communication materials and the communication channels that will be used. Essentially, the decisions made in Step 5. Consider not only what, but also who will be developing these communication items.
  - Key communicators who will help with the rollout.
  - Distribution.
  - Timeline/dates.
  - Quality control.
  - Obtaining feedback on initial reaction of employees.
- Reinforcement—Determine how the message will be clarified and/or reinforced to the audience.
  - Think about how to obtain feedback from employees.

Step 7: Implement the Campaign

The implementation process requires several steps. First, preintroduce your message:

- Determine who needs to know about the message in advance of the general employee population (e.g., human resources managers, line managers, service center representatives).
- Build interest in the message.
- Conduct an understandability test before the release of the message.
- Develop a theme for the message.
- Determine other organizational tie-ins for the message.

The basic release of your message should include the:

- Identification of who will deliver the message.
- Timing for its distribution.
- Quality control procedures for its distribution.
- Introduction of the theme.
- Distribution of the message.

After the basic release of your message, the final steps of implementation are its journey through informal networks, solicited and unsolicited feedback from employees, and reinforcement. These last steps are often a continual cycle, especially if the message is complex. So, determine up front how you plan to reinforce your message by repeating and clarifying it.

Step 8: Evaluate the Campaign

Just as audience research is necessary in the design phase of a communication campaign, it is also critical in the evaluation phase. Obtain feedback from employees through questionnaires, focus groups, interviews, and the company's informal network. When appropriate, compare "before" and "after" responses from the same employees.

Determine the strategy effectiveness by researching whether the communication pieces targeted the right audiences and considering whether the chosen media were the most suitable.

Ascertain whether the original communication objectives were achieved by reviewing the SMAART objectives. If the SMAART objectives have not been met, analyze how your campaign fell short of them (e.g., bad targets, bad media choices, etc.).

The communication campaign can be adapted by creating additional communication vehicles to address employee questions or clarify misrepresentations; for example, a web site that accepts questions and posts answers, or a toll-free telephone number for employees to call. By evaluating employee comprehension, future pieces can be modified so they better explain and reinforce areas employees have found difficult to understand.

Evaluation and modification of the communication campaign will strengthen your total rewards program through increased employee understanding, awareness, and expectations for your company and its programs. Evaluation is a continual process. Begin the assessment at the initial rollout, and, at the very least, further evaluate its success four to six months later.

COMMUNICATING THE PROGRAM'S RICHNESS

Because total rewards encompasses everything the employee perceives to be of value from the employer, value should be created for all compensation, benefits, work-life, performance and recognition, and development and career opportunities programs. One of the best ways to create value is to ensure that programs both meet employees' needs and that employees are fully aware of everything the employer offers to them. Remember: An underutilized program is an ineffective employee incentive for which the company still must pay.

Also, employees may develop an entitlement mentality regarding certain total rewards programs. For example, employees may begin to expect yearly cost-of-living increases, company-paid health and welfare benefits, and company-paid job training.

Instead, you want your employees to:

- Understand that company success generates more opportunities for employees to experience personal career growth.
- Link the company's business goals with their individual efforts so they recognize the achievement of those goals not only as higher company profits, but as higher profits for themselves, as well.

No matter how rich a total rewards program might be, without effective communication these goals cannot be achieved. (See Figure 5.9.)

FIGURE 5.9 Total rewards communication goals.

- Reduce entitlement mentality.
- Persuade employees to change behaviors and choices.
- Build trust between employer and employees.

Compensation

There are several innate challenges to communicating compensation programs. Not surprisingly, the lowest level of employee satisfaction revolves around understanding pay systems. The problem is further complicated by the great variance of corporate cultures and human resources philosophies. Most important, compensation is an emotional issue. (See Figure 5.10.)

Employees' sense of self-esteem may be attached to pay, including merit increases and incentive plans. Because the value of compensation may be affected by employees' perceptions of their self-worth, employers should provide employees with comfort that their pay is based on the value of the "jobs," not the value of each individual. Also, total rewards professionals should be particularly sensitive to how pay changes are communicated.

Knowledge or perception of pay in the marketplace also may affect employees' spheres of experience. When limited or no information is provided regarding pay, employees will often seek to find data to fill this void. Unfortunately, their findings may be inaccurate or incomplete.

Employer communication has an enormous influence on employee knowledge about pay systems and employee feelings about their pay systems, employers, jobs, and themselves.

Depending on an organization's total rewards and compensation philosophy, it may choose to develop communication campaigns for base pay, variable pay, and performance management programs. (See Figure 5.11.) The law also requires that employers communicate certain information to employees. For example:

FIGURE 5.10 Compensation communication strategy.

- Is knowledge about pay systems open or closed?
- Will salary grades and ranges be made available to employees? If so, how?
- Will merit ranges and performance standards be published?

FIGURE 5.11 What to communicate.

Base Pay	Variable Pay	Performance Management
• Salary administration programs, grades, and bands • Merit policy and timing of increases	• Eligibility • Objectives linked to business strategy, payout terms, and eligibility • Targets, quarterly progress, and expected payouts • Vesting, risks, and tax implications for equity plans	• Objectives, policies, and expected behaviors • Specific rewards for various levels of performance

- Minimum wage, labor, and hour laws must be conspicuously posted.
- Form W-2s must be given to all employees.
- Proxy data for top officer salaries must be disclosed.

Benefits

While compensation communication often is procedural, benefits communication tends to be explanatory, educational, and centered around events. *Employment-oriented* communication occurs after an event related to an individual's employment. *Needs-centered* communication occurs at the time of an individual need.

With the high cost of benefits, effective communication is essential to help both employees and employers manage costs while still retaining the highest value from their plans. Good communication can positively influence plan participation, plan usage, and plan costs. For example, education regarding urgent care may prevent overusage of emergency rooms.

There are, however, many challenges to communicating benefits.

In the past, employers led employees to view benefits as an entitlement instead of part of the broader context of total rewards. So, the shifting of benefits costs to employees has affected employee trust and requires extra sensitivity.

Benefits information also can be complex. There are technical details, complicated formulas, and, often, multiple considerations. Legal requirements also govern the documentation, administration, financing, and communication of benefits plans.

While not exhaustive, the following list includes the basic legal requirements with which a communication program must comply. (See Figure 5.12.)

Finally, employers must communicate benefits programs to an audience larger than their current employees. Spouses, family members, retirees, as well as new and former employees, also may need to receive and understand benefits information. The employee is not always the one who makes the benefits decisions or uses the plan the most. So, consider audience demographics carefully when deciding on communication delivery.

Work-Life

Work-life is composed of offerings in the total rewards package that address the unique individual needs of the employee. These offerings are important to the employee but may be less tangible than compensation and benefits:

- Caring for dependents.
- Supporting health and wellness.
- Creating workplace flexibility.
- Financial support programs.
- Creative use of paid and unpaid time off.
- Community involvement programs.
- Culture change initiatives.

Work-life programs satisfy *intrinsic* needs, such as control over one's work environment. (See Figure 5.13.)

Details of work-life programs are often distributed in an organization's employee handbook, recruiting materials, and orientation materials. They also might be

FIGURE 5.12 Legal requirements for benefits communication.

Law	Employer General Requirements	Implications for Communication
Legislation/ case law	State that a plan may be amended or terminated. Describe how a plan is amended. Be aware that, regardless of mitigating language, an error in a summary plan description may still be binding.	At a minimum, a disclaimer plainly stating that the plan may be amended or terminated must be published with each communication, and your internal or external legal counsel should approve this language.
Consolidated Omnibus Reconciliation Act of 1985 (COBRA)	Notify employees of cancellation of insurance coverage and offer continuation of that same coverage.	COBRA packages may be sent out from an employer directly or by a COBRA administrator. Review the materials your plan administrator intends to send. Even if you do not customize the entire package, you may want to customize a cover letter to ensure your employees fully understand their decisions.
Family and Medical Leave Act of 1993 (FMLA)	Notify employees of their legal rights when they take a qualifying leave of absence.	Employees need to understand how FMLA works in conjunction with other leaves, such as short-term disability. Provide examples in employee communication to show employees how these benefits work alone or together.
Health Insurance Portability and Accountability Act of 1996 (HIPAA)	Provide employees with a certificate of credible coverage when health insurance coverage ends. Communicate new rules applicable to personal health information.	In addition to summary plan descriptions, you may want to publish language about this act in your benefits handbook or enrollment materials to educate employees about how these benefits work with your medial plan.
Women's Health and Cancer Rights Act of 1998 (WHCRA)	Provide employees with a notification of their rights under the act upon enrollment and annually thereafter.	Notifications may be communicated as a regular part of the company's benefits enrollment package or in a benefits newsletter.

(continued)

FIGURE 5.12 (*Continued*)

Employee Retirement Income Security Act of 1974 (ERISA)	Provide employees with summary plan descriptions, summary material modifications, and summary annual reports. Provide other information upon request.	Recent court cases have favored employees in situations in which they have claimed to not have understood or received required communication materials. Required ERISA communications always should be carefully drafted by ERISA experts and reviewed by legal counsel. Creating compliant communication is not the final step; you should ensure your chosen delivery method is appropriate so employees are sure to receive materials.
Securities Act of 1933 and Securities Exchange Act of 1934	Provide employees with prospectuses (usually an S-8) when company stock is offered or sold under total rewards program. Provide employees with annual, quarterly, and periodic reports and proxy statements when they hold stock under total rewards statements.	There is potential for tremendous cost savings by using electronic media for dissemination of these materials. SEC rules permit you to incorporate your summary plan description into your S-8 prospectus. But, if you do so, plan changes must be reflected in the summary plan description immediately, rather than in accordance with normal Department of Labor timing rules.

FIGURE 5.13 What to communicate about work-life.

- Program objectives
- Eligibility
- Benefit for employees
- Benefit for the organization

promoted in special announcements, such as the introduction of a tuition reimbursement program or a new training program.

These programs may be recommunicated based on internal or external events. For example, during high-stress times, many organizations remind employees about employee assistance programs.

Performance and Recognition

Performance and recognition programs are unique to each organization. Each must be designed and implemented with the unique characteristics of the organization in mind. What works for one organization's employees may not work well in a different organization. However, there are some basic principles to follow when deciding how these elements will be used to support the business strategy and meet organizational goals.

- Performance involves the alignment and subsequent assessment of organizational, team, and individual effort toward the achievement of business goals and organizational success. Organizational, team, and individual performances are assessed in order to identify what was accomplished and how it was accomplished.
- Recognition acknowledges or gives special attention to employee actions, efforts, behavior, or performance.

Development and Career Opportunities

Development and career opportunity programs allow employees to continually upgrade and build new skills and capabilities. Employee levels of performance and personal job satisfaction can increase.

- Development comprises learning experiences designed to enhance employees' applied skills and competencies. Development engages employees and encourages them to perform more effectively.
- Career opportunities involve a plan for an employee to pursue his or her own career goals and may include advancement into a more responsible position in an organization. The organization supports career opportunities internally so that talented employees are deployed in positions that enable them to deliver their greatest value to the organization.

SPECIAL SITUATIONS

The employee population or an organization's development may force total rewards professionals to take special circumstances into account when developing a communication campaign.

Communicating with Various Levels of Employees

The detail and emphasis of communication should be correlated with the level of the audience. Take into consideration what needs to be communicated to whom and at what level of detail. (See Figure 5.14.)

Mergers and Acquisitions

Along with downsizing, rightsizing, and restructuring, mergers and acquisitions present significant communication challenges. Total rewards professionals should

FIGURE 5.14 Communicating with various levels of employees.

Executives	Managers	Employees
General explanation	Thorough explanation	Fairly detailed explanation
Emphasis on strategic implementation	Emphasis on development and motivation	Emphasis on process and policy
Executive rewards explained in detail		Workings of specific rewards programs

FIGURE 5.15 Communicating negative change.

- Be honest and open.
- Tell employees about the situation the employer faced.
- Outline the alternatives and choices.
- Explain how and why the business decision was made.
- Give employees a coping strategy.
- Provide facts early and often.
- Make information accessible; offer resources for answering questions.

take extra care when preparing for and anticipating employee concerns during such a time of significant organizational change. Planning and professional execution of the communication strategy for any restructuring is essential. Employees are especially hungry for information during times of change—so communicate early and often. (See Figure 5.15.)

Communicating in a Union Environment

The number one reason that employees unionize is perceived lack of management response to employee concerns. Consequently, a unionized audience may have a sphere of experience that makes them less receptive to communication from management than other employees.

Also, your company may have differing total rewards programs for unionized and nonunionized workers that can cause friction.

Special care must, therefore, be taken to properly communicate total rewards programs within a union environment, and, in particular, you should take into consideration any contractual obligations that have previously been negotiated.

Off-Shift, Off-Site, and Remote Location Employees

Off-shift, off-site, and remote location employees may not be able to attend meetings, focus groups, or other events. Communicating to these employees may require special meetings or targeted communication. For example, you may need to present information to these employees in special formats, such as CD-ROMs, audiotapes, or web tools. Carefully consider your delivery channels to ensure that all employees have access to required communication.

Global Communications

What is considered appropriate in one country may not be appropriate for employees in other countries. Be sensitive to the following issues:

- Word-for-word translations, mistranslation, and colloquialisms.
- Cultural customs, including greetings, gestures, and public manners.
- Compensation, benefits, and work experience expectations unique to each country (e.g., team compensation, differing holidays and work days, etc.).
- Different communications processes that may take longer because of translation, legal review, obtaining and evaluating feedback, and physical distribution.

MEDIA CONSIDERATIONS

Selecting the appropriate media can make or break your communication campaign. Decision guides, personalized statements, posters, e-mail announcements, CD-ROMs, and web sites all can be used to convey messages. The appropriate medium depends on the situation, audience, and corporate culture, but all media choices should support and enforce the company's brand.

Branding

Branding is the proprietary visual, emotional, rational, and cultural image that one associates with a company or a product. While most people are familiar with external branding from advertising campaigns such as Nike's "Just do it," the successful communication of total rewards requires an equally provocative brand.

Nike's product is footwear. Your products are compensation, benefits, and the work experience. Like Nike, if you take a marketing approach to your products, which have a greater impact on people's lives than any single consumer product, you can create a platform that resonates deeply with employees.

Employer Branding

Employer branding is how an organization wants its employees and potential employees to see it; it makes the company recognizable and attractive as an employer. It is important to understand the overall company brand and philosophy so you can establish or support an appropriate human resources brand within your organization.

A CASE STUDY: SOUTHERN COMPANY

In 2002, Southern Company undertook a communications campaign to:

- Link all of its retirement benefits and position them as a comprehensive, competitive retirement program.

- Provide fundamental retirement planning and investor education.
- Promote a basic understanding of how each retirement plan works.

The first step in developing the communications campaign was to create an identifiable theme that would represent Southern Company's total retirement program in the minds of employees. Southern Company used the visual and thematic identity, "Power Tools." This branding tied into Southern Company's industry—the power industry—and conveyed the message that retirement benefits are not a finished product but a comprehensive and powerful set of tools employees can use to build a good retirement from their own blueprints.

The communications program's success can be measured by the following results:

- More than half of the employees felt that the retirement program compared well in relation to other companies' programs.
- Two-thirds of the employees were satisfied with the company's retirement program.
- More than 80 percent of employees rated their understanding of the retirement program as good or high.
- Ninety percent of surveyed employees completed retirement worksheets and two-thirds understood that they would need more than 70 percent of their preretirement income to maintain their standard of living.

Importantly, in the last quarter of 2002, annualized 401(k) plan "catch-up contributions" amounted to more than $4.5 million, 401(k) contribution levels increased by 2 percent for the same period, and requests for pension estimates increased by one third.

TOTAL REWARDS BRANDING

Total rewards branding includes the packaging of benefits, compensation, work-life, performance and recognition, and development and career opportunities initiatives into a specific, integrated set of symbols and key messages. Total rewards branding should:

- Link to business objectives.
- Support organizational values and culture.
- Align with the company's total rewards philosophy.

The importance of TR branding:

- People awareness and strategic communications are key drivers of employee commitment.
- Employees are critical to translating business strategy into future success.
- Higher-performing organizations place greater emphasis on formal communication strategies and communication of the company's values, culture, and business goals.

An organization cannot create an employer brand image without communication—that's where HR comes in!

- HR's role—responsible for developing, communicating, and maintaining the employer/TR brand image.

FIGURE 5.16 Advantages of branding.

- Improved employee attraction and retention
- Greater employee satisfaction and pride in association with the organization
- Recognizable corporate/employee culture

FIGURE 5.17 Elements of total rewards branding and communication.

- Graphics, copy, and theme that complement and reinforce the overall corporate mission and values
- Concepts drawn from the organization's total rewards philosophy
- Repetition of key words or phrases that convey the total rewards philosophy
- Use of a total rewards logo
- Common colors, typefaces, and images

- Elements of TR branding and communication may include:
  - Surveys to determine appropriate appeals.
  - Concepts drawn from the total rewards philosophy.
  - Distinctive copy and graphic themes.
  - Implications that carry through a wide variety of HR initiatives.
  - Use of a TR logo.
  - Common graphic themes.
  - Common colors, typefaces, images, etc.
  - Repetition of key words or phrases that convey the TR or rewards philosophy. (See Figure 5.16.)

Creating a total rewards brand that complements and supports your corporate brand is intrinsic to effectively communicating your total rewards programs. (See Figure 5.17.) Not surprisingly, organizations with formal strategies in place to communicate company values, cultures, and business goals consistently perform better than those without. Communications integrity is associated with a 4-percent increase in a company's market value, and it is one of the main vehicles through which total rewards professionals can contribute to their organization's profitability.

But branding may fail for many reasons. If it is poorly planned or executed, based on themes or concepts that do not stand the test of time, geared to the wrong audience, not reinforced, used inconsistently, or, at worst, offensive to the receiver, branding is unlikely to be successful.

MEDIA CHOICES

After establishing the brand and your objectives, consider the communication vehicles that will most effectively communicate your messages.

Written Communication

Written communication is most effective for complex information to which employees must refer over time. (See Figure 5.18.) It also is effective for any audience size. The reader sets the pace and may refer to the details of the material at any later date. There is, however, no guarantee that employees will read or understand written communications.

To use this medium successfully:

- Eliminate needless words.
  - Keep sentences short.
  - Keep paragraphs short.
- Use personal tone.
  - Use "you" and "we."
  - Write the way you talk.
  - Write to express, not to impress.
- Use words the reader can understand.
  - Avoid abbreviations and jargon.
  - Avoid definitions.
  - Do not assume expertise is uniform.
  - Consider reading level and the reader's primary language.
- Ensure that the reader understands what he or she is being asked to do.
  - Give the date, time, and place for required responses.
  - Include a contact name, phone number, and e-mail address in case the reader has additional questions.
- Tie in with the reader's experience.
  - Use examples of how individuals will benefit or have benefited.
- Use active voice.
- Think creatively.

Written communication encompasses not just words, but also the graphics, charts, and colors used to convey meaning. There are four principles of design you should keep in mind when creating written materials:

FIGURE 5.18 Advantages and disadvantages of written communication.

Advantages
- Effective for any audience size
- Reader sets the pace and may reread the information
- No leader required
- Effective for communicating technical/legal information

Disadvantages
- May be misinterpreted by the reader
- No guarantee the audience will read the communication
- Language barriers/illiteracy
- Does not allow for interaction

- *Contrast.* Contrast is created when two elements are different. If two items are not exactly the same, make them very different. For example, contrast large type with small type.
- *Repetition.* Repetition develops organization and strengthens unity. Repeat some consistent aspect of the design throughout the entire piece. For example, use the same font for all newsletter headlines.
- *Alignment.* Alignment unifies and organizes the page. Many communication pieces use an underlying grid system to ensure visual consistency and harmony. Create a set of rules for the page setup of your publication. For example, establish that body copy will always be two columns, left justified, with mastheads and subheads aligned. Repeat your logo on each page in the exact same place.
- *Proximity.* Proximity groups related items together. Create proximity by ensuring a visual beginning and end to each group of ideas. Use three to five units per page. (See Figure 5.19.)

One of the best ways to achieve greater employee appreciation and understanding of a total rewards package is to prepare personalized annual statements that quantify the total value of each employee's compensation, benefits, work-life, performance and recognition, and development and career opportunities programs available to them.

Technology-Based Communication

The use of electronic communication, such as web sites and e-mail, is continually increasing. Electronic communication tools now are the standard, not the exception. This shift has been fueled by:

- The growing number of employees with access to computers.
- The cost and administrative efficiency it can provide to human resources.
- New legislation.
- 9 out of 10 organizations report that more than half of their workforce has access to the Internet or Intranet.

The Taxpayer Relief Act of 1997 required the Internal Revenue Service (IRS) and Department of Labor (DOL) to issue guidance on the use of new technologies by plan sponsors and administrators to fulfill the notice, election, consent, disclosure, and recordkeeping requirements of the Internal Revenue Code and ERISA. This legislation also requires the Internal Revenue Service to clarify the extent to which

FIGURE 5.19 Tips for success with visual design.

- Imitate what employees see on television and in magazines.
- Use pictures of people.
- Use color.
- Allow for white space.
- Keep it simple.

the writing requirements under the Internal Revenue Code concerning retirement plans permit paperless administration of those plans.

The Electronic Signatures in Global and National Commerce Act ("E-sign") validates the use of electronic signatures, contracts, and records. E-sign, as well as IRS and DOL regulations require employers to provide participants and beneficiaries with paper copies of required notices and communications on request as a fail-safe.

The following figure summarizes the Internal Revenue Service and Department of Labor rules for the use of electronic media. (See Figure 5.20.)

Most electronic communication can be considered a specialized form of written communication to which many of the same usage rules apply. There are, however,

FIGURE 5.20 Electronic administration of benefits plans.

	According to the Internal Revenue Service	According to the Department of Labor
What Can Be Electronic	• Participant enrollments • Contribution elections • Beneficiary designations (other than those requiring spousal consent) • Direct rollover elections • Investment elections for allocating future contributions • Investment elections to reallocate past balances • Inquires about general plan information (e.g., investment options and distribution options) • Inquiries about account information (e.g., current account balances and current investment allocations) • § 411(a)(11) notice of distribution options and right to defer distribution • § 402(f) rollover notice • § 3405(e)(10)(B) withholding notice (including the abbreviated notice described in § 35.3405-1T, Q&A d-27) • § 3405(e)(10)(B)(i)(III) annual notice to recipients of periodic payments	• Summary plan descriptions • Updated summary plan descriptions • Summaries of material modifications • Summary annual reports • Individual benefit statements • Investment-related information concerning so-called 404(c) plans • COBRA notifications • QDRO notifications • QMCSO notifications • Participant loan information • Information required to be furnished or made available for inspection in response to a request by a participant of beneficiary • Notification of benefit determinations

	• The electronic transmission of participant consent to a distribution under § 411(a)(11) • §§ 411(a)(11) and 402(f) notices more than 90 days before a distribution if the plan provides a summary of the notices no less than 30 days and no more than 90 days before the distribution	
To Whom It May Be Distributed Electronically	• To participants and beneficiaries with reasonable access to the electronic media	• To participants who have effective access to electronically furnished documents at the workplace • To participants and beneficiaries outside the workplace who consent to receive notices electronically • The individual must be advised that he or she can request, at no charge, a paper copy of the transaction
What Electronic Media Is Permissible	• The electronic medium must be reasonably accessible to participants and beneficiaries • The electronic notice or communication must be no less understandable than a written paper document • The electronic notice or communication must advise participants and beneficiaries of their right to a paper copy at no cost	• The plan administrator must take measures to ensure that documents are actually received, e.g., e-mail return receipt or system notification of undelivered e-mails • Electronic documents must be prepared and furnished in a manner consistent with the applicable style, format, and content requirements • Recipients must be provided with a notice informing them of the documents being furnished, the significance of the documents, and their right to receive paper copies without charge

some specific issues to consider when creating a human resources web site. While many web sites began as a place to post information, they have evolved into places at which employees can transact and interact. (See Figure 5.21.)

Content

A survey conducted by WorldatWork and Buck Consultants looked at common practices in electronic communication of benefits, compensation, and the work experience. Benefits information was the most prevalent, with more than half of organizations surveyed reporting benefits information online, including 401(k) plan, health care plan, and summary plan descriptions (SPDs), among their electronic offerings.

Compensation information, on the other hand, has not made it online for the mainstream of companies. Less than 20 percent of organizations surveyed said compensation information was available online; further, 75 percent said they had no plans to make it available in the future.

Online total rewards statements can be a very effective tool to show personalized pay, benefits, and other HR program value. More than 40 percent of organizations surveyed report they have online statements available or in development.

Before going ahead with the creation of a site, take the time to consider appropriate content.

- Balance business needs with employee needs.
- Put the highest cost or highest value benefit online first.
- Make the site easy to use through a blend of *static* and *interactive* components.
  - Static components only allow employees to retrieve information and should be used sparingly for reference information.
  - Interactive sites allow employees to perform tasks (e.g., plan enrollment and changes, retirement account transactions, email questions, etc.).

Resources and Priorities

Depending on your organization's internal expertise on information technology, a site may be created and maintained internally, externally, or via a combination of

FIGURE 5.21 Web site content.

Post	Transact	Engage
• Employee directory	• Annual enrollment	• Career planning
• Orientation materials	• 401(k) account transactions	• Personal development
• Summary plan descriptions	• Training sign-up sheets	• Personal financial planning
• Newsletters	• Employee surveys	
• Job postings	• Personal data changes	

both resources. Identify resources, priorities, and your budget before beginning to build or redesign the site.

User Feedback

Solicit user feedback regularly and track site usage. Knowing how employees are using and want to use the site will help in deciding what should be added to it.

Adding Information

Regularly refresh the site with new content. Develop a plan for periodic review of its contents and for updating it as needed. For example, once you have launched a new plan and posted the information about it, you should update the site over time to delete references to the "new" plan and keep dates or features current.

"Three Clicks" Rule

Ensure that it takes no more than three mouse clicks to get to the information an employee needs.

Graphics

Limit the use of elaborate graphics. Consider download time for all elements and make it as short as possible. (See Figure 5.22.)

Verbal Communication

Studies show that the actual words used in verbal communications are less important than the facial expressions, body movement, and vocal qualities that accompany them. (See Figure 5.23.) The following tips are more important with large groups, but can affect any verbal communication:

- Prepare and practice.
  - Familiarize yourself with the material.
  - Be prepared to answer questions.
  - Practice using visual aids.
- Stick to the basics.
- Use your voice effectively.

FIGURE 5.22 Tips for a successful web site.

- Develop the vision first.
- Pilot, test, and refine.
- Track utilization.
- Continually update and refresh content.
- Emphasize action.
- Follow the "three clicks" rule.

FIGURE 5.23 Advantages and disadvantages of verbal communication.

Advantages

Individual Meetings
- Easy to ask/answer questions
- Instant feedback
- Highly personalized
- Safe setting encourages questions about personal issues

Small Groups
- Easy to ask/answer questions

Large Groups
- Communicates same message to a large audience
- Communicates a message that must be understood in its entirety

Disadvantages

Individual Meetings
- Time-consuming and costly if large number of meetings is required
- Inconsistency from one meeting to another

Small Groups
- Time-consuming and costly if large number of meetings is required
- Inconsistency from one meeting to another

Large Groups
- Limited audience involvement
- Requires leader with effective presentation skills
- Inconsistency from one meeting to another

- Speak loudly enough so the entire audience can hear you.
- Speak slowly enough so the entire audience can understand you.
- Use rhythm and stress important words or phrases.
- Make eye contact to both convey openness and honesty, as well as to encourage energy.
- Use your hands.
- Open hands (with palms up) convey honesty and openness.
- Use simple sentences and avoid long words.
- Repeat words or key phrases to stress ideas and increase audience retention.
- Smile.

Audiovisual Communication

Visual aids make verbal communications more effective, especially when detailed information or numbers are involved. Audiotapes or CD-ROMs, on the other hand, can be used as companion pieces to written or verbal communication. They are most effective for walking employees through enrollment processes, providing plan highlights to specialized audiences, or sending motivational messages from management. (See Figure 5.24.)

Videos are more effective for conveying emotional content to a dispersed audience. (See Figure 5.25.)

FIGURE 5.24 Tips for success with audio.

- Use professionals.
- Keep it short.
- Think creatively.
- Use a script.
- Record a voice.

FIGURE 5.25 Tips for success with video.

- Use professionals.
- Feature people.
- Keep it short.
- Think creatively.
- Use a script.
- Do not use for details or data.
- Put the most important content at the end.
- Represent the diversity of the workforce.

IMPLEMENTATION

The final step in the effective communication of total rewards is making certain you have a team with the required skill sets in place to efficiently manage the development and implementation of the campaign. Complex information must be understood. Language barriers must be overcome. The needs of varying audience levels must be met. Cost considerations must be satisfied. To meet these challenges, total rewards professionals should be able to:

- Identify and define tasks.
- Create strategies for managing internal and external contributors.
- Develop plausible time frames.
- Measure the return on investment of a total rewards program.

PLANNING A CAMPAIGN

As with most projects, two of the biggest pitfalls in implementing a communication campaign are poor planning and poor management. Good planning and management, on the other hand, can make the most of even scant resources.

Project Management

A project manager or leader is essential for a successful campaign. Good project management skills go a long way toward ensuring that it will be effective, on time, and within budget. Your project manager also should possess the leadership skills

FIGURE 5.26 Use the communication process.

- Analyze the situation.
- Define objectives.
- Set realistic goals.
- Determine key messages.
- Conduct audience research.
- Select media.
- Determine who, what, and when.
- Decide how to measure success and return on investment.

to work effectively with other team members. These leadership skills include the ability to:

- Communicate with the team regularly so that all members are aware of deadlines and any necessary changes.
- Monitor progress and completion of tasks to ensure that the project is completed on time and within budget.
- Manage any changes in the campaign that might result from changes within the organization.
- Determine which factors will indicate that the campaign is successful and how to measure them.
- Celebrate successes at each milestone of the campaign. (See Figure 5.26.)

Project Planning

Build a project team. Include appropriate members from throughout the organization (e.g., human resources, information technology, corporate communications, and managers from key departments). Also include external team members, such as consultants or vendors. Ensure that your team has the time to meet deadlines and gives the project the necessary priority. The project team will need to:

- Assess available resources.
- Create a budget.
- Establish a timeline.
- Carry out the plan.

MANAGING A CAMPAIGN

Actively manage your campaign by including some or all of the following steps during the development and rollout of your program. (See Figure 5.27.)

Preintroduce the Communication Campaign

By preintroducing your campaign, you can lessen the possibility of mixed messages. Begin by obtaining senior management approval, and then brief your line management and human resources personnel to obtain their buy-in, as well as to ensure consistent answers to employee questions. Finally, make an initial announcement

FIGURE 5.27 Seven steps to success.

1. Communicate with your team.
2. Actively manage the process.
3. Obtain management buy-in from the start.
4. Test ideas and communication pieces.
5. Treat all communication as ongoing.
6. Expand beyond communicating facts to communicating their relevance to the receiver.
7. Ensure team commitment and resources.

using either the grapevine or with teasers in newsletters, e-mail, or posters that announce meetings or materials.

Communication during Program Rollout

Communicate your program through several complementary media to reinforce your messages. For example, provide employees with written materials such as announcement letters, decision guides, and plan documents. Depending on the complexity, cost, and importance of the program, decide whether it makes sense to personalize the materials for each employee. Other things to consider include:

- Holding employee meetings throughout the campaign.
- If possible, presenting the new program to all employees at once.
- After initial introduction, holding small group or departmental meetings to encourage employee discussion and answer any questions about the program.
- If necessary, addressing individual issues in individual meetings.

Promote other resources that are available to employees for questions and decision making. These resources include tools and conveniences such as:

- Interactive enrollment or financial modeling on the human resources web site.
- The capability for employees to place transactions through a call center.
- Your library of detailed documents and forms.
- Frequently asked questions and answers ("FAQs").

Gathering and Responding to Employee Feedback

There are a variety of methods to gather feedback:

- Talk to managers and group presenters to find out how the program was received.
- Talk to key employees regarding their perceptions.
- Coordinate focus groups.
- Monitor frequently asked employee questions.

Respond to the feedback you gather through follow-up communications. Responding to employee concerns in a timely fashion will help you reinforce your messages and eliminate noise. The following media are good choices for follow-up:

- Targeted materials to management explaining issues employees had difficulty understanding.
- Questions-and-answers bulletin board on company intranet.
- Articles in upcoming employee or manager communications.
- Added information on company intranet.
- Confirmation statements.

These communications should be as well thought out as your initial campaign. Take the time to decide which media will best address the feedback you have received.

Evaluation

Meet with your project team periodically to review your initial objectives and determine whether these goals have been met or whether continuing communication is needed. If it is needed, repeat the communication process. If not, determine how often periodic reinforcement of your key messages will be needed and set up a schedule for it.

Working with an Internal Communication Department

Depending on your organization, it may be best to include a member of the corporate communication department on your project team either as a contributor, or, at a minimum, as a reviewer. Because an internal communicator will have both communications expertise and knowledge of your company's culture, this team member is invaluable. An internal communicator can confirm that the total rewards program is consistent with corporate messages, as well as see that it is properly integrated into the timing and release of company-wide communications.

If your program requires the aid of a group of communication specialists, assign a specific communication project manager or main contact person. Decide on the most effective means of regularly communicating with this team within your team so that buy-in on all objectives can be obtained at the outset of the project and materials can be routed through one source. (See Figure 5.28.)

FIGURE 5.28 General tips for success.

- Prepare for audience reaction.
- Give examples.
- Let employees know what you want them to do.
- Fix mistakes quickly.
- Follow the "Rules of Seven."
  - An audience may need up to seven repetitions before a message registers.
  - The average person's short-term memory can retain only up to seven items.

Working with External Specialists

When enlisting the services of outside communication specialists and vendors, establish a good working relationship by integrating them into your team and clearly outlining roles and your expectations of them.

The skilled specialist will research your company's history, core values, and historical communication practices. In turn, you should supply your partners with the relevant material and access to team members that an outsider would need to understand your objectives and accomplish them with you.

Then, to ensure smooth interaction among all the parties, create an upfront review process to make the flow of material between vendors, the company point person, and internal reviewers smooth and effective. Involve the vendors in every step of the communication process so they understand the big picture of your campaign.

Finally, follow up after project completion by conducting a feedback meeting with your vendors to discuss the process, the project's success, and any room for improvement.

MEASURING RETURN ON INVESTMENT

After your company has successfully rolled out its communication campaign, the project team should analyze the return on the company's investment.

Define Measurements

Begin by reviewing the SMAART objectives created for the project. Remember that you should have determined up front what you would consider success at the project's end. Stick to your initial SMAART objectives to define what success means for your organization.

Track Statistics

Compare your most current data regarding the measurements chosen with the historical data for those same measurements. For example, if your goal was to increase "paid fairly" perceptions among managers from 56 percent to at least 70 percent, survey managers to determine what percentage of them now believe they are paid fairly following the education campaign you designed to establish pay criteria and build manager knowledge.

Investigate Cost Savings

Research whether there were any direct or residual cost savings from implementing and communicating the total rewards program. Identify areas in which the company may have saved money such as recruitment, training/orientation, human resources labor, or other expenses associated with the program.

CRITICAL OUTCOMES

While prognosticating always has risks, there seems little reason to doubt that total rewards will not only survive, but thrive as a meaningful framework for employers to manage their total investment in employees.

Fifty years ago, rewards were synonymous with compensation; as the workforce aged and entered the twenty-first century, benefits took on new importance. As that workforce once again morphs to reflect global diversity, the importance of the work environment will be paramount. The flexibility of the total rewards framework will enable employers to deliver attractive and relevant rewards at a sustainable cost and help ensure that employees perceive they are receiving appropriate value from the company in exchange for their contributions to its success.

Regardless of each organization's unique total rewards approach, the desired end result is the same: a satisfied, engaged, and productive group of employees who, in turn, create the desired business performance and results. Employee satisfaction and engagement, on one hand, and business performance and results, on the other, are critical outcomes that depend upon one another.

The final return on investment is a total rewards program that is difficult for competitors to duplicate. This creates a leading-edge HR environment and contributes—through the attraction, motivation, and retention of employee talent—to the achievement of organizational goals and objectives.

New demands are being made on all human resource programs, and, as never before, human resource professionals are expected to be active contributors to business success. It is no longer enough for human resources to keep administrative machinery running smoothly. Now human resources must constantly prove that the rewards offered to employees are helping to achieve the organization's business targets.

There is no question whether you need to communicate with employees about total rewards programs offered by your organization. Your programs can only be as successful as your communication campaign.

The keys to addressing this challenge are to develop measurable objectives for communication, to professionally implement communication campaigns, and to follow through by analyzing the data concerning your initial objectives. Using this process ensures that you can demonstrate the return on investment that effective communication provides to the organization.

6 Compensation Fundamentals

At one time, compensation systems were the exclusive domain of the compensation experts. In today's world of pay transparency, managerial self-service, and shared services, compensation systems are well on their way to being recognized as managerial programs and processes.

In large organizations with shared-services models or centralized compensation functions, HR generalists may broker compensation services on behalf of their business unit or division. In such an environment, the HR generalists must be able to clearly articulate the organization's business strategy, as well as design and implementation challenges that must be addressed, often with individuals in another time zone who may or may not have ever studied the business needs in detail. In such environments, comprehensive strategies and programs may be designed without ever holding a face-to-face meeting.

In smaller organizations, HR generalists may be expected to assume overall responsibility for everything from developing pay strategy to overseeing pay administration for the local employee workforce. In either case, it is essential for the HR generalist to understand the language of pay.

The following discussion focuses on the "nuts and bolts" of traditional pay programs as they are practiced today in large organizations. New approaches and ideas are constantly being tested; the key, as always, is to ensure that the final system meets the organization's needs.

THE FOUNDATION: A COMPENSATION PHILOSOPHY

Successful compensation programs are the result of well-defined and closely managed systems. A compensation philosophy provides the foundation to ensure that each of the different programs and systems is working in harmony with the others. A compensation philosophy should explain:

- Who the organization defines as labor competitors.
- How the organization prefers to set pay levels for its various job titles compared to the market (at the market, ahead of the market, at the market, on a total compensation basis, etc.).
- What the balance is between internal and external equity.
- The roles of managers, compensation, and HR in managing pay.
- What technology or systems will be used to manage pay.
- Frequency and timing of key events, such as merit increases (annual or semi-annual, etc.).
- The type of incentives in use, as well as eligibility.
- The type of organizational culture and/or business results desired by the company, and how the compensation systems will support each.
- ROI (return-on-investment) requirements for different types of programs.
- Sunset dates for any key programs, if applicable.
- The scope and type of programs used (e.g., extent of variable pay).
- The role of quasi-compensation systems, such as rewards and recognition.

These collective areas provide insight and direction to senior management and the compensation function, as well as the entire HR organization. In some cases, a compensation philosophy is a written document, often summarized in employee handbooks. In other cases, the philosophy is less documented, and instead is a recognized set of practices. An edited compensation philosophy statement is outlined in Figure 6.1. See Figure 6.2 for sample questions to ask to understand an organization's compensation philosophy.

FIGURE 6.1 Sample compensation philosophy.

ABC believes in creating a high-performance culture for our employees. In our belief, a motivated and engaged workforce will provide job satisfaction for our employees, above-average shareholder returns, and sustain our high-performing culture. We offer a wide variety of programs to motivate employees, depending on the location and business unit. Please check with your manager, or HRNow! (our online reference tool) for information for plans in your location.

In general, all of our programs have the following components:

- Base salary is based upon local market conditions and targeted to be just below market.
- Incentives are offered to all employees, with the opportunity to achieve a higher-than-market total compensation level based upon payout of the incentive.
  - All management employees participate in a plan that pays out based on achievement of company-wide financial performance.
  - Exemplary customer satisfaction scores can increase the payout by up to 50 percent.
  - All other employees participate in local productivity incentive programs based upon local objectives.
- All employees are eligible for annual merit increases, which are designed to be competitive with other manufacturing employers of our size.

- We offer a competitive benefits package, which is designed to be generally comparable to our market competitors for labor.

The corporate compensation group develops overall strategy in alignment with the company's total rewards strategy, initiated in 2004. Business-unit compensation develops local strategies based upon approval from corporate compensation. Line managers are responsible for setting individual pay levels.

FIGURE 6.2 Understanding the organization's compensation philosophy.

Q: What is the organization's compensation philosophy?
This is an important question for several reasons. A good compensation philosophy indicates where the organization prefers to position its pay level against competitors; what amount of pay will be fixed and what amount is variable; and whether it prefers to gear pay more toward internal equity or external competitiveness. Also, a good philosophy ties pay closely to the organization's overall business strategy.

Q: Does the organization determine bonus eligibility based on salary grade or on position responsibilities?
Some companies determine bonus eligibility by grade, which makes the process of understanding how a job is placed in a specific grade extremely important. Other organizations use job responsibilities to determine bonus eligibility. Both techniques have advantages and disadvantages. Job levels are easier to explain, but this approach can lead to perceptions of inequity among employees who are below the "magic" cutoff level. Job responsibilities will be inequitable if employees with similar job levels but different duties participate in different bonus plans.

Q: What decisions need to be approved by the compensation function? When?
Each organization makes pay-related decisions based on staffing, philosophy, and degree of centralization. In more stable organizations, job values have been established, and HR's role is to determine which existing job classification is the most appropriate. Many organizations centralize the evaluation of new jobs and determination of who is eligible for incentive pay. In some companies, HR designs new pay systems; in others, HR only administers pay.

Q: How many years does it take for a high performer to reach the midpoint of the salary range?
Most organizations have a rough guideline of how they expect top performers to be paid. In high-growth, high-movement organizations, position in range is not always important because small promotional increases are an integral part of the culture. In other organizations, position in range is more important, and, thus, there are many tools available to accelerate position in range. Knowing the organization's philosophy will help in recruiting and retaining high-quality employees.

Q: What changes in the compensation system are expected during the upcoming year?
Compensation programs change often. Forewarned is forearmed!

Q: What is the compensation calendar, and what roles do line managers, line HR, corporate compensation, and local compensation play?
Knowing this will help to plan work in relationship to the overall calendar and ensure that each of the different groups concerned is adequately involved.

CHARACTERISTICS OF COMPENSATION PROGRAMS

The following "ideal" characteristics are necessary for every compensation program in order to attract, motivate, and retain qualified employees. (Note: These characteristics are primarily for all positions except single incumbent senior management positions.) These characteristics are the foundation for an ideal pay structure:

- *Internal Equity.* A measure of how an organization values each of its jobs in relation to one another.
- *External Competitiveness.* A measure of an organization's pay structure compared to that of its competitors.
- *Affordability.* A measure of how costly a compensation program is to a company. If pay structures are not developed responsibly, an organization could incur labor costs that exceed what it can afford to pay.
- *Legal Defensibility.* Compensation programs must adhere to specific laws designed to provide fairness in how employees are paid. These laws are discussed in Chapter 7.
- *Understandable/Saleable.* To be accepted and understood, compensation programs must be well communicated.
- *Efficient to Administer.* With increased pressure to improve productivity and reduce costs, it is important that an organization's compensation program be as simple and straightforward as possible to maintain and administer. A balance needs to be struck between what appears to be the "best" program and what is efficient, effective, and easiest to administer.
- *Safeguard Organizational Resources.* The compensation program should reward performance fairly without conflicting with the interests of company stakeholders. Rewards should reflect both individual employee and company performance. HR should be seen as an investment that should be protected, as well as optimized.
- *Flexible.* Pay programs are necessary tools to compete for labor in the marketplace. As such, they must be flexible and capable of changing as needed without requiring a redesign every time a new need arises.
- *Meets the Organization's Unique Needs.* To some degree, each company is unique within its own industry or geographical area. Unique characteristics need to be recognized and addressed when designing compensation programs, and, particularly, pay structures.

Most compensation programs will not include all of these characteristics. In fact, some of these characteristics may be in conflict. For example, it may not always be possible to maintain internal equity when a company is trying to be externally competitive. Therefore, it is important to recognize the possibility of such conflict and review the business strategy to determine the appropriate balance of all features of the compensation program.

Although compensation is the largest component of the rewards system and a major cost factor for organizations, many employers have not had a formal strategy in place to ensure that compensation dollars are used wisely. Additionally, the broader concept of directing employees' behaviors to desired outcomes through rewards usually has not been integrated into an organization's strategic plan.

ELEMENTS OF COMPENSATION

Compensation can be characterized by two basic elements:

- *Base Pay.* Nondiscretionary compensation that does not regularly vary according to performance or results achieved.
- *Variable Pay.* Discretionary compensation that is contingent upon performance or results achieved.

Compensation Programs at a Glance

Base Pay

- Salary, hourly, or piece rates.
- Knowledge- or skill-based pay.
- Competency-based pay.
- Differentials.
  - Shift.
  - Weekend/holiday.
  - Expatriate.
- Pay increases.
  - Merit increases.
  - Lump-sum increases.
  - Step-rate increases.
  - General increases.
  - Cost-of-living increases.
  - Equity-based adjustments.
  - Market-based adjustments.

Variable Pay

- Based on organizational, group/team, or individual performance.
- Profit-sharing plans.
- Performance-sharing plans.
- Group/team incentives.
- Individual incentives.
  - Short-term incentive plans.
  - Sales incentive plans/commissions.
  - Executive incentive plans.
- Discretionary bonuses (annual or spot).
- Equity-based compensation.
  - Stock options.
  - Stock grants.
  - Restricted stock.
  - Performance unit plans.

Much of the innovation in compensation is occurring in the variable-pay element. Companies are making greater use of variable-pay programs by expanding them to a significantly broader portion of the workforce than they have in the past.

THE BASICS: BASE PAY

Every organization must decide how much to pay each of its employees, but HR generalists and compensation specialists often have different viewpoints about how to manage this process. Generalists tend to think first about the requirements of the person, while specialists tend to think first about the requirements of the job.

Edward E. Lawler III, Ph.D., Director of the Center for Effective Organizations at the University of Southern California's Graduate School of Business Administration, wrote in his book, *Strategic Pay:* "Organizations hire individuals, but once individuals join most organizations, the amount they are paid is determined primarily by the type of job they do." Therefore, it is important for HR generalists to understand the steps required in job-level pay determination, as well as individual-level pay determination. Job-level pay determination includes job analysis, job evaluation or job worth determination, salary structure placement, incentive pay determination, and performance management.

JOB ANALYSIS

The first step in determining base pay under any pay system is to understand the job and its requirements. This process is formally called job analysis, which is sometimes accompanied by a job description or job summary.

The depth of the job analysis is dictated by time, economics, and whether the analysis will be used for purposes other than compensation. At one time job analysis was conducted for all positions; some organizations analyzed jobs on a regular cycle, such as every two to three years. Entry-level compensation specialists and/or HR generalists completed this work by interviewing incumbents or managers or reviewing completed structured questionnaires. In recent years this practice has fallen by the wayside as organizations have looked for ways to streamline their processes and reduce headcount.

Currently, most organizations have streamlined methods of analyzing jobs, including matching to position surveys, using prewritten job descriptions, requesting thumbnail descriptions of job duties and accountabilities, or analyzing job content only when the position is being evaluated or reviewed for compensation purposes. As job analysis has become more abbreviated, job description preparation has declined. Many organizations have eliminated job descriptions, or only prepare them if required or requested to do so. Others have moved to high-level job summaries, which outline key accountabilities with little specificity. However, companies with internal-worth job evaluation systems, described later, typically will use a proscribed format for job descriptions to ensure that all meaningful data are compiled.

Despite its decline, there is a role for job analysis, which provides meaningful information for staffing and recruiting and performance management, as well as compensation decisions. As Figure 6.3 indicates, there are a number of approaches to obtain job-analysis information, each of which has advantages and disadvantages.

FIGURE 6.3 Primary sources of job-analysis information.

Approach	Major Advantages	Major Disadvantages
1. Direct observation	■ Helps job analyst understand work being performed	■ Time-consuming
2. Individual interview	■ Not dependent on incumbent's written communication skills	■ Time-consuming
3. Group interview	■ Same as above, but less time-consuming to interview several incumbents at once	■ May inhibit individual response in group setting ■ May misclassify two jobs as one
4. Technical conference	■ Same as above	■ Same as above
5. Diaries/logs	■ Can provide complete picture of job	■ Time-consuming
6. Open-ended questionnaire	■ Quick turnaround time ■ Inexpensive ■ Flexible design ■ Can serve multiple purposes ■ Can support other job-analysis methods	■ Sometimes difficult to get them all returned ■ Limited usefulness with unskilled/semiskilled employees who have limited language skills ■ Incomplete/inaccurate response requires follow-up ■ Watch for inadequate responses or deliberate misstatements
7. Highly structured questionnaire	■ Can provide HR data for many purposes ■ Level of detail may aid credibility of results	■ Time-consuming ■ Expensive to develop or purchase

In any of its guises, job analysis is typically performed when a position is first created, or when job content changes in a substantial way. Streamlined job analyses are most common when an organization reorganizes, downsizes, or changes its overall scope and direction. Some jobs are so stable that the analysis remains stable over time, or only minimal revisions are required.

As corporate human resources departments downsize, many organizations have begun to shift the responsibility for job analysis from compensation to HR generalists to line management. This can create challenges when the compensation department requests specific information required for determining job worth, which line management or line HR have not gathered. Therefore, it is important to understand the depth of job analysis required for your organization under different circumstances.

JOB EVALUATION

In many organizations the job analysis phase is either very short, or in some cases, nonexistent. Therefore, the first visible step for many generalists or line managers is job evaluation. There are two major schools of job evaluation: market-driven systems and job-worth systems.

Market-Driven Systems

In a market-driven compensation system, the "going rate" for the position is the primary determinant of pay. (See Chapter 8 for further discussion on the subject.) Under this system, inequities can be created by labor shortages, which can drive up salaries substantially beyond their value to the organization. We have all experienced times that pay for a specific position has been inflated by scarcity or high demand, such as enterprise resource planning (ERP) programmers or project managers. A market-driven system is perfectly designed to manage and reflect pay escalation, as well as decreases in pay. In those cases where pay has moved dramatically either upward or downward, market-driven systems will yield results that are not reflective of perceived internal equity. As a result, line managers often struggle with implementation.

Market-driven systems should be monitored closely to track changes in pay. The move from one set of external comparisons to another can result in substantial changes in recommended pay levels. For example, not-for-profit organizations typically pay less than general industry for secretarial and clerical jobs. Changing the market reference point from services to manufacturing could imply that the whole compensation system is out of whack when it is not. With enough time and attention, inequities that arise from a market-driven pay system can be corrected. (See Figure 6.4.) However, line managers are often frustrated by inequities with the market, especially when a hot candidate for a hard-to-fill job is being recruited or when there are numerous long service employees in low market value positions.

Job-Worth Systems

In a job-worth system, the primary determinant of pay is the value of the job to the organization. In some cases, a job-worth system can result in pay differences from the external marketplace. Again, managers may struggle with implementation as they attempt to find a way to reflect the market without violating the spirit of the internal job-worth system. At one time, companies were attempting to find neutral ground between internally and externally driven systems, using complex multiple regression models. Over time, such systems have fallen into disfavor because of their administrative complexity. In addition, such systems mitigate the problems associated with either a purely market-driven or purely internally driven system; they do not eliminate them.

Job-worth systems typically grant points for the presence of various factors such as the skills required to perform the job, the effort required to achieve results, the

FIGURE 6.4 Key elements of a market-driven compensation system.

It is based on the "going rate" for a job.

The quality of external comparisons is critical.

External comparisons may not exist for all positions; in these cases, determining job worth is difficult and slotting may be required.

Pay levels can jump substantially in a particular year due to labor shortages; most organizations prefer to wait out these changes rather than immediately increasing pay.

A job's market value does not always reflect internal equity, so some organizations may be reluctant to pay competitively for scarce technology or knowledge.

number of employees supervised, and the size of the assets managed. At one time, many U.S. organizations used the same or largely identical factors to determine job worth. In Canada, pay-equity laws require the use of four generic factors: skill, effort, responsibility, and working conditions. A maximum number of points are available for each factor, leading to the name "point-factor system." As the needs of organizations have become more complex, more comprehensive job-evaluation systems have been developed to reflect overall organizational values and goals. Thus, job-worth systems with 10 or more factors are more common, as are points for strategic organizational goals such as quality, teamwork, and customer satisfaction. (See Figure 6.5.)

Differences between Market-Driven and Job-Worth Systems

Market-driven and job-worth systems yield different results. In the case of a discrepancy, internally driven job-worth systems will err on the side of maintaining internal equity, and external, market-driven systems will err on the side of reflecting how the outside world pays the position. Figure 6.6 demonstrates the differing results that can be yielded by the two systems.

The debate regarding the appropriateness of either system has gone on for some time. Internal-equity proponents speak about the scarcity of appropriate market data reference points and the need to address employees' ongoing efforts to compare worth internally. Market proponents point to the differences between internal job evaluation systems and the marketplace, with differences of 5 percent to 20 percent not uncommon. In the end, the key issue is to ensure that the final system meets the organization's needs. Seniority-driven companies with long service employees may benefit from the stability of an internally driven job-worth system. Organizations with

FIGURE 6.5 Key elements of a job-worth compensation system.

> **Results depend heavily on the factors selected and the weights used to evaluate these factors.**

> **Internal equity is more important than external market conditions.**

> **Each salary range encompasses a range of evaluated positions; positions within a pre-established range of points are considered to have the same value and are placed in the same range.**

FIGURE 6.6 Comparison of market-driven and job-worth compensation systems.

Market-Driven System

Senior Database Management: Analysis and Design	$66,300
Senior Budget Analyst: Planning and Analysis	$55,000

Job-Worth System

Job Title	Knowledge	Problem-Solving	Working Conditions	Total
		Ratings (Points)		
Sr. Database Mgmt.	50	50	10	110
Sr. Budget Analyst	50	40	10	100

■ Under the market-driven system, the jobs are placed one salary grade apart.
■ Under the job-worth system, the jobs are placed in the same salary grade.

higher turnover and numerous external hires may benefit best from a market-driven system. A key responsibility of those designing and/or managing a compensation system is to ensure that line managers do not attempt to pick and choose between the two approaches in order to obtain the most favorable results.

The Future Is Now

Because of the differing results between market-driven and job-worth systems, the majority of organizations have moved to a market-driven pay system. This has placed enormous emphasis on the need for accurate and timely external market comparison data. In addition, many organizations have begun to shift the responsibility for determining job worth to the line. In major organizations, including those with limited corporate or shared-services compensation staffs, local HR is required to determine the worth of the position by matching directly to databases of surveys or internal reference points. Organizations with managerial self-service models accompanied by extensive technological support often require managers to identify job worth through selection of a salary grade with only minimal oversight from HR.

Regardless of which kind of system is used, the results of a job evaluation will indicate the salary grade in which a job will be placed.

MARKET ANALYSIS

Whether an organization uses an internally or externally driven pay system, it is important to compare pay practices to the external market. Most organizations participate in regular surveys that gather data from a specific set of competitors and release overall averages on an annual basis. Typically, however, every position is not included. Those positions that are included (often called benchmarks) typically exist in most organizations with fairly similar responsibilities.

Salary surveys with national and geographic data may be purchased from numerous organizations, including all of the major consulting firms such as Mercer, Towers Perrin and Watson Wyatt. Most of the major survey providers have set up web-enabled access allowing for instantaneous access to data. However, companies often find that it is impossible to match all of their positions, and thus need to conduct custom surveys to gather specific information. (See Sidebar 6.1.)

Sidebar 6.1: Conducting a Salary Survey

Sometimes it is important to gather survey data on what local competitors are doing. Before beginning a custom survey, check to see if a survey already is conducted in the area; WorldatWork or local compensation and benefits groups can help identify existing surveys, saving organizations the time, effort, and expense of conducting their own. If a custom survey is necessary, the following steps can prove useful:

- Decide on the depth of the information that needs to be gathered and what jobs should be included. Asking about base salaries when total compensation data are needed will only provide part of the answer. Prepare job descriptions or summaries for each position to be surveyed.
- Contact the competitors with whom the organization would like to work. Selecting the wrong competitors in a market-driven system can be a major mistake, yielding results that are unusable. Volunteer to analyze data fully, in the format the survey participants would like to see, and promise a quick response in providing results. Often, an external

(continued)

Sidebar 6.1 *(Continued)*

consultant, who can guarantee confidentiality, can perform data analysis effectively. The use of a third party to gather and analyze data is essential in some industries where the exchange of salary data can give the appearance of collusion and raise antitrust issues.

- Ask for a wide range of data such as salary range minimums, midpoints, and maximums as well as current average pay levels and typical starting salaries. The more data that is collected, the better the chance of making a true comparison. If an organization has an average pay level that significantly exceeds the midpoint because of high tenure in a particular job, data on the typical starting salary for that job can help prevent a misleading comparison. It also is useful to ask about incentive targets, typical payouts, and descriptions of what incentive plans reward. If an organization pays for skills or knowledge, it should ask about the number of steps used by other organizations and the requirements to progress through each step. If an organization uses salary bands, it should ask about the range widths of each band used by other organizations.
- Be sure to "age" all collected data. Salary ranges summarized in November will probably change in January. Be sure to adjust appropriately to ensure that true apples-to-apples comparisons are made.
- Share the survey results quickly, including data from the organization conducting the research. Everyone appreciates a prompt reply, and responsiveness can help ensure that these organizations participate in future surveys.

Compensation departments at large organizations usually participate in a number of surveys annually, and are requested to participate in custom surveys on an ad-hoc basis throughout the year. Typically, organizations participate in annual market studies that often are tied to the end of the fiscal or calendar year. Published surveys have their own timelines that are set by the firm that compiles and analyzes the data.

SALARY RANGES

Salary range is one of the most important determinants of pay on a daily basis. Understanding the fundamentals of a salary range is critical.

Every salary range has a minimum, midpoint, and maximum. Some companies divide their ranges into thirds; others use quartiles. In all cases, the difference between the minimum and the maximum is often referred to as the "spread." The minimum and/or the lower portion of the structure are often used as the starting salary. Most compensation systems gear merit increases to move employees closest to, or within 10 percent of, the midpoint of the salary range. The maximum is the highest rate paid for a position in that grade. Employees above the maximum often are "red circled," meaning that their pay is frozen until salary-range adjustments place current salaries below the maximum. Employees hired below the minimum are referred to as "green circled" and often receive accelerated increases to move them into the range as quickly as possible.

Typically, salary ranges are reviewed and updated annually. Most often, the entire range is moved upward by a selected percentage, although in some cases organizations may elect to increase different salary grades by different levels to fine-tune their relationship to the market or to fix existing problems.

Regardless of range width, the midpoint is geared to the marketplace as much as possible. The focus on midpoints can often cause problems for line managers and employees, who rightfully look at the entire salary range as their pay potential. Many employees question why they are unable to move up in their ranges, or always are compensated at approximately the same place in the range. It is important to remember that in a market-driven system, an employee who is at the maximum of a 50-percent wide range is being compensated 25 percent more than the going rate for that job. (See Figure 6.7.) In a market-driven system, jobs are placed into grades based upon the market. The position is slotted into the grade with the midpoint closest to the market value of the position. In an internally driven system jobs are placed into grades based upon point values.

FIGURE 6.7 Example of salary ranges.

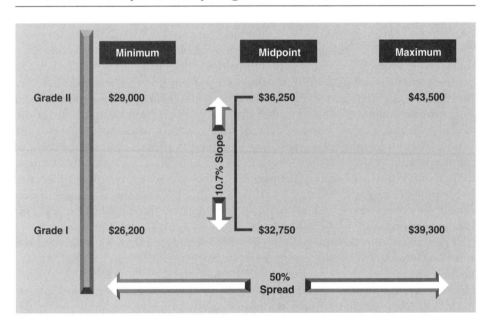

Organizations may try to tie the difference between each range midpoint (called the "slope") into the increases given to employees at the time of promotion. Thus, if the slope is 5 percent, an organization might try to give promotional increases of close to, or more than, that amount to ensure that promoted employees are not always paid at the minimum of their salary ranges. However, with the current trend toward wider salary ranges with midpoints that are 10 percent to 15 percent apart, this practice is less likely to occur. It is becoming more common to find that promoted employees receive a 10 percent increase, or an increase to the minimum of the appropriate salary range, whichever is higher.

In the late 1980s and 1990s, the move to market-based pay systems and the desire for flexibility caused many organizations to embrace salary bands, rather than traditional salary grades. Salary bands gained popularity as organizations attempted to overcome the difficulties created by traditional salary ranges. These difficulties include the following:

- Employees and supervisors tend to view salary ranges as a career ladder, thus creating ongoing requests for job re-evaluations or promotional increases for relatively small changes in job duties.
- Traditional salary ranges are seen as inflexible.
- It is difficult to keep salary ranges current with an ever-changing market.
- Salary ranges do not promote skill enhancement through lateral moves as readily as bands.
- There is a desire to reduce administrative burden associated with managing grades.
- The increase in organizational restructurings, such as mergers or divestitures, creates the need for flexible systems with little administration.

A quick glance at a salary band suggests that bands are simply very wide salary grades, because most bands are more than 100 percent in width. However, salary bands are fundamentally different from salary grades in several ways. Typically, organizations will use only a handful of salary bands, rarely more than 10. In some organizations, all pay grades have been collapsed into as few as five pay bands. In many systems, each position has its own "band within the band," reflecting its competitive market, often referred to as the competitive zone.

These changes raise the need for solid and ongoing communication. Thus, employees and line managers must be educated to understand that their salary band encompasses numerous positions, and that the most relevant comparison for the employee is the comparison to market, or their competitive zone. In some organizations, the competitive or market zone is defined as plus or minus 10 percent of the market; other organizations elect to target competitive pay with plus or minus 20 percent. For many line managers and employees, the relatively tight difference between beginning and ending of market reference points implies that pay opportunities have been decreased, in comparison to more traditional salary ranges. This misconception must be carefully managed.

The shift from traditional salary ranges to pay bands is a significant change, and must be thoroughly communicated. Even so, many organizations find that it takes as long as three or four years of ongoing communication and education before employees and supervisors clearly understand the new system. Often, many managers will desire to move back to a traditional salary range system simply because it is familiar to the manager. Although broad bands are still in use, the trend toward implementing broad bands has declined as the job market has cooled and the war for talent has become less prevalent. A common compromise is to use wide ranges of 50 percent or more and to attempt to manage pay within informal market or competitive zones rather than moving completely to bands.

At one time, it was common for companies to have different salary ranges for various types of positions, differentiating between nonexempt and exempt jobs, for example. Although this practice still exists, it is not in vogue in today's environment of teamwork and cooperation among employees of all levels. Where separate ranges exist, there often is an attempt to bridge the difference by designing salary grades that overlap. (See Figure 6.8.) However, different salary ranges for hourly and salaried positions are still very prevalent. In addition, it is not unusual to see different salary ranges for different business units or segments, although the trend is toward standardization to enhance transferability and ease managerial self-service.

FIGURE 6.8 Example of overlapping salary ranges.

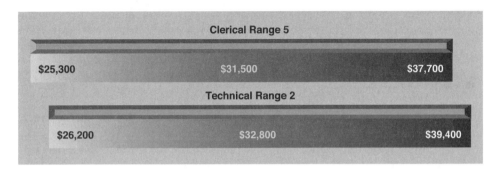

Salary ranges also are used to determine the size and frequency of merit increases. The most typical tool is a compa-ratio, which represents the individual's salary divided into the salary range midpoint. Many companies strive to have their consistently high-performing employees paid between 90 percent and 110 percent, or 95 percent to 105 percent, of the midpoint. To accomplish this, high-performing employees with low compa-ratios receive larger pay increases than high-performing employees with higher compa-ratios. This will move the high-performing employee's pay relatively quickly to the middle zone of the range. However, in organizations with very wide ranges and modest merit budgets of 2.5 percent, it is not uncommon for even a high-performing employee to take five years or more to reach the middle zone of the salary range.

Organizations using salary bands determine merit increases based upon the width of the competitive zone and the organization's overall merit budget. Similar to salary ranges, organizations will attempt to keep employees' competitive pay within a specified percentage of the relative market. High performers receive larger increases than average performers. Employees whose pay is significantly less than market will be targeted for special increases, which are sometimes incorporated within the overall merit budget, and most often treated through a special adjustment budget targeted to address market inequities. Although this concept works well in the abstract, it has become increasingly difficult to manage pay effectively with merit budgets of 2 to 3 percent. Automated tools ease the administrative burden, yet still leave the most onerous task untouched—determining how to allocate a limited budget. HR generalists play a critical role in helping line managers to make sound merit decisions, rather than succumbing to the pressure to simply offer everyone the same amount. Forced distributions and forced ranking are becoming prevalent as companies try to control costs and top-grade talent at the same time.

COMPETENCIES

The 1990s saw the emergence of competencies as a new tool in HR's tool kit. Competencies reflect the bundled together skills, traits, and abilities that are required to help an organization reach marketplace success. Competencies can be created to reflect overall organization needs, or the specific technical skills required for a position or job family. At one time, many organizations experimented with competency-based pay systems, which moved employees through the salary range, or their salary band, based upon the acquisition of an increased level of proficiency within mission-critical competencies. However, the majority of organizations have moved away from competency-based pay because of the complexities inherent in such a system, and are instead focusing on using competencies as a key element in their selection systems, performance management systems, and employee development systems. Many organizations view the integration of competencies into a performance management system as competency-based pay.

INCENTIVE PAY

Incentive plans represent the best, most consistent method to pay for performance, enabling an organization to deliver targeted results while rewarding employees who are responsible for those results. Incentive plans can be designed to focus on three levels of performance: individual, team, and organization.

Individual incentives are the most prevalent, and they have been used for many years. At the same time, increasing numbers of organizations are recognizing team and group incentives as an effective way to build cooperation and reward teamwork. Team and group incentive plans will incorporate the same design parameters as plans for individuals, but they have the added complexity of measuring performance for a group of individuals rather than just one person.

DESIGN ELEMENTS

Regardless of the level being targeted, an incentive plan will include the following elements:

- *Eligibility.* This portion of the plan decides who is eligible to receive a payout and who is not included. Eligibility will include how long an individual needs to be employed at the organization, other criteria used to determine eligibility, and whether payouts will be given to people who leave the organization or otherwise become ineligible. Many HR managers have approved or recommended lateral transfers from one position to another, only to find out later that the new position is not incentive-eligible. Therefore it is important for HR generalists and line managers to understand incentive programs eligibility requirements. (For more information on transfers, see Sidebar 6.2.)

Sidebar 6.2: Comparing Total Compensation Packages

Helping people move along in their careers is one of most important—and rewarding—roles played by HR generalists. One component of this role is to ensure that an employee's total compensation remains appropriate when the employee changes positions. To make an appropriate analysis, consider the following questions:

- Is either position eligible for the incentive plan? If so, what is the amount of the potential payouts? Does eligibility or payout timing change?
- Are there any perquisites tied to either position that could change, such as use of a company car? How much do these perquisites add to the total compensation package?

- Does the new position require a move? What are the provisions of the organization's relocation policy? Are there different tax implications in the new location? Employees who are transferred between divisions sometimes find that their Social Security withholding starts again if the divisions are different legal entities. Some locations are subject to state or local income tax; others are not.
- Are there any special pay practices tied to either position that could change?
- What will the employee's new position in range be? Will this make the employee eligible for a merit increase sooner?
- Does this change affect eligibility for benefits? Eligibility for the pension plan or 401(k) plan?

- *Target payout.* Each plan sets a target payout level that often is expressed as a percentage of pay or midpoint, although it also can be expressed in terms of dollars. Sometimes there is a minimum or maximum amount that will be paid. Occasionally plans will specify that minimum payouts will occur even if the plan's performance requirements are not met. Such a design is rare, but is sometimes considered in organizations that are substituting incentive pay for merit increases or other increases in base pay. In such cases employees quickly begin to view minimum guaranteed payments as deferred base pay. A more effective approach is to fund the plan based on actual performance, and to set the funding at a level that requires stretch, but not impossible, performance levels. Maximum payouts are typically designed to control costs and prevent windfalls. (See Figure 6.9.)
- *Performance criteria.* The best incentive plans measure and reward behaviors that are specific, measurable, and within the participants' control. Designing plans that are within the participants' control often is the most troublesome part of developing or managing an incentive plan. In many cases, the behavior that managers want to encourage is beyond the employee's control.

  For example, many line managers desire to implement broad-based employee stock programs, feeling that organizational success will follow if all employees are focused on increasing the stock price. However, many employees do not perceive a clear line of sight between their own behavior and the company's stock price, and thus, such plans often fail to engage the hearts and minds of employees. In other organizations, such as high-tech or high-growth companies, stock ownership is a fundamental portion of the total rewards program. For example, PepsiCo's much-publicized SharePower program has been a success for many years. In addition, broad-based programs are difficult to implement in global organizations because of country-specific tax ramifications. Thus, broad-based stock programs remain in the minority.

  In some incentive plans, performance criteria consist of financial measures; in others operational measures such as the accomplishment of individual objectives are used. In addition, plans tied to the achievement of key goals such as customer satisfaction are increasingly prevalent. Often, plans will have financial and operational measures with a weight assigned to each. Many middle-management incentive plans base 50 percent of the payout on organizational performance against a financial objective and 50 percent on the manager's performance against assigned objectives.

FIGURE 6.9 Example of a target incentive award.

Job Level	Salary Range Midpoint	Target %	Incentive Award
10	$50,000	20	$10,000
11	$60,000	22.5	$13,500
12	$72,000	25	$18,000

- *Duration.* Each plan sets a time for measurement of performance and payment of bonuses. Typically, incentive plans are most effective when rewards are given soon after the results are measured, although longer time frames tend to be used for higher-level jobs. Management incentive plans generally are paid out annually, with ties to the organization's fiscal-year results. Lower-level employees, such as hourly workers, may have quarterly incentives. Typically, incentive plans are most effective when rewards are paid out as soon as possible after the results are measured. Many companies pay out incentives in separate checks to highlight the reward.

REASONS FOR FAILURE

Incentive plans typically fail when employees are not motivated or cannot influence results. Lack of motivation may be owing to a number of reasons:

- *Award size.* Awards that are too small will serve as irritants, not motivators. In general, 10 percent of pay is considered the smallest possible amount that can lead to changes in behavior. As merit budgets decline to the 2- to 3-percent range, this belief is being challenged and a 5-percent payout level is becoming more acceptable.
- *Plan complexity.* Any plan should be simple and easy to understand. Plans that measure three, four, or more things often fail, either because employees cannot understand what is expected or because employees perceive that their efforts in any one given area will not lead to a significant reward.
- *Control over results.* Incentives that are based on the wrong things can lead to an atmosphere of entitlement (i.e., rewards are "automatic") or windfalls (i.e., rewards are "unpredictable"), not motivation.
- *Senior-level support.* Senior managers may change their minds about what behaviors they want to motivate, or they may eventually come to believe that the

amount they are paying to motivate performance is too much. In some cases, managers will not want to oversee a plan that creates a total compensation package that is higher than their own. Each of these factors can lead to a plan that is not supported by senior management, and, thus, does not succeed.

Equally there are many reasons why employees may not feel that they can influence the results, including:

- The plan uses funding measures (such as Economic Value Added) that are complex, and difficult to measure.
- The company sets performance targets too high.
- A high-performing group or division reports into an underperforming business unit with business unit–wide performance incentive plan funding.

Incentive plans can be highly effective, but there are as many plans that underperform as plans that perform on target. Working closely with line managers and testing the plan to see how it fits the overall compensation program can minimize the risk of creating a plan that does not perform. Finally, incentive programs are more difficult to take out than to put in, therefore it is important that HR generalists spend time to think through the ramifications of implementing a plan.

MANAGEMENT OF PAY FOR PERFORMANCE

Some companies house the responsibility for performance management design work within the compensation department while others house the responsibility within the organizational development group. This reflects the unique role of performance management systems: to improve organizational performance while rewarding individual efforts. There are two key components to the compensation-related side of managing a pay-for-performance system: designing a merit increase matrix and overseeing salary management.

Designing a Merit Increase Matrix

Although the design of a merit increase matrix is sometimes centralized and performed by compensation specialists or experts, many organizations will request that HR generalists help develop merit guidelines or adjust an overall matrix to meet their business unit needs. Following are the major steps required to design and cost a traditional matrix:

- *Use published surveys to determine what size of increases other firms are giving.* World-atWork's annual *Salary Budget Survey* is an excellent source of information; large consulting firms and other regional organizations also produce surveys each year. Identify the appropriate comparison group for the organization by industry sector and location.
- *Select appropriate data sources, which consist either of projected merit budgets or average salary increases given in the past.* This data will serve as the starting point for employees who perform on target at the middle of their salary ranges, with compa-ratios between 90 and 100, or 95 and 105.
- *Analyze how performance distributions have been reported in the past.* Examine these distributions with respect to salary grade as well as by position in range.

- *Determine where the organization pays in relation to the market.* An organization with traditional salary ranges and high turnover will have many employees near the lower ends of its salary ranges. In addition, an organization that pays far below the market may need a higher-than-normal merit matrix to increase pay to the appropriate levels.
- *Prepare a first draft of the merit matrix, using as an external norm the increase for an employee in the middle of the salary range who is performing as expected.* Build the middle section first, including all employees in the middle of the range. Top performers should receive increases that are significantly higher than employees who are performing on target. Best practices research suggests that top performers should receive at least two times the amount given to average or on target performers, in order to create meaningful pay differentials over time. Employees who are significantly below performance expectations generally do not receive increases. Employees who are slightly below target may receive a nominal increase or in many organizations, no increase.
- *Build the other portions of the merit matrix, ensuring that employees who are below the midpoint receive increases that are the largest.* Do not worry too much about the actual amounts given at this point; there are likely to be two or three versions of this process before it is done.
- *Cost the matrix, calculating what the total dollars would be and the average increase given.* This calculation is based on the past distribution of ratings and the first draft of increases. Adjust as needed to meet the organization's overall budget. For an example of a completed merit increase matrix, see Figure 6.10.

It is increasingly common for HR to recommend an overall merit budget that is substantially higher than what the business is willing to fund. As a result, many companies prefer to start with the organization's budget and build a matrix that supports it. This

FIGURE 6.10 Sample merit increase mix.

Performance Rating	Position in Range before Increase			
	1st Quartile or Below	2nd Quartile	3rd Quartile	4th Quartile
Outstanding	9-10% 6-9 months	7-8% 9-12 months	5-6% 10-12 months	3-4% 12-15 months
Consistently Exceeds Standards	7-8% 8-10 months	5-6% 10-12 months	3-4% 12-15 months	2-3% 15-18 months
Meets Standards	5-6% 9-12 months	3-4% 12-15 months	2% 15-18 months	0
Does Not Fully Meet Standards	0-2% 12-15 months	0	0	0

SOURCE: Steven P. Seltz, CCP, and Robert L. Heneman, Ph.D., *WorldatWork How-to Series for the HR Professional*, 2004.

approach, although practical, obscures the real issue, which is the amount of money that truly needs to be spent to match the marketplace. An organization can never identify or fix its long-term compensation-related problems without calculating the true cost of an appropriate merit matrix. Hence, it is important for the creator of the merit matrix to work closely with the finance department to create a long-term plan for reaching market parity, as well as creating a merit matrix that is appropriate for the short term.

Overseeing Salary Management

Along with ensuring that salary increases are given on time and that performance appraisals are accurate and timely, it is important to ensure that overall salary levels are appropriate. Therefore, it is important once a year to review the equity of the organization, division, or group to determine if there are any pay problems that need resolution. Many companies complete this step concurrent with preparation of the merit matrix. The following steps may be taken:

- *Analyze the pay for all employees, sorted by salary level and job title.* Request the average salary, average compa-ratio, and number of people in each portion of the salary ranges. The report also should detail each person's salary, time of service, last performance rating, date placed in current position, position in range, last increase amount, and next increase date.
- *Scan the report for inequities.* An employee who has long-term service in the job and a solid performance history but is paid at the minimum of the range or at the bottom of his or her competitive zone should be considered for a special increase. In addition, look to see if individuals performing the same job are paid equitably. A report that can help identify problems lists position in range, sorted by sex and equal employment opportunity (EEO) code. Finally, look to see if there are any "compression" problems (i.e., too little difference between an individual's pay and that of his or her supervisor). Although the days of maintaining higher salaries simply because of supervisory responsibilities are over, compression problems must be reviewed and explained.
- Prepare an initial analysis of what kind of special pay adjustments are necessary to fix any inequities, including the amount of the increase and timing. Revise as necessary. Decide whether to request special pay increases all at one time, or whether they should be phased in at the time of service anniversaries or salary reviews.

This analysis is often combined with a diversity program analysis, which reviews actual or perceived inequities between various groups and/or individuals.

EFFECTIVE COMPENSATION MANAGEMENT

Every employee receives a paycheck and translates that paycheck into a lifestyle. Understanding an organization's compensation program is critical in developing HR strategies that help employees feel motivated, recognized, and rewarded. Failing to understand compensation can lead to a disjointed effort in human resources, which in turn can minimize an organization's overall success. (See Figure 6.11.)

A variety of HR programs exist to help support the basic mission of human resources: to attract, motivate, and retain an effective workforce. Compensation programs are just one element of fulfilling this mission. When compensation programs are developed,

FIGURE 6.11 Do's and don'ts of compensation.

Do:

- Anticipate that changes will occur regularly in the compensation system—salary ranges are reviewed annually along with merit budgets and incentive plans, and new programs are continually proposed.
- Expect to sometimes manage programs based on data and sometimes based on principles. Inequities will exist, and it is important to identify and minimize them.
- Read all documents that are distributed to employees about the compensation system.
- Ensure that the information provided is clear and specific (i.e., avoid vague explanations such as "compensation made the decision").
- Do consider all existing pay programs while designing a new type of program, such as a spot incentive plan.

Don't:

- Design a spot bonus or recognition program with a higher payout than the incentive system.
- Compromise on "principle-driven" compensation systems. It is essential to use consistent guidelines for all employees.
- Make compensation decisions in isolation without considering the interaction between compensation, benefits, and perquisites as important components of the organization's compensation philosophy.

administered, communicated, and managed in isolation, misalignment occurs and significant organization resources are spent without corresponding results. HR generalists are uniquely positioned to help bridge the potential gap because of their broad exposure to all facets of the organization as well as to employee perceptions and emerging issues. Thus, it is critical that HR generalists learn compensation basics.

A number of HR issues show up on all practitioners' "to do" lists. Work-family balance issues, effective team management, reducing turnover, and increasing employee commitment are examples of the myriad of employee-related issues that have reached the boiling point during the past few years. Although organizations are creating compensation and benefits programs that address these and similar issues, such programs are not yet as well understood and institutionalized as more traditional compensation programs, such as incentive plans. Therefore, many companies leap to pay as a solution for every employee relations problem. HR generalists can play an active role in ensuring organizational fit by carefully assessing whether new pay programs are an effective solution, or simply the easiest solution.

Changing organizational models and HR's desire to integrate fully into the business as a business partner have caused HR generalists to take on new responsibilities, including setting compensation strategies for divisions and business units. As line managers take on more responsibilities for activities that were previously in HR's domain solely, such as attending job recruiting fairs and determining starting salaries, they in turn are pushing HR generalists to focus more intently on ensuring that total rewards strategies are in sync. Thus, we can expect that HR generalists will face increased needs to understand and apply compensation principles. This move will help HR generalists to serve in a value-added capacity for their businesses, and truly serve as a business partner to line management.

7 Regulatory Environment: The FLSA and Other Laws That Affect Compensation Practices

One of the most important aspects of a compensation system is that it complies with existing laws and regulations, and that it be legally defensible in this era of litigation. It is critical for compensation experts and HR professionals to work closely to ensure that the organization's pay system is defensible and that everyone who works with compensation understands the relevant regulations. Figure 7.1 summarizes some of the existing laws that affect compensation practices, the most prominent (for pay program design purposes) being the Fair Labor Standards Act of 1938 (FLSA).

FAIR LABOR STANDARDS ACT OF 1938

The Fair Labor Standards Act of 1938 (FLSA) was born of the Great Depression and Franklin D. Roosevelt's "New Deal" administration. Roosevelt sent the bill to Congress in 1937 with a message that the United States should be able to give "all our able-bodied working men and women a fair day's pay for a fair day's work."

After a long, hard-fought battle, the FLSA was signed into law on June 25, 1938, and took effect on October 24, 1938. Its primary objective was workers' rights, and it was intended to eliminate detrimental working conditions, establish a minimum wage rate, and protect the educational opportunities of youth.

During his fireside chat right before the implementation of the act in October, Roosevelt commented that, with the exception of only the Social Security Act, the FLSA was the most far-reaching, far-sighted program for the benefit of the workers that had ever been adopted. He went on to say that, without question, this act started the United States toward a better standard of living and increased purchasing power to buy the products of farm and factory. Roosevelt then admonished some business leaders by saying that the American people should not let any "calamity-howling executive" with an income of $1,000 a day, who has been turning his employees over to

FIGURE 7.1 Compensation regulation.

Rule	Details	Governing Body
Railway Labor Act	Grants the right of non-managerial and airline employees in the private sector to bargain collectively with their employers on questions of wages, hours, and work conditions	National Mediation Board National Board of Adjustment
Davis-Bacon Act	Establishes wage and fringe-benefit standards for laborers and mechanics for federal public construction projects that exceed $2,000	U.S. Department of Labor
Walsh-Healey Public Contracts Act	Establishes wage, hour, overtime pay, child-labor and safety standards for employees of manufacturers or suppliers of goods for federal contracts in excess of $10,000	U.S. Department of Labor
Fair Labor Standards Act (FLSA)	Deals with minimum wages, overtime pay, equal pay for both sexes, child labor, and recordkeeping for employees engaged in interstate commerce or in production of goods for interstate commerce, or employed by an enterprise engaged in interstate commerce or production of goods for interstate commerce	U.S. Department of Labor
Equal Pay Act (EPA)	Prohibits wage differentials based on sex for employees engaged in commerce or in production of goods for commerce, or who are employed by an enterprise engaged in commerce or production of goods for commerce	Equal Employment Opportunity Commission (EEOC)

Title VII of the Civil Rights Act (Equal Employment Opportunity Act)	Prohibits discrimination based on race, color, religion, sex, pregnancy, or national origin for employers with 15 or more employees and whose business affects commerce; employment agencies; labor organizations engaged in an industry affecting commerce; the federal government; and the government of the District of Columbia	Equal Employment Opportunity Commission (EEOC)
Service Contract Act (SCA)	Establishes wage and fringe-benefit standards for employees of suppliers of services to the federal government in excess of $2,500	U.S. Department of Labor
National Foundation Arts and Humanities Act	Establishes wage and working-condition standards for professionals, laborers, and mechanics directly engaged in working on projects receiving funding from the foundation	U.S. Department of Labor
Age Discrimination in Employment Act (ADEA)	Prohibits job discrimination in hiring, firing, or conditions of employment against individuals aged 40 or older for employers of 20 or more individuals, employment agencies, and labor organizations	Equal Employment Opportunity Commission (EEOC)
Americans with Disabilities Act (ADA)	Prohibits discrimination against individuals with disabilities in employment, public services, public accommodations, and telecommunications for employers with 15 or more workers	U.S. Department of Labor (DOL) Equal Employment Opportunity Commission (EEOC) Federal Communications Commission (FCC)

(continued)

FIGURE 7.1 *(Continued)*

Civil Rights Act of 1991	Establishes two standards of discrimination under Title VII: disparate treatment and disparate impact	Equal Employment Opportunity Commission (EEOC)
Internal Revenue Code	Defines deductibility and tax treatment of compensation for all employees and all employers	Internal Revenue Service (IRS)
Securities and Exchange Commission (SEC) regulations	Regulate plans that provide employer stock to participants for all publicly held companies	Securities and Exchange Commission (SEC)
State laws	Affect minimum wage, hours, overtime pay, discrimination, and taxes for various employers	Vary by state

the government relief rolls in order to preserve his company's undistributed reserves, tell you that a wage of $11 a week is going to have a disastrous effect on all American industry. Roosevelt closed his comments about the FLSA by declaring that this type of executive is a rarity with which most business executives most heartily disagree.

Hence, the FLSA became the principal federal statute that affects the design of direct compensation programs. In the beginning, only about one-fifth of the working population was affected by the act, which established a minimum wage of 25 cents per hour and a maximum workweek of 40 hours, or $11 per week. In its current state, after several amendments over the years, the act now covers more than 90 percent of all workers in the United States and the current minimum wage is $5.15, but the maximum workweek is still 40 hours.

The most recent changes to the act, which took effect August 23, 2004, deal specifically with Section 541 (most commonly referred to as the white-collar exemptions). This section was last modified in 1975—when the salary levels were updated. In the early 1990s, an amendment was added that dealt with computer professionals, and, in 1997, the minimum wage was raised to $5.15. That is where it remains today. (See Figure 7.2.)

What Is the FLSA?

Congress enacted the Fair Labor Standards Act of 1938 (FLSA) to establish a floor for minimum wage, overtime, recordkeeping, and child labor for employers nationwide. When first enacted, this piece of legislation affected about one-fifth of the workforce. Today, after many amendments, the FLSA applies to more than 90 percent of the U.S. workforce.

Since it was enacted, a preponderance of case law has helped us to better understand the concept of the FLSA. However, recent amendments and interpretations

FIGURE 7.2 History of the minimum wage.

1938	1956	1974	1980	1991	1997
$.25	$1.00	$2.00	$3.10	$4.25	$5.15

by the courts have made it extremely important to understand the language of the FLSA. Moreover, because today's workforce and workplace are very different from what they were in 1938, it has become a challenge to comply with the FLSA while still meeting business needs. (See Figure 7.3.)

Who Does the FLSA Affect?

Today, the FLSA covers employers who are involved in interstate or foreign commerce. Coverage is broadly interpreted and includes nearly all employers of all sizes. Amendments in 1966 and 1974 expanded coverage to include more than 90 percent of the U.S. workforce. However, certain employees are considered exempt from the provisions of the FLSA. All other employees—designated as nonexempt—are subject to the provisions of the act. The classification topic area includes the tests used to decide who is included in which category.

The major provisions of the FLSA cover rules for:

- The determination of a minimum wage and a regular rate of pay to be used in the calculation of overtime.
- The determination of which activities shall constitute hours worked.
- Who is classified as exempt.
- Child labor restrictions.
- Recordkeeping requirements.

What Is Covered?

Minimum Wage

An amendment mandating the current minimum wage of $5.15 per hour was signed into law and became effective September 1, 1997. Employees under the age of 20 can be paid $4.25 per hour for the first 90 consecutive calendar days of employment. Certain full-time students, student learners, apprentices, and workers with disabilities may be paid less than the minimum wage under special certifications issued by the U.S. Department of Labor (DOL).

Tipped employees must be paid a cash wage of at least $2.13 per hour. This rule applies to employees who receive at least $30 per month in tips. However, if an employee's tips combined with the employer's contribution of $2.13 per hour does not equal the minimum wage of $5.15 per hour, the employer has to make up the difference to meet minimum wage.

Hours Worked

On any given day, hours worked are defined as the time when an employee begins or is required to be available to begin his or her principal activities of work until the

FIGURE 7.3 FLSA timeline.

1938	Section 13(a)(1) is included in the original FLSA. Later that year, 26 CFR Part 541 is issued.
1939	Duties test revised (Stein Report).
1949	Duties test revised (Weiss Report).
1954	Salary basis test updated.
1958	Salary levels revised (Kantor Report).
1961	Congress eliminates language limiting exemptions in retail to "local retailing capacity" to cover all retail and service enterprises. Employees in these positions can still qualify as exempt executive, administrative, or professional employees if they meet the qualifications for these exemptions, and Congress relaxes the duties tests solely to make it easier for such firms to meet the exemption requirements.
1966	Elementary and secondary schools are made subject to the FLSA. Teachers and academic administrative personnel are added to exemptions.
1972	Educations Amendments of 1972 make the Equal Pay provisions (Section 6[d] of the FLSA) applicable to employees who are otherwise exempt from Section (a)(1).
1975	Salary levels updated. This is intended to be an interim adjustment.
1981	Revisions to increase the salary levels issued at the end of the Carter administration are stayed indefinitely by the incoming Reagan administration.
1985	Based on petitions from industry groups, the U.S. Department of Labor (DOL) begins a more comprehensive review, leading to an Advanced Notice of Rulemaking that reopens the public comment period and broadens the review to all aspects of the regulations.
1990	New regulations permit computer systems analysts, computer programmers, software engineers, and similarly skilled professional workers to be exempt, including those who are paid on an hourly basis if they are paid at least six-and-one-half times the minimum wage ($4.25), or $27.63 per hour.
1992	Exemption requirements are modified to state that otherwise exempt public sector employees do not lose exempt status under a regulated public sector pay and leave program that requires partial-day or hourly deductions from pay for employee absences not covered by accrued leave, or for budget-driven furloughs.

1996	Congress increases the minimum wage to $5.15 per hour and enacts Section 13(a)(17) exemptions for computer employees. The compensation test for computer-related employees is capped at $27.63 per hour.
1999	The General Accounting Office (GAO) recommends that the Secretary of Labor perform a comprehensive review and update of the FLSA.
2002	The DOL convenes a series of stakeholder meetings, asking for suggestions from more than 40 interest groups representing employees and employers.
2003	The DOL proposes rules to define and delimit the exemptions for executives, administrative, professional, outside sales, and computer employees. Public comments on the proposed rules are accepted. The Senate and House vote on measures to block the DOL from making changes to the FLSA. Congressional and labor union opponents cease efforts to block changes.
April 20, 2004	The DOL announces final changes to the *Federal Register*. Changes include overtime protection for all white-collar employees who earn less than $23,660, blue-collar workers, police officers, firefighters, paramedics, emergency medical technicians, and licensed practical nurses. There also is an exemption for a "highly compensated employee" who earns $100,000 in total compensation but may not meet all of the exemption standards as an executive.
April 23, 2004	The DOL publishes the FairPay Final Regulations in the *Federal Register*, with an effective date of 120 days after publication (August 23, 2004).
August 23, 2004	FairPay Final Regulations in the *Federal Register* become effective. All organizations, from this date, have two years to become compliant with the new rules.
August 23, 2006	All organizations need to abide and be in compliance with the FairPay Final Regulations in the *Federal Register*.

conclusion of the employee's workday (when he or she ceases to perform the principal activities of work). The workday does not necessarily equate to the "scheduled workday" for the employee and can be much longer or shorter.

Workweek

A workweek is defined as seven consecutive, regular, recurring 24-hour periods totaling 168 hours. This is the unit of measurement used to determine compliance with minimum wage and overtime provisions. Each workweek stands alone and:

- Can begin on any day of the week and at any hour.
- Does not have to coincide with the duty cycle or pay period, or with a particular day of the week or hour of the day.

- Once the beginning and ending time of the work period is established, it remains fixed regardless of how many hours are worked within the period.

The beginning and ending of the work period may be changed, provided that the change is intended to be permanent and is not designed to evade the overtime requirements of the act.

Rates of Pay and Overtime Calculations

The U.S. Supreme Court defines the regular rate of pay as the hourly rate paid to the employee for the normal, nonovertime workweek for which he or she is employed. Under the FLSA, the regular rate is the hourly rate. However, the act does not require employers to compensate employees on an hourly basis.

The FLSA allows that the regular rate of pay should be an hourly measurement of all straight-time compensation received by the employee. The types of compensation that may be excluded from the hourly measurement define this "regular rate":

- Discretionary bonuses and gifts.
- Reimbursement for expenses.
- Payments for idle time.
- Benefit plan contribution.
- Overtime premiums.
- Third-party payments for insurance, pensions, etc.

The FLSA also explains how to calculate hourly rates of pay for multiple specific payment contexts (e.g., piecework rates and commissions). Calculated rates of pay are used for specifying overtime payments for nonexempt employees. While the general rule for overtime pay requires employers to pay at least one-and-one-half times the regular rate of all hours worked over 40 in each week, the FLSA provisions provide specifics for varying cases.

Child Labor Restrictions

The FLSA was created in part to protect the educational opportunities, health, and well-being of the youth in the United States. The following provisions apply to the employment of children ages 14 to 16, and provide rules for the periods and conditions of employment:

- Work must be outside of school hours.
- The child may not work more than 40 hours in any one week when school is not in session, and no more than 18 hours when school is in session.
- The child may not work more than eight hours in any one day when school is not in session, and no more than three hours when school is in session.
- The child may only work between the hours of 7 A.M. and 7 P.M. in any one day, except during the summer when the evening hour is extended to 9 P.M.
- There is a special exemption for minors ages 14 and 15 who are employed to perform sports-attending services at professional sporting events.

The provisions ban children ages 14 to 18 from work considered hazardous. The following provisions define "hazardous work":

- Occupations in or about plants or establishments that manufacture or store explosives or articles containing explosive components.

- Coal mine occupations.
- Logging occupations and occupations in the operation of any sawmill, lath mill, shingle mill, or cooperage stock mill.
- Occupations involved in the operation of power-driven woodworking machines.
- Exposure to radioactive substances and ionizing radiations.
- Occupations in the operation of power-driven meat processing machines.
- Occupations involved in the operation of bakery machines.
- Occupations involved in the manufacture of brick, tile, and kindred products.
- Occupations in roofing operations.

Recordkeeping Requirements

Employers are required to keep records on wage, hours, and other information for all employees. These records must be saved for at least three years. No particular form is required with regard to exempt employees, but the following records must be maintained for nonexempt employees:

- Name, home address, and birth date if the employee is younger than 19 years.
- Sex and occupation.
- Hour and day when the workweek begins for the employee.
- Regular hourly pay rate for any week when overtime is worked.
- Hours worked each workday and total hour worked each workweek.
- Total daily or weekly straight time earnings.
- Total overtime pay for the workweek.
- Deductions or additions to wages and total wages paid each pay period.
- Date of payment and pay period covered.

What Is Not Covered?

The FLSA does *not* require payment for time not worked, such as:

- Vacation pay.
- Holiday pay.
- Severance pay.
- Sick pay.
- Meal periods of 30 consecutive minutes or more, duty free.
- Rest periods (breaks) of more than 20 consecutive minutes if the employee is completely relieved of duties.

Also, the FLSA does *not* mandate:

- Time clocks to record hours worked.
- Any kind of special pay or premiums for Saturday, Sunday, holiday, or sixth- or seventh-day work.
- That employees be paid at premium rates for hours worked in excess of eight hours per day, unless the employer chooses and is eligible for the 8/80 option.
- That an employer differentiate between exempt and nonexempt employees in any way other than minimum wage payments, overtime premiums, and records.
- The beginning and ending of a workweek in terms of starting and stopping on a specific calendar day or time.

- Meal period and rest period requirements (note: the FLSA *does* mandate the ability to exclude such time in the calculation of regular rate).
- The frequency in which employees receive compensation (note: though the FLSA does not set specific intervals for pay periods, most states have regulations regarding the timing and payment of wages).
- Limitations on the number of hours in a given workweek (note: the FLSA does state that any work in excess of 40 hours in the workweek will be treated as overtime and compensated at one-and-one-half times the regular rate of pay).
- Pay for travel time outside of normal work/business hours when travel is overnight.
- That employers compensate employees on an hourly-rate basis (note: earnings may be determined on a piece-rate, salary, commission, or other basis, but the FLSA *does* require that overtime calculations be based on the regular *hourly* rate of pay.

Did You Know?

- Tipped employees can be paid a minimum wage of $2.13 per hour as long as they receive at least $30 per month in tips.
- Some states have higher minimum wage standards than those required by the FLSA. If a company employs workers in those states, it must comply with state regulations.
- The workday does not necessarily equate to the "scheduled" workday for the employee and can be much longer or shorter.
- The FLSA does not require employers to compensate nonexempt employees on an hourly basis.
- "Waiting to be engaged" and "engaged to wait" have different meanings under the FLSA.
- Employees must be paid for all hours worked, even if a supervisor did not approve the time worked.
- Employees must be paid for the time they take to seek medical attention for on-the-job injuries.
- Children 14- to 16-years-old cannot start work before 7 A.M. and must end work by 7 P.M. on any given workday (the time is extended to 9 P.M. in the summer).
- The FLSA requires employers to save pay records for at least three years.
- Meal and rest periods are not required under the FLSA.
- The FLSA does not mandate overtime pay for more than eight hours worked in one day. State and local regulations or union contracts may require daily overtime rates.

Classifications

Exempt and Nonexempt Categories

The FLSA divides all employees into two categories: exempt and nonexempt. Exempt employees are not covered under the same rules as nonexempt employees.

Therefore, classifying employees into one of these categories is of major importance when deciding how to implement the FLSA statutes.

There are five categories in which a worker may qualify as exempt:

- Executive.
- Administrative.
- Professional.
  - Learned.
  - Creative.
- Computer.
- Outside sales.

Employees classified in one of these categories are exempt from minimum wages, overtime, and certain recordkeeping requirements. It is important to note that job titles alone do not determine if a position is exempt or nonexempt. Employers need to be cognizant of employees' job duties to ensure that those duties fall within the range of the regulations.

Determination Tests for Classifying Exempt Employees

The DOL has established tests to determine whether an employee fits into one of the five exempt groups. An employee is exempt from minimum wages and overtime regulations only if he or she meets all the requirements of one of the following tests. These tests apply to the employee—not the position title assigned to the employee. As such, the employee can be exempt one week and nonexempt the next depending on the actual job duties performed each week.

On April 23, 2004, the DOL published new Section 541 requirements for exemption. The new regulations replaced the previous short and long duties tests and salary requirements, putting in place a new, standardized test of each exemption and an increase in weekly salary for the salary basis. The regulations became effective on August 23, 2004—120 days from the date they were published in the *Federal Register.* Essentially, there are three tests: the salary limit test, the salary basis test, and the duties test.

Salary Limit Test

For an employee to be classified exempt, he or she would need to pass the salary limit test. This test is the same for all exemption categories (except for outside sales and positions in American Samoa), and has been raised from $155 per week (per the long test) to $455 per week, equaling $23,660 per year.

Basically, any employee earning less than $23,660 in base salary per year is classified as nonexempt, regardless of the duties performed. By increasing the floor to $455 per week, employers can utilize a more realistic salary in determining exemption.

The salary limit is effective for the United States and its territories, except for American Samoa. For employees in American Samoa, the lower limit is $380 per week.

Salary Basis

Salaried means an employee is paid the full salary for the workweek regardless of the number of hours worked, the quality of work, or the quantity of work during that workweek. The only exception to this is for the computer professional.

Duties Tests

Under the pre-August 2004 regulations, each exemption had both a short and a long test to determine exemption. Under the FairPay Final Regulations, the DOL established a standard test for each exemption.

One of the most conspicuous changes to the exemption tests was the complete elimination of the "time spent on nonexempt work" provision. Found in the long test section of the old regulations, employers tried to apply that percentage of work when using the short tests.

Did You Know?

- There are five categories in which a worker may qualify for exempt status under the FLSA.
- An employee can be exempt one workweek and nonexempt the next workweek without moving into a new position.
- If an exempt employee is docked for partial pay absences, it may jeopardize the status of the position (defined as under the same manager in the same region).
- An employee—not the position—must meet *all* requirements of the applicable exemption test to be exempt from minimum wage and overtime regulations.
- The minimum salary requirement for computer professionals is $455 per week or $27.63 per hour, which is six-and-one-half times $4.25, not six-and-one-half times the current minimum wage of $5.15.
- There is no salary test for outside salespeople.
- Many computer professionals do not qualify for the professional exemption solely based on job content, but they may meet the administrative exemption.
- There is a $100,000 salary test for employees who perform one or more exempt duties (e.g., executive, administrative, professional).

Rates of Pay

Regular Rates of Pay

The U.S. Supreme Court defines "regular rate" as the hourly rate actually paid to the employee for the normal, nonovertime workweek. The regular rate under the FLSA does not require employers to compensate employees on an hourly rate basis. The law defines the regular rate by listing the types of compensation that can be excluded:

- Discretionary bonuses and gifts.
- Reimbursement for expenses.
- Payments for idle time.
- Benefit plan contributions.
- Overtime premiums.
- Third-party payments (for insurance, pensions, etc.).

The regular rate should be an hourly measurement of all straight-time compensation received by the employee, including agreed-upon wages and any additional earnings that cannot be excluded from the regular rate per the FLSA. This includes production bonuses, travel time, set-up time, etc. The FLSA does not require employers to compensate employees on an hourly basis. However, the FLSA *does* require that, for purposes of overtime pay, the straight-time earnings must be converted to an hourly equivalent.

Types of Pay

The FLSA does not require the employer to compensate an employee by one particular method. Employers have commonly used one of many different types of pay.

Hourly Rate

An employee is compensated on a predetermined hourly rate of pay. The regular rate would be calculated like the preceding example.

Piece-Rate

There are two acceptable methods for computing overtime for employees paid by the number of pieces they produce:

- Average piece-rate earnings over the workweek.
- Paying "piece-and-one-half" for the pieces produced during overtime hours.

The regular rate is computed by dividing the total earnings (except statutory exclusions) by the total number of hours for which earnings were paid. If the piece-rate earnings constitute straight-time pay for all hours worked, only additional half-time needs to be paid for hours over 40.

Piece-and-one-half may be computed for pieced produced during overtime hours. The intent is to simplify the method of computation while ensuring that employees receive substantially the same amount for overtime worked.

Day Rates and Job Rates

An employee is paid a flat sum for a day's work or for doing a particular job without regard to the number of hours worked in the day or at the job. If the employee receives no other form of compensation for services, the regular rate is determined by totaling all the sums received at such day rates or job rates in the workweek and dividing by the total hours actually worked. The employee is entitled to extra half-time pay for all hours worked in excess of 40 in the workweek.

Salary Basis

An employee who is paid solely on a weekly salary basis has a regular rate that is calculated by dividing that salary by the number of hours for which the salary was intended to compensate.

When a salary covers a pay period longer than a workweek (e.g., monthly, bi-weekly, or semimonthly), it must be broken into its workweek equivalent.

Fixed Salary for Fluctuating Hours

Work hours fluctuate from week to week and the employee receives a salary that remains constant. The employee has entered into an understanding with the employer that the fixed amount is straight-time pay for whatever hours the employee is called upon to work in any given workweek and the employee will receive half time (0.5 times straight-time pay) for any hours worked in excess of 40 in a workweek. To simplify, it is the payment of straight time (which can also be the regular rate) *plus* half time for hours worked in excess of 40.

This salary arrangement is permitted by the FLSA when there is a clear and mutual understanding between employer and employee that the fixed salary is compensation (apart from overtime premiums) for the hours worked each workweek, rather than for 40 hours or some other fixed weekly work period. The fluctuating workweek method of overtime payment may not be used unless the salary is large enough to ensure that there will never be a workweek in which the employee's average hourly earnings fall below the minimum wage.

Employees Working Two or More Rates

Different pay rates occur when an employee is engaged in multiple jobs that provide different agreed-upon base rates during any one workweek. These base rates must be at least the equivalent of the applicable minimum wage. The regular rate for that workweek is calculated as the weighted average of those different rates.

Commission Payments

Payments for hours worked must be included in the regular rate, whether based on a percentage of total sales, sales in excess of a specified amount, or on some other formula. This is true whether the commission is the sole source of the nonexempt employee's compensation or is paid in addition to a guaranteed salary or hourly rate, or on some other basis. It also is true regardless of the method, frequency, or regularity of computing, allocating, and paying the commission. It does not matter if the commission earnings are computed daily, weekly, biweekly, semimonthly, monthly, or at some other interval. If the commission is paid on a basis other than weekly, and the payment is delayed for a time past the employee's normal payday or pay period, the employer is not excused from including this payment in the employee's regular rate for the period covered.

Commissions Paid on a Workweek Basis

Commission is paid on a weekly basis and is added to the employee's other earnings for that workweek (except overtime premiums and other payments excluded as provided by the FLSA). The total is divided by the total number of hours worked in the workweek to obtain the employee's *regular rate* for purposes of overtime calculations. The employee must be paid extra compensation and one-half of that regular rate for each hour worked in excess of 40 hours in the workweek.

Deferred Commission Payments

The calculation and payment of the commission cannot be completed until after the regular payday for the workweek in which the commission was earned. In this case, the employer does not include the commission when originally calculating the *regular rate* for that workweek. When the commission can be computed and paid to the employee, the employer then recalculates the regular rate by including the commission for the workweek in which it was earned versus paid.

If it is not possible or practical to allocate the commission to a particular workweek(s) of the commission period, another reasonable and equitable method must be adopted.

Did You Know?

- The regular rate of pay isn't necessarily an employee's hourly wage.
- Travel time, production bonuses, and set-up pay all must be included when calculating the regular rate.
- An employee can be paid based on the work he or she produces and not on the number of hours it takes to complete the job.
- There are two types of pay rates based on salary for nonexempt employees.
- Employees paid on a "fixed salary for fluctuating hours" actually have their regular rate go down the longer they work. This salary method cannot be used unless the salary is large enough to ensure no workweek dips below minimum wage requirements.
- Employees can be compensated at two or more rates by the same employer in the same workweek.
- Employees who are compensated at two or more rates by the same employer in the same workweek have their regular rate for that workweek calculated by weighted average.
- Under the FLSA, a commission payment paid other than weekly that is delayed from the normal pay period does not excuse the employer from including this payment in the employee's regular rate.
- It does not matter whether commission earnings are computed daily, weekly, or by some other interval.
- Employers must recalculate the regular rate for the periods that deferred commission payments cover.
- An employer can choose to allocate commissions over the workweek or by the hour depending on the circumstances.

Overtime

Overtime and Regular Rates of Pay

The FLSA does not require employers to compensate employees on an hourly rate basis. Earnings may be determined on a piece-rate, salary, commission, or other basis, but, in such cases, the overtime compensation due to employees must be computed as an hourly rate. This hourly rate must be recomputed each workweek based on the regular rate for that specific workweek.

Remember: The regular rate means the rate at which the employee is actually employed. It may not be less than the statutory minimum wage. Special premiums are *not* included in the regular rate calculation as long as these premiums are at time and one-half.

Special (or overtime) premiums would be compensation provided for hours worked in excess of a daily or weekly standard. These include:

- Premium pay for hours in excess of a daily or weekly standard.
- Premium pay for work on Saturdays, Sundays, and other "special days" (i.e., holidays or sixth and seventh days of rest for those who typically work Saturday or Sunday in their regular schedule).
- "Clock pattern" premiums, which include payment for work outside what is determined to be the basic, normal, or regular workday (not exceeding an eight-hour maximum).

Time of Overtime Payment

The FLSA does not require overtime compensation to be paid weekly. The general rule is that overtime compensation earned in a particular workweek must be paid on the regular payday for the period in which such workweek ends. When the correct amount of overtime compensation cannot be determined until after the regular pay period, FLSA requirements will be satisfied if the employer pays the overtime compensation as soon as is practical.

- Payment may not be delayed for a period longer than is reasonably necessary for the employer to compute and arrange for payment of the amount due. Under no circumstances may payment be delayed beyond the next payday after such computation can be made. When retroactive wage increases are made, retroactive overtime compensation is due at the time the increase appears in the employee's paycheck.

Overtime Calculation

The FLSA does not permit averaging of hours over two or more weeks, even if the average of the two workweeks is within the 40-hour maximum.

If an employee works 30 hours in one week and 50 hours in the next, the employee must receive overtime compensation for the 10 hours worked in the second workweek over the 40-hour maximum set by the statute.

The individual work schedule and timing of wage payment does not affect this standard. This also is true for piecework and commission-based employees. For purposes of computing pay under the FLSA, the workweek may be established for a plan or other establishment as a whole, or different workweeks can be established for different employees or groups of employees.

There is a notable exception to the 40-hours-in-one-week maximum. In health care settings, the 8/80 rule may be used. This rule allows the amount of hours in two weeks to be combined, but any hours over 80 are eligible for overtime.

Hourly Rate Employee Overtime Calculation

The employee is compensated on a predetermined, agreed-upon hourly rate of pay. If more than 40 hours are worked in a workweek, any hours over the initial 40 are paid at one-and-one-half times the regular rate

Nonexempt Salaried Employees Overtime Calculation

An employee who is paid solely on a weekly salary basis has a regular rate that is calculated by dividing that salary by the number of hours for which the salary was intended to compensate.

Day Rates and Job Rates

Employees who earn day or job rates are paid a flat sum for a day's work or for performing a particular job, regardless of the number of hours worked in the day or at the job. These employees receive no other form of compensation for services. The regular rate is calculated by totaling all the sums received at such day rates or job rates in the workweek and by dividing by the total hours actually worked. The employee is entitled to extra half-time pay for all hours worked in excess of 40 in the workweek.

Two or More Rates

When an employee works two or more different types of work with different pay rates in a single workweek for the same employer, the regular rate for that workweek is the weighted average of such rates.

Piecework Calculations

There are two methods of calculating overtime payments for piece-rate overtime hours:

- Average piece-rate earnings over the workweek, or paying "piece-and-one-half" for the pieces produced during the overtime hours. The regular rate is computed by dividing total earnings (except statutory exclusions) by the total number of hours for which earnings were paid. If the piece-rate earnings constitute straight-time pay for all hours worked, only additional half-time need be paid for work over 40.
- Piece-and-one-half may be computed for pieces produced during the overtime hours. The intent is to simplify the method of computation while ensuring that employees receive substantially the same amount for overtime work.

Commissions in Overtime Calculations

Commissions Paid on a Regular Weekly Basis

The regular rate is calculated by adding the employee's other earnings for that workweek (except special premiums and other payment excluded as provided by the FLSA) and dividing by the total number of hours worked in the workweek to obtain the employee's regular rate for the purposes of overtime calculations. Then, the employee must be paid extra compensation at one-half of that rate for each hour worked in excess of the applicable maximum-hours standard.

Deferred Commission Payments

If the commission calculation and payment cannot be completed until after the regular workweek payday, the employer may disregard the commission in computing the regular hourly rate until the amount of commission can be determined. Until that is done, the employer may pay compensation for overtime at a rate of not less than one-and-one-half times the hourly rate paid the employee, exclusive of the commission. If it is not possible or practical to allocate the commission on a workweek basis, some other reasonable and equitable method must be utilized. The following methods have been recommended by the DOL:

- Allocation of equal amounts to each week.
- Allocation of equal amounts to each hour worked.

When the commission can be computed and paid, additional overtime compensation must be included in the payment. To calculate this additional overtime compensation, the commission should be allocated over the workweeks for the period during which it was earned. The employee then receives additional overtime compensation at not less than one-half the new regular rate for each workweek in the period in which the employee worked in excess of 40 hours.

Overtime Pay and Special Cases

In certain special cases (e.g., hospitals and nursing homes), an employer can use more than 80 hours in a two-week period rather than 40 hours per week. This 8/80 rule allows for greater scheduling flexibility in a two-week period, but does require paying overtime for all hours over eight worked during any given workday.

Remember: Always check whether state and local regulations are more generous than the federal statute.

Common Problems in Computing Overtime

Overlapping Workweeks

Overlapping work time when a change of workweek is made can make computing overtime tricky. The beginning of a workweek may be changed for an employee or a group of employees if the change is intended to be permanent and is not designed to evade the FLSA's overtime requirements. A change in the workweek necessarily results in a situation in which one or more hours or days will fall (or be counted in) both in the "old" workweek and the "new" workweek.

Thus, if the workweek for an employee in the old workweek began at 7 A.M. Monday and in the new workweek begins at 7 A.M. Sunday, all the hours worked from 7 A.M. Sunday to 7 A.M. Monday will be both the last hours of the old workweek and the first hours of the new workweek for the pay period of the workweek change.

Retroactive Pay Increases

When a retroactive pay increase is granted to an employee, it increases the regular rate of pay for the employee for the period of its retroactivity. Therefore, if an employee is awarded a retroactive increase of $2 per hour, under the FLSA the retroactive increase of $3 would apply to each overtime hour the employee worked during the period for which the retroactive pay applies.

A retroactive pay increase in the form of a lump sum for a particular period must be prorated back over the hours of the period to which it is allocable to determine the resultant increase in the regular rate, in precisely the same manner as a lump-sum bonus.

Overtime Averaging by Pay Period

The FLSA does not permit averaging of hours over two or more workweeks, even if the average of the two workweeks is within the 40-hour maximum. For many employers, a biweekly or semimonthly pay period may be the norm. In those instances, it is not permissible for the employer to blend the hours from one workweek into the other, even if the wages are all paid in the same pay period.

Exclusions from Overtime Payment

The following are excluded from use in the rate of pay when creating calculations for overtime payments:

- Discretionary bonuses.
- Pay for certain idle hours.
- "Call back" pay.
- Payment for hours not worked.
- Profit-sharing, thrift, savings plans.
- Gifts, holiday, and special occasion bonuses.
- Stock options.

Did You Know?

- The FLSA requires that straight-time earnings be converted to an hourly equivalent for purposes of overtime pay.
- There are two acceptable methods of computing overtime for piece-rate employees.
- The FLSA requires employers to pay all nonexempt employees not less than one-and-one-half times the regular rate for all hours worked over 40 in each workweek.
- The FLSA has no limitation on the number of hours an employee may work in a given workweek.
- Nothing in the FLSA relieves the employer of its obligations under a collective bargaining agreement.

(continued)

- Earnings may be determined on a piece-rate, salary, commission, or other basis, but, in such cases, the overtime compensation due to employees must be computed as an hourly rate.
- Overtime payments may not be delayed for a period longer than is reasonably necessary for an employer to calculate the amount due.
- Discretionary bonuses are excluded from the calculation of the regular rate of pay for overtime purposes.
- The FLSA does not permit averaging of hours over two or more weeks, even if the averaging is within the 40-hour maximum.
- Individuals paid a day rate or job rate are entitled to extra half-time pay for all hours worked in excess of 40 in the workweek.
- In special cases, such as hospitals and nursing homes, employers can use an 80-hour standard over a two-week period versus the statutory 40 hours in a single workweek.
- The FLSA does not allow employees to carry over hours from one workweek to the next.
- Overlapping workweeks and retroactive pay increases are common computing problems for overtime.

The FLSA/FMLA Interplay

An employee's exempt status may be jeopardized in light of changes in the way the court approaches interpreting pay deductions in relation to the Family and Medical Leave Act of 1993 (FMLA).

Basic FMLA Provisions

The FMLA was enacted as a federal law in February 1993 and became effective for most employers in August 1993. The FMLA provides for unpaid, job-protected leave to eligible employees so they may care for their families or themselves under specified family and personal medical conditions.

The FMLA provides eligible employees with up to 12 weeks of unpaid leave in a 12-month period for:

- The birth, adoption, or foster care placement of a child.
- Care of a spouse, son, daughter, or parent with a serious health condition.
- Care for an employee's own serious health condition that causes an inability to work.

If an employee qualifies and has unused FMLA leave time, an employer cannot deny FMLA leave except under very specific situations.

The FLSA and FMLA Regulatory Background

If an employee is otherwise exempt from minimum wage and overtime requirements of the FLSA, providing unpaid FMLA-qualifying will not cause the employee to lose the FLSA exemption. Subsequently, an employer may make deductions from the employee's salary for any hours taken as intermittent or reduced FMLA leave within a workweek without affecting the employee's exempt status. The DOL regulation provides the following examples of deductions employers can and cannot make, consistent with exempt status:

- An employer cannot make pay deductions for absences to a lack of available work.
- An employer cannot make deductions for absences occasioned by jury duty, testimony as a witness, or temporary military leave, but may offset any amounts received by the employee for these services against the salary otherwise due.
- An employer can make pay deductions for absences of a day or more (full days) due to personal reasons other than sickness or disability.
- An employer can make pay deductions for absences of a day or more (full days) due to sickness or disability (or work-related accidents) if such deductions are made under a bona fide sickness or disability policy.
- An employer can make deductions for penalties imposed in good faith for violations of safety rules (of major significance).
- An employer can make deductions for violations of workplace conduct of a day or more (full days) if the violation was against written policy.
- An employer is not required to pay full salary in the employee's initial week of employment (can pay a prorated salary) or last week or employment (due to termination).
- An employer is not required to pay the full salary for weeks in which an employee takes unpaid FMLA leave.

The effect of making a deduction, which is not permitted under the aforementioned scenarios, depends on the facts of the particular case. During several decades, the regulatory facts and circumstances test in the provisions meant that no single deduction or deduction policy could wholly determine exempt status. These regulatory facts and circumstances have supported that an "occasional deduction for partial-day absences, as opposed to a regular pattern of such deductions, would not defeat an employee's exempt status except in the workweek the deduction was made."

Special Calculations

Employers can use special calculations for salaried nonexempt employees who are paid on a fluctuating workweek. Employers can modify the salary agreement for an employee who is on FMLA leave. An employee on a fluctuating workweek is paid a set salary regardless of the number of hours he or she works. Any hours over 40 in the workweek are compensated at half-time. If an employee is on FMLA leave and the employer does not want to continue compensating the employee for the full salary, the salary can be changed to an hourly equivalent so the employee is paid for actual hours worked. Any hours worked in excess of 40 would be paid at time-and-one-half for the duration of the leave. The employer who chooses this modification must be consistent in applying this change to all employees who have fluctuating workweeks and are on FMLA leave.

Court Rulings

Present Approaches in Court Interpretations

Newer court interpretations look at partial-pay docking as a rationale for losing exempt status. The issue is one of interpreting how absence from the workplace should be credited toward leave time. While the DOL interpretation has not changed, the evolving workplace and various court decisions are calling the DOL position into question.

In the past, a loss of exempt status was limited to the actual docking of pay. A single deduction would not change one's status, as long as it was an isolated, non-recurring event.

Employees covered under the FMLA are required to make and maintain records pertaining to their obligations under the FMLA, in accordance with FLSA record-keeping requirements and FMLA regulations. Employers must maintain records for at least three years and make them available upon request for inspection, copying, and transcription by the DOL. The FMLA applies the compensable hours of work standard of the FLSA when determining whether an employee has worked 1,250 hours. If an employer fails to maintain adequate records of the hours worked, the DOL and courts will presume the employee has satisfied the 1,250 hours service requirement.

Safe Harbor

Under the August 23, 2004, FLSA provisions in the salary basis test, exemption may still apply if the employer can show, among other things:

- A deduction was inadvertent.
- A deduction was made for a reason other than lack of work.
- There is a policy in place to pay on a salary basis, and that policy and corresponding recordkeeping procedures are communicated (i.e., distribution of policy upon hire, employee handbook, company intranet).
- An improper deduction was reimbursed in a timely fashion.
- If an employer is found to have made an improper deduction of an exempt employee's salary, exemption loss is restricted to:
  - The period in which the improper deduction was made.
  - Only the employee who received the improper deduction.
  - Only employees working for the same manager making the deduction.

Did You Know?

- An employer can make partial-day deductions from an exempt employee's paychecks for leaving work early without jeopardizing their exempt status under the FLSA.
- An employer can make pay deductions for exempt employee absences of a day or more for personal reasons other than sickness or accident.
- An employer cannot make pay deductions for absences caused by lack of available work for exempt employees.

- An employer can make pay deductions for absences of a day or more for sickness or disability if such deductions are made under a bona fide sickness or disability policy.
- If an employer fails to maintain adequate records for the number of hours worked by an employee, the DOL and courts will presume that the employee has satisfied the 1,250 hours of service requirement under the FMLA.
- Employers who have covered employees must maintain records for at least three years and make them available for inspection under the FMLA.

FLSA Violations and Penalties

The DOL's Wage and Hour Division is responsible for enforcing the FLSA. The FLSA provides that authorized representatives from the Wage and Hour Division may conduct an audit to investigate and gather data regarding wages, hours, and other employment conditions and practices. Employers may not retaliate against employees who exercise their FLSA rights, and employees cannot voluntarily waive their FLSA rights.

Employers who violate the FLSA's minimum wage and overtime provisions are subject to both civil actions and criminal prosecution. Civil actions include:

- Civil suit by the DOL to collect unpaid minimum wages and overtime due employees, plus an equal amount as liquidated damages.
- Civil suit by the DOL to enjoin further violations. The DOL can request the court to enjoin the interstate shipment of goods produced in violation of the FLSA and can request back pay for affected employees.
- Injunction.

Criminal prosecution by the Justice Department includes:

- Conviction that may result in fines of up to $10,000 per violation, and, for second-time offenders, imprisonment of up to six months per violation.
- Barring of federal contractors from federal contract work if found guilty of willful violations.

Violation-Related Definitions

Willful Violation

"Willful" applies to situations in which the employer should have known or clearly should have sought out advice from the DOL or counsel before implementing the plan or program that is found to be noncompliant. A willful violation occurs when an employer knows its conduct is prohibited under the FLSA or shows reckless disregard for FLSA requirements. An employer's conduct will be considered "knowing" if the DOL had earlier advised the employer that its actions were unlawful. The willful violation provision also applies if the employer should have inquired further into whether its conduct was in compliance with the FLSA and failed to do so.

Repeated Violations

A repeated violation is established when an employer has a prior finding against it by the DOL, court, or another tribunal with authority to make such a finding. A prior finding could be established if the employer has failed to file an appeal or if an appeal has been concluded. A multiestablishment employer can be fined for violations at different establishments under its control.

Good Faith Defense

An employer may escape back pay or liquidated damages liability if it relied in good faith on a written interpretation of the FLSA from the Wage and Hour Division. An employer may reduce its liquidated damages liability by showing it had a good faith defense based on other sources for its belief that it was not violating the FLSA. An employer's good faith is not a defense to an action for an injunction.

Statute of Limitations

Actions to enforce nonwillful violations must be started within two years of the cause of the action. Actions to enforce willful violations must be started within three years of the cause of action.

Effect of Improper Deductions from Salary

There are few instances in which an employer can deduct from an exempt employee's salary. If an employer makes improper deductions and it is determined that the employer did not intend to pay the employee on a salary basis, the employee could lose the exemption. The factors considered in these instances include, but are not limited to:

- Number of improper deductions (especially compared to employee discipline issues).
- Time period.
- Number of employees affected.
- Geographic region of employees affected (the DOL looks for patterns by using geographic regions).
- Number of managers making improper deductions.
- Geographic region of managers making improper deductions.
- A policy permitting (or prohibiting) improper deductions clearly communicated by the employer.

The employer might not lose the exemption if the improper deduction was inadvertent or an isolated case.

What Prompts an Audit?

There are three ways in which the DOL prompts an audit.

Employee Complaint

Employee complaints to the DOL are probably the most common reason for an audit. When an employee feels taken advantage of, he or she may call the local DOL office and register a formal complaint. Even if the employee's complaint has no merit, DOL auditors will review information that extends beyond the complaining employee's records.

Random Audit

The intention of the random audit by the DOL is similar to the use of sampling for quality. The DOL looks at several employment sites to establish the compliance level.

Industry/Geographic Target

Two examples:

- The fast food industry is periodically targeted, especially for child labor compliance issues.
- Geographic targeting can be seen when there are large numbers of immigrants and the DOL is looking for minimum wage and overtime, as well as recordkeeping requirements.

Common FLSA Violations

Compensatory Time Off

For the majority of employers, there is no such thing as compensatory time off for nonexempt employees. The simplest way to ensure FLSA compliance is to pay nonexempt employees for all hours worked in the week that they are worked. If those hours exceed 40, the employer should pay the appropriate overtime premium for all such hours.

Failure to Pay for Unauthorized Hours Worked

Telling an employee to leave his or her workstation for lunch and to not show up early or leave late does not reduce an employer's responsibility. The FLSA specifies that an employer must pay an employee for all hours the employer "suffers, permits or allows" the employee to work.

Bonus Pay Exclusion from Regular Hourly Rate

With the growing interest in variable pay, at-risk pay, gainsharing, lump-sum merit bonuses, etc., it is critical that legal counsel and/or the DOL be consulted before a plan is implemented. An audit is not the time to discover that an employer has not included bonus earnings in the regular rate of pay. There is a strong likelihood that the DOL would consider this not only a violation, but a willful violation of the FLSA provisions.

Failure to Pay for All Recorded Hours

A risk of using time clocks is that employees do not clock in at precisely the shift start time. The time represented on the official time card versus the time for which the employer actually pays the employee may differ and serve as an area of contention. Even for those companies that do not use time clocks, if the practice is to not pay for lunch time but an employee only records his or her "start" and "stop" times, the official record of time will differ from the actual hours paid.

Inaccurate Records

Inaccurate records can occur in many ways. Failure to pay for all recorded hours is one way that time records are inaccurate. Employees making changes, supervisors altering records, lost records, someone else recording (or punching in) for another employee, are all ways that recordkeeping can become suspect. Care must be taken to ensure that all recording of time and payment of nonexempt employees is handled correctly. Remember: These are legally required documents.

Employee Misclassification

The DOL will take great care to confirm the criteria an employer used to establish exemption. In actuality, the DOL is looking for attempts by employers to avoid the overtime penalty.

Improper Payment for Break Time

Any break of 5 to 20 minutes must be considered hours worked. Breaks that last more than 20 minutes are not hours worked. Bona fide meal periods of 30 minutes or more are not hours worked.

On-Call Time

When the employer requires an employee to be on-call and the employee is not free to pursue the majority of his or her normal nonwork activities, the on-call time is considered hours worked.

Training Time

The hours spent in training and some amount of study time must be considered hours worked if one of the following occurs:

- The time spent in training is during the regular work hours.
- Any job-connected work is produced during training.
- The training is considered a requirement for the ongoing employment relationship (i.e., training is not voluntary).

Travel Time

A nonexempt employee traveling on company business must be paid within the framework of the FLSA provisions. Many employers think that nonexempt employees are grateful for the opportunity to travel and have the company pay for the airplane ticket. This innocent misperception could prove embarrassing.

Did You Know?

- Employees cannot voluntarily waive their FLSA rights.
- Employers who violate the minimum wage and overtime provisions of the FLSA are subject to both civil and criminal prosecution.
- The FLSA is subject to both civil and criminal prosecution.
- Civil action includes inhibiting interstate shipment of goods and can require back pay for affected employees.
- Criminal prosecution includes imprisonment for second-time offenders and the barring of federal contractors from federal contract work if found guilty of willful violations.
- A willful violation occurs when the employer knows its conduct is prohibited under the FLSA or shows reckless disregard for FLSA requirements.
- A repeated violation occurs when an employer has a prior finding against it by the DOL court or another authoritative agency.
- An employer may reduce its liquidated damages liability by showing a good faith defense.
- An employer's good faith is not a defense to an action for an injunction.
- If an employer is found to have a nonwillful violation of the FLSA, wages and penalties can be calculated back over the past two years.
- If an employer is found to have a willful violation of the FLSA, wages and penalties can be calculated back over the past three years.

SHERMAN ANTITRUST ACT OF 1890

The Sherman Antitrust Act of 1890, as amended, prohibits every contract, combination, or conspiracy in restraint of trade and allows for the imposition of substantial penalties for violations thereof. Named after Sen. John Sherman, the act was proposed to address growing concern over the rapidly increasing prominence of large corporations, corporate trusts, and business combinations in the U.S. economic landscape toward the end of the nineteenth century. Set forth as Title 15, §§ 1–7 of the U.S. Code, the Sherman Act is based on Congress' constitutional power to regulate interstate commerce and was enacted at a time when the only similar laws were state statutes governing intrastate business.

Though the Sherman Act had immediate potential to aid the Federal government in addressing concerns over increasing corporate power, its potential was not realized for several years. Initially, Supreme Court decisions effectively prevented its use by the Federal government. Thereafter, Congress gradually put in place the supporting legislation and agencies necessary to successfully challenge anticompetitive activities. This building process began in 1904 when President Theodore Roosevelt launched his "trust-busting" campaigns and the Supreme Court found in favor of the Federal government, dissolving the Northern Securities Company.

The Sherman Act's reach increased during the Taft and Wilson administrations with the enactment of the Clayton Antitrust Act and the establishment of the Federal Trade Commission in 1914. Further, the addition of supplementary legislation, such as the Robinson-Patman Act during President Franklin Roosevelt's administration, continued to improve the Federal government's ability to challenge corporate actions on antitrust grounds. Finally, as federal antitrust agencies began broadening their interpretations of the antitrust statutes in the 1980s and 1990s, antitrust enforcement reached new heights, beginning with the 1982 breakup of the AT&T monopoly and culminating with the widely publicized Microsoft case, which ended in 2002.

Virtually since its inception, antitrust has been controversial. Proponents have seen it as a preserver of competition and a protector of consumers, while critics have viewed it as being based on flawed economic assumptions and as a destroyer of free markets and property rights. Figure 7.4 provides a summary of these conflicting views.

Although the law prohibits contracts or conspiracies that result in trade restraint, the specific practices that are illegal are not spelled out in the law. Instead, they are left to the courts to decide, based on the facts and circumstances of each case. For example, the Supreme Court decided long ago that contracts or agreements that restrain trade "unreasonably" are prohibited, with the definition of "unreasonable"

FIGURE 7.4 Conflicting views of antitrust.

General Views of Supporters
- The historic goal of the antitrust laws is to protect economic freedom and opportunity by promoting free and open competition in the marketplace.
- Combinations, trusts, and monopolies tend to restrict output, and thus drive up prices.
- Antitrust prohibits business practices that unreasonably deprive consumers of the benefits of competition, resulting in higher prices for inferior products and services.
- Antitrust laws protect competition.
- Antitrust laws protect consumers.
- Certain agreements and exchanges of information between competitors are frowned upon.
- Antitrust laws preserve economic freedom and our free-enterprise system.

General Views of Critics
- The Sherman Antitrust Act was never intended to protect competition as such.
- It was a protectionist act designed to shield smaller and less-efficient businesses from their larger competitors, all at the expense of consumers.
- Breaking up large companies and preventing mergers damages the free market and raises prices for consumers.
- Only government, not private business, can create monopolies and legal barriers to entry.
- Antitrust violates property rights and destroys economic freedom.
- Antitrust is immoral, as it punishes the successful for being successful.
- Antitrust laws are fluid, nonobjective and often retroactive, punishing a company for an action that was not legally defined as a crime at the time of its commission.
- Antitrust is based on a static and unrealistic view of the market.
- A narrow definition of the "relevant" market can make any firm a "monopolist."
- Business rivals and their allies wield antitrust law in the political arena.

being left to the courts to decide. Some practices, such as price fixing, have been declared unreasonable per se.

Enforcing Antitrust

Antitrust enforcement primarily is handled by two government agencies: the Antitrust Division of the Department of Justice (DOJ) and the Federal Trade Commission (FTC). The DOJ concerns itself primarily with "conspiracies," "monopolies," and the like, while the FTC directs its attention to "unfair trading practices" in pricing, sales practices, etc.

These two antitrust organizations operate in a somewhat different fashion. The DOJ by itself cannot issue an order to impose a penalty. It must initiate a suit through the courts. The defendant may demand a jury trial. The FTC, however, is an autonomous administrative agency: It is complainant, judge, jury, and prosecutor all in one, and it can issue its own cease-and-desist orders. At no time is there a jury trial in an FTC procedure.

In either type of antitrust action, the defendant may appeal the verdict to higher courts. However, in a case that may involve thousands of pieces of evidence in the form of vouchers, receipts, purchase orders, etc., the courts tend increasingly to rely on "expert" government testimony as to what is "unfair" or "monopolistic." The Supreme Court, in particular, usually upholds the government's case.

DAVIS-BACON ACT OF 1931

Under the provisions of this act, passed in 1931, federal contractors and their subcontractors are to pay workers employed directly upon the site of the work no less than the locally prevailing wages and fringe benefits paid on similar projects. The Department of Labor maintains a very helpful web site with more detailed information related to this act located at http://www.dol.gov/dol/compliance/comp-dbra.htm.

NATIONAL LABOR RELATIONS ACT

The National Labor Relations Act (NLRA) of 1935 was enacted with the intention of creating a better environment for collective bargaining. The NLRA was created to provide a more equitable environment for labor and management dispute resolution, and covers all employers involved in interstate commerce (with the exceptions of airlines, railroads, agriculture, and the government). The NLRA guarantees the right of employees to select or reject third-party representation, as well as the rules for bargaining in good faith and controlling against unfair labor practices. The enforcing agency of the NLRA is the National Labor Relations Board (NLRB). It is interesting to note that neither the federal courts nor the U.S. Department of Labor have jurisdiction in matters concerning the NLRB.

WALSH-HEALEY ACT

The Walsh-Healey Act, passed in 1936, provided general employment regulations for employers holding manufacturing or supply contracts with the Federal government in excess of $10,000. While originally requiring payment of overtime rates (time-and-one-half) for hours worked in excess of 8 per day or 40 per week, the law was amended in 1986 to eliminate the requirement to pay overtime rates after eight hours in a work day. Although the law requires employees to be paid the minimum prevailing manufacturing wage established by the Secretary of Labor, the secretary has, as a result of litigation, issued the minimum wage as the "prevailing" wage since the 1960s. The law also established certain child labor and safety standards. The U.S. Department of Labor (DOL) is the enforcing agency for the Walsh-Healey Act.

SERVICE CONTRACT ACT

Passed in 1965, the Service Contract Act applies to federal contracts for services in excess of $2,500 and requires service contractors to pay minimum wages and fringe benefits as established to be prevailing by the Secretary of Labor. As with the Davis-Bacon Act, pay scales are based upon "prevailing" wages, which is typically interpreted by the government as union equivalent wages and benefits in the local labor market. The act also includes certain safety standards. The U.S. Department of Labor is the enforcing agency of the Service Contract Act.

Recordkeeping and posting requirements, government investigations and hearings, court actions, and blacklisting of violators have been established as enforcement mechanisms for the Davis-Bacon, Walsh-Healey, and Service Contract Acts.

ANTI-DISCRIMINATION LAWS

The Federal government enacted a number of statutes in the 1960s that were designed to ensure the fair treatment of specific segments of the population in regard to their rights as individuals and employees. The most important of these are the Equal Pay Act of 1963 and Title VII of the Civil Rights Act of 1964.

Equal Pay Act of 1963

As early as World War II, the National War Labor Board was created as the arbiter of salary disputes between labor and management. In 1942, it issued an order for salary adjustments to "equalize the wage or salary rates paid to females with rates paid to males for comparable quality and quantity of work on the same or similar operations." A bill requiring "equal pay for comparable work" performed by males and females was introduced in Congress in 1945 and rejected, as were several similar bills for the next 18 years.

The Equal Pay Act, which prohibits gender-based compensation discrimination, was successfully enacted in 1963. Specifically, the act prohibits an employer from discriminating "between employees on the basis of sex by paying wages to employees . . . at a rate less than the rate at which he pays wage to employees of the opposite sex . . . for equal work on jobs that require equal skill, effort, and responsibility, and are performed under similar working conditions." There are, however, four exceptions (affirmative defenses). Unequal payments can be based on (1) a seniority system, (2) a merit system, (3) a system that measures quantity or quality of production, or (4) any other factor aside from sex.

The act, an amendment to the Fair Labor Standards Act, was originally enforced by the Wage and Hour Division of the Department of Labor, and employers subject to the FLSA were subject to the provisions of the Equal Pay Act as well. In 1979, the Equal Employment Opportunity Commission (EEOC) became the enforcing agency.

Plaintiffs who file lawsuits under the Equal Pay Act must show that they are paid less than a person of the opposite sex for doing substantially equal work (in the same job family) that requires substantially equal skill, effort, and responsibility and is performed under similar working conditions. Once the *prima facie* case has been established, the burden shifts to the employer to prove that the pay difference is based upon a seniority system, a merit system, a system that measures earnings by quantity or quality of production, or some other factor aside from gender.

The bottom line of the Equal Pay Act for pay program design and administration is that if, on the average, men and women are paid different rates when they perform work that is substantially the same, these differences must be shown to be attributable to one of the "allowable differences."

The effects of the Equal Pay Act have been far-reaching and include the revision of employee benefit programs to eliminate gender-based differentials, greater emphasis on written job descriptions, greater emphasis on job-content-oriented procedures for assignment of pay grades and ranges to specific jobs, and greater emphasis on written policies and procedures.

Title VII of the Civil Rights Act of 1964

The most comprehensive of the civil rights statutes, this legislation was created to prohibit discrimination by employers on the basis of race, color, religion, sex, or national origin, in the hiring, firing, training, compensation, or promotion of employees. On the last day of debate, sex was added as a prohibited basis of discrimination, creating overlap with the Equal Pay Act.

For cases subject to this overlap on sex-discrimination in pay, the Senate added the Bennett Amendment that (ambiguously) states, "It shall not be an unlawful employment practice under Title VII for any employer to differentiate upon the basis of sex in determining the amount of the wages or compensation paid to employees of such employer if such differentiation is authorized by the provisions of the Equal Pay Act." Regardless of how the amendment is interpreted, differences in pay may be defended if attributable to work that is not substantially equal, or is based on seniority, merit, or quantity and quality of work.

The Civil Rights Act is enforced by the EEOC, which was created by the act. Virtually all employers with 15 or more employees are covered.

Employees who file lawsuits under the act must demonstrate either "disparate treatment" or "disparate impact." Under "disparate treatment," the plaintiff must prove that the employer deliberately discriminated, based on the employee's race, color, religion, national origin, or sex. If this is done, the employer must demonstrate a legitimate nondiscriminatory basis to justify the practice; then, in order to prevail, the employee must prove that any such "justification" is just a pretext for discrimination.

Under "disparate impact," the employee must establish a *prima face* case showing adverse impact on a protected class. Then the employer must validate the challenged practice by demonstrating a business necessity for the practice and proving that no alternative exists that would produce a less adverse impact.

The bottom line of Title VII for pay program design and administration is that pay programs should produce pay rates that treat all classes of employees similarly, and any differences should be attributable to job-related, defensible causes (seniority, performance, and the like). Case law resulting from litigation under Title VII created the concept of "bona fide occupational qualifications" (BFOQ). This concept specifies that job qualifications imposed by employers must be defensible and necessary in order for an employee to perform the job.

Age Discrimination in Employment Act of 1967

The Age Discrimination in Employment Act, passed in 1967 and amended in 1978 and 1986, protects workers aged 40 and older from employment discrimination. While it prohibits discrimination in all terms and conditions of employment, it has been applied principally in cases involving retirement, promotions, and layoff policies.

The purpose of the act is to "promote employment of older persons based on their ability rather than age, to prohibit arbitrary age discrimination in employment, and to help employers and workers find ways of solving problems arising from the impact of age on employment."

The law prohibits mandatory retirement (with some exceptions, generally involving public safety), limiting or classifying employees in any way related to their age (such as with maturity curves), reducing any employee's wage in order to comply with the act, and indicating any preference based on age in notices of employment. Individual state laws sometimes are more restrictive than the federal law.

The act applies to employers of 20 or more persons, as well as to federal, state, and local governments. Employment agencies serving covered employers, and labor unions with 25 or more members, are also included under the provisions of the act.

There are several statutory exceptions to the ADEA:

- Bona fide executives who are entitled to $44,000 per year or more in retirement benefits from employer contributions. Also, there is a mandatory retirement age of 65 that is allowed.
- Elected (or high level appointed) officials in the government are not covered.
- Bona Fide Occupational Qualifications (BFOQ), which can be defined as an occupational qualification that is reasonably necessary to the normal operation of the employer's business. Employers may discriminate on the basis of age if it is reasonably necessary.
- Seniority systems.

The EEOC has been charged with the enforcement of the act since July 1979. The plaintiff must prove that he or she is a member of a protected group and that he or she has been adversely affected by a personnel policy or action (*prima facie* case). Once this is established, the burden shifts to the employer, who may argue that the adverse treatment occurred on the basis of considerations other than age or that the decision or policy was *rightly* based on age (e.g., if age is a BFOQ for the job).

Executive Order 11246

This Presidential Order, signed by President Johnson in 1965, requires companies holding federal contracts or subcontracts in excess of $10,000 not to discriminate in their employment practices (which include pay practices) on the basis of race, sex, religion, or national origin, and to take affirmative action to ensure that their employment decisions are made in a nondiscriminatory manner. For service and supply contracts in excess of $50,000, contractors must also develop and implement written affirmative action plans that include goals and objectives of increasing minority and female participation in their workforce.

The Executive Order is enforced by the Office of Federal Contract Compliance Programs (OFCCP) in the U.S. Department of Labor, which investigates complaints of discrimination and also conducts on-site compliance reviews to determine federal contractors' compliance with the Executive Order mandates.

Vocational Rehabilitation Act of 1973

The act covers persons employed by, or seeking employment from, federal departments and agencies or businesses performing federal contract work in excess of $2,500. Recipients of federal assistance are also protected from discrimination based on any mental or physical disability that substantially limits one or more major life activities. Section 503 of the Act applies to private industry and Section 504 applies to institutions receiving federal grants. Discrimination in employment is prohibited in all terms and conditions of employment, which certainly includes compensation.

The act is enforced by the OFCCP, which requires covered employers to utilize affirmative action to employ and advance qualified handicapped individuals. The act also requires employers "to make reasonable accommodation to the known physical or mental limitations of an otherwise qualified, handicapped applicant, employee or participant." Further, the act requires the elimination of physical barriers, to ensure that the "facility is readily accessible to and usable by qualified handicapped individuals."

Charges under the act proceed in exactly the same way as Title VII. If, for example, a human capital policy or action has an adverse effect on a handicapped person, the employer must then show that the adverse treatment was based on considerations other than the handicap (e.g., seniority or performance) or that the handicap was a legitimate basis for such policy or action. This last defense is rare in compensation cases.

Vietnam Era Veterans Readjustment Act of 1974

The Vietnam Era Veterans Readjustment Act requires companies holding federal contracts or subcontracts of $10,000 or more to take affirmative action and not to discriminate in the employment and advancement in employment of qualified special disabled veterans and veterans of the Vietnam era.

The act is also enforced by the OFCCP, which investigates complaints and checks for compliance with the act during on-site investigations.

Americans with Disabilities Act of 1990

The Americans with Disabilities Act (ADA) of 1990 was enacted to include any company involved in interstate commerce with 15 or more employees. The act is enforced by the EEOC and dictates that the charge of discrimination must by filed within 180 days of the alleged discriminatory act.

A disability can be defined as an impairment that substantially limits or restricts a major life activity such as hearing, seeing, speaking, breathing, performing manual tasks, walking, caring for oneself, learning, or working. Any employee or job applicant who meets the following criteria may be covered under the ADA:

- Has a physical or mental impairment that substantially limits one or more of the major life activities.
- Has a record of any such impairments.
- Is regarded as having such impairments.
- Is associated with anyone having such impairments.
  - This provision is designed to protect any qualified individual, whether or not they are disabled, from disability-related discrimination.

It is important to note that the individual must be qualified for the job and must be able to perform the essential functions of the job. Essential functions can be defined as those functions that include the following criteria:

- Reason the position exists is to perform the function.
- Limited number of other employees available to perform the function.
- Degree of expertise or skill required to perform the function.

Under the ADA, if an employer can reasonably accommodate a request by a disabled employee (or applicant), the person is required to accept it. A reasonable accommodation is any change or adjustment to a job or work environment that permits a qualified applicant or employee with a disability to participate in the job application process, to perform the essential functions of a job, or to enjoy benefits and privileges of employment equal to those enjoyed by employees without disabilities. It is a violation of the ADA to fail to provide reasonable accommodation to the known physical or mental limitations of a qualified individual with a disability, unless to do so would impose an undue hardship on the operation of the business. Undue hardship means the accommodation would require significant difficulty or expense. The act specifies three criteria to measure reasonableness of accommodations:

- The size of the business.
- Number (or type) of facilities.
  - Budgetary constraints.
  - Type of operation.
  - The composition.
  - The make-up of the workplace.
- Nature and cost of accommodations.

8   Market Pricing

Being aware of prevailing wage rates in the external marketplace is critical to an organization's success. Employers need to keep a watchful eye on fluctuating pay rates and market price their jobs to maintain competitiveness. *Market pricing* is defined as the process of analyzing external salary survey data to establish the worth of jobs, as represented by the data, based upon the "scope" of the job (company size, industry type, geography, etc.). Market pricing has become the most common method of valuing jobs. More than 80 percent of companies use market pricing as their primary job evaluation method, surveys show. When jobs are market priced, the external market is the key determinant of job value that influences pay philosophy.

In this method, job rates are set based on the organization's best estimate of the typical wage rates in the external market place for that job. Job descriptions are used to match appropriate jobs. Market data are analyzed and benchmark jobs are arranged into a job-worth hierarchy. Jobs with no market data are slotted using relative worth.

With so many salary surveys available, where does one begin sorting through the maze of data to arrive at competitive market rates? Where can employers find sound, unbiased data that correspond to the jobs they need to market price? How should an organization communicate its pay program to employees? These seemingly never-ending questions can make a compensation analyst's head spin.

The successful execution of pay programs calls for a delicate balance between often-competing objectives; for example, the desire to attract and retain the best-qualified employees versus competitive constraints on labor costs. Organizations need to weigh the cost of the compensation program against other factors, such as being less competitive in the labor market to improve operating margins.

WHERE DO YOU BEGIN?

To maintain a competitive edge, organizations should make pay adjustments according to job market fluctuations. So, where should the compensation professional begin? First, the organization's pay structure should be examined. Salary structures are the foundation of most employee compensation programs. They represent job hierarchies and pay ranges within an organization. The salary structure may be expressed in terms of job grades, job points, pay lines, or any combination of these. These structures reflect the internal job value hierarchies and external job value relativity.

It is understood that the greater the relative worth of the job—as determined by job content and labor market analysis—the higher its pay grade and range. Pay grades and ranges are determined by market rates for comparable jobs (external competitiveness), in conjunction with management's judgment about the relative worth of the job's content (internal equity).

The process of developing a pay structure involves the following steps:

- Job analysis.
- Job documentation.
- Job evaluation.
- Collecting and analyzing labor market data.
- Establishing pay rates or ranges.

JOB ANALYSIS

Job analysis is a systematic process for obtaining important and relevant information about the duties and responsibilities that make up the job content. For compensation purposes, this includes clarifying the nature of the job, including tasks and responsibilities, as well as the level of work being performed. This also may include specific skill or knowledge levels required to perform all aspects of the job at a competent level. The first step is to determine what information needs to be collected. Data should include the extent and types of knowledge, skill, mental and physical effort, and responsibility required for the work to be performed.

The Many Uses of Job Analysis

- Document work methods and process for training purposes.
- Provide a basis for performance appraisal based on job-related standards.
- Identify job families, career paths, and succession planning.
- Identify qualifications required to perform work for purposes of job posting, recruiting, and candidate selection.
- Provide a basis for legal and regulatory compliance.
- Determine if a job should continue to exist in its present form.
- Develop a job-worth hierarchy.
- Identify organization design elements and success in planning processes.
- Reveal why one job may be more valuable than another in the market.

JOB DOCUMENTATION AND JOB DESCRIPTIONS

Job descriptions are narrative statements of the nature and level of work being performed by persons occupying a job, along with specific duties, responsibilities, and specifications necessary to perform the job. Increasing legislation and employee litigation have made job documentation a must. Most formalized pay programs use written job descriptions to document job content. A job description should describe and focus on the job itself and not on any specific individual who might fill the job.

From a market-pricing standpoint, job documentation is needed to evaluate the content of a job in relation to other jobs in the marketplace. Job documentation also is needed for the following HR administration purposes:

- Ensure that employees are assigned to appropriate jobs.
- Facilitate job-content evaluation.
- Facilitate salary-survey exchanges (if job matching).
- Explain, and, when necessary, defend certain pay-program decisions to employees and others.
- Assist in attraction and selection efforts.
- Establish performance standards.
- Facilitate organizational design.
- Assist in establishing career paths.

JOB EVALUATION

Job evaluation is a formal, systematic process for determining the relative worth of a company's jobs. It is used to ensure that a company's compensation system is equitable. The job, not the employee, is evaluated and rated.

Two basic methodologies have been used in developing a job-worth hierarchy: one starting with and emphasizing market data; the other starting with and emphasizing job content. In both cases, job content is important—the difference is in the starting point. Each employer must determine which approach suits the organization's needs. To a great extent, this will be determined by the number of distinct jobs in the organization, and the necessary resources for the pay program's design, installation, and maintenance. The nature of the labor market also is critical.

BENCHMARK JOBS

Market pricing begins with the selection of benchmark jobs, which serve as market anchor points. Although most pay programs recognize the market's role in ranking jobs, some existing formal systems use market rates as the primary basis for establishing job worth. Benchmark jobs are chosen, priced from survey data, and assigned relative values based on market levels. All other jobs then are positioned in relation to these benchmarks. At least 50 percent of jobs should be benchmarked.

Benchmark jobs closely resemble other jobs performed in other organizations and/or across industries. Benchmark jobs should:

- Be well-represented positions in the marketplace.
- Be important in the organization's internal hierarchy.

- Represent many organizational levels or grades in the salary structure(s) utilized by the company.
- Be matched to 70 percent or more of the duties found in the survey jobs.
- Generally have multiple incumbents with the exception of managerial and executive-level positions within an organization.

Benchmark jobs also serve as internal anchor points for nonbenchmark jobs. For example, a bookkeeper and an administrative assistant assigned the same pay grade and salary range now become the anchor points for assigning other positions without market data matches. Assignments of nonbenchmarked jobs is called slotting because it involves comparing or evaluating the value of the job, not based on market factors or points, but on the job's relative worth compared to other jobs that were evaluated.

COLLECTING THE RIGHT DATA

Now that you've identified, analyzed, documented, and evaluated the jobs that need to be market priced in your organization, it's time to collect market data for your selected benchmark jobs. The process of collecting this data is part of market pricing.

Many employers establish their job-worth hierarchy primarily on the basis of external market data, such as salary levels paid by other employers for jobs similar to their own. To use market data properly to establish the job-worth hierarchy, employers must identify the relevant markets and be able to collect external pay data on at least 50 percent of their organization's jobs. All remaining jobs will then be slotted into the pay structure as appropriate.

The overall purpose for collecting market data is to make informed decisions about the organization's compensation program. These decisions involve pricing jobs, analyzing pay trends, identifying pay practices, and establishing a job-worth hierarchy. A variety of data collection methods and factors is available to help determine the method that should be used.

Caution: In gathering and analyzing salary survey data, a determination should be made as to whether jobs described in the survey are comparable to jobs in the organization. If so, it is valid to use the survey data. If job documentation is inaccurate, incomplete, or outdated, invalid comparisons and decisions may result.

DECISION FACTORS IN COLLECTING MARKET DATA

Organizations should take the following factors into consideration when deciding which data collection source to use:

- *Cost.* Is the cost of the survey reasonable for the number of positions for which you will be able to market price and the number of employees represented in the data? Do you have the budget for the survey?
- *Time.* If you are considering conducting your own survey or having a customized survey completed for you, how much lead time do you need? How old are the data reported in the survey?
- *Reliability/accuracy.* Is the source of the data credible? Have the data been verified for accuracy? Is the sample size significant enough to accurately represent the marketplace?

- *Availability.* How easy are the data to access? How open was the survey for participation? Can you purchase the survey even if you didn't participate?
- *Confidentiality.* Is the information collected in the survey kept confidential?

Tread with Caution: Beware of Antitrust Implications

The Sherman Antitrust Act of 1890 originally was established to ensure competition and eliminate monopolies. So, what does this have to do with compensation surveys?

It has been determined through the courts, the Department of Justice (DOJ), and the Federal Trade Commission (FTC) that conducting your own surveys could be deemed anticompetitive price fixing when the element of collusion to "fix the cost of labor" is present. Included in the elements of collusion are the current average pay rates (deemed to be historical data) combined with merit budget estimates (deemed to be projective of the future).

Exxon, nursing groups in Utah and Connecticut, along with the Federal Reserve Bank of Boston, have been accused of price fixing salaries based upon surveys they have devised. Both the DOJ and the FTC have established some basic steps to follow to ensure you are not impeding the free market for labor through survey design. These following steps are called the *antitrust safety zone:*

- An independent third party (consultant, academic institution, government agency, or trade association) should manage the survey. The DOJ and the FTC allow some exchange of information without a third party, depending upon the use and the anticompetitive effect. *When conducting your own survey, seek legal counsel.*
- Data provided by survey participants must be more than three months old.
- Use at least five survey participants, with no individual participant's data representing more than 25 percent weighted basis of a given statistic.
- The results must be reported so recipients cannot determine specific participant data.

KNOW THE MARKET: HALF THE BATTLE

Knowing the organization's relevant labor market is key in selecting and participating in the right surveys. The relevant labor market can be defined in terms of "employee sources and destinations," which could be described as the markets from which the organization draws employees and the markets to which it loses employees. These markets can be defined in terms of industry, organization size, and/or geographic location. Figure 8.1 lists types of labor markets that might be identified for three job groups in a pharmaceutical firm with annual sales of $2 billion.

FIGURE 8.1 Sample labor market—large pharmaceutical firm.

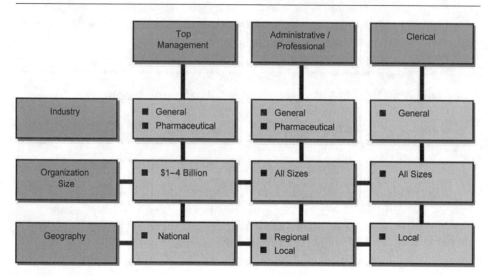

There are numerous valid and reliable methods of market pay data collection and analysis. Before collecting pay data, an organization should define its relevant labor market, which may consist of:

- Similar organizations in the local labor market (i.e., similar size or comparable industry).
- All employers in the local market.
- Similar organizations in the regional or national market (i.e., similar size or comparable industry).
- All employers in the regional or national market.

Employers will want to use surveys that include data from competing organizations in the labor market. Therefore, this survey sample may vary widely between different groups of jobs. Typically, considerations include the geographic area, size of the organization (number of employees), revenue, industry, and other factors deemed pertinent to the group being surveyed.

GATHERING VALID DATA

There is no exact market rate for any job. Compensation professionals must rely on market data to determine going market rates for jobs, but a plethora of available surveys can be mind-boggling. It's also a double-edged sword. On a positive note, there is an abundance of information from which to choose. On the flip side, wide-scale availability can lead to careless survey selection and inappropriate data.

Factors, such as sample size, participant base, statistical analyses, survey methodology, and job-matching procedures, impact the accuracy of the final market rate composite for a benchmark job. As a rule of thumb, salary information is expected to be reflective of the marketplace within plus or minus 10 percent. Consequently, a market index of 95 percent to 105 percent can be viewed as fully meeting competitive market pay levels.

In addition, availability of pay data on the Internet is growing. Employees with a roving eye are swayed easily by the extensive salary information that's available on web sites devoted to listing salaries by job title and location. However, not all posted data are reliable or validated. Before using this data, organizations need to ask:

- What is the targeted audience for the web site?
- What is the data source?
- Are the data from employer-based surveys or from individuals who enter the site?
- How is the web site maintained?

To ensure collection of the relevant data, organizations first should determine:

- What compensation data need to be collected?
- For what jobs are salary data needed?
- From which labor markets are survey data needed?
- Does the data focus exclusively on base pay or does it include target incentive pay?

An organization should conduct a needs assessment to reveal the type of surveys required for its job market pricing effort. This appraisal shows what data need to be in the surveys, which jobs need to be reported, and what industry and regional breakdowns are needed. Multiple surveys, when available, help to cull all of the pertinent data and ensure a more accurate picture of the relevant labor market.

DATA SOURCES

Purchase Published Surveys

There are thousands of published surveys available for purchase. The purchase price varies by survey source, survey scope, type of analysis, and overall sophistication of the final product. Also, most survey providers give a substantial discount to survey participants. Employers will want to use surveys that include data from competing organizations in the labor market. Therefore, this survey sample may vary widely between different groups of jobs. Typically, considerations include the geographic area, size of organization, revenue, industry type, and other factors deemed pertinent to the job group being surveyed.

Caution: When using the same survey source from year to year, ensure that changes in the survey participant group do not unduly influence changes in market rates.

Be aware that incumbent numbers may have a dramatic impact on the survey averages. A large employer who is hiring many people may report a lower average per job compared to last year because of new hires who are brought in at a lower rate than more senior incumbents. Conversely, a company downsizing may show higher pay rates year-over-year if layoffs tend to cull the less senior and lower-paid workers.

By carefully identifying the organization's needs and researching a wide variety of available surveys, you can accurately select the ones that will deliver the most relevant data to your company. The following information will be useful in your survey search.

Survey Content Checklist

Before purchasing a survey, ask the following questions:

- What information was collected? Is it consistent with your needs?
- What companies were surveyed? Do they match your needs?
- How much data are available for each job or role?
- Are the appropriate statistics reported? (For example: average, weighted average, median, percentiles, bonus/incentive, total compensation/total cash)
- What is the effective date of the data in the survey? Is it current enough for your needs? Can the data be aged easily?
- How expensive is the survey? Is there a price advantage for survey participants? Can nonparticipants purchase the survey?
- Has the survey been conducted by a reputable third-party survey provider? Does the survey have a history of providing credible information?
- Can the survey organization provide additional data analyses? Can you do additional analyses?
- In what form is information available (books, CD-ROM, web site, etc.)?

Conduct Your Own Survey through a Third Party

After thorough investigation of the data collection alternatives, an organization may decide to conduct its own survey, ranging from formal and comprehensive to a quick, informal phone or fax survey for limited data. Conducting your own survey allows you to gather data that meet your specific needs. The company will have more control over the data collection and analysis if it conducts the survey itself, although it may be the time-consuming choice.

Compensation surveys can range from quick phone surveys covering readily available information to highly complex studies involving sensitive information and requiring sophisticated mathematical analysis. A survey can be conducted by the following methods:

- Telephone interviews.
- A mailed questionnaire.
- A personal visit to the company to be surveyed.
- Any combination of the above.

Regardless of the method used to collect data, be specific and consistent about the information you are gathering. Make sure you're getting the *same type of information* from all participants: range, starting rate, number of incumbents in the job, etc.

The cost of gathering data is important and must be taken into consideration. Parameters should outline time constraints, reliability of the data, the need to control the quality of the data collected, and the necessity to keep the data confidential. Data access is another consideration. Many companies choose to only provide survey data through a third party (versus another employer) for a number of valid business reasons.

The third party can be a professional association, graduate students from a local university, or a consultant—anyone who is knowledgeable about survey methodology and research. In many cases, participants in a survey sponsored by an individual company pay nothing to receive a copy of the survey results. The advantage of using a third party is the company can target its competitors and may receive a higher participation rate because of third-party confidentiality.

Use Free Sources

Many consulting organizations have web sites containing sample survey data. Before using such data, you should be sure the information is current and includes adequate descriptions on the benchmark jobs. The Bureau of Labor Statistics (BLS) offers free downloadable information on salaries and wages. The home page address is http://www.bls.gov.

Collecting public information (e.g., proxy statements) is another reliable source of free information.

CAPTURING COMPETITIVE MARKET DATA FOR HIGH-DEMAND JOBS

In light of the shortcomings of traditional surveys, how do you measure the market for high-demand, hot-skills jobs? Remember, hot skills are needed in the market, but are in short supply and in high demand; for example: nurses, engineers, IT, telemarketers, etc. Some techniques include:

- Shift the focus from the more broadly defined job role to individual employees with specific skills (e.g., SAP application developer) needed to do the work.
- Create high-technology skill and skill-level definitions.
- Define base skills and capture compensation data on them to serve as a reference point for determining the premium for high-technology skills.
- Capture a richer array of survey data by blending data to get a "feel" for the job.
- Conduct the survey more frequently than once a year. Some skills are in high demand and the market will adjust rapidly.

In the case of IT pay, companies are finding market data useful in determining appropriate pay ranges for their employees, and also for valuing worker's knowledge and skills acquisition. Like base pay, the market value for skill-based pay is driven by supply-and-demand economics. However, unlike salaries, skill-based pay tends to fluctuate more dramatically from quarter to quarter in reaction to the market.

CRUNCHING NUMBERS

Now that the survey data have been selected, it is time for data analysis. Interpreting published survey data is complicated by the fact that survey administrators can choose different approaches to collecting and displaying survey results. The challenges are in making sound decisions about the data that need to be extracted from a particular source and interpreting these data appropriately when they are analyzed across several sources. Although numbers and formulas can seem intimidating, "easy does it" is the rule of thumb with this simplified process.

Survey data analysis is not a science; it's more of an art. The key to interpreting data successfully is to understand how statistics are computed in any given survey and blend that information into your own organization's compensation philosophy. If this information is not documented in the survey report, contact the survey publisher to verify computations.

Several issues should be considered when analyzing survey data:

- Options for measuring central tendency.
- Percentiles.
- Aging data.
- Weighting market data across survey sources.

OPTIONS FOR MEASURING CENTRAL TENDENCY

What's the best measure of a job's going market rate? Most surveys provide multiple measures of central tendency, or the measure of the "center" of all data collected for the data set. The common measures of central tendency are *median* (exact middle point in the data), *mean* (average), and *mode* (the most frequently occurring single data point in the data set). In most surveys, the common measures of central tendency are reported as the *unweighted average,* the *weighted average,* and the *median.* The best one to use depends on the information being sought. *Unweighted average* gives equal weight to every organization represented in the data. It answers the question: "On average, what are companies paying for this job?" (See Figure 8.2.)

- *Weighted average* gives equal weight to every salary represented in the data. It answers the question: "On average, what are incumbents in this job paid?" You can weight by number of companies (n = 136), or number of employees (n = 150).
- *Median* identifies the middle rate in the data set. It answers the question: "What is the exact middle salary in a set of ranked salaries?" For example, if the data set contains the ranked salaries of 51 accountants, the middle salary would be the 26th ranked salary because there are exactly 25 salaries ranked below it and 25 salaries ranked above it. A large difference between mean and median statistics can be the result of a sample that is skewed high or low by a few unusual cases. Means, or averages, can be affected dramatically by such skewing; medians are

FIGURE 8.2 Unweighted average by number of surveys.

Survey	Number of Companies Represented	Number of Employees Represented	Base Salaries Reported
1	56	60	$47,500
2	47	55	$53,100
3	33	35	$55,400
	136	150	Total: $156,000
			Average: $52,000 ($156,000/3)

FIGURE 8.3 Weighting by number of employees.

Survey	Number of Companies Represented	Number of Employees Represented	Base Salaries Reported	Weighted Average of Base Salaries Reported
1	56	60	$47,500	$2,850,000
2	47	55	$53,100	$2,920,500
3	33	35	$55,400	$1,939,000
	Totals:	150	$156,000	$7,709,500
			Weighted Average:	$51,397 ($7,709,500/150)

less susceptible to data extremes. Which statistics to use is still a matter of choice. However, unless you have a high degree of confidence in the sampling representation and the data analyses, the median is likely the best estimate of the "typical" pay for the job. In Figure 8.3, the median salary is $53,100.

PERCENTILES

Surveys also may provide information in the form of a percentile, which defines the value below which a given percentage of data fall. For example, if a salary survey shows $60,000 or the 90th percentile for the data, then 90 percent of survey respondents pay below $60,000 and 10 percent of survey respondents pay above $60,000. The 10th, 25th, 75th, and 90th percentiles are the most often reported. The data point at the 50th percentile also is the median of the data set. Percentiles may be important to an organization whose philosophy is to pay above market or track market leaders.

AGING DATA TO A COMMON POINT IN TIME

It is important to age published survey data to one common point in time so that accurate and consistent market comparisons can be made between the market and internal average pay. You can combine data from multiple surveys to reflect a common point in time by determining the annual aging factor.

Important considerations in selecting an annual aging factor and the date to which you want to age the data include:

- *Compensation levels increase at different rates in the marketplace.* For example, the rate of increase in executive pay generally exceeds the rate of increase in nonexempt pay on an average annual basis. Consequently, you should research market movement based on such considerations as:
  - *Industry type:* health care, finance, manufacturing, service, etc.
  - *Job level:* nonexempt, exempt, or executive.
  - *Geographic location:* Southern, Eastern, Western, Central.
  - *Type of compensation:* base salary or total compensation.

- To select an appropriate annual aging factor (e.g., increase nonexempt data by 4 percent and executive data by 5 percent), you can review surveys that present data on annual-increase budgets, such as the annual WorldatWork *Salary Budget Survey*. This approach assumes that actual pay in the labor market increases by the budgeted increase amount.
- The year-over-year increase in mean/median market rates within a single survey source often is reported in the survey's introduction or executive summary. This change in mean/median market rates is potentially one of the more accurate measures of market movements. However, the increases are historical rather than projected.
- To age data across two calendar years, you should develop a separate aging figure for each year, and then combine the two percentages.
- The lead, lag, or lead-lag structure policy will determine to what point in time you should trend your survey data for purposes of establishing competitive pay structure midpoints. For example, if your fiscal year is January through December and your policy is lead-lag, you will trend all data to July 1.

WEIGHTING MARKET DATA ACROSS SURVEY SOURCES

A decision regarding weighting survey data will be a function of a number of criteria, including:

- *Compensation strategy.* You will weight surveys in your industry more heavily if you have established a strategy that defines your competitive labor market as industry-specific.
- *Quality of surveys.* The statistical analyses provided—participant base and number of cases per job, among other factors—contribute to the perceived quality of a survey. Based on judgments about this quality, some surveys will receive more weight than others. For example, if one of your sources is an in-house survey, you may choose to weight this source more heavily than sources obtained externally.
- *Quality of job match.* Certain job matches are more appropriate than others based on job content, and market data can be weighted accordingly. This job-specific weighting factor can supplement or override previously established survey source weights. To generate an objective weighting factor at the job level, the number of cases (employees or companies) can be used to weight the raw data. Surveys that most accurately capture your labor market and best reflect your jobs' contents—and provide accurate and appropriate statistical analysis—are those to which you will give the most weight.

DEVELOPING MARKET INDEX OF COMPETITIVENESS

The market index will reflect market-pricing decisions already made in selecting appropriate surveys and survey statistics and in matching your jobs to survey jobs. How do you develop an analysis of your organization's overall pay competitiveness?

Use the following formula to calculate the market index of competitiveness:

Market Index = Company Average Salary ÷ Market Average Salary.

FIGURE 8.4 Company salary versus market salary.

Job	Market Average Salary	Company Average Salary	Market Index
A	1,300	1,400	1.08
B	1,430	1,450	1.01
C	1,570	1,500	0.96
D	1,730	1,600	0.93
	6,030	5,950	0.99

For example, according to Figure 8.4, Job D is the least competitively paid relative to the market. What else do you notice about company salary versus market salary? What is the overall market index?

How do you know if jobs and incumbents are paid competitively? Answering these questions correctly requires thoughtful review and interpretation of the data in relation to these issues:

- *Nature of the job.* Some jobs serve as entry-level positions through which employees pass quickly. Thus, job tenure is low and turnover is high. If employees typically are hired at grade minimum or low in the range, the job will have a low market index—a situation that is both expected and acceptable, assuming you can attract adequate numbers of qualified candidates.
- *Type of job evaluation plan.* If the company uses a "market pricing and slotting" evaluation plan, a job with a high or low market index can be reslotted into a different grade based on market pricing results. If, however, the company uses a quantitative evaluation system, such as job content or point factor method, a job with a very low or very high market index may have to be "green circled" or "red circled" to ensure the continued internal equity of all jobs. (See Sidebar 8.1.)
- *Number of incumbents in the job.* It is more typical for a heavily populated job to have a normal distribution of pay, and, therefore, to be paid closer to the market rate composite. Consequently, in a bank, a market index of 83 percent for the teller job will be of greater concern than the same index for the single-incumbent accounting manager job.
- *Individual incumbent characteristics.* Employee factors such as education, skill, ability, seniority, and individual performance must be considered when interpreting the comparison of market rate composites with internal pay levels. It is acceptable and desirable to pay incumbents above or below market on the basis of individual characteristics.

Sidebar 8.1: Green Means Go; Red Means Stop—Even in Compensation

Green-Circle Rate

A green-circle rate is below the minimum of the range rate and usually occurs when the wage structure is changed upward and the employee was at the

(continued)

Sidebar 8.1 *(Continued)*

bottom of the salary range. To rectify this situation, the employer can raise the pay immediately or in a couple of steps. All green-circle rates should be examined for discrimination.

Red-Circle Rate

A person paid above the maximum of the range for his or her job receives a red-circle rate. A red-circle rate is above the established range maximum assigned to the job grade. This situation is more difficult to deal with than a green-circle rate. Solutions vary from doing nothing to reducing the pay to the top of the range. Per company policy, an employee may not be eligible for further base pay increases until the range maximum surpasses the individual pay rate.

Market Adjustments

If you completed a market study for a position that already exists, you may recommend the position to be assigned to a different salary grade and/or recommend pay adjustments for current employees in the job. This action is called a market adjustment.

If a pay grade change is not recommended, you may suggest pay increases to employees who are not being paid close to or over the midpoint, or market rate, for the job. In this instance, the decision to provide pay increases will be based, in large part, on how difficult it is to fill the position, how important the position is to your business, and your company's compensation philosophy.

Below New Range

When an employee's salary is below the new range, the organization may select from a variety of methods to bring the salary within the new range. However, the amount of the increase will be affected by the amount by which the employee is below the minimum and the number and the size of increases it would take to get to the minimum.

For example, if your organization has a policy limiting the amount of any one increase or the total annual increase in pay, it will be necessary to determine if one increase will close a large percent gap, or if two or more increases will be required.

Caution: Although there is no federal law pertaining to the payment of employees below salary ranges, one must be cognizant of the employees below the range. Some organizations might have a policy stating that it is acceptable to have employees below the range; however, it is the organization's responsibility to ensure the policy is administered consistently and does not adversely affect any one employee or groups of employees.

MARKET BLIPS—A WORD OF CAUTION

Typically, "blips," or unusual swings of the market, are associated with a "hot-skills" job or a tight labor market in a specific location. They usually occur when the demand for a specific job increases because of an external event, or, on a smaller scale, when an organization is new to the area and it pays above market to initially attract critical talent.

Beginning in the late 1990s, organizations paid computer programmers "extra" increases and perks to ensure the systems would have a smooth transition from 1999 to 2000. During this time, market wages for this "hot skill" began to climb. However, market wages are starting to stabilize after the transition. In this scenario, an organization that adjusted all of its salary grades upward to accommodate this "blip" for some specialized positions now is reassigning some employees into a lower grade. In some instances, the organization is red-circling employees who now are paid over the new range maximum.

Before seeing a "blip" in the market for jobs that you have priced:

- Consider delaying a change in salary grade for the position and communicate to the hiring manager the ability to hire-in at midpoint of the range or above.
- Consider removing the range maximum for these "hot-skills" positions that are difficult to recruit but whose wages are temporarily inflated.
- If you are beginning to see a trend in market data over time for a position that is not classified as "hot skilled," review data over a three-year period to see if a grade movement is appropriate.

Get creative! If you're keeping a close watch on your compensation budget, you can add to the compensation of "hot-skills" individuals without adding to their base salary with lump-sum merit increases, recruitment bonuses, and retention bonuses.

APPROACHES TO PROGRAM COSTS

Compensation professionals need to understand how pay program design and administration methods affect program costs or budgets. The design of successful compensation and benefits programs calls for a delicate balance between often-competing objectives: Employers want to attract, motivate, and retain the most qualified employees, while facing competitive constraints on labor costs. To accomplish these objectives successfully, employers need to weigh the cost of the compensation program against other factors, such as being less competitive in the labor market to improve operating margins.

Whether market pricing individual jobs based on a job evaluation process or conducting a market analysis of benchmark positions to determine salary structure and pay competitiveness, determining the compensation program's cost is an important part of the planning process.

Costing of compensation programs can be as simple or as sophisticated as you choose to make it. It is important, however, to identify both first-year costs and any ongoing costs associated with the program. In many industries, labor costs account for 50 percent of all operating costs. With typical merit and salary programs, costs are compounded because the base salary of the employee is not fixed but keeps growing over time with each new merit increase awarded. To determine the costs of compensation decisions, you will need specific information regarding three key elements:

- Size of the average increase if looking at structure adjustments and amounts of actual increases if looking at market adjustments.

- Number of employees receiving increases (participation), including the length of time between increases (frequency).
- Timing of when the increases become effective (effective period).

There are three primary approaches.

All-at-Once Approach

The simplest option is to increase pay to eligible employees who are paid below market by giving those employees a salary increase in an amount that will move them up to market rate. In doing so, the initial cost of the increase will be higher than other options, but each employee will immediately be paid at market rate. However, it will be important to work with your finance department to ensure that by doing this, you will not impact your company's profit margins significantly.

Phase-In Approach

Although giving all employees a salary increase at one time is fairly straightforward and easy to administer, not all organizations have the available funding to support this type of increase in the first year. A way to administer the same increase, but lower the first-year cost, is to phase in the increase throughout the first year. This is accomplished by staggering the increases over a longer period of several months (or longer) to lower the first-year costs.

Wait-and-See Approach

The wait-and-see approach is another way to address a group of employees paid below market rate. Occasionally, the demand for a job or group of jobs may increase. This increase could lead to a temporary higher market wage for this group of employees.

With the wait-and-see approach, the compensation professional will "wait and see" what the market does before any increases are given. By waiting a set period of time, the market wage may either stay at the new higher level or decrease to a previous level. If the market wage decreases to a previous level, then the wage increase witnessed was a temporary increase based on external or unusual market conditions. If the wage increases continue, then the compensation professional will follow one of the two previous methods (all at once or phased-in) to implement a salary increase.

If you notice that the market wages for a particular position have remained relatively flat for an extended period of time and then appear to spike, you may want to take a wait-and-see approach. However, be aware that the wait-and-see approach may cost you more than wages if the market is paying a premium for skills and you are not. Some of your employees may be lured away to the highest bidder, which could cause higher turnover in those hard-to-fill positions.

HOW TO KEEP EMPLOYEES IN THE LOOP

Pay delivers a strong message. Research indicates that the most financially successful companies are more likely to communicate pay information to their employees, as well as provide training to first-line supervisors on pay communications.

Employees have a desire to know what methods are used to define and determine the value of jobs within their organization. In the context of this book and as stated previously, pay is calculated through market pricing according to the organization's compensation philosophy. Openly communicating pay policy and strategy helps build trust in the employer-employee relationship and breaks down any misconceptions about pay that may have arisen.

Who Should Communicate the Message?

The person who communicates the pay information to employees should not be a fellow employee in the same department. The communicator should be chosen based upon the specific pay action and audience and could be any of the following individuals:

- Supervisor.
- Department manager.
- HR manager.

To relay pay messages to employees in a lasting manner, the supervisor is the most effective channel and should be at the center of the communications effort. Employees' perceptions about the organization's pay system are shaped through dialogue with their managers and via formal and informal communications programs.

As ongoing communication with employees enhances the effectiveness and acceptance of the pay program and helps reduce misperceptions, it is critical that the communicator is equipped with the right information. "Train the trainer" sessions will help supervisors communicate the most accurate and up-to-date pay information to employees.

Managers can't afford to guess about competitive compensation in the marketplace. A ballpark answer is not good enough. They need to communicate precise answers to head off any employee concerns. If the compensation program is to contribute effectively to the overall employee relations program, employees in the organization must perceive that their level of total pay is fair and competitive. Although employees may argue for pay adjustments based on comparisons with only the highest-paying employers, they usually recognize that an employer responds to labor market averages. They will not become seriously dissatisfied unless they perceive their total compensation level as lower than that of a significant majority of employees performing similar jobs through the relevant labor market.

What Information Should Be Communicated?

The supervisor or manager should communicate pay adjustments simply and concisely from the employee perspective, while focusing on the main elements of the pay action, including:

- What is the reason for the pay action?
- How will the pay action be processed?
- When will the pay action become effective?
- Is the pay action a one-time adjustment?
- Will the pay action be in a lump sum or a periodic action?

OPENING THE PAY DIALOGUE

A major part of every manager's or supervisor's job is answering questions about the compensation program. In today's competitive business environment, many companies have abandoned secrecy about their pay program in favor of openly conveying information to their employees. Increasingly, organizations are making public information about pay ranges and merit budgets.

For example: After performing a market pricing analysis for an accounting clerk position, it is decided there will be a pay adjustment. When communicating this information to employees who will be granted the increase, the manager or supervisor should be prepared to answer a variety of employee questions and observations, including:

- "Why can't I receive the full increase now?"
- "Why didn't I receive an increase when my coworker, who has not been here as long I as have, received an adjustment?"
- "What do I need to do to get the increase?"

Being aware of potential questions and appropriate answers is key to effective communication. It is a good idea to brainstorm possible questions and answers with coworkers. In doing so, you will be able to anticipate problem areas and be prepared to address employees' questions and concerns. An open exchange of dialogue will enhance communication, understanding, and reinforce employees' trust in the organization.

9 Salary Surveys: A Snapshot

Market data obtained from salary surveys create the foundation for a viable compensation strategy. When combined with economic statistics and business strategy, they create the infrastructure of an organization's salary practices. Just as DNA provides information used to construct, identify, and operate the human body, market data obtained from salary surveys are used to construct and operate organizations' pay programs.

Market data evolve from salary surveys that are compiled and analyzed periodically to determine how well the company pays relative to the market. How the company statistically analyzes, charts, and uses the data is a function of its corporate compensation strategy. Then, pay is delivered to employees through base salary and bonus/commission programs and maintained using salary administration guidelines and other pay delivery systems. Critical to this effort is effective communication of all components of pay to earn the most satisfaction from employees, and, ultimately, high productivity and success for the company.

THE BIG PICTURE

Where do salary surveys fit in? Why do we use them?

An organization has many resources to achieve its goals. Even though these resources include land, material, capital, and people, it is only people who make decisions about and do things with the land, material, capital, and the people. An organization's goals are accomplished only through people. Hence, the major challenge of any organization is to attract, retain, motivate, and align the types and numbers of people it needs to achieve its goals.

This is accomplished through a *value exchange*—a situation in which the company and the employee give value to the other in exchange for value received to achieve their

FIGURE 9.1 Value exchange pie charts.

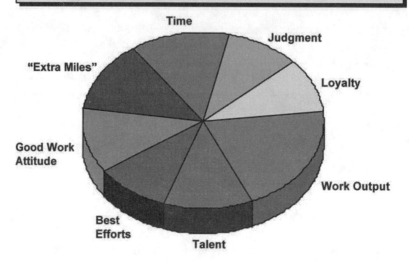

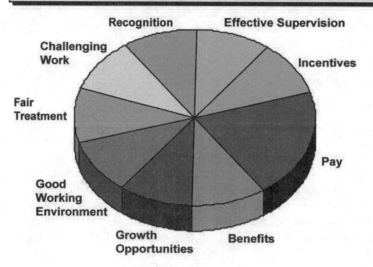

respective self-interests. This notion can be summarized by the phrase, "Value given for value received." Figure 9.1 shows some of the items involved in the exchange.

Many items given by the employee to the employer are not quantitatively measurable, but they are present and are very important to the company. The items from the employer to the employee may differ from one employee to the next with regard to what is of value. Indeed, even the relative size of the pieces differs among employees and individuals during a lifetime. For example, a relatively new employee may value growth opportunities more than an employee near retirement. Likewise, an individual might feel pay is very important today but tomorrow, when a new baby joins the family, benefits become more important. This shows that pay is just one component of the exchange.

When an employer decides how much to pay an employee, several factors usually are considered:

- Business strategy.
- Internal value of job/skill.
- Market pay.
- Individual factors.
  - Experience.
  - Education.
  - Performance.
  - Contribution.
  - Skills.
- Balance with benefits, stock, work environment, etc.
- What the company can afford.
- Compensation philosophy.
  - Desired market position.
  - What the company wants to pay for.

The focus of this chapter is market pay. What the market pays for a job or a skill isn't the only factor in deciding the monetary worth of a job or skill, but it's a key one. Salary surveys provide important information in the decision-making process of deciding pay.

DEFINITION AND PURPOSES

A salary survey is a statistical description of what organizations pay for certain _____. "Jobs," "skills," "experience," "education," or any combination of these could fit in that blank. Surveys have three main purposes:

- Identify a company's market position and form a basis for a salary increase budget.
- Create a salary structure or structures.
- Develop targets for individual pay levels.

Some desired features of a salary survey include:

- Desired jobs, companies, and locations.
- Good job descriptions and job matches.
- Large amounts of data, screened data, and data integrity.

- Confidentiality.
- Flexibility.
- Sound survey design.
- Easy data submission.
- Useable and user-friendly results.
- Interpretation.
- Timeliness.
- Availability of special analyses.
- Value received for cost.
- Helpful and knowledgeable customer service.
- Responsiveness.
- Continuous improvement.

Because of the importance of surveys, many companies use some surveys for analysis—primary surveys—and other surveys for reality checks—secondary surveys. Secondary surveys may not have the right companies or locations, but they provide an important perspective.

Surveys can solicit and gather information via telephone, mailed hard copy questionnaires, e-mailed or web-based electronic questionnaires, and personal interviews. An organization, a large third-party consulting firm, or a boutique third-party consulting firm can conduct the survey.

BENCHMARK SURVEYS

The remainder of this chapter focuses on benchmark surveys (surveys that describe what companies pay for certain jobs). Other types of surveys not covered are skills surveys, which measure what companies pay for certain skills, or maturity surveys, which measure what companies pay for experience and education in certain work areas.

Which Jobs to Survey

Several criteria act in concert when deciding which jobs in your organization to survey. The jobs that should be surveyed:

- Span levels in the organization.
- Span functions.
- Span families.
- Have a large number of incumbents.
- Are mission-critical.

A sufficient number of jobs with a sufficient number of incumbents should be surveyed to make a compensation practitioner feel comfortable that he or she has surveyed enough to achieve the survey's purpose. Specific numbers are decided on an individual basis, but some rough guidelines are:

- Number of jobs matched—one-third to two-thirds of jobs.
- Number of employees in matched jobs—one-half to three-quarters of employees.

Of course, the more jobs, the better but time and budget constraints often are limiting. Further, some jobs may be so unique that there is no similar job match in any other organization. Remember: The quality of job matches is more important than the quantity of jobs surveyed.

Survey Job Descriptions

Job descriptions for surveys vary from short paragraphs to a full page and often include an organization chart or description of reporting relationships. Jobs that tend to be standard among organizations often can be described briefly, such as an assembler or a file clerk. New jobs or jobs that are similar but have a high degree of variation tend to be described more fully, such as a marketing development manager. Regardless, the survey job descriptions should have the main thrust of the job, along with the principal functions or key responsibilities, and the job title should be descriptive.

When reporting relationships (e.g., reports to the president) or scope (e.g., revenue of the company or number of direct and indirect reports) are important in valuing the job, these factors should be included. If certain qualifications or certifications are required (e.g., master electrician's license), these criteria should be included.

Use caution when describing education and experience requirements. With education, rather than stating, for example, that a college degree is required, instead state what that degree represents, such as "the theoretical knowledge of the field or discipline is required," because someone may have gained the needed knowledge through experience. This is the "or equivalent" notion of formal education.

With experience, remember that when a description says, for example, "10 years of experience," it usually means experience with increasing levels of responsibility. However, you may have an incumbent with one year of experience 10 times over, who is not really doing the level of work in the description. When years of experience are part of benchmark survey job descriptions, it unfortunately directs too much attention on that one factor and not enough on the work described.

Which Companies to Survey

Part of a company's compensation philosophy should include a designation of the external reference for compensation program purposes. The reference usually describes other companies defined as competition. Examples include local major employers to compare office and clerical nonexempt jobs or local manufacturers for assemblers. For professional and supervisory jobs, companies often look to employers in their industry and national employers of similar size or revenue in their industry for upper management and executive jobs. Criteria to define a company's competition include companies that:

- Do the same thing.
- Are the same size.
- Are in the same locations.
- Hire and lose employees to one another.

It is important to ask managers who they think is relevant competition. Figure 9.2 offers some discussion starting points.

There may be a situation in which the reference point is not actual competition, but a realistic and stable basis for the compensation program. For example, there is a company near Dallas that draws its employees locally, not competing with the suburbs around Dallas for nonmanagerial jobs. But those suburbs are the only source

FIGURE 9.2 Determining the competition.

Executives
Similar size in same industry
Middle Management
Similar size in same industry
Industry-Specific Professionals and Supervisors
Any size in same industry
Nonindustry-Specific Professionals
Any size
Office and Administrative, Skilled and Unskilled Labor
Any size in same location (local market)

of survey data, so they are used as a reference point for compensation program purposes. The company decided that not having to commute to the Dallas suburbs was worth about 10 percent, so its average pay is 10 percent below the reference point.

Data to Be Gathered

The type of data needed flows from the survey's purpose and an organization's pay strategy. Choices include:

- Base salary.
- Total cash (base plus bonus/commission).
- Equity (stock).
- Benefits.

Typical statistics include:

- Averages (weighted, unweighted).
- Percentiles (10th, 25th, 50th, 75th, 90th).
- Raw data (after decoding to preserve confidentiality).
- Various summaries of scope data.

General information often includes:

- Current salary increase budget.
- Policy information.
- Design information.

Compensation practitioners need to decide what they want to seek, or they need to create a survey that satisfies individual needs.

More Than Just Salaries

The typical salary survey has more than base pay reported on benchmark positions. Because companies manage compensation using a total rewards strategy, there usually is trend information, including general questions about merit budgets, salary structure movement, and benefits provided. For example, the WorldatWork annual *Salary Budget Survey* includes questions on trends in variable pay, types of incentives, and other popular innovations in compensation.

Review the Survey Database

Companies often neglect to review their survey database to determine if it is providing adequate coverage of jobs and sampling the right companies and industries. By reviewing the coverage of jobs and looking for alternative data sources, a company ensures it has comprehensive intelligence of the labor landscape. Figure 9.3 illustrates a survey job matrix, which is a useful tool for ensuring the right coverage. Some additional rules of thumb include:

- Have at least two sources of surveys for key jobs. This provides validation of one survey against another.
- Review the makeup of the companies included to ensure the competition is represented.

FIGURE 9.3 Salary survey job matrix.

Create a salary survey matrix and review coverage of job categories included in your survey database. Also, review the survey participation list for each survey to ensure there is a cross-section of your competitors included in the specific survey. This can be misleading as some companies alternate which surveys they choose to participate in from year to year.

Survey Name	Survey Cost	Date Published	Executive	Middle Management	Professional	Admin	Hourly	Discipline, Function, or Industry
Survey A	$XXX	June	☑	☑				Executive
Survey B	$XXX	June		☑	☑	☑	☑	Call Center
Survey B	$XXX	Sept.		☑	☑			Engineering
Survey B	$XXX	August	☑	☑	☑	☑	☑	IT
Survey D	$XXX	Spring	☑	☑	☑	☑	☑	Finance
Survey E	$XXX	Fall		☑				Middle Mgmt.
Survey F	$XXX	January		☑	☑	☑	☑	Chemical
Survey G	$XXX	March	☑	☑	☑	☑	☑	Energy
Survey H	$XXX	July	☑	☑	☑	☑	☑	High Tech

- Be cautious of surveys in which some respondents participate every other year or sporadically; consistent data is important when monitoring trends in pay for critical positions.
- Don't look at "base pay only" for jobs that typically are eligible for other forms of variable or equity pay.
- Ensure salary surveys are supplemented with equity compensation surveys and incentive survey data to get the big picture.
- Get data from companies in the same industry for technical jobs, but use general industry data for administrative positions, such as accounting, legal, and HR.
- Review the strategy annually and look for new, improved, or different surveys, if appropriate.
- While it is valuable to look at trends reported year to year for some surveys, don't overlook other valuable surveys that might enhance or supplement market analysis.
- Periodically review the surveys used to ensure that quality and consistency are maintained.
- Conduct a review of survey results and develop a strategy for participation on a going-forward basis.

When to Conduct an Ad Hoc or Special Survey

Sometimes it's impossible to find a ready-made survey that reflects the right jobs or companies—all surveys do not provide everything for every job. This is the time for the company, or a third-party vendor, to conduct a custom survey. Sometimes, special circumstances dictate that a special survey be conducted, such as:

- The company is relocating its headquarters to a new city.
- There is a short supply of special skills.
- There is a dramatic shift in the economy, creating a shortage of certain knowledge workers.
- A special industry survey is needed for a specific geographic location.

Recently, a major financial services company sponsored a special customer service representative survey in one of its markets. There are more than 500 call centers in that specific market, and competition for these skills is tremendous.

The financial services company found that paying above market still was not drawing the right kind of talent, so the organization decided to find out what the market really required without having the data "filtered" through a general survey. The company commissioned a third-party consulting firm to conduct a special survey. Confidentiality was maintained for the raw data, but the company was able to select competitors to participate in the survey. This offered first-hand information on a job group that was critical to the company's success.

JOB MATCHING

After finding or creating the needed surveys, the most critical aspect of salary surveys comes into play: job matching, or the process of comparing a company's jobs to the survey jobs. When they are comparable, this constitutes a match.

Job matching is, without a doubt, the most important component of a salary survey because this is where compensation practitioners match apples to apples to ensure they are obtaining the right market data. Often, when managers challenge the results of survey analyses, they are thinking that, "My people do so much more than the survey jobs," which translates to a disagreement with the job matches made.

There are two issues to address concerning job matching: Who does it and how it is done.

Those familiar with or knowledgeable about the work should do the matching. Ideally, managers or subject matter experts should match jobs. If this isn't possible, compensation practitioners do the matching based on their knowledge of the jobs, which they have gained by interviewing incumbents and managers, or reading internal job descriptions. Another approach is to review survey job descriptions with managers, comparing internal jobs or job descriptions to them, and then reaching agreement on the matches.

There is one maxim that must be adhered to for a survey analysis to have any validity: *Jobs must be matched on job content, not job titles.* Match the jobs and the work people are doing, not the title or the people themselves (rising stars or falling duds). An underlying assumption is that the incumbents are performing the job at a solid, competent level and are not beginners or superstars. Note that a valid match means the job essentially has the same function as the survey job, and the incumbent performs the same, if not all of, the typical duties in the survey job. If the comparison is not obvious, don't force a match. Also, if incumbents match more than one job, select the job in which they spend most of their time.

The matching process can take one of several forms:

- *Matching Meetings.* In this process, survey groups consisting of line managers and compensation practitioners from different companies convene and present their matches to the survey jobs. Meeting participants obtain clarification or challenge matches perceived as inappropriate. In these meetings, the group often is asked, "If this company makes the proposed match, the results will contain data for that job; is that what you want?" The result of such a discussion should be a consensus on the matches.
- *One-on-one Discussions.* In these discussions, matches are made with either a participant or survey consultant conducting the discussions with participants. Sometimes, these discussions are made by telephone/conference call.
- *No Dialogue.* Sometimes, just reading the survey job descriptions and comparing jobs to them—without any dialogue—makes the match.

When matching jobs, the following job components should be considered and discussed:

For All Jobs

- Principal function.
- Typical duties.
- Reports to.
- Location on organization chart.
- Relevant scope data.
  - Revenue.
  - Number of employees supervised.

FIGURE 9.4 Issues that arise during job matching.

Value Hierarchy
 The relative importance of different aspects of the job (e.g., "Which is more important in a technical sales job: Sales or technical skills?").

Semantics
 The meaning of words, such as the meaning of "complex" and how it compares with "very complex" and "highly/extremely complex."

Matching Family Levels
 When an organization has a different number of levels than reflected in the survey (e.g., the survey has four levels of engineers and the company has six), does the compensation practitioner try to have exact matches and just match four levels, or should he or she combine some of the company's levels to match the survey descriptions? Different survey groups handle this differently.

Match Adjustments
 When a job is a close—but not exact—match, are any adjustments or notations made to the data?

For Jobs in a Family

- Primary function of the family.
- Typical role at each level.
- Progression criteria.
- Approximate distribution among levels.
- Career path.

It is important to realize that job matching is a judgment process and sometimes not clear-cut. Take special note of the issues outlined in Figure 9.4. There are no single right answers to these issues, but compensation practitioners should be aware of them and be comfortable with the determined resolution.

JOB TITLE AND CHARACTERISTICS

A key concern with market pricing is job titling—ensuring the definition of a job is the same as the surveys being used. A job title is defined as "a descriptive name for the total collection of tasks, duties, and responsibilities assigned to one or more individuals whose positions have the same level." Job titles should describe the nature and level of work performed.

For this example, the total idea of a job and its responsibilities is broken into five types of jobs:

1. Support staff.
2. Professional.
3. Supervisory.
4. Managerial.
5. Executive.

(See Figures 9.5, 9.6, and 9.7.)

FIGURE 9.5 Example of five job classes.

Support Staff: Usually nonexempt hourly employees. Main job responsibilities are to offer varying forms of support to all levels of the organization.

Professional Staff: Usually exempt-level salaried professionals. Some college experience or on-the-job knowledge of a specific field. Main responsibilities are in a specific field of knowledge and ensuring day-to-day portion of that field is completed.

Supervisory: Usually exempt-level salaried professionals; however, could be nonexempt-level hourly employees. Main responsibilities include ensuring operations of a small group of employees doing similar tasks are completed. Has some coaching and disciplinary responsibilities. Could possibly also do a subordinate's job if the situation is needed.

Managerial: Exempt-level salaried professionals. Advanced college or on-the-job knowledge of specific field. Main responsibilities include ensuring operations of a group of employees doing varying tasks in the same field are completed. Has understanding of interpersonal skills and problem-solving ability.

Executive: Exempt-level salaried professionals. Advanced college and/or on-the-job knowledge of multiple business units. Main responsibilities include ensuring operations of multiple business units are completed. Has advanced interpersonal communication skills and application of problem-solving ability.

FIGURE 9.6 Characteristic definitions.

Title: Job position being defined.

Class: Organizational position.

Exemption: Possibility of exemption as defined by the exemption tests of the Fair Labor Standards Act (FLSA). In order to classify specific position, exemption tests must be followed as written in the FLSA.

Supervision: Amount of supervision needed for specific position.

Typical Duties: Average minimum tasks an employee may do in this position.

Difficulty of Job: Average level of complexity for all tasks completed.

Responsibility Level: Average organizational importance of decisions being made.

Direct Reports: Amount/level of supervisory responsibility.

Knowledge: Job knowledge learned by performing job responsibilities.

Education: Minimum formal education requirements (high school, college, etc.).

Computer Skills: Minimum required computer skills.

Budget Responsibility: Portion of the organizational budget position for which employee is responsible.

Additional Information: Any additional applicable information pertaining to duties, tasks, or job-specific responsibilities.

Position Description: Brief description of a typical position found within the job title.

Position Examples: Examples of complete job titles found in organizations.

FIGURE 9.7 Example job title with characteristics.

Senior Vice-President/Executive Director

Class: Executive.

Exemption: Exempt (executive test).

Supervision: Minimal.

Typical Duties: In charge of daily operations of a percentage of the organization.

Difficulty of Job: High.

Responsibility Level: High.

Direct Reports: Yes.

Knowledge: In-depth understanding of inner workings of multiple business units and the organization.

Education: Four-year college education or equivalent.

Computer Skills: Advanced knowledge, application, usage, and understanding of office-type and organizational-wide programs.

Budget Responsibility: High—Responsible for reviewing percentage of organizational budget and issuing first approval. Will submit to Executive Committee for final approval.

Additional Information: Has demonstrated in-depth knowledge and understanding of multiple business units and the organization along with understanding of interpersonal communications and advanced in-depth understanding and application of problem-solving ability. Oversees operations of multiple business units and a percentage of the organization.

Position Description: Oversees daily operations of a percent of organization. Responsible for reviewing, approving, and ensuring compliance to long- and short-term organizational goals and objective. Will ensure units are implementing cost-saving measures and increasing production levels, compliant with organizational goals. Reviews subordinates' reports and takes all issues into consideration for daily operations and meeting long-term objectives.

Position Examples: Senior Vice-President of Operations, Executive Director of Total Rewards.

SURVEY FREQUENCY

How often should a survey be conducted? The usual survey cycle is annual, but the answer to this question really depends on the market movement and the jobs or skills involved; different markets move at different speeds. The market sometimes moves quite quickly for skills or jobs that are mission-critical to the organization, such as the case in recent years with various computer programming language skills, where the market for these skills moved at two to three times the rate for most other jobs. One major survey was created and conducted every six months to fill the demand for information on those skills. Other surveys also were created that reported quarterly or "real-time" information.

Because most organizations conduct salary budgeting annually, it makes sense to get survey data annually. If for some reason an organization goes longer than two years to gather survey data, the aging assumptions needed for survey analyses become tenuous and salary increase budget decisions are built on shaky ground.

To maximize the benefits of surveys, employers need to commit to and budget for surveys, and then participate every year or cycle. Not only will this keep data current, but participation also enhances survey stability. A high participant churn creates results that are somewhat unreliable, and, ultimately, will cause the survey to fail.

Finally, when compiling market data from surveys that may be as much as six months to one year old, do a reality check of the current market. Organizations' recruiting staffs should be questioned on trends that they have observed in attracting talent in key professional, technical, service, and unskilled job categories. Markets sometimes shift suddenly in certain geographic areas and for key "hot jobs." The survey might say an accountant can command annual pay of $50,000, but there may not be any qualified candidates willing to accept the job for less than $55,000. Good business sense needs to come into play when evaluating survey data, and one should not rely solely on reported data without doing a reality check with the appropriate job market.

STRETCHING THE SALARY SURVEY BUDGET

Surveys vary considerably by price, based in part by how the survey is conducted and what information is available:

- Some surveys have group job matching meetings while others just expect job matches to be made by reading descriptions.
- Some surveys have results meetings; others do not.
- Some surveys furnish sophisticated statistical analyses and many options, while others do not.

Compensation practitioners, of course, do not have unlimited resources. Following are some helpful hints for stretching the salary survey budget dollar:

- Form industry network groups to share trends.
- Participate in surveys sponsored by other companies.
- Join local compensation associations to network and share trends.
- Research articles that reference salaries (e.g., trade journals or www. careerjournal.com, published by *The Wall Street Journal*).
- Check competitors' web sites for job listings and starting salaries.
- Submit survey data early to get available "early-bird" discounts.
- Prioritize your needs; participate in surveys with the broadest job coverage.
- Participate in free salary budget surveys that list trends.
- Subscribe to surveys that report entry-level professional data from colleges and universities. Even if a particular employer doesn't hire graduates, compression and inequities can result if the business doesn't keep pace with the supply-and-demand issues for certain professions.

BEHIND THE SCENES

Companies often will participate in surveys conducted by third-party consulting firms. A consulting firm typically goes through the following process when conducting a salary survey.

Preparation

There are many steps in planning and preparing for a salary survey. Decisions or confirmation are made on:

- The survey's objective.
- The jobs to be surveyed.
- The data and information to be collected.
- The format for the final results.
- The job-matching process.

It is equally important to:

- Identify any necessary survey processing software development or revisions.
- Create or revise job descriptions.
- Identify prospective participants.
- Develop solicitation and marketing strategy.
- Prepare and send solicitation and marketing materials.
- Prepare the survey questionnaire.
- Send the survey questionnaire.
  - Hard copy.
  - Electronic.

Gather Data

There is a lot of down time here, as it typically takes from three to six weeks from the receipt of the questionnaire to the submission of data from participants. More complex surveys can take longer. If there is a formal job-matching process, it takes place here. Also, the consulting firm often has to remind slower participants to submit their data on time.

Creating the Master File

Different consulting firms may have different names for this file, but this step involves making sure the data are good before any reports are created. Only good data go into the master file. In determining whether data are good, the following is considered:

- Missing values (e.g., reporting an average salary but no number of incumbents).
- Wrong codes (e.g., the directions said "E" for exempt and "N" for nonexempt. One participant submitted "Q." What does that mean?).
- Inversions (e.g., "low" salary higher than the "high" salary, or the senior level being paid less than entry level).
- Outliers (e.g., a salary that is many standard deviations from the mean).
- Numbers that don't make sense (e.g., a $100 bonus for the CEO, or a $100,000 bonus for the janitor).
- Large or unusual changes from last year (e.g., a large increase or decrease in the number of incumbents or in the pay levels for a job).

In each of these instances, someone must call back or e-mail the original source of the information to verify data and matches. Half the time a consulting firm spends conducting a salary survey is spent screening data to create a master file to ensure that good data form the basis for the survey results. When compensation practitioners receive calls from the firm about data, they should feel comfortable about the consultant's validation processes and the resulting data.

Initial Reports

Once the master file is created, this intermediate step is taken to look at the data in aggregate. In the previous step, the data were examined on a participant basis; now they are examined on a job and job-family basis to identify possible anomalies, and, if needed, more calls or e-mails are made to the sources.

Final Results

This is the moment for which everyone has waited—the *results*. At this stage, the consulting firm will:

- Publish the final reports in hard and electronic copy.
- Produce special analyses requested by participants.
- Conduct results meetings and discussion forums as appropriate.
- Gather evaluation feedback from participants for survey improvement.

The results usually contain some core elements:

- Job descriptions.
- Descriptive statistics for each job.
- Participating companies.
- Date of the data.
- General questions and summarized responses.

THE COMPENSATION PRACTITIONER'S ROLE

Compensation practitioners have several roles in the salary survey process:

- Decide the jobs and surveys.
- Match the jobs.
- Submit data.
- Extract data to create an individual survey database.
- Use the data.

When compensation practitioners submit data, it is important to leave a trail. This will help to easily correct any data errors in case the consultant calls as part of the screening process. This also helps when participating in subsequent years to "remember" what was done in the previous survey. Consider keeping the following on file for each job submitted to a survey:

- Department.
- Job code.
- Job title.
- Grade.
- Family.

- Structure.
- Data submitted.
  - By incumbent.
  - By job.
- Date of the data.
- Survey code.
- Survey name.
- Survey job code.
- Survey job title.
- Page of job description.
- Level, if in a family.

Extracting Data

Before analyzing survey results, compensation practitioners need to:

- Verify the job matches with the published descriptions as a quality check.
- Decide the type of data to be extracted. This is a function of the type of analysis being conducted.
  - Base pay.
  - Total cash.
  - Equity.
- Decide the statistics to be extracted.
  - Weighted average.
  - Unweighted average.
  - Median.
  - Other percentiles.

Finally, as with submitting data, it also is vital to leave trails during this stage, not only to help find data that seems out of line during analysis, but also to *remember* where you got the data. In addition to the type of identification recorded for submitted data, keep the following on file for each job in which you extract data from a survey:

- Date of the data.
- Page of salary data.
- Survey data cuts.
- Salary data extracted.

There are two additional steps beyond the statistical analysis: synchronizing surveys with economic data and communicating appropriately to employees.

Synchronizing Surveys with Economic Data

Ongoing review and maintenance of the data and statistics derived from the data must be synchronized with events in the marketplace and economy. Though most companies don't revise salary structures and programs more than once a year, a dynamic job market or volatile economy can affect past decisions and cause companies to rethink pay strategies and merit increase budgets.

For example, the terrorist attacks on September 11, 2001, had devastating effects on the economy and commerce in general, and many companies reigned in salary increase budgets and plans for higher salary structures.

Just a year earlier, the market was like a runaway train. At that time, high-tech organizations were revising pay plans and participating in salary surveys for technology workers as often as every six months.

Factors (other than salary surveys) that influence pay decisions include:

- Labor supply and demand.
- Company's ability to pay.
- Threat from competition.
- Merit budget trends.
- Employment cost index (ECI).
- Industry trends.
- Unemployment rate.
- Global business environment.
- Cost of living in key office locations.
- Budget constraints.
- Stock market volatility.
- Mergers and acquisitions.
- Downsizing/rightsizing.
- Unions.

Communications

A thorough marketing approach to communicating employee pay and salary administration usually leads to more satisfied employees. Even in a bad economy, well-paid employees can be dissatisfied with the efficacy of pay for performance. In fact, when merit budgets are in the 3 percent to 4 percent range, employees scrutinize pay increases more heavily because their increases are so small. Employee opinion surveys often reveal that employees don't understand a company's compensation strategy, don't feel that recognition programs are adequate, and feel that performance management is unfair. This is true even at companies that pay at the 75th percentile of market because they do a poor job of communicating total rewards.

Just as DNA is a mystery to laypeople, salary programs are an enigma to the average employee. Building an effective marketing campaign that communicates pay program information to employees can go a long way to building credibility and morale, reducing turnover, and ultimately improving productivity. The best-designed pay program and compensation strategy can fail to attract, retain, align, and motivate top performers if it is not communicated well or understood by employees.

SALARY SURVEY GUIDELINES

WorldatWork recognizes the professional imperative of acquiring and using valid, timely and noncollusive salary survey data. WorldatWork also believes that while survey data is a vitally important tool for the practitioner and often is the dominant tool, by no means should surveys be the sole source used to determine an organization's pay ranges and compensation packages. In addition to salary surveys, other sources such as government labor statistics, association resources, SEC disclosure reporting, proxy statements, and an organization's own written or unwritten total rewards philosophy should be considered in establishing compensation packages.

The following set of guidelines for survey selection and characteristics of a good survey should be considered a starting point for the practice of using salary surveys.

Best Practices In Survey Selection

1. *Assess why you need salary survey information.* A thorough needs assessment is an imperative first step in determining the need for salary surveys. Determine what data are needed, for which jobs, and what jobs need to be listed in the survey data. Start thinking about the appropriate markets factors to use in comparison, including geography, industry, etc.
2. *Make sure management is supportive.* Gain a thorough understanding of your organization's compensation philosophy—whether written or unwritten—and verify that management is supportive of the use of salary survey data. Without this support, time, effort, and perhaps even expense may go unappreciated and perhaps even overruled.
3. *Use reputable sources to find reputable surveys.* There are numerous catalogues of salary survey sources and information about survey providers. These are excellent sources to begin the search for the right surveys for your organization.
4. *Make sure the survey(s) selected match the desired labor market and job category.* Comparing apples to apples is vitally important in job pricing. Important market factors to consider in job pricing include geography, industry, job function, and the maturity level of the organization, to name a few. Also critically important is the matching of actual job functions and duties, not just job titles.
5. *Don't put all your eggs in one basket.* Carefully consider how many data sources are appropriate for your organization's unique compensation situation. Some organizations use just a single source or survey, while others believe that more is better. Using more survey sources yields a larger database and helps avoid the potential bias or idiosyncrasy of a single source. Ultimately, the number of sources used by an organization in determining pay scales is a matter of preference.

Characteristics of Good Salary Surveys

1. *Good surveys adhere to antitrust safe harbor guidelines in the collection of and reporting of data.* The U.S. Department of Justice has issued guidelines suggesting parameters for the appropriate and legal collection and reporting of salary survey data. Reputable survey data providers adhere to both the spirit and letter of these guidelines.
2. *Good surveys have an adequate sample size.* Surveys with small samples have less statistical validity and can provide skewed data. It is difficult for the practitioner to know whether the data are skewed on the low side or on the high side.
3. *Good surveys contain timely data.* In the age of hyperfast business cycles and "hot-skill" positions popping up every few months, the timeliness of survey data is obviously important. However, despite the desire for up-to-the-minute data, government antitrust guidelines suggest the use of data that are at least three months old to avoid any appearance of collusive behavior.

4. *Good surveys have no secrets.* All high-quality, credible salary surveys readily disclose such items as the date of data collection, term definitions, statistical methods, position descriptions, and information about the sample and sources. These elements, in addition to a consistent methodology, are inherent in all reputable surveys. In addition, data screening and verification techniques are readily disclosed, and reputable surveys always are open to revealing the source of their sample to show the data are both valid and accurate.

5. *Be cautious with free online survey information.* Numerous issues may affect the reliability and validity of the information reported in free online survey data. A key concern is how data are collected and reported. As noted in No. 4, good surveys readily identify the source of all data and disclose details about how they were collected, the sample(s) solicited, and other important information about survey methodology.

10 Job Analysis, Documentation, and Evaluation

The process of building a base pay structure and determining the value of a job begins with job analysis. As stated in Chapter 8, job analysis can be defined as the systematic process for obtaining important and relevant information about each distinct role played by one or more employees. This would include duties and responsibilities of the job as well as the required behaviors, competencies, and worker characteristics.

One of the first questions to ask when beginning the job analysis process is, "Who in the organization should be involved?" Should it be limited to only those in human resources or compensation? How about department managers? What about incumbents?

All of the aforementioned groups would be a great addition to a team. For job analysis to be accepted as a valid analysis, you should include a team of representatives outside of the human resources function to conduct the job analysis. The incumbents are valuable because they would have the most detailed information about their own duties and responsibilities. The compensation department could provide a more objective approach and would add consistency if involved in the job-analysis process. The department managers could help the team both validate the incumbent's comments and the intent of the job.

And, although typically, a true job analysis only would be concerned with the current job, by determining the intent of the job, an analyst could analyze the job further and determine knowledge, skills, and ability requirements for the job.

When starting the process of job analysis, it is important to first determine what information to collect. This typically is based upon the method of job evaluation to be used. (See Figure 10.1.)

For internal job evaluation purposes, it is important to gather information that will help the compensation department effectively and efficiently evaluate jobs based upon the plan's predetermined critical factors. With most internal evaluation

FIGURE 10.1 Methods of job analysis.

Direct Observation—Observing workers in order to understand job duties, responsibilities, tasks, and task elements.

Individual Interview—Structured, one-on-one review of job content by a job analyst with the incumbent or supervisor.

Group Interview—A structured review of job content between a job analyst and a group of incumbents.

Technical Consultation—A structured review of job content between a job analyst and several experts.

Open-Ended Questionnaires—A written set of questions regarding job content that requires the incumbent to prepare a narrative response.

Highly Structured Questionnaires—A written set of questions regarding job content that limits responses to a predetermined set of answers.

plans, another output of the job evaluation process would be to develop some form of detailed job documentation to help effectively establish the job's position within the job-worth hierarchy. Secondly, it is important to determine which sources and methods will be used and who will be collecting this information.

When conducting a job analysis, it is necessary to identify, collect, and analyze critical data about the job. Typically, the critical data collected will fall into two categories—the nature of work and the level of work. The nature of work usually refers to the duties and responsibilities of the incumbent in the job. The level of work refers to the skill required for the job, any mental or physical effort needed, levels of responsibility/accountability, and various working conditions (basically the generic factor groups identified in the Equal Pay Act of 1963).

Several sources of information can be used to identify and analyze job-critical data. This data can be collected from both primary and secondary sources. Primary sources refer to information obtained directly from the incumbent or supervisor, and typically will be obtained by using one of the methods of job analysis listed previously. Secondary sources refer to any information obtained from sources other than the incumbent or supervisor. (See Figure 10.2.) Secondary sources are very helpful in the understanding of the job as a whole, without any possible bias that might exist with the incumbent or supervisor. It is useful to study existing secondary source information about the job or process to be reviewed.

To accomplish the goal of establishing a valid, reliable, and defensible job-evaluation system, the job analysis must have employee acceptance. If the compensation department has done an inadequate job of communicating the purpose of the job analysis, employees may have a negative view of the process. In addition to communication, it is vital that the methods of data collection and analysis are valid. Some of the barriers of validity include:

- Sampling errors.
- Incumbent bias.
- Incomplete information.
- Illogical question order and sequence.
- Inadequate communication.
- Misinterpretation of the questions.

FIGURE 10.2 Secondary sources for job analysis.

Work-flow studies may have been conducted in an attempt to analyze which jobs can be automated.

Policies and procedures materials of the group can sometimes be an indication of the work process, training, and knowledge requirements of various job groups.

Organizational charts can provide some indication of the level of the job and reporting relationships.

Existing job documentation is an effective way to obtain background information on the job.

Organizational goals or objectives discuss the responsibilities and achievements that are measured for performance purposes.

Industry association materials can be useful, as some associations have standard job descriptions to provide benchmark information.

Salary surveys have some generic job descriptions in the survey materials.

Government publications are generally inexpensive and comprehensive in sampling a large number of jobs (O*NET, Dictionary of Occupational Titles, Occupational Outlook Handbook).

- Bias in recording the information.
- Faulty interpretation of results.

By carefully reviewing the methods of data collection and the means used to analyze the data, and communicating these methods in simple terms to the employee population, the chances of a successful implementation are greatly increased. With a valid job analysis in hand, the compensation department then can move into the next phase of the job process—job documentation.

JOB DOCUMENTATION

When most people hear the words "job documentation," the first thing that comes to mind is a job description. Unfortunately, the second thing that often comes to mind is how out-of-date their organization's job descriptions are, if they exist at all. How important are job descriptions? Are job descriptions the only form of job documentation? Why do organizations use job documentation? What is the purpose?

Job descriptions are perhaps the most widely used form of job documentation, although certainly not the only form used by organizations today. Any written information about job content typically resulting from a job-analysis effort could be considered a form of job documentation. Job documentation usually takes one of several forms:

- *Job-analysis questionnaires*—in many cases, questionnaires completed by incumbents contain more specific and extensive data about a particular job than a formal job description.
- *Job-family matrices*—information on multiple levels within the same job family.
- *Job descriptions*—a formal documentation of duties and responsibilities as well as job specifications.

Job descriptions can be defined as the following:

- A job description is a summary of the most important features of a job, including the general nature of the work performed (duties and responsibilities) and level (e.g., skill, effort, responsibility, and working conditions) of the work performed.
- It typically includes job specifications that detail employee characteristics required for competent performance of the job.
- A job description should describe and focus on the job itself and not on any specific individual who might fill the job.

With the passage of the Americans with Disabilities Act of 1990, job descriptions began to take a more prominent role within organizations. Although not specifically required by the act, most employers use job descriptions as a way to identify essential functions of the job. An essential function can be defined as:

- The reason the job exists.
- A limited number of employees available to distribute the work.
- Functions that are highly specialized and require expertise.

There is no universal format for job descriptions. In fact, because job descriptions are not specifically required, a job documentation document can take any form. However, most job descriptions contain similar information.

A job title should be the first item listed on any job description. The job title defines the general nature of the job and the level of work performed, and is the main identifier of the job. It is important to include the job title for classification purposes as well as using it as a placeholder in the job-worth hierarchy.

The exemption status of the position is also typically found on a job description. In most job descriptions, it is indicated whether the job is exempt, or not exempt, from the hours worked and the overtime provisions of the FLSA. Because some organizations group like jobs together, the exemption status listing could assist with that grouping. Additionally, by listing the exemption status on the job description, employees will know if they are overtime eligible (or not).

A listing of reporting relationships is another section found on most job descriptions. In this section, both whom the employee reports to and who reports to the employee are identified. This identification could be textual or on occasion a graphical representation may be included.

The first main task identifier found on a job description is the general summary. This section is intended to give some idea of the level of skill and responsibility found in the job. It is a brief summary (just a few sentences) and is provided as a general overview of the general nature, level, and purpose of the job.

After the general summary, the job description typically contains a principal duties and responsibilities section. This section generally contains the essential functions of the job with the duties and responsibilities listed in some rank order of importance. Any duties or responsibilities that account for more than 5 percent of time or are critical to the successful performance of the job are usually included. Sometimes each duty/responsibility will have the percent of time it would encompass the incumbent's time listed, which will help in the evaluation process of the job.

After the duties and responsibilities are identified, a section containing job specifications usually can be found. This section identifies the knowledge, skills, abilities (KSAs) and behaviors needed to perform the job competently. This section usually notes the minimum specifications required to perform the job. If a bona fide occupational qualification (BFOQ) exists, it would be noted in this section.

In some job descriptions, a working conditions section is included. The working conditions section lists any hazardous or unpleasant (or pleasant) working conditions that may be encountered on the job. The information provided will entail the level of intensity, frequency, and duration of the adverse working conditions.

The final section found on most job descriptions is the disclaimer. A typical disclaimer section will cover any instance when an incumbent might be asked to do a duty that is not listed on the job description. Because of these unforeseen occurrences, many descriptions contain a disclaimer statement that states: "may perform other duties as assigned."

Although job descriptions can be written by anyone in an organization, it is recommended that the job descriptions maintain the same "look and feel" for all jobs in the organization. Human resources, the supervisor/manager, or even the incumbent could write the descriptions. Regardless of who writes the job descriptions, the job descriptions should be unbiased and kept up-to-date.

WHAT IS A JOB?

In practice, the terms *job* and *position* often are interchanged. However, there is a difference. A job consists of a collection of duties and responsibilities, which can be further divided into specific tasks and further into task elements. (See Figure 10.3.) Using an "executive assistant" job as an example, a task element is the simple motion of setting up a word processing document. A task is typing the minutes of a particular meeting. A duty is having to maintain a record of those minutes from a series of meetings. A responsibility of this job is having accountability for the recording, typing, dissemination, and maintenance of the record. When there are enough duties and responsibilities to require the employment of a worker, a position exists. Consequently, an organization has as many positions as it has current workers and job openings (vacancies). When more than one worker is employed in the same or similar position(s), a job exists.

FIGURE 10.3 Hierarchy of terms.

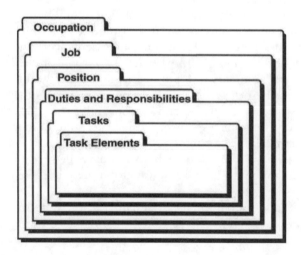

For example, when two workers are employed as administrative assistants, and their duties and responsibilities are essentially the same, there are two administrative assistant positions but only one administrative assistant job. Of course, there are also single-incumbent jobs (e.g., the chief executive officer). Jobs that are common to many organizations are known as occupations. For example, most organizations employ administrative assistants and accountants; thus, both are occupations.

A work group or team exists when a worker interacts with others to produce a component of a product or service for sale or consumption (Figure 10.4). The emphasis is on the human element involved in the production, not the mechanical or automated processes involved, except to understand how the worker interacts with or affects them. The focus of work analysis is on how worker interactions add value during the process. It consequently serves as the first step in identifying teams. Single-job analysis actually can be part of work analysis, depending on the ultimate objective of the analysis project. Job or work analysis is a step-by-step process.

JOB ANALYSIS: A STEP-BY-STEP PROCESS

Step 1: Obtain Management Approval

Before beginning a major undertaking in any organization, be sure to obtain top management support. The human resources department should not unilaterally initiate a job analysis effort. Support is won more easily when management is aware of its legal liabilities under the Fair Labor Standards Act (FLSA), ADA, Equal Pay, and all of the various local, state, and federal civil rights laws (in Canada, the Human Rights Act and pay-equity laws). Consequently, it may be necessary first to educate management about the critical role job analysis has in minimizing liability under these laws. Job analysis also is the first step to ensure that jobs are classified

FIGURE 10.4 Work team.

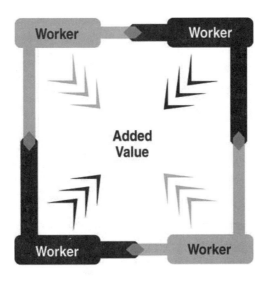

properly as either exempt or nonexempt, that "essential job functions" are identi-fied, and that hiring requirements (i.e., job specifications) are clear and defensible. Moreover, performance appraisals can lead to lawsuits under state and federal anti-discrimination laws. Legally, a performance appraisal is a type of selection proce-dure or employment test. The basis for developing standards of performance is the job description, which is developed from a detailed job analysis. Consequently, job analysis is critical to developing a sound performance management system.

When coupled with work analysis, there are many aspects of job analysis that also are of interest to management. All organizations want to ensure that roles and re-sponsibilities are clearly understood, that there is no duplication of effort, and that work flows smoothly and efficiently from one department or function to another. In an era when organizations are seeking to achieve the "right" size, job and work analysis also can establish the basis on which staffing decisions can be made. Tech-nology has greatly impacted the design of work and efficiency of workers. An up-to-date job analysis ensures management that job content, job descriptions, and so on accurately reflect how work is being performed and what skills are required. It also ensures them that correct job matching occurs when benchmark jobs are priced against relevant labor markets. Job analysis is also necessary to develop a successful training program for workers assigned to jobs that require formal training. Job and work analysis give management a clear picture of who is doing (or not doing) what, and they provide the basis for ensuring that the company's limited compensation dollars are properly spent.

To institute effective quality management programs, it is imperative that the work dynamics be understood before any realistic improvements can be made. However, management's desire to make things better is not enough; employee acceptance also is needed.

Step 2: Gain Employee Acceptance

Employee acceptance is crucial. If management has done an inadequate job of com-municating what the job analysis or work-study effort is all about and the reasons for it, negative employee relations may result.

Because of the recent downsizing trend in American business, employees natu-rally will view job or work analysis efforts with suspicion. To mitigate any negative impact of the job analysis process, an upbeat communication campaign should be developed to explain to employees why the study is being done (e.g., imple-mentation of an incentive program, compliance with ADA, re-evaluation of jobs, development of the strategic plan, development of total quality management programs, etc.).

Emphasize the benefits to the employee as well—a clearly defined job that will be the basis for developing performance standards and evaluating the job's worth, or the creation of opportunities for employee participation in the production process to increase quality and efficiency, and to enhance employee satisfaction. Potentially, the study could result in determination of required competencies and training de-veloped for employees in those competencies that employees might now fall below new standards. The latter may particularly be the case with new/upgraded technol-ogy. Communicate how employees can help the process by properly filling out ques-tionnaires, responding to interview questions with detailed information, making suggestions for work improvement, and identifying problem areas.

Emphasize to employees how critical it is to get good information about their jobs. If the job-analysis effort is the first step in a project to re-evaluate jobs, the organization should promise to communicate the results—consistent with management's philosophy on communicating compensation matters. To maintain credibility in the future, it is imperative to honor that promise.

If the work-study is intended to result in a realignment of workers into teams or to implement quality improvements, explain to participants that their input at the outset is vital, and that the final work redesign plan will be presented to them first for their suggestions. Employees must believe that their participation is welcome and will make a difference.

Gaining Union Support

In a union environment, gaining the union's cooperation and support is always important. However, even without that support, management has the right to collect important information about jobs. Fortunately, union support frequently is forthcoming because job-analysis information is helpful in defining jobs in contracts and in conducting pay surveys. However, job descriptions sometimes become work "rules" and handcuff management's flexibility in union environments.

Work-studies may be opposed if a union perceives it to be the first step in job eliminations. However, in today's competitive, global economy, unions understand the need for efficiency and quality. It is on this basis that their cooperation can be solicited, especially if they are invited to participate in the process so everyone is working toward a common goal—a profitable and stable organization that produces a quality product.

Step 3: Decide Who Will Conduct the Analysis

Job or work analysis can be performed by anyone in the organization who has been trained or who is familiar with the work being analyzed. Of course, it is always best to ask trained job analysts from the human resources department or elsewhere to conduct the study. This is not always practical, however, because of time constraints, geographic limitations, or company size.

To be efficient, especially when many jobs need to be analyzed, organizations ask supervisors, job incumbents, human resources staff, outside consultants, and others to perform the analysis. The best results come from directly involving supervisors and incumbents. Most important, mutual concern for working efficiently and enhanced communication between worker and manager often result. If everyone is not trained in the analysis techniques discussed in this book, the results will be inconsistent, and, consequently, of limited value.

Whoever is chosen to do the analysis should have good interpersonal skills, good writing skills, and knowledge of how the organization functions. In addition, successful analysts will be inquisitive by nature and objective in their business dealings.

Step 4: Think in Terms of Work Flow

In all organizations, whether profit or nonprofit, public or private, work "flows" from one area to another. (See Figure 10.5.) Whether it is manual or intellectual work that is being analyzed, think of work flow in these terms: The worker will receive work from someone (or somewhere), will add value by doing something to it, and then will pass it on to the next worker. If no value is added (this may frequently be the case, particularly in bureaucratic organizations), the activity should be reviewed to determine the implications of discontinuing it. If it is discontinued, the worker should be reassigned, if possible.

In a quality management environment, workflow focuses heavily on the "added-value" component. Workflow on an assembly line, for example, might involve one worker passing a semifinished product to the next worker on the line, who adds another part and then passes it on, and so on until completion.

In quality management, workflow is scrutinized from two standpoints:

- From within the job itself.
- Through the entire process of the workflow.

Workflow is not simply lateral. In knowledge work, workers receive a project assignment from their bosses, or a request from another department, or a report from a subordinate. A job analyst's concern is what the worker does with the assignment. Therefore, workflow can be vertical (work assignments are passed upward or

FIGURE 10.5 How work flows.

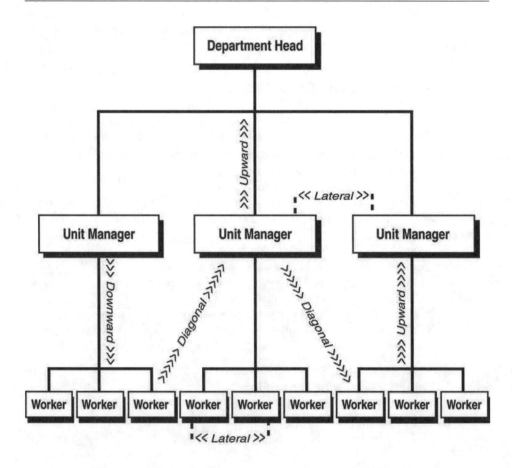

downward in the organization), lateral (work assignments are received from and sent to peer departments), or diagonal (work is requested from or sent to incumbents who are in other functions and at different levels in the organizational hierarchy). Often, the formal chain of command is not followed, and workflow speed increases; this is important to remember in conducting workflow analysis, especially if the ultimate goal of the analysis is to reorganize job incumbents into teams.

While review of workflow is important for both quality management and job evaluation purposes, the process differs for each purpose. For job evaluation, it is important to understand a specific job and its relationship with other jobs in the job-worth hierarchy (the value organizations place on individual jobs). In quality management, workflow is scrutinized from two standpoints:

- From within the job itself, by having the job incumbent ask questions for each activity, such as: From where or from whom does the work come? Are there any changes in how the work is provided to me that would make my job easier or faster? How could I enhance the work I provide to others to expedite the next step in the workflow? By asking such questions, the worker is trained to think in an analytical way about what is being done and why.
- Through the entire process of the workflow, to determine if a major activity can be accomplished more effectively and efficiently through reassignment or through modification of one or more tasks or responsibilities, not only across job functions but also across departmental lines. If the purpose of the work-study ultimately is to enhance teamwork, the analysis will focus additionally on identifying the best cluster of workers, or "team," that adds value to the product or service being produced.

Step 5: Consult Secondary Sources First

Before beginning to conduct the actual job or work analysis by approaching a worker or a supervisor, it is always useful to study existing secondary-source information about the job or process to be reviewed. Many sources of information are already available about the work being performed.

Internal Sources

The most obvious and perhaps most useful piece of information available is the existing job description. Instead of starting from scratch, it is possible simply to update the job description based on additional information gathered from the job incumbent, supervisor, or both. Focus on "what has changed" rather than rewriting the job description from the beginning. Again, technology has greatly influenced how work is done, and it is imperative that these changes are captured through a current job analysis. Generic job descriptions provided in salary surveys of benchmark jobs are another good secondary source of information.

Other sources can offer quite a bit of information about the job, about the unit in which the job or work group is located, and about workflow. In terms of workflow, the most useful source is the organization chart. It tells where the worker function is located within the organization, and it provides a good idea of where the work comes from and where it goes after the unit has added value.

Many organizations design company phone books that reflect their structure. For example, the head of a department is shown at the top of the page, indented below is a list of the major functional units within that department, and further indented are the specific names and titles of workers in each unit. When current formal organization charts are not available, the phone book can be a valuable substitute, but keep in mind that it may not reflect actual reporting relationships accurately.

Today's organizations often use the management-by-objectives (MBO) approach to communicate the key contributions expected from each department on an annual basis. These usually are broken into specific objectives for each worker, and they will indicate the expected contribution(s) of the job being analyzed. Organization or department strategic plans and annual budget write-ups also can provide helpful, though indirect, information. These are important models to use while conducting the "reality test" in Step 10.

In an attempt to understand which functions can be automated, systems analysts often prepare work-studies and procedures manuals. To do so, they will ask job incumbents to keep diaries and logs for a period of time. Certain types of work need to be performed in an orderly and consistent manner, and many organizations develop training or procedures manuals that instruct the worker on how to perform specific tasks. These documents all should be consulted to gain an understanding of the nature of the work that is being performed before actually conducting a job analysis. If parts of the workflow have been outsourced, the outsourcing contract will usually contain specific "Service Level Agreements" that spell out in detail the work to be performed and the level of quality to be achieved by the external entity.

External Sources

Source material also may be found in government publications, books, magazines, and other material published by industry or professional trade associations. *The Dictionary of Occupational Titles (DOT)*, published by the federal government, provides information on more than 20,000 job titles. The government also publishes *The Occupational Outlook Handbook (OOH)*, which is cross-referenced to the *DOT* and provides extensive information about jobs and the outlook for related careers. Both are valuable sources and especially are useful when the analyst has little knowledge of the jobs to be studied. Both *DOT* and *OOH* are accessible online.

In addition, many professions such as law, accounting, and human resources have associations that gladly will supply information about the nature of work performed by their membership, including model job descriptions. Usually, they also publish magazines and newsletters that, although technical or narrow, certainly can provide valuable insight to a job analyst. In addition, do not forget the local bookstore or library, where information can be found about the type of work that is to be analyzed, including textbooks in the subject field.

The idea is to use any or all of these sources, as necessary, to gain at least a general understanding of the job before moving to the next step. Moreover, the customer may be the most critical source of information regarding the quality or lack of it that represents the outcome of the work performed.

Step 6: Decide Method and Collect Data

When deciding how to collect the information needed to analyze work, it is important to take into account the scope of the project and the time, staff, and costs involved. There are three primary methods of collecting information about jobs: observation, interviews, and questionnaires. Each has advantages and disadvantages.

Observation Method

The observation method is most appropriate for manual and repetitive production work. For example, in the case of an assembly line worker attaching simple handles to pieces of equipment, two or three observations would be sufficient to learn where the work comes from, what the assembler does with it, and where the work goes after the operation is complete.

In-depth questioning of the worker, or having the worker maintain a detailed log for several days, would not be necessary to understand what is being done and how it is being done. For a more complicated or protracted process, it might be necessary to observe several cycles or to observe them piecemeal. The cycles may occur over days or weeks, so it is important to know if the entire function or just part of it is being observed.

How to Observe

Do not assume that the worker knows why the observation is occurring. Remember, the best job analysis occurs in an atmosphere of trust. Once the observation begins, be as unobtrusive as possible so as not to interfere with the process. While observing production jobs, it is important to be aware of the effort the worker exerts in doing the job and the physical environment in which the work is performed. Record noise, heat, moving machine parts, and the weight of parts or equipment handled. Pay special attention to the work environment, for example, heat, noise, etc. If the work is performed outside, weather and other factors may also be important. Note any exposure or handling of hazardous materials, safety equipment required as well as the physical demand on the worker, for example, ability to lift objects weighing more than 50 pounds. Thank the worker when finished with the observations. It is always a good idea to discuss observations with a supervisor. Summarize any notes taken soon after the observation so important details are not forgotten. If complete, notes are a form of job documentation, even though they usually are developed into a more formal job description.

The observation method is not limited to single-job analysis. It is useful in following a product or service from raw material to finished product, especially if the process is predominantly manual in nature. In fact, it is a valuable first step in total quality management to walk through the entire production process before any changes are contemplated. "Walk-throughs" are also a valuable step when the purpose of the study is to identify appropriate members of work teams.

Observation and Interviews

Observation can be used in conjunction with questionnaires by having workers complete them before observation of the production process. When observing a more sophisticated process, ask the worker a few questions to clarify the observations. For example, suppose an assembler sometimes opens the casing before attaching the handle and makes some adjustment to the internal mechanisms. Observation in this case does not tell the whole story. It is necessary to ask the assembler why the adjustments are being made to some machines and not others, what the adjustment actually is, and how long the average adjustment takes. In a workflow study; ask what could have been done in a previous operation to make the worker's job more efficient, or what the worker could do to streamline the next operation in the process. Try not to interfere with the worker or the process; questioning between cycles is best. If it seems that part of the picture is missing, talk to a supervisor.

Observations: Advantages and Disadvantages

Observation is time-consuming and costly, and it requires observers to be trained properly. By itself, it may not be a sufficient approach to job analysis because the observer might "miss" something important. In a more thorough work analysis, an analyst will have to question why things are being done. Consequently, the analyst will have to discuss his or her observations with a worker's supervisor or other technical experts. While it can be expensive, observation is not as costly as the next method, one-on-one interviewing.

One-on-One Interviewing

The observation method becomes less useful toward the higher end of the organization hierarchy. Watching a financial analyst poring over numbers or executing a computer program will not tell much about what actually is being done, nor will it indicate the skills required to do it. An in-depth discussion with the job incumbent will provide information about what is being done, how and why. A useful analogy often has been drawn between a job analyst doing an interview and a newspaper reporter whose job is to find out who, what, where, when, why, and how. As mentioned before, consult secondary sources first to ensure that interview questions are informed and insightful.

Starting an Interview

The most important part of the interview is the beginning. (See Figure 10.6.) It is always important to put the job incumbent at ease by engaging in informal chitchat to break the ice. Then, as the formal part of the interview begins, it is imperative to explain why the meeting is taking place, what will be discussed, and what will occur after the interview is over. If the job incumbent still seems unsure about why the interview is taking place, it is even more important to provide an adequate explanation. Otherwise, the interviewee will be guarded and the interview will be difficult. Remember, the best interview occurs in an atmosphere of trust and mutual commitment to fact-finding.

Start the actual interview with broad, general questions: On what do you spend most of your time? What are your major responsibilities, from the most important to the least important?

If there are no up-to-date organization charts, start by asking the incumbent to describe the department and the chain of command. Keeping the concept of workflow in mind, probe from the general to the specific as the incumbent begins to answer questions. Listen actively by nodding when the incumbent emphasizes certain points. Use eye-to-eye contact frequently and ask insightful and clarifying questions; it demonstrates genuine interest in the job.

FIGURE 10.6 How to conduct an interview.

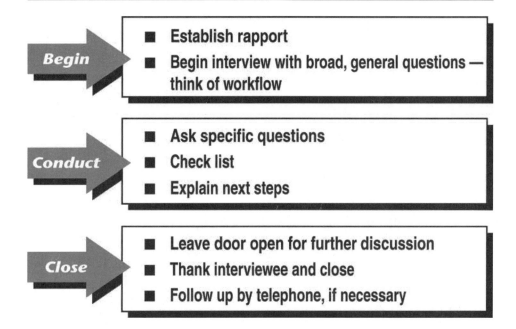

Learn to listen "between the lines." Avoid closed-ended questions that can be answered with simple "yes" or "no" answers. The mission is to obtain as much information about the job as possible.

Writing a Job Description

If the goal is to write a job description from the interview that will be used for job evaluation, it is necessary to know beforehand what the evaluators will be looking for in the job description—that is, what "compensable factors" they will be using to evaluate the job. Compensable factors are ones for which an organization is willing to pay. The specific factors and how they are measured should be explained in the job-evaluation plan being used.

It is important to have a solid understanding of the compensable factors in order to ask pertinent questions or to probe deeper for clarification. Let's take a compensable factor such as "freedom to act," for example, and assume it is measured by the degree of sign-off authority an incumbent has. In the interview, ask: "What is your expenditure approval authority? Is it $1,000? $10,000? $1 million?"

Note that the answer to this question is expressed in numbers, or dimensions. *Dimensions* are statistics that help quantify the scope of the job and the impact that the incumbent performing it has on the bottom line. Frequently requested dimensions include dollar sign-off authority, number of subordinates reporting, budget, dollar-value of plant and equipment, sales volume, revenues, expenses, assets under management, and so on.

Some organizations are moving toward defining jobs in terms of "competencies," the technical and behavioral skills inherently needed to perform the job well. Competencies focus on what people are or can do; they identify traits, knowledge, skills, and abilities.

How to Ask Questions

Not all questions will be direct or specific. Figure 10.7 gives a list of suggested questions that can be modified to create a specific checklist that ensures all-important topics have been covered. With practice, it is possible to develop a reliable list of questions and a sequence for asking them. Remember to ask questions that pertain to quality management and workflow. (See questions 9 through 14 in Figure 10.7.)

Each interview is unique, and some will be easier (and more interesting) than others. Do not try to hold the job incumbent to a preset notion of the order in which things should be discussed. Remember to direct the interview, not control it. A free-flowing dialogue can reveal much. However, to make sure all important issues have been explored, double-check the question list toward the end of the interview.

During the interview, it is acceptable to admit that something is unclear. Every profession has its jargon and acronyms, and professionals often talk in "code," forgetting that the uninitiated do not understand. When unsure of something, stop the interviewee and ask, "What does that mean?", or, "Could you please explain?" Also ask for examples. If a financial analyst talks about a complicated report, ask to see a copy of it. Being able to touch the report physically to see how lengthy and

FIGURE 10.7 Suggested interview questions.

1. To whom do you report?
2. Who reports to you?
3. What are your budget accountabilities—both budget dollars and the value of assets under your control?
4. What are your principal duties and responsibilities?
5. What is the most important task you perform?
6. How do you spend most of your time?
7. On whom do you rely for information necessary to do your job?
8. To whom do you routinely provide information?
9. What tasks should be completed before the work comes to you?
10. What do you do to add to the quality of the product (or service)?
11. What tasks do you feel are redundant or unnecessary?
12. How can workflow be improved?
13. How would you change the workflow to expedite the process without decreasing quality?
14. What could be handled differently to reduce expenses or costs?
15. Are there any formal guidelines, regulations, policies, etc., that you must follow in fulfilling your job responsibilities?
16. About what decisions would you consult or notify your boss before taking action?
17. How does this job challenge your creativity and problem-solving abilities?
18. With whom do you have regular contact, both inside and outside the organization? What is the reason for the contact?
19. What qualifications would your replacement need, in terms of knowledge and experience, to perform your job at a competent level?
20. Describe the physical conditions in which you work (if appropriate).
21. How would you answer the question, "Why does my job exist?"

involved it is (or is not) will provide a more complete picture of the work as well as the knowledge, skills, and abilities required to do it.

Closing the Interview

Closing the interview is as important as beginning it. Explain the next steps in the process. (For example, a draft of the job description will be prepared and sent for the incumbent's review and comments within five business days.) Give the incumbent a business card and invite him or her to call if there is anything that should have been discussed but was not. Find out when the best time is to contact the job incumbent with follow-up questions, if necessary.

Most organizations separate the responsibility for job analysis from the responsibility for job evaluation. However, someone in the awkward position of being both analyst and evaluator should not be forced during the interview into giving an indication of the evaluation. Emphasize the current fact-finding role; explain that evaluation decisions will be postponed until the job description is finished and can be reviewed in the context of the larger picture. If the interview was conducted as part of a work-study, explain that the job and the value it adds will be assessed when the whole process has been analyzed.

Often, the incumbent will find that the interview was a valuable experience. Don't be surprised if the incumbent says afterward, "You know, I never stopped to think about how much I actually get involved with around here."

When finished with the interview, take time immediately to summarize and organize notes, especially if there is more than one interview a day or if a time lapse of a day or two is expected before it is possible to write the job description or work-analysis report. Time has a way of eroding the understanding and recall of important details.

Group Interviews

Interviewing is not limited to a single job incumbent. It is possible to conduct a "group interview," where several incumbents are interviewed at the same time. The guidelines presented earlier apply. At times, especially in total-quality programs, it may be desirable to bring several experts from different disciplines together to discuss the work, usually because it is highly technical.

For example, consider an assembler who has to stop occasionally to make an adjustment before attaching the handle. Perhaps there is a problem with the previous operation. By bringing the supervisor, quality-control manager, and parts department together, the problem can be identified and resolved. If not, at least there will be an adequate explanation made of why the adjustment is necessary on some machines but not every machine, and a conclusion can be drawn that there is nothing more to be done to prevent it at this time. Such meetings are known as "technical interviews" because they tend to focus on very specific items. Technical interviews are critical in a total-quality study because they help enhance communications, clarify the source of problems, and identify possible solutions.

Interviewing Customers

Although a different set of questions may be used to interview customers, the questioning techniques will be similar. However, more emphasis will be placed on product quality and customer needs and wants.

Interviewing: Advantages and Disadvantages

Interviewing is the most costly method of job and work analysis, especially when there are many jobs to be analyzed. For one thing, interviewing occupies two people simultaneously in a single-job analysis, or several in a technical interview or quality review. For another, interviewing takes a lot of time.

Interviewing can be inefficient if the analyst and the interviewee(s) are ill prepared to engage in a meaningful discussion of the work. This can happen if the purpose of the meeting is not explained adequately, if the analyst does not consult secondary sources, or if there is resistance to the job or work analysis underway. What adds to cost is the additional time the job analyst spends organizing notes and actually writing the job description or a thorough workflow study. However, the benefits from accurate job descriptions, improved quality, cost savings, efficiency, and enhanced communication often far outweigh the costs involved in the interview method.

Questionnaires

When many jobs are to be analyzed, questionnaires often are used in place of interviews. Questionnaires are interviews on paper. They set forth a list of questions that attempt to capture the same information that would be pursued in a one-on-one interview.

Questionnaires are flexible because they can be tailored to the job population being analyzed, especially when the nature of the work is very different. For example, a questionnaire for production jobs most likely would be modified for professional jobs and further modified for executive-level jobs. Such questionnaires are great devices for preparing a job incumbent for an interview. By sending the incumbent a questionnaire a week or so ahead of the actual interview, the chances of a successful interview are increased greatly because the incumbent has a chance to think through the questions and to gather relevant materials.

Frequently, when there are a number of incumbents (positions), analysts will select a sample of individuals to interview after they have received the completed questionnaires. Often, a manager will help the analyst in deciding whom to interview. Usually, it is best to interview the most experienced job incumbents, and the best performers. A combination of completed questionnaires and selective interviewing can be a highly effective way of conducting a thorough job analysis, and it can provide the analyst with a solid basis for developing an accurate and complete job description or a thorough workflow study.

Open-Ended Questionnaires

There are essentially two types of questionnaires. For most professional, managerial, and executive-level jobs, an "open-ended" questionnaire is appropriate. It is called open-ended because the questions are structured to allow the job incumbent much latitude in responding—the same technique as used during an interview. The questionnaire form should provide a sufficient amount of blank space for job incumbents to complete their answers. (For an example, see Figure 10.8.)

The responses to open-ended questionnaires may be inadequate for a complete job analysis. Frequently, it is necessary to follow up with the job incumbent to clarify or elaborate on responses; this process can be handled easily over the phone.

FIGURE 10.8 Position-analysis questionnaire.

NAME _____ DATE _____

JOB TITLE _____ DEPARTMENT _____

DIMENSIONS Describe any specific measures of your job responsibilities (e.g., budget accountability, operating revenues, number of customers, geographic areas of responsibility, assets under management, etc.)

ORGANIZATION CHART

Your job title [_____]

Job titles reporting to you

Indicate the primary function of each area below

DUTIES AND RESPONSIBILITIES Please group your job duties into major areas of responsibility and list them, in order of importance, beginning with the most important.

% time required	Major areas of responsibility

(Attach any additional information you believe is relevant.)

CONTACTS

A. With what other jobs in the company do you have regular contact, and what is the purpose of these contacts?

B. Describe the nature and purpose of any external contacts required by your job.

C. From where do your work assignments come, and where or to whom do you send completed work?

EFFICIENCY AND QUALITY

A. What tasks should be completed before work comes to you?

B. How can workflow be improved?

C. What specific value do you add to the quality of the product or service?

DECISION MAKING

A. List any formal guidelines, technical manuals, regulations, etc., with which you must comply in fulfilling your job responsibilities.

B. What issues would you refer to your boss before you took any action?

C. What do you consider to be the major challenge(s) of your position?

JOB SPECIFICATIONS — Summarize the specific knowledge, skills and abilities your job requires. (If you were recruiting to fill a job identical to yours, what background would you expect a successful job applicant to have?)

1. Knowledge of:

2. Skill in:

3. Ability to:

4. Describe any previous work experience required to perform your job.

POSITION OBJECTIVE — In one or two sentences, answer the question: "Why does my job exist?" (Focus on end results.)

Approved: _____
         Manager

         Date _____

Reviewed: _____
          Corporate Compensation

          Date _____

If the majority of the incumbents in the job population being analyzed have weak language and writing skills, their responses will be of limited value. This is why open-ended questionnaires often are not used for lower-level jobs. On the other hand, highly creative incumbents may enhance responses so the analyst believes their jobs have a much greater impact on organizational success than they actually do, or the analyst may not notice redundancies or inefficiencies.

Closed-Ended Questionnaires

Closed-ended questionnaires, which focus mainly on the frequency of tasks or responsibilities, typically are used for lower-level, production-type jobs. They measure simply whether an incumbent has responsibility for performing a certain task, and, if so, how frequently. Two sample questions from a closed-ended questionnaire are shown in Figure 10.9.

Closed-ended questionnaires are often designed to be analyzed by computers. The mere fact that a worker does or does not perform a task usually does not address the issues an analyst is trying to uncover in a work-study. The analyst's goal is to improve efficiency and quality, and questionnaires generally are considered to be of limited use in workflow analysis.

There are highly sophisticated closed-ended questionnaires tailored to specific organizations, and some questionnaires are very effective for job evaluation for most levels in an organization because they are behavioral- rather than task-based. These questionnaires are very expensive to develop, and they are processed using computers and statistical techniques. They, too, do not lend themselves to workflow analysis.

Questionnaires: Advantages and Disadvantages

Because the questionnaire method can be used to analyze large numbers of jobs in the least amount of time, it is considered the most efficient method of single-job analysis. However, questionnaires by themselves often result in incomplete, confusing, or insufficient answers. If the language and writing skills of the population are inadequate, the results will be weak. If the job population being studied includes employees who do not read or write English, the English version of the questionnaire will have to be translated and the answers interpreted, adding to the cost.

Using questionnaires may be a necessary step, but it probably will not be a sufficient step in documenting work for purposes of a quality study. Follow-up interviews, most likely technical interviews, will be required.

FIGURE 10.9 Closed-ended questionnaire.

Job-related experience required for competent performance of this job. (Check one.)	Maintain effective customer relations. (Check one.)
	Not part of job
No experience required	Little time spent performing this task
Up to one month	Moderate time spent performing this task
Over 1 month, up to 12 months	Substantial time spent performing this task
Over 1 year, up to 3 years	Little time spent supervising this task
Over 3 years up to 5 years	Moderate time spent supervising this task
More than 5 years	Substantial time spent supervising this task

SOURCE: Materials for WorldatWork Certification Course C2: Job Analysis, Documents, and Evaluation, 2007.

Step 7: Document the Analysis

When data gathering is complete, job documentation already has been created, regardless of the data-collection method or combination of methods used. Notes taken during an observation or an interview are a form of job documentation, as are completed questionnaires.

FIGURE 10.10 Example of a human resources manager job description.

JOB TITLE: Human Resources Manager

REPORTS TO:	Director of Human Resources
JOB INCUMBENT:	J. Doe
LOCATION:	ABC Division
DATE:	January
JOB ANALYST:	VCW

JOB SUMMARY

This position is accountable for managing the implementation of human resource policies and practices, programs, processes and procedures for three sites affecting approximately 600 employees, under the direction of the Director of Human Resources, consistent with corporate policies and procedures.

DIMENSIONS: Employee Relations Administrators (3)
Recruiter (1)
Personnel Assistant (2)
Secretary (1)
Employees (600)

1. Provides direction to Employee Relations Administrators to ensure accurate, equitable implementation of human resource policies and procedures.

2. Reviews policies, procedures and education programs provided by corporate headquarters; educates managers and establishes communication programs for employees.

3. Oversees personnel file maintenance for division, including processing of salary increases, job changes, terminations and other personnel actions. Ensures integrity of human resources database information.

4. Provides advice and counsel to division managers concerning employee relations, hiring, progressive discipline, termination, promotions, workers compensation and other human resource actions.

5. Manages recruiting effort for new/replacement jobs to ensure openings are approved, managerial strategy is determined, job is described properly and appropriate recruitment sources are used. Oversees orientation of new employees.

6. Ensures proper termination procedures are followed regarding employees leaving the company.

7. Provides accurate, timely demographic information to corporate, including employment statistics for Affirmative Action programs.

8. Coordinates with Division Safety Manager to maintain safe, productive employee environment.

9. Works with corporate training staff to develop and implement managerial and employee training programs.

10. Develops, recommends and implements employee welfare programs such as stress management, health screenings, etc., and employee activities such as the company picnic, intramural sports leagues and entertainment discounts.

JOB SPECIFICATIONS

Knowledge
Requires English written and verbal communications knowledge; general knowledge of business operations; sufficient employment law, employee relations, and personnel policy knowledge to advise managers; and sufficient knowledge of basic salary administration and benefits programs to ensure accurate implementation.

Skills and Abilities
Strong interpersonal skills to counsel managers and employees, and the ability to communicate effectively in verbal and written form to keep employees and managers apprised of current human resource programs and employee relations issues.

Ability to collect, analyze and interpret statistical data to make recommendations to management regarding utilization of human resource programs.

Ability to manage and develop subordinates.

Ability to travel to three separate locations at least weekly and extend work day into second-shift hours as needed. Ability to respond to emergency calls from second shift at each location.

Knowledge and skills identified above typically are acquired through undergraduate-level studies in human resources, industrial psychology or business administration and five years' progressively responsible human resources experience, including six months with the company for knowledge of company-specific plans and programs.

DISCLAIMER
This job description indicates the general nature and level of work expected of the incumbent. It is not designed to cover or contain a comprehensive listing of activities, duties or responsibilities required of the incumbent. Incumbent may be asked to perform other duties as required.

Approved: _____
Director of Human Resources

Date _____

Reviewed: _____
Corporate Compensation

Date _____

Job descriptions are the most common, complete, and usable form of job documentation because they attempt to record the important aspects of a job in an organized, narrative fashion. (See Figures 10.10, 10.11, and 10.12.) Because job descriptions vary from organization to organization, there is no widely agreed-upon format. However, descriptions usually contain the following sections:

FIGURE 10.11 Example of a department administrative assistant job description.

JOB TITLE: Department Administrative Assistant

REPORTS TO:	Controller
JOB INCUMBENT:	S. Jones
FLSA:	Nonexempt
DATE:	January
JOB ANALYST:	VCW

JOB SUMMARY

This position is accountable for providing administrative support to the Corporate Controller and the department professional staff, including routine and specialized administrative services.

PRINCIPAL DUTIES

1. Transcribes machine-recorded dictation involving general business vocabulary or a limited range of specialized accounting terminology.

2. Uses word processing software to produce correspondence, reports, tables, financial schedules, etc., from rough drafts, and edits grammar, punctuation or spelling.

3. Assembles and completes a variety of routine reports for approval by Controller, posts data to records and logs, and maintains established files.

4. Responds to routine inquiries from telephone callers and visitors, redirecting calls or providing routine information requiring a detailed knowledge of department functions.

5. Performs routine administrative functions, such as responding to inquiries with a standard letter or arranging meetings and conferences.

6. Maintains Controller's calendar, schedules appointments as directed and arranges travel schedules, as necessary.

7. Sorts, opens and distributes mail directed to department.

8. May take and produce minutes of department meetings.

9. Performs other duties as required.

JOB SPECIFICATIONS

1. Work requires written communication skills to edit and proofread business correspondence and reports.

2. Work requires the ability to type accurately and efficiently from rough draft and machine transcription involving a standard business vocabulary or a limited range of specialized, recurrent accounting terminology using word-processing software.

3. Work requires a thorough knowledge of department policies, practices and operations, and oral communication skill to perform routine administrative duties such as arranging meetings, responding to routine inquiries from telephone callers or visitors, and gathering background information for routine reports.

4. Work requires the ability to analyze routine administrative details of limited complexity such as resolving minor scheduling conflicts, redirecting mail, etc.

5. Work requires ability to read and concentrate via typing and proofreading activities, including numbers, up to 50 percent of time.

6. Work is typically sedentary, but may require standing and walking for up to 10 percent of work time; occasional bending and stooping while accessing files.

The above knowledge and skills normally are acquired through completion of a high school education, plus a two-year vocational office education program or equivalent work experience and nine months related company experience, in addition to one month on-the-job training.

DISCLAIMER
This job description indicates the general nature and level of work expected of the incumbent. It is not designed to cover or contain a comprehensive listing of activities, duties or responsibilities required of the incumbent. Incumbent may be asked to perform other duties as required.

Approved: _____

      Controller _____

      Date _____

Reviewed: _____

- *Heading:* Important organizational information is provided here (e.g., title, department, FLSA status, current date, job incumbent, reporting relationships, job analyst, etc.).
- *Job Summary:* Two to four sentences usually are written to answer a single question: "Why does this job exist?" It is advisable to write the job summary only after the rest of the job description has been written and the entire job—including the required knowledge, skills, and abilities—has been "thought through."
- *Principal Duties:* This section lists the major duties and responsibilities of the job incumbent. It can be organized a number of ways: from the most important responsibility to the least important, most time spent to least time spent, or in order of sequence. For lower-level jobs, it is a good idea to indicate the percentage of time spent on each responsibility, making sure the percentages, of course, total 100.

Because of the ADA, "principal duties" should be divided into two subsections: essential functions and nonessential functions. Many organizations include a disclaimer statement such as, "Performs other duties as required." This type of disclaimer becomes particularly important as organizations expand the content of jobs and provide more lateral experiences for job incumbents. In a union environment, however, the disclaimer statement might not be permitted, and under the ADA it should pertain only to nonessential functions.

- *Working Conditions:* The physical environment in which the work is performed is described here. Adverse environmental conditions such as noise, heat, and fumes are detailed along with the frequency of exposure. Most professional and executive job descriptions do not include this section because work is

FIGURE 10.12 Example of a human resources manager, human capital team, job description.

TITLE: Human Resources Manager

TEAM:	Human Capital Team
LOCATION:	ABC Division
DATE:	January
JOB ANALYST:	VCW

TEAM OBJECTIVE

The objective of the Human Capital Team is to ensure that appropriate human resources strategies are in place to maximize the division's human capital in support of the business plan.

HR MANAGER TEAM RESPONSIBILITIES

1. Analyzes and determines skills and abilities of existing workforce vis-á-vis the five-year business plan and recommends staffing and development strategies to meet the human capital needs of the division.

2. Advises team on training and development needs of the work force, including the cost-benefit analysis of developing and conducting training in-house vs. engaging outside sources.

3. Develops staffing strategies to meet the division's labor needs.

4. Develops compensation strategies that support the business plan.

5. Serves as knowledge expert regarding HR policies, procedures and practices, and recommends revisions as appropriate to support business objectives.

6. Advises team on applicable local, state and federal employment-related statutes.

TEAM MEMBER SPECIFICATIONS

Requires the ability to interpret five-year business plans into human capital needs and to develop appropriate strategies to meet those needs and knowledge of company human resources policies, practices and procedures. Knowledge and skill are usually acquired through undergraduate-level studies in human resources, industrial psychology or business administration and five years of progressively responsible human resources experience.

assumed to be performed under normal office conditions. If it is not, the section should be included.

- *Job Specifications:* Commonly referred to as hiring or background requirements, job specifications tell the reader what specific knowledge, skills and abilities a worker needs to perform the job at a satisfactory level. Avoid simply stating, "B.A. or B.S. required." Instead, list the specific areas of knowledge the incumbent must have, and then conclude (if it is reasonable to do so) that what is listed is "equivalent to a B.A. or B.S." in a specific subject area.

Use the financial analyst job as an example. A specification might read as follows: "This position requires knowledge of accounting, financial analysis and forecasting techniques, as well as quantitative methods acquired through formal education and two to three years of on-the-job application. Also required is computer proficiency in spreadsheet software and word processing, and strong writing and verbal skills to prepare management reports and presentations. Equivalent to a B.A. or B.S. in finance or business administration."

If the objective of the analysis is the "big picture," it probably will be necessary to submit a work-study report. The format of such a report will, of course, depend on management's preferences and the person preparing the report. A work-study report usually includes the job descriptions in an appendix, but the body of the report will describe the workflow, opportunities for improvement, quality pitfalls, inefficiencies, and staffing redundancies or inadequacies. Diagram the workflow and highlight the opportunities for improvements. If appropriate, include recommended team rosters.

Step 8: Obtain Necessary Approvals

No job description is complete without the review and approval of the immediate supervisor. If the organization culture supports it, have the job incumbent review a first draft for accuracy, and then submit the revised version to the supervisor for review and approval. Have the supervisor sign and date the description.

Job documentation should be anchored in time so future readers will know exactly when the analysis was done. If someone other than a trained job analyst prepared the job description, have the human resources department review it for content and format consistency. Most organizations require human resources review of the job description.

Obtaining approval for a work-study report might not be straightforward because the recommendations might point to perceived failures on the part of some departments. However, if the whole initiative was positioned as a team effort with substantial participation from line managers and workers, then the final recommendations (Step 11) should be everyone's, not just those of the report's author.

Step 9: Test for Legal Compliance

After summarizing the observation or interview notes—or obtaining a completed questionnaire—ask some questions. Are the job specifications defensible? Does the job content described support the knowledge, skills, and abilities required? Will the job content pass an exemption test under the FLSA?

Throughout the observations and interviews, be aware of equipment or processes that would prohibit a disabled person from performing a particular activity, and determine if that activity is "essential" to the performance of the job. Ask whether the activity is necessary to achieve the end result(s) of the job, or whether it is an "add-on" activity that easily could be reassigned to another worker. While going through this analysis, think of ways a disabled worker could perform the activity with the aid of special equipment or with a schedule change.

If appropriate, have the individual responsible for plant safety review the documentation for compliance with the Occupational Safety and Health Act (OSHA). Also, if the final product is a work-study report that recommends substantial organizational changes affecting people's jobs—especially if it results in staff reductions—the EEO specialist should conduct a population analysis to determine if any adverse impact will result from implementation of the recommendations.

Step 10: Conduct a Reality Test

In addition to testing the job documentation for legal considerations, it is always a good idea to step back and look at the big picture. Even if the specific mission was only to analyze single jobs and write job descriptions, a good job analyst always questions the work design to identify opportunities for improvement. Are the analyzed jobs designed to meet departmental objectives identified in the secondary sources? Is the flow of work consistent with meeting those objectives efficiently? Are the right workers interacting regularly to ensure quality? Would establishing a team approach greatly improve efficiency? Is there any duplication of effort? Are there enough quality checkpoints? Are roles and responsibilities defined clearly? Do all workers understand their jobs? Are expectations communicated clearly? Are accountabilities understood? Does everyone in the process take ownership of the end result?

These are just sample questions. More specific questions, depending on the goal of the study, also might be required. The ultimate objective is to realize the maximum from efforts to analyze individual jobs and to examine workflow. The most important question is: What specific suggestions or recommendations can be made to management that would improve quality and efficiency, enhance communications, expedite workflow, reduce costs, empower workers, and so on?

Step 11: Formulate Specific Recommendations

If the analyst's role was limited to single-job analysis for the purposes of job evaluation, Step 11 is not required. However, if the end product is a work-study report, organize the opportunities identified in Step 10 into a final report to the appropriate member of management. Include workflow charts and final job descriptions or team rosters to illustrate recommendations.

Step 12: Keep Up-to-Date

The world is changing constantly. New technology, new products, new markets, and reorganizations make existing job documentation obsolete quickly.

Organizations become bureaucracies when old methods and processes become entrenched. Consequently, these methods and processes need to be reviewed much more frequently than in the past. Initially, the task of conducting job and work analysis and creating job documentation is onerous. However, a comprehensive analysis of all jobs does not need to be repeated every time the organization changes. If a procedure is established for keeping job descriptions and other forms of documentation up to date, a total reconstruction of the job-documentation library is not necessary. Establish a "tickler" file that ages job descriptions so that every two or three years a job description (or questionnaire) can be sent to the incumbent and supervisor for review and comment. Many organizations ask managers and subordinates to review job descriptions annually as performance reviews are conducted. This approach serves the dual purpose of updating the description and focusing both parties on appraising performance on the basis of job responsibilities.

Organizations are reorganizing and creating new jobs continually, and managers frequently approach the human resources department for job re-evaluation. As these events occur, job documentation should be updated. With the powerful word-processing capability that exists today, keeping job descriptions or questionnaires up to date is not as burdensome as it was in the past. Also, there are many software packages on the market that are designed to facilitate the job description and questionnaire process.

When reorganizations occur, processes change, new technology is introduced, or new products are added, the work-study should be updated so opportunities for efficiency and improved quality are not missed. Even if there is no major change, follow-up studies should be scheduled to ensure that the efficiencies and quality improvement initially predicted are occurring.

JOB AND WORK ANALYSIS: WEIGHING COSTS AND BENEFITS

Having a system for managing the job documentation library will ensure that an organization is on top of job and work analysis, and it will strengthen further the organization's position should it be challenged on the employment-law front. Good job documentation, however, is not simply a preventive measure. It also greatly assists an organization's efforts to achieve efficiency and quality, and it facilitates the creation of an equitable job-worth hierarchy. Furthermore, job documentation is used in many other initiatives: hiring, training and development, and succession planning, for instance.

Work analysis provides the basis for quality management programs to assess where processes need to be improved through a change in human behavior such as a job redesign and incentive program, or training in new/enhanced competencies. It also helps determine where processes can be eliminated or streamlined. The review should take place at the individual job level, within a department and across functional lines, and it should follow the product or service from raw material to customer usage. In addition, work analysis can assist an organization to determine if certain elements of the workflow should be considered for outsourcing to increase productivity and/or reduce cost.

Initially, job or work analysis appears to be a monumental undertaking, but if approached in an organized way, the effort can yield a tremendous return to the organization over the long term. Perhaps the most important benefit is in improved communications: Job or work analysis can help translate an organization's strategic plan into specific roles and responsibilities.

JOB EVALUATION

Job evaluation can be defined as a formal process used to create a job-worth hierarchy within an organization. The two basic approaches are market data and job content. The job-content approach can be further broken down into nonquantitative methods and quantitative methods.

The process used for mapping the job process is fairly distinct, and to be a valid and defensible process, each step should feed into the next step. If the job analysis is done properly, it will feed into the job documentation; if the job documentation is accurate and up-to-date, it will help ensure a valid evaluation of the job. When the job is evaluated, it will fall within the job-worth hierarchy of the organization. When each component of this process is correctly completed, all of the necessary information to complete the next component is at hand.

INTERNAL JOB EVALUATION—NONQUANTITATIVE METHODS

Two major objectives of job evaluation are to develop internal standards of comparison and measure relative job values within the organization. For many organizations, the relative value of jobs internally is just as important as external competitiveness.

This may be based on the organization's compensation philosophy or on a compensation strategy that seeks to ensure that employees feel they are being compensated fairly in relation to their peers, both internally and externally.

The third component of the job-mapping process is to evaluate the job. As stated previously, an organization either can use job content–based evaluation systems or market-based evaluation systems. A job content–based evaluation is a systematic approach designed to help establish the relative value of jobs within a specific organization. The focus of job-content evaluation is on the actual content of the job. Job content can be evaluated using specific, quantifiable measures of job value (quantitative methods) or by other means where no attempt is made to obtain quantitative measures of job value (nonquantitative methods).

The ranking method of job evaluation is the simplest form of job evaluation. Basically, the organization would use a whole job comparison approach and rank order the jobs within the organization from highest to lowest. It is important to note that ranking only gives an organization an indication of how each job fits within the job-worth hierarchy; ranking does not provide any insight as to the relative degree of distance between the various jobs.

Ranking jobs within an organization typically follows three steps:

1. Analyze and document job content.
2. Identify selected groups of jobs (also known as job sets).
3. Rank order jobs within the sets.

The first step with any evaluation process is to determine the job evaluation criterion; by comparing whole jobs, the criterion used is the job itself. The job analysis and documentation steps will provide the organization with a description of the job, which will then be used to compare the jobs with each other. For ranking purposes, the comparison is based on the job as a whole, not its component parts.

The second step in the ranking process is to identify selected groups of jobs (job sets). If the organization has a small number of jobs, all jobs could be ranked at one time; however, this is not always feasible. When an organization has a large number of jobs, they should be broken into groups or job sets. Job sets can be established using any set of criteria (e.g., clerical, supervisory, director, etc.). However, the job sets should assist with the creation of a job-worth hierarchy. The main goal of establishing job sets is to simplify the ranking process, so that one does not need to compare 100 jobs, but 5 sets of 20 jobs, for example.

After the job sets are created, the next step is to rank order the jobs within each set. After each set is ranked, the job-worth hierarchy is established. (See Figure 10.13.)

The paired-comparison approach is the second nonquantitative approach. This approach is more effective than ranking when evaluating a larger number of jobs. The paired-comparison approach to job evaluation compares every job to every other job within the organization. Each job is individually compared to every other job and the job that is most valuable from each pairing is noted. The job-worth hierarchy is then established by the number of times a job was selected during the comparison phase. With pair-comparison, it is completely feasible and possible that some jobs could have been selected the exact same number of times; if further ranking is needed for these jobs, whole job ranking can be used.

The paired-comparison approach typically follows the following four steps:

1. Determine number of pairs required.
2. Compare each pair and select the stronger job.
3. Determine the number of times each job was selected.
4. Rank order the jobs.

The first step uses a formula to assist with determination of the total number of pairs required. The formula used is number of pairs $\times$ [(number of jobs to be ranked) $\times$ (number of jobs to be ranked minus 1)]/2. For example, if an organization had 50 jobs, the number of pairs would be [(50) $\times$ (49)]/2 or 1,225 pairs, for paired-comparison.

The second step would be to compare each of the pairs and select the stronger job. Each job will be compared to every other job during this step.

FIGURE 10.13 Job-worth hierarchy using ranking.

Title	Rank
Director of Accounting	1
Director of Human Resources	2
Senior Manager of Advertising	3
Manager of Accounting	4
Senior Compensation Analyst	5
Senior Human Resources Analyst	6
Senior Financial Analyst	7
Financial Analyst	8
Supervisor, Accounts Payable	9
Accounts Payable Clerk	10
Human Resources File Clerk	11

Pairs	**Selection**
Job 1 vs. Job 2	Job 2
Job 1 vs. Job 3	Job 1
Job 2 vs. Job 3	Job 2
Job 3 vs. Job 4	Job 4
Job 1 vs. Job 4	Job 1
Job 2 vs. Job 4	Job 2

The third step of the paired-comparison approach is to determine the amount of times each job was selected during the comparison. Remember, it is possible to have some jobs selected the same number of times. In the example above:

- Job 1 was selected two times.
- Job 2 was selected three times.
- Job 3 was not selected at all.
- Job 4 was selected one time.

The final step in the paired-comparison approach is to rank the jobs and establish a job-worth hierarchy. In the instances that two (or more) jobs have been selected the same amount of times, whole job ranking would determine the hierarchy. Following the example, the job-worth hierarchy of the organization would look like:

- Job 2.
- Job 1.
- Job 4.
- Job 3.

Using the ranking or paired-comparison approach to job evaluation has its advantages and disadvantages. In most cases, both ranking and paired-comparison approaches are easy to administer, inexpensive, and require little training of all the people involved. However, because the jobs are compared "wholly," several disadvantages exist. One of the most significant drawbacks is the potential of inconsistent judgment across raters. Documentation may not be collected to record differences, so it could be difficult for different evaluators to evaluate the same. Additionally, in cases where the jobs are very similar, important aspects of the job might be overlooked because the details of the job should be ignored.

The final method of nonquantitative job evaluation is the classification method. The best example of classification being used today is in the government. This is a true classification system where jobs are compared on a whole-job basis with predefined class descriptions established for a series of job grades. The jobs then are placed in the classification grouping that best describes the job.

Using the classification approach typically follows five steps:

1. Analyze/document job content.
2. Identify and cluster benchmark jobs.
3. Develop preliminary generic definitions.
4. Compare jobs to definitions.
5. Assign remaining jobs to classification levels.

First, the job analysis and documentation steps will provide the organization with a job description that will be used to compare the jobs with each other. For classification purposes, the comparison is based on the job as a whole, not its component parts.

The second step is to identify benchmark jobs that appear to be similar and cluster them. The similarity used is typically an aspect of the job—nature, scope, or level. This will enable the evaluator to note the similarities and provide that information for the next step.

The third step is to develop preliminary definitions of each cluster. These definitions will be the basis for the generic comparison factors used in classification. This step defines the classification levels or pay grades.

The fourth step is a review step. In the classification model it is important to review the job clusters and ensure that the preliminary definitions match the jobs within the clusters. If they do not, benchmark jobs might be moved to a cluster that better represents the job, or the preliminary classification levels can be adjusted to match the jobs within each level.

The final step is to slot the nonbenchmark jobs into the classification levels. Typically this step is done by comparing the nature, scope, or level of each nonbenchmark job to the classification levels that best fit. This final step ensures that a job-worth hierarchy is created with all jobs in the organization.

INTERNAL JOB EVALUATION—QUANTITATIVE METHODS

As opposed to nonquantitative methods of job evaluation, quantitative methods use measures that lend themselves to precise definition and assessment, with very little room for variability of data. When conducting a quantitative job evaluation, it is important to ensure that the factors selected to determine job value do not discriminate against a specific group or class of employees. Additionally, it is important to balance complexity and/or flexibility of a given method against the needs of the organization. This section will discuss the selection and definition of compensable factors.

Compensable factors are the key to quantitative methods of job evaluation. They can be defined as:

- Any criterion used to provide a basis for judging job value in order to create a job-worth hierarchy.
- The elements used to measure a job's worth.
- Intrinsic elements in jobs that add value to the organization and for which it wants to pay.

Generic compensable factors are skill, effort, responsibility, and working conditions. These generic factors are outlined in the Equal Pay Act of 1963 as the key criteria for determining whether jobs are substantially equal and thereby requiring equal pay.

Most organizations that use quantitative methods of job evaluation use a derivation of the four generic compensable factor groups, which are also known as the level of work. Typically each group is further divided to determine the true worth of the job.

The first generic factor, skill, usually requires a short description when used in a job evaluation plan. This is because skill factors include:

- Experience—which typically relates to actual experience performing the job, either gained through the employer or through previous employers.
- Knowledge—refers to the educational knowledge needed to perform the job. This usually is the minimum knowledge needed to perform the job.

- Manual dexterity—relates to specific movements required.
- Analytical ability—if the job requires the incumbent to analyze, decipher, or explore other possibilities.
- Creativity—typically found in jobs of a creative nature (web design, graphic design, marketing manager, advertising).
- Communication.
  - Verbal—refers to the level of verbal communication needed to perform the job (a phone customer service representative may require a higher level of verbal communication than a janitor).
  - Written—refers to the level of written communication needed to perform the job (a journalist would need a higher level of written communication than a cashier).
- Complexity of the job—defines the overall use of specific skills needed to perform the job. It is important to note complexity of the job does not always relate to the level of the job; a machinist job could potentially be more complex than an administrative assistant.

The effort factors usually refer to:

- Physical demands of the job—how much exertion is need for this job (lifting, walking, running, sitting).
- Mental exertion required—relates to the amount of mental effort required to perform the job. This could contain both decision making and/or concentration.

Responsibility factors include:

- Supervisory duties—how many direct reports the position has could potentially place the job higher within the job-worth hierarchy.
- Budget—the amount of budgetary responsibility the incumbent has could reflect a higher position within the hierarchy.
- Decision making—this typically relates to the impact of the decisions made to the organization.
- Accountability—refers to the amount of liability the incumbent has on decisions made.
- Impact job has on the organization—how important is the incumbent's position to the organization.

Working conditions refer to:

- Hazardous environment—refers to the amount of time an incumbent could be exposed to potentially hazardous conditions in the workplace.
- Temperature conditions—relates to the variance of temperature an incumbent might face (e.g., for a person who works on a fishing boat, the day could be sunny or rainy or cold or warm).
- Odors—what adverse odors might an incumbent be exposed to (e.g., smells that could be generated in smelting plants).
- Loud noises—will the incumbent be exposed to loud noises, and how long in duration will the noises last.
- Or lack of hazardous environment—refers to incumbents who are not exposed to potentially hazardous conditions (office environment).

When evaluating a job on the generic factor groups, each group is divided into specific factors. Factors can be defined as an individual component aspect of job content within the generic factor groups. For example, analytical ability is a factor of the skill generic factor group. (See Figure 10.14.) Additionally, each factor would be measured in varying degrees on levels of complexity.

When conducting a job evaluation, it is important to select the appropriate compensable factors for the organization. For example, the service industry might determine that the working conditions factor does not really apply to its industry, whereas, the manufacturing industry would place high importance on working conditions. In determining which factors would best fit the organization, it is vital to identify the organization's internal values. What does the mission statement say? What about the business strategy? These will help the evaluator determine what is important to the organization, and therefore which factors would most support the stated mission and strategy. Going back to the service industry example—if the strategy of the organization is to provide the best customer service while responding to customer inquiries in an efficient, timely manner—the skill generic factor group would be very important, and the communications factor would appear to be vital. Determining the strategy of the organization will help in selecting compensable factors.

The next step in selecting compensable factors is to review the job content of the work group to be evaluated. This is an important step because it will help establish what factors are important to each work group, thus helping to establish an organization-wide evaluation system. Typically, one would examine the results from the job analysis and job documentation relating to each work group. When analyzing each work group, common characteristics usually surface. Additionally, unique aspects of each job or the diverse characteristics of the jobs should be noted.

To use the service example: If the call center work group were reviewed, it would be important to review aspects of the job. For example, how often do they talk on the phone to customers? What about e-mail? How much product knowledge is required? Is there a need for physical exertion? All of these observations/questions will help in determining which factors need to be considered.

When selecting compensable factors, is there a limit on the number of factors to be used? It is important to include enough factors to establish a value differential. That is, if too few factors are selected, it will be difficult to gauge a difference in the value of each job; if too many factors are selected, it will be too administratively

FIGURE 10.14 Terms—generic factor group: _skill_.

Specific Factor Name: Experience

Specific Factor Description: This factor measures the time normally required on related work and on-the-job training for the job being evaluated for an individual to attain satisfactory performance standards under normal supervision.

- 1st degree—less than 3 months
- 2nd degree—3 months, up to and including 12 months
- 3rd degree—more than 1 year, up to and including 3 years
- 4th degree—more than 3 years, up to and including 5 years
- 5th degree—more than 5 years

burdensome to conduct the evaluation. Usually, 5 to 12 factors should be brought to upper management to determine which ones best reflect what the company values. Bringing the factors to upper management and asking for assistance on the selection process will add the buy-in component to the process. This will help with obtaining management support and stakeholder acceptance.

After receiving input from upper management, the next task is to determine the specific factors to be used. Effective factors should:

- Differentiate job value. For purposes of internal job evaluation, measuring the same of similar job characteristics more than once should be avoided.
- Have a logical relationship to overall job value to the organization.
- Cover all major aspects of job requirements for which the organization is willing to pay.
- Be manageable. It is important to limit the factors used to a reasonable number.

Failure to consider these factors increases administrative time without adding meaningful information and may create systemic bias for (or against) certain jobs. During this process, it is vital to include all important factors. If any important factors are not included, there may be an inadvertent discrimination for (or against) certain jobs, or it may produce a job-worth hierarchy inconsistent with internal values.

After the compensable factors have been selected, the next step is to define the factors. This basically means to develop a clear and comprehensive definition for each factor and define the highest and lowest levels of each factor present in the work group to be covered by the plan. (See Figure 10.15.) After the highest and lowest levels are determined, the intermediate levels can be identified, typically in a lowest to highest progression using a logical approach. This ensures that the factors reflect reasonable differences.

Because the goal of compensable factors is to establish a job-worth hierarchy that is consistent with management's perception of relative job worth, selecting the correct compensable factors is important. The appropriate number of factors and the corresponding levels will assist in construction of the job-worth hierarchy. If too many levels are selected, it may force artificial distinctions between degree levels, as well as increase administrative time. Additionally, having too many levels would require highly detailed job documentation; this increases the possibility of additional requests for re-evaluation of jobs, which, in turn, may result in "grade creep." If too few levels are selected, it may not fully cover the range of work performed and not adequately differentiate important aspects of job value.

FIGURE 10.15 Factor definition and levels: mental/visual strain and fatigue.

The degree of this factor is determined by the amount of mental/visual strain and fatigue caused by performing this job. AuQ 1

1st degree—rarely (15% or less of work time)
2nd degree—occasionally (16–35% of work time)
3rd degree—frequently (36–50% of work time)
4th degree—often (51–75% of work time)
5th degree—constantly (75% or more of work time)

Overlapping levels is another issue to consider. With overlapping levels, it becomes difficult to select the correct level for the job because the adjacent level descriptions are too similar.

Weighting is the final step concerning compensable factors. In this step, weights are based upon the value of each compensable factor to the organization. The more a factor drives the organization's business strategies and objectives, the higher is the weight value associated to the factor. For example, in a call center environment, factors relating to skill and communication will carry more weight than a factor relating to hazardous work environment. (See Figure 10.16.) Determining how much more value the communication skill has versus the hazardous work environment is a very important step in the process.

When establishing the weighting of the factors, it is very important to consider the nature of the work performed by each job group and the appropriate measures. The next step is to rank them in order of importance to the organization. (Please note: This process refers to the larger factor and not the degrees within each factor.) After the factors are rank ordered, the initial factor weights need to be developed. The process of developing the initial factor weights could encompass statistical analysis and/or management judgment. The last step in this process is to review the weights with key management and stakeholders and make any changes as required.

FIGURE 10.16 Call center environment.

Factor
Verbal Communication
Hazardous Work Environment
Written Communication
Prior Work Experience
Product Knowledge
Analytical Ability
Physical Demand

Factor	Rank
Verbal Communication	1
Written Communication	2
Prior Work Experience	3
Product Knowledge	4
Analytical Ability	5
Hazardous Work Environment	6
Physical Demand	7

Factor	Factor Weights
Verbal Communication	30%
Written Communication	20%
Prior Work Experience	15%
Product Knowledge	15%
Analytical Ability	10%
Hazardous Work Environment	5%
Physical Demand	5%

The factors and the weights potentially could vary by job group, depending upon the organization's business strategy. In cases where the factors and weights would vary, this process would be repeated for each job group, based upon the nature of work from each job group.

INTERNAL JOB EVALUATION—POINT FACTOR

A factor comparison method is one of the most commonly used methods of internal job evaluation. It values specific aspects of the job and compensable factors, and assigns a weight and level to that job.

The point factor method, which assigns point totals to each compensable factor, is the most widely used method of factor comparison.

It started in the mid-1930s when Edward Hay began development of one of the first point factor plans. He first installed a job-evaluation program in a bank in the 1940s. He went on to found Hay & Associates in 1943 and continued work on this evaluation methodology. In the 1950s, organizations using this methodology wanted Hay to develop a linkage between internal equity and market pay. Hay was the first to make this linkage through market surveys based on job content versus title matches that were the prevailing practice at the time. Today, this methodology is the most broadly used in the world, with linkages of job evaluation to market pay in more than 40 countries. (See Sidebar 10.1.)

Sidebar 10.1: Hay Point Factor Plans

The Hay Guide Chart Profile Method of job evaluation is considered the benchmark of point factor/factor comparison job-evaluation plans. In the mid-30s Edward Hay began development of this method to determine how to value jobs based on common compensable elements of job value. The Hay plan today typically contains three to four factors (the fourth factor, working conditions, is most typically applied when evaluating nonexempt jobs):

1. **Know-how** is defined by using the following critical areas of applied knowledge and skill:

   a. Technical
   b. Managerial
   c. Human relations.

2. **Problem solving** is defined by the following criteria:

   a. Thinking environment
   b. Thinking challenge.

3. **Accountability** is defined by the following criteria:

   a. Freedom to act
   b. Magnitude
   c. Impact.

(continued)

Sidebar 10.1 *(Continued)*

4. **Working conditions** is defined by criteria such as:

   a. Physical effort
   b. Working environment
   c. Sensory attention
   d. Physical risks.

In addition, a unique characteristic of the Hay method is that it incorporates a principle called *profile* where the weight and relationship of the factors is indicative of the size and nature of the job. For example, accountability is the most important factor for a top executive position, while know-how is weighted more heavily for an entry-level professional. Further, accountability is weighted more heavily than problem solving for line jobs and the reverse is true for research jobs.

The Hay method is the first one to make the linkage of internal job value to external market value through surveys that utilize job content in addition to job titles and organization size as the fundamental criteria for market pricing.

As stated, factor comparison models value jobs based upon specific compensable factors and the importance of those factors to the organization. In the beginning, factor comparison models were entrenched in statistics and mathematics. Many organizations felt these models were very accurate, but extremely difficult to administer and even more difficult to communicate. As factor comparison plans evolved, point factor plans came to the forefront to solve these administration and communication problems, and are one of the most prevalent internal job-evaluation methods.

Point factor plans can be defined as a quantitative form of job content evaluation that uses defined factors and degree levels within each factor (usually five to seven levels, also defined). Each factor is weighted according to its importance to the organization. Job content descriptions are compared to definitions of the degree levels and the corresponding points assigned to the appropriate level are then awarded to the job and summed for all factors to determine the total job score. The total scores are used to create a job-worth hierarchy.

Although organizations have the ability to purchase off-the-shelf versions of point factor plans, some organizations create and use their own version. Designing and developing a customized point factor plan may not be as difficult as one might think, and custom designing a plan that fits the organization can produce a plan that better reflects the organizational values than an off-the-shelf version.

One of the first steps involved in developing a point factor plan is to select and weight the compensable factors that most reflect the organizational strategy. The weighing process would entail defining the factors and degree levels within each factor—each factor should be weighted as a percent, with all factors equaling 100 percent. This process is very important in ensuring that what the organization values will be used to establish the job-worth hierarchy. For example, in a call center environment, if the factor of adverse temperature conditions is selected and assigned a high weight, most employees would receive a lower score because adverse temperature most likely would not be encountered in a call center.

FIGURE 10.17 Weighing compensable factors.

Factor	Max Points	% of Possible Points
Skill	**(62.6%)**	
Knowledge	120	14.6%
Work Experience	135	16.4%
Analytical Ability	110	13.3%
Independent Judgment	150	18.3%
Effort	**(9.4%)**	
Mental/Visual Strain and Fatigue	77	9.4%
Responsibility	**(21.9%)**	
Contact	75	9.1%
Supervision	105	12.8%
Working Conditions	**(6.1%)**	
Physical Working Environment	50	6.1%

In Figure 10.17, the organization has deemed that skill (62.6 percent) is the most important generic factor, and independent judgment (18.3 percent) is the highest-rated factor. It also appears that the jobs covered under this plan have a significant amount of supervision responsibility (12.8 percent), whereas they would not have a lot of supervision. Based upon the distribution of points, this plan was designed for a position group with the following characteristics: (1) high level of education and work experience; (2) high level of analytical ability; (3) high level of independent judgment; and (4) high level of supervision. This could be a financial, accounting, or managerial position.

The next step would be to determine the number of degree levels and assign points to each of those levels. This step adds complexity to the development process. Typically you assign points to the structure by dimension and progression. Dimension refers to the number of factors with which each point relates. Progression refers to the way the numbers increase as the level increases.

There are two ways to look at dimension: single and multiple. Single-dimension factors relate to instances when the factor is dependent on only one variable (e.g., years of experience). (See Figure 10.18.)

Multiple-dimension factors relate to when the factor is dependent on multiple variables (e.g., business judgment is dependent on both decision making and scope). When multiple-dimension factors are used, each subfactor must be evaluated as it relates to the main factor. (See Figure 10.19.)

As with dimension, there are also two ways to look at progression: arithmetically and geometrically. With arithmetic progression (typically used in the single-dimension factor approach), each level of the dimension receives a number. (See Figure 10.20.) The increase between levels could be as simple as 10, 15, 20, etc. With geometric progression (typically used in the multiple-dimension factor approach), each level receives a percent increase over the previous level. (See Figure 10.21.) As a percentage, the points assigned to each dimension progressively increases, thereby allocating more points for increasing knowledge.

After the point factor plan is constructed, the next step is to begin evaluating the jobs within the organization. In order to get an accurate evaluation of jobs within

FIGURE 10.18 Single-dimension factor.

Factor A	Knowledge

Knowledge refers to the minimum level of knowledge required for the job. Knowledge is basically acquired through formal education versus on-the-job training.

Degree	Definition	Point Value
1	Work requires basic understanding of reading and writing principles, as well as basic arithmetic. Ability to communicate verbally through use of multiple and complete sentences as well as written communication using sentences and paragraphs. Ability to read, interpret, and understand use of decimal and fractions. Able to complete nontechnical reports and records (including maintenance reports, payroll reports, etc.).	15

FIGURE 10.19 Multiple-dimension factors.

Factor G	Mental/Visual Strain and Fatigue

The degree of this factor is determined by the amount of mental/visual strain and fatigue caused by performing this job.

Percentage of Time	Intensity		
	Minor Exposure	Low Moderate Regular Exposure	Significant High-Intensity Exposure
Rarely Less than 15% of time	10	14	20

the organization, accurate job analysis and documentation must be completed. It is important that all job descriptions are both up-to-date and jobs are described in terms of the selected compensable factors. If the job descriptions are up-to-date but not in a format that is usable for evaluation, the jobs either will be difficult to evaluate or lead to an inaccurate job-worth hierarchy. (See Figure 10.22.)

With the evaluation process, each job (job description) will be compared to the degree definitions. The process of evaluating jobs entails looking at each job's compensable factor and comparing that to the compensable factors in the point factor plan. (See Figure 10.23.) For each of the compensable factors defined in the plan, the role of the evaluator is to determine which degree definition of each factor best fits the job and assign the respective point values. When the process is completed, each job will have a total number of job evaluation points. These points will then be used in creating the job-worth hierarchy.

FIGURE 10.20 Arithmetic progression.

Factor A	Knowledge

Knowledge refers to the minimum level of knowledge required for the job. Knowledge is basically acquired through formal education versus on-the-job training.

Degree	Definition	Point Value
1	Work requires basic understanding of reading and writing principles, as well as basic arithmetic. Ability to communicate verbally through use of multiple and complete sentences as well as written communication using sentences and paragraphs. Ability to read, interpret, and understand use of decimal and fractions. Able to complete nontechnical reports and records (including maintenance reports, payroll reports, etc.).	15
2	Work requires the level of knowledge typically attained through a brief period (typically fewer than six months) of specialized technical training.	30
3	Work requires knowledge typically acquired through a four-year high school diploma, or equivalent. Can express complex thoughts clearly in writing, perform complex algebraic calculations and deal effectively with other people.	45

FIGURE 10.21 Geometric progression.

Factor G	Mental/Visual Strain and Fatigue

The degree of this factor is determined by the amount of mental/visual strain and fatigue caused by performing this job.

	Intensity		
Percentage of Time	Minor Low Exposure	Moderate Regular Exposure	Significant High-Intensity Exposure
Rarely Less than 15% of time	10	14	20
Occasionally 16–35% of work time	14	20	28
Frequently 36–50% of work time	20	28	39

FIGURE 10.22 Job description.

Title:	Course Developer
Department:	Product Delivery and Training
Classification:	Exempt
Reports to:	Director of Training and Development

General Summary
Responsible for the design, development, maintenance, and improvement of instructor-led and computer-based training for clients on DNS products.

Duties and Responsibilities
- Responsible for designing and developing instructor-led and computer-based training for clients on DNS products.
- Develop and maintain course manuals, instructor guides, and handouts.
- Train the trainers for instructor-led courses.
- Respond to feedback by completing product updates and course improvements.
- Conduct needs assessments and compare to generally accepted body of knowledge to determine training needs/gaps.

Job Specifications
- Basic understanding of network management systems.
- Technical writing and product-management skills.
- Ability to identify training needs and translate into effective courses for clients.
- Knowledge of web-based training application software.
- Excellent oral/written communication skills.
- Well-developed presentation skills.

Education/Training/Experience
- Master's degree in education, instructional design, or a related field.
- Three years of experience administering client product training or one year of experience developing client training in a network management environment.
May be required to perform duties outside of those listed above.

It is important to note that there is always some inherent bias in any system used to evaluate jobs. As several different evaluators review the same job, it is possible (even likely) that some jobs might receive different point totals. If the job descriptions were written so that they reflect the compensable factors listed on the point factor plan, some of the differences could be eliminated.

Regarding Figure 10.22, based upon the job description and review of the position, the position of course developer is worth 546 points out of a total of 862 points. This position's location on the job-worth hierarchy would be higher than those with fewer than 546 points and lower than those with 547 points or more. But what exactly does this mean to the organization? How does one determine how much to pay a course developer with 546 points? What about someone with 347 points? How does point factor equate into a grade/midpoint structure?

As stated earlier, point factor plans will help an organization with the development of an internally driven job-worth hierarchy. After each job is evaluated and point totals are assigned to each job, a hierarchy can be established.

FIGURE 10.23 Job evaluation plan: professional and technical employees.

ABC Corporation

Job Evaluation Plan: Professional and Technical Employees

Factor G	Mental/Visual Strain and Fatigue

The degree of this factor is determined by the amount of mental/visual strain or fatigue caused by performing this job.

	Intensity		
Percentage of time	Minor—low exposure to fatigue	Moderate— regular exposure to fatigue	Significant— high intensity and levels of fatigue
Rarely—15% or less of work time	10	14	20
Occasionally—16%–35% of work time	14	20	28
Frequently—36%–50% of work time	20	28	39
Often—51%–75% of work time	28	39	55
Constantly—over 75% of work time	39	55	77

FIGURE 10.24 Job-worth hierarchy (point totals).

Job Title	Points
Director of Human Resources	790
Senior Manager of Marketing	753
Senior Manager of Tax and Accounting	748
Buyer	697
Manager of Finance	686

Remember, when utilizing a job-worth hierarchy based upon internal evaluation, the hierarchy will be established based solely upon organizational criteria and organizational value. These values and placements might not reflect what the market is paying, but how the organization values the positions. In Figure 10.24, the buyer is a highly valued position within the organization (higher than the manager of finance). If the organization does a market analysis on the positions within the organization, they might find a buyer position is valued much lower in the marketplace. These discrepancies are common when using internal valuation over external valuation. The key to making this successful is to have a solid structure and be confident in the plan used to value these jobs.

To determine the appropriate way to pay a position once the hierarchy is established, an organization can take several approaches. Most often, organizations

FIGURE 10.25 Regression analysis.

Position	Points	Market Rate
Administrative Assistant	335	$31,000
Recruiting Manager	470	$45,000
Mail Clerk	190	$22,400
Human Resources File Clerk	210	$25,000
Executive Assistant	430	$42,000

Regression

X	Y
31000	335
45000	470
22400	190
25000	210
42000	430

Straight Line Equation—Derived from the Regression Analysis (will vary based upon salary and data points; this equation is solely based upon the numbers above)
Salary = (78.9)Points + 7286
Verify that the equation works—solve for a point total already known
Recruiting Manager   470 points $45,000 salary
Salary = (78.9)Points + 7286
Salary = (78.9)470 + 7286
Salary = 37,083 + 7286
Salary = $44,369.00
$44,369.00 is approximately equal to $45,000 market rate; therefore, the equation is valid.
To determine the "dollar/point," plug in one (1) for point in the above equation
Salary = (78.9)Points + 7286
Salary = (78.9)1 + 7286
Salary = $78.9 + $7286
For the equation above, each point is worth approximately $78.90, with an additional $7,286 added to each evaluation.

market price benchmark jobs and determine a "dollar/point" value using a statistical technique called regression analysis (more on this later). Other methods would be to utilize consultants, government sources, or any other mean to establish a dollar/point value.

Using market data might seem a little strange, as the entire idea behind using a point factor plan is to value jobs internally, without regard to external data. This is true; in fact, before market rates are added to the system, the jobs are evaluated based upon the compensable factors used within the point factor plan. Because each job is assigned a point value, and each job is slotted in the hierarchy based upon that value, the market position of the various jobs should not alter the positioning of these positions.

FIGURE 10.26 Groupings (or clusters).

Position	Points
Director of Finance and Accounting	801
Director of Human Resources	790
Senior Manager of Web Development	789
Senior Manager of Marketing	753

In the example above, the first three positions (Director of Finance and Accounting, Director of Human Resources, and Senior Manager of Web Development) appear to form a grouping. Those positions could potentially be in the same grade, which could be defined as:

Grade 10	**(785–815)**

The first step in conducting a market pricing analysis would be to determine the benchmark jobs within the organization. A benchmark job can be defined as jobs that closely resemble other jobs performed in other organizations and/or across industries. A benchmark job should:

- Be well represented in the marketplace.
- Be important in the organization's internal hierarchy.
- Represent many organizational levels or grades in the salary structure utilized by the organization.
- Be matched to 70 percent or more of the duties found in the survey jobs.
- Generally have multiple incumbents (with the exception of managerial and executive-level positions) with an organization.

After the organization collects and analyzes market data for the benchmark positions, the next step is to perform regression analysis on the data collected. Regression analysis is the statistical method in which a straight line is created depicting a model of a Y (dependent) variable as a function of one or more X (independent) variables using the method of least squares. (See Figure 10.25.) Regression analysis allows the evaluator to create a base pay policy line. This line will be used to determine the dollar/point value. For point factor examples, the Y (dependent variable) will always be market rates (salary) and the X (independent variable) will always be the job points. The simplest way to calculate a regression line would be to use a spreadsheet program that will calculate the value for you (Excel can do this calculation once the Data Analysis ToolPak is activated).

Based upon the equation in Figure 10.25, the course developer (545) in Figure 10.22 would be worth approximately $50,286.50:

$$\text{Salary} = (78.9)\text{Points} + 7286$$
$$\text{Salary} = (78.9)545 + 7286$$
$$\text{Salary} = 43,000.50 + 7286$$
$$\text{Salary} = 50,286.50.$$

How does point factor relate to grades and midpoints? Point factor plans can be used in typical salary structure environments, grades and midpoints, or they can be constructed to have each point be its own grade. Typically with point-type hierarchies, there are two methods used to place a job into a grade. The first method would be to place jobs into grades prior to the market rate analysis. With this method, right after the job-worth hierarchy is constructed, the evaluator will look for groupings (or clusters) of points and use those groups as initial grades. (See Figure 10.26.)

The second method would be to conduct the market analysis of the positions, establish the grade structure and slot the positions into the grade that has the closest midpoint. (Although this is a simplified explanation of the process, this is what typically happens in a market pricing environment.)

Another way that point factor plans can utilize a structure would be if each point total had its own minimum, midpoint, and maximum. Although having 862 grades (as in the example of course developer) would appear to be an administrative nightmare, it really is not. With today's technology and the use of spreadsheets, it is relatively easy to set up this sort of structure, and when the structure moves, the formulas can be entered to automatically adjust when one structure is adjusted.

As mentioned previously, it is important to ensure that job documentation (i.e., job descriptions) is used appropriately to accurately reflect the responsibilities of the job and to accurately place the job within the hierarchy. Job evaluation systems, in general, if not managed properly, can lead to both level creep and job description inflation.

11 Base Pay Structures

Compensation deals with establishing a meaningful and acceptable relationship between work and rewards. Work performed by employees should help organizations achieve their objectives. These objectives are derived from the organization's overall business strategy, which supports the company's mission statement.

When designed and administered appropriately, a company's compensation program is an effective management tool for supporting the organization's overall business strategy. A series of steps is used in the process of designing sound compensation programs. (See Figure 11.1.) This process is not a one-time event. It involves constant review and refinement in light of changing business needs.

PAY STRUCTURES

A pay structure consists of a series of pay ranges, or "grades," each with a minimum and maximum pay rate. Jobs are grouped together in ranges that represent similar internal and external worth. (See Figure 11.2.)

The midpoint or middle-pay value for the range usually represents the competitive market value for a job or group of jobs. The company's base-pay policy line connects the midpoints of the various pay ranges in the pay structure.

In recent years, pay policy lines have been developed to reflect base salary midpoints and also to take into consideration variable compensation. For the purpose of this discussion, the design and development of pay structures will be confined to base salary, representing all positions except single-incumbent senior management positions.

FIGURE 11.1 Determine strategy before structure.

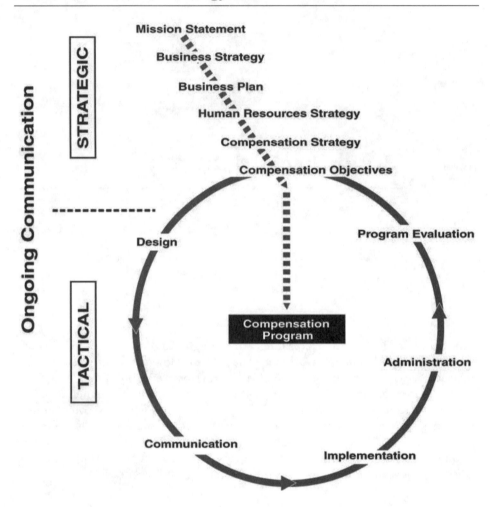

GENERAL AND SPECIFIC FACTORS AFFECTING PAY STRUCTURES

Pay structures are influenced by the following *general* factors:

- *Corporate culture and values.* An organization's pay structure usually reflects the way employees' work is valued. For example, does an organization always look for the best and brightest employees? If so, the pay line may be positioned to lead the market. If the organization encourages and values prudent risk-taking, the total pay line may have an additional risk/reward component.
- *Management philosophy.* Narrow pay ranges and more grades allow for more frequent promotions—and a greater perception of "growth and advancement"—than wider ranges and fewer grades. However, if management believes in promoting employees only when duties and responsibilities change significantly, the distances between midpoints of ranges may be as substantial as 15 percent or more.

FIGURE 11.2 Pay structure example.

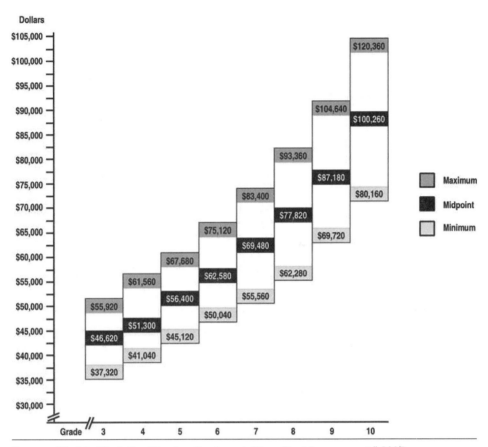

SOURCE: WorldatWork Certification Seminar 4: "Base Pay Management," 2007.

- *External economic environment.* Varied supply and demand for certain skills may necessitate a multistructured pay program. Technical professionals such as engineers may have special pay structures when there is a high demand for their skills. However, these special structures may be merged into the general structure when there is an increase in the supply of engineers in the market. Other external factors that may be reflected in pay structures include inflationary fluctuations and cost-of-living indices such as the Consumer Price Index (CPI).
- *External sociopolitical and legal environments.* The steps in the pay structure are likely to be more narrow and rigidly administered in a union environment than in a nonunion environment. Pay structures also are affected by regulations such as the FLSA, which mandates the minimum wage for most jobs and thereby determines the lowest possible pay scale.

Several other factors that influence pay structures relate directly to the operations and culture of a *specific* organization:

- *Centralized compensation policy.* A corporate compensation policy may call for the organization's overall competitive posture to always be ahead of the market. This will be reflected in the pay policy line being higher than the market at every point on the salary range. On the other hand, the strategy could be to hire employees at a rate always higher than the market but over time to bring them in line with the market. This would mean steadily fine-tuning the pay ranges at different levels.

- *Decentralized compensation policy.* An organization's goal may be to compete within the top quartile of its competitors in a particular functional segment (e.g., sales/marketing) or product segment (e.g., jet engines or disability income insurance). In this case, the pay structure may be different for those particular functional and product segments within the organization.
- *Short-term vs. long-term orientation.* A company with long-term orientation is most likely to have well-designed pay structures with career-path capabilities and smooth transitions from range to range. The ranges themselves will be developed after much thought and research. Short-term or temporary problems need to be taken care of with temporary solutions. Solving temporary problems with long-term solutions should be avoided. Employees generally have an entitlement mind-set with respect to compensation, and it may be difficult to "undo" prior actions, even though the original reasons for such actions no longer exist.

ANATOMY OF A PAY STRUCTURE

A pay structure has multiple pay or salary ranges. Every pay structure has key components that are critical to its overall design. The following section defines and describes these basic elements.

PAY RANGES AND RANGE SPREADS

A "pay range" has a minimum pay value, a maximum pay value, and a midpoint or central value. The difference between the maximum and the minimum is the "range spread," or the "width" of the range. Range width usually is expressed as a percentage of the difference between the minimum and maximum divided by the minimum. For example, in Figure 11.3, the range spread in dollars for Grade 10 (from Figure 11.2), where the maximum is $120,360 and the minimum is $80,160, is $120,360 − $80,160 = $40,200. The percentage is about 50 percent, or $40,200 divided by $80,160.

FIGURE 11.3 Illustration of a pay range and a range spread.

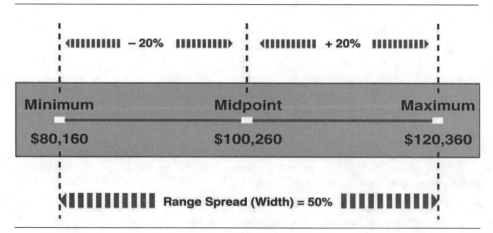

Note: Numbers have been rounded. Actual range spread is 50.15 percent.

To calculate the spread on either side of the midpoint, use the formulas shown in the Formula 11.1 box (where $100,260 is the Grade 10 midpoint in Figure 11.2).

A pay range with a 50-percent range spread will have a 20-percent spread on either side of the midpoint. (See Figure 11.3.) That is, $80,160 is 80 percent of $100,260, and $120,360 is 120 percent of $100,260.

While all the ranges in Figure 11.2 have a range spread of 50 percent, the spread does not have to be uniform throughout the pay structure. Figure 11.4 lists common range spreads and their corresponding spreads on either side of the midpoint.

Example 11.1 shows how to calculate the spread on either side of the midpoint. To perform the calculation, one of the three points (minimum, midpoint, or maximum) on the pay range needs to be specified along with the range width.

Using a range spread of about 50 percent and a minimum of $66,800, the maximum and midpoint are calculated as in Example 11.1.

Some Practical Considerations

Range spreads vary based on the level and sophistication of skills required for a given position. Entry-level positions that require skills that are quickly mastered usually have narrower pay ranges than supervisory, managerial, or higher-level technical positions. Individuals in lower-level positions not only master the requirements of the job sooner, they also have a greater number of opportunities over time to be

Formula 11.1

Calculation of Spread on Either Side of Midpoint

$$\frac{\text{Midpoint - Minimum}}{\text{Midpoint}} = \frac{\$100,260 - \$80,160}{\$100,260} = -20\% \text{ of Midpoint}$$

$$\frac{\text{Maximum - Midpoint}}{\text{Midpoint}} = \frac{\$120,360 - \$100,260}{\$100,260} = +20\% \text{ of Midpoint}$$

FIGURE 11.4 Common range spreads.

Range Spread	Spread on Either Side of Midpoint
20%	± 9.1%
25%	± 11.1%
30%	± 13.0%
35%	± 14.9%
40%	± 16.7%
45%	± 18.4%
50%	± 20.0%

Note: Under a broadbanding system, range spreads may reach 100 percent or more.

Example 11.1

USING A 50-PERCENT RANGE SPREAD

➡️ Maximum = Minimum x (1 + Range Spread) = $80,160 x 1.50 = $120,360*

➡️ Midpoint = $\dfrac{(\text{Maximum} + \text{Minimum})}{2} = \dfrac{(\$120,360 + \$80,160)}{2} = \$100,260$

➡️ Spread on either side of the midpoint =

$\dfrac{(\text{Midpoint} - \text{Minimum})}{\text{Midpoint}} = \dfrac{(\$100,260 - \$80,160)}{\$100,260} = -20.0\%$ of midpoint

or

$\dfrac{(\text{Maximum} - \text{Midpoint})}{\text{Midpoint}} = \dfrac{(\$120,360 - \$100,260)}{\$100,260} = +20.0\%$ of midpoint

* Numbers in this equation have been rounded. Actual range spread is 50.15%

---

promoted to higher-level positions. Senior-level positions require a longer learning curve and often have limited opportunities for advancement. The following are typical range spreads for different kinds of positions:

- 20–25 percent: lower-level service, production, and maintenance.
- 30–40 percent: clerical, technical, paraprofessional.
- 40–50 percent: higher-level professional, administrative, middle management.
- 50 percent and above: higher-level managerial, executive, technical.

Care should be taken when deciding pay-range width. Assuming a constant midpoint, changing range spreads also changes the minimum and maximum. Notice in Example 11.2 that as the ranges get wider, the maximums increase, the minimums decrease, and the midpoints are constant.

Ranges should be designed to provide midpoints that reflect the "going rate" and are reasonably close to what the market establishes as the minimum and maximum for the job. Minimums that are too low will result in a company needing to pay

---

Example 11.2

Range Spread	Minimum	Midpoint	Maximum
30%	$27,826	$32,000	$36,174
40%	$26,667	$32,000	$37,333
50%	$25,600	$32,000	$38,400

an employee higher in the range in order to pay competitively. This narrows the position's long-term earning potential. In turn, a high maximum may provide long-term earnings opportunities that are higher and more costly than what are needed to be competitive.

MIDPOINTS

The midpoint is a key element in pay administration. It is often used as a reference point in salary administration decisions as a point or "target." The midpoint is usually the reference used because it is typically set to equal the market average or median. It should not be an organization's only market reference point.

Related to the midpoint is the compa-ratio, a statistic that expresses the relationship between base salary and the midpoint, or between the midpoint and market average. Figure 11.5 illustrates the calculation of compa-ratio for the same job as well as for the market average. Compa-ratios can be calculated for individuals, groups of individuals, and the company as a whole.

Most companies strive to have the overall workforce paid at or around a compa-ratio of 100 percent. Individual compa-ratios vary according to how long the individual has been in the job, previous work experience, and job performance. A mature, long-service workforce will tend to have a higher compa-ratio (often above 100 percent) than a younger group of employees with a shorter service record.

It is important for a company to be able to explain the reasons for its current compa-ratio. Businesses monitor compa-ratios because they recognize them as an important tool for managing compensation costs. In some cases, companies cap pay at the midpoint for the purpose of paying "at market" for base salaries. The remainder of the range is available only to high performers and often is paid on a lump-sum basis from year to year. These companies increase base salaries only when range midpoints move and their compa-ratios drop below 100 percent.

FIGURE 11.5 Illustration of compa-ratios.

	Within Company				Outside Company
	Person 1	Person 2	Person 3	Average	
Base Salary	$22,500	$25,000	$27,500	$25,000	$24,500 Market Average
Midpoint	$25,000	$25,000	$25,000	$25,000	$25,000 Market Average
Compa-Ratio $\left(\frac{\text{Base Salary}}{\text{Midpoint}}\right)$	90%	100%	110%	100%	98%

RANGE PENETRATION

Another way of tracking an organization's compensation is to view employee pay in relationship to the total pay range. This is known as range penetration. Unlike compa-ratios, which are calculated using a grade's midpoint, range penetration is calculated using the minimum and maximum of a salary range. Range penetration is shown in Example 11.3.

Often range penetration is a preferred tool because it does not focus on one number alone, the midpoint. Instead, it refers to how far into the range a particular individual's salary has penetrated. Range profiles often are used in conjunction with either the compa-ratio or range penetration to describe where employees should expect their pay to fall in relationship to their pay range over time. (See Figure 11.6.)

Example 11.3

Given a minimum of $80,160, a maximum of $120,360 and an incumbent salary of $102,000, what is the range penetration?

$$\text{Range penetration} = \frac{(\text{Incumbent Salary - Range Minimum})}{(\text{Range Maximum - Range Minimum})} =$$

$$\frac{(\$102,000 - \$80,160)}{(\$120,360 - \$80,160)} = 54.3\%$$

FIGURE 11.6 Ilustration of range penetration.

Year	Minimum	Midpoint	Maximum	Salary	Range Penetration
1	$15,360	$19,200	$23,040	$15,360	0.00%
2	$15,744	$19,680	$23,616	$16,282	6.83%
3	$16,138	$20,172	$24,206	$17,260	13.90%
4	$16,541	$20,676	$24,811	$18,294	21.19%
5	$16,955	$21,193	$25,432	$19,393	28.76%
6	$17,382	$21,724	$26,068	$20,555	36.56%
7	$17,813	$22,266	$26,719	$21,788	44.64%
8	$18,258	$22,823	$27,388	$23,095	52.99%
9	$18,715	$23,393	$28,072	$24,481	61.62%
10	$19,182	$23,978	$28,774	$25,950	70.56%
11	$19,662	$24,577	$29,494	$27,508	79.80%
12	$20,154	$25,192	$30,230	$29,159	89.36%
13	$20,658	$25,822	$30,986	$30,907	99.24%

$$\text{Range penetration} = \frac{(\text{Salary - Minimum})}{(\text{Maximum - Minimum})}$$

Constant Range Width: 50%

Constant Annual Range Movement (Structure Change): 2.5%

Constant Salary Increase: 4%

Given the above constants and a starting salary of $12,800, it would take:

- *8 years* to exceed the *midpoint* ($22,823) of the range
- *13 years* to reach close to the *maximum* ($30,986) of the range

> By changing any one of the three constants, the extent of range penetration could be increased or decreased. The actual progression in the range is determined by the difference between range movement and the amount of salary increase.

MIDPOINT PROGRESSION

Midpoint progression refers to the percentage difference between pay-grade midpoints. The larger the midpoint progression, the fewer the number of grades within a pay structure. Conversely, the smaller the midpoint progression, the larger the number of pay grades within the pay structure.

Three Approaches to Developing Midpoints

One approach to developing midpoints is the present value–future value formula, which may be used to determine the percentage between midpoints, assuming the highest and lowest midpoints and the number of grades are known. Formula 11.2 may be used, or the calculations may be performed on a business calculator.

Suppose a company wishes to develop a pay structure with six grades that has a highest midpoint of $77,820 and a lowest midpoint of $46,620. What is the midpoint progression?

Using Formula 11.2, the midpoint progression is calculated to be 12.5 percent. The resulting pay structure looks like Figure 11.7.

There are two other approaches to developing midpoints and the resulting midpoint progression. The first is to use the average of the market pay rate for different jobs within benchmark-job groupings. The resulting midpoint progression would have varying percentage differences between midpoints, which reflect the market more closely than constant differences. An organization's pay structure need not have a constant percentage progression—it may remain uneven without being smoothed. In such instances, it should be recognized that promotional increases may be uneven and sometimes difficult to administer because of the following reasons:

- If the percentage difference between midpoints is too high, the result could be costly promotional increases.

Formula 11.2

Present Value – Future Value Formula

$$PV = \frac{FV}{(1 + i)^n}$$

	DEFINITION	VALUE
PV	Present value (midpoint of lowest pay grade)	$46,620
FV	Future value (midpoint of the highest pay grade)	$77,820
n	Number of desired grade intervals (one less than the total number of grades in the structure)	4
i	Percentage difference between midpoints	To be determined

Using these values, i = 12.5%

FIGURE 11.7 Example of midpoint progression.

Grade	Midpoint	Midpoint Progression
3	$46,620	12.5%
4	$51,300	12.5%
5	$56,400	12.5%
6	$62,580	12.5%
7	$69,480	12.5%
8	$77,820	12.5%

Note: Numbers have been rounded.

- If the percentage difference is relatively low, the result could be salary compression problems between supervisory and subordinate positions and difficulty in matching promotions with appropriate compensatory rewards.

The other approach to developing midpoints in a pay structure is the use of regression analysis. The advantage of this approach is it helps align market rates more closely with company policy. Regression analysis works well when job-evaluation points are used to develop pay structures. With the advent of more sophisticated technology, much of the statistical work can be done with the use of computers or powerful calculators.

PAY GRADES

The purpose of grades is to be able to refer to a compensation range that groups together multiple jobs with similar value based on internal comparisons and external market data. Grades need not always be numerical; alpha grades can serve the purpose just as well. Pay grades can be established by a number of methods.

There are many grades or levels within a pay structure. The number of grades used by a particular organization will vary based on findings from market research as well as the company's compensation policy. Does the policy call for frequent "promotions," or does it allow for real promotions when the major functions in the new job are of a higher value to the employees? Does the company want a "flat" organization, or does it prefer multiple levels within the organization?

Segmentation of Pay Grades

A pay grade may be segmented or subdivided in many ways—thirds, quartiles, quintiles, and so on. These segments may or may not overlap. They serve as reference points for cost control and pay administration. The number of segments within a pay grade varies by company, and it often reflects the company's merit pay process and pay administration philosophy.

Using segments within a pay grade instead of only midpoints provides more flexibility to managers in pay-related decisions. These segments serve as miniranges within the main range. Exercising salary judgments within a segment often is easier and more practical than focusing rigidly on a single point within the salary range, such as the midpoint.

Pay-Grade Overlap

Pay grades usually overlap. Except for the minimum of the lowest grade and the maximum of the highest grade, minimums and maximums usually fall within adjoining ranges. The width of the pay grade and the midpoint differentials determine the amount of overlap between adjoining grades. Grade overlap is minimal when midpoint differentials are large and range widths are small. (See Figure 11.8A.) Grade overlap is significant when midpoint differentials are small and range spread is large. (See Figure 11.8B.) Figures 11.8C and 11.8D are illustrations of moderate grade overlap.

In a pay-for-performance or merit system, grade overlap allows high performers in lower pay ranges with longer time-in-grade to be paid more than a relatively new (and/or lower) performer in a higher pay range. However, overlapping more than three or four pay grades generally should be avoided. Too much overlap limits the difference between midpoints, which in turn places limits on potential earning ability and can cause differentiation problems between supervisor and subordinate pay.

Multiple Pay Structures

An organization may have many pay structures within its overall structure. The number of structures is primarily a function of the market and the company's compensation philosophy. For instance, the ranges for certain professionals such as information systems and technology and investment management may call for a separate structure that cannot be force-fit into atypical "corporate" structure.

Different labor markets with different levels of supply and demand may necessitate multiple pay structures. Such pay structures allow greater flexibility in pay administration. Different groupings of positions such as clerical, blue-collar jobs versus technical and professional jobs usually reflect different labor markets depending on supply and demand. Therefore, the slope of the pay lines could be different for different job families.

DEVELOPING A PAY STRUCTURE

There are two basic considerations to factor into the design and development of pay structures: internal equity and external competitiveness.

Internal Equity

Internal equity refers to the relative values assigned to different jobs within an organization and how reasonable those values are, both within job families and

FIGURE 11.8 Illustrations of grade overlap.

11.8A Illustration of a minimal grade overlap. In this illustration, the differential between grades is 15 percent and the range width is 10 percent. There is no grade overlap. The maximum of any grade falls only within one grade. (Example: $14,000 falls only within the first grade.)

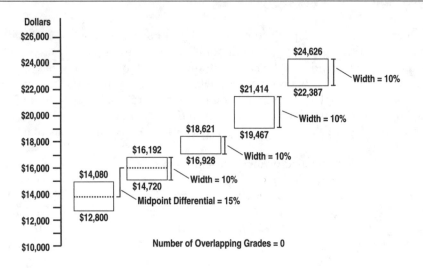

11.8B Illustration of a significant grade overlap. In this illustration, the differential between grades is 5 percent and the range width is 60 percent. There is a five-grade overlap. (Example: $20,000 falls within the five grades shown.)

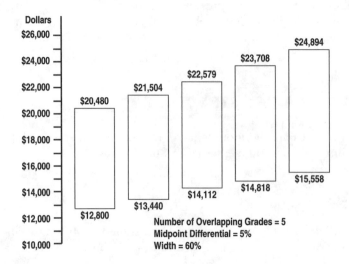

11.8C Illustration of a moderate grade overlap. In this illustration, the differential between grades is 5 percent and the range width is 10 percent. There is a two-grade overlap. (Example: $14,000 falls within the first two grades.)

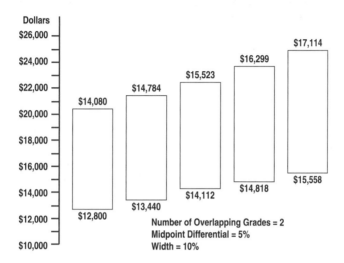

Number of Overlapping Grades = 2
Midpoint Differential = 5%
Width = 10%

11.8D Illustration of a moderate grade overlap. In this illustration, the differential between grades is 15 percent and the range width is 60 percent. There is a four-grade overlap. (Example: $20,000 falls within the first four grades.)

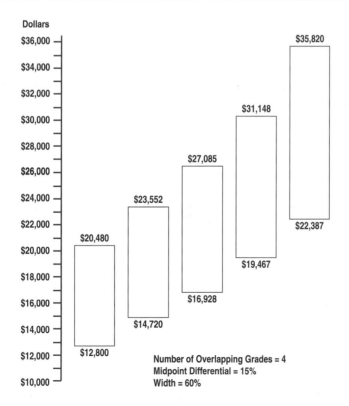

Number of Overlapping Grades = 4
Midpoint Differential = 15%
Width = 60%

among comparable jobs throughout the organization. Internal equity can be examined horizontally and vertically, as shown in Figure 11.9. In this example, Departments A and B demonstrate horizontal internal equity in all three jobs because the salaries are fairly close. These departments also demonstrate vertical internal equity because there is a similar progression within the job hierarchy. Department C, however, demonstrates neither horizontal nor vertical internal equity.

Although horizontal and vertical internal equity are presented as two separate concepts, in reality they are interrelated. While it is appropriate to pay Secretary Level III more than Levels I and II, how much more is determined by what is being done in the other two departments. (There are other factors that also must be factored in, such as performance and time-in-grade.)

The purpose of this illustration is to emphasize the importance of equity in salary administration and also to point out the different perspectives from which equity needs to be viewed. Internal equity is a key consideration in developing pay structures not only within a job family, as shown in the illustration of secretarial positions, but also among various job families that have common job grades. The first step in establishing internal equity is job evaluation.

External Competitiveness

The other basic consideration in the design and development of pay structures is external competitiveness, or external equity. Businesses compete in a free market for products and services. The costs of these products and services include labor, which is never constant. Companies need to closely monitor labor costs to make sure that they neither overpay (leading to a higher cost than necessary in providing a product or service) nor underpay (possibly leading to higher turnover, which could hurt productivity).

The labor market is subject to the same external pressures as the product and services market. Organizations have to respond quickly, appropriately, and consistently to survive constant changes in the labor market. It is important that the company's pay structure be capable of accommodating such changes.

FIGURE 11.9 Internal equity example.

	Position	◀▪▪▪▪▪▪▪▪▪▪▪ **Horizontal** ▪▪▪▪▪▪▪▪▪▪▪▶ (Across departments or organizational units)		
		Department A	**Department B**	**Department C**
▲▪▪▪▲ **Vertical** ▪▪▪ (Within departments or organizational units) ◀▪▪▪▲	**Position**	Salary	Salary	Salary
	Secretary Level I	$25,000	$26,000	$29,000
	Secretary Level II	$30,000	$31,000	$25,000
	Secretary Level III	$35,000	$36,000	$50,000

Defining Competition

In researching a company's competitive posture, the first step is the definition of "competition." During times of low turnover, it may be more difficult to identify organizations that compete for labor. Low turnover should not lead to the false conclusion that there are no competitors for labor or that the compensation program is working perfectly for a given organization.

Turnover statistics may show which skills are in demand—and, in turn, which special pay structures may be necessary. However, turnover statistics by themselves may not reveal much about competitiveness. Terminations may be taking place for many reasons, both personal and professional. If employees are leaving particular companies for reasons other than increased pay—for example, to start their own businesses—these companies should be excluded from the defined list of competitors.

Once it is established that employees are moving to other companies, it is time to gather data on these businesses. In the final analysis, a company's human resources strategic plan must tie directly to the data gathered on any defined competition. In general, companies tend to survey other businesses similar to themselves in all or some of the following characteristics: size (usually reflected by total assets), industry type (products, services), geographical location, revenue/income size, and required job skills. Here are three ways to obtain data:

- *Refer to published surveys.* Before using published surveys, carefully review their usefulness and applicability to the organization. It may be possible to examine the survey input documents as well as an extract of survey output.
- *Participate in customized surveys.* When possible, participate in customized surveys conducted by other companies of similar size or industry type.
- *Conduct a survey.* If data are required in a hurry, a telephone survey may be conducted. However, telephone surveys are not recommended for multiple jobs because the amount of phone time required may not be convenient for all participants.

Before a company decides to conduct its own survey, there are obvious considerations such as time, costs, usefulness of data, and survey purpose. There also are some hidden concerns, such as the difficulty of convincing potential peer organizations to participate.

KEY STEPS IN DESIGNING AN EFFECTIVE PAY STRUCTURE

The following set of steps describes the specific ways in which internal equity and external competitiveness both play a role in establishing pay structures and job hierarchy. (See Figure 11.10.) These steps are based on the assumption that the organization is using a point-factor job-evaluation plan, one of the many methods of establishing the value of a job internally.

After the description of each step, key issues pertaining to that step are highlighted and questions to be asked regarding each issue are indicated. Specific answers to these questions are not given because they would differ from organization to organization. Note that the first five steps relate to the establishment of internal equity. The last five steps relate to external competitiveness. In general, as the job level increases, the reliance on external market data—as opposed to internal considerations—also increases. (See Figure 11.11.)

Step 1: Review Overall Point Differentials

This step is often referred to as "sore thumbing" because it involves reviewing all of the job-evaluation points to see if any evaluations stand out from the group. If necessary, points are changed to better reflect the internal value of the job before proceeding to the second step.

FIGURE 11.10 Internal equity vs. external competitiveness.

Internal Equity	External Competitiveness
Review overall point differentials	Incorporate market data
Rank order jobs by total evaluation points	Review market inconsistencies
Develop job groupings	Smooth out grade averages
Develop preliminary point bands	Review differences between midpoints and market averages
Check intrafamily and supervisory relationships	Resolve inconsistencies between internal and external equity

FIGURE 11.11 Internal versus external equity as applied to the hierarchy of jobs.

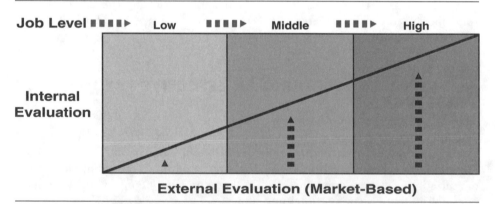

Note: In the process of establishing job levels, the proportion of internal evaluation and external evaluation used usually varies with the level of the jobs within the hierarchy of jobs in the company. As the level of the job increases, the reliance on external market data increases.

Key issue: Do any job evaluations appear to be "out of place," either with their peers across functions or with their superiors or subordinates?

Key questions to ask: Do the evaluators fully understand the jobs? Is the job description or questionnaire complete? Is the job being compared to the correct peer group? Is the rater evaluating the job or the person?

Step 2: Rank Order Jobs by Total Evaluation Points

Rank all jobs in ascending or descending order as shown in Example 11.4.

Key issue: Does the hierarchy of positions make intuitive sense?

Key questions to ask: Does the hierarchy reflect the differences in the functions of the various positions? Has any position been overrated or underrated? Do the differences in points reflect the degree of differences between positions?

Example 11.4

Rank Order	Job Title	Points
13	Claims Officer	565
12	Accounting Systems Control Officer	550
11	Employee Relations Officer	545
10	Team Leader	470
9	Senior Accounting Consultant	425
8	Project Coordinator	405
7	Accounting Technician	355
6	Accounting Consultant	355
5	Records Management Specialist	345
4	Reconciliation Technician	335
3	Service Center Coordinator	260
2	Copy Center Worker	210
1	Mail Clerk	140

Step 3: Develop Job Groupings

While developing groupings, look for point breaks. Make sure that the number of levels identified is compatible with the number of levels within the organization. Possible job groupings using natural point breaks are shown in Example 11.5.

Key issue: How to develop job groupings that are meaningful rather than contrived.
Key questions to ask: Where are the natural point breaks? How many levels should there be to accommodate levels within the organization?

Step 4: Develop Preliminary Point Bands

Salary-grade point bands, or ranges, can be developed as either "absolute" point spreads or as percentage-based point spreads between point-band maximums. Table 11.1 is an example of an absolute point spread based on some of the jobs in the preceding examples. Notice that 39 points is the absolute value between point-band maximums. However, the percentage spread varies.

A variation on the absolute point spread is to increase the point spread when moving up the salary-grade structure. Companies may choose to do this in recognition

Example 11.5	
Job Groupings	
Claims Officer	565
Accounting Systems Control Officer	550
Employee Relations Officer	545
Team Leader	470
Senior Accounting Consultant	425
Project Coordinator	405
Accounting Technician	355
Accounting Consultant	355
Records Management Specialist	345
Reconciliation Technician	335
Service Center Coordinator	260
Copy Center Worker	210
Mail Clerk	140

of the broader range of skills represented within higher salary grades. Table 11.2 is an example.

An alternate approach is to develop point bands with percentage-based point spreads between point-band maximums. The percentage spread can remain constant or vary. Tables 11.3 and 11.4 are examples.

TABLE 11.1 Constant Absolute Points

GRADE	POINT BANDS		CONSTANT ABSOLUTE POINTS	VARYING PERCENTAGE SPREAD (rounded)
	MINIMUM	MAXIMUM		
1	137	178		
			39	22%
2	176	217		
			39	18%
3	215	256		
			39	15%
4	254	295		
			39	13%
5	293	334		
			39	12%
6	332	373		

TABLE 11.2 Absolute Points Increase as Grades Become Higher

GRADE	POINT BANDS		VARYING ABSOLUTE POINTS	VARYING PERCENTAGE SPREAD (rounded)
	MINIMUM	MAXIMUM		
1	140	165		
			15	9%
2	166	180		
			35	19%
3	181	215		
			35	16%
4	216	250		
			40	16%
5	251	290		
			40	14%
6	291	330		

TABLE 11.3 Percentage Spread Constant

GRADE	POINT BANDS		VARYING ABSOLUTE POINTS	CONSTANT PERCENTAGE SPREAD (rounded)
	MINIMUM	MAXIMUM		
1	126	145		
			22	15%
2	146	167		
			25	15%
3	168	192		
			29	15%
4	193	221		
			33	15%
5	222	254		
			38	15%
6	255	292		

TABLE 11.4 Absolute Points and Percentage Spread Vary

GRADE	POINT BANDS		VARYING ABSOLUTE POINTS	VARYING PERCENTAGE SPREAD (rounded)
	MINIMUM	MAXIMUM		
1	126	145		
			22	15%
2	146	167		
			25	15%
3	169	192		
			33	17%
4	199	225		
			38	17%
5	230	263		
			50	19%
6	275	313		

Key issue: Determining the width of each point band.

Key questions to ask: Wider point bands will require fewer grades, and they will group a larger number of jobs together. Is this in line with the company's corporate policy? Are jobs with similar skill, effort, and responsibility being grouped together?

For the purposes of this example, a salary structure will be constructed with 11 grades. It is important to remember that this decision is not purely objective. It takes into account an organization's internal values and other practical considerations such as the desired number of grades or a set policy regarding the number of grades between supervisor and employee. Most important, the structure should work for the company.

The point bands in Example 11.6 were developed using job evaluations and the natural breaks between jobs. A minimum of 137 points was set for the lowest grade, which is occupied by the Mail Clerk job (evaluated at 140 points). Each grade's point-band width is a constant 39 points between point-band maximums. The 11 grades, shown in Example 11.6, are designed to accommodate the lowest-level job—Mail Clerk—to the highest-level job—Claims Officer.

Step 5: Check Intrafamily and Supervisory Relationships

The last step in the internal equity process is to check the evaluations to ensure they represent all the levels and reporting relationships within the organization. It is important to determine whether jobs of similar skill, effort, responsibility, and working conditions are within the same salary level. The structure should be reviewed to ensure that dissimilar jobs are not placed within the same level, and that subordinate and supervisor positions are not placed within the same grade.

Key issue: Peer and subordinate/superior relationships.

Key questions to ask: Are there enough levels between supervisor and subordinate positions? Do the set levels accurately reflect levels within job families?

Step 6: Incorporate Market Data

Based on the preliminary ranking performed in Steps 4 and 5, market data are added to identify differences in how your company and the market value a particular set of jobs. Table 11.5 is an example.

Example 11.6

Grade	Point Bands
11	527 +
10	488-526
9	449-487
8	410-448
7	371-409
6	332-370
5	293-331
4	254-292
3	215-253
2	176-214
1	137-175

TABLE 11.5 Use of Market Data

GRADE	POSITION	MARKET AVERAGE
11	Claims Officer Accounting Systems Control Officer Employee Relations Officer	$57,000 $53,000 $49,000
10	Open	
9	Team Leader	$36,000
8	Senior Accounting Consultant	$31,600
7	Project Coordinator	$29,200
6	Accounting Technician Accounting Consultant Records Management Specialist	$25,600 $24,300 $23,000
5	Reconciliation Technician	$23,000
4	Service Center Coordinator	$20,300
3	Open	
2	Copy Center Worker	$18,000
1	Mail Clerk	$15,300

Key issue: How to obtain the best fit between internal evaluation and market value.

Key questions to ask: Are the market numbers reliable? Are the job matches appropriate? How many open grades are needed to meet future needs? Is it possible to keep the market comparisons current?

At this point in the process, differences between a company's internal values for a job and the market's values become apparent. In Example 11.7, note that there is only a 20-point difference between the evaluations for the Employee Relations Officer and the Claims Officer but an $8,000 difference in pay.

Step 7: Review Market Inconsistencies

At this point, the organization must decide the importance of the internal values that have been placed on its positions. It also must decide whether it can afford to pay differently than the market. Can the organization risk the internal integrity of the compensation program by relying more heavily on the market value of these

Example 11.7		
Job Title (Grade)	**Points**	**Market Average**
Claims Officer (11)	565	$57,000
Accounting Systems Control Officer (11)	550	$53,000
Employee Relations Officer (11)	545	$49,000
Open (10)		
Team Leader (9)	470	$36,000
Senior Accounting Consultant (8)	425	$31,600
Project Coordinator (7)	405	$29,200
Accounting Technician (6)	355	$25,600
Accounting Consultant (6)	355	$24,300
Records Management Specialist (6)	345	$23,000
Reconciliation Technician (5)	335	$23,000
Service Center Coordinator (4)	260	$20,300
Open (3)		
Copy Center Worker (2)	210	$18,000
Mail Clerk (1)	140	$15,300

positions? Are there enough positions within a job family to justify establishing a separate salary structure to address these problems?

Once any inconsistencies between the internal and external markets have been resolved, "raw" averages for jobs in each of the salary grades are calculated. These averages are simple means calculated from the market data. (See Table 11.6.)

Key issue: The company must decide whether it can accept a salary structure with varying percentages between its midpoints.

Key questions to ask: Is the number of grades selected (11) still acceptable? Can the differences between midpoints be smoothed out without affecting the integrity of the market competitiveness? How important is it to be close to the market?

Step 8: Smooth Out Grade Averages

While smoothing out grade averages, a decision has to be made on where it is most important to be competitive and where the most payroll dollars are at stake. Then test to see which midpoint-to-midpoint percentage increment is the most logical to use.

Example 11.8 has made use of 13.229-percent increments, which allow for use of the 11 grades proposed earlier. (These increments may be derived using the "present value" formula discussed in Formula 11.2.)

Key issue: The company must decide whether there is an "ideal" midpoint-to-midpoint percentage spread.

Key questions to ask: Is smoothing out always necessary or desirable? Because the smoothing-out process is one of trial and error, at what point is it advisable to stop so that the salaries generated by the structure are competitive and at the same time payroll dollars are not used ineffectively or irresponsibly?

TABLE 11.6 Calculation of Raw Averages

GRADE	RAW MARKET AVERAGE	% DIFFERENCE
11	$53,000	
10	Open	
9	$36,000	
		13.9%
8	$31,600	
		8.2%
7	$29,200	
		20.2%
6	$24,300	
		5.7%
5	$23,000	
		13.3%
4	$20,300	
3	Open	
2	$18,000	
		17.6%
1	$15,300	

Example 11.8

Grade	Proposed Midpoints
11	$53,000
10	$46,807
9	$41,338
8	$36,509
7	$32,243
6	$28,476
5	$25,149
4	$22,211
3	$19,616
2	$17,324
1	$15,300

Step 9: Review Differences between Midpoints and Market Averages

The key to this step is to identify any large differences between proposed midpoints and individual job-market averages. (See Table 11.7.)

Key issue: The company must determine the percentage factor that should be used to smooth out the midpoints.

Key questions to ask: Which jobs have the greater need to be competitively paid? Can any jobs be underpaid without affecting the company's ability to attract and retain employees? Can the company afford to overpay some jobs?

Step 10: Resolve Inconsistencies between Internal and External Equity

The proposed salary structure shows how each of the evaluated positions relates to one another internally as well as how each job relates to the market. Most companies are comfortable if the proposed midpoints are within 10 percent of the competitive market. Using this as a rule of thumb, the following positions are most out of line with the market:

- *Reconciliation Technician:* 24 percent.
- *Records Management Specialist:* 24 percent.
- *Accounting Consultant:* 17 percent.

TABLE 11.7 Differences Between Proposed Midpoints and Individual Job Market Averages

GRADE	POINT SPREAD	POSITION	POINTS	MARKET AVERAGE	PROPOSED MIDPOINT	COMPA-RATIO	$\left(\dfrac{\text{PROPOSED MIDPOINT}}{\text{MARKET AVERAGE}}\right)$
11	527 +	Accounting Systems Control Officer	550	$53,000	$53,000		100%
		Claims Officer	565	$57,000			93%
		Employee Relations Officer	545	$49,000			108%
10	488-526	Open		–	$46,807		–
9	449-487	Team Leader	470	$36,000	$41,338		115%
8	410-448	Senior Accounting Consultant	425	$31,600	$36,509		116%
7	371-409	Project Coordinator	405	$29,200	$32,243		110%
6	332-370	Reconciliation Technician	335	$23,000	$28,476		124%
		Records Management Specialist	345	$23,000			124%
		Accounting Consultant	355	$24,300			117%
		Accounting Technician	355	$25,600			111%
5	293-331	Open		–	$25,149		–
4	254-292	Service Center Coordinator	260	$20,300	$22,211		109%
3	215-253	Open		–	$19,616		–
2	176-214	Copy Center Worker	210	$18,000	$17,324		96%
1	137-175	Mail Clerk	140	$15,300	$15,300		100%

With these proposed midpoints, the company will pay above the going rate in the market. If internal equity is a greater concern, then the additional money spent may not be a significant issue. However, another possibility to consider is pulling these jobs out of the proposed pay structure and paying them separately. The grade level would stay the same to provide internal job level equity, but the pay midpoints would represent the market more closely.

Decisions of this nature must be made after reviewing the inconsistencies. Each company must take into account its corporate culture and ability to pay when deciding what adjustments to make in the balance between internal values and external competitiveness. The key goal, as always, is to develop an acceptable pay structure that will aid the company in attracting, retaining, and motivating qualified employees.

Key issue: Determining what is more important—internal or external equity.

Key questions to ask: What is the company culture? What is its stance on the consistent treatment of its employees? Is there high turnover in the company? Is it in a low-level job family or a high-level job family?

PITFALLS AND PRECAUTIONS

A pay structure is not an end in itself. In fact, it is possible for a company to pay its employees without having a formal pay structure. While pay structures help create a systematic and equitable system of cash-compensation management, it is important to keep in mind that they are only tools. Pay structures actually will burden a company unless the following issues are considered:

- *Competitive posture.* What is the competitive posture of the company? How much above or below the market should the company pay or can it afford to pay?

- *Decision making.* Who will make the critical decisions underlying the pay structure? (For most companies, senior management tends to make these decisions.)
- *Monitoring.* How frequently will the pay structure be monitored and assessed for currency and appropriateness?
- *Flexibility.* Is the pay structure flexible enough to handle dynamic situations? This is critical in this age of constant change in corporations and in the economic environment, particularly the labor market.
- *Resources.* Can the company afford to allocate sufficient resources (including technology) to build and maintain current and relevant pay structures related to data?
- *Communication.* Is the company willing to allocate the required effort and resources to communicate the pay structures to employees and educate management in the proper use of pay structures?

Many companies currently are considering the *broadbanding* of salary ranges where applicable and appropriate. Broadbanding is the combining of existing ranges by expanding range width and reducing the number of grades. This usually is done for many reasons to benefit the organization and its employees. These reasons include the following:

- Paying for performance and allowing managers greater flexibility in salary administration.
- Ease of moving people within the company.
- Reduction of the demands of job evaluation as well as the time and effort required to make organizational changes.

Broadbanding is only one approach to pay administration in general and pay structures in particular.

Pay structures should be developed from the organization's mission and business strategy. Strategy should always precede structure development. Many internal and external environmental factors determine a company's pay structure. The pay structure has to adopt the same positive characteristics of a company's overall compensation program.

While designing a pay structure, a balance between internal and external equity must be maintained. Constant fine-tuning should take place. Developing pay structures is more an art than a science, although many mathematical techniques and processes may be used. While it is important to be specific about structural features such as the range spread, midpoint progression, and so on, the key element of an effective pay structure is its value in functioning as a tool for managing pay.

BROADBANDING

Broadbanding has been a part of the HR field since the late 1980s and early 1990s and was developed to compress many salary grades into fewer, wide pay "bands." Those organizations that implemented such a system were driven by the need to adapt salary administration systems and procedures to meet a new business climate and create a flatter organization.

Broadbanding can be defined as a pay structure that consolidates a large number of pay grades and salary ranges into much fewer broadbands with relatively wide salary ranges, typically with 100 percent (or more) differences between minimum and maximum. Simply stated, broadbanding refers to the collapsing of job clusters or tiers of positions into a few wide bands to manage career growth and deliver pay.

Broadbanding was created to help achieve several objectives, namely:

- Develop broader workforce skills.
- Encourage career development among employees.
- Reduce administration with job evaluation, salary structure, and merit pay.

Broadbanding usually appeals to fast-moving organizations that are undergoing persistent change. Such organizations that want to be quicker and more flexible in the marketplace have implemented broadbanding. They have found that broad-bands complement processes designed to increase company speed, flexibility, and risk taking.

Some or most of the career ladder rungs were removed and employees were encouraged to earn more by adding value to the company. This could be accomplished by developing new skills or competencies and/or participating in a variable pay system with a line of sight to the company's performance.

Broadbands support this evolving organizational dynamic by providing less formal structure. The traditional compensation approach emphasizes internal equity, focused employees' attention on the world inside the firm, and helps them experience an internal culture that more closely reflects the external, competitive marketplace. It helps make it easier for them to reorient themselves to the marketplace.

In broadbanding, there is no automatic progression to the midpoint because there is no midpoint. The marketplace for talent is no longer represented by highly defined salary structures, but rather mirrored by loosely defined, ambiguous broad-bands that do not apply directly to an employee's position. (See Sidebar 11.1.)

STARTING RATES OF PAY

When pay ranges have been formally established, it is the policy of most employers to pay new hires, who appear to have only the minimum qualifications for their jobs, at or near the range minimum. The objective is to avoid paying them at rates that are too close to those paid to more experienced employees in the same job. Occasionally, supply and demand conditions are such that new hires with relatively little experience must be paid substantially above the range minimums. Additionally, individuals with substantial experience (or otherwise superior qualifications) frequently are hired at higher levels in the rate ranges.

INCREASES TO BASE RATES OF PAY

Today's employees typically are eligible for several types of base pay increases, such as general (or across-the-board) increases, cost of living increases, promotional increases, step increases, and merit increases.

General (or across-the-board) increases are those that are granted in equal percentages or equal dollar amounts to all employees in an eligible group. For example, all employees might receive pay increases equal to 25 cents per hour, or 3 percent of their current pay. Employers might specify that some employees

---

Sidebar 11.1: Broadbanding Is Not for Everyone

Broadbanding is not a panacea for all organizations. One potential disadvantage is that broadbanding's delayered approach to salary administration may not fit the culture of heavily level-oriented companies. The need to manage salaries also does not go away. Market pricing becomes even more important because it is used extensively to identify salary targets.

When broadbanding is implemented, an organization may also have to re-examine such things as management incentives, perquisites, and other items tied to the conventional salary grade. Line managers also may need to be retrained to make compensation decisions while being persuaded to accept new or greater responsibility for employee career development.

As some companies have found, pay systems are most effective when they support organizational change, not when they lead change. Some theorize if an organization is not ready for broadbanding, it will likely fail.

Other potential pitfalls exist:

- It could be possible to flatten the pay structure to the extent that supervisors and their subordinates are in the same band.
- The question of inflation arises, both of pay and of expectations, when employees are put in bands with potentially higher maximums than their previous grade maximums.
- It becomes more difficult to compare jobs to the marketplace and maintain external equity.

(e.g., those who exceed the maximums of their rate ranges or those whose performance is unacceptable) are to be excluded from receiving such increases. General increases are not conceptually compatible with pay-for-performance programs, and the use of general increases has diminished as performance-based programs have expanded.

A *cost of living increase* is a specific type of general increase that is typically awarded in equal cents per hour or percentage terms to all employees in a pay program or structure. Cost-of-living allowance (COLA) increases, however, are intended to protect employees' purchasing power against erosion caused by inflation. These increases typically relate to increases in the Consumer Price Index (CPI). Thus, all cost-of-living increases are general increases, but not all general increases are cost-of-living increases.

Promotion increases are increases granted to employees who are promoted from one job to another job with a higher pay grade and range. The size of increase is usually influenced by the magnitude of the promotion (as measured by the difference between the pay ranges assigned to the promotee's old and new jobs) and the pay relationships among the promotee's peers, superiors, and subordinates.

Within-range increases are types of base pay increases that move employees forward in the pay ranges assigned to their jobs. Within-range pay increases are virtually always determined by some combination of the employees' length of service and performance. The two principal types of within-range increases are:

1. *Increases based primarily on length of service* (though differences in performance may also be reflected). These may be *step increases,* whereby the pay ranges are divided into a number of pay rates with increases related to length of service. The step increase concept is used most commonly for nonexempt employees, and there are several different approaches to this concept:

   a. The first is for *length of service only.* Here the employee receives single-step increases up to the range maximum, which is usually at or just above the competitive market rate. If performance is unsatisfactory, the increase is denied and probation, demotion, or dismissal may result.

   b. The second reflects both *length of service* and *performance.* One approach is illustrated in the following chart:

Performance	Rating Pay Action
Outstanding	2-step increase
Exceeds standards	1-step increase; may accelerate timing of next review
Meets standards	1-step increase
Does not meet standards	No increase

   c. Another approach involves *two or three performance tracks* through which the employee progresses to a performance zone maximum. The number of steps can be increased to allow for smaller percentage steps.

   d. Finally, it is possible to add *timing* differences. This further accentuates differences in pay level based upon differences in performance.

2. *Increases based on merit* usually are administered in the form of a range of percentages for varying levels of performance. As mentioned earlier, they also may be used in combination with step progression increases.

Inherent in most merit increase programs are the notions that:

- The speed with which employees move through pay ranges will be determined principally, if not solely, on the basis of their job performance.
- Performance will also determine how far employees are allowed to progress in their pay ranges.

Thus in determining merit increases, many organizations consider the performance of the individual and his or her current rate in the pay range. As a result, the merit increase may vary in size and timing.

Many organizations use a fixed frequency and vary the increase's size. The fixed frequency may vary by job level, but the most typical frequency at all levels is 12 months. Timing of increases is sometimes based on the pay policy year (focal point) or the anniversary (anniversary date) of the employee's service or last increase date.

A smaller but significant percentage of organizations vary the size of the increase and the frequency. A minority of organizations fix the size of the increase, but vary the frequency.

The size of the increase (typically measured as a percent increase) generally varies directly with the individual's performance (the better the performance, the bigger the increase), and, inversely, with the employee's position in the pay range (the lower the position in the range, the bigger the increase as a percent of current pay). It is common practice to provide supervisors and managers with increase planning guidelines. These guideline charts include a range of options, to allow managerial flexibility.

A final variation on the previous methods involves either step progression or percent merit guideline increases to the range midpoint, with a lump sum bonus given that varies in amount, depending upon performance.

There are, of course, many variations of these pay increase approaches. Basically, however, all known variations of in-range pay increases are some combination of these two basic approaches—step increases or merit increases.

MERIT PAY CONSIDERATIONS

Compensation professionals believe certain conditions generally must exist for performance-based pay increase programs to be successful:

- Individual differences in job performance should be measurable.
- Individual differences in job performance must be significant enough to warrant the time and effort required to measure them and relate pay to them.
- The pay range should be sufficiently broad (35 percent to 50 percent) to allow for adequate differentiation of pay based upon performance, and/or level of experience and skill.
- Supervisors and managers must be trained in employee performance planning and appraisal.
- Management must be committed, and employees must be receptive to making distinctions in pay based upon performance.
- Managers must be adequately skilled in managing pay.
- Sufficient control systems must be implemented to ensure that merit increase guidelines are followed.

There are potential productivity and incentive benefits to be derived from the implementation of a performance-based pay increase program. However, this type of program is more complex to administer and requires more difficult management decisions. Compensation professionals must ensure that their merit pay programs measure performance as objectively as possible. Management must carefully evaluate performance and make judgments regarding pay differentials. Significant commitments of time and effort are required by all involved in this process.

PERFORMANCE APPRAISAL CONSIDERATIONS

For a performance-based pay system to meet its objectives, a well-designed and properly administered performance management system must exist. An effective performance management system includes the following characteristics:

- Performance is appraised on the basis of direct measurement of each employee's output or results. For example, the quantity and quality of work is assessed rather than the employee personality traits. Employee behavior is considered only to the extent that it is job-related and affects job results.
- Supervisors are trained in the concepts and the process involved in appraising performance.
- Measures or criteria used are as objective and quantitative as possible, to minimize the potential for varying interpretations by different reviewers.

- Objective performance standards are established for various levels of employee performance when practical.
- The relative importance (weight) of each of the performance criteria is established.
- When practical, employees are involved in the determination of performance criteria, standards, and weights to ensure greater acceptance of the program.
- Performance criteria, standards, and weights are communicated to the employee at the beginning of the appraisal period, and periodically reviewed and updated for timeliness, relevance, and utility.
- The appraisal is written, and discussed by the employee and supervisor. The employee is involved in the process prior to finalizing the written appraisal. (Many organizations make a copy of the written appraisal available to the employee and provide an appeals mechanism for reconciling differences between employee and supervisor.)
- Finally, the appraisal process is audited routinely and frequently, to identify and eliminate potential problems.

MAINTAINING AND AUDITING THE PAY PROGRAM

Maintenance of pay programs is one of the most critical elements of sound base pay administration. Unless programs are properly maintained, errors occur and inequities will eventually undermine program effectiveness. The maintenance of pay programs is inherently difficult, because of:

- Continual changes in the content of the various jobs in an organization.
- Continual changes in the going market rates for jobs.
- Frequent changes in organizational structure and staffing levels.
- The ever-evolving and expanding regulatory framework governing pay programs.
- The inevitable turnover within the compensation function itself.

KEYS TO SUCCESSFUL PAY PROGRAM MAINTENANCE

There are five keys to the proper maintenance of pay programs:

- Clearly stated objectives, policies, and procedures are established and communicated.
- Proper controls are operative to ensure policies and procedures are being consistently applied.
- There is adequate support for the compensation function itself—including provision of sufficient staff and other resources, as well as the top management support necessary to ensure that the pay program is administered with fairness and integrity.
- The compensation staff properly performs administrative activities.
- The pay program is routinely audited for effectiveness and efficiency.

The next sections focus on the ongoing administrative activities necessary for maintaining pay programs and the types of audits that can be conducted to ensure that the programs are functioning properly.

ONGOING ADMINISTRATIVE ACTIVITIES

The proper maintenance of base pay programs requires continual analysis of the content and requirements for the various jobs in an organization. The information collected in the course of these ongoing analyses requires careful documentation by job descriptions, completed position analysis questionnaires, or some combination thereof.

Changes in organizational structure and staffing levels also affect the content of jobs and their relative worth to the organization. Unless job documentation is properly maintained and jobs are properly evaluated, employees may be assigned incorrect job titles, pay grades, and/or pay ranges. To ensure ongoing program success, some organizations undertake regular reviews or "desk audits" of various organizational components. Others attempt to verify job-content information throughout the process of performance planning and appraisal.

Compensation professionals also continually monitor the position of the organization's pay levels vis-à-vis those of the competition. Thus, compensation professionals participate in, purchase, and extract data from pay surveys. This compiled data, plus the organization's pay philosophy and ability to pay, combine to produce decisions regarding changes in pay structures and budgets. If the monitoring of the market is neglected or poorly performed, an organization's pay rates and/or rate ranges may be too high (causing excessive financial costs) or too low (causing excessive employee relations costs) when compared with those of competitors.

In addition to pay structure maintenance activities, compensation professionals create pay increase budgets, planning documents, authorization procedures, and guidelines that combine to support the organization's pay philosophy. They also prepare periodic reports for top management regarding pay program results and costs.

PAY PROGRAM AUDITS

Systematic pay program audits can be invaluable for ensuring an organization's compensation program is being properly administered and maintained. Observers of human behavior have noted "people do what is inspected, not necessarily what is expected." In the absence of audits, policies may become wishes and pay programs may be rendered ineffective because of inconsistent practices and resultant inequities, charges of illegal discrimination, employee dissatisfaction, or excessive costs.

Five Steps to Prepare for and Conduct Pay Program Audits

Step 1: Decide What to Audit

In general, pay program audits include some combination of four different types of measures:

- *Process measures* are used to determine the extent to which the pay program is being smoothly and efficiently administered. Some sample measures would be:
  - Productivity of staff.
  - Satisfaction of line managers with the administration of the pay program.
  - Cost of analytical/data collection activities.
    - Job analysis.
    - Job documentation.

- Job evaluation.
- Survey data.
- Amount of management time required for pay program administration.
- Cost of data processing/consulting support.
- Error rates in databases.
- Backlog of requests for evaluations/re-evaluations.
- Timeliness of pay increase planning and processing.
- Timeliness and quality of performance appraisal data.
- *Policy compliance measures* are used to determine if the pay program is being administered in accordance with policy. Several examples would be:
  - Actual rates and ranges versus market position specified by policy.
  - Pay position in range.
  - Percent of employees outside pay ranges.
    - Green circle.
    - Red circle.
  - Extent of compliance with salary increase policies.
  - Extent of compliance with starting rate policies.
  - Job title congruence with actual job content.
  - Validity of job evaluation data.
  - Consistency of pay grade and range assignments with job evaluation results.
  - Compliance with performance appraisal policies and procedures.
  - Quality of performance appraisal information.
- *Documentation adequacy measures* are used to determine the extent to which the program is committed to putting it in writing. For example:
  - Percent of jobs for which accurate and up-to-date documentation exists.
  - Percent of jobs with accurate job evaluation documentation.
  - Percent of jobs with valid pay grade assignments.
  - Percent of employees' files containing current performance appraisal documents.
  - Compliance with Fair Labor Standards Act (FLSA)/Equal Pay Act (EPA) recordkeeping requirements.
  - Existence of written policies regarding:
    - The design and operation of the job evaluation procedures.
    - The operation of performance appraisal procedures.
    - Pay increases.
    - Structure adjustment procedures.
    - Re-evaluation procedures.
- *Overall results measures* are used to assess how well pay programs achieve the established goals, such as:
  - Attraction and retention of qualified employees.
    - Number of openings.
    - Duration of openings.
    - Quality of employees.
    - Number of terminations (voluntary and involuntary).
  - Compliance with applicable laws and regulations.
    - Grievances.
    - Lawsuits.
    - Statistical analyses.
  - Results of performance-based pay polices.
    - Turnover by performance level.

- Percent of payroll allocated in a performance dependent manner.
- Correlation between pay and performance levels.
- Protection of the organization's financial resources.
  - Pay as a percent of operating budget.
  - Historical.
  - Product competitors.
  - Organization rates versus market rates.
- Employee perceptions of
  - Internal equity.
    - In the same job.
    - In different jobs.
  - External equity.

Step 2: Select the Participants

Participants should understand audit principles and processes and possess well-developed analytical, writing, and interpersonal skills. In addition, they should be disinterested parties that have no stake in a particular audit outcome.

Step 3: Develop a Data Collection and Analysis Plan

Interviews or opinion surveys can be used to determine how various parties view the pay program. Auditors also can examine a wide variety of internal and external records and reports, including human resource records, payroll data, pay survey data, accounting records, and compensation databases.

Step 4: Assemble the Necessary Data to Support the Analysis

Step 5: Analyze the Collected Data and Develop Findings and Recommendations

The audit report should present findings in an objective manner and provide adequate information to give readers the proper perspective.

Management's role is to:

- Review audit results and recommendations.
- Prioritize the improvements that are required.
- Allocate the necessary resources.
- Follow up to ensure that the work is completed.

Organizations often find that audits are useful tools for educating management groups about the intricacies of pay program administration, thus increasing their understanding and support for the pay program.

Considering the size of base pay expenditures in many organizations, it is generally appropriate to conduct comprehensive audits at least every two years. This approach will ensure organizations are continually aware of the extent to which pay programs achieve their objectives, so problems can be identified and resolved as quickly as possible.

12 Sales Compensation Fundamentals

The degree of an HR department's involvement with sales compensation plan design and implementation varies from company to company. In some companies, HR's involvement is actively sought by the sales department. In others, HR's involvement is discouraged or prevented. HR professionals frequently ask, "What can I do to play a more meaningful role in plan design and implementation at my company?" This question is not surprising, because having limited or no involvement in the process of shaping and launching a sales compensation plan means that companies miss the opportunity to use the expertise of their HR staff in key people-management areas. These key areas include ensuring that a company's sales compensation plan is designed to attract, retain, and reward talented salespeople who can win and keep customers. It is clear that developing and using a compensation plan that helps a company achieve that goal should draw upon the expertise of the HR function. This chapter describes the aspects of sales compensation plan design and implementation in which the HR professional can play a meaningful role. Further, it provides suggestions about actions that an HR professional can take to perform that role effectively.

WORKING WITH THE SALES ORGANIZATION

At many companies, the business partner role defines how HR is expected to work with its assigned organizational client. The assigned client may be either a business unit that includes the sales organization or it may be only the sales organization. When the business partner role is the prevailing model for providing HR services, the HR generalist is faced with a broad range of duties and responsibilities. However, an HR professional's No. 1 priority should be to gain and continually build a thorough understanding of the assigned client's business. When the assigned client is the sales organization, that understanding should include:

- Customer markets served and the product/service offerings provided.
- Sales channels deployed and the jobs operating within those channels.
- Current year's business plan, sales strategies, and sales financial goals.
- Sales leadership's operational style (e.g., centralized versus decentralized management) as it pertains to various sales management programs—territory assignment, quota allocation, sales crediting—that impact compensation.

Some senior HR professionals have said that an up-to-date understanding of the four areas itemized is the entry or "ante into the game." As in many business situations, the key to success is the quality of one's relationships with the individuals in senior leadership positions. Relationships built on trust, confidence, and respect are acquired over time. HR professionals who have successfully developed effective working relationships with senior sales leaders did so through regular, proactive, and meaningful interactions with the sales organization. Figure 12.1 itemizes activities in which an HR/compensation professional should

FIGURE 12.1 HR professional—sales compensation plan involvement.

Who	What (Illustrative Interactions)
• Sales leaders, i.e., top sales executive and regional sales executives (e.g., North America, Europe, Asia/Pacific)	• Regular conversations (monthly, quarterly) about effectiveness of current plans—what's working, what's not; early ideas for change in the future • Participation in sales leadership meetings related to future business planning; implications for sales compensation • Review/discuss with sales leadership teams: quarterly sales results and impact on sales incentive compensation payments, e.g., percent of sales team earning under the plan, percent of sales team achieving target incentive earnings; overachievement earnings; individual sales performance and general staffing concerns
• Field sales managers, e.g., first-level sales managers	• Occasional "work withs" to understand challenges faced by field sales managers in their jobs; role sales compensation plays in motivating and managing their sales team • Regular calls to selected field sales managers to gain feedback on current plans—what's working; what's not • Issues/challenges with current plans—what are the most common questions or problems members of the sales force are experiencing under the plan • Needs relative to managing with the plan, e.g., reports, response to special requests

• Sales staff, e.g., sales operations or administrative executives	• Regular conversations with sales staff supporting the plans to understand their perspectives on what's working, what's not and why; early thoughts about opportunities for plan improvement in subsequent year • Periodic meetings to confirm system capabilities, abilities to meet management information needs
• "Sellers," e.g., sales representatives, account managers, sales specialists	• Occasional "ride withs" to understand sales roles and jobs, i.e., how members of the sales force go about their work, influence they have on customer buying decisions, service work they perform; how sales compensation plan influences their behavior and performance • Periodic sales force surveys to understand what members of the sales force like best/least about current plans

engage to demonstrate a willingness to learn how the sales organization operates. Through these activities, an HR/compensation professional can develop a first-hand understanding of the needs and requirements of the sales organization for compensation support.

Taking the initiative to understand how the sales organization operates assumes that sales leaders are receptive to having HR involved with the sales organization overall, and with the sales compensation plan in particular. Because in some cases this is not a valid assumption, Figure 12.2 indicates some of the more common objections to HR involvement with the sales compensation plan and provides suggestions for overcoming those objections. These suggestions should be helpful to an HR professional in convincing the top sales executive that his or her involvement with the sales compensation plan will be helpful to both the sales organization and the company.

Whether HR is considered an internal consultant or a policy gatekeeper, involvement of the HR professional with the sales compensation plan is important to business success. Meaningful involvement is most likely to take place in situations where the HR professional has developed a thorough understanding of how sales operates and has built an effective working relationship with key sales leaders throughout the sales organization. Additionally, HR/compensation professionals must develop and improve upon their knowledge of sales compensation principles, practices, and techniques. Every HR/compensation professional with responsibility for sales compensation should ask, "What am I doing to continually improve my mastery of the tools and techniques required to provide innovative compensation solutions to the sales challenges faced by my company?"

This chapter's overall goal is to provide you with the tools and knowledge required to support the sales organization through compensation solutions. In particular, the goal of this chapter is to describe some of the competencies that require mastery in today's business environment. Included in this list of competencies are:

• Knowing how to help sales executives address and resolve sales compensation problems as they arise during the course of a year.

FIGURE 12.2 Overcoming resistance to HR involvement with sales compensations.

Objections—Sales Executives	Suggested Response—HR Professional
• No relevant experience	• Describe experience in sales compensation plan design and design of management-incentive plans • Explain role in process and key contributions acknowledged by others • Describe seminars or courses taken in sales compensation
• No understanding of our sales channels, process, jobs	• Ask for the opportunity to develop that understanding by visiting field locations, doing "work withs" with field managers, going on sales calls with sales reps
• No time	• Explain that priorities have been adjusted to make time available to work on sales compensation
• Don't know where it would make sense to involve you	• Suggest a process; offer ideas about specific tasks that HR could undertake and complete; describe outcomes and benefits

- Knowing how to assess the effectiveness of the sales compensation plan and therefore how and when to help sales executives make plan changes in order to increase sales effectiveness through compensation.
- Having the ability to lead or participate in a design process that includes advising management on which jobs should be eligible to participate in the sales compensation plan, the appropriate level of pay for those jobs, what type of plan is appropriate, and how the incentive arrangement should be structured.
- Developing a holistic understanding of the company's sales management programs and the role their interdependence plays in the company's achievement of its sales goals.
- Understanding how communication strategies and tactics are created and executed in order to ensure that a new or changed plan produces the expected business results.

SIX AREAS OF SALES COMPENSATION PLAN INVOLVEMENT

HR professionals should be proactive in seeking opportunities to become involved with the sales compensation plan. A solid understanding of how the sales organization operates and the respect of sales leadership are important prerequisites for gaining involvement with the sales compensation plan. Once those prerequisites are established, it is equally important to be confident about where and how HR involvement with sales compensation is beneficial to a company and its sales force. HR involvement is most often desired and/or needed in the following six areas:

1. Problem Resolution

Many HR professionals indicate that their first significant involvement with the sales compensation plan was the result of a major problem that sales leaders believed was caused by the plan. This can often occur in companies in which HR's involvement with sales compensation is either a new or emerging responsibility. In such a company, an HR professional might be invited to help address a problem with the plan because there is a new awareness among sales executives that HR can bring an objective perspective and fresh thinking that could help address and resolve the problem. This, of course, means that the HR professional must have the knowledge, skills, and experience to make a meaningful contribution to a solution. HR professionals are too frequently not asked for their involvement because they are seen as not having adequate experience and skills in sales compensation. They are further perceived as not possessing a sufficiently intimate knowledge of the business to be of help to the sales organization. The old adage of "be prepared" is quite relevant here. An HR professional must possess applicable knowledge, skill, and experience in order to make a value-added contribution.

Common examples of plan problems that HR professionals are frequently asked to investigate include: (1) sales employee dissatisfaction with the plan, (2) exceptions to either payout calculations or plan rules, (3) overpayments or underpayments, and (4) turnover either higher or lower than internally expected, industry benchmarks, or both. Seasoned HR professionals should be equipped to help the sales organization address problems such as these.

Most experienced HR professionals understand human motivation and how to tap into the workforce through interviews and surveys in order to determine root causes of job dissatisfaction. Many HR professionals have also acquired analytical skills that can be applied to determining the turnover rate and its relationship to overall industry conditions. The important point is this: Because the problems just mentioned are common sales compensation problems, a thoughtful HR professional should be able to respond with a plan of action when called on for help by the sales organization. This book is one source of information that can help HR professionals develop that action plan.

Generally speaking, the exact cause of the perceived sales compensation problem is less important than how one goes about helping sales leaders address and fix the problem. Two hallmarks of success in resolving such problems, at least from the sales function's perspective, are a willingness on the part of HR to act swiftly and authoritatively to identify the root causes of the problem and the ability to help sales leaders formulate practical alternative solutions that can be implemented quickly. It is worth mentioning, however, that HR should take great care in identifying and isolating the root cause of the problems associated with sales compensation. In a majority of cases in which sales compensation is blamed for shortcomings in its overall effectiveness, the root cause of the problem actually lies elsewhere.

Consider this common situation. When members of the sales force are not earning their incentive compensation opportunity under the plan, field sales managers may report that their people are dissatisfied with the plan. However, the dissatisfaction may have little to do with either the incentive opportunity or the payout formula mechanics. The real problem may well be overly ambitious sales growth targets reflected in sales quotas that may be unachievable by a disproportionately high percentage of the sales force. The important point here is this: It is easy to attach blame to the sales compensation plan, but rarely will a fix to the sales compensation plan solve a performance problem that has its root cause elsewhere.

2. Design and Implementation Process

Companies are increasingly following a documented process for the design and implementation of their sales compensation plans. Most processes include the following four major activities:

1. *Assessment:* How effective is the current sales compensation plan; what evidence is there to suggest that the plan may require modification or may need to be replaced by a completely new plan, for example, change in business strategy; implementation of new or restructured sales channels; jobs; or both; new product launch?
2. *Design and testing:* What changes could be made to incentive pay mechanics— that is, linking performance to pay; will such change redirect sales behavior in the areas management requires for achievement of the coming year's business results; can such changes be supported with sales financial data (i.e., costing and individual performance modeling) that show a proposed change will result in a material improvement in business results?
3. *Implementation:* How will plan changes or a completely new plan be introduced to the sales force so that it will produce maximum motivational mileage and thus contribute to achievement of desired business results?
4. *Monitoring:* What actions are taken to confirm that the sales force has received its plans, that it understands the plans, and that field sales managers are managing effectively with the new plans?

It is easier to lay out these activities than to actually execute them effectively. There are three common flaws in the plan design and implementation process that you should watch out for at your company.

1. The first type of flaws are those that are present both in the underlying process used to assess the current plan and in the process to either design new plans or modify current plans. There are three common process errors: (1) executing design tasks out of sequence (e.g., modifying the incentive formula without first assessing how well the current plan is working, understanding what the new business objectives may be, or both); (2) limiting design work to a single function such as Sales, when the design process would actually benefit from a multifunctional approach that includes Sales, Finance, HR, and others; and (3) misunderstanding how long the design process takes and thus either spending too little time (the most common mistake) or too much time on it.

    It is frequently the HR professional's role to ensure that one or more of these three process flaws does not encumber the design process. To do so, HR (or the designated process owner) should pull together representatives from all of the functions that currently have involvement with the plan and agree on the safeguards that will be put into the process—for example, agreeing to a defined project Work Plan with regular check-point meetings—to ensure that none of these flaws will be allowed to creep in to the design process.

2. Design errors are the second most common category of flaws that occur during the process. Common design errors include: salary/incentive ratio that is inappropriate for a particular sales job, leverage (i.e., upside incentive opportunity) that is either too little or too high, performance measures that cannot be influenced or accurately tracked and credited to members of the sales force, and sales quotas (goals) that do not appropriately reflect the sales potential in sales force territories. Here, too, the HR professional should take an active role in confirming with others who are involved with the sales compensation plan that these types of design flaws are common and should be avoided in the process.

3. Ineffective implementation and ineffective monitoring of performance represent the third set of common flaws that occur when changes are made to a sales compensation plan. Examples of ineffective implementation include: no formal process for communicating plan change, no defined/assigned change accountabilities, and lack of a clear leadership message about change (what will change, why change is important now, and how change will benefit customers, salespeople, and the company). Examples of ineffective monitoring of the new plan's impact on the business include: no predefined measures of plan success, no set time period (e.g., after first payout, after first quarter, mid-year) for assessing success, and no reports provided to field sales managers so they can see how the sales force is performing under the plan.

HR typically plays an important role in developing materials for communicating the compensation plan to the sales force. Employee communications is a key competency of many HR professionals. This is therefore one area where help is usually welcomed. However, HR generally plays a less active role in monitoring the effectiveness of new sales compensation plans. This should not be the case. Because the sales compensation plan can play an important role in sales force performance management, the HR professional should be proactive in helping sales leaders define how success under the new (or revised) plan will be assessed and measured.

3. Sales Compensation Guiding Principles

Guiding principles are the main values that best-practice companies follow in order to design effective and successful sales compensation plans. Guiding principles are based on and support the company's philosophy of pay. However, these guiding principles are rarely documented and assembled in one place for ready reference and use. There are two disadvantages to not using a set of documented guiding principles during a plan design process:

1. The absence of guiding principles is analogous to trying to shoot at a target in the dark. How do you know when you have hit the bull's-eye? The answer, of course, is that you don't know. Thus, guiding principles set forth the standards against which a plan or plans are designed. The principles provide each of the participants in the plan design process with the same understanding of what the design team is shooting for at a conceptual level and in terms of the design results. A statement of sales compensation guiding principles typically includes the following topics: (1) business strategy, (2) competitive

compensation positioning, (3) plan types, (4) performance management, and (5) administrative considerations, for example, desire for plan simplicity, management commitment to effective communication.

2. The second disadvantage of not having and using guiding principles is that it is virtually impossible to know the extent to which a new plan has contributed to business success. For example, the statement of guiding principles typically defines the expected performance distribution under the sales compensation plan. Without the benefit of a specific expectation in this area, it is difficult to determine if the plan paid more or fewer salespeople than expected.

An HR professional involved with a sales compensation plan should encourage the design team to formulate and use a set of guiding principles for the plan design and implementation process. Using guiding principles will provide the design team with a blueprint that both sets forth clear direction and can save time during the process itself.

4. Competitive Pay Assessments

In most companies, sales executives look to the compensation plan to help attract and retain the caliber of people they need to successfully sell to and interact with customers. Because attracting and retaining top-notch talent is one of the most persistent challenges faced by sales organizations, HR has an opportunity to make a major contribution to the sales compensation plan through competitive pay assessment. HR's role is to assure sales executives that pay levels are externally competitive and internally equitable (or otherwise consistent with the organization's compensation objectives based on the roles and responsibilities of the jobs).

It is typically HR's job to assemble labor market data that can be used in making decisions about where to set sales pay levels. This means that HR is responsible for identifying and selecting reliable labor market surveys for use in job pricing. A company will usually rely on two to four survey sources for competitive labor market data. It is commonly a company's HR professional who has been given the responsibility to select and purchase the survey data and to assist with or manage the data submission from the company.

HR should help management determine the appropriate competitive position (e.g., median, 75th percentile) in the labor market for use in pricing a company's particular sales jobs. This is an important contribution to the sales compensation plan because the total cash compensation level for each sales job must be large enough to attract, motivate, and retain top-notch talent as well as pay for the performance that drives desired business results.

5. Industry Trends and Practices

Sales executives are vitally interested in how various practices affecting the sales compensation plan compare to others in their industry. The HR professional, through participation in industry networking groups and compensation survey job-matching sessions, can be in an excellent position to gain an understanding of trends and practices that may affect the sales compensation plan. Thus, the HR professional should be a member and active participant in industry and survey groups.

Sales leaders are also typically interested in knowing about changes taking place in sales channels and sales coverage in the markets in which they compete for customers. Job-matching sessions in industry survey groups are often one place to learn about how others in the industry are covering the market. For example, if new jobs that your company does not have are surfacing in either the surveys or the job-matching sessions, that may be an indication of a trend in sales coverage that should be brought to the attention of sales leadership.

A third area of interest to sales leaders is how the operation of the sales compensation plan is affected by administrative practices. For example, draws, sales crediting, and splits (duplicate crediting) are all topics of great importance to sales leaders as they consider the effectiveness of a current plan. An HR professional involved with sales compensation should consistently make every effort to learn about industry trends and practices that are likely to impact both the thinking about and the planning for sales compensation and share those findings with sales leaders. Doing so increases the value that the HR professional provides to the sales organization.

6. Plan Effectiveness Assessment

At most companies, sales compensation return on investment (ROI) is an important topic. In fact, a recent WorldatWork survey reports that 86 percent of the respondents indicated that how to determine sales compensation plan ROI is a top priority at their company.[1] The reason for this interest is that companies have begun to think of sales compensation as an investment in improving overall sales effectiveness instead of thinking about it as an expense to be minimized. Thus, they have shifted their outlook and view sales compensation as a means of achieving increased volume and quality of sales. This shift in thinking provides an opportunity for the HR professional to help sales leaders also rethink their approach to plan assessment.

One of the reasons for the difficulty of assessing plan effectiveness is the existence of unclear expectations for sales compensation. The best time to gain an understanding of what sales leaders expect to accomplish through the compensation plan is at the time the plan is being formulated. The key question is: What are the outcomes that sales executives (and, in turn, top management) anticipate from a new compensation plan? These outcomes are the quantifiable results that management wishes to derive from its investment in cash compensation for the sales force.

The selection of assessment metrics, including ROI, is determined by the goals of the business and the priorities set for the sales organization by top management. Thus, the actual metrics used are situational; that is, they should be tailored to a company's particular situation and should be set at the beginning of the new sales compensation plan year. The optimal environment is one in which the HR professional is a very active participant in the assessment of a current sales compensation plan's effectiveness.

LEARNING A NEW LANGUAGE

Learning about sales compensation can be like learning a new language, a language that has its own unique key concepts and terms. One of the most difficult challenges of working on sales compensation within your organization is ensuring that everyone is using the same language. Your knowledge of the fundamental concepts of the language of sales compensation will add to your ability to effectively participate in your organization's sales compensation plan design and implementation.

COMPENSATION TIED TO TOTAL REWARDS

It is important to first understand the charter and scope of sales compensation. The amount of pay called "sales compensation" typically cannot fulfill all of the attraction, motivation, and retention requirements of a total rewards strategy by itself. In fact, most companies suffer from using sales results and sales compensation earnings as the only indicators of a sales professional's performance. Many companies fall into the trap of overemphasizing the pay results to the point that sellers say, "If it's not in the sales compensation plan, then I'm not paid for it." While no one can argue that these factors do not matter, other results are also important, and may not be built into the sales compensation plan or performance management evaluation. This fact becomes even more important when your company asks talented sales professionals to tackle more challenging sales assignments or when your sales organization is integrated into a merged or restructured organization. An important responsibility of the HR professional is to help the company learn to accept and communicate that "total compensation," including all of the aspects of the rewards of work, is used to reward "total performance."

WorldatWork defines total rewards as "All of the tools available to the employer that may be used to attract, retain and motivate employees. Total rewards include everything the employee perceives to be of value resulting from the employment relationship." The *Rewards of Work* study[2] describes the five types of rewards shown in Figure 12.3. As you work with the sales organization, it is important to have a common understanding of what is included in all the reward types as they pertain to a sales force. This common understanding will help ensure that all components of the total rewards system are appropriately aligned with the company's expectations for sales jobs.

Direct and Indirect Financials (Total Pay)

In some companies, a significant amount of time and energy is devoted to determining the total pay plan for the sales force. Elements of total pay include:

- Base salary.
- Incentive compensation—bonus, commission.
- Special performance incentive for the field force (SPIFF)s, including sales contests.
- Recognition/Overachievers Club.
- Benefits.
- Perquisites.

While total pay is very important in attracting, motivating, rewarding, and retaining a highly effective sales force, putting too much attention on it could create a culture that is counter to business success. Sales leaders in high-performing sales organizations increasingly seek to strike the right balance between total pay and the other types of rewards.

FIGURE 12.3 Types of rewards.

Affiliation

It is critical for most employees to belong to an admirable organization. All employees are interested in the company's vision and strategy. For the sales force, however, such interest is particularly strong because its members "face" company customers regularly. Thus, the following elements of "affiliation" are particularly important:

- Business vision and aspirations.
- Company image and reputation, for example, how customers feel about the company.
- Top management's support and recognition of the sales force.
- Consistent sales performance management activities.
- Support and mutual respect of peers.
- Openness of communication.
- Ethics—commitment to doing business honestly.

Affiliation can have a significant impact for sales organizations in which many sellers are remote or home-based employees. Extra efforts may be required to ensure they remain advocates of the company rather than solely advocates of customers to whom they are closest.

Career

Most sales employees welcome the opportunity to grow in their career, although many find a role as an individual contributor highly satisfying. For the sales force, key elements of individual and career growth include:

- Performance management and coaching style.
- Opportunities for career advancement within Sales and other areas of the company (e.g., sales operations or product development and marketing).
- Opportunities for individual development and growth.

Work Content

Finally, the quality and content of the job is now more important than ever. With that in mind, sales employees at all levels have heightened interest in the quality of the job and the workplace. Key elements of that building block include:

- Meaningful involvement of first-line sales management.
- Working relationships (trust and commitment) with colleagues in other functions.
- Effectiveness and efficiency of the selling process.
- Effective sales support tools (e.g., customer relationship management [CRM], mobile computing, quote/configuration automation), and resources.
- Innovation and commitment to new products.
- Investment in training—market, products, and selling skills.

You probably hear most often that the sales compensation plan is the "most important tool" the company possesses for the purpose of attracting, retaining, and motivating its sales force. However, work content and other intangibles are often more influential than pay, especially for those in complex selling roles. Understanding how the sales compensation plan fits into total rewards at your company is a key element in working to develop a philosophy and guidelines for the program. While all five areas of the total rewards model are important, most companies fail to excel in all. In advising your company, you should evaluate which areas provide the best competitive differentiation for your current and prospective talent pool and place strong emphasis in those areas.

VARIABLE PAY PLAN CATEGORIES

Before addressing the details of plan design elements, it is important to understand that there are three basic variable pay or rewards plan categories in which customer-facing employees might participate: Individual, Team and Corporate. These plan categories might be short-term or long-term, and can use cash or non-cash as the reward. The right type of incentives must be aligned with each role to ensure an effective total rewards strategy. Appropriate incentives balance the degree of salesperson impact and the company's ability to measure that impact so that the program or plan is fair, equitable, and manageable.

Individual Incentives create payouts based on the results of an individual relative to their assignment. While there may be team members (on the account team, for example) sharing in those results, the individual's pay is based solely or primarily on how their accounts or territories achieve. Companies typically use this kind of plan for individual contributors (sales reps, account managers, product specialists) as well as sales management.

Team Incentives are based on how a group of similarly functioned or similarly tasked people performs collectively. The plan combines all results, and the members of the team receive payment on the total result. Although on occasion there is some modification at the individual level, the team results drive the payouts. This kind of plan best fits pooled resources assigned to support a range of sellers, in which individuals do not always have direct control over the specific assignments or opportunities to which they are assigned and may work across multiple opportunities.

Corporate Incentives represent broader plans based on total company or division performance. This typically occurs through some funding process that may or may not allow for differentiation at the individual level. Companies typically implement this kind of plan for a variety of roles in the company beyond customer-facing jobs. This may include sales support functions that have minimal customer contact, support a wide range of sales professionals, or have many other duties outside of sales support.

"Sales compensation" generally describes individual or team incentives, or a combination of both. Rewards are shorter-term (the measurement period is typically one year or less) and the reward currency is cash.

SALES COMPENSATION PHILOSOPHY

To develop an effective sales compensation program, the design should be consistent with your company's compensation philosophy. This philosophy is frequently both undocumented and informal. It is therefore very helpful to confirm and document the company's compensation philosophy in order to support alignment across all related programs. Elements of the framework for a sales compensation philosophy are:

1. Objectives: Confirmation of the strategic foundation of the programs.
   - Legal and regulatory requirements.
   - Business and financial alignment.
   - Personnel objectives.
2. Labor Market Comparison: Appropriate companies and jobs.
3. Competitive Positioning: Percentile positioning and relationship to other jobs in the company based on the skills, competencies, and focus required to successfully perform in each role.
4. Salary/Variable Pay Ratio Factors: Based on the company's philosophy of risk versus reward.
5. Base Salary Determination: Elements/programs that will be used.
6. Short-Term and Long-Term Incentives: Eligibility/type.

GUIDING PRINCIPLES

Once the sales compensation philosophy is defined and documented, various guiding principles related to plan design can be determined. These principles are based on key elements of the philosophy. They can be used throughout the organization to test decisions as sales compensation plans are developed or revised in order to ensure that the plans are consistent with the company's philosophy. Examples of guiding principles are provided in Figure 12.4.

Once the conceptual groundwork has been established, it's important to understand the criteria for determining who should participate in the sales compensation plan and the key components of any sales compensation plan framework: target earnings, the mix of fixed and variable pay, upside earnings potential, performance measures, and performance standards.

ELIGIBILITY FOR SALES COMPENSATION

When your company is going through a change initiative, and the result is new jobs, new products, or new processes, it is critical to validate the eligibility of relevant jobs for participation in the sales compensation plan. Whether the job is direct-to-consumer (like a retail clerk), or business-to-business, the key criterion is the role each job plays in the sales process, particularly the degree to which the job is involved in persuading a customer to buy the company's products or services. To validate the eligibility of relevant jobs for participation in the sales compensation plan, the team must understand the sales process (whether it has been formally documented or can be defined specifi-

FIGURE 12.4 Example of guiding principles.

- Plans are aligned with the company's business strategy and primary goals—sales growth, profitability, new product sales, and other strategic initiatives (as highlighted in the business plan).
- Plans are designed to the specific accountabilities of each job.
- Plans differentiate various levels of performance.
- The absolute number of performance measures is limited (i.e., up to 3) within a specific plan, and the capability to track and report results is confirmed prior to plan finalization.
- The goals of the sales force are based on optimal performance distribution. This means that threshold and excellence performance levels are realistically achievable; that is, they will be set so that at least 90 percent of the sales force achieves threshold, 60–70 percent achieves/exceeds quota, and 10–15 percent achieves/exceeds excellence.
- The company is committed to using plans that are simple, flexible, and self-calculating by plan participants. Approved plans are ones that can be administered in a timely and cost-efficient manner with minimal requirements for manual intervention.
- Management at all levels of the organization is committed to clearly communicating the plans and to providing the support required to enable the sales force to succeed under the compensation plan.

cally based on case example) from developing and qualifying leads to persuading the customer to buy and then fulfilling the order.

In recent years, there has been an increasing tendency to make more service- and fulfillment-related jobs eligible for sales incentive pay. However, one key differential between sales incentive pay and other variable pay is the degree to which target incentive pay is included in the calculation for market-rate competitive pay. For many jobs, the base wage, or base salary, is considered 100 percent of the target pay for that job, and incentive earnings are added on. As the HR expert on the team, your job may include the need to challenge eligibility assumptions in order to ensure that jobs are treated equitably, consistent with market/industry practice and generally accepted principles of compensation plan design. Three primary criteria for eligibility to be on either individual or team sales plans are:

1. The primary responsibility of employees in designated sales jobs is customer contact and persuading the customer to do business with the company.
2. Employees can affect sales results and may have assigned sales goals.
3. Sales results can be tracked and accurately measured at the employee level.

Target Earnings

Three key compensation terms used in sales compensation are defined in Figure 12.5. The target cash compensation (TCC) for a job includes the base pay that is available for "expected" or "acceptable" performance (either a fixed base salary for the job or the midpoint of the salary range for the job) plus the at-risk pay available for achieving expected results (e.g., the quota). As you work with the sales organization, it is important to remember that TCC is a broadly accepted term, but specific industries may use different terms to describe it. Other names used for TCC include the high-technology term on-target earnings (OTE), and total target compensation (TTC), which is frequently used in the services industry.

Possibly the single most critical factor to use in determining the appropriate TCC for a job is confirmation of that job's role, not simply the title given to that job in

FIGURE 12.5 Key sales compensation terms and definitions.

- Target cash compensation (TCC): The total cash compensation (including base salary and incentive compensation) available for achieving expected results.
- Salary/Incentive Mix: The relationship between the base salary and the planned (or target) incentive amounts in the total cash compensation package at planned or expected performance. The two portions of the mix, expressed as percentages, always equal 100 percent. For example, an 80/20 mix means that 80 percent of the TCC is base salary and 20 percent is incentive pay at target performance.
- Leverage: The amount of increased or upside incentive opportunity—in addition to target incentive pay—that management expects outstanding performers to earn. Leverage may be expressed as a ratio of upside to target (e.g., 2 : 1), as a multiple of the target incentive (e.g., 2 times target), or as a total of the target incentive opportunity plus the multiple of target at upside (e.g., triple leverage).

your company. Titles vary significantly from company to company, but the job role (e.g., telesales, counter sales, geographic sales, technical specialist) is the designator used to match your company's job to externally available data about how companies pay jobs having the same role.

The process of confirming the TCC for a sales job is essentially the same process used to benchmark other jobs in your company: Once the job has been confirmed, both external market data and internal structure and equity are used to establish the parameters of the job value. The WorldatWork *Survey Handbook & Directory*, as well as booklets in the WorldatWork *How-to Series for the HR Professional*, provide a helpful set of tutorials and summaries on how to obtain and use market data. See Figure 12.6 for a brief summary of several factors you, or the person on your team charged with market pay determination, should consider.

The results of the competitive/market analysis will need to be balanced against your own internal compensation structure and programs as well as equity requirements across similar job levels in different functions. This can be done on either a "base pay plus" or "total cash compensation" basis, but is generally required to ensure internal equity and consistency with legal requirements. It is also a tool that is helpful during the dreaded "FLSA audit" that you or someone in HR is typically responsible for periodically completing. It is sometimes quite a challenge to confirm (or determine) the appropriate FLSA status for sales jobs, both inside and outside; however, this should always be done in light of the actual requirements of the job rather than a perceived lack of internal standing if job status changes.

Salary/Incentive Ratio and Target Upside

Sellers are willing to accept putting a degree of their pay at risk if there is significant upside pay available for achieving or exceeding expectations or average productivity. Several behavioral theories underlie the concept of "risk and reward":

- *Achievement Need:* D. C. McClelland defines achievement need as the desire to perform in terms of a standard of excellence or as a desire to be successful in competitive situations.

FIGURE 12.6 Using survey results.

- Have at least two survey sources for key jobs.
- Ensure the competition is represented (in the participant list).
- Verify job matches with the published descriptions (work with sales management to ensure matches are accurate).
- Based on the company's pay philosophy, decide on the statistics to be extracted (e.g., 50th or 75th percentile, median, weighted average).
- Extract data for each compensation level and productivity analysis (base salary, incentive pay, target cash compensation, quota).
- Use discrete data points instead of using averages or blending different data sources for sales compensation surveys—participants and job matches differ as does quality of data.
- Synchronize the survey data with economic data (events in the marketplace and the economy).

- *Reinforcement Theory:* As demonstrated through many studies, most notably those of B. F. Skinner, the frequency of a behavior is likely to be increased when a valuable reward is directly linked to that behavior.
- *Expectancy Theory:* This theory of employee motivation suggests that the sales force makes decisions based on the degree of perceived attractiveness of the outcome.

These theories come into play for two important aspects of sales compensation plan design: incentive mix and upside opportunity (leverage). Setting them correctly is important to a successful process.

Salary/Incentive Ratio (Mix)

While the target cash compensation (TCC) for a job is, of course, very important to the job incumbents, *salary/incentive mix* has at least equal importance because it

FIGURE 12.7 Target cash compensation and mix.

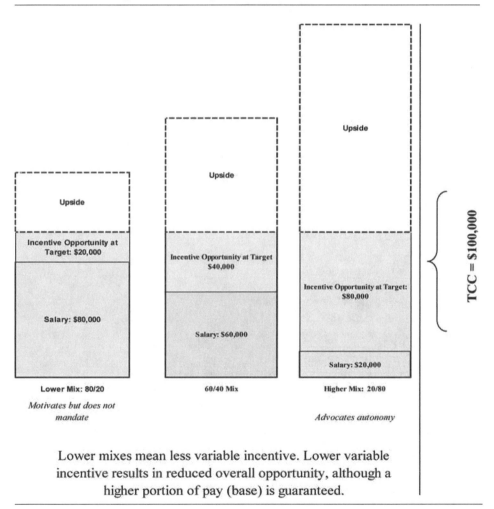

Lower mixes mean less variable incentive. Lower variable incentive results in reduced overall opportunity, although a higher portion of pay (base) is guaranteed.

Note: Lower mixes mean less variable incentive. Lower variable incentive results in reduced overall opportunity, although a higher portion of pay (base) is guaranteed.

directly impacts take-home pay and cash flow. Incentive mix is typically expressed as a ratio (e.g., 50/50 or 70/30) in which the first number represents the percentage of target pay in base salary and the second number represents the percentage of target pay at risk for achieving expectations or target performance. Some companies describe mix by stating variable incentive as a percentage of base. While this is a fairly simple mathematical calculation, it does not visibly express the concept of at-risk pay as an element of the total cash opportunity.

Because mix indicates the proportion of pay at risk, a job with an aggressive mix (50 percent or more of the TCC is incentive pay) has less predictable cash flow, while a job with less aggressive mix (e.g., with 25 percent or less of the TCC as incentive) has a much more predictable cash flow associated with it. Many of the same factors that were used to help you determine the most appropriate TCC for each job also apply as you consider the right mix of base pay and at-risk or incentive pay as well as the amount of upside (or over-target incentive pay) that should be available. Figure 12.7 provides an illustration of mix.

Several job- and sales process-related factors, in addition to market practice data, should be used to determine the proportion of pay that is base and the proportion that is incentive pay, as shown Figure 12.8.

The most critical element is the role of the seller. The incentive mix should reflect the degree of influence the sales professional has over the purchase decision and the value of that transaction. The more important and influential the seller, the higher the mix (higher percentage put into variable compensation).

Industry surveys indicate that the overall market average mix for sales positions is 70/30. Therefore, a job with a 50/50 mix or less implies that the role places sig-

FIGURE 12.8 Factors that impact salary/incentive mix.

Sales Process
- Transactional (more pay at risk)
- Consultative (less pay at risk)
- Product-focused (more pay at risk)
- Relationship-focused (less pay at risk)
- Many, frequent sales (more pay at risk)
- Few, large sales (less pay at risk)
- Long sales cycle (less pay at risk)

Role in the Process
- Team member (less pay at risk)
- Key impact on decision to buy (more pay at risk)
- Provides leads/access or fulfillment only (less pay at risk)
- Provides key expertise in product, customers, or segments (less pay at risk)
- Limited expertise required for sales success (more pay at risk)

Type of Product or Service
- Commodity (more pay at risk)
- Specialty or custom (less pay at risk)
- Sold on price (more pay at risk)
- Sold on value (less pay at risk)

nificantly more emphasis on the selling skills and influence of the seller as factors that cause the customer to buy. A 90/10 mix would imply that the salesperson is only one of many factors affecting the customer's buying decision or the absolute volume purchased.

Based on the factors shown in Figure 12.8, establishing or confirming the mix applied to the TCC for each job requires an accurate and current definition of the job. While input from Sales and other functions is useful to confirm roles and processes, as the HR professional on the team, this task is likely to be your responsibility as well.

One final consideration for mix is how it is expressed and the effect of that on merit pay increase. While mix is the proportion of base versus variable pay as proportions of 100, there are several ways to implement the concept. (See Figure 12.9.)

FIGURE 12.9 Implementing mix.

| Method | Description of Components | | Illustration ($100,000 and 50/50 mix) |
	Salary	Incentive	
Uniform Base/Uniform Incentive: Mix is actual and uniform for all job incumbents	Uniform salary for all incumbents in the same job	Uniform incentive opportunity *as a discrete dollar amount* for all incumbents in the same job	$50,000 base + $50,000 incentive
Base Range/Uniform Incentive: Mix varies by individual; less aggressive (less pay at risk as a percent of the total) for those higher in the range	Salary range is implemented consistent with practice in other functions; salary midpoint used to determine mix	Uniform incentive opportunity *as a discrete dollar amount* for all incumbents in the same job	$40,000–$60,000 base range, $50,0000 midpoint + $50,000 incentive
Salary Plus Percentage of Salary: Mix is actual and uniform for all job incumbents	Salary range is implemented consistent with practice in other functions	Incentive opportunity *as the same percent of the individual's salary* for each incumbent in the same job	$50,0000 base + 100% of base incentive

How mix is expressed for your sales organization has direct effects on the way merit increase is handled. As discussed previously, merit pay is a useful financial tool for rewarding total performance; however, merit pay increases may also have unforeseen consequences. If merit increases are used with your sales organization, it is important to add dollars to salary while ensuring that this change does not dilute the importance of the variable component of the sales compensation plan. As such, increased dollars should be spread across both base and incentive at the desired ratio to ensure the intensity of focus on the sales results desired.

Target Upside (Leverage)

Once the value of the incentive opportunity has been established or verified, that is, the TCC and the mix have been confirmed, the leverage (the amount of upside pay earned at some defined level of performance above 100 percent) needs to be determined. Mix and leverage are strongly linked in the minds of most sales compensation plan participants; the reason is fairly simple—the more pay there is at risk, the greater the upside opportunity. An important note: Definition of the "leverage" does *not* necessarily mean that a plan is "capped" (i.e., that earnings are limited). However, determination of the additional pay available at levels of performance above expected performance will help immensely when it comes time to design the formulas in the plan.

While upside affects all individuals who overachieve target expectations, the upside/leverage ratio reflects the opportunity available for your sales organization's top performers (typically the top 5 percent to 10 percent of your sales force on a job-by-job basis). The amount of upside available is based on the role of the sales job, the ability to overachieve, and financial affordability. For example, sales teams, account managers with very large quotas, and senior sales managers have little opportunity to significantly overachieve their target numbers. In these situations, the upside ratios tend to be lower, which puts more pressure on setting more aggressive target compensation levels for meeting expectations. Figure 12.10 provides an overview of the relationships of role to upside/leverage ratio across industries.

There are several ways to express leverage: as a ratio of upside to target (e.g., 2 :1), as a multiple of target (e.g., 2 times target), or as a total of the target incentive opportunity plus the multiple of target at upside (e.g., triple leverage). The term you should

FIGURE 12.10 Typical relationship of upside to role/sales job.

- Direct Seller Territory—Highest
- Account Manager—Many Accounts—Highest
- Account Manager—Single/Few Accounts—High
- Outbound Telesales—High
- Inbound Telesales—Medium to low based on job focus
- Channel Account Manager—Medium
- Overlay Sales Specialists—Medium
- First-Line Sales Management—Medium
- Second-Line and Above Sales Management—Low

use is the one that has been used in your company in the past—the one that your team finds easiest to use and to explain to others. Figure 12.11 illustrates leverage and how each term could be used to describe the same upside opportunity.

Figure 12.12 shows the impact of a change in leverage on total upside opportunity.

Plan Measures and Performance Standards

Once the percentage or amount of variable compensation and upside are determined, your company must then select the most financially and strategically important measures for which to pay these dollars as well as the range of performance used in calculating payout.

Performance Measures

The following factors are used when deciding on the most appropriate performance measures:

- *Job:* Measures should reflect job accountabilities, and the salesperson must be able to influence the outcomes.
- *Business drivers:* Measures should be consistent with the financial drivers associated with successful achievement of the business plan.

FIGURE 12.11 Leverage illustration.

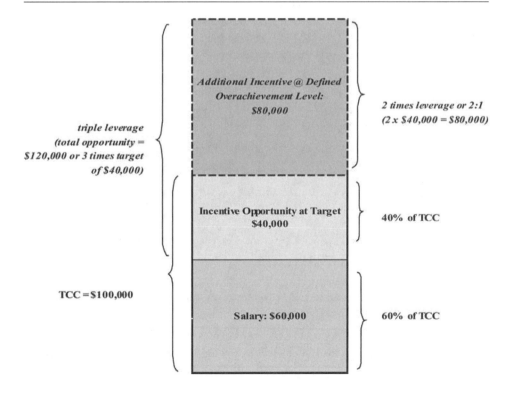

FIGURE 12.12 Impact of upside on earnings opportunity.

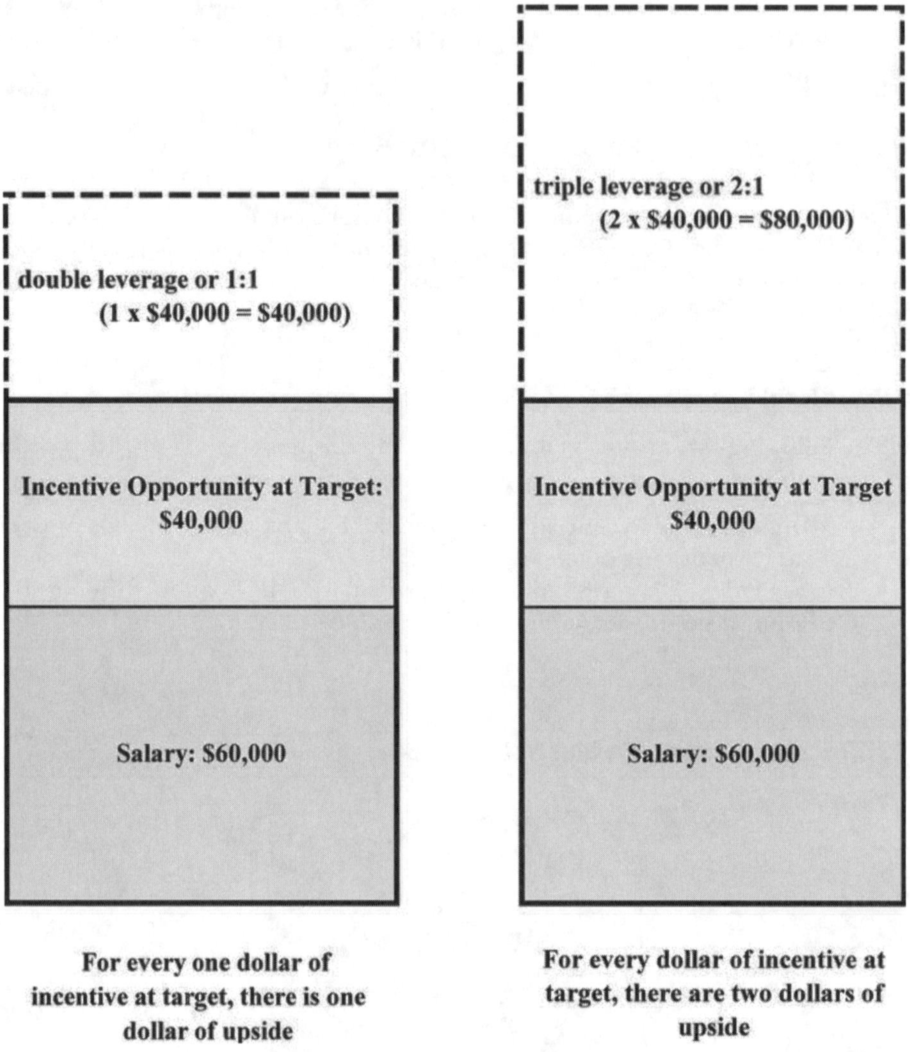

double leverage or 1:1
(1 x $40,000 = $40,000)

Incentive Opportunity at Target:
$40,000

Salary: $60,000

For every one dollar of
incentive at target, there is one
dollar of upside

triple leverage or 2:1
(2 x $40,000 = $80,000)

Incentive Opportunity at Target
$40,000

Salary: $60,000

For every dollar of incentive at
target, there are two dollars of
upside

- *Focus:* To ensure focus and meaningful payout opportunity for each measure, it is best to use no more than three performance measures in a sales compensation plan.
- *System capabilities:* If it cannot be tracked and measured today, it does not belong in the sales compensation plan. Inaccurate or late payouts and reports greatly diminish the motivational power of sales incentive compensation.

Performance measures selected for use in calculating payouts fall into two broad categories:

1. *Financial:* Because sales jobs are focused on top-line growth, and, in some cases, on profitable growth, one measure of success in these jobs must be financial. Financial measures are generally one of two types: volume and profitability.

They may be measured against expected productivity or quota. Your rule of thumb should be that between 60 and 100 percent of the sales compensation opportunity is based on a sales volume or productivity component. Using this rule ensures that the focus on the sellers is on meeting the company's fiscal plan.

Examples of financial performance measures include:

- *Sales revenue:* overall, by segment or channel, for specific products.
- *Growth:* overall, by customer, account, channel, segment.
- *Absolute volume:* that is, number of units or transactions.
- *Gross profit:* percent, dollars.

Any dollars taken away from financial success reduce the impact of the sales compensation plan on achievement of quantifiable results and thus must be justified as secondary or strategic measures that are critical to the "quality" or nature of financial achievement.

2. *Nonfinancial:* Nonfinancial measures may be either quantitative or qualitative. Quantitative measures such as market share or share of account are relative rather than absolute and are used in situations where growth is achieved by "taking business" from competitors. Activity measures such as number of calls are quantitative in theory, but qualitative in practice, because only effective activities lead to achievement of financial objectives.

Management by objectives (MBO), also known as key sales objectives or key performance objectives, are examples of nonfinancial, potentially qualitative objectives. This type of a component is usually point-based and relies on a manager to develop or select from a menu of possible objectives for the seller to achieve over a defined period of time (typically a quarter or half-year). As a rule, these objectives create an averaging of pay for all participants and thus they fail to differentiate superior performance. The larger the population for which they are utilized, the less effective and more administratively burdensome they become. They can then be short-lived inside a well-designed sales compensation plan for a large sales force.

While there are several drawbacks to MBO-like measures, they can be more effective with smaller teams in which the manager is well trained in objective setting and evaluation. Further, they force a conversation between the seller and the sales manager about what strategic activities need to occur. They are best used to reward for activities or results that have a high probability of creating a booking or billing in a future period but for which the seller will get no sales credit in the current period (e.g., design wins in an original equipment manufacturer [OEM] sales model).

Number of Measures

As stated earlier in this section, a rule of thumb is that no sales compensation plan should have more than three components. Using more than three measures/components detracts from the value of each measure and the true driving impact of the plan on total sales results. As an adviser to your company, you must always reflect on whether or not the dollars are significant enough to support more than three measures (especially when those dollars are divided by pay frequency and taxes are subtracted). Too many measurements in a plan often indicate either that a company is trying to design one plan for multiple distinctive roles or that management lacks agreement on the objectives of the particular sales job.

Performance Standards

Another consideration for performance measures used in the sales compensation plan is *performance standards.* One important task in designing plans is confirming expected performance and establishing two other reference points: one below "expected performance," and one significantly above "expected performance." These three achievement levels are:

- *Threshold:* The minimum level of performance that must be achieved before an incentive can be paid.
- *Target:* Expected level of sales results or individual performance. (This is the point at which the target incentive opportunity is earned.)
- *Excellence:* Individual sales performance that is in the 90th percentile (top 10 percent) of all performance measured. (This is the point at which the defined "leverage" or upside is earned.)

Once these three levels are established in a quota-based plan (either bonus or commission), it is then possible to complete the plan payout formula as well as various analyses such as aggregate plan cost and expected return on investment. Remember: Many people new to sales compensation assume that a defined "excellence" point means that a plan is capped. This is not the case! It simply means that the value of each percent achievement above 100 percent can have a defined value; it does not mean that there is an achievement level above which people cannot earn more sales compensation dollars. When you are working with a design team, or with sales management, it sometimes helps the discussion to refer to the "excellence" point as a "design reference point" that is used for the purpose of developing a payout line and value.

Sales Crediting

One requirement for successful use of any volume measure in the sales compensation plan is well-articulated and well-understood crediting rules. To establish these rules, the sales management team must first have a relatively clear understanding of what customer segments and which products are required to meet the financial plan. Using crediting rules ensures that results that are affected by the salesperson and that support the achievement of your company's business objectives are being tracked and measured. Second, management must take a look at the nature of sales transactions by seller type and consciously determine if all aspects of the transaction provide sales credit toward the volume achievement objective as well as whether they should all be treated equally. In today's complex selling world, all transactions are not alike, and transactions may or may not include all products or services. Further, some transactions are one-time deals instead of ongoing business, which can be paid all at once or over time. Companies thus must know what they need to accomplish and must examine the range of deals that exist in order to determine how to implement crediting toward sales achievement in the core volume component of their plans. Figure 12.13 provides definitions and typical applications of the three kinds of sales credit.

FIGURE 12.13 Sales crediting.

Type	Definition	Application
Single	One sales resource receives full credit: 100% credit to one person.	One salesperson completes the entire sales process.
Multiple	Full credit provided to two or more sales resources; more than 100% is credited.	A team is required to complete the sale; it is not possible to distinguish the unique contribution of a single resource; the financial impact can be predicted and managed.
Split	The credit is divided in some way among two or more sales resources; 100% credit in total is provided.	Multiple resources or channels may be required to close a sale, but it is relatively easy to distinguish each resource's contribution; additional financial liability is not acceptable.
Partial	A portion of the full credit is allocated to one or more sales resources; less than 100% credit is given in total.	Resources involved in the sale did not contribute as required and full credit is an unacceptable financial liability.

TIMING CONSIDERATIONS

Two timing considerations need to be confirmed for the sales compensation plan. The first is the *plan performance period,* the period of time for which the company assigns objectives and measures performance for the purpose of earnings. A plan performance period might be annual (with annual objectives), semiannual, quarterly, monthly, or weekly. In general, the more complex the selling activities and sales cycle, the longer the plan period.

There are two alternative approaches to measurement: cumulative and discrete. A performance measurement is cumulative when the performance of the incumbent is measured over subsequent performance periods. As an example: "While payouts are made each month, performance is cumulative because it is measured from the start of quarter to date." Performance measurement is discrete when the performance of the incumbent is limited to a defined performance period without any connection to past or future performance periods. As an example: "Each month is discrete, because performance is measured for that month and payout is made for that month independent of past or future performance."

The second timing consideration is *payout frequency,* how often a payout is made. Alternatives range from weekly (generally for those jobs that are paid 100 percent commission) to less frequent payouts (quarterly, for example). The decision to pay more or less frequently should be made after a review of such factors as length of sales cycle, motivational value, and the ability of systems to handle payout calculations.

ALTERNATIVE MECHANICS

The math or formulas used to calculate the payout under the sales compensation plan can be as simple or as complex as the designers wish. Of course, "simpler is better" is a cardinal rule. However, there are many alternatives to consider as the formula is developed. These include both the type of plan that is suitable for the job and the formula modifiers that can be used to ensure that the plan is motivational and financially viable.

Plan Types

The formula by which payout is delivered can be based on two types of plan: commission or bonus. One or both types of plan may be used in the incentive formula, based on the message that management wants to deliver about performance requirements, competitive practice, and key business objectives. A commission generally focuses on volume, while a bonus focuses efforts on achievement of one or more specific goals.

Commission is compensation paid as a percentage of sales measured in either dollars or units. A quota can be used with a commission structure but is not required. The following approaches can be used when designing a commission plan:

- *Single or flat-rate commission:* This is the simplest commission to develop and explain. A fixed rate is applied to all relevant sales in order to calculate the commission payout; for example, 4 percent of sales or $100 per unit. This type of commission is most often used in new companies, companies with very small sales organizations, companies with "open" territories (territories that have no geographic boundaries), or for a new product for which there is no sales history. The theme is, "The more you sell, the more you make."
- *Individual commission rate (ICR):* This approach results in a unique commission rate for each seller. This approach has two key characteristics in common with a bonus type plan: It has the effect of "evening out" territories in terms of pay, and it is always used with a quota. The theme is, "Every salesperson has the same opportunity to earn his or her target incentive, no matter how large or small the territory."
- *Tiered (or "ramped") commission structure:* A single rate is determined for "target" achievement and different rates are provided for sales below target or above target. "Target" may be a specified sales volume, or a percent of quota achievement. If a tiered commission rate is used, the plan can be cumulative or each range can be discrete. If the plan is cumulative, incentive paid versus incentive earned is recalculated at defined intervals. If the plan is discrete, then the new rate is applied only to dollars associated with the new range of achievement. The theme is, "Sales below target are less valuable than sales at and above target."
- *Adjusted (or "variable") commission rate:* This approach to commission is used if several types of products, or types of transactions, will be prioritized in the commission structure. The rate applied to each transaction is adjusted based on the priority or importance of the product or transaction. The theme is, "Some sales are more important than others."

Illustrations of each type of commission plan are provided in Figure 12.14.

A bonus is a percent of base pay, or a fixed dollar amount, for accomplishing objectives. A quota or some other kind of goal is generally associated with this type of plan. The three basic approaches to a bonus are:

- *Single or fixed-rate bonus plan:* One incentive opportunity is available for achieving the specified objective.
- *Interpolated bonus plan:* A formula to calculate a defined dollar value for each percent achievement is used.
- *Step-rate bonus:* A tiered bonus structure, with no interpolation between tiers, is used; each tier is discrete.

Examples of each type of bonus plan are provided in Figure 12.15.

FIGURE 12.14 Types of commissions.

Type	Examples	
Flat Commission: Rate $\times$ Volume	3% $\times$ ($s) $100/Unit	
Individual Commission Rate (ICR): Individual's Incentive Target Divided by Individual's Quota	**Rep 1:** $100,000 incentive target/$1,000,000 quota = 10% rate applied to sales volume **Rep 2:** $100,000 incentive target/$1,500,000 quota = 6.7% rate applied to sales volume	
Ramped: Rate Adjusted Based on Achievement of Sales Volume or Quota	0%–100% of quota achieved	5% rate
	>100% of quota achieved	7.5% rate
Adjusted: Rate Varies Based on Characteristic Other Than Volume or Quota	Product A	5% Base Rate
	Products B and C	7.5% Rate (Base Rate $\times$ 1.5)

FIGURE 12.15 Types of bonus plans.

Type	Example	
Fixed	$25,000 for 100% achievement of quota	
Interpolated	0%–100% of quota achieved	$250 per percent achieved
	>100% of quota achieved	$275 per percent achieved
Step	50%–99% of quota achieved	$5,000 (no matter where achievement falls in the range)
	99.1%–102% of quota achieved	$20,000

Modifiers

In addition to selecting the type of plan or plans that will be used in the incentive formula, there are other tools that can be used to adjust how payout is calculated. These include how measures relate to each other for the purposes of payout and how payout is modified (up or down).

Linkage is the factor that relates one measure to another. Measures are linked if payout for one measure depends on attaining another objective. *Unlinked* plans (i.e., plans in which payout for each measure is discrete and has no relationship

FIGURE 12.16 Linkages.

"Hurdle"

Measures	Sales vs. Quota Bonus	Margin Gate
Total Sales vs. Quota Bonus	120% of Quota	$40,000
Strategic Product Hurdle	100% of Quota	$30,000
	80% of Quota	0

Margin Gate: 100% of Strategic Product Quota Must Be Achieved Before Total Sales Bonus Over Target Will Be Paid

"Multiplier"

Measures	Sales vs. Quota Bonus	
Total Sales vs. Quota Bonus	120% of Quota	$40,000
Strategic Product Hurdle	100% of Quota	$30,000
	80% of Quota	0

×

Strategic Product Multiplier	
>100% of Quota	$40,000
100% of Quota	$30,000
< 100% of Quota	0

"Matrix"

Measures

Total Sales vs. Quota
Strategic Product vs. Quota

Total Sales				
	120%	$20,000	$35,000	$40,000
	100%	$10,000	$30,000	$35,000
	80%	-0-	$10,000	$20,000
		80%	100%	120%

Strategic Product Sales

to achievement in other areas) may indicate to the salespeople that they should base their own selling priorities on their own earnings expectations. Plan designers should consider linking performance measures in the incentive formula if it is desirable for the sales force to focus on more than one key area and if they use metrics that compete (like market share vs. profitability, etc.). Three mechanisms, as shown in Figure 12.16, can do this:

1. A *hurdle* (also known as a *gate*) requires some defined level of achievement in one performance measure before payout is made for another measure.
2. A *multiplier* adjusts payout on one performance measure based on some level of achievement of another measure. Positive adjustment is generally preferred, although adjustment up or down can be used to ensure financial viability of the plan.
3. A *matrix* is the most stringent mechanism, because performance in two areas is used; achievement of one measure is mathematically related to achievement of another to determine payout.

Modifiers include both *payout accelerators* and *payout limiters*. While a plan formula could deliver payout on a linear scale, or with a single rate, most plan designers use both payout limitation and payout acceleration tools to modify the incentive formula.

Payout limitation tools are used to manage cost relative to productivity and are frequently used when a company is new to using sales compensation, setting business goals, or allocating quota. The two approaches to payout limitation are: a *decelerating payout rate* (the rate for achievement above some defined level decreases) or a *cap* (there is a defined maximum payout available). If a cap is used, it can be applied either to each transaction or to the total payout.

FIGURE 12.17 Questions to ask about your company's sales compensations.

- Is everyone on the same sales compensation plan regardless of sales job?
- Do people in similar sales jobs have the same amount of target pay or different amounts? If different, which parts differ—salary, target incentive, or target total compensation?
- Of the target compensation, how much is delivered through base salary versus target incentive?
- How many different components or performance measures are used in the sales compensation plan? What are they? What is the relative importance of each plan component in each plan?
- What percentage of the sales compensation plan is based on sales volume? Is the sales volume component based on quota achievement or absolute dollars?
- For other components, is payout based on quota achievement?
- Is there a minimum or maximum achievement level at which pay begins or is capped? For which component or components?
- What type of plan (commission or bonus) is used to calculate payout for each component?
- Are any of the plan components or measures linked? If so, how?
- How frequently is each component of the sales compensation plan paid?

Payout acceleration tools are used to enhance payout above a linear rate for defined levels of overachievement. Acceleration is generally accomplished using specific multipliers against the target incentive opportunity, including adjusted commission rates. In practice, acceleration is the mathematical application of leverage or upside.

Some modifiers may act as either a *decelerator* or *accelerator* depending on achievement levels. For example, a multiplier may adjust payout up or down, based on achievement of the related performance measure. In some cases, additional acceleration is available only if quota is achieved on another measure; payout otherwise remains flat, or has less attractive acceleration. One typical example of this approach is a plan with a financial measure related to quota achievement and another milestone objective such as Design Wins. The qualitative measure would have little or no upside associated with it; however, if it is achieved, the acceleration on over-quota payout is greater.

UNDERSTANDING HOW SALES COMPENSATION FITS

Understanding how sales compensation fits into the total rewards philosophy of your company is a very effective starting point in your involvement in design or redesign efforts. The key concepts begin with a well-documented and clearly communicated philosophy and guiding principles. The amount of pay available, performance measures, plan formulas, and timing of payout are all elements that you will hear about and use in each design process. Figure 12.17 gives you a series of questions that provide a framework for structuring your understanding of how the sales compensation plans at your company now work.

13 Executive Compensation: An Introduction

A well-designed executive compensation plan is important because it rewards both executives and shareholders, whereas a poorly designed one wastes corporate resources without motivating the executive. At the extreme, a poorly designed incentive system can cause the executive to take actions that reduce shareholder value—for example, cutting back on long-term profitable investments (a.k.a. positive net present value projects) to increase current compensation.

Research has shown that when the corporation is performing poorly, shareholder proposals on executive compensation are likely to be made (Thomas and Martin 1999), with most of these proposals calling for limits on amounts paid to executives. Other research shows that stock prices react positively to initiation and/or amendment of compensation plans (Morgan and Poulsen 2000; Brickley, Bhagat, and Lease 1985; Tehranian and Waegelein 1985), indicating that shareholders believe the plans will motivate executives to increase shareholder value.[1]

Executive compensation is also important because it affects compensation levels and composition throughout the organization (Gomez-Mejia 1994). It affects the level of compensation because lower-management compensation is often a function of upper-management compensation, and it affects the composition of their compensation package because the same goals may be applied as well.

Underlying the need for, and importance of, executive compensation plans is the separation of ownership from the control of the modern corporation (Berle and Means 1932; Jensen and Meckling 1976). Thus, the goal of the executive compensation plan is to align the interests of executives and stakeholders, commonly assumed to be shareholders.

OWNER-MANAGER CONFLICT: AGENCY THEORY

Understanding the executive compensation package and its role in the modern corporation requires a basic understanding of corporate governance. (See Sidebar 13.1.) In the modern, and sometimes not-so-modern, corporation, the ownership and management functions are separated. This separation can arise from two situations. In the first situation, there are individuals with preexisting businesses who either do not have the desire and/or skills required to manage the business. In the second, there are individuals with good ideas/products that may not have the funds necessary to bring those products to market and/or sustain themselves through the startup period and thus must seek outside investors. Our capital markets, both public and private, allow these individuals to meet and transact business in a way favorable to both. Public capital markets include domestic and international, stock and bond markets (e.g., the New York and Tokyo Stock Exchanges). Private capital markets include venture capitalists, banks, friends, neighbors, and relatives. Given the freedom to contract, or not to contract, it is generally assumed that contracts are entered into only when both parties expect to be better off.

This separation of the ownership and management functions can lead to conflicts. For example, while the owner(s) are concerned with the maximization of the value of their stake in the corporation, the executive(s) are concerned with the maximization of their well-being, which involves a trade-off between maximizing their wealth and minimizing their effort. At the extreme, owners bear the risk that executives will transfer the assets to themselves, which is to say, they will steal the assets. While not a major risk in countries with well-developed legal systems, the risk does exist.[2]

A more likely scenario is that executives, while not stealing the assets, may not manage them in a value-maximizing way. That is, they might pass up profitable investments because taking those investments would require increased effort on their part. They might also overconsume the perquisites of their position, for example, purchase a corporate jet rather than fly commercial airlines.

Academics refer to the costs arising from the separation of the ownership from the management of the corporation as agency costs (see Jensen and Meckling 1976). If these costs can be reduced, the gains can be shared between the owners and executives. Therefore, owners and executives have the incentive to minimize these costs.

The mechanisms for controlling the incentive conflicts arising from the separation of the ownership and control of the corporation include, but are not limited to:

- Monitoring by large shareholders and the board of directors.
- Equity ownership by executives.
- The market for corporate control.
- The managerial labor market.
- Compensation contracts that provide incentives to increase shareholder value.

In publicly held corporations, shareholders elect a board of directors, which in turn has the power to hire and fire executives. They also have the responsibility of setting executive compensation. The board may have a committee devoted to compensation issues, a committee sometimes referred to as the "compensation committee."

Monitoring by the board of directors has its limitations. For example, the board cannot review every decision the executive makes, and even if it could, it may lack the firm- and/or industry-specific expertise to evaluate those decisions.[3] Further, given that most directors have limited investment in the corporations on whose board they sit, directors' incentives also may not be aligned with those of shareholders. The existence of a large shareholder, be it an individual or institution, can mitigate this problem as the large shareholder has both the incentives and the financial resources to monitor management.

Ownership by executives mitigates the incentive conflicts by aligning the interests of executives with those of shareholders. It does so by making the executives shareholders in the corporation. As such, they, like other shareholders, are interested in seeing the corporation's share price increase. Unfortunately, given that most executives have rather limited resources when compared to the market values of their employers, executives own rather small amounts of their employers. Further, when the executive wealth constraint is combined with risk aversion, it may not be in the best interests of other shareholders for an executive to have a large amount of his or her wealth tied up in the corporation's stock.

The market for corporate control, in theory, provides executives with incentives to increase shareholder value. The reason is that if executives manage the corporation in a suboptimal way, the value of the corporation's shares will be low, and if a group of individuals or another corporation believes it could manage the corporation more efficiently, it has the incentive to purchase the corporation to obtain the increase in value from the improved management. If such a purchase were to occur, it is highly likely that the new owners would fire the executives it believed were managing the corporation suboptimally in the first place.

The managerial labor market, or market for a particular executive's services, mitigates the incentive conflicts by providing executives with the incentive to perform well, thereby increasing their market value, that is, their value to other potential employers. Unfortunately, some of the techniques used to retain executives, such as noncompete agreements, also reduce the incentives provided by the managerial labor market. That is, an executive with a noncompete agreement is contractually prohibited from working for some potential employers for a period of time after he or she leaves his or her current employer. Thus, that executive has less motivation to be concerned about his or her value to other employers.

The compensation package can also be used to align the interests of owners and executives. Properly designed, the compensation package can be a tool for mitigating the conflict between owners and executives. It does so by rewarding executives for taking actions that increase shareholder value. Unfortunately, owners (and directors) have incomplete information about the actions of executives. Further, they may not have the expertise to evaluate those actions, even if the actions are observable. Thus, it is difficult to base compensation on actions alone. Rather, compensation is often tied to measures that are positively correlated with managerial effort, for example, accounting income, share price, or market share.

OTHER THEORIES THAT EXPLAIN AND INFLUENCE EXECUTIVE COMPENSATION

Under agency theory, the compensation package is important because it is used to provide the proper incentives to executives, and hence, mitigate the conflict between owners and executives. While the majority of this chapter and many academic studies are grounded in agency theory, other theories, both competing and complementary, exist to explain the composition and importance of the executive compensation package. These theories include *class hegemony, efficiency wage, figurehead, human capital, marginal productivity, prospect, social comparison,* and *tournament* theories.

Class hegemony theory argues that executives share a common bond, and that through boards composed primarily of CEOs, executives are able to pursue their own goals and interests (and not those of shareholders). In particular, Gomez-Mejia (1994) notes "board input is primarily used to legitimize high executive pay, reflecting a shared commitment to protect the privileges and wealth of the managerial class."

Efficiency wage theory (Prendergast 1999) suggests that executives are paid a premium to provide them with the incentive to exert effort to avoid being fired. This premium leads them to put forth effort, because of the consequences of being fired (i.e., having to accept another position at a lower wage). In theory, this effort increases executive productivity and reduces turnover.

Ungson and Steers (1984) argue that the CEO, unlike an operational manager, should not be paid based upon operating results, but rather for his or her role as leader or political figurehead *(figurehead theory)*. As such the CEO is both a symbol and representative of the corporation, representing the corporation at ceremonial events and political functions, and managing interactions with owners, employees, government, and the general public.

Under *human capital theory*, the value of the executive, and hence, his or her compensation, is based upon his or her accumulated knowledge and skills. Agarwal (1981, p. 39) explains the logic behind human capital theory:

> The amount of human capital a worker possesses influences his productivity, which in turn influences his earnings. The same general reason should hold for executives as well. Other things being equal, an executive with a greater amount of human capital would be better able to perform his job and thus be paid more.

Managerialism theory argues "that the separation of ownership and control in modern corporations gives top managers almost absolute power to use the firm to pursue their personal objectives" (Gomez-Mejia 1994). They could then use this power to increase the level, and reduce the risk, of their compensation.

Under *marginal productivity theory*, in equilibrium, the executive should receive as compensation his or her value to the corporation. Gomez-Mejia (1994) defines this as the "observed performance of the firm minus what performance would be if the next best alternative executive was at the helm, plus the pay that would be necessary to acquire the latter's services."

In contrast to agency theory, which assumes risk aversion, *prospect theory* focuses on the executive's loss aversion (Wiseman and Gomez-Mejia 1998). That is, in certain circumstances, for example, to avoid losses or missing goals and/or targets, the executive is actually willing to take risks. In contrast, the executive is unwilling to take risk once he or she has achieved his or her performance goals, as the benefit (to the executive) of increasing performance is more than offset by the possibility of falling below target.

Under *social comparison theory*, board members use their own pay as a reference point when setting pay of executives (O'Reilly, Main, and Crystal 1988). Under *tournament theory* (Lazear and Rosen 1981; Rosen 1986), executive compensation is set to provide incentives, not to the executives themselves, but rather to their subordinates. The executive may in fact receive no incentives from the package, and may be overpaid relative to his or her marginal product or value to the corporation. The incentive is for lower-level executives to work hard, win the tournament, and be promoted, whereby they will receive that higher level of compensation. Rosen (1986, p. 714) claims "Payments at the top have indirect effects of increasing productivity of competitors further down the ladder."

EXTERNAL INFLUENCES ON THE EXECUTIVE COMPENSATION PACKAGE

A number of items external to the corporation and the executive influence both the amount and composition of the executive compensation package. For example, different components of the compensation package have different financial reporting treatments. That is, while items like salary and bonus reduce reported accounting income when earned by the executive, prior to 2006, most stock options did not reduce reported accounting income. Given the desire of executives to report a higher level of income, this differential accounting treatment may have caused them to design compensation packages that included more stock options, and less other compensation, than would otherwise be optimal. Starting with fiscal years beginning after the June 15, 2005, Statement of Financial Accounting Standards No. 123 (revised), Share-Based Payment (SFAS) requires the expensing of all option grants, thereby eliminating the accounting incentive to issue stock options. Consistent with this leveling of the accounting treatment, over the past few years we have seen a decrease in the use of stock options.[4]

Similarly, components of the compensation package are not treated equally for tax purposes. For example, Section 162(m) of the Internal Revenue Code limits the deductibility of compensation to the CEO and the next four highest-paid executives to $1 million per individual, with an exception allowed if compensation is "performance-based." Whereas salary can never be performance-based, bonus plans can be modified to meet the exception, and, in most cases, stock option plans are performance-based by definition. Thus, the tax code provides incentives for corporations subject to this constraint to shift compensation from salary to bonus and stock option plans. Consistent with these incentives, research has found these shifts have occurred.

Finally, the political environment surrounding executive compensation has the potential to influence the level and composition of the compensation package because of the potential "political costs" that may be imposed upon the executive and the corporation. Narrowly defined, political costs are the costs imposed upon the executive and the corporation by the government's ability to tax and regulate. An example would be Section 162(m) of the Internal Revenue Code, which limits tax deductions, and hence, increases the after-tax cost of executive compensation.

Political costs also include actions taken by nongovernment regulators, for example, the Financial Accounting Standards Board, which, after multiple attempts, finally passed a standard requiring that corporations recognize an expense for the stock options granted to employees. Broadly defined, political costs include the costs imposed upon the executive and the corporation by interested parties, which include, but are not limited to, politicians, regulators, unions, suppliers, and customers. These parties have made periodic accusations that executive compensation is excessive and unrelated to corporate performance. In theory, the pressure and costs imposed by these parties could reduce the level of executive compensation, and/or cause a shift from the components of compensation that are not based upon corporate performance (e.g., salaries and pensions) toward components of compensation that are based upon corporate performance (e.g., bonuses and stock options).

In practice, political pressure may lead firms to attempt to hide compensation (e.g., shifting compensation from items that are clearly reported in the proxy statement like salary and bonus to items that are harder to value like pensions).[5]

However, that practice is now less likely because of new disclosure rules for executive and director compensation that were proposed and adopted by the Securities and Exchange Commission (SEC) at the end of 2006. The extensive amendments to the disclosure rules are intended to provide investors with a clearer and more complete picture of executive and director compensation than existed under prior disclosure rules, which were criticized as being too rigid in terms of format and inadequate in terms of all inclusiveness.

SOURCES OF DATA ON EXECUTIVE COMPENSATION

Data on executive compensation are contained in proxy statements mailed to shareholders and filed with the SEC. The SEC then makes these statements publicly available, both in their offices and online, via their Electronic Data Gathering, Analysis, and Retrieval system (EDGAR) at http://www.sec.gov/edaux. Section §229.402. Item 402, of SEC Regulation S-K, requires and governs disclosure of compensation for the CEO, CFO, the next three highest paid executives, and potentially two additional individuals for whom disclosure would have been required but for the fact that the individual was not serving as an executive officer of the registrant at the end of the last completed fiscal year.

The SEC requires disclosure of the following information in a summary table for the most recent three-year period: salary, bonus, stock awards, option awards, non-equity plan incentive compensation, change in pension value and nonqualified deferred compensation earnings, and all other compensation.

This new summary table, which went into effect for filings after December 15, 2006, provides several items not previously required. First, the firm is now required to incorporate the value of the change in pension value and nonqualified deferred compensation earnings. Additionally, the firm now must provide a summary number for total compensation in the last column of the table.

In addition to the summary compensation table, the SEC requires a series of additional tables, with three focusing on equity compensation. The first (equity) table requires disclosure of grants of plan-based awards, in particular the estimated future payouts, including threshold, target, and maximum payouts for plans where the payouts depend on future outcomes, and the number of fixed share and option awards (and the exercise price of those options). The second table will disclose the status (i.e., vested versus unvested), amount, and value of share awards outstanding at year end, while a third table discloses options exercised and shares vested, including the value recognized for each.

Whereas previously firms provided one or more tables that in theory allowed investors and others to estimate the amount of pension payouts, the revised regulations require a table where the firm needs to disclose the present value of each of the named executives' accumulated benefits. The firm also needs to provide a table detailing nonqualified deferred compensation, including executive contributions, firm contributions, earnings and withdrawals during the last fiscal year, and the accumulated balance at the end of the year. Both of these tables, in addition to the summary compensation table, make it easier for interested individuals to identify the true compensation earned in the current year, as well as the firm's future obligation.

An additional tabular disclosure is required for director compensation. Akin to that required for executives, the firm must disclose a summary number for total compensation including cash earned, and the value of options and stock granted during that year, and changes in the present value of pensions and other nonqualified deferred compensation plans.

In addition to the tables discussed previously, the new disclosure regulations require a substantial amount of qualitative disclosure about compensation arrangements, for example, employment contracts. A central location, but not the only location for these disclosures, is Compensation Discussion and Analysis, where the compensation committee of the board of directors discusses the corporation's compensation policies applicable to executive officers, the specific relationship of corporate performance to executive compensation, and the criteria on which the CEO's pay was based.

COMPONENTS OF EXECUTIVE COMPENSATION

The executive compensation package can, and most often does, contain many components. These components have differing effects on employee motivation and risk, as well as different costs for the corporation. A well-constructed compensation package must make trade-offs between these components to maximize the net benefit[6] to both the corporation and the executive.

The major and most common components of executive compensation are:

- Salary.
- Bonus.
- Stock options.
- Stock grants.
- Other stock-based forms of compensation.
- Pensions.
- Benefits and perquisites.
- Severance payments.
- Change-in-control clauses.

To start, let's define these components.

Salary

Salary is the fixed contractual amount of compensation that does not explicitly vary with performance. However, it can be affected by performance, as good performance can lead to higher salary in future periods.

Bonus

Bonus is a form of compensation that may be conditioned upon individual, group, or corporate performance. For most executives, bonus is both based upon group performance and determined as part of a plan covering a larger group of employees. Thus, their individual employment contract may only specify their participation in the plan or a minimum bonus they are guaranteed. The performance conditions used to determine the bonus can be implicit or explicit, objective or subjective, and financial or nonfinancial. In some cases, bonuses can be based upon one factor (e.g., net income or sales), whereas in other cases, they can be based upon a combination of factors. In addition, bonuses can be based upon short-term or long-term measures.

Stock Options

Stock options allow their holder to purchase one or more shares of stock at a fixed "exercise" price over a fixed period of time. They have value if the corporation's share price is greater than the exercise price. As the exercise price is normally set at the share price on the date of grant,[7] the ultimate value of the option depends upon the performance of a corporation's share price subsequent to the date of grant. That is, they can be extremely valuable when the share price rises dramatically, but can also expire worthless if the share price declines.[8] As with bonuses, in most cases the executive participates in a stock option plan along with other employees. Thus, the employment contract only specifies that the executive will participate in the plan and not the amount of the executive's grant. While all options have expiration dates, the norm is 10 years. Hence, the longer the life, the more valuable the option.

Stock Grants

Stock grants occur when corporations give shares to their employees. They differ from stock options in that they have no exercise price. Whereas a stock option only has value if the corporation's share price is above the exercise price, a stock grant has value as long as the share price is above zero. Consequently, a stock grant is always worth more than an option grant for the same number of shares.

Stock grants can be unrestricted or restricted. An example of a restriction imposed upon a stock grant might be that the employee cannot sell the shares until he or she has worked for the corporation for a period of time. Another example of a restriction is one based upon performance. Performance-based restrictions have become more common in recent years and will probably become even more common in the future. Consider the following discussion, which is contained in the Pepsico Performance-Based Long-term Incentive Award plan, of forfeiture of restricted stock units if performance conditions are not met.

> 3. *Forfeiture of Restricted Stock Units.* The number of Restricted Stock Units that are payable shall be determined based on the achievement of performance targets. Subject to the terms and conditions set forth herein, the Restricted Stock Units shall be subject to forfeiture as follows:
>
> (a) The payment of one-third of the Restricted Stock Units shall be determined based on the achievement of specific {Year} performance targets. The specific performance targets and the percentage of the one-third of the Restricted Stock Units that shall be forfeited if such targets are not achieved shall be established by the Committee in the first ninety (90) days of {Year}.

(b) The payment of one-third of the Restricted Stock Units shall be determined based on the achievement of specific {Year+1} performance targets. The specific performance targets and the percentage of the one-third of the Restricted Stock Units that shall be forfeited if such targets are not achieved shall be established by the Committee in the first ninety (90) days of {Year+1}.

(c) The payment of one-third of the Restricted Stock Units shall be determined based on the achievement of specific {Year+2} performance targets. The specific performance targets and the percentage of the one-third of the Restricted Stock Units that shall be forfeited if such targets are not achieved shall be established by the Committee in the first ninety (90) days of {Year+2}.[9]

These restrictions can be binding. In a series of Form 4s[10] filed with the Securities and Exchange Commission on February 3, 2006, executives at the Pepsi Bottling Group, including John T. Cahill, Chairman and CEO, reported the forfeiture of restricted stock because of failure to meet performance targets. For Cahill, the number of shares forfeited was 63,830,[11] which valued at that day's closing price of $56.81 were worth $3,626,182.

Other Stock-Based Forms of Compensation

While not as popular as stock options and grants, some companies grant *stock appreciation rights, phantom stock,* and/or *equity units.*

Stock appreciation rights, sometimes called SARs, are the right to receive the increase in the value of a specified number of shares of common stock over a defined period of time. Economically, they are equivalent to stock options, with one exception. With a stock option, the executive has to purchase and then sell the shares to receive his or her profit.[12] With a stock appreciation right, the corporation simply pays the executive, in cash or common stock, the excess of the current market price of the shares over the aggregate exercise price.[13] Thus, the executive is able to realize the benefits of a stock option without having to purchase the stock. In most cases, stock appreciation rights are granted in tandem with stock options where the executive, at the time of exercise, can choose to exercise either the stock option or stock appreciation right.

Phantom stock are units that act like common stock, but that do not constitute claims for ownership of the corporation. They entitle the executive to receive the increase in common stock prices *and* any dividends declared on common stock. They are often used in privately held corporations, or publicly held corporations, where the owners do not want to dilute existing ownership.

Equity units entitle the holder to purchase common stock at its book value, and then resell the stock to the corporation at its book value at a later date. The owner also gets the dividend payments on the stock. Like phantom stock, equity units are often used in privately held corporations, or publicly held corporations where the owners do not want to dilute existing ownership.

Pensions

Pensions are a form of deferred compensation, whereby after retirement from the corporation, the employee receives a payment or series of payments. These payments may be defined by the pension plan,[14] or based upon the amounts accumulated in the employee's personal retirement account.[15] If the payments are defined by the plan, they can be based upon a number of factors including, but not limited to, number of years with the corporation, earnings while working, and level within the corporation. Pensions can be structured in many ways; for example, the payments can be fixed in amount, or they can be adjusted for inflation. Because of Internal Revenue Code limitations, in most cases, executives are covered by more than one plan. That is, they participate in a primary "tax-qualified" plan along with other employees, and have at least one "supplemental" nonqualified plan. The second plan is necessitated by Internal Revenue Code limitations on payments from a qualified plan. That is, in order to qualify for favorable tax treatment, the plan must be nondiscriminatory, that is, the benefits cannot be skewed in favor of highly paid employees, *and* the corporation cannot consider compensation in excess of a threshold, which was $220,000 for the year 2006 (Section 401(a)(17)), in determining pension benefits, nor make payments in excess of $175,000 (Section 415(b)). Most top executives make substantially larger sums. Thus, the supplemental plan or plans provide additional benefits without limitation.[16]

Benefits and Perquisites

In addition to receiving salary, bonuses, stock-based compensation, and pensions, executives receive a variety of *benefits* and *perquisites,* whose value must be reported in the proxy statement.[17] These items include corporate cars; the use of corporate airplanes and apartments; special dining facilities; country club memberships; health, dental, medical, life, and disability insurance; and the ability to defer compensation at above market rates of interest.

Rajan and Wulf (2006) report that 66 percent of the employers in their sample offer their CEO access to the company plane, 38 percent chauffer service, 56 percent a company car, 47 percent country club membership, 48 percent lunch club membership, 17 percent health club membership, 70 percent financial counseling, 65 percent tax preparation, and 59 percent estate planning. In the past, many corporations (Sessa and Egodigwe 1999) would offer their executives interest-free loans to finance their purchases of corporate stock; however, Section 402(a) of the Sarbanes-Oxley Act of 2002 generally prohibits loans to executives and directors.

Generally, it will be unlawful for an issuer to extend credit to any director or executive officer. Consumer credit companies may make home improvement and consumer credit loans and issue credit cards to their directors and executive officers if it is done in the ordinary course of business on the same terms and conditions made to the general public.

Severance Payments

Severance payments are fairly common and have become very controversial. Severance payments occur when an executive leaves the company under pressure or is fired without cause; consequently while they are sometimes included in the executive's employment contract, severance payments, at most, happen once at the end of the executive's tenure with the company.

Change-in-Control Clauses

Change-in-control clauses are also standard in the executive compensation contract. A change-in-control payment occurs when the company is acquired by another company and is a way to provide the executive with some insurance should he or she lose his or her job as a result of the merger, which often happens.

MAKING THE OFFER ATTRACTIVE

To illustrate the decisions a corporation must make in designing a compensation package, consider the corporation that wishes to hire an executive from outside the corporation. First, the corporation must make the compensation package lucrative enough to entice the targeted executive to take the position. That is, the value of the compensation package offered to the executive should exceed his or her next best opportunity, or "opportunity cost." This may be his or her current compensation package, or the compensation package being offered by another potential employer. However, simply exceeding the executives' current compensation package may not be enough. Changing jobs is a gamble, and executives, as risk-averse individuals, need to be compensated for taking chances. To induce them to take that chance, a substantial premium may be involved. As mentioned previously, to reduce that premium and to combat the natural risk aversion of the executive, the firm may also have or choose to include a severance provision in the contract to minimize the financial risk to the executive.

It should be noted that the value of the compensation package to the executive includes both pecuniary and nonpecuniary factors. An executive may be willing to accept a lesser-paying position if the corporation's headquarters is in a preferred location. Alternatively, an executive might be willing to accept less compensation to work for corporation A than for corporation B because corporation A is viewed as more prestigious and/or has more growth potential.

PROVIDING THE PROPER INCENTIVES

The corporation wants to design the contract to encourage the CEO to act in a way consistent with its objective, presumably value maximization. In doing so, the corporation recognizes that the different components of the compensation package have different effects on CEO incentives, risk, political costs, and tax payments, and on its own financial reporting, political costs, and tax payments.

To make things simple, and minimize contracting costs, the corporation could offer to pay the CEO a salary, which would fix compensation regardless of performance. However, in that situation, the CEO has little financial incentive to maximize shareholder value because he or she does not benefit from doing so.[18] And considering that economists view most individuals as work averse (although there are many who would argue that individuals who make it to the executive suite are not work averse, but rather workaholics), the CEO would have incentive to shirk and/or overconsume perquisites. Alternatively, the corporation could offer the CEO a contract whereby his or her compensation is solely based upon corporate performance. While this would provide the CEO with incentive to maximize shareholder value, it would impose substantial risk on the CEO.[19] As most economists assume individuals are risk averse, the CEO would be unwilling to take the contract unless there was a substantial premium built into it to compensate for the risk involved. For example, the CEO might be willing to accept $1 million if compensation was fixed, but require an expected payout of $3 million if compensation were totally based upon performance. The corporation would then have to decide if the increased performance that could be expected under the performance-based contract would warrant the extra costs of the contract.

In practice, few contracts are either totally fixed or variable. More commonly, compensation packages include both fixed and variable components. Fixed components are included to reduce the risk to the CEO and guarantee a standard of living, whereas variable components are included to provide incentives and align the interests of management and shareholders. Assuming that the compensation package the corporation designs will include fixed and variable components, the corporation then has to decide how much of each to include, and what forms they should take.

Fixed components might include salary and benefits, such as employer-paid life insurance, health care, and pensions. Variable components might include bonuses, where the payout may be based on reported accounting numbers, market share, or customer satisfaction; and stock compensation, where the payout is based on stock prices. Each has differing effects on CEO incentives and has differing costs to the corporation.

Referring to the incentives, consider salary and the pension benefit, both nominally fixed in amount. While nominally fixed in amount, both provide certain incentives and can influence the decisions the CEO makes, both personally and for the corporation. For example, while salary is nominally fixed in amount, it can be renegotiated *upward or downward*, although the latter is less frequent than the former. And a defined benefit pension plan can be structured so that it does not vest immediately and/or the benefit increases with the individual's tenure with the corporation. Both give the CEO incentive to remain with the corporation. However, if the pension is not fully funded, the CEO has the incentive to reduce the risk of the corporation, which could involve forgoing otherwise profitable projects.[20] Why? Because if the corporation goes bankrupt, not only does the CEO lose his or her job, but also to the extent his or her pension is not fully funded, he or she becomes an unsecured creditor of the corporation. Why not then simply make the fixed component all salary? One reason is that our tax code provides incentives for employers to provide things like life insurance, health care, and pensions.[21] Sometimes the tax incentives even exist for the employee to defer salary to future periods.[22] To the extent that the compensation package can be structured to minimize taxes, or more formally, the joint tax burden of the corporation and CEO, both parties can be made better off.

When a corporation is determining the variable components of its compensation plan, that is, determining whether variable compensation should include bonuses, stock compensation, or both, it must also realize that different forms of variable compensation provide different incentives. The corporation should also realize that the structure of an incentive plan can yield very specific orientation and behaviors. A bonus plan based upon accounting numbers may lead to higher reported accounting income, but not necessarily lead to higher shareholder value, as management may make cosmetic changes to its financial statements to increase its bonuses. Similarly, if managers are rewarded for increasing market share, the corporation may get increased market share, but at the cost of reduced profits and reduced shareholder value. In contrast, stock compensation only increases in value when value (narrowly defined as share price) increases, but subjects the manager to market risks, for which he or she will want to be compensated. Theoretically, this market risk can be controlled for with a market-adjusted option whereby the exercise price of the option can be adjusted up or down depending on market movements. However, corporations do not seem to grant market adjusted options.[23] Separately, recent research has shown that tying compensation to stock prices may lead to some unethical behavior, for example, backdating.

If stock compensation is used, the corporation must decide if it should take the form of stock grants or stock options. Stock grants are valuable as long as the share price is above zero, whereas stock options are only valuable if the share price is greater than the exercise price (the price at which the option allows the holder to purchase shares). In general, stock options will provide the CEO with more incentives to take risks than stock grants. Yet certain companies, such as Philip Morris, grant restricted stock "in an effort to retain its executives in the face of a steep drop in the company's share price," arguing that options do not "work well for tobacco companies, whose share prices now are influenced more by what happens in courtrooms than by whether management is meeting its goals."[24]

In practice, corporations include both bonuses and stock-based compensation in the compensation package, as a way of reducing the risks to the executive (Sloan 1993). Alternatively, the bonus might be used as a way to reward the executive regardless of performance.

DESIGNING THE CONTRACT TO RETAIN THE EXECUTIVE

To minimize recruiting and training costs, and avoid the downtime associated with an open position, corporations would like to ensure that the executive being recruited stays with the corporation. There are two, nonmutually exclusive tracks it can take. The first approach would be to provide monetary incentives to stay, for example, compensation that vests over a period of time and hence is forfeited if the executive leaves before the end of the vesting period. This track, which involves long-term components of compensation, such as restricted stock, stock options, and pensions, could be referred to as the "golden handcuffs" approach. However, if the new employer is willing to reimburse the executive for amounts forfeited when leaving the old employer, the employment contract loses its retentive effect.

The second approach is to limit the executive's alternative employment opportunities with noncompete, nondisclosure, and nonsolicitation provisions. These provisions are fairly standard in executive contracts.

RESTRICTIONS

Employees, in general, and high-level executives, in particular, build up a certain level of corporation- and industry-specific knowledge. Hence, a manufacturing executive at an automaker would be more valuable to a rival automaker than to a computer manufacturer. Thus, preventing executives from taking positions (through the noncompete provision) at rival corporations makes them less likely to leave. Further, even if the executive were willing to take a position not in competition with his or her former employer, he or she would be prohibited, through the nonsolicitation provision, from hiring any of his or her former colleagues. While this example pertains to a CEO, similar provisions can be designed for a broad base of executives. Of course, if a corporation wants an executive badly enough, it can negotiate with the executive's former employer to release the executive from these restrictions.

A third approach, if the first two do not work, is to use the legal system to deter potential competitors from hiring your executives. Thurm (2001) discusses some of the legal steps companies have taken to prevent employees from working for competitors, including forcing former employees already working for competitors to leave their new positions.

MINIMIZING COSTS TO THE CORPORATION

In addition to making the package attractive enough to entice the individual under consideration, and structuring the package so that the individual has the appropriate incentives, the corporation has to take into consideration a multitude of costs, some of which are not generally thought of as costs. First, consider the financial costs of different forms of variable compensation. Bonuses normally require the payment of cash, whereas stock compensation only requires the issuance of previously unissued shares, a trade-off that may be important for cash-strapped corporations. Also, the accounting and tax treatments differ between bonuses and stock compensation, and different types of stock compensation. For example, while bonuses are normally recognized as an expense for financial reporting purposes in the period earned, stock compensation is normally recognized as an expense over the vesting period. Furthermore, under the Internal Revenue Code, bonuses are both taxable to the employee and deductible by the employer in the period paid. However, if stock option grants meet certain conditions, they are not taxable to the employee until they are exercised *and certain options are not even taxable then!*

While stock options are treated favorably under the Internal Revenue Code, other forms of compensation are not looked upon as favorably. In particular, subject to certain exceptions, Section 162(m) of the code limits tax deductions for compensation paid to the top five executives of the corporation to $1 million per executive per year. Thus, while not limiting the amount of compensation a corporation can pay its executives, Section 162(m) affects the after-tax cost to the corporation. As with other financial decisions, the corporation must take into account the after-tax cost when designing the compensation package.

Nonfinancial costs have to be considered too. One such cost would be equity. For example, it would be insulting to the outgoing CEO if the new CEO were to make more than he (or she) did. Not only would this be insulting, it would breed resentment and not bode well for a working relationship between the two, with the latter possibly retaining the Chairman position, or at least a position on the Board of Directors.

Similarly, a large gap between the newly hired CEO and the remainder of the executive group would add insult to injury, as not only were they passed over in favor of an outsider, that individual is also being paid much more than they are. While in many cases those passed over for the top slot leave the corporation, it is also true that in many cases the corporation, while not wanting to make them CEO, would like to retain them.[25] These concluding points illustrate that while explicitly a contract is being designed for one person, there are ramifications beyond that person that must be taken into consideration.

Sidebar 13.1: Applying a Good Governance Model to Compensation

"The fox is guarding the henhouse." This cliché captures some of the concerns of both HR and Finance regarding the effectiveness of compensation, sales compensation, and executive compensation plans. Crediting issues, gaming opportunities, pay inflation, and extra expense can be interwoven so tightly in the final compensation plan that it is almost impossible to address and resolve them after the fact. On top of this, shareholders and Congress impact the process through Sarbanes-Oxley. Now, the CEO and CFO can go to prison if errors that are deemed unethical occur in the compensation plans and it is found that there was knowledge of these errors or "inadequate controls." That fact alone has driven management to exert increased control and *governance* over compensation.

While terms and conditions (T&Cs) have always been a fundamental element of a well-designed compensation plan, they focus primarily on explaining various administrative and employment aspects and are often not enough by themselves to support governance. Governance implies that a system for authoritative control is in place related to the program. While some executives may perceive governance as excessive control, in fact, a good governance model can be applied to compensation without robbing the organization of its flexibility to respond to labor markets, customer needs, and competitive opportunities. In some cases, it may even benefit employees, as T&Cs are beefed up to include formally documented dispute and exception processes.

With that in mind, this section has two objectives. First, it describes the challenges associated with effective compensation governance. Second, it explains how you can address and resolve those challenges at your company. Examples and techniques are provided that have been successfully used by leading companies.

Compensation Governance

Governance associated with compensation programs begins at the highest level of control. *Board governance* is essentially the checks, balances, and due diligence necessary to ensure that C-level (CEO, COO, CFO, CXO, etc.) executives do not make short-sighted decisions that benefit themselves at the expense of shareholder value. Because of the complex legal, accounting, and reporting issues that must be considered, the compensation committee of the board of directors typically handles executive compensation packages for top executives.

Several aspects of compensation plans require sound governance principles because compensation design and administration is a complex cross-functional exercise. If any one participant becomes too strong in the process, or if ideological gaps exist between participants, governance becomes critical.

(continued)

Sidebar 13.1 (*Continued*)

Communication and Process Gaps

A sound governance model helps overcome four basic gaps. Because these are the places where corporate strategy and policies can lose their meaning and power if companies are not careful, you should be familiar with these gaps and how to close them at your company. They include:

1. The gap between senior management and front-line managers.
2. The gap between functions (such as HR, Sales, and Finance).
3. The gap between business units (BUs) with distinct profit & loss (P&L) responsibility.
4. The gap between geographies that may or may not have different laws and subsidiaries (legal entities).

Gap between Senior Management and Front-Line Managers

The gap between senior management and front-line managers typically is a problem of communication and alignment.

Communication. If senior managers do not take pains to communicate strategies and tactical plans out to the field, it can be expected that there will be deviation, malicious or not. It takes many repetitions of simple concepts to build a unified vision. Therefore, an investment of time is necessary. However, field communications is an area in which there is significant underinvestment by senior management.

Alignment. Alignment of plans is important to ensure that top management's equity and profit-based plans do not compete entirely with middle management's cash and revenue-based plans and the front line's revenue and activity-based plans. This is a check that is often best performed after distinct role-based compensation plans have been designed. It is also something to be wary of if management's compensation plans are designed in a separate effort from the front-line plans. Both communication and alignment are areas where you can have considerable impact as the compensation plan is being designed and during rollout and ongoing follow-up. Poor communication and alignment put governance in a deficit position from the start.

Gap between Functions

The gap between functions is generally one of communication and expectations; this is one of the most difficult tactical issues to control during the compensation design process. Different functional goals may result in competing agendas, and intelligent compromise may be difficult to achieve. Clearly defined functional roles and accountabilities are critical to closing any difference in expectations. The concept of segregation of responsibilities is important to good governance. If the aforementioned functions are the last accountable reviews for various distinct metrics and conditions, the organization can feel somewhat more comfortable that irregularities have been ironed out and a consensus solution for the common good has been achieved.

Gap between Business Units

The gap between business units (BUs) is a more delicate matter. The use of business unit P&L responsibility to empower leaders yet hold them accountable for results is a powerful management tool. However, these BU leaders may not have a good view of the complete picture of success for the corporation as a whole. On top of that, their management skills may not be as strong as those of the corporate leadership team. They may lean heavily on a few management tools (such as the incentive pay plan) or capitalize on approaches or models that do not make the most sense for the company as a whole or for the long term. These leaders are often internal customers of shared corporate services that must work with them to deploy compensation plans. Strong operating principles and design frameworks that provide reasonable local flexibility with some centralized control are necessary to bridge this gap. The same governance principles must apply to the growth segments as well as the mature lines of business, regardless of how much more challenging their performance goals might be.

Gap between Geographies

The gap between geographical regions within a multinational corporation is still a sensitive issue despite years of moving toward globalization. The business practices accepted in some countries may appear flawed at best when taken out of context and printed on the front page of *The Wall Street Journal*. HR professionals have long recognized the difficulty of deploying consistent compensation plans across geographical and political boundaries. Whether it is the tax treatment of bonuses in Canada or the advance notice of intended changes required by the Works Councils in Europe or the less aggressive pay mixes dictated by some Asian cultures, it has always been challenging to manage across these complex organizations.

True, resources in these countries are becoming more receptive to traditional North American pay-for-performance structures. But in spite of U.S–based businesses' recent focus on business ethics and governance, some remote regions do not always feel a sense of urgency to get on board. Corporate governance processes should be in place that can be used with appropriate adjustments across geographies as those regions are ready to implement a formal control system.

Demystifying Sarbanes-Oxley

In 2002, Congress passed the Sarbanes-Oxley Act as a response to scandals at Enron, Tyco, and other public companies. The act is intended to "protect investors by improving the accuracy and reliability of corporate disclosures."

(continued)

Sidebar 13.1 (*Continued*)

In reality, House Resolution 3763 is 66 pages of well-meaning but vague legalese. (See Figure 13.1 for a list of its contents.) Many of the act's 11 "titles" (chapters) address issues such as auditor independence and increased penalties for corporate fraud. These have very little impact on the HR professional's involvement in compensation design and administration. The sections that do have implications are fairly isolated and short:

Section 302, Corporate Responsibility for Financial Reports: This section states that the CEO and CFO must certify each annual or quarterly report. It then goes on to state what they are certifying—"that . . . the report does not contain any untrue statement of a material fact or omit to state a material fact necessary to make the statements . . . not misleading," that "the signing officers are responsible for establishing and maintaining internal controls . . . designed . . . to ensure that material information . . . is made known to such officers," and that there will be an "audit . . . [to identify] all significant deficiencies in the design or operation of internal controls." Essentially, this

FIGURE 13.1 Contents of Sarbanes-Oxley act.

Title I—Public Company Accounting Oversight Board (establishes this body with its composition, funding, and authority)

Title II—Auditor Independence (sets rules for selection and rotation of independent auditors for public companies)

Title III—Corporate Responsibility (outlines the responsibilities of the audit committee, insider trading issues, and penalties)

Title IV—Enhanced Financial Disclosures (sets a code of ethics for top executives and establishes new reporting requirements to demonstrate internal controls)

Title V—Analyst Conflict of Interest (establishes new rules for securities analysts and the relationships they can have with publicly traded companies)

Title VI—Commission Resources and Authority (further outlines authority and practices of the Commission)

Title VII—Studies and Reports (reviews impacts of accounting firm consolidation and investment bank restructuring)

Title VIII—Corporate and Criminal Fraud Accountability (establishes criminal penalties for altering documents, protection for whistle-blowers, and sentencing guidelines)

Title IX—White Collar Crime Penalty Enhancements (increases penalties for mail and wire fraud, violation of ERISA)

Title X—Corporate Tax Returns (establishes that all corporate tax returns must be signed by CEO)

Title XI—Corporate Fraud and Accountability (addresses additional rules and guidelines for document tampering and other offenses by corporate officers or board members, increases penalties established under the Securities Exchange Act of 1934)

is stating that there is no plausible deniability when it comes to the kinds of mistakes described previously in a public company's financial statements.

Section 401, Disclosures in Periodic Reports: This section states that a company must disclose off-balance sheet transactions that have a "material current or future effect on financial condition." This could be construed as impacting several types of sales transactions that include related binding promises or financing.

Section 404, Management Assessment of Internal Controls: This section is very similar to Section 302, but adds the responsibility for "adequate" internal controls and management's responsibility for assessing and reporting on the controls' adequacy.

A Detailed Governance Model

A more detailed outline of "adequate controls" is necessary, primarily because (as with most government legislation) it isn't spelled out for the concerned executive anywhere else. Three basic concepts should be addressed for governance to be adequately addressed:

Accountability: It must be clear which functions and people within the organization are accountable for which results and adherence to which policies. This accountability should be reinforced by the organizational structure, performance metrics, performance evaluation, and compensation plans themselves. This should ensure that the intended results are built into each person's job description and that only people who follow the rules and deliver the intended results receive positive evaluations and target (or higher) bonuses. The organizational structure issue is more a function of removing obstacles and improving "lines of sight" than of developing any groundbreaking design.

Alignment: The strategies and goals of the organization must be clear and must deliver value to shareholders. The processes and systems required to support them must align with those objectives. Where necessary, explicit decision support tools should supplement the processes. Overall, implementation of this alignment creates a cultural expectation that all activity must drive real, substantial shareholder value (not just short-term increases that allow top executives to exercise their options). This culture should be intolerant of fraud and supportive of whistle-blowers.

Accuracy: Data to support financial reporting and sales compensation crediting must be accurate from all regions and channels. There should be a paper trail to support auditing of that data. Rules and regulations should be accurately communicated and enforcement and penalties accurately applied. Performance evaluation must be based on an accurate picture of that performance and payout formulas accurately applied and calculated.

As complex as this may sound, it is merely a representation of sound business practices when displayed in its basic state. (See Figure 13.2.) Documentation of these activities and programs is the element that is often missing.

(continued)

Sidebar 13.1 (*Continued*)

Companies tend to view documentation as important to the degree that they have had issues with enforcement. Companies without a history of legal problems or with strong cultures of accountability may keep basic electronic and paper files of meeting minutes, votes on key decisions, and reported metrics. However, companies negatively impacted in the latest round of investigations have committed to go the extra mile and document every step of every process.

Excluding enforcement of generally accepted accounting principles (GAAP), many of these activities or concepts are within HR's scope of expertise, and you should work with Finance or the internal audit team to assess each area (looking for conflicts of interest, weak systems, or undocumented processes) and to make recommendations for improvement. The deadline for responding to Sarbanes-Oxley has come and gone, and many companies are still struggling to demonstrate "adequate controls."

Leadership

Ultimately, the accountability comes back to executive leadership. Companies that are best prepared to deal with compensation governance issues are companies that have top executives who will stand up, accept ownership, and

FIGURE 13.2 Three-sided governance model.

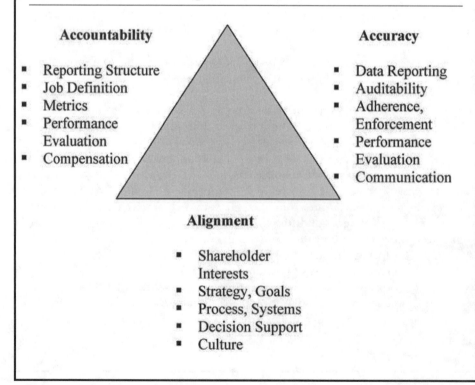

Accountability

- Reporting Structure
- Job Definition
- Metrics
- Performance Evaluation
- Compensation

Accuracy

- Data Reporting
- Auditability
- Adherence, Enforcement
- Performance Evaluation
- Communication

Alignment

- Shareholder Interests
- Strategy, Goals
- Process, Systems
- Decision Support
- Culture

champion the program. HR has as much potential to lead this effort as any function. (Note: A powerful ally for HR in this effort may be Legal if it is willing and able to exert an opinion on compensation governance.) The ideal executive champion should:

- Have some experience with the motivational power and potential complexity of compensation.
- Be able to influence and marshal resources from other departments.
- Represent decisions made by the compensation team and outline the supporting arguments for those decisions to outsiders.
- Have the authority to restructure the composition of the compensation team as deemed necessary to execute the company's strategy and governance model.

Keep in mind that one trade-off with a strong leader is the increased importance of checks and balances for approvals. If your organization is still struggling with the deployment of effective governance processes and practices, look first to the leadership of the effort for serious commitment and the other characteristics described here.

Central versus Local Control

A strong, central, corporate leader of compensation, while a tremendous asset, will also sometimes lead to questions about centralized versus local control in compensation. The presence or absence of regional leaders who share a strong sense of accountability, alignment, and value of accuracy will further complicate these questions. The most successful companies typically have structured a framework that explicitly retains certain decision rights for central corporate resources while empowering local resources to make other specific decisions to suit their unique business environment and strategies. These decision rights should be documented in both the governance framework and the compensation T&Cs. A logical division of these might be:

Centralized: Market benchmark percentile, role eligibility (there must be an objective standard as to the skills and experience necessary to be assigned to a role, and participants should not be able to make that judgment themselves), performance measures, some formula mechanics, quota-setting process, most crediting rules (typically matching the quota-setting principles regarding duplicate or split credit), key policies concerning employment status (e.g., transfer, leave of absence), pay administration.

Localized: Pay level, pay mix, upside, weightings of performance measures, some formula mechanics, pay frequency, individual quotas, supplemental policies.

Additional responsibilities can be moved in either direction as manpower and culture warrant. As more activities and decision rights are moved toward the local geographies or BUs, the central corporate lead will want to consider the need for "satellite" design teams to parallel the design work and process taking place at headquarters. This assumes that there are local/regional

(continued)

Sidebar 13.1 (*Continued*)

resources in Finance, Marketing, and HR that are up to the task. Likewise, as responsibility moves outward to local regions or BUs, most companies will increase investment in the audit side of the equation. Empowerment is smart, and scrutiny is smarter. An inability to implement tailored tactics is a symptom of a compensation program that is too centralized. Plan proliferation, increased cost, and loss of control are symptoms of a program that is too decentralized.

Meetings, Voting, Notes, Documentation

As your organization works through a carefully structured and documented process, you will have several scheduled or ad hoc meetings to confirm plan issues from the assessment, plan change objectives, expense budgets, system capabilities and testing requirements, communication strategies, mid-period plan (or quota or territory) changes, and emergent issue resolutions. To conform with good governance principles, you should make sure that these meetings are attended by the full team (sometimes a tremendous challenge in schedule management—you may need to literally cancel meetings that are partially attended). Key decisions that require a vote of the team members should be explicitly stated as requiring a single authority to approve, a majority to approve, a super-majority (67 percent), or full consensus. The results of any votes should be documented in meeting minutes and the minutes should be filed (electronic and paper copies) for future reference and auditability. Meetings of regional design teams, corporate governance councils, and/or steering committees should have established distribution lists for decisions and documentation so that information is flowing in the right directions to provide consistent governance.

Summing Up

Governance is a concept that sounds complicated but is really a reinforcement of sound management principles. If you have established explicit, documented compensation philosophies, design and administration processes with assigned roles and responsibilities, and cross-functional design teams and steering committees, you are already more than halfway toward a sound compensation program with a foundation of good governance. To complete the model, decision rights and results must be documented and you must be diligent in your analysis of plan performance and process reinforcement. Disputes and issues in both design and administration must be escalated to the correct authorities who must act without conflict of interest.

The biggest obstacles in the quest for improved compensation governance may be your corporate culture or the inertia of some executives. Sarbanes-Oxley, while not creating radically new thought in terms of governance structure, may well be the impetus for change with its increased accountability and penalties for top management.

REFERENCES

Agarwal, Naresh C. "Determinants of Executive Compensation." *Industrial Relations* 20 (Winter 1981): 36–46.

Balsam, Steven, and Wonsun Paek. "Insider Holding Requirements, Stock Options and Stock Appreciation Rights." *Journal of Accounting, Auditing and Finance* 16 (Summer 2001): 227–48.

Bebchuk, Lucien, and Jesse Fried. *Pay without Performance: The Unfulfilled Promise of Executive Compensation.* Harvard University Press, 2004a.

———."Stealth Compensation via Retirement Benefits." *Berkeley Business Law Journal* 1, no. 2 (Fall 2004b): 291–326.

Berle, Adolf Augustus, and Gardiner Coit Means. *The Modern Corporation and Private Property.* New York: Commerce Clearing House, 1932.

Brickley, James A., Sanjai Bhagat, and Ronald C. Lease. "The Impact of Long-Range Managerial Compensation Plans on Shareholder Wealth." *Journal of Accounting and Economics* 7, nos. 1–3 (1985): 115–30.

Fairclough, Gordon. "Philip Morris to Pay Special Bonuses to Executives, Citing an 'Unusual Year.'" *Wall Street Journal* (March 14, 2000): A22.

Gomez-Mejia, Luis R. "Executive Compensation: A Reassessment and a Future Research Agenda." *Research in Personnel and Human Resources Management* 12 (1994): 161–222.

Jensen, Michael. J., and William H. Meckling. "Theory of the Firm: Managerial Behavior, Agency Costs and Ownership Structure." *Journal of Financial Economics* 3 (1976): 305–60.

Lazear, Edward P., and Sherwin Rosen. "Rank-Order Tournaments as Optimum Labor Contracts." *Journal of Political Economy* 89, no. 5 (1981): 841–64.

Leggett, Karby. "Small Investors Rail against China." *The Wall Street Journal* (December 28, 2000): C1, 10.

Lublin, Joann S., Matt Murray, and Rick Brooks. "Home Depot Nabs GE's Nardelli as CEO." *The Wall Street Journal* (December 6, 2000): A3.

Maremont, Mark, and Laurie Cohen. "How Tyco's CEO Enriched Himself." *Wall Street Journal* (August 7, 2002): A1, 20.

Matsunaga, Steven R. "The Effects of Financial Reporting Costs on the Use of Employee Stock Options." *The Accounting Review* 70, no. 1 (1995): 1–26.

Miller, Merton H., and Myron S. Scholes. "Executive Compensation, Taxes and Incentives." In *Financial Economics: Essays in Honor of Paul Cootner,* ed. W. Sharpe and C. Cootner. Prentice-Hall, Englewood Cliffs, NJ, 1982.

Morgan, Angela G., and Annette B. Poulsen. "Linking Pay to Performance—Compensation Proposals in the S&P 500." Working Paper, Clemson University and the University of Georgia, 2000.

O'Reilly, Charles A., Brian G. Main, and Graef S. Crystal. "CEO Compensation as Tournament and Social Comparison: A Tale of Two Theories." *Administrative Science Quarterly* 33 (1988): 257–74.

Prendergast, Canice. "The Provision of Incentives in Firms." *Journal of Economic Literature* 37 (1999): 7–63.

Rajan, Raghuram G., and Julie Wulf. "Are Perks Purely Managerial Excess?" *Journal of Financial Economics* 79 (2006): 1–33.

Reingold, Jennifer. "An Options Plan Your CEO Hates." *Business Week* (February 28, 2000): 82–87.

Rosen, Sherwin. "Prizes and Incentives in Elimination Tournaments." *The American Economic Review* 76, no. 4 (1986): 701–15.

Sessa, Danielle, and Laura Saunders Egodigwe. "Incentive Plans Can Fuel Insider Buying." *The Wall Street Journal,* January 13, 1999, C1.

Silverman, Rachel Emma. "The Jungle/What's News in Recruitment and Pay." *The Wall Street Journal* (August 1 2000a): B12.

———. "The Jungle/ What's News in Recruitment and Pay." *The Wall Street Journal* (October 31, 2000b): B18.

Sloan, Richard. "Accounting Earnings and Top Executive Compensation." *Journal of Accounting and Economics* 16 (1993): 55–100.

Tehranian, Hassan, and James F. Waegelein. "Market Reaction to Short-Term Executive Compensation Plan Adoption." *Journal of Accounting and Economics* 7, nos. 1–3 (1985): 131–44.

Thomas, Randall S., and Kenneth J. Martin. "The Effect of Shareholder Proposals on Executive Compensation." *University of Cincinnati Law Review* 67 (1999): 1021–81.

Thurm, Scott. "No-Exit Strategies: Their Outlook Bright, Fiber-Optics Firms Put Job-Hoppers on Notice." *The Wall Street Journal,* February 6, 2001, A1.

Ungson, Gerardo Rivera, and Richard M. Steers. "Motivation and Politics in Executive Compensation." *Academy of Management Review* 9, no. 2 (1984): 313–23.

Wiseman, Robert M., and Luis R. Gomez-Mejia. "A Behavioral Agency Model of Managerial Risk Taking." *Academy of Management Review* 23, no. 1 (1998): 133–53.

14 Linking Pay to Performance

Merit pay, commonly called "pay for performance," is perhaps the most widely used means by which U.S. organizations determine employee pay increases. The purpose of merit pay is to reward employees for individual contributions and to encourage the best performance possible. In theory, if all employees operate at peak efficiency relative to their capabilities, the organization will thrive.

The logic behind merit pay is straightforward: If pay is made contingent upon performance, then employee motivation to achieve high performance is increased. (See Figure 14.1.) The key to merit pay is founded in three motivational theories:

- Reinforcement theory states that merit pay should motivate improved performance because the monetary consequences of good performance are made known—the better one's performance, the greater the pay increase will be.
- Expectancy theory states that merit pay should motivate improved performance because performance is instrumental to the attainment of a pay increase—improved effort to perform leads to increased pay.
- Equity theory states that merit pay should lead to improved performance because a pay raise is seen as a fair outcome for one's performance input—the more one contributes to the organization, the greater the pay increase.

A successful merit pay program will:

- Reward employees for achieving performance results and exhibiting behaviors aligned with the objectives of the organization, which often are linked directly to the strategic business plan and mission of the organization.
- Provide rewards commensurate with contributions (i.e., bigger pay increases for stronger performers).
- Be communicated easily to employees.
- Be understood readily by employees.

FIGURE 14.1 Linking pay to performance.

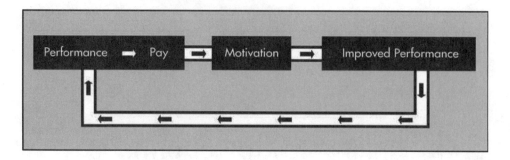

- Recognize "bottom line" considerations and the organization's ability to deliver pay increases.
- Be rational, structured, and administered in a logical manner.
- Conform to legal requirements.
- Use a well-founded, credible means of evaluating performance.
- Conform with and support management philosophy.

As with most business programs, a merit pay plan should be planned carefully to achieve these goals. If an organization takes the time to design its merit pay plan carefully, it will establish a strong link between pay and performance.

DETERMINING WHAT TO REWARD

Before a merit pay plan can be designed, the first steps are to determine:

- What the organization values.
- Which types of individual employee contributions should be rewarded.
- The organization's ability to pay.
- The organization's ability and willingness to communicate the plan.
- The organization's ability to administer the plan.

Some organizations make these determinations through the planning efforts of senior management, who refer to the overall business strategy and mission. Other organizations use a structured human resources planning effort, which relies on formal performance-planning and goal-setting activities. Other organizations make informal determinations. Some additional steps to getting started on a merit pay plan are listed in Figure 14.2.

Without a clear understanding of the organization's values and expectations, it is possible that employee contributions that are contrary to the organizational objectives will be rewarded. A successful plan requires that individual goals be aligned with the organization's:

- Identity, which relates to whom the organization serves and what products and services are provided.
- Strategic plan, which relates to how the mission of the organization is accomplished.
- Objectives, which relate to what corporate goals have been established.

FIGURE 14.2 Getting started on a merit plan.

Verify that key prerequisites are in place:

- Top-management support
- An established performance-management system that is reliable, valid, fair, flexible, and credible

Conduct research to verify that merit pay is appropriate and workable for the organization:

- Review of prior merit pay theory and research
- Collection of information on other employers' experiences with merit pay, focusing on those that are regarded as highly successful and highly unsuccessful as well as those that are similar in management style and organization
- Evaluation of the effectiveness of the merit pay program by establishing a baseline of employee attitudes and perceptions about pay

Form an employee task force to oversee the development of the plan and ensure work-force "buy-in," with the following functions represented:

- Line management
- HR professionals
- Employees representing different "levels" in the organization
- Nonexempt employees, if appropriate for the organization's culture

Once the link between individual and organizational objectives has been defined, merit pay can be used to align individual goals with those of the organization. When used properly, merit pay will reinforce the accomplishment of individual contributions that are in line with the identity, strategic plan, and objectives of the organization.

Merit pay also must be consistent with regard to the business environment of the organization. Business environment characteristics that support or detract from merit pay are shown in Figure 14.3.

DOCUMENTING PERFORMANCE STANDARDS

The second step in developing a merit pay plan is to devise a system that establishes and evaluates performance against individual objectives. Performance standards, also known as performance goals or objectives, are written statements that help determine the extent to which employees have contributed to the mission of the organization. These standards establish the basis on which employee contributions are evaluated, and they define the expected level of performance. Various ratings systems can be used to describe how successful an employee has been in attaining

FIGURE 14.3 How business environment characteristics relate to merit pay.

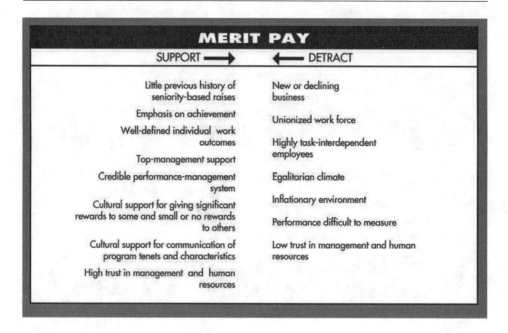

objectives. Some examples of common performance standards are shown in Figure 14.4.

While establishing performance standards, determining which standards best meet an organization's needs is critical. Objective standards—such as quality and quantity of work performed—should be assessed as well as more intangible, subjective aspects of the job such as teamwork, cooperation, and customer service.

Documentation of work standards is an essential part of the performance-evaluation process. Typically, this is an annual event in which supervisors and subordinates discuss goals and objectives for the coming year while evaluating the prior year's performance. In some organizations, determining and documenting work standards is a cooperative effort between managers and employees. Other options include:

- Having managers determine objectives and then communicate them to the employee.
- Having employees present goals to their managers for discussion.

However work standards are established in an organization, obtaining employee "buy-in" is essential. If employees cannot comprehend the standards or accept their reasonableness, they are unlikely to perform in a manner that is consistent with the mission of the organization. To help ensure that employees accept and act upon performance standards, three actions should be taken:

- Emphasize results and behaviors rather than traits. Performance standards should reflect what the person produces (results) or what the person does (behaviors) rather than personality characteristics (traits). For example, it is

FIGURE 14.4 Examples of common performance standards.

Quality
Demonstrates work quality by producing goods or services that meet or exceed preset, measurable standards (e.g., less than one defect per thousand items).

Quantity
Meets or exceeds specific production quotas within a given period of time.

Communications
Effectively expresses thoughts verbally, in writing and nonverbally. Listens attentively and makes productive use of acquired information. Gains agreement and acceptance of plans, ideas or activities being discussed while incorporating others' good suggestions.

Creativity and Innovations
Conceives, encourages, develops and applies imaginative concepts that improve operating procedures and efficiencies, or that make better use of company assets.

Interpersonal Teamwork
Works well with others toward the accomplishment of goals. Earns respect and trust. Makes a contribution to the team's achievements. Shows consideration for the feelings and needs of others.

Planning and Organizing
Defines and prioritizes objectives. Installs a thorough, appropriate plan of action. Establishes procedures to monitor progress toward task completion. Can manage multiple projects, priorities or deadlines to accomplish long- and short-term goals.

Problem Analysis
Identifies problems, secures relevant information and relates data from different sources to determine possible causes of problems.

better to measure the quality of performance by using a result such as "number of customer complaints" or a behavior such as "is always courteous to customers" than it is to use a trait such as "is nice to people."

- Employees should participate in setting standards. For employees to act upon performance standards, they must be committed to them, which means that they need to have a sense of ownership in the process. When employees are given an opportunity to help establish performance goals and objectives, they are more likely to feel as if they "own" the process and to protect their ownership interests by meeting the standards.
- The standards should be flexible. It is the nature of work and organizations to be in a constant state of flux. Consequently, performance objectives and standards that are viable now may—because of influences outside the control of the employee—become obsolete. An organization should be willing to modify standards as shifting demands dictate.

ESTABLISHING A MERIT BUDGET

A fundamental feature of any merit pay plan is an established budget that has been endorsed by management. Every year that a merit pay plan is in effect, the budget process should consist of two key activities:

- Determining the size of the budget.
- Allocating funds to business units within the organization.

DETERMINING BUDGET SIZE

Typically, salary-increase budgets will be established each year based upon many factors, including:

- Actual or anticipated organization financial results.
- Cost-of-living and/or inflation.
- Industry trends.
- Competitive factors such as retention rates and recruiting successes.
- Cost of labor and the competitive position of the organization's pay in the marketplace.
- Group (e.g., division or department) performance and needs.

In most organizations, it is common to obtain or develop salary budget surveys each year that show expected increase rates for similar employers. WorldatWork and many of the major compensation consulting groups conduct annual salary budget surveys and publicize their findings widely.

On the basis of survey information, and after taking into account the organization's financial situation, senior management ordinarily will approve a not-to-be-exceeded "bottom line" increase budget computed as a percentage of current payroll. During the past 10 years, merit-increase budgets have averaged approximately 5 percent annually.

DETERMINING BUDGET ALLOCATION

The next step in the budget process is to determine how funds are to be distributed to business units within the organization. A simple and commonly used method of allocating merit pay dollars is to use a uniform budget. Under this procedure, merit pay budgets are distributed to divisions or departments as a percentage of "eligible payroll," which is defined as the aggregate base salaries of all employees who are eligible to participate in the merit pay plan.

Eligibility may be driven by a calendar date. Some organizations include only those employees who have exceeded a minimum service requirement such as six months at the time of their expected date of increase. Other organizations will include all employees on payroll, but will prorate increases for those employees with a partial year of service.

Using the uniform-budget approach, every business unit in the organization shares proportionally in the amount of money available for salary increases. Figure 14.5 is an example of a uniform-budget allocation.

Use of uniform budgets fails to take into account that some business groups are more or less successful than are others. Furthermore, in organizations with geographically dispersed business activities—some of which may be located in areas with different cost-of-living, inflationary, or competitive pressures with respect to the work force—a uniform budget may be inappropriate.

To respond to differing achievement levels of the various business units or the need to pay different wages in certain locations, some organizations use a flexible-budget approach. The flexible-budget method introduces a level of complexity into the budget process that is not a factor in uniform merit budgets. Unlike uniform budgets, flexible budgets require sound measures of business-unit performance and geographic pay differences to distribute budget dollars. Many organizations are

FIGURE 14.5 Example of a uniform-budget allocation.

Department	Total Payroll Dollars	Merit Budget Percentage	Merit Budget Dollars
Finance	$2,450,500	4.0%	$98,020
Human Resources	$1,750,900	4.0%	$70,036
Marketing	$4,375,055	4.9%	$175,002
Production	$7,980,250	4.0%	$319,210
Totals	$16,556,705	4.0%	$662,268

ill-prepared to track or calculate these differences accurately. Figure 14.6 is an example of a flexible-budget allocation. Note that budget percentages have been rounded.

SETTING MERIT PAY POLICY

The essential goal of a merit pay plan is to link pay to performance that is consistent with the mission of the organization. To cement this link, pay increases must vary according to the level of an employee's contributions and efforts. There are two required conditions:

- Variations in employee performance must be measurable and measured.
- Managers must be provided with the necessary "tools" to determine the appropriate rewards.

These tools are to be found in the established guidelines or policies that govern pay increases as well as in the process for implementing these guidelines.

POLICY DECISIONS

Key factors in creating a merit pay policy are the size, timing, and delivery of merit increases.

FIGURE 14.6 Example of a flexible-budget allocation.

DEPARTMENT	TOTAL PAYROLL DOLLARS	MERIT BUDGET PERCENTAGE	MERIT BUDGET DOLLARS
Finance	$2,450,500	3.1%	$75,966
Human Resources	$1,750,900	3.6%	$63,032
Marketing	$4,375,055	4.3%	$188,099
Production	$7,980,250	4.2%	$335,171
Totals	$16,556,705	4.0%	$662,268

Size: Absolute vs. Relative

The size of pay increases is a critical component in merit pay programs. Two conditions are necessary to motivate employees most effectively to meet and exceed performance standards for their positions:

- The absolute size of the merit increase must be significant enough to make a noticeable difference to employees (e.g., the increase must not be so trivial as to be deemed inconsequential).
- The relative size of the increase must be significant enough that real differences in performance are recognized by meaningful differences in rewards.

A successful merit pay program will ensure that increases awarded to the "best" contributors will be substantially greater than increases awarded to average or less-than-average performers. If differences among pay increases are deemed by recipients to be trivial, the merit pay program will be undermined because employees will not be motivated to improve their performance. For example, a merit pay program that provides additional 2-percent increases for "exceptional" performers is likely to be perceived by employees as not providing significantly different rewards. However, a merit pay program that offers an additional 4- or 5-percent increase for exceptional performance is more likely to alter employee behavior and be motivational.

Timing: Anniversary vs. Common Review

Another issue that must be addressed is the date merit-increase decisions are made. Survey data suggest that common review dates are used by almost two-thirds of organizations while one-third stagger increases, mostly by providing them on anniversary dates.

Using an anniversary-date approach spreads the administrative burden (tasks such as completing performance reviews, making increase decisions, and processing pay increases) throughout the year for managers and human resources staff. Payroll increases also are staggered, reducing the financial impact that accompanies a single jump in salaries. Also, the anniversary-date approach focuses the performance evaluation and increase on an individual employee, ideally leading the employee to believe the process is focused specifically on him or her.

A disadvantage of an anniversary-date approach is that relative performance (e.g., comparative appraisal ratings), which often is a basis for merit-increase decisions, may be hard to judge, particularly if performance is evaluated at different times for all employees. Another disadvantage becomes evident when conservative budget management accentuates the natural tendency of many managers to "save" money until year-end. When this occurs, employee increases at the beginning of the year may be smaller than increases at the end of the year, and the result may be to penalize some employees unfairly.

A common (i.e., annual) review date consolidates the administrative burden for management and human resources, and increases can become part of the yearly budgeting process. Furthermore, because increases for all employees are determined at the same time, appraisal ratings for all employees can be collected and relative performance can be factored into the decision more easily. If the merit budget is based on business-unit performance, the linkage among business-unit performance, individual performance, and merit increases can be clearer with a common date.

Disadvantages of common review dates are that the workload may be onerous if the timing of the salary-increase program coincides with other major efforts (such as year-end financial closings, open enrollment for benefits, and departmental budgeting), and cash-flow implications for the organization may be extreme when all increases occur simultaneously.

Neither an anniversary-date nor a common-review-date approach is the "right" way to administer merit increases. The approach should be determined by several factors, including availability of performance data for employees and for organizational units, and availability of management and human resources.

In organizations where budgets for salary increases are allocated based upon organizational performance during a fixed period of time, employee and departmental performance also may be evaluated during the same time period. In such cases, a common review date may make sense. Anniversary-date increases may be more appropriate in organizations that stagger appraisals of performance or that permit little or no increase-budget variability among departments and in organizations that want to emphasize the individual's performance against absolute standards instead of emphasizing relative performance.

Another issue is whether to permit variability in time between increases in the pay program. In some organizations, the time between increases is not uniform for all employees; rather, performance differences are reflected not only in the size of increase but also in frequency. Excellent performance may be rewarded with larger and more frequent rewards. For example, top contributors might receive relatively large pay raises every 6 to 9 months, while average performers might wait 12 to 15 months for a lesser increase.

Delivery: Base vs. Lump Sum

Under traditional merit pay plans, merit increases are built into employees' salaries for as long as they remain with the organization. Hence, the increases are permanent, and their values are compounded over time as additional increases are granted.

One alternative to base-salary increases that recently has become more popular is the use of lump sum increases. Lump sum increases are one-time payments made in lieu of a traditional base-pay increase, and they typically are delivered annually via the merit pay program. Similar to a "bonus" payment, a lump sum must be re-earned each year based on performance—it is not built into base salary. Often, lump sum payments are provided to employees who are near, at, or over the maximum of their salary range (often called "red circle" employees).

The advantages of lump sum increases for the organization are clear: While retaining a pay-for-performance relationship, payroll costs over time are lessened because of the lack of a compounding effect. Also, the "sanctity" of pay ranges is protected because the number of red-circle employees can be controlled. In organizations where employees are at or over the maximum of their grade, but are not permitted to receive increases, lump sums provide a mechanism to continue to reward and motivate strong but highly paid contributors.

There are fewer advantages of lump sums for the employee, though receiving the annual increase at once rather than having it paid out over 12 months—as is the case with a base-pay increase—may appeal to some. For long-term and highly paid employees, who may be near the top of their salary range with no room to grow, lump sums provide a means to continue to receive rewards.

Frequently, lump sums issued in lieu of merit increases concern many employees because their gross (base) pay will be less over time. Longer-term employees approaching retirement typically exhibit the most concern. Many employers allay this concern by counting lump sum awards toward final average-earnings pension calculations. Similarly, such payments often are tied to benefits. For example, benefits such as life insurance, which are linked to salary, will reflect lump sum payments in addition to base salary. This solution addresses a number of issues:

- The motivational link between performance and reward can be maintained.
- The organization reaps the benefit that lump sum payments provide in controlling total compensation costs.
- Employee benefits entitlements are not seriously reduced.

However, caution should be used with this approach because employees may react negatively when their base salaries do not change or grow relatively slowly over time.

POLICY IMPLEMENTATION

A merit pay policy answers the following questions about salary increases: How much? When? How? How frequently? These decisions can be summarized in a simple compensation tool called a merit pay matrix.

A merit pay matrix details the amount and timing of increases for various levels of performance at various locations in the pay grade. A merit pay matrix may be interpreted as an operational statement of an organization's pay-for-performance theory or policy. It spells out the contingency between pay and performance in specific terms.

Merit pay matrices range from the simple to the complex, depending on the number of variables upon which pay is made contingent. Generally, there are three alternatives for issuing merit increases:

- Based only on performance.
- Based on performance and position in range.
- Based on performance and position in range using variable timing.

Performance

This method, which uses the simplest form of merit matrix (Figure 14.7), is most common in organizations without well-defined salary grade structures. Pay increases are granted based solely on performance, resulting in top performers receiving bigger increases than lower performers. Typically, salary increases are calculated as a percentage increase in base pay.

Note: The matrices displayed in Figures 14.7, 14.9, and 14.10 use ranges of increases rather than single percentages. This provides for more managerial discretion in awarding increases, and it more closely links pay and performance. In some companies, however, each cell of the matrix is occupied by only a single number.

Basing merit increases on performance alone ignores internal pay comparisons. Within a performance class, higher-paid employees receive greater absolute increases, even though the merit percentage reward is the same. This has the effect of perpetuating pay inequities that might exist, and it may reward long-tenured and/or highly paid employees disproportionately.

FIGURE 14.7 Linking merit increases to base pay.

Performance Rating	Fixed Increase Amount	Discretionary Increase Amount
Outstanding	8%	6–10%
Consistently Exceeds Standards	5%	4–6%
Meets Standards	3%	2–4%
Does Not Fully Meet Standards	0%	0–2%

An alternative is to calculate merit increases as a percentage of the employee's salary-grade midpoint rather than their base pay. This approach provides larger relative dollar increases to employees within a performance class who are paid lower in their salary range than it does for employees who are high in their range. (See Figure 14.8.) Over time, inequities in salaries of employees in the same salary grade will be reduced as lower-paid employees are accelerated toward midpoint and higher-paid employees are "slowed down." This method reduces some of the bias toward long-term/highly paid employees that may be inherent in a performance-only merit matrix.

FIGURE 14.8 Linking merit increases to salary-grade midpoints.

Increase as a Percentage of Base Pay

Employee	Current Pay Rate	Increase Percentage	Increase Dollars
A	$25,000	4.0%	$1,000
B	$35,000	4.0%	$1,400
C	$45,000	4.0%	$1,800

Increase as a Percentage of $35,000 Midpoint

Employee	Current Pay Rate	Increase Percentage of Midpoint	Increase Dollars	Effective Increase Percentage
A	$25,000	4.0%	$1,400	5.6%
B	$35,000	4.0%	$1,400	4.0%
C	$45,000	4.0%	$1,400	3.1%

The advantage of either approach to calculating merit increases based only on performance is that the method is:

- Simple to budget.
- Easy to administer.
- Straightforward to communicate.

Performance and Position in Range

Organizations with more traditional and/or sophisticated grading structures commonly introduce the practice of basing increases on both performance and position in range, which is commonly defined by quartiles, or, if greater precision is required, by compa-ratios. This practice is based on the concept that the midpoint represents a "competitive" or "fair" wage for a particular set of skills in the marketplace, and that, over time, employees with a similar level of sustained performance should be paid an equivalent amount. Thus, a merit-increase guide chart similar to Figure 14.9 will cause employees with the same performance to converge, over time, on a target point (typically the midpoint) by awarding bigger increases to employees lower in their range and smaller increases to employees higher in the range.

This merit-matrix approach has several advantages:

- The tendency is reduced to perpetuate tenure-based pay inequities and to continue to "overpay" (relative to market) highly paid employees.
- The approach is more likely to be deemed "fair" by the work force because, over time, employees with similar performance in the same salary grade will tend to be paid comparably.

FIGURE 14.9 Linking merit increases to performance and position in range.

Performance Rating	Position in Range Before Increase			
	1st Quartile or Below	2nd Quartile	3rd Quartile	4th Quartile
Outstanding	8–9%	6–7%	4–5%	3–4%
Consistently Exceeds Standards	6–7%	4–5%	3–4%	2–3%
Meets Standards	4–5%	3–4%	2–3%	✕
Does Not Fully Meet Standards	0–2%	✕	✕	✕

Basing merit increases on both performance and position in range introduces a level of complexity into the process not found in the simpler performance-only model. It is more difficult to administer and communicate.

Performance and Position in Range Using Variable Timing

A more complex model for administering merit increases involves the concept of variable timing. The guide chart shown in Figure 14.10 demonstrates how the size and frequency of increase can be varied based upon performance and position in range. In this model, top performers receive bigger and more frequent increases, while average and below-average contributors wait longer for smaller increases.

There are several advantages to this approach:

- Top performers will receive bigger rewards with greater frequency, yielding significant increases because of the compounding effect.
- During times of tight budgets, rather than issuing "below market" increases at regular intervals, "normal" increases can be granted at moderately delayed intervals. For example, rather than granting a 3.5 percent increase at 12 months, an organization may prefer to grant a 4.7 percent increase at 16 months.

The disadvantages of variable timing are:

- It is much more complicated to administer.
- It is difficult to track and maintain budgets.

FIGURE 14.10 Linking merit pay to position in range using variable timing.

| Performance Rating | Position in Range Before Increase | | | |
	1st Quartile or Below	2nd Quartile	3rd Quartile	4th Quartile
Outstanding	8–9% 6–9 months	6–7% 9–12 months	4–5% 10–12 months	3–4% 12–15 months
Consistently Exceeds Standards	6–7% 8–10 months	4–5% 10–12 months	3–4% 12–15 months	2–3% 15–18 months
Meets Standards	4–5% 9–12 months	3–4% 12–15 months	2–3% 15–18 months	
Does Not Fully Meet Standards	0–2% 12–15 months			

- It is difficult to monitor the consistency of application throughout the year.
- It is more complex to communicate.

A successful merit pay plan requires more than well-developed policy statements and a conceptually sound design. It also requires administrative processes and procedures that are logical and easily understood. Some of the administrative issues that should be given consideration to ensure that a policy is implemented as intended are communication, training, and perceived fairness.

MANAGING A MERIT PAY PLAN

The merit pay "equation" is simple: Significant performance efforts yield significant rewards, which in turn motivate significant performance efforts. However, this equation relies on trust to enforce the contract between employees and the organization. Employees must trust the organization to fulfill its commitment that today's efforts will be compensated fairly tomorrow, and the organization must trust that employees will be motivated by performance-based rewards.

As in any relationship, trust can be promoted through openness and candor or thwarted through secrecy and obfuscation. Honest, open communication between management, human resources, and employees serves as the means by which the messages of merit pay can be conveyed and reinforced.

Traditionally, many organizations have been unwilling to share much of their compensation-related data. Usually, these organizations have the mistaken belief that employees neither want nor need to know about such matters, and that providing "too much" information to employees somehow reduces management's ability to exercise flexibility and discretion.

In recent years, many organizations have come to believe that no matter how carefully designed or well founded a compensation program might be in theory, success requires adequate communication. Thorough communication permits employees to test the validity of the organization's promises while conveying to them that the organization has nothing to hide. It also establishes opportunities for dialogue on issues of critical importance, enhances credibility by obtaining employee buy-in, and promotes overall trust.

A successful communication program requires a careful balance between an insufficient amount of information and too much information. Management should release enough information about the plan to demonstrate its faith in the process, but not so much information that its ability to exercise managerial discretion is impeded. Employees should be provided enough information about the merit pay plan that it serves as a performance motivator without breaching their right to privacy.

How much to communicate to employees will be influenced by many factors, including the organization's culture, management's willingness to share information that traditionally may have been confidential, and the readiness and ability of human resources to support the communications effort. Some of the key elements often introduced in a comprehensive communications program are:

- General information about the performance-appraisal program and process.
- General information about the organization's compensation program (e.g., how pay is determined, how jobs are evaluated, and what the salary ranges are).

- More specific information about the merit pay program (e.g., salary-increase budgets, performance-rating distributions, and merit matrices).
- Size of an individual's increase, minimum and maximum raises granted, and average size of merit increases.

TRAINING

Implementation of a successful merit pay program requires managers to make two key sets of decisions:

- Evaluation of performance.
- Allocation of increase awards.

An accurate, reliable, and credible performance-appraisal program is the foundation of a successful merit pay program, and it is imperative that managers and supervisors be capable of evaluating employee behaviors and results objectively and critically.

The skills required to appraise performance, assess employee contributions, and assign rewards are not intuitive. To ensure adequate interpretation and understanding of program requirements and consistent application of program tenets, training should be provided for all managers who are given the task of implementing the merit pay program. Training should include the following components:

- How to plan performance that links individual efforts and accomplishments to business plans and strategies.
- How to measure and evaluate performance fairly and consistently.
- How to provide feedback through intrinsic (e.g., coaching and praise) and extrinsic (e.g., pay increases and incentive payments) rewards.
- How to use the merit matrix to allocate rewards.
- How to communicate the assessment of performance and the allocation of rewards to employees.

PERCEPTION OF FAIRNESS

Program credibility is key to gaining a favorable response among employees to merit pay. Employees need to feel that increases and the process used to derive the increases are accurate and fair. To help ensure the perception of fairness, the merit pay program should incorporate the following tenets:

- Relevant laws and regulations must be followed (e.g., Title VII, the Civil Rights Act, the Fair Labor Standards Act, and various tax laws).
- Employees should participate in the setting of performance goals and standards, they should know what performance is expected of them, and they should be able to control the specific aspects of their performance on which their pay will be based.
- Employees should know and understand how the pay program works, and they should be encouraged to raise concerns, ask questions, and seek clarification of their increases.

- An appeals process should be established to provide employees with an opportunity to discuss their performance evaluation and their increase with an authority other than their direct supervisor.

HOW COMPUTER TECHNOLOGY CAN ASSIST ADMINISTRATION

The most conceptually and theoretically sound merit pay program is burdensome and inefficient to administer. Consequently, anything that contributes to simplifying planning and administration will help ensure the program's success.

Computer technology can assist in the management of the merit pay plan in a number of ways:

- Budget planning can be facilitated by generating different increase-matrix models, testing various options, and deriving forecasts of the economic impact of alternatives.
- Data can be probed to evaluate the effectiveness, impact, and equity of the merit pay plan. Increases, performance distribution, and other factors can be analyzed by department, position, organization, or individual.
- Employee records can be stored, monitored, and analyzed over time.
- Data can be managed to formulate cost projections based on salary-structure changes, the impact of inflation, and other financial factors.
- Summary reporting can be streamlined for internal and external purposes, tedious administrative tasks and reporting efforts can be automated, and productivity can be improved by reducing the amount of time, labor, and expense involved in managing the pay program.

EVALUATING A MERIT PAY PLAN

To ensure that a merit pay plan is operating as intended and is effective in meeting an organization's compensation needs, a systematic, post-implementation evaluation of the plan should be conducted regularly. This often-overlooked step is critical to the ultimate success and acceptance of the program. Many factors can be analyzed to assess plan effectiveness:

- Employee satisfaction with the pay program.
- Employee job satisfaction.
- Employee perception that pay is based on performance.
- Employee acceptance of and trust in the performance-appraisal process.
- Employee trust in management.
- Employee and organizational performance (e.g., productivity improvements).
- Employee commitment to the organization as demonstrated through reduced turnover and absenteeism rates.
- Correlation between actual performance ratings and actual merit increases.

Measurement of these success factors before and after implementation of a merit pay plan is likely to yield the most meaningful information, and it can be accomplished through various means: controlled empirical studies, employee-attitude surveys, focus-group discussions, and management and employee anecdotal feedback. Employee attitudes and perceptions ideally should be evaluated by collecting survey data from employees before the introduction of a merit pay plan and again after the program has been introduced and employees have received their first merit increases.

Some organizations attempt to gauge the success of newly introduced merit pay plans by measuring productivity and/or performance improvements over time and then correlating that information with appraisal ratings and salary increases. Also, turnover and absenteeism rates can be tracked and correlated with performance and salary increases. These data could be used to modify development of the plan, but it should be remembered that many other factors, including industry and economic trends, also may affect these factors. For example, high unemployment rates will tend to drive down turnover rates, regardless of employee satisfaction with corporate pay plans.

Because employee perception of fairness is so important in determining the success of the merit pay program, one analysis that should be performed is to test how accurately, fairly, and consistently the program has been administered throughout the organization. Some common employee questions that need to be addressed to demonstrate the fairness of a merit pay plan are:

- Does where or for whom you work mean more than how well you perform? Do some departments rate employee performance disproportionately high, and are some supervisors unfairly critical while others are unreasonably generous?
- Are all employees afforded a relatively equal opportunity for high performance ratings and commensurate increases? Is the plan free from racial, gender, and age bias?

MERIT PAY ADVANTAGES AND DISADVANTAGES

While merit pay remains a popular means of determining pay increases, the potential drawbacks of the approach should be clear before implementation. Once these drawbacks are recognized, an organization can appreciate the advantages of merit pay and how it will improve employee perceptions of work and rewards. (See Figure 14.11.)

FIGURE 14.11 Advantages and disadvantages of merit pay.

MERIT PAY	
ADVANTAGES ➡	⬅ DISADVANTAGES
Helps improve employee satisfaction with work and pay as well as individual performance	Rewards individual performance, not group performance
	Depends highly upon a sound performance-appraisal system
Rewards performance rather than seniority or skills	Clashes with organizational emphasis on tenure
Clarifies performance expectations	De-emphasizes intrinsic work rewards while possibly discouraging "average" and "below average" performers
Attracts and retains highly motivated employees	

As is the case with any reward system, merit pay must be compatible with an organization's culture and philosophy if it is going to be effective. For example, merit pay will not work for an organization that values tenure over performance. Also, merit pay may be inappropriate for a growing number of organizations that are trying to emphasize group performance instead of individual performance. By rewarding individuals, merit pay can help undermine the cooperation and interdependency that are needed in a team environment. However, it may be possible to preserve the best elements of a team environment while rewarding the highest-performing individuals by integrating group-based incentives with some form of merit pay system.

Merit pay will not work unless an organization has a sound system of measuring individual employee performance that is accepted by the work force. Even if a good performance-appraisal system exists, merit pay may be discouraging to "average" or "below average" employees, who typically will fail to qualify for high pay raises. By tightly linking pay and performance, merit pay also can de-emphasize the intrinsic rewards and satisfaction gained simply from doing a job.

By linking a merit pay program with a sound communications strategy, an organization can clarify its performance expectations and create an atmosphere of trust between employees and management. This atmosphere tends to increase overall employee satisfaction with work and pay, and it is likely to lead to improved individual performance.

The main reason an organization chooses a reward system is to enhance its competitiveness, productivity, and bottom-line results. Positive financial results are more likely when an organization places emphasis on employee performance instead of tenure, and highly motivated employees are more likely to be attracted and retained when their efforts are rewarded regularly. A merit pay system can help ensure that an organization's rewards policy fits the performance-based philosophy it needs to survive and prosper.

LINKING RESULTS AND COMPETENCIES TO BUSINESS STRATEGY

A performance management system functions as a management tool to help ensure that employees are focused on organizational priorities and operational factors that are critical to the organization's success.

Most organizations operate from business strategies that include critical, measurable success factors. These may include:

- Financial success (e.g., return on investment, return on sales).
- Productivity (e.g., cost per labor hour, units per day).
- Quality standards and customer service (e.g., customer satisfaction scores, waste and reject indices).
- Work environment (e.g., attitude survey scores, employee grievances).

An organization's critical success factors form the basis for key result areas for the measurement of organizational, department, team, and individual performance. Key result areas define what is to be accomplished (e.g., the job's end results, which in turn reflect the job's primary purpose) and generally are defined as key responsibilities, one-time or periodic projects, or annual objectives. Examples of key result areas are:

- Types and proofreads department correspondence and reports.
- Researches leading practices in the area of real estate acquisition.
- Develops and implements a new purchasing management system.

In addition to key result areas, an organization may include the identification of competencies that focus on *how* results are to be attained.

Competencies generally are defined as the knowledge, skills, and abilities exhibited by individuals as they work to accomplish key result areas. Competencies may be developed universally for the organization, for job families, or for individual jobs. Competencies often are selected to reflect an organization's values and may include some or all of the areas listed in Figure 14.12. These factors should be included in the performance management process and used as input when evaluating performance at the end of the assessment period.

While using competencies, it is important to identify specific behaviors associated with them. For example, associated behaviors for teamwork may be communicating openly with others and achieving win-win solutions while working with peers. Generally, organizations identify 5 to 10 competencies to focus employees on key organizational priorities.

If an organization has developed comprehensive performance measures that are evaluated and used regularly to manage overall organizational performance, these measures should be included in the system so all employees can focus their priorities and energies on these strategies. For example:

- If an organization has established a company-wide quality or customer service performance measure, it should be incorporated into individual performance plans at all levels.
- If teamwork is a key organizational value, the performance management system should hold each employee accountable for behaviors identified with teamwork.

FIGURE 14.12 Examples of competencies.

Teamwork

Achievement orientation

Customer service orientation

Relationship building

Analytical thinking

Developing others

- If maintaining a positive environment and high employee morale are organizational priorities, managers should be held accountable for the environment and the morale in their work units.

DETERMINING THE PERFORMANCE MANAGEMENT CYCLE

Any performance management system is an ongoing cycle. For most organizations, the typical performance period cycle is one year, although this period may vary depending on business cycles and probationary periods for new hires, promotions, and transfers. The cycle also may be determined by the link to organizational measurements of success. For example, if financial measurements are included in the system, the performance cycle may be tied to the fiscal cycle. If an employee is involved in a project team with specific target dates for various stages, the performance management cycle may reflect the project's schedule.

The design team should consider the typical performance management cycle within the organization. This cycle is likely to consist of three phases: planning performance for the upcoming period, coaching performance and giving feedback throughout the period, and evaluating performance for the just-completed period.

Phase I: Planning Performance for the Upcoming Period

Planning performance for the period includes defining key results for each position as well as establishing performance standards against which key result areas are measured. The design team should consider the most appropriate approach to conducting the performance planning process, focusing on the roles that will be played by HR, immediate supervisors, and employees.

In many organizations, HR will be responsible for working with line management to devise a framework for developing key result areas and performance standards. HR also typically is responsible for developing training materials to communicate the approach to line management and employees and for training line management and employees in the performance planning process. After training has been completed, HR often works with line management to ensure that performance plans are developed appropriately. This function also may be accomplished by appointed performance planning teams that include employees from all levels of the organization who have been trained to help facilitate the performance planning process.

Because the performance planning process requires detailed knowledge of job responsibilities and performance expectations, line management should play a significant role in the process and be ultimately accountable for the performance plans of their employees.

The advantages of having managers and/or employees define key results and establish performance standards each period include:

- Managers and/or employees can structure each job to the individual's and the department's best advantage, increasing flexibility in what is measured.
- Managers and/or employees are more knowledgeable about their department's day-to-day needs.
- Job responsibilities and standards can be modified to reflect special projects or assignments for the period.

At the same time, HR can play a key role by providing coaching and training, and by ensuring consistency of key results and standards throughout the organization.

Typically, each position should list 5 to 10 key results that support the organization's business strategy. If more results are listed, they no longer are likely to include only "key" results of the job. If fewer results are listed, the full scope of responsibilities may not be closely defined.

In most cases, all key results do not have equal impact on the job. It is common practice to assign a weight of importance to each key result based on impact, frequency, and relative significance to the overall list of responsibilities as well as to the department and the organization. Weights may be determined informally and discussed when planning performance for the period. Weights also may be assigned to each key result using:

- Percentage weighting (adding up to 100 percent).
- Numerical weighting (1 = highly significant, 2 = significant, 3 = moderately significant, 4 = insignificant, 5 = highly insignificant).
- Word descriptions (critical, important, etc.).

The design team should decide how weighting will be handled, keeping in mind both the organization's culture and the desired goals of the system. Results that best meet the organization's overall goals generally should be assigned the greatest weight.

Phase II: Coaching Performance and Giving Feedback throughout the Period

An important step for the design team involves the concept of open, honest, positive, two-way communication between supervisors and employees throughout the period. The goal of a performance management system should be to improve employee performance, not to find an easier way to terminate an employee for poor performance. Therefore, a system should emphasize coaching and feedback from the supervisor as well as feedback and input from the employee throughout the performance period.

The design team should plan structured feedback throughout the period, including mid-period, quarterly, or monthly progress reviews. A more structured feedback approach works especially well for poorly performing employees who require more frequent monitoring and coaching. Feedback, which should include constructive criticism, should be offered in a private, formal setting. In addition, the system should encourage supervisors to give informal feedback throughout the period. This is especially true for positive feedback, which may include a pat on the back or even a brief suggestion to "Try doing it this way next time." Employees should be encouraged to ask for frequent feedback from their supervisors.

Phase III: Rating Performance for the Just-Completed Period

One of the most challenging aspects of developing an individual performance management system is developing the approach for rating employee performance. When identifying an approach, it is important to focus on the characteristics of the organization and the objectives of the performance management system. For example, a traditional hierarchical organization tends to focus on judging employees' past performance. An organization oriented toward total quality management might focus less on judging past performance and more on strategies to improve future performance.

PERFORMANCE RATING APPROACHES

The number of categories in the rating scale probably is one of the most controversial issues in performance management design. On the one hand, the more levels of performance that are identified, the more accurately performance may be evaluated. For example, rating an employee on a scale with five performance levels (e.g., consistently exceeds expectations, exceeds most expectations, meets expectations, does not meet most expectations, does not meet any expectations) seemingly differentiates performance more accurately than does a three-point scale (e.g., exceeds expectations, meets expectations, does not meet expectations). On the other hand, how does one objectively differentiate performance at each of the five levels?

If one is measuring units of production in a factory or words typed per hour, objectively identifying performance at all five levels may be possible. However, in a service-based work environment, it often is not feasible to implement performance standards at five levels. Evaluating performance then becomes the subjective judgment of the supervisor, and it is difficult to communicate so that employees understand the performance expectations at different rating levels.

For example, within a manufacturing operation in which five performance levels may be appropriate, making five units per hour may be considered level-five performance, making four per hour may be considered level-four performance, and so on. When evaluating performance in this environment, there is little or no interpretation as to the performance rating that should be given.

However, in an environment in which it is difficult to compare performance against established standards, such as a service or white-collar environment, the question is whether it is acceptable for supervisors to make subjective judgments among the different levels of performance. Furthermore, although most supervisors believe they can make this differentiation, they find it virtually impossible to communicate these distinctions to employees in a way that employees can understand and accept. For example, if one of an administrative assistant's responsibilities is to make travel arrangements through a travel agency, how will a supervisor identify and communicate the five levels of performance so they will be accepted by the employee?

In addition, it is a common perception among employees in most organizations that it is unacceptable to be rated more than one level below the top rating. In fact, supervisors often rate employees one level below the top to minimize conflict and avoid spending a significant amount of time attempting to justify the performance rating. For example, in the five-point rating scale, a rating of "meets expectations" has the connotation of "average" and would generally be perceived as unacceptable, even though it is acceptable. Because of these perceptions and an increasing focus on improving future performance, the trend is toward using fewer rating categories when using rating scales—in many cases, as few as three. With the three-point scale, only one level of performance falls above "meets expectations" or acceptable performance.

When determining ratings levels, it is important to focus on definitions that compare performance to performance expectations, such as "consistently meets expectations" or "frequently exceeds expectations." It is equally important to avoid ratings that compare employees, such as "average" and "above average."

Many organizations today favor not only fewer performance rating levels, but also nonquantified ratings systems. Although it may be tempting to view performance management as an objective and precise process that can be weighted and scored, in most cases it is a subjective process based on supervisors' judgments that are difficult to communicate. Many organizations have concluded, therefore, that performance management systems should include rating levels that are fewer in number and that are qualitative.

Using Summary Ratings

The design of a summary rating should focus on the objective of the system. With that in mind, the design team may consider three options:

- *Summary point scores.* In a weighted and scored system in which the rating of each key result is assigned a number (consistently exceeds expectations = 5, exceeds most expectations = 4, meets expectations = 3, etc.), the overall rating is a point score. The issue, then, is to convert the overall point score back into a rating category.
- *Summary labels.* If the purpose of the system is primarily to judge past performance, and if the method for evaluating performance is fairly objective, then the use of rating categories, or "labels," may be appropriate. These labels may be the same as those used to rate each key result: "consistently exceeds expectations," "exceeds most expectations," "meets expectations," and so on.
- *Summary statements.* To reduce the subjectivity of performance management systems and increase the focus on continuous improvement, organizations have tended to move away from rating categories or labels toward summary statements that are behavior oriented and more focused on future improvements. For example, suppose Joe's performance occasionally fails to meet expectations for the job. Joe meets most standards and exceeds one of them, but he needs to increase his typing speed. This overall level of performance is acceptable this year because Joe is a new employee; however, he will be expected to increase his output next year. Assuming most employees generally meet performance expectations, it is much easier for the supervisor to focus on strategies for improving future performance when there are no summary labels. With this approach, the challenge for supervisors is to communicate the performance evaluation clearly to employees so there are no misunderstandings when employees are—or are not—considered for promotions or transfers, or when they are terminated for poor performance.

Employee Responsibility

The role of the employee is an important aspect of the evaluation process. As organizations flatten and the scope of supervision expands, it becomes increasingly difficult for supervisors to interact with employees to judge performance. Looking at this situation along with organizational initiatives to empower employees, the design team should consider the extent to which employees may be involved in the evaluation process. This involvement may include:

- Evaluating their own performance.
- Completing a self-evaluation that includes identifying development plans and career objectives.
- Gathering performance-related information.
- Scheduling evaluation sessions.

Employee involvement in performance evaluations can facilitate the evaluation process. If used as part of a multirater assessment process, employee involvement can allow supervisors to function more as coaches and less as judges of performance.

MULTIRATER ASSESSMENT

One question for the design team to consider is who will rate performance. In an organization focused more on developing future performance, that development includes a high degree of involvement by those other than the supervisor, including the employees themselves. Under these circumstances, a technique known as multirater assessment, "360-degree feedback," might be used. With multirater assessment, employee performance evaluations are compiled by several—usually five to nine—people who come in regular, direct contact with the employee, including peers, internal and external customers, supervisors, and subordinates. Most important, employees are able to evaluate their own performance.

The advantage of the technique is that the larger number of sources of evaluative input is likely to provide a more complete, well-rounded picture of the employee's performance, and employees often view this picture as more credible than single-source assessments conducted only by the supervisor. (See Figure 14.13.)

The disadvantage is that the process involves greater administration to collect, compile, and distribute feedback while ensuring the anonymity of evaluators and the confidentiality of results. Because one rater who deviates from the others can significantly affect an employee's evaluation, many organizations opt to discard the highest and lowest ratings before compiling results. Furthermore, it can be helpful to provide feedback to raters who deviate significantly from others so they may modify their techniques and provide more consistent evaluations in the future. With a

FIGURE 14.13 Advantages of using multirater assessments.

Some Users Perceive Multirater Assessment as More:
- Fair: less rating inflation, less adverse impact on diversity, and more process and technology safeguards
- Accurate: less bias and more balance
- Credible: more believable because of respect for the opinions of multiple work associates
- Valuable: more specific feedback and greater distinctions among performance criteria
- Motivational: more encouragement for constructive behavior change because of peer pressure and the desire to be recognized by the team.

multirater system in place, supervisors can assume greater roles as performance coaches rather than acting simply as performance judges.

Although research has indicated that it is possible to obtain more objective performance feedback from multiple sources, the design and implementation of a multirater feedback system often depends on the level of employee trust that the feedback will be handled confidentially and that it will be used appropriately. Many organizations begin by providing performance feedback only to the individual employee; during this time, the system is focused on improving performance rather than rating performance. Once an appropriate level of employee trust has been established, the multirater system can evolve so both supervisors and employees receive the information. Both can use it for evaluating performance and providing feedback for individual development. (See Figure 14.14.)

LINKING PERFORMANCE MANAGEMENT AND PAY DELIVERY

When designing a performance management system, the design team should consider whether and how the system will be linked to employee compensation or to the determination of pay increases. Traditionally, an overall rating—either numerical or a rating summary—has been developed that determines a pay increase from merit guidelines. Although this approach directly links performance and pay, it may cause budget overruns unless the guidelines are based on an analysis of past performance-rating distributions. Supervisors may tend to overrate employees' performance to justify larger merit increases for them.

When there is a direct link between the performance evaluation and merit pay increases, especially when the two are done at the same time, the performance evaluation system is likely to be perceived as part of the pay system. The evaluation often is focused on the "judgment" of past performance instead of on a positive discussion of an employee's strengths and weaknesses and on how performance should be developed in the future. Furthermore, management may lower performance ratings in some cases to ensure that merit increases do not exceed budget, which obviously causes negative reactions from employees.

One solution may be to separate performance appraisal ratings and pay increases by de-emphasizing the "judgment" aspect of point scores or overall rating labels and shifting to a narrative statement that summarizes overall performance. The performance appraisal may be further separated from the pay increase by changing the timing of the two activities or by changing the appraisal and pay cycles. For example, the performance evaluation may be given on each employee's anniversary date and pay increases may be given on a common date, perhaps based on the fiscal period.

Another solution may be to provide a merit budget to department heads and require them to allocate pay increases to their employees on the basis of relative performance. Department heads then have to determine who their top performers are in order to allocate merit money without exceeding budget.

Because a performance management system is most useful when it is used to manage performance, organizations need to consider carefully how pay will be linked to a performance rating as well as the impact this linkage will have on the operation of the performance management system. If the primary objective of the system is to determine ratings for pay increases, the system should be designed to differentiate performance levels. Organizations that are more interested in using performance

FIGURE 14.14 Sample multirater evaluation questions.

Rater #1	EVALUATION		
	Not Satisfactory	Satisfactory	Highly Satisfactory
COMMUNICATION SKILLS			
Keeps others informed of specific issues affecting them	1	2	3
Listens attentively to others	1	2	3
Participates effectively in meetings	1	2	3
DEVELOPING SUBORDINATES			
Provides subordinates with detailed performance feedback on a regular basis	1	2	3
Empowers subordinates by delegating responsibility and authority whenever possible	1	2	3
Provides subordinates with the resources needed to get the job done	1	2	3
LEADERSHIP			
Leads by example	1	2	3
Considers customer/client satisfaction to be a top priority	1	2	3
Challenges people to extend themselves to the fullest	1	2	3
PROBLEM SOLVING AND DECISION MAKING			
Is open to new and creative suggestions when solving problems	1	2	3
Analyzes situations to get to the root causes of problems	1	2	3
Develops step-by-step solution to problems	1	2	3
KNOWLEDGE AND TECHNICAL COMPETENCE			
Keeps up to date with developments in his/her field	1	2	3
Is knowledgeable about a number of fields related to his/her specialty	1	2	3
Is expert at performing the specific tasks and technical skills required of his/her job	1	2	3

(Rater #2 and Rater #3 evaluation forms appear stacked behind Rater #1.)

management as a tool to develop their employees may want to separate the performance management and pay delivery systems to prevent either system from having a negative impact on the other.

Although performance may be an important factor in determining pay increases, there may be other contributing factors such as the rate at which salaries are increasing in the marketplace, internal equity factors, or an employee's position within the salary range. When the two systems are directly linked, employees may assume there is a one-to-one relationship between performance and pay and not recognize the impact of these other factors, which is often difficult to communicate to them. A pay system may be designed to target an employee's pay at a certain position within the salary range that is consistent with the employee's contribution to the organization. For example, employees who consistently meet expectations may have their pay targeted toward the middle of the salary range while employees who consistently exceed standards may have their pay targeted toward the top. Once employees reach the middle of the range or the market value, future increases may be limited, or they may be delivered as variable pay in lump sums.

In general, the design of the performance management system should be compatible with the pay delivery system philosophy and should support that philosophy. At the same time, how performance management is linked, or not linked, to pay will send a strong message to the work force about organizational priorities and values. The decision as to how performance management and compensation will be related should not be made lightly.

15 Cash Bonus Plans and Recognition Programs

In today's high-performing organizations, total rewards professionals are charged with supporting the attainment of corporate objectives through the development and implementation of strategies, which ensures that key employees feel valued and rewarded for their efforts. For rewards professionals focused on creating attraction and retention programs, cash bonuses are effective tools and remain among the most frequently used variable pay plans.[1]

Used correctly, a cash bonus can be a quick, easy, and valuable tool to promote employee satisfaction and commitment. But, used incorrectly, it can be a waste of precious dollars and a source of discontent in the work force.

Cash bonus plans—specifically sign-on, referral, spot, and retention bonuses—can be designed to reward performance and behaviors that are tied to the company's bottom line, instilling pride in the organization. Employers readily implement these tools to communicate a fresh commitment from the employer to the employees and remind employees how much they are appreciated.

Each of these bonus vehicles is highlighted below and discussed in detail.

WHAT IS A SIGN-ON BONUS?

A sign-on bonus is a premium compensation incentive that is given up front and is not based on performance. It is useful in marketing the company to large numbers of potential candidates to motivate them to apply for job openings and for recruiting talent that is in high demand, especially in technical and scientific professions. In fact, competitive practices in certain industries and locations may all but require that an upfront bonus or other inducements be included in compensation packages for candidates with high-demand skills or key talent requirements, such as R&D engineers.

Even in today's volatile economy, companies still need to sweeten the compensation pot to entice desirable candidates. With the reduction of the use of stock as a sign-on tool, many companies increase the use of a cash bonus as a bargaining tool.

The signing bonus can enhance the compensation package without distorting the salary structure, thereby averting the internal compression and equity problems that sometimes result from escalating salaries in a competitive marketplace. Such a bonus often can help employers avoid higher, ongoing fixed compensation costs. It also can be an effective vehicle for attracting attention and securing an initial willingness to join the company.

When money talks, people frequently listen. Companies often use a sign-on bonus as their final trump card in negotiating an employment agreement with the right job candidate. Of course, their main concern is how much they should offer as a sign-on bonus.

SIZE OF SIGN-ON BONUS

The amount of the bonus varies based on the job position and level in the job hierarchy. Sign-on bonuses are designed to encourage a new hire to take a position as soon as possible. For example, for companies in urgent need of employees with specific skills and expertise, the hiring manager may say, "If you say 'yes' and can start work in one month, we will give you an extra $5,000." In another example, a hiring manager may say, "If you stay with the company for six months, you will receive an additional $5,000."

A sign-on bonus provides extra impetus to get employees on board for difficult-to-hire positions and/or help with relocation expenses.

Will all employees in a specific employee group receive the same amount for a sign-on bonus? It depends on the scenario, taking into consideration the difficulty in recruiting the best candidates for the position. In the following cases, the sign-on bonus may be outlined in a bonus policy:

- When the job candidate requests a salary that is above the maximum, and a sign-on bonus may make up the difference.
- When senior management says, "Pay whatever it takes to get the desired candidate on board."
- When the job prospect has a comparable position at another organization in the industry and needs to be lured away.
- To help mitigate the financial loss a potential employee would incur by walking away from a plan with his current employer.

On the other hand, if a job candidate has been laid off and desperately needs employment, the company may offer a sign-on bonus less than originally anticipated or not at all, thus saving money for the organization.

The well-designed signing bonus can do triple duty as:

- A recruitment device.
- A performance incentive.
- An equity or equity-like vehicle.

Treated in this manner, the sign-on bonus serves as a retention tool by motivating and directing the new hire's performance and creating an ownership stake in the business. To accomplish these goals, organizations should take a look at the design features for signing bonuses:

- *Payout period.* Configure the bonus as a restricted grant with retention features. Pay only a portion of the bonus at the time of hire. Additional payouts can be made in 6- or 12-month increments, conditional upon continued employment over a one- to three-year period (depending upon level of the position and bonus size). The size of incremental payments even can be "back-end loaded," with larger amounts payable later in the restriction period for maximum retention value.
- *Payout criteria.* Configure as a performance incentive by providing a "kicker" to the "baseline" payout amount if the employee achieves, within a specified time frame, performance goals or other measurable contributions linked to the critical skills for which he or she was hired.
- *Payout vehicle.* Use restricted stock awards in combination with cash payouts sufficient to cover income tax obligations on the stock award to both increase the retention and create a sense of ownership in the enterprise. If actual stock is not available, a simple form of equity simulator can be used to replicate the performance of stock.
- *Size of bonus.* Because the new hire carries a greater risk of not getting full payout on a hiring bonus with this configuration, payment being contingent upon several outcomes, the size of the bonus may need to be somewhat higher than levels typically used. However, this incremental cost will more than pay for itself by assuring that the company spends the money only in return for the desired outcomes.

This configuration reinforces long tenure, high performance, and alignment of high-demand employees' values with those of the company. It also results in greater perceived equity on the part of other employees, since some portion of the bonus now stands at risk, being paid out only upon "delivery" of specific results (continued employment and performance contributions).

CLAW BACK CLAUSE

Consider this scenario: An employee receives a sign-on bonus at the time of employment and then leaves the company within six months. What can a company do if the employee agreement was for 18 months? How should the payment amounts be structured?

The key question is the legality of the employment agreement and what recourse provisions are available. To counter the perils of the signing bonus, some companies attach restrictions to the bonus, usually in some form of service requirement ranging from six months to two years. Companies can leverage this strategy in three ways:

- Require a specified period of service before the payment of the signing bonus.
- Prorate the repayment of the bonus if a specified period of service is unfulfilled.
- Make bonus payments over a specified period of time.

First, the company needs to look at the alternatives and consider the use of a claw back clause. A claw back clause stipulates that employees must pay back all or a portion of the bonus if they don't stay at the organization for a specified period of time.

When a company offers a sign-on bonus, it has the option to:

- Pay the bonus up front with no claw back clause.
- Pay the bonus up front and include a claw back clause.
- Pay one-half of the bonus at the time of hire, include a claw back clause in the employment agreement, and pay the remaining half after one year of service (or some other specified period of time).

ALIGNING THE SIGN-ON BONUS WITH TOTAL REWARDS

More than economic inducements are necessary to assure that these employees develop and sustain a commitment to the company. Other companies will continue to lure coveted employees away. The intrinsic motivators—commitment and loyalty—are the best defense against the extrinsic rewards any courting company can offer.

Building employee commitment requires a company to understand the key drivers or commitment and be willing to modify or tailor its interactions with its work force to activate and reinforce those drivers.

As companies continue investing dollars to enhance their success in recruiting people with high-demand skills, they also should examine how they are performing on the higher-order issues affecting commitment and retention of all employees. Otherwise, companies may find they have wasted time and money on unhappy employees who quickly exit for the next signing bonus or remain in the organization unmotivated to optimize their contributions or unable to achieve their potential.

Attracting candidates with hiring packages that are sweetened with signing bonuses will not be a successful strategy unless the total offering is in line with the values of the target audience. Therefore, organizations may want to consider structuring and integrating the signing bonus with other elements of a total rewards package to create an effective motivational framework for the new hire. This also ensures the company's return on its higher investment in the critical-skill employee.

EXECUTIVE SIGN-ON BONUS

A company may use hiring bonuses to entice executives into accepting employment by compensating them for concerns that are not related to specific job qualifications or experience, such as relocating into less-desirable geographic locations or for accepting a lower initial base salary, offsetting the loss of annual incentives or invested stock awards, or simply for agreeing to accept the position.

Golden Hellos

The latest aspect of executive pay to come under the microscope is upfront payments to newly hired chief executives. These so-called golden hellos are a twist on the signing bonus, which has been around for decades. The upfront payments are not linked to performance and appear to be getting bigger and more prevalent. Upfront payments are made in cash, stock, additional contributions to supplemental retirement plans, or in a combination of forms.

POTENTIAL PITFALLS

Using signing bonuses to attract critical-skill employees may produce a short-term effect at best and, when used alone, may result in a relatively low return on investment. A sign-on bonus does not guarantee a loyal and committed employee.

Newly hired employees may leave the company after a short tenure to accept an offer at another organization for yet another signing bonus or higher salary. Or they may stay, but never fulfill their promise in terms of high performance and significant contributions to the business. In either case, a company is left with little or no return on its investment and with disgruntled existing employees who did not receive a sign-on bonus and view these "no strings attached" bonuses as giveaways. With one or two bad experiences under their belts, companies are beginning to examine the effectiveness of signing bonuses.

Although sign-on bonuses are great recruiting tools, there may be some drawbacks. Employers need to take the good with the bad in offering sign-on bonuses, taking into consideration possible resentment among existing employees, extraneous expenses such as relocation costs, return on investment, and taking a risk with a new employee.

Causes Resentment among Existing Employees

Sign-on bonuses can have a negative effect on the company's current employees. New hires may be receiving the same rate as someone who has been there six months or a year. Employees may think that if new candidates are being offered what they are earning, there is no incentive for them to stay.

Relocation Expenses

Another issue job candidates may have to deal with is substituting a sign-on bonus for relocation expenses. These two issues should be addressed separately. If many candidates are competing for positions in the organization, they will drive the sign-on bonus market down.

Lack of ROI Data

Return on investment (ROI) is difficult to measure, for example, for call center reps who have little or no experience in the business. Call volume drives the hiring of call center reps—the company needs to get warm bodies in chairs as orders increase. A company may decide to pay lower-level employees one-half of the bonus up front, and the remaining half after six months.

Taking a Risk

For higher-level positions, a claw back clause usually is included in negotiating the employment contract and, as explained earlier in this chapter, comes in handy when an employee leaves the company before a specified period of time and must return part or all of the funds received as part of the sign-on bonus. Engineers usually have impressive resumes, and it generally is understood by both parties (employer and employee) that the incumbent is capable of delivering a certain level of performance.

COMMUNICATING THE SIGN-ON BONUS

For any recruitment tool to be effective, communications should run up and down the corporate ladder. Total rewards professionals should continually communicate to upper management for their initial buy-in and to keep them sold on it. The HR department and anyone else involved in the recruiting process should be aware of the details of the sign-on bonus, since it is a powerful attraction incentive.

The sign-on bonus is just one recruitment tool available to the hiring manager to be used in the negotiation process. When the recruitment process comes down to a few final candidates to fill the positions, that's the time to pull out all stops, sell the company perks to potential employees, and dangle the sign-on bonus carrot in front of their nose. If it's enticing enough, you'll have job seekers chomping at the bit.

Although the hiring manager should be aware of the availability of a sign-on bonus as an attraction tool, it often comes down to the discretion of HR and the compensation manager to determine the dollar amount of the bonus and incorporate it in final employment package negotiations. Regardless of who crafts the employment offer, use of a sign-on bonus should be kept strictly confidential for higher-level and professional employees. However, the sign-on bonus should be made public to recruit lower-level employees.

WHAT IS A REFERRAL BONUS?

Companies are realizing that the best way to recruit new talent is through referral bonus programs with current employees. A referral bonus is an incentive for employees to go out and make an extra effort in looking for a good job candidate. Companies have long recognized that referred job candidates usually are better employees because quality people know quality people.

If every employee knows how to articulate the company's mission, business drivers, and values, they can give strength and breadth to the recruiting force. And paying out a decent referral bonus can cost considerably less than months of professional recruiting and agency fees.

Companies are turning to more creative and progressive recruiting and retention strategies to appeal to job candidates and create differentiation from their competitors. A critical aspect of recruitment is to have "curb appeal" for the specific demographics of potential incoming employees. Beyond the basic of competitive compensation, companies need to offer benefits that appeal to the specific age groups, genders, cultures, and lifestyles of their current and target work force, for example, leave benefits, education, development, and work-life effectiveness. And who but an employee can more accurately convey the total picture of a company to a possible job candidate?

If you give employees the opportunity to make referrals, they automatically suggest high-caliber people because they are stakeholders in the company. There's a stronger sense of ownership when employees refer candidates. Cost-effectiveness is a primary benefit of implementing an employee referral program.

If you want to improve an existing employee referral program or start a new one, you should first ask the following questions:

- How much money does the company spend now on the total recruiting costs?
- Could the company reduce some cost areas and improve the quality of hires?
- Are you using outside agencies instead of your own internal headhunters?
- How many hires does the company expect the employee referral program to produce?
- What cost-per-hire numbers would you like to minimize in your overall recruiting program?
- What metrics will be used to measure the impact of employee referrals?
- How will you track the employee referral program costs versus ROI?

The answers to these questions will help you build a budget for referral bonuses or reallocate money in the company's existing salary budget.

How do companies get their hands on the most effective advertising for a job? Many companies will use a "hire-by-source" or "media effectiveness" measure, which simply is counting up applicants and determining where they came from. Over a period of time, a company can figure out where it's getting the most value for its dollars and eliminate or restructure those avenues that aren't paying off.

Even though companies tighten their budget belts in response to economic uncertainty, referral bonus programs typically are not cut. Companies realize how important it is to both preserve and build human capital in good times and in bad. For high-level employees, referrals are a lot less costly than bringing in a headhunter or recruitment firm.

ELIGIBILITY

In most companies, only employees in certain levels of the organization are eligible to participate in the employee referral bonus program. Other employee referral programs are unusual in that all employees, regardless of their position within the company, are eligible for the cash awards, including vice presidents and higher. HR professionals also may be included, as long as they are not directly involved in any part of the recruitment process for a specific job. (See Figure 15.1.)

TIMING OF CASH AWARD DISTRIBUTION

The time when a cash award is paid to a referring employee also varies among employers. For example, because turnover is high among call center personnel, payments usually are stretched over a year's time. The payments, however, are "grossed up" so employees actually receive a total of $1,000 after taxes have been applied. The first payout is made 30 days after the referred employee's start date. Other incremental payouts are made based on the new employee's length of service, such as at 90-day, 6-month and 9-month intervals. The final payment is made when the referred employee is employed for one year.

Often, time is of the essence. When the payout is immediate, employees obtain a real sense of gratification. Another company may pay 50 percent of its referral cash award on the day a new employee starts work. The remaining half is paid when the new employee reaches 90 days of service. Other companies do not give the referral bonus until the employee has been employed for a specified period of time, such as 2 weeks, 1 month, or 90 days. There's a drop-off in interest if the referring

FIGURE 15.1 Sample referral bonus policy.

Introduction: Beginning January 1, 2008, BioKing will implement an Employee Referral Bonus Program. This program will pay eligible associates a bonus amount for referring an applicant for hire to BioKing. If the applicant is hired, the associate will be eligible for a bonus between $500 and $1,500, depending on the referral position.

Bonus Amounts: The amount received by the associate will be between $____ and $_____ based on the position being filled. The associate will receive half of the bonus after the candidate has worked for 30 consecutive days, and the other half after the candidate has worked for 180 consecutive days.

Eligibility: In order for the associate to be eligible to receive a referral bonus, the associate must be employed with BioKing for 180 consecutive days and must be currently employed on the date the bonus is distributed.

The referring employee will not qualify for a referral bonus if the applicant was a former employee or contractor of BioKing.

The referring employee must be actively at work, on benefit time, or on authorized leave at the time the referred applicant submits his/her employment application and on the referral's start date to be eligible to receive the referral bonus. Also, the referring employee must be actively at work, on benefit time, or on authorized leave at the time the bonus is paid.

Process: The associate must inform Human Resources, using the Employee Referral Form, prior to the candidate applying for the position with BioKing. Human Resources will then track the candidate through the hiring process and, if hired, will trace the candidate for bonus purposes. After the candidate has been employed for 30 consecutive days, Human Resources will distribute a check for one-half the bonus amount. After the candidate has been employed for 30 consecutive days, Human Resources will distribute a check for the remaining one-half portion of the bonus amount.

Taxes: The referral bonus is considered taxable income. The bonus payment will be included as part of the employee's regular paycheck and taxed at the employee's W-4 rate. The bonus will be noted on the employee's check stub as "referral." The bonus amounts will be distributed as a lump sum and will be subject to both federal and state taxes, possible higher than current payroll taxes.

Length of Program: This program will be reviewed periodically and may be cancelled at BioKing's discretion.

employees have to wait 90 days to receive an award payment. Whatever the timing, administration is critical: Pay when you say!

PROMOTING AN EMPLOYEE REFERRAL PROGRAM

Here are some handy guidelines for promoting a referral program internally:

- *Create a theme.* Spending the time and money to create a themed program provides unexpected advantages and promotes employee interest. A catchy name, accompanied by an identifiable character, is an attention-grabber.

FIGURE 15.2 Sample referral bonus rules.

Any employee, except a manager or director of the executive team, is eligible to participate in the referral bonus program. If you would like to refer someone to BioKing, send an e-mail message to human resources. This e-mail notification must precede receipt of a resume or other expression of interest by the candidate. Your e-mail message should include the name of the person you are recommending for employment; how to contact this person; and your recommendations about the nature of the contribution you think this person could make to BioKing.

BioKing receives more applicants than we can employ. As an employee referring another person for employment, it's important that you understand that we value your referral, whether or not a candidate you refer is immediately offered a position. Your referral reflects positively on your status at BioKing. We recognize that personal relationships often are involved in referrals. As such, BioKing will ensure that all applicants are treated with professional courtesy as well as with sensitivity toward your contribution.

A candidate may offer valuable skills for which BioKing does not have a current job opening. BioKing's hiring needs are continuously changing. As a result, candidates who are not immediately hired may eventually be offered a position. In this instance, the referring BioKing employee still may be eligible for the referral bonus at the time of hire.

Candidates who are referred through this program will be treated in a manner consistent with other job candidates. The selection process will be consistent, and evaluations will be made on the basis of merit. Regular team members who refer candidates will not be involved in the selection process for that candidate. This clarification will be made to the candidate, as well.

A $500 bonus will be paid on the first day following the 90-day anniversary of the new employee.

- *Keep employee referral programs alive and kicking.* This is one of the biggest challenges employers face. Informing participants of the status of their referrals and keeping the benefits of the program highly visible are key components to the program's success.
- *Post a list of job openings.* A list of current job openings with corresponding referral bonus rates posted in an employee lunchroom or other prominent location will spark interest and serve as a reminder that the bonus program is alive and kicking.
- *Publicize successful hires.* In many companies, all employees, with the exception of recruiting staff and senior personnel, are eligible to participate in the referral program. An all-staff e-mail announcing the new hire and the referring employee will fuel continued interest in the program.

Use the company newsletter or intranet to publicize the referral program.

- *Keep the program rules simple.* (See Figure 15.2.) Complex submission rules will discourage employee participation. Create guidelines that are easily understood, but make sure you address problematic issues, such as how to deal with a situation in which two employees claim to have referred the same candidate who is ultimately hired.
- *Document each referral.* You can reduce potential problems by time-stamping each resume, accompanied by the referral information. Keep data that list the

FIGURE 15.3 Sample referral bonus form.

Effective Date:

Directions: To be eligible to receive a referral bonus, employees need to submit a completed Employee Referral Form to Human Resources prior to the candidate's application for a position with BioKing.

Date of Referral: _____

Your Name:_____

Your Title:_____

Your Work Phone:_____

Name of Applicant:_____

Title of Position Applying for:_____

For Office Use Only

Date Received:_____

Received by:_____

Did the referral result in a hire to the position in question? ____ Yes   ____No

Hire Date:_____

First Payment of $_____, distributed on _____

Second Payment of $_____, distributed on _____

Date Completed:_____

---

referring employee, the date, the job candidate's name, a copy of the resume and application, and a copy of the referral form. (See Figure 15.3.)

- *Add pizzazz to job postings.* Spice up written job postings with savvy and style. Give employees easy access to openings and job descriptions.

Kick off the employee referral program with an annual company-wide event.

- *Use frequent giveaways to boost communication.* Build program awareness with posters, T-shirts, water bottles, desk calendars, or other small items, in addition to regular cash awards. Even e-mail can help build awareness.

- *Offer bounty bonuses.* Boost the referral bonus for especially difficult-to-fill positions.
- *Establish appropriate payout guidelines.* Stipulate when referring employees will receive their referral bonus for recruiting new employees (e.g., upon date of hire or three months from date of hire). An additional award also could be made contingent upon the recruited individual remaining employed with the company beyond some specified period (e.g., one year).
- *Build momentum.* Offering prize drawings on a quarterly basis is a popular tool. The number of referral submissions will climb when a prize is being offered, such as a hotel stay or gift certificates.
- *Introduce the referral program to employees at the new-hire orientation program.* Many employers use this opportunity to communicate more thoroughly about employees' recruiting efforts. Follow-up information can be included via the paycheck envelope or through a separate mailing to the employee's home.

WHAT IS A SPOT BONUS?

A company can applaud employee performance by awarding a spot, or recognition, award. A spot award is intended to acknowledge and demonstrate immediate and spontaneous appreciation and recognition for the exceptional contribution of individuals or teams. Recognition rewards usually are relatively small and are given at the time of achievement.

In most cases, managers typically can give spot awards based on direct observation and/or feedback from others of exceptional effort or exceptional results. They might come in the form of a cash award, a thank-you note, movie passes, sporting event tickets, dinner vouchers, etc. An outstanding accomplishment by an individual or team may warrant monetary reward and recognition above and beyond a company's regular pay and bonus programs. Larger rewards usually are bestowed at a formal recognition event or ceremony. For all intents and purposes, this book will focus on *cash* spot bonuses.

In the high-flying days of mid-2000, companies were eager to award spot bonuses to quality employees for fear that they may jump ship. Now, with the job market easing and money tighter at many companies, organizations still see the importance of rewarding top performers for a job well done to keep them around. Companies that have tightened their salary budget belt find that when pay increases aren't feasible, a spot bonus is an affordable option that makes an employee feel valued and appreciated.

Spot bonuses award employees for a "job well done" and have stayed in vogue because of their direct link of showing employee appreciation. They serve as motivational tools to inspire high-level performance.

At management's discretion, employees are recognized for making material contributions to a project or task that adds value to the organization, for example:

- Meeting or exceeding project goals and expectations ahead of schedule.
- Increasing productivity and efficiency.
- Cost-saving ideas implemented.
- Improvements in the quality of teamwork.
- Excellent customer service.
- Effectively handling a particularly complex and/or sensitive issue.

Employees also can be recognized for:

- Performance.
- Productivity.
- Safety.
- Sales.

There are many reasons to offer a spot bonus, but equally important are the business drivers, which may include:

- Using it as a recruiting tool to demonstrate a performance culture to prospective employees.
- Rewarding positive contributions to product or service quality.
- Recognizing improvements in productivity.
- Positively impacting morale and loyalty to the organization.
- Retaining qualified employees by providing spot bonus recognition.

The most common strategies of recognition programs are:

- Rewarding employees for making exceptional contributions above and beyond their daily job functions.
- Strengthening employee morale.
- Increasing retention.
- Tying performance to the company's mission.

SIZE OF SPOT BONUS

Spot bonuses are nonbase pay and generally range from $50 to $250. However, some spot bonuses aren't just a few extra bucks in the employee's paycheck—many companies regularly award between $1,000 and $2,500 for a job well done. For executives and upper management, awards greater than $10,000 are not uncommon. The amount awarded should be commensurate with the achievement or contribution. The presentation of the award should be personalized and made as soon as possible following the employee's accomplishment.

SPOT RECOGNITION PROGRAM GUIDELINES

Spot bonuses have elements that fit with both a formal and informal recognition program. A spot cash bonus provides immediate recognition much like an informal program but still has definitive structure like a formal program.

A spot recognition program is relatively easy to implement, and training time is minimal for participants. Simply follow these eight easy steps:

Step 1: Define the program's purpose. This does not have to be a complicated defined purpose but should state simply what the program is trying to accomplish. For example: "The purpose of the informal recognition program is to recognize those actions by employees that can be readily observed and immediately rewarded."

Step 2: Determine who will be eligible. All employees usually are eligible to participate in a spot bonus program. Generally, administrative staff and possibly department directors are excluded. Some organizations also exclude temporary, casual, and contracted employees from the program.

Step 3: Establish monetary and program guidelines. The recognition should be meaningful, but also stay within established program boundaries: For example, recognition should be given only for performance considered over and above established standards (e.g., excellent customer service); cash bonuses will not exceed $1,000 for any recognition event; the program will not duplicate any current total rewards program.

Step 4: Establish program expectations. The expectations should be built around areas where the organization is seeking to make improvements. Examples include customer service, organizational morale, team development, productivity, and personal development. The following expectations are an example and are not as well defined or developed as what is generally seen in a formal recognition program.

- Increase management visibility with employees and provide them with a tool to reward positive work performance.
- Provide a positive work environment that recognizes employees for their contributions.
- Gratify employees who will feel good about their work and contributions.
- Recognize those employees who provide exceptional customer service.
- Encourage similar performance by the employee in the future.
- Recognize those employees who provide meaningful contributions to the organization.

Step 5: Define what behavior and actions are eligible for recognition. The following bullet points are the types of behavior and actions that would warrant recognition. The difference between these behaviors and those listed in the spot recognition policy (see Figure 15.4) is that managers still have some discretion when using an informal approach to recognition.

- Behavior or action that resulted in a compliment from an internal or external customer.
- Employee exceeds expectations on a project or work assignment.
- Employee displays an unusual cooperative spirit in working with other team members or with other work areas.
- Employee's actions enhance the organization's image.
- The manager/supervisor observes the employee engaging in actions that will improve morale or enhance the organization's image.
- Employee goes above and beyond the call of duty without being asked to do so.
- Employee makes a work improvement or changes a process that will increase productivity or efficiency.
- At the supervisor's discretion, any action that in her/his estimation adds significant value to the organization should be recognized.

Please note that it is often difficult to define exactly what will be rewarded. Often, it is easier to define what is *not* rewarded, for example, not awarding a spot bonus to an employee who is doing his job as expected.

Step 6: Identify exclusions, if appropriate.

Step 7: Establish who has the ultimate responsibility for administering the program (i.e., human resources department, recognition committee, program coordinator). What approval processes, if any, need to be followed? When approval is granted, the timing of awarding bonuses is critical.

Step 8: Establish the program procedures and guidelines that will be used to recognize an individual. The recognition should reflect what is important to the organization's culture. For example, if the culture is mature and conservative, a more traditional approach, such as certificates of appreciation and cash awards, may be more appropriate. In younger organizations, departmental parties, gift certificates, and other types of public recognition may be needed. What works best for your organization?

FIGURE 15.4 Sample spot recognition policy.

Policy Statement: It is a policy of BioKing to provide a spot cash bonus to reward employees immediately for exceptional performance or who provide exceptional customer service. The recognition committee is responsible for coordinating the spot recognition program.

Purpose: The purpose of the spot recognition program is to reward employees immediately. The monetary value of spot recognition awards can be as high as $1,000. Awards of $50 or less do not require approval.

Definition: Employees will be recognized for meaningful contributions that exceed expected levels of performance, which are detailed in the employee's job description and/or the employee's performance evaluation. Spot recognition should be timely and immediate and encourage similar performance or behavior in the future.

Eligibility: All employees, with the exception of department directors and higher-level positions, are eligible for the spot recognition program.

Eligible Actions/Behavior: The following guidelines should be used to determine if the performance or behavior qualifies for spot recognition:

The employee's performance exceeded normal expectations for the job.

The employee's action(s) or behavior(s) enhanced the organization's image.

The employee's action(s) or behavior(s) delighted a customer.

The employee's action(s) or behavior(s) exceeded the supervisor's expectations.

The employee's action(s) or behavior(s) exhibited an entrepreneurial/intrapreneurial spirit in resolving a problem or handling a customer concern.

Exclusions: (1) If the employee is already being compensated or rewarded for the performance or effort, the employee will not be eligible for spot recognition, for example an employee who agrees to work an alternate work shift and receives additional compensation for working the shift; (2) The employee performs a duty that is expected or that is not beyond normal work expectations, for example directing a customer to the appropriate office for service.

Program Guidelines: (1) Any employee can nominate or recommend another employee for spot recognition. The recommendation can be presented to the employee's supervisor or to a member of the recognition committee. (2) A customer also can recommend an employee for spot recognition. (3) The supervisor/leader will present the recognition to the employee. (4) The recognition should be documented and sent to the Human Resources Department for inclusion in the employee's personnel file. (5) Items that can be used for spot recognition can be obtained from HR.

Be careful to monitor the culture for the department or work team that may be significantly different than the organization's culture. The supervisor should identify those unique characteristics present in their work area and work with the recognition committee to build an effective recognition program.

HOW TO EFFECTIVELY USE SPOT RECOGNITION

A spot bonus program should effectively align with the organization's business strategy. This only happens when the program is built on trust and credibility. Informal programs can be severely impacted if it becomes an approach used on a "hit-and-miss" basis. It should be consistently applied and continuously communicated to employees. Informal recognition programs have five basic principles:

- *Acknowledge and recognize employees in a timely manner, using specific and concrete examples of the positive performance.* Employees want to know what they did right. They also want to be able to receive recognition in conjunction with the contribution. This adds value to the employee and to the achievement.
- *Bridge the recognition with organizational goals and business strategy.* If the recognition is not focused on the organization, it will appear disjointed and unimportant to participants. The message to employees should be that the organization values their contributions and wants them to be a partner in meeting goals. For example, excellent customer service is often a focal point for the organization. When employees are recognized for good customer relations skills, it emphasizes that customer service is valued and appreciated by the organization.
- *Center the program on the organization's culture and values.* As discussed previously, this means matching recognition with the culture.
- *Develop positive performance skills in employees by recognizing their achievements.* The recognition should reinforce positive work behavior.
- *Enlist support from all program participants.* The recognition should focus on how to keep the program meaningful and still meet the needs of all participants.

These principles provide a foundation from which to administer a successful program. The following obstacles should be avoided if the program is to be taken seriously by employees and other key stakeholders.

POTENTIAL PITFALLS

The following obstacles should be addressed up front to ensure that the program does not stall. The last two bullet points, in particular, should be scrutinized since they often are responsible for the program's long-term failure.

- Inconsistent and infrequent application of the program.
- Failure to match the reward with the achievement.
- Failure to adapt the recognition to the individual's preferences.
- Poor communication by the supervisor/leader with the employee.
- Person doing the recognition has a low level of trust and credibility with employees.
- No clear definition of what actions/behaviors are being recognized.
- Lack of understanding by participants of what the program is trying to accomplish.
- Failure to communicate tax implications of some rewards.
- Inadequate time allotted by the supervisor/leader when recognizing the individual.
- Failure to keep the program fresh and fun.
- Lack of enthusiasm for the program by participants.

CONDUCTING THE RECOGNITION EVENT

According to Ken Blanchard and Spencer Johnson in *The One-Minute Manager,* "You can never over recognize, the more you recognize people, the more productive they'll be." If this is true, why do so many leaders avoid recognizing employees? The problem is that leaders are uncomfortable telling employees that they did a good job. The recognition event is the cornerstone of the recognition process. The leader should be fully prepared when communicating the recognition to the employee. The following guidelines should be used to plan and communicate the recognition to the employee.

- Select an appropriate time and place.
  - Individual meeting. Use this approach when the employee does not like public recognition.
  - Departmental meeting or group setting. Use this approach to publicly celebrate the recognition.
  - Hold meeting at the beginning of the workday. This allows the employee to feel good all day.
  - Allow enough time to appropriately recognize the employee.
  - Recognition should be as immediate as possible.
  - Avoid negative locations when conducting the recognition. Some examples include the supervisor's office, the employee's work area, or a public location.
- Document the recognition if possible.
  - Use a congratulatory citation, thank-you card, or certificate of recognition.
- Communicate the recognition brightly and clearly.
  - Choose positive statements to communicate the recognition (e.g., "I appreciate the long hours and quality of work you put into this project," as opposed to, "This certainly was better than the last project you were assigned").
  - Use nonverbal cues that positively reinforce the recognition.
  - Maintain eye contact with the individual.
  - Use positive facial expressions such as smiling to indicate approval.
  - Use an open body stance.
  - Warmly greet the individual with a firm handshake.
  - Voice tone should communicate positive reinforcement.
  - Avoid sighing and long periods of silence.
  - Maintain a moderate pitch level.
- Be specific about the achievement.
  - Provide clear and specific facts and examples of why the individual is being recognized.
- Encourage input from the employee.
- Leave something tangible with the employee.
  - Thank-you card.
  - Cash award.
  - Gift certificate.

If at all possible, the recognition should be done face-to-face by the supervisor/leader. In this electronic age, some leaders like to use the Internet and e-mail to recognize employees. The recognition's impact may be less in those cases. Some of the guidelines would still apply for electronic recognition. The key to electronic recognition is to personalize the recognition and use active verbs to indicate excitement and enthusiasm to the reader. After completing the recognition event, document the specific achievement and the recognition event.

DOCUMENTING RECOGNITION

A well-documented recognition event helps the leader link it with the employee's performance evaluation. The documentation also is important to employees when they are seeking a promotion or job transfer. An employee who has a history of being recognized as an outstanding performer will have an easier chance of moving up in the organization. Documented recognition reinforces and encourages the employee to repeat his/her outstanding performance. It is a template for employees to use for future work behavior.

- Focus on specifics.
- Cite the performance standard or organization goal that was exceeded if appropriate.
- Describe in detail the achievement: Who was involved? List the names and individuals involved. What happened? Describe exactly what the employee achieved that was extraordinary.
- When did the achievement occur?
- Where did the achievement occur?
- Why is this event being recognized (e.g., exceeds a departmental goal, an example of exceptional customer service)?
- Comments of appreciation by the individual giving the recognition should be included in the documentation.
- Date the recognition was given should be documented.
- Indicate type of recognition approach used, if appropriate.
- Provide a copy of the documentation to the employee.
- Place a copy of the recognition in the employee's personnel file.

COMMUNICATING THE SPOT PROGRAM

Employees, senior leadership, and the board of directors should be kept apprised about how the program is doing. A summary of program usage should be provided to senior leadership and to the board of directors, including the following elements:

- Total number of employees recognized with spot bonuses.
- Program costs.
- Impact on organizational morale, if known.
- Impact on customer satisfaction.
- Impact on productivity if it can be tied to recognition.
- Impact on attraction, retention, and employee development.

Who Does the Recognizing?

Often, the dollar amount of the spot bonus corresponds with the level of the individual who will recognize and honor an employee with a spot bonus. For smaller bonus amounts, a manager or supervisor may bestow the honor (and the check). For larger spot bonuses, department heads, directors, or the CEO may be involved.

LEGAL AND TAX REQUIREMENTS

A lump sum may be paid out as a one-time payment or in the employee's regular paycheck. Spot bonuses are subject to all federal and state taxes as income, and are not included in the base rate for nonexempt overtime calculation.

Determining Tax Liability

There are a number of Internal Revenue Service (IRS) and federal regulations that govern recognition programs. The regulations governing spot bonus programs focus on the following criteria:

1. *Cash awards.* Programs granting a direct cash award are always subject to direct taxation.
2. *Nominal value of the noncash award.* The IRS determines the definition of nominal value. Currently, this definition is unclear and unresolved by the IRS. Proposed guidelines (i.e., Section 274–8(c)(5)(ii)) state that $50 is nominal value for tax purposes. To be eligible for exclusion at all, the award should be given under the guidelines established by a written plan or program in any given year. If an award is defined as nominal, it can be excluded from the total award costs used to determine the average cost per recipient. The average cost per recipient determines the tax liability of the plan and cannot exceed established IRS limits.
3. *Qualified versus nonqualified.* According to the Internal Revenue Code, a qualified plan is an employee achievement award that is awarded as part of an established written plan or program that does not discriminate in favor of highly compensated employees (Note: This is currently set at an annual income of $85,000 or more). An employee recognition program will not be treated as a qualified plan for any taxable year if the average cost of all employee award programs provided by the employer during the year exceeds $400 per recipient.
4. *Written versus nonwritten plans.* Written plans have more favorable tax treatment and meet the criteria established for qualified award plans. Nonwritten plans generally are not given favorable tax treatment unless the value of the award has a "de minimis" benefit value.

Legal Compliance

The biggest compliance challenge in developing recognition programs is that many of the plan designs closely resemble existing employee benefits plans. For example, tying recognition to specific payout formulas could result in additional legal compliance problems. While there certainly is nothing wrong with granting cash recognition or tying it to a payout formula, the cash is not only subject to taxation but also to certain pay laws, such as the Fair Labor Standards Act (FLSA).

According to the FLSA, any nondiscretionary bonus paid to nonexempt employees needs to be included in calculating the regular rate for determining overtime compensation. A nondiscretionary bonus is an incentive or bonus paid out based on predetermined formulas, established criteria, or based on a stated performance goal.

Discretionary bonuses are not based on predetermined criteria or prior agreement. Such bonuses represent payments made at the sole discretion of the employer.

FIGURE 15.5 Rules for developing written communications that comply with regulatory guidelines.

- *Develop written criteria.* What is the program's purpose? Who is eligible?
- *Identify program exclusions.* What performance or behavior is excluded from recognition? Identify expected performance standards, if appropriate.
- *Determine monetary limits for the program.* Identify de minimis awards. Establish dollar limits for cash and noncash awards. Clearly identify formula-based limits.
- *Clearly spell out the procedure for taxing awards.* Identify under what conditions the award will be taxed, if appropriate.
- *Identify areas of legal compliance (if appropriate).* FLSA overtime requirements. Regulatory reporting requirements, if appropriate. Federal, state, and local regulations, if appropriate.
- *Identify the types of awards.* Cash awards, noncash awards, tangible recognition items, intangible recognition, formal, and informal programs.
- *Develop procedures for conducting recognition.* How can the employee be recognized? Who can recommend the employee for recognition? Document the recognition event and specify award ceremonies (formal or informal presentation).
- *Identify Responsible Parties.* Identify persons responsible for overall program administration. Who is responsible for conducting the recognition event? Who is responsible for program review and approval? Who is responsible for resolving program complaints and concerns?
- *Establish a sunset provision.* What is the program review process? A sunset provision establishes under what conditions the program will be continued or terminated. For a formal recognition program, which is built around cash or awards with significant tangible value, it is important to review them at least annually. Informal programs that have de minimis or intangible awards generally do not need a sunset provision. These programs can be discontinued at any time.
- *How frequently is the program reviewed?* Under what circumstances can the program be terminated or continued?

Although such bonuses are taxable, a discretionary bonus is not included in overtime calculations. (See Figure 15.5.)

It is important to design written communications that meet the intent of the law but also can be easily understood by all participants. All communications should be reviewed before sending them to employees. Once the program is in writing or a policy format, employees can use it against the organization in the case of a legal challenge.

Legal and tax requirements should not be a deterrent to implementing a spot bonus program. Most recognition approaches require generally few regulations. The organization should be more concerned about successfully communicating the program. If the program is successfully communicated, then employees and supervisors will see the program as an important tool in the workplace.

WHAT IS A RETENTION BONUS?

A retention bonus is a contractual promise to pay an employee a certain dollar amount upon the occurrence of a specific event or date. Retention bonuses have become popular vehicles used by buyers or sellers to retain critical employees during a transition period, such as a merger or acquisition. These compensation arrangements are highly varied, with monetary rewards ranging from a few extra weeks of severance pay to hefty multiples of six-figure salaries. The employees covered by these plans can be limited to top executives or extended throughout the ranks. The individual circumstances and requirements surrounding each transaction drive rewards levels and eligibility. (See Figure 15.6 for sample guidelines.)

Maintaining a business during transitional periods, whether it's a spin-off, acquisition, merger, turnaround, or reorganization, is a difficult task when key employees decide to pursue greener pastures. Retention rewards should be large enough to entice key employees to stay through the transition. Employees should be assured that they will receive total payout even if they're laid off.

The company needs to ask: What operational issues will we face if key talent leaves? In most cases, it's too expensive in cash and time to hire other top performers to fill those newly vacant positions during a transition and, besides, top performers are hard to find. But when money talks, nobody walks. Retention bonuses can make an organization's dollars speak volumes.

In the environment of mergers, acquisitions, and divestitures, designing and staging compensation programs to hold key staff can be exciting as well as tension filled. Well-crafted plans can avoid undue stresses on negotiations and can sometimes be a key factor in consummating the deal. A well-designed retention plan can:

- Keep the current business operating.
- Maintain employee focus.
- Control customer defections.
- Manage Wall Street and investor perceptions.
- Motivate employees when incentive plans no longer are achievable.

BUILDING A BUSINESS CASE

But simply offering more money to employees isn't always the answer. Few employees will remain loyal if you're simply correcting outdated compensation practices or if you fail to provide other nonmonetary incentives such as continuing education credits, onsite day care, health club memberships, flexible vacation policies, and so on.

Nevertheless, bonuses can be an important element in a comprehensive retention strategy. A retention program that delivers monetary payouts needs an underlying strategy that is linked to an anticipated outcome (e.g., spin-off, acquisition, merger, turnaround, or reorganization). A retention program should be supported by upper management, marketed to key stakeholders, and tied directly to business goals.

The board of directors needs to understand the importance of a good retention plan, particularly when it comes time to discuss cost. The argument becomes cost versus value and, if the board sees value in a retention plan, it's easier to digest the associated cost. After the board realizes the retention plan's value, the CEO and senior management team need to develop the retention strategy. Business unit leaders should establish specific goals and measurements, then communicate those up and down the employee line.

Next, HR and the finance department should collaborate to develop the awards and payment schedule, which will be sent to the board for approval. Finally, it's time to define a "key" employee.

FIGURE 15.6 Sample retention bonus guidelines.

Introduction

Retention bonuses are an available tool for retaining employees critical to BioKing. They are especially applicable during facility shutdowns, divestitures, mergers and acquisitions, and other periods of organizational restructuring, but also may be used, as necessary, in support of regular ongoing operations. Retention bonuses must be approved by the appropriate management function and are to be paid using business/functional operating funds.

Note that during periods of organizational restructuring the primary retention tool remains the applicable Severance Benefits Program (SBP). Thus, use the retention bonus policy only when the SBP is not likely to apply or is deemed unlikely to be effective (generally due to the short tenure of the employee and a corresponding SBP amount that is relatively nominal). These guidelines describes the following:

- When to use a retention bonus.
- When *not* to use a retention bonus.
- Guidelines on award size.
- Bonus payout procedure.
- Nomination process.

When to Use a Retention Bonus

Retention bonuses should be used on a highly selective basis and only when the following two criteria are satisfied:

- Retention of the employee is **critical** to the business/function.
- The employee is **vulnerable** to leaving the company.

Critical employees are typically those who: (a) possess skills absolutely vital for completing an activity essential for the company (e.g., plant shutdown; merger-related transaction, etc.); and (b) could not be readily replaced with other employees or available outside talent should they decide to leave the company before their necessary work is completed.

Vulnerable employees are those who, without some intervention, are likely to leave the company. The particular situation creating this vulnerability can vary, but most often is related to outside employment opportunities or personal/family reasons that have been divulged voluntarily by the employee to company management. *Note: Employees eligible for a significant severance benefit, should their jobs be eliminated, usually would not be considered vulnerable as these employees would be expected to stay until their last day of work in order to be eligible for severance benefits.*

Also note that the retention bonus is generally intended to retain employees for a relatively short period (typically one year or less) and in most cases the employee is unlikely to remain with the company after the retention period. Longer-term retention where continued employment with BioKing is likely is more appropriately treated through career development and, if necessary, the special recruitment, recognition, and retention stock option program.

When *Not* to Use a Retention Bonus

Because retention bonuses should be used sparingly, it is useful to provide a few examples that illustrate when a retention bonus generally would *not* be appropriate.

Example 1 (The SBP Case): A highly skilled and experienced engineer with 20 years of BioKing service is critical to an essential facility shutdown and has highly marketable skills. This employee, while critical, would normally not be considered vulnerable due to eligibility for a severance award equal to 80 percent of his or her annual base pay.

Example 2 (The Multiple Employee Case): During a merger integration, including the reorganization of the legal function, three attorneys who are likely to lose their jobs due to the reorganization are critical to completing the merger transaction. All possess highly marketable skills. Two are long service, but the third attorney has only been with the company for two years. Although the natural inclination of some managers might be to provide retention bonuses to all three employees, it is generally only appropriate to provide the short-service employee with the bonus. This is because the two long-service employees would not be considered vulnerable due to their eligibility for significant severance benefits under the terms of the SBP.

Example 3 (The Project Completion Case): A team of software programmers is key to a major computer systems project. After the project, the employees on the team likely will return to their existing jobs within the company or be assigned to another project. While it is critical that the team be retained for the project's duration, a team-based project completion bonus tied to project milestones probably is more suitable than a retention bonus. This is especially true given that the employees likely will remain with the company after the project is completed.

Example 4 (The Long-Term Retention Case): The company would like to retain longer term a research scientist with key skills; there is no ongoing restructuring and no immediately critical project or activity. Rather than a short-term retention bonus, the more appropriate treatment in this case is through career development and potentially a special stock option award.

Guidelines on Award Size

The business/function can determine the size of the retention bonus. This determination should be based on consideration of the guidelines outlined below.

- In most cases the award size should be based on: (1) an assessment of the criticality and vulnerability of the employee; and (2) the duration of the retention period. The assessment of vulnerability should include consideration of the current labor market.
- A guideline for retention bonuses is one month's salary for each month of the retention period. However, this is just a guideline and variations for business reasons may be necessary.
- Human resources leadership within each business/function should monitor the size of retention bonuses to ensure that the criteria for determining award sizes are consistently applied. For example, two employees who both need to be retained for the same time period where both are deemed to be equally critical to the business and equally vulnerable to leaving the company should receive the same size retention bonus.
- The retention bonus should be expressed as a multiple of the employee's base salary; the maximum award is 12 months' base salary.
- An employee may receive more than one retention bonus (e.g., if the original retention period is extended), but under no circumstance may receive total retention bonus awards of greater than 12 months' base salary.

Bonus Payout Procedures

- Payment is to be made at the end of the retention period and is to be paid from business operating funds.
- The retention bonus is forfeited if the employee resigns or is terminated for cause or performance-related reasons prior to the end of the agreed upon retention period *(please see the Retention Bonus Agreement for a full explanation of this provision)*.

(continued)

FIGURE 15.6 *(Continued)*

• If the company decides to shorten the retention period after the period begins, the employee is entitled to the full agreed-upon retention bonus, unless the company's decision is based on performance reasons as noted above.

Nomination Process

1. Candidates should be nominated by the HR business manager and approved by the appropriate leadership council member.
2. The HR business manager forwards a copy of the completed Retention Bonus Questionnaire via e-mail to the law department. The questionnaire should include a statement of the rationale for the bonus and indicate that the appropriate leadership council member has approved it.
3. The law department will develop a Retention Bonus Agreement and return it to the submitting HR business manager for the appropriate signatures. Employees will have five business days to sign and return the agreement.
4. The HR business manager returns the signed original Retention Bonus Agreement to the law department and retains a copy for HR records.

These guidelines are not a contract, and may be modified or eliminated at any time by the company.

The company needs to identify which employees it wants to retain, clarify how the company will retain them, and discover what the organization needs to retain them. It is critical to define key talent because they are the experienced employees who keep the company running. The "who" and "how many" have to be tied to the business plan. So, although an employee may do an excellent job, that doesn't mean management should rush to offer him or her a retention bonus.

Industry experts place the cost of replacing an employee between one and three times the incumbent's annual salary. When you figure in the cost of recruiting and training a replacement, not to mention the financial impact of delaying an important project for lack of expertise, it often seems smarter to shell out the extra bucks for the talent you already have on hand.

Instrumental in Meeting Organizational Goals

Well-designed bonus plans can help the organization meet retention goals. For example, the vice president of research and development tells the head of research and development that if the team meets its operational goals and also introduces another product into testing within a certain time period, then the company will award each team member $750. They achieve the goal, receive the bonus, and are publicly recognized, which motivates them as a team. Team-based rewards reflect the achievement of the group and encourage top performers to interact with others to achieve mutually desirable goals.

Combating Turnover

When a valued employee is offered a hefty increase at another company, what should the employer do? To convince him to stay, the manager can entice the employee with a raise and reassign him to a more interesting project. Often, the employee will consider the money a nice gesture, but will jump at the chance to get back on the career track that was originally promised.

The bonus may buy a few more months of the employee's time before another employer lures him away with a further increase in pay, a more attractive locale, and the promise of more exciting projects.

Monetary rewards cannot stand alone. Critical and hot-skills employees will go where the pay is best and where they think they can get continued skill-building. If you can't create an environment that combines all those attractions, it very difficult to keep and even recruit people, no matter how much money you throw at them.

Offering bonuses often is a knee-jerk reaction to turnover. But outdated compensation aside, turnover is often a sign of other underlying problems, such as ineffective managers, limited opportunities for professional growth, and a hostile corporate culture. If you want to attract and retain good people, don't forget the fundamentals. In addition to fair compensation, you have to create an environment that nurtures career development.

RETENTION BONUS Q & A

How does a retention bonus differ from a severance plan?
The key difference is that a severance payment is only payable upon termination of employment. A true retention bonus is payable regardless of whether the employee remains employed following the scheduled payment date. An employer may choose to combine a retention and severance program so that an employee who remains employed through the closing date of a business transaction, for example, will be entitled to a retention bonus as well as a severance payment if thereafter terminated.

Who should be covered?
Most retention bonus plans are limited to officers, managers, and/or key technical personnel, particularly in fields where there are severe labor shortages. Executive change-in-control agreements cover top officers and senior management. Retention bonuses cover large group of employees that are not at risk due to a change in the structure of the business. Few retention bonus plans cover all employees. Often, retention bonus plans will be coordinated with other severance compensation agreements. Because retention bonus plans are not subject to ERISA and do not receive any special tax treatment under the Internal Revenue Code, such plans are not subject to any nondiscrimination rules and employers may pick and choose among those individuals eligible for the benefit.

Does a retention bonus plan or policy have to be in writing?
An employer may choose to enter into individual agreements or adopt a broad-based policy. If the latter approach is undertaken, then the employer should coordinate the policy with any individual agreements. For example, the retention policy should make it clear that any person who has an individual agreement would not be entitled to benefits under the general policy unless the employer intends to the contrary.

How much should be paid and how should that amount be determined?
An employer has unlimited discretion to determine the amount of the retention bonus to be paid to an employee. Typically, the bonus amount is determined as a percentage of the employee's pay, with the percentage increasing over time. Alternatively, an employer may choose to pay a flat sum amount, which may or may not differ depending upon the employee's employment classification.

Examples

In the context of a deferred signing bonus, an alternative to lump sum payment upon the attainment of a certain date may be to impose a graded pay-out schedule similar to a graded vesting schedule used in the context of qualified retirement plans. For example, the retention bonus could be structured based on the following schedule:

Period of service	Percentage of retention bonus paid
Fewer than three months	0 percent
Three months to six months	25 percent
Six months to one year	75 percent
One or more years	100 percent

An employer also may choose to apply different percentages depending upon the employee's employment classification (for example, executives may be entitled to a retention bonus of 75 percent of pay, mid-level management employees 50 percent of pay, and all others 25 percent of pay).

In the context of a business transaction, the retention bonus may be determined as follows:

Time to closing or completion of project	Percentage of retention bonus paid
Within six months	50 percent
Six months to one year	75 percent
More than one year	100 percent

Other alternatives to consider are an employee's years of service and/or the sales price of the transaction.

What form of payment?

After specific employees have been identified to receive a retention bonus, the next step is to determine the retention amount for each employee level. The majority of retention bonuses are paid as lump sum cash payments. Some companies, however, use staggered retention payments to sustain peak performance over a critical period. In the case of a business transaction, payment may be made in installments if the employee is required to remain employed beyond a closing date. The obvious advantage that the installment method has over a lump sum payment is that the former approach has an additional built-in retention incentive because each installment would only be paid if the employee were employed on the scheduled installment payment date.

In some cases (most typically with respect to senior executives), stock options also may be awarded as part of the retention bonus with the option becoming exercisable following the closing.

What conditions need to be met before payment is made? should there be any exceptions?

There are two critical conditions to payment of benefits. First, payments should always be conditioned upon the satisfactory performance of the employee's service. In that regard, the employer may want to include a definition of "termination for cause" as part of the bonus agreement. Second, the employee must be employed on the scheduled payment date. An exception may be made to this latter condition if the employee is discharged without cause or, in the case of a business transaction, if the transaction fails to close. In either case, the employer may choose to pay a reduced bonus.

Other Conditions.

As an additional condition of payment, an employer may choose to include a confidentiality provision and/or noncompete agreement. If the retention bonus is combined with a severance plan, the employee also may be required to execute a release and waiver of claims.

ERISA Implications

A retention bonus plan is generally exempt from the Employee Retirement Income Security Act of 1974 (ERISA) by virtue of the fact that it constitutes a "payroll practice" rather than an employee benefits plan. However, if the plan in practice results in the deferral of income to termination of employment or additional retirement income (for example, the employer offers a retention bonus to only those individuals who are age 60 and expected to retire on or around the time the bonus is to be paid), the retention bonus plan may be an ERISA plan. In addition, if the retention bonus plan is designed and implemented in connection with a severance plan, then the plan may be an ERISA welfare benefits plan (not a pension benefits plan). The consequence of being an ERISA plan is that the employer will have additional disclosure, reporting, and fiduciary obligations. One advantage of ERISA status is that a court may apply a deferential standard of review with respect to any decision or interpretation of the plan made by the plan's administrator, provided that the plan specifically reserves the exclusive power of interpretation and construction to the administrator.

An ERISA-covered "employee pension benefits plan" includes any plan, fund, or program that is established or maintained by an employer or employee organization to the extent that such plan, fund, or program provides retirement income or results in a deferral of income by employees for periods extending to termination of employment or beyond [ERISA § 3(2), 29 U.S.C. § 1002(2)]. The Department of Labor regulations provide that such term does not include payments made by an employer to some or all of its employees as bonuses for work performed unless such payments are systematically deferred to the termination of covered employment or beyond or so as to provide retirement income to employees [29 C.F.R. §2510.3–2(c)].

When should you offer retention bonuses and how much?

In special cases like plant closings, retention bonuses (with a tie to performance) are effective. Target employees, such as IT people, who are at risk. Their value changes rapidly and they also tend to be less tolerant when career growth slows. If the company does not want to pay retention bonuses, it has two other options:

- In lieu of retention bonuses, ask an outside consultant to assess who is underpaid and/or at risk. Adjust employees' pay accordingly and do a quarterly update to ensure that you maintain competitiveness.
- Assume that some degree of turnover is natural and prepare "backfill" bench strength for each key position. Make it a requirement that every position has a trained replacement ready in case of a termination.

POTENTIAL PITFALLS

Poorly designed retention plans can backfire, delaying negotiations or killing the merger, acquisition, or turnaround deal. If the situation is poorly handled from the start, it tends to set off a domino effect of negative consequences that can severely disrupt the affected business unit. For example, key management may jump ship, morale may decrease, and productivity may decline.

Retention bonuses usually work, if they are large enough, to keep targeted employees on board. Unfortunately, there could be some unintended consequences:

- The company retains an employee who really doesn't want to be there, but couldn't refuse the handsome retention bonus.
- The retained employee enjoys ultimate job security. The company now can't fire this highly paid person and everyone else knows it.
- A retention bonus doesn't motivate the employee to continue performing at a high level.
- The retained employee will use company time to prepare for his next job.
- A retention bonus cultivates resentment between the employee who received one and those who didn't.
- Some employees will prolong their stay at an organization in hopes of receiving a retention bonus. Unfortunately, their productivity levels are likely to be low in the interim.
- Paying people for staying sends a message that performance doesn't matter. If the wrong employees are retained, they may add little value after the merger.
- Retention bonuses do not require unhappy workers to be quiet. They will still complain.

COMMUNICATING THE RETENTION PLAN

Discretion should be applied in communicating bonuses. A step-by-step communications plan should be created and implemented to ensure the success of the bonus program. The following steps are essential for establishing a successful plan:

- Who will be affected?
- What is going to be communicated?
- What are the tax and legal implications?
- Where are the stakeholders located who should be aware of the program (multiple locations, all work shifts, specific departments, etc.)?
- When do employees and other key stakeholders need to know the information?
- Why do employees and stakeholders need to be informed? Is the program a new component of the total rewards program?
- How will the organization communicate the program to employees and key stakeholders?

CASH BONUSES IN THE TOTAL REWARDS MIX

In examining the make-up of the WorldatWork total rewards model in Chapter 1, it is easy to assume that cash bonus plans fall under the compensation portion of the model. And, given the general nature of these plans, they obviously provide compensation to employees. Cash compensation is critical to attract and retain the desired quality of employees requisite to support the company's business strategy. However, it also should be obvious that cash bonus plans play a role in the performance and recognition component of total rewards. By being an incentive tool that builds a sense of company pride in employees, cash bonus plans are an important part of a company's culture and provide recognition to employees and groups who accomplish their goals.

Even sign-on bonus plans, which would not seem to have a connection to a company's culture, affect that culture indirectly. By attracting individuals to work for a company, sign-on bonuses are an essential foundation in building the culture because they are part of employees' first impression of the company.

The total rewards philosophy is based on the premise of making every aspect of working for a company rewarding to an employee. By ensuring that an employee takes home enough pay to live a decent life, has a benefits plan to account for any health issues, and enjoys work-life effectiveness, companies can build a reputation as a place where people want to work. This is an important distinction for companies striving to fill their ranks with qualified employees.

Referral bonus plans play directly on that philosophy by rewarding current employees for bringing in qualified people who fit in with the philosophy, drive, and attitude of the company. In a nutshell, the employee is rewarded for bragging about the company and convincing someone else that it's a great place to work. Partnered with a sign-on bonus for the new employee, the bonus plans work full circle in building company commitment.

16 Equity-Based Rewards

Many U.S. employers rely on equity-based rewards to inspire their employees to reach new heights of performance. Based on existing company practices, equity-based rewards account for much of the marked increase in executive pay, and many employees still participate in stock option plans despite the less favorable accounting treatment that is the result of sweeping regulatory changes, which will be covered later in this chapter.

Equity rewards take many forms. Within the total rewards package, some companies consider equity to be a form of compensation and others consider it to be a benefit. For the purpose of this chapter, we will cover equity rewards under both umbrellas.

- *Compensation.* Some equity rewards are used as long-term employee incentives, which are a form of variable pay. Equity rewards that may be considered compensation include stock options, stock awards/grants, and stock alternatives.
- *Benefits.* Some types of equity rewards are used for the purpose of providing income protection, assisting employees with wealth building and retirement planning. Examples include employee stock purchase plans (ESPPs), retirement plans such as employee stock ownership plans (ESOPs), and other defined contribution plans. Equity-based rewards programs are more likely to be considered benefits programs when they are tax-qualified and cover a broad employee population.

BUSINESS STRUCTURES

The types of equity-based rewards used by different organizations are highly dependent upon the business structure under which organizations operate. Some organizations do not have equity (stock) to use for these programs. Some of the more commonly known business structures are as follows:

- *Sole proprietorship.* The sole proprietorship is the simplest structure, with one individual owning the company. For legal purposes, the individual and the company are the same, with the individual accepting liability for all of the company's debts and declaring the income from the company as personal income. Although a sole proprietorship does not have stock, it may use certain stock alternatives (discussed later) to reward employees in a manner similar to other equity-based programs.
- *Partnership.* A partnership is similar to a sole proprietorship from a legal standpoint as the owners (partners) share in the profits and losses and are personally liable for the debts of the business. The partnership does not issue shares to represent ownership
  - *General.* Two or more owners share in the operation and finances.
  - *Limited.* Limited partners may invest in the partnership, but limits are set on their role in the operation and liability for the debts of the business.
- *Closely held company.* A closely held company may have stock that is not publicly traded. Regarding equity-based rewards, some closely held companies may use stock alternatives or offer ESOPs.
  - An *S corporation* is a corporation that passes the taxes through to the owners, as if it were a partnership. It can have no more than 75 shareholders.
  - A *limited liability company* (LLC), permitted in some states, is a combination of a partnership and a corporation. Unlike a partnership, the owners of the LLC are considered a different legal entity from the company, limiting their liability. This business structure enjoys some of the same tax advantages as an S corporation, although it is not subject to S corporation IRC requirements.
- *Publicly held corporation.* A publicly held corporation has stock that is traded on a public exchange or "over-the-counter." The owners of publicly held companies are the shareholders, who, for legal purposes, are considered a separate entity from the company, limiting their liability to their investment in the company. Publicly held corporations have the greatest flexibility and number of alternatives related to equity-based rewards. The majority of the information in this chapter focuses on the equity-based rewards available to employers that operate as publicly held corporations.
- *Not-for-profit corporation.* A not-for-profit corporation cannot issue stock or pay dividends. It is exempt from certain taxes under IRC Section 501(c)(3). The individuals who operate not-for-profit corporations, subject to certain exceptions, have limited liability for the corporation's debts. As a result, creditors are entitled only to the assets of the corporation in the event of bankruptcy. Because a not-for-profit corporation cannot issue stock, the equity-based rewards programs it may offer are limited to those that do not require the use of company stock (e.g., stock alternatives, 403[b]).

COMPENSATION PLANS USING EQUITY

Equity rewards that may be used as part of the compensation package for the employee include:

- *Stock options:* rights to purchase company shares at a specified price during a specified period of time.

- *Stock awards (also known as stock grants):* plans that provide stock to employees without any cost to them (usually with corresponding restrictions).
- *Stock alternatives:* plans that do not involve the actual ownership of shares or right to shares, but whose potential value to participants parallels value of ownership.

BENEFITS PLANS USING EQUITY

The use of equity in employee rewards does not stop at compensation. Many benefits plans involve employee ownership of the employer's stock and/or other equity vehicles, such as:

- *Employee stock purchase plan (ESPP):* a program whereby stock is offered at a fixed price (usually below market) and paid for in full by employees; typically implemented via payroll deduction.
- *Defined contribution (DC) plan:* a plan that provides for future income from an individual account for each participant, with benefits based solely on the amount contributed to the account and any income, expenses, gains, losses, and forfeitures allocated to that account.
- *Employee stock ownership plan (ESOP):* a plan that enables qualified employees to receive shares that they accrued as plan participants upon retirement or separation from the organization.
- *401(k) plan:* a defined contribution plan that enables employees to make pretax contributions through salary reduction agreements within the format of a cash or deferred arrangement (CODA).
- *Other:* other defined contribution retirement plans that are invested in equity.

Q&A
Aren't employee stock purchase plans considered compensation?

It depends on whom you ask. Some companies consider these plans to be compensation, particularly if the stock is offered to employees at a discount. Other companies consider ESPPs to be an employee benefit, particularly if they are tax-qualified and feature broad-based eligibility, covering most of the company's employees. The bottom line: Categorize the plan according to what you do at your employer. The information presented here on ESPPs is not affected by whether the plans are considered compensation or benefits.

EQUITY TERMINOLOGY

Some of the terms that will appear in this chapter are defined below:

Equity: As an employee reward, equity represents ownership in a company. Ownership typically is in the form of stock (also known as shares, securities).

Company stock: Shares in the stock of the employer.

Stock class: Refers to the type of stock issued (common, junior common, or preferred).

Common stock: The most prevalent form in which an owner's interest is represented (most equity rewards use common stock). Appreciation and dividends are not fixed or guaranteed.

Preferred stock: Equity securities in which an owner's rate of return is fixed (via a guaranteed dividend). Preferred stock receives a higher priority to be paid back than common stock in the event of liquidation or bankruptcy.

Stock split: A change in the number of shares issued by a company by adjusting the number of shares to existing shareholders. For example, a two-for-one split would double the number of shares owned by a stockholder. A reverse stock split of one-for-five would decrease the total number of outstanding shares.

Liquidity: An indicator of a company's ability to generate cash to meet short-term financial obligations.

Dividends: Payments to shareholders by a corporation, paid from the company's retained earnings and not deductible as an expense to the company.

Yield: The rate of return on an investment, expressed as a percentage. The *total return* on a security is a combination of the capital gain and the dividend yield (annual dividend rate/current price per share).

Downside risk: The potential for losing money when a downturn in the market or the stock price negatively affects the value of one's stock holdings.

Public securities market: The "market" or exchange where stocks are publicly sold/traded. Exchanges such as the New York Stock Exchange (NYSE), American Stock Exchange (AMEX), Tokyo Stock Exchange (NIKKEI), and the National Association of Securities Dealers Automated Quotation system (NASDAQ) are also known as *secondary markets* in that shares of corporations are sold between investors rather than directly from the corporation to the investor.

Initial public offering (IPO): A company's initial sale of its shares to the investing public.

EVOLUTION OF EQUITY-BASED REWARDS

Since the founding of the New York Stock Exchange in 1792, stocks have had a significant influence on American society. That influence, however, has evolved, especially with regard to employee rewards, as evidenced by the passing of the following two acts:

- In 1933, the *Securities Act* was passed, which regulates company offers to buy or sell its stock. It also contains Rule 144, requiring an executive to hold stock not registered in accord with this act for two years before selling it on the open market.

- In 1934, the *Securities Exchange Act* was passed, which regulates insider trading and requires disclosures on executive compensation. The Securities and Exchange Commission (SEC) is responsible for the establishment and enforcement of rules for reporting financial and business results to shareholders of publicly owned companies.

EVOLUTION OF STOCK OPTIONS

Stock options, which initially gained popularity in the 1920s, were once reserved for the executive level of the organization. As early as 1952, one company, Pfizer, began offering stock options to all employees. In the 1990s, due in part to the emergence of New Economy companies, options were expanded to all levels in many organizations. The National Center for Employee Ownership (NCEO) defines broad-based plans as those where at least 50 percent of employees are eligible.

In the early 2000s, the issue of and ensuing debate over expensing of options became heated. As companies began to treat options as an expense on the shareholder books, there was a shift in their advantages and disadvantages versus other equity-based rewards. Subsequently, there were cutbacks and changes in the use of stock options, particularly broad-based programs. The use of stock options will continue to evolve as companies adapt to mandatory expensing and its effect on stock options and other equity-based reward vehicles.

EVOLUTION OF BENEFITS PLANS USING EQUITY

ESPPs

The Revenue Act of 1964 modified the statutory stock options introduced in 1950 (Internal Revenue Code [IRC] Section 422) and added statutory stock purchase plans (IRC Section 423). FAS 123(R) modified the conditions whereby ESPPs will not incur a compensation cost and corresponding charge to earnings.

ESOPs

ESOPs have primarily been used as a vehicle to transfer stock ownership in closely held or private organizations from owners to employees. Covered under IRC Section 401, ESOPs date back to the early 1950s. As opposed to stock options, which were initially available only to key executives, ESOPs have a more inclusive history.

The Employee Retirement Income Security Act of 1974 (ERISA) has ensured broad employee participation in the plans. In 1974, only 200 companies within the United States offered ESOPs to their employees. The number increased dramatically in the 1980s as a result of favorable tax treatment. (A leveraged stock ownership plan [LSOP] purchases the stock with loans/debt.)

Since Congress eliminated some tax incentives in 1989, the number of U.S. companies offering plans has leveled off at more than 11,000, according to 2005 statistics from the Resource Library of the ESOP Association (www.esopassociation. org).

A change in the Internal Revenue Code in 1978, known as 401(k), resulted in a major shift in the retirement planning of millions of Americans. Today, there are more than $2 trillion in assets held in the accounts of millions of participants nationally. The 401(k) plan has become the most commonly offered employer-sponsored retirement plan, with the number of plans and participants increasing every year. With the decline in defined benefit plans, this trend is expected to continue and/or accelerate.

WHY EQUITY IS USED TO REWARD EMPLOYEES

Organizations use equity to reward their employees for a number of reasons, including:

- *Align management/employees with shareholders.* Employee interest in the profitability and success of the company is often limited to the desire for job stability.

Equity rewards help to create an ownership culture in which employees take a greater interest in the factors driving business success. It should be noted that many employees sell their ownership interest as soon as the rules and regulations allow them to do so.

- *Build motivation.* Many components of the total rewards package can be used to motivate employees. Money is one of the most powerful motivators available. Equity rewards programs offer employers effective methods to financially motivate employees.
- *Conserve resources.* In many cases, equity rewards allow companies to provide competitive compensation without depleting other assets, such as cash.
- *Wealth creation.* The actual realized gain can create significant opportunity for employee wealth creation.
- *Tax advantages.* Equity reward programs may offer tax advantages to the employee and/or the employer. In some cases, employers may significantly reduce their tax obligations through the use of various equity reward programs.
- *Attraction and retention.* Creative use of equity rewards, coupled with the right mix of other total rewards components, may provide the competitive edge to attract, motivate, and retain key talent.
- *Capital accumulation.* Positive cash flow from employee stock purchases provides a mechanism for the company to raise capital.

LEGAL, TAX, AND ACCOUNTING ISSUES

One of the "facts of life" of equity-based rewards programs is that they are highly regulated. This can be a plus in that much of the legislation created over the years has given rise to innovation in equity rewards.

With regard to taxation, equity-based reward programs vary widely in the tax implications on both the employer and the employee. The effect of taxation can drive plan selection depending on employer objectives.

The following section examines the impact of the legal environment on the evolution of equity rewards and the tax implications of the various programs.

IMPACT OF LEGISLATION ON EQUITY-BASED REWARDS PROGRAMS

Regulation of equity rewards spans many government agencies, including the IRS, SEC, and Department of Labor (DOL). (See Figure 16.1.) Legislation specifically addressing equity rewards dates back to the 1920s and has been instrumental in the creation and revision of many programs. (See Figure 16.2.)

Internal Revenue Code

In its simplest sense, the Internal Revenue Code (IRC) refers to the tax laws passed by Congress and administered by the IRS. Of all the legislation affecting the design and implementation of equity-based rewards programs, the IRC is arguably the most far-reaching, affecting most plans in one way or another. See Figure 16.3 for a partial list of the IRC sections affecting various equity-based rewards programs.

FIGURE 16.1 Governing agencies.

- *Securities and Exchange Commission:* a federal agency (part of the Treasury Department) that enforces the Securities Act of 1933, the Securities and Exchange Act of 1934, and other securities acts and issues rules and regulations on related matters, such as insider trading and required disclosures on executive compensation.
- *Financial Accounting Standards Board:* the private sector organization that issues the "generally accepted accounting principles" (GAAP) that govern accounting for publicly held U.S. companies. The SEC recognizes the principles developed by the FASB.
- *International Accounting Standards Board:* independent, privately funded organization that issues global accounting standards.
- *Department of Labor:* responsible for the administration and enforcement of more than 180 statutes, including ERISA.
- *Internal Revenue Service:* the agency of the federal government responsible for interpretation of tax laws, collection of income tax, and enforcement of the Internal Revenue Code.

FORMS OF TAXATION: EMPLOYEE

An understanding of the impact of various equity-based rewards programs begins with a review of some basic tax information.

Ordinary income tax refers to an individual's tax on earnings from wages, tips, and all other sources except capital gains. Current federal rates range from 10 percent to 35 percent of taxable income.

Capital gains taxes, in certain cases, allow individuals to pay lower tax rates than those imposed on ordinary income. Capital gains tax refers to the tax on gains realized from the sale of capital assets, such as real estate or shares of stock.

The tax rate on *short-term capital gains* (assets held for 12 months or less) is the same as ordinary income tax rates. The tax rate on *long-term capital gains* (assets held for one year and one day or longer) is 15 percent for individuals in the 25 percent to 35 percent brackets.[1]

The Jobs and Growth Tax Relief Reconciliation Act of 2003 (JAGTRRA) introduced a new *dividend tax rate* equal to the capital gains tax rate that dramatically lowered taxes on dividends.

Some equity-based rewards can create so-called tax preference income (TPI) for recipients. This income may be subject to the *alternative minimum tax* (AMT), which was introduced in the tax act of 1969 to impose potential tax liability on high-income taxpayers who may not have been required to pay taxes under the regular tax system because they benefited from various tax preference items.

Congress has changed the rates and application of the AMT on numerous occasions since 1969. The current maximum rate is 28 percent. (The first $175,000 of income is taxed at 26 percent. Income above $175,000 is taxed at 28 percent.)

The AMT currently is a separate tax system from the regular tax system. Individuals are required to keep separate records for purposes of regular and alternative minimum tax.

FIGURE 16.2 Legislative timeline.

- **1950 – Revenue Act** introduced statutory stock options.
- **1959 – The Accounting Principles Board**, funded by private industry, was created to establish accounting standards.
- **1964 – Revenue Act** led to the creation of ESPPs and qualified stock options.
- **1972 – Accounting Principles Board, Opinion 25 (APB 25)** ruling established the *measurement date principle*, requiring measurement of the compensation expense at the point where the price/share and number of shares in an award are first known.
- **1973 – Financial Accounting Standards Board (FASB)** replaced the APB.
- **1973 – Fisher Black and Myron Scholes developed a method** to value stock options for the purpose of comparison with other elements of compensation. (Note: Black-Scholes is not legislation. However, it is a method used by many companies to comply with certain reporting requirements.)
- **1974 – The Employee Retirement Income Security Act (ERISA)** was designed to ensure the security of company pension plans. Until this time, workers were at risk of losing company pensions. Events such as the 1963 closing of the Studebaker auto plant in South Bend, Indiana, resulted in the loss of pension benefits for thousands of workers.
- **ERISA impact on equity rewards** – ESOPs, 401(k) plans and other qualified retirement plans that defer payment until retirement or termination are subject to ERISA requirements, in addition to the requirements of the Internal Revenue Code (IRC).
- **1976 – Tax Reform Act** eliminated qualified stock options.
- **1978 – 401(k)** amended the IRC and opened the door to the now widespread retirement plan.
- **1981 – Economic Recovery Act** introduced ISOs, reviving qualified stock options eliminated in 1976.
- **1995 – FASB issued Financial Accounting Standard 123 (FAS 123),** allowing the earnings impact of stock options to be reported under a present value method (e.g., Black-Scholes) or by APB 25 with a footnote on present value in financial statements.
- **2000 – FASB issued Interpretation No. 44**, affecting the repricing of stock options under APB 25. It had a huge impact on repricing until the revision of FAS 123.
- **2001 – Economic Growth and Tax Relief Reconciliation Act (EGTRRA)** included pension reform provisions that allow employers to enhance benefit plans and offer more options to employees.
- **2002 – Sarbanes-Oxley Act** was enacted to restore investor confidence. Among other things, it prohibits loans to executive officers and directors and subjects them to additional restrictions on transactions of company securities.
- **2002 – FASB issued FAS 148**, providing more favorable transition methods for companies adopting FAS 123.
- **2004 – American Jobs Creation Act** affected equity-based arrangements that previously had not been considered deferred compensation plans (e.g., stock appreciation rights and ESPPs). This led to the establishment of IRC section 409A.
- **2004 – FASB revised FAS 123** (now referred to as FAS 123[R]), requiring expensing of employee stock options and eliminating APB 25.

FIGURE 16.3 IRC sections affecting various equity-based rewards programs.

- Stock options: 56, 83, 162, 409A, 421, 422, 423, 424, 6039
- Stock grants: 83, 404
- Stock alternatives: 83
- ESPPs: 414, 421, 423
- ESOPs: 1042
- Stock bonus plans: 1042
- Money purchase pension plans: 402(a), 403(a), 404(a), 501(a)
- 401(k) plans: 401
- 403(b) plans: 403, 501(c)(3)
- 457 plans: 457

The failure of Congress to make adjustments to the AMT that account for inflation, plus reductions in regular tax rates, has dramatically increased the number of taxpayers who are subject to AMT.

FORMS OF TAXATION: EMPLOYER

The amount of tax paid by the employer can be affected in different ways by various equity-based rewards programs.

Companies are required to pay a corporate income tax of 35 percent (maximum) on their pretax profits. This number can be reduced by a variety of methods including write-offs of depreciated corporate assets, tax credits (e.g., research and development), and tax deductions (e.g., compensation expense, 401[k] matching contributions).

ACCOUNTING BASICS: FINANCIAL STATEMENTS

Equity-based rewards affect the company's financial reports in varying ways. To understand their impact, it is necessary to have a basic understanding of financial reports, such as:

- *Annual report:* a required report that details a company's financial position. It includes information on company financial operations and the following four financial statements:
  - *Income statement:* outlines the revenues and expenses of the organization over a specified period of time; also known as a *profit and loss statement.*
  - *Balance sheet:* lists the company's assets and liabilities, as well as its net worth, at a particular moment in time.
  - *Cash flow statement:* reports cash received and cash spent during the fiscal year.
  - *Statement of shareholders' equity:* shows the same basic information as the statement of retained earnings, but also shows changes in all shareholders' equity accounts.
- *10-K report:* a required annual SEC filing for a public company that provides certain financial and related business information. It is more detailed than the annual report and has a filing deadline.[2]

FIGURE 16.4 Sample company income statement.

Consolidated Income Statement for the Year 20XX

(A)	Net sales	$767,000
(B)	Cost of goods sold	$535,000
(C)	*Gross margin (A − B)*	$232,000
(D)	Operating expenses	
(E)	Depreciation and amortization	$28,000
(F)	Selling, general, and administrative expense	$96,804
(G)	*Total operating expenses (E + F)*	$124,804
(H)	Operating income (C − G)	$107,196
(I)	Dividends and interest income	$5,250
(J)	*Income before income taxes (H + I)*	$112,446
(K)	Provision for income taxes	$39,356
(L)	Net income (J − K)	$73,090
(M)	Average common shares outstanding	28,650
(N)	*Earnings per share (L / M)*	$2.55

- *10-Q report:* a quarterly SEC filing that provides a review of a company's financial performance for the first three quarters of the company's fiscal year.

Income Statement

The income statement provides a picture of the company's profitability for the designated year, expressed as net income and earnings per share. (See Figure 16.4.)

Compensation expense (excluding that which can be charged to the cost of goods sold) is included in the selling, general, and administrative (SG&A) section. Operating income is often an important factor in measuring division performance, as it excludes interest and income tax costs. Some companies use income before tax in incentive measures; while others use net income.

The accounting basis upon which revenues and expenses are recorded can be either:

- *Accrual accounting:* recording revenues and expenses in the time period to which they apply regardless of cash flows.
- *Cash accounting:* recording revenue when cash is received and expenses when cash is disbursed.

For income tax reported, the maximum marginal federal tax rate is 35 percent. However, accounting rules for shareholders and for the IRS are substantially different in many respects, thus the provision for income tax in the annual report is seldom 35 percent. It may be more or less.

ACCOUNTING FOR EQUITY-BASED REWARDS

For years, companies had different choices to account for equity-based compensation. These choices, as discussed below, were removed with FAS 123(R), which became effective in 2005.

APB 25 (1972) was the initial accounting standard used to determine the expense for equity-based rewards. FAS 123 (1995) was the accounting standard introduced in 1995 that was voluntary when first introduced. Under the original FAS 123, companies had the option of adopting FAS 123 or continuing to account for equity-based rewards under APB 25. If companies continued to use APB 25, they were required to disclose the equity-based compensation expense in the footnotes of their financial statements. Once a company elected to use FAS 123, it could not later change back to accounting under APB 25.

FAS 123(R) (2004) is now the mandatory accounting standard; it supersedes APB 25 and was effective for public companies at the beginning of the next fiscal year after June 15, 2005.

APB 25

Historically, most companies had used APB 25 because it presented company financial results in the most favorable light. Advantages included:

- *Valuation methodology.* Stock awards were valued on the date of grant and expensed over the service period.
- *Definition of intrinsic value.* APB 25 based the compensation expense of an equity-based reward on its intrinsic value at grant, which was the difference between the fair market value and the purchase price.
- *Applications*
  - *Fair market value (FMV) options.* FMV options, those with a purchase price equal to the fair market value at grant, had an intrinsic value of $0, resulting in no compensation expense.
  - *Employee stock purchase plans (ESPPs).* Under APB 25, ESPPs were considered noncompensatory provided that certain requirements were met (Section 423 plans qualified).

FAS 123(R)

FAS 123, as released in 1995 and revised in 2004 as FAS 123(R), changed the valuation methodology from intrinsic value to fair value.

- *Valuation methodology:* All equity-based compensation must be accounted for based on its fair value.
- *Definition of fair value:* The definition of fair value under FAS 123(R) focuses on stock options, since the fair value of full value shares such as restricted stock is more certain. For stock options, the fair value must be estimated with an option-pricing model that uses six standard assumptions.
- *Applications*
  - *Fair market value (FMV) options:* Compensation cost is measured at grant and recognized over the requisite service period.
  - *Employee stock purchase plans:* ESPPs create an earnings charge unless they meet certain criteria.

Equity Accounting Continuum

Deciding what type of equity-based rewards program to implement can depend upon how it will or may affect the bottom line. At one end of the spectrum are

FIGURE 16.5 Equity accounting continuum.

Open-Ended Liability
Variable Charge to Earnings
↓   ↓   ↓   ↓
Performance unit plans
Cash-settled:
   - Performance shares
   - Stock appreciation rights
   - Phantom stock
Fixed
Charge to earnings
Fixed
Charge to Earnings
↓   ↓   ↓   ↓
FMV stock options
Restricted stock
Stock-settled:
   - Performance shares
   - Stock appreciation rights
   - Phantom stock

equity-based rewards programs with an open-ended or variable charge to earnings. The company is unable to predict the hit that the financial report will take. At the other end are programs that are charged to earnings, but the amount charged is "fixed" at grant. (See Figure 16.5.)

Impact of Mandatory Expensing

Mandatory expensing of stock options has many implications for equity-based rewards. First, it levels the playing field by making the true cost of stock options more transparent and allowing comparisons to other rewards that create an expense on company financial statements. Second, although there are many reasons to use different equity-based rewards, a compelling reason to use stock options (favorable accounting treatment) has been eliminated, which may motivate companies to make changes to their rewards programs as other criteria take priority.

Shareholder Issues

Many equity-based rewards programs require an increase in the number of shares outstanding in order to make shares available for the program. Shareholders sometimes take issue with this, as it results in dilution. Dilution is the decrease in the ownership percentage of current owners when additional shares of stock are issued. The methodology to calculate diluted earnings per share on the company financial statement is shown in Figure 16.6.

FIGURE 16.6 Example of dilution.

We start with this as the existing net income and shares outstanding.

Existing

Average shares outstanding			28,650,000
Net income			$73,090,000
EPS calculation	$\dfrac{\$73,090,000}{28,650,000}$	=	$2.55 / share

Issue additional shares 1,000,000

The addition of 1,000,000 shares in this case dropped the earnings per share (EPS) by 8 cents, or about 3.1%.

Additional Shares Outstanding

Net income			$73,090,000
Additional shares issued			1,000,000
EPS calculation	$\dfrac{\$73,090,000}{29,650,000}$	=	$2.47/ share
Dilution %	$\dfrac{\$2.55 - \$2.47}{\$2.55}$	=	3.1%

The *net* dilution effect of equity-based reward programs such as stock options may be reduced if the company uses the option proceeds and any tax benefits to buy back shares.

OVERVIEW OF STOCK OPTIONS

Regardless of the different accounting treatment, stock options today still have a place in many companies as part of a balanced incentive portfolio, while some companies are now weighing options versus other vehicles and fine-tuning the design of incentive packages to maximize the value to the corporation relative to the expense.

Stock options are a right given by an organization (grantor) to a person (optionee) to buy (exercise) a specified number of shares of company stock at a set price (grant/exercise price) during a prescribed period of time (exercise period). Broadly granted stock option plans are generally found both in smaller, closely held companies (often entrepreneurial, high-growth firms) and in large public companies. While there has recently been a decrease in the number of organizations offering stock options and a reduction in the number of eligible employees, stock options continue to be the most widely used stock-based form of compensation.

Key Dates

There are five dates that are of particular importance with regard to stock options, defined as follows:

- *Grant date:* refers to the date on which the options are first given to the optionee.
- *Vesting date:* refers to the *first* date on which the optionee actually holds the option and may buy the stock from the company.

- *Exercise date:* refers to the *actual* date on which the optionee buys the stock from the company (exercising the option).
- *Disposition date:* refers to the date on which the optionee sells, exchanges, or transfers the stock.
- *Expiration date:* refers to the date on which an optionee's ability to exercise options ends.

Stock Option Characteristics

Stock options, regardless of type, share some common characteristics:

- Stock options provide employees with the opportunity to build wealth by choosing to exercise the options and buy the stock at a set *exercise price* (typically the price of the stock on the grant date), but the purchase takes place on a later date (the exercise date) when the value of the stock on the market has (hopefully) appreciated.
- Employees recognize immediate financial gains measured by the difference (also known as spread) between the exercise price and the value of the stock on the exercise date.
- Employees meet vesting requirements. Typically, there are time requirements defining when an optionee can receive the potential benefit of options (also known as vesting period).
- Employees avoid the downside risk faced by stockholders because they do not actually own the stock unless they decide to exercise their options.
- Employers have an effective way to provide attractive compensation packages to employees without the use of cash resources.

Q&A
What's the difference between the grant price and the exercise price?

Grant price (also known as strike price) and exercise price are sometimes used interchangeably. Technically, the grant (or strike) price refers to the price, set at grant, at which the employee is entitled to purchase his or her options at some point in the future. The exercise price refers to the price that the employee pays on the exercise date, which is usually the same as the price that was set at grant. So are the grant price, strike price, and exercise price the same? Yes, in most cases, the grant price (strike price) and exercise price will be the same. Note: The grant price and exercise price can differ for indexed stock options, discounted stock options, and performance-based stock options.

Advantages of Stock Options

Stock options hold advantages for both employees and employers, such as:

Employee

- Receives a financial interest in the appreciation of the company's stock.
- Can realize financial gain while still employed.
- Is not required to make an upfront investment (at grant).

- Depending on plan design, can receive assistance in financing the exercise.
- Has the ability to time taxation.

Employer

- Provides employees with substantial rewards without the use of cash resources.
- Can increase cash flow and provide a tax deduction.
- Can target key employees, rather than all employees.
- Has a powerful motivator in companies with strong growth potential.
- Provides an increased ability to attract and retain key talent.
- Provides a balanced perspective between short-term and long-term business goals.

Disadvantages of Stock Options

Employee

- Employee investment required (at exercise or sale, depending on type).
- Tax liability (discussed later).

Employer

- Charge to earnings with no immediate perceived value by the participant.
- Increased dilution.
- A fall in stock prices can lead to worthless employee stock options (underwater), negatively affecting employee morale.

TYPES OF STOCK OPTIONS

There are two broad categories of stock options that vary depending on whether the tax treatment favors the employee (ISOs) or the employer (NQSOs). These and other differences will be discussed.

- *Incentive stock options (ISOs)* are also known as qualified or statutory stock options and must satisfy requirements set forth in IRC Section 422 for preferential tax treatment.
- *Nonqualified stock options (NQSOs)* are also known as nonstatutory stock options and do not satisfy the requirements of the IRC for preferential tax treatment.

Incentive Stock Option (ISO)

ISOs are subject to IRC requirements. Options meeting these requirements are qualified for favorable tax treatment (employee tax is deferred until the date the shares are sold) under IRC Sections 421 and 422. Section 422 (b)(5) restricts the transferability of ISOs.

ISO Requirements

Because ISOs are qualified for preferential tax treatment under Section 422 of the IRC, they are subject to several requirements including:

- Plan.
    - The specified number of shares issued and employees eligible.
    - Awards being made contingent upon shareholder approval within 12 months.
    - A vesting limit of $100,000 per year, per employee, as measured by the option price multiplied by the number of shares.
- Grant.
    - ISOs may be granted to employees only. Nonemployee directors, consultants, independent contractors, and so forth, are not eligible.
    - The exercise period is limited to 10 years.
    - The option price may not be less than 100 percent of the fair market value (FMV) at grant. (Owners of 10 percent or more of company stock must pay 110 percent of FMV or higher and are limited to a five-year exercise period.)
- Exercise: The exercise date is affected by certain events, including the following:
    - Termination: must exercise options within 90 days.
    - Retirement: must exercise options within 90 days.
    - Disability: must exercise options within one year.
    - Death: subject to terms of plan.
- Sale: ISOs are subject to a holding period in order to qualify for long-term capital gains treatment. The optionee must hold the stock until two years after the grant date and one year after the exercise date.

ISO Tax Implications for the Employee

As stated earlier, ISOs are qualified stock option plans with tax implications that are favorable to employees. These include (1) deferred taxation until date of disposition (sale, transfer, gift, exchange); (2) capital gains tax rate rather than the ordinary income tax rate; and (3) the alternative minimum tax (spread between the grant/exercise price and the FMV *on the exercise date* may be subject to the AMT).

To maximize the tax benefits available with an ISO, the employee must ensure that the stock is sold under certain conditions. In a qualifying disposition, an employee pays *capital gains tax* if he or she holds the stock until two years after the grant date and one year after the exercise date. In a disqualifying disposition (ISO requirements have not been met), an employee pays *ordinary income tax and capital gains tax* if he or she does not meet the required holding period specified above.

The tax is as follows:

- FMV on exercise date – FMV on grant date = Ordinary income.
- FMV on disposition date – FMV on exercise date = Capital gain.

ISO Tax Implications for the Employer

In the case of ISOs, there is no tax deduction unless the employee makes a disqualifying disposition. In a disqualifying disposition, the employer takes a deduction for the amount recognized by the employee as ordinary income. There also are no withholding requirements even though the employee may recognize ordinary income upon a disqualifying disposition. Additionally, a disqualifying disposition is not considered wages for FUTA or FICA withholding.

Nonqualified Stock Option (NQSO)

Nonqualified stock options tend to be more flexible in terms of plan design and consequently are more prevalent than ISOs. "Nonqualified" refers to the inability of the plan to qualify for preferential tax treatment under the Internal Revenue Code.

NQSO Tax Implications for the Employee

If the option does not have a readily ascertainable fair market value at grant, the optionee recognizes ordinary income on the spread between the exercise price and the FMV of the stock at exercise. After exercising the option, the optionee recognizes capital gains on any additional appreciation from the exercise date to the disposition date. There is *potential* (but unlikely) taxation at grant if the option has a readily ascertainable fair market value.

Note: An option not actively traded on an established market has no readily ascertainable fair market value unless its fair market value can otherwise be measured with reasonable accuracy. See Treasury Regulations Section 1.83–7(b) for an explanation of the four required conditions for fair market value that can be measured with reasonable accuracy.

NQSO Tax Implications for the Employer

As opposed to ISOs, the employer may take a tax deduction for NQSOs. The employer must also withhold taxes. A tax deduction for the employer is allowed in the same amount and in the same year as the ordinary income recognized by the employee. In some cases, employers have been able to significantly reduce their tax obligation by doing so.

Overall, because the employees are recognizing ordinary income, the withholding requirements for employment tax are the same as if the employees were receiving wages.

NQSO Limitations

Many of the limitations of ISOs (eligibility, holding period, pricing, etc.) are actually advantages of NQSOs. Without these limitations, employers may use NQSOs to achieve objectives that cannot be achieved with ISOs. For example, employers receive significant tax advantages with NQSOs; however, the tax treatment for recipients is not as favorable (as with ISOs), so as a result, NQSOs may be a less effective attraction/retention tool.

TYPES OF STOCK AWARDS AND ALTERNATIVES

Stock awards (also known as "whole value" or "full value" awards) are plans that provide stock to employees without any cost to them, except for tax liability.

Two types of stock awards include performance shares and restricted stock award (RSA) plans. Other alternatives covered in the rest of this chapter include restricted stock units (RSUs), performance accelerated restricted stock award plans (PARSAPs), stock appreciation rights (SARs), phantom stock, and performance unit plans (PUPs).

Performance Share Plan (PSP)

A performance share plan (PSP) is a stock grant (or stock unit) award plan contingently granted upon the achievement of certain predetermined external or internal performance goals. These goals must be met during a specified period (e.g., three to five years) before the recipient has rights to the stock. Further, the share value is linked to either the fair market value of the employer's stock or a specific book/formula value. Thus, there is a double incentive for the grantee: Achieve the goals established and work toward a higher stock price.

Performance shares are unique because they combine the accomplishment of set performance targets and the stock performance. Recipients want to meet or exceed the set targets and see the stock price appreciate. If designed with the appropriate performance measures, PSPs can become an optimal motivational vehicle.

PSP Tax Implications for the Employer

- There is no tax deduction at grant. Instead, the employer gets a tax deduction when the employee receives the award and recognizes ordinary income.
- Any amounts paid are subject to both federal and state withholding taxes.

PSP Tax Implications for the Employee

- There is no tax at grant.
- Upon payment of the award, the award is taxed as ordinary income.

PSP Accounting Considerations

Under FAS 123(R), the performance shares may be valued using the option pricing model on the date of grant. This is a significant change from APB 25, where PSPs were variable market to market. However, the goals have to be nonmarket (stock)-related. If shares are forfeited, the company can back out the charge.

PSP Pros and Cons

The following advantages make the PSP a long-term incentive plan worth considering:

- There is a double-ended incentive for the employee to achieve performance targets and increase the stock price.
- If settled in stock, there is a fixed charge to earnings.
- Award is highly performance oriented.

- Executives' tax liability can be paid out of the award.
- Vesting requirements are an effective means of retaining recipients.

Disadvantages include:

- Performance goals may be difficult to determine.
- If paid in stock, dilution is a consideration.

Restricted Stock Award (RSA)

Restricted stock awards (RSAs) are a stock grant by an employer to an employee whereby the employee's rights to the stock are subject to some type of restriction and risk of forfeiture. Restrictions often include an employment or length-of-service restriction, and such stock awards are known as time-lapse restricted stock (i.e., vesting over a three- to five-year period). Typically, the employee may not pledge, sell, or transfer the shares of stock until the restrictions lapse; however, the employee receives dividends and voting rights during the restriction period. Once the stated restrictions lapse, the employee obtains full ownership of the unrestricted shares, which may be pledged, sold, or transferred. In the event the employee does not meet the stated restrictions, the shares are forfeited.

Companies may choose to offer RSAs to selected employees because they:

- Attract and retain.
- Provide dividend payments to employee stockholders.
- Increase stock ownership.
- Support performance goals.
- Diversify long-term incentive awards.
- Supplement other pay practices.

RSA Tax Implications for the Employer

The company only receives a matching tax deduction when an employee recognizes ordinary income and is taxed accordingly. The company does not receive a tax deduction at the time of grant, but does receive a tax deduction equal to the employee's ordinary income at the time the restrictions lapse. If the employee does not meet the holding requirements to qualify for long-term capital gains treatment upon sale of the stock, the company receives a tax deduction equal to the ordinary income received by the employee. If the employee makes an 83(b) election and pays the required taxes in the year of the award, the company receives a matching tax deduction for the income recognized by the employee.

RSA Tax Implications for the Employee

Under current federal income tax rules, a restricted stock award recipient is not taxed at the time the award is granted; liability for taxes occurs when the restrictions lapse (when vesting occurs). The amount of income subject to tax is the fair market value of the shares at the time of vesting less any amount paid for the shares. When the employee holds the stock for one year and a day after the date of vesting (and after paying the initial ordinary income tax on the value of the stock upon vesting less any amount paid to purchase the stock), the recipient qualifies for long-term capital gains treatment for any subsequent stock price appreciation between the vesting date and sell date.

83(b) Election

Internal Revenue Code section 83(b) allows the recipient of a restricted stock award the option to make an election within 30 days of the grant date to recognize and pay ordinary income tax. The amount of income is determined by the fair market value of the shares on the date of grant. When the recipient holds the award for one year past the date of grant, all subsequent appreciation is considered long-term capital gains and is taxed accordingly.

If a taxpayer who made an 83(b) election and paid the subsequent taxes in the year of the award forfeits the shares (e.g., is terminated), the taxpayer is not permitted to claim a tax loss on the forfeiture of those shares. Additionally, if the price of the stock decreases after a taxpayer made an 83(b) election and paid the subsequent taxes, the taxpayer is not permitted to claim a tax loss on the difference in the price of the stock on the award date and vesting and/or sale date.

RSA Accounting Considerations

Following the implementation of FAS 123R, the accounting for restricted stock continues to use the same method as was used in the past under APB 25.

The total charge to earnings for a typical grant of restricted stock is a straightforward calculation—the product of the number of shares in the award and the price of the stock at the grant date. Any subsequent appreciation of the shares is not charged to earnings. This total earnings charge is fixed at grant, thus making restricted stock easily budgeted and a friend of the finance department. The big picture of the accounting is consistent for the various types of restricted stock grants discussed in this chapter, including RSAs, RSUs, and performance-accelerated RSAs. However, where they differ is in the amortization of the total charge over the vesting period.

162(m) Considerations

Companies awarding restricted stock to their top executives should be mindful of Internal Revenue Code section 162(m). In short, section 162(m) does not allow companies to deduct the compensation expense for nonperformance-related compensation in excess of $1 million provided to the CEO and/or the next four highest paid executives of a publicly traded company.

Specifically, if one of the top five executives of a publicly traded company is awarded restricted stock with a value in excess of $1 million, and the only restrictions are time-based, the company will not be able to deduct the compensation expense. Additionally, section 162(m) gives companies three years after an initial public offering to be in compliance, and one year for a company spinning off from a public company.

RSA Pros and Cons

The following are some advantages of restricted stock:

- It promotes immediate stock ownership.
- The charge to earnings is fixed at the time of grant and can be budgeted and more easily planned for.
- Dilution is set at the grant date and does not vary as restrictions lapse.

- Fewer shares are required to deliver greater value (compared to options).
- If the stock price appreciates from the date of grant, the company's tax deduction may exceed the fixed charge to earnings.
- It immediately aligns employee's interests with those of shareholders.
- It allows employees to receive dividends and voting rights.
- It is immediately recognizable to employees.
- If an employee terminates and forfeits shares, the shares then are available to be used as an attraction vehicle for someone else.
- It offers employees potential long-term appreciation as the company grows.
- The award retains value even if the stock price drops.

The disadvantages of restricted stock include:

- There is a charge to earnings.
- There is immediate dilution of earnings per share.
- The employee incurs tax liability as shares vest, not at the exercise or sell date.
- If the stock price depreciates, the company's fixed-earnings charge exceeds the actual value delivered to the employee and the subsequent tax deduction.
- Unless performance accelerators are utilized for vesting, there are no performance-related criteria, except vesting, for receipt of the award.
- Possible 162(m) issues could apply.

Restricted Stock Unit (RSU)

Restricted stock units (RSUs) are the newest version of restricted stock and were widely publicized by Microsoft's 2003 announcement. RSUs are very similar to RSAs but have a few key differences.

An RSU is an agreement to issue underlying stock at the time of vesting. No shares are delivered until the employee satisfies the vesting schedule. Once vested, the taxes owned are netted (deducted) out of the available units before the employee receives the units. By using units instead of the traditional RSA, a company secures additional advantages such as:

- Eliminating the need for 83(b) elections and all the associated administrative and communication issues.
- Facilitating the payment of taxes at vesting with an automatic withholding of shares.
- Postponing shareholder dilution until vesting/payout.
- For companies with multinational operations, RSUs often are better for participants than RSAs because of tax timing.

Performance Accelerated Restricted Stock Award Plan (PARSAP)

A twist to the traditional time-vested RSA is its "performance-vesting" counterpart known as a performance accelerated restricted stock award plan (PARSAP). Under this type of plan, the restriction can be stretched over a longer period of time than usual (10 years instead of 3 years) to add retention value. It spreads the profit and loss charges out, but with an enhanced motivational feature of accelerating or lifting of restrictions if certain predetermined performance criteria are achieved.

This simple "twist" significantly boosts the retention and motivational aspects over a traditional RSA. Combine this with the better accounting consequences and the PARSAP may prove beneficial in a company's LTI program.

Stock Appreciation Right (SAR)

A stock appreciation right (SAR) is a long-term incentive vehicle whereby the corporation grants an executive the right to receive a dollar amount of value equal to the future appreciation of its shares. Typically, an SAR is exercised by the grantee after a specific vesting period. U.S. companies operating in foreign countries where the tax and/or other local laws preclude the use of stock options have used SARs extensively.

Typically SARs, like any other type of long-term incentive, are granted to employees in an effort to attract, retain, and motivate. Although available to anyone, participation is usually reserved for those key employees who actually create value over the long term. It is not unusual for the plan document to specify who is included, but it will usually reserve participation to whomever the compensation committee or board of directors specify.

SARs typically are granted as a stand-alone right. However, it is not without precedent that they sometimes are granted in tandem with other long-term incentive awards, especially if there is a corresponding need for cash at exercise—for example, for purchase and/or tax purposes.

SAR Tax Implications for the Employer

- The corporation will receive a deduction for compensation expense when the SARs are exercised, and the employee is in constructive receipt, on the value of the appreciation from grant.
- Any amounts paid are subject to both federal and state withholding taxes.

SAR Tax Implications for the Employee

- There is no tax at grant.
- If proceeds are paid in cash when exercised, the employee recognizes ordinary income upon exercise.
- If proceeds are paid in stock or other property, the employee is taxed on the fair market value of the stock received.

SAR Accounting Considerations

Because the number of grants that will be granted to an employee and/or the price of the shares are not determined until the actual exercise date, plus when settled in cash, there is a variable, open-ended charge to earnings. The company must take a market-to-market charge for positive and negative changes in the company's stock price.

To calculate the charge to earnings, the company calculates the amount of stock appreciation each year and applies it to the percentage of the award that is vested. The accrual equals any appreciation in the stock price over the SAR grant price multiplied by the number of vested shares.

SAR Pros and Cons

There are several key advantages that make the SAR worth considering, specifically:

- The employee benefits from the appreciation in the corporation's stock without having to make an actual purchase.
- The SAR has built-in exercise flexibility so that the employee is in a position to get better utility from it—from both cash flow and tax perspectives.
- Vesting requirements are an effective means of retaining key employees.
- SARs can provide the cash needed for the exercise (purchase) of stock options.
- No purchase or set-aside of shares is necessary; therefore, SARs are nondilutive and often are used when there are no additional shares to grant.
- SARs are particularly useful for corporations with operations overseas where stock options are not practical.
- The company retains voting rights and ownership privileges.

SARs have the following disadvantages:

- SARs, if settled in cash, result in an open-ended and unpredictable charge to earnings if the stock appreciates up until the time it is exercised by the employee.
- SARs that are paid in cash can result in cash flow problems if not planned for properly.
- SARs are not actual ownership in the company and might not be as motivational as actual stock awards.
- The stock price for the reward may not reflect improved company performance, but may be because of a strong market.

Phantom Stock

Phantom stock is an arrangement whereby the executive receives the appreciation in the book, fair-market, or formula value over a set period of time. Phantom shareholders do not own actual stock and typically do not have voting rights; however, they are usually eligible to receive dividends or their equivalent. Phantom stock is used by privately held companies that want to be competitive but cannot or do not want to grant actual stock to executives.

Phantom stock plans typically are useful in privately held companies where the ownership desires key management to be motivated and to share in the increase in value of the company without diluting the ownership structure. It is unusual for a publicly traded company to use phantom stock (opting instead for stock appreciation rights).

Phantom Stock Tax Implications for the Employer

- The corporation will receive a deduction for compensation expense when the phantom shares are exercised, and the employee has constructive receipt on the value of the appreciation from grant.
- Any amounts received by the employee are subject to both federal and state withholding taxes.

Phantom Stock Tax Implications for the Employee

- There is no tax at grant.
- When the phantom shares are cashed in, the employee recognizes ordinary income.

Phantom Stock Accounting Considerations

Because phantom stock is a contingent cash-based plan, there is an open-ended charge to earnings. The appreciation of the phantom stock and dividends paid are a charge to earnings and must be accrued on a quarterly basis as compensation expense. Unless capped, the overall charge will be unknown and therefore could be a concern to the company—especially if there is any contemplation of going public.

Phantom Stock Pros and Cons

The following are advantages of phantom stock:

- No executive investment is required.
- Vesting requirements are an effective means of retaining key employees.
- The company retains voting rights and ownership privileges.
- Employees are motivated and benefit from the appreciation in the corporation's stock, or formula set, without having to make an actual purchase.
- Phantom stock is useful for corporations that wish to remain private.

The following are disadvantages of phantom stock:

- It is usually paid in cash and therefore can result in a cash flow problem if it is not planned for and budgeted in advance.
- There is no actual ownership, so it may not be as motivational as actual stock awards.
- The exercise date usually is stated in the document and not left to the discretion of the executive.
- Phantom stock results in an unpredictable/open-ended charge to earnings, which usually is not critical to a private company unless it is contemplating an initial public offering (IPO).
- Depending on the valuation formula used, it can be difficult for an executive to know his value in the plan at any given moment.

Performance Unit Plan (PUP)

A performance unit plan (PUP) is a unit award plan contingently granted on the achievement of certain predetermined external or internal performance goals over a specified period (typically three to five years) before the recipient has a right to the unit. Unlike a performance share plan (PSP), the unit value rarely has any tie-back to stock price, and the actual award payment is typically paid in cash.

PUPs were initiated in the early 1970s when the stock market had stalled and options were the primary source of wealth creation for executives. With the decline in the options value, motivating and retaining talent was in jeopardy. For companies still meeting key strategic and financial goals, PUPs were a great way to recharge and refocus key executive talent on working toward the long-term viability of their companies.

These plans remained very popular until the bull market that began in 1983, when they were replaced by options. In light of today's market volatility, PUPs may prove to be a great LTI vehicle for consideration.

PUP Tax Implications for the Employer

- The corporation will receive a deduction for compensation expense when the PUPs are paid and the employee has W-2 income.
- Any awards paid are subject to both federal and state withholding taxes.

PUP Tax Implication for the Employee

- There is no tax at grant.
- On the date amounts are paid, the award is taxed as ordinary income.

PUP Accounting Considerations

The value of the performance units granted is charged to earnings, but only to the degree that the goals are being achieved over the performance period. The charge is capped since there is a maximum amount possible.

PUP Pros and Cons

The following are advantages of PUPs:

- No executive investment is required.
- The payouts are tied directly to performance achieved.
- Tax withholding can be deducted directly from the award.
- The maximum charge to earnings is fixed at grant.
- PUPs are useful for corporations that want to diversify an executive's compensation package and get focused on key strategic issues other than market price appreciation.
- There is no dilution to shares outstanding unless paid in stock.
- PUPs, like SARs, can provide cash needed for the exercise (purchase) of stock options.

The following are disadvantages of PUPs:

- There is a charge to earnings.
- Sometimes it is difficult to set appropriate long-term performance targets.

Typical Performance Metrics of PUPs

Goals of PUPs typically are financial in nature, but it is not a requirement. Metrics like earnings per share (EPS), return on equity (ROE), and return on assets (ROA) are very popular. However, the PUP user should know what metrics fit the industry and the company. Service firms will differ from manufacturing companies; energy companies will differ from financial institutions, and so on.

THE USE OF EQUITY IN BENEFITS PLANS

The total rewards model defines benefits as focusing on two broad areas: income protection and pay for time not worked. Income protection can result from various benefits plans designed to protect the employees' standard of living and cash flow while employed and upon leaving the workforce.

Equity benefits plans address these needs, creating wealth-building opportunities that may either supplement employees' income during employment or build nest eggs that will produce income at retirement. Additionally, tax-qualified plans with broad-based employee eligibility tend to be part of the benefits package. In general, equity benefits plans tend to be broad-based, available to all or the majority of the workforce. This is because these plans are usually qualified, meeting IRC requirements that ensure a range of participation.

EMPLOYEE STOCK PURCHASE PLAN (ESPP)

Many companies classify the employee stock purchase plan (ESPP) as an employee benefit. Companies may establish ESPPs as an optional benefit for employee wealth building that allows them to share in the organization's performance.

An ESPP is a program under which employees buy shares in the company's stock by authorizing payroll deductions for a specified period of time. A qualified ESPP meets IRS statutory requirements and results in more favorable benefits and tax treatment for the employee, provided that the employee meets certain holding period requirements. A nonqualified ESPP does not result in favorable tax treatment for the employee, but permits a tax deduction for the company and may include any terms (e.g., discounts below statutory IRS limits).

Under FAS 123(R), ESPPs lose attractiveness because they now must be expensed unless they meet certain conditions. These conditions include a "safe harbor" discount of no more than 5 percent from fair market value and no look-back features.

According to 2005 estimates by NCEO, the number of participants in ESPPs is around 15.7 million in the United States. Companies, even before new accounting rules were issued, began eliminating or modifying their plans.

ESPPs allow employees to purchase company stock at a discounted price, often via payroll deduction. Because ESPPs are governed by Section 423 of the Internal Revenue Code, they are frequently referred to as "Section 423 Plans."

Statutory Requirements

In order to qualify as a Section 423 plan, an ESPP must meet several statutory requirements, including the following:

- *Eligibility*
  - Only employees are eligible to participate (IRC Section 423[b][1]). Participants must be employed continuously by the granting corporation from the grant date until at least three months prior to the exercise date (IRC Section 423[a][2]).
  - Employees possessing 5 percent or more of the corporation's voting power are ineligible (IRC Section 423[b][3]) to participate.

- *Shareholder approval.* The plan must be approved by shareholders within 12 months before or after the plan is adopted (IRC Section 423[b][2]).
- *Purchase price.* The purchase price may not be less than the lesser of 85 percent of FMV at grant or 85 percent of FMV at exercise (purchase) (IRC Section 423[b][6]). Note that purchase prices less than 95 percent may result in a charge to earnings under FAS 123(R).
- *Disposition.* As with ISOs, in order to qualify for preferential tax treatment for the employee, ESPPs may not be disposed of (sold) within two years after the grant date or one year after the transfer (purchase/exercise) date (IRC Section 423[a][1]).

ESPPs require that employees use their own resources to purchase the stock, thus creating a true ownership relationship. The employee risks his or her own cash in purchasing the shares and therefore takes the financial risk for the outcomes of the share performance. For each calendar year, the employee may purchase up to $25,000 in company stock, measured by the fair market value determined on the date of grant.

ESPP Pro and Con

The following is an advantage of ESPPs:

- ESPPs are attractive to employers because they provide a mechanism for employees to purchase shares without requiring a charge on the income statement for the discount (subject to the 5 percent discount limit established by FAS 123[R]).

The following is a disadvantage of ESPPs:

- Because employees' personal funds are at risk, ESPPs could lose their motivational effect if the stock price drops. To minimize this risk, many plans offer same-day sell provisions.

ESPP Tax Implications for the Employee

ESPPs share some characteristics with ISOs. A notable similarity is the ability of the plans to be qualified under the IRC for favorable tax treatment. As such, the tax treatment of ESPPs is similar to that of ISOs. The tax implications for an employee, as documented by NCEO, are as follows:

- Capital gains tax treatment at disposition unless either of the following two situations exists, resulting in ordinary income tax:
  - The purchase price is below FMV at grant (i.e., the purchase price is less than FMV on the purchase date). In this case, the employee would pay ordinary income tax upon disposition on the lesser of the discount he or she received at the time of grant or the total gain (i.e., the spread between the purchase price of the stock and the price at the time of sale). All additional gain upon the disposition/sale of the stock is subject to capital gains tax treatment.
  - The employee makes a disqualifying disposition, selling the stock prior to the required holding period (same as ISOs). In this case, the employee recognizes at disposition ordinary income on the bargain element and capital gains on appreciation above the bargain element.

ESPP Tax Implication for the Employer

- There is no deduction unless the employee makes a disqualifying disposition, in which case the employer can take a deduction in line with the ordinary income realized by the employee.

DEFINED CONTRIBUTION PLANS

Defined contribution plans are retirement plans. While ESPPs provide more latitude for employees to sell their shares early, defined contribution plans place more limitations in this area. Defined contribution plans vary in the percentage of the plan that may be invested in company stock. On one end of the spectrum are ESOPs, invested primarily in company stock. On the other end are 403(b) plans, offered by institutions that have no company stock.

Employee Stock Ownership Plan (ESOP)

An ESOP is a qualified defined contribution plan that enables employees to receive company shares that they accrue as plan participants upon retirement or separation from the organization. With an ESOP, the employer makes a defined annual contribution that accumulates to produce a benefit that is not defined in advance, as opposed to defined benefit retirement plans, which define the benefit in advance. Tax qualification of these plans ensures broad-based participation.

ESOPs are more common in closely held companies. One reason for this is that they provide retiring owners with a means of cashing in on the company's equity without selling to outsiders. They are less common in newer companies because owners are not at the point where they are considering selling their interests.

Contrary to the above, the majority of employees covered by ESOPs are employed in public companies. This is because public companies offering ESOPs typically have more employees than private companies.

ESOP Requirements

The nature of the ESOP is that employees' retirement funds are comprised mostly of company stock. As a result, the IRC places certain repurchase obligations on companies with ESOPs.[3] The first of these obligations refers to the need for nonpublicly traded companies to provide their employees with a market for their shares. This is done through a put option. With a put option, employees may sell their stock back to the company at independently appraised fair market rates. Similar to stock options, the put option is *exercised* by the employee during a specified exercise period, typically 60 days from the date of distribution.

A similarity between ESOPs and other equity rewards is the lack of diversification. To protect retirees from this risk, the code requires that companies must provide cash to the ESOP so that participants may diversify their accounts as follows:

- A 55-year-old participant with 10 years of participation can diversify 25 percent of his or her account in the 5 years after his or her 55th birthday.
- A 60-year-old participant with 10 years of participation can diversify as much as 50 percent of his or her company stock as of his or her 60th birthday.

Distributions can be made in a lump sum or in installments over several years. Publicly traded organizations can sell distributed shares in the stock market, but as noted earlier, privately held companies are required to offer the employees a put option on the stock for 60 days after distribution. If the employee chooses not to sell during that 60-day period, the organization then must give another put option for a second 60-day period beginning one year following the distribution date. After the second 60-day period, the employer (or ESOP trust) is no longer obligated to buy the shares from the employee.

Privately held companies may restrict ESOP participants from selling company stock received from the ESOP.[4] This "right of first refusal" allows the employer to make the ESOP distribution in cash or to mandate the employee to sell distributed stock back to the company. Additionally, the ESOP may allow the employer the right to match any third-party offer to purchase the stock.

ESOP vs. Stock Options

Some may confuse ESOPs with stock options, but in reality, the two plans are quite different. In addition to the fact that stock option plans are not defined contribution plans, the differences between these equity reward programs are illustrated in Figure 16.7.

ESOP Tax Implications for the Employer

Qualified defined contribution plans such as ESOPs defer the tax consequences to the employee, while the tax deduction for the employer is immediate. Company contributions to fund the ESOP are tax deductible up to certain limits. Dividends paid on ESOP-held stock are also tax deductible.

Under the Economic Growth and Tax Relief Reconciliation Act of 2001 (EGTRRA), employers may reinvest dividends in the plan and still take a deduction, provided that employees are given the option of receiving the dividend in cash or reinvesting it.

Money Purchase Pension Plans

Money purchase pension plans, which are common in union environments, are used when the employer contributes to the employee's account based upon a formula (e.g., equal to 5 percent of pay), regardless of profits.

FIGURE 16.7 ESOPs vs. stock options.

	ESOP	Stock Options
Retirement Program	Yes	No
Owned by Employee	At distribution	At exercise
Utilization	Established companies	Start-ups and established companies
Participation	Broad	Broad or limited

Money purchase pension plans do not allow pretax contributions and are used less frequently than other programs. They provide for specific retirement plan contributions, unrelated to profits or what an employee may contribute. They may not be included with a 401(k) plan feature (unless plans are separate and distinct) and the funds may be invested in company stock.

401(k) Plans

A 401(k) with solid investment options, a good company match, and reasonable vesting and eligibility requirements can be a helpful tool in attracting, motivating, and retaining employees. Multiple investments with a higher earnings potential than traditional savings accounts, the power of compounding, and tax-deferred earnings are some of the reasons the 401(k) provides a significant opportunity for employees to build a retirement nest egg.

Named after a section of the Internal Revenue Code that permits investments using pretax dollars, the 401(k) is perhaps the best-known defined contribution (DC) plan. A retirement planning vehicle, it allows tax-deferred savings in multiple investment options (including company stock). Employers may provide some or all of the employer matching contributions in company stock.

Key Features of the Basic 401(k) Plan

- The 401(k) plan may be offered by publicly or privately held companies.
- Employee is allowed to make contribution and independent investment choices among several investment alternatives.
- Company *often* matches contribution, typically with a maximum (e.g., company will match 50 percent for every dollar contributed by the employee up to 6 percent of employee's earnings).
- Investments are made in differing money markets, annuities, stocks—including company stock, bonds, etc.—ranging from low-risk to high-risk, high-return investments.
- Beginning with the 1999 plan year, a 401(k) plan may not require more than 10 percent of an employee's elective deferrals to be invested in employer stock. This restriction does not apply to employer matching contributions.
- Loans may be permitted from the 401(k) accounts and repaid through payroll deduction depending on plan design.

401(k) Tax Implications

Tax implications for 401(k) plans are similar to those for ESOPs.

- Employee
  - No taxes are paid on plan contributions.
  - Low- and middle-income participants may be eligible for a tax credit, in addition to pretax benefits of savings (EGTRRA).
  - Earnings on investments accumulate on a tax-deferred basis.
  - Distributions are taxable as ordinary income.
- Employer
  - Employer contribution is tax deductible at the time of contribution (IRC Section 404).

403(b) Plans

403(b) plans (and related 457 plans) are defined contribution plans that employers unable to offer 401(k) can provide as a retirement benefit to their employees. A 403(b) is a tax-sheltered annuity plan for nonprofit and public sector organizations (e.g., 501[c][3] organizations and educational institutions).

Though similar in many ways to the 401(k) plan, the 403(b) plan has distinct differences as well. The biggest difference between the two plans is who can participate. Both plans are devised for participants to save for retirement on a tax-deferred, pretax basis. Both plans are named after the IRC section governing their existence. Unlike the 401(k), 403(b) plans do not allow participants to invest in individual stocks. Typical investment options for 403(b) plans include:

- Insurance company annuity contracts.
- Mutual fund custodial accounts.
- Retirement income accounts for churches.

17 Employee Benefits Basics

To attract, motivate, and retain good workers, companies need to define what an employee wants from the employment relationship. One way to define employee needs is to consider "total rewards," which are everything an employee perceives to be of value resulting from working for the company.

Benefits are a core element of the WorldatWork total rewards model. (See Figure 1.3 in Chapter 1.) Benefits include health and welfare plans and retirement plans designed to help protect and ensure employees' financial security, as well as programs providing pay for time not worked. Over a period of time, employee benefits have evolved from basic "fringe benefits" of insurance coverage and a few perquisites to a comprehensive range of benefits that strike a balance between employees' personal and professional lives.

The ever-growing package of offerings has evolved, along with some compensation programs, into a separate element of the total rewards model, work-life. Can some programs of work-life be considered benefits? Yes, many organizations still consider them benefits. The total rewards model takes into account the fluidity of the relationship between compensation, benefits, and work-life. It will be up to each individual organization to define precisely where the various programs will be categorized.

HISTORICAL PERSPECTIVE OF BENEFITS

The world of employee benefits is drastically different than just 5 years ago, let alone 15 to 20 years ago. What is not new is that employees need benefits and companies need employees. However, due to the escalation of benefit costs, employers have started to re-examine the *employees'* role in the selection, payment, and management of benefits.

FIGURE 17.1 Historical influences—the benefits timeline.

Late Nineteenth Century
- U.S. economy changed from agricultural to industrial
- First pension plan established in 1875 by the American Express Company

1900s—World War I
- New workers entering United States
- Social safety nets; no financial safety nets
- Department of Labor (DOL) formed by Congress in 1913
- Homogeneous workforce (male, sole wage earner)

1920s—Riding High until Stock Market Crash
- Few disability benefits available to workers retired, injured, or killed on the job
- First Blue Cross plan established at Baylor University Hospital
- Kaiser Health Maintenance Organization (HMO) established
- Revenue Acts of 1921, 1926, and 1928 encouraged private, employer-sponsored retirement plans

1930s—Depression
- Public safety net began to develop
  - Workers' compensation
  - Unemployment insurance
  - Social Security (1935)
- National Labor Relations Act (NLRA)
  - Collective bargaining for pay and benefits

1940s—World War II
- National Labor Relations Board (NLRB) formed in 1948
- Huge growth in unions—unions demanded more for employees
- Women entered the workforce—"Rosie the Riveter"
- Family care issues emerged
- Private pension plans grew significantly

1950s—Post–World War II
- Fringe benefits emerging
- Employers began competing with benefits to address the wage freeze
- Simple benefits packages met the needs of the traditional family—major medical, life, disability, pension plan
- Low costs

1960s—Kennedy Assassinated; Vietnam
- Changing demographics
  - Divorce became more common; break-up of families
  - Working mothers (sole income) unsupported with benefits
  - More transient workforce
- Medicare and Medicaid established
- Title VII of the Civil Rights Act of 1964

1970s—Watergate; Oil Crisis
- Economic downturn—high inflation, slow economic growth
- More than 20 major pieces of legislation affecting benefits plans—specifically the Employee Retirement Income Security Act of 1974 (ERISA), IRC Section 125, 401(k), HMO Act
- Initial corporate response to changing workforce
  - Working mother issues began to take force
  - Single fathers became an issue

1980s—Computer Commonplace; Space Shuttle Challenger Explosion
- Benefit costs skyrocketed
- Gradual development of flexible benefits
- Announcement: Social Security is broke
- Cost shift to employees
- Consumer education
- Employers moving to "self-insurance" of health plans
- Beginnings of managed care (utilization management)

1990s—Information Technology; Internet
- Focus on benefit value and personal responsibility—optimizing the value for each dollar spent
- Performance orientation of benefits plans consistent with corporate goals
- Flexible benefits expanded, addressing the needs of a diverse workforce
- Employer accountability to expand choices for employees
  - Segmented benefits for different demographics
- Greater employee accountability for decision making
- Emerging shift in definition of dependent
  - Domestic partner, aging parents, elder care, adoption
- Consolidation of health care industry

2000s—Focus on Corporate Accounting/Governance; Concern for Lack of Health Care Coverage; Social Security Solvency
- National annual health expenditures projected to reach $3.1 trillion in 2012; gross domestic product (GDP) projected to reach 17.7 percent by 2012
- Health care costs on the rise again
  - Prescription drug costs soar
- Movement away from "entitlement" (paternalism) to partnership and shared accountability between employers and employees
- Consumer-driven health plans expand; consumerism opportunity provided by technology
- Wellness initiatives expand
- Funding for Social Security coverage debated
- Triple whammy: child-care, elder-care, and retirement planning at the same time
- Uninsured and underinsured increases; issue of universal health care coverage debated

Historically, employers handled all aspects of benefits. This was the era of providing "cradle to grave" benefits. Employers selected and paid for benefits. Employees had minimal to no input in any benefit-related decision. Benefits were considered "fringe" and employees viewed benefits as "entitlements." (See Figure 17.1.)

Today, initiatives from the U.S. government (involving Medicare) and employers are placing more responsibility and accountability on employees for benefit decision-making and cost responsibilities. Businesses and government still have important roles. But the trend is for employers and government to share the platform with benefit recipients. Some call this *shared accountability.*

ELEMENTS OF BENEFITS

Benefits programs may be categorized into the following two elements: (1) income protection programs; and (2) pay for time not worked programs. (See Figure 17.2.)

FIGURE 17.2 Benefits programs at a glance.

Income Protection Plans (Mandatory)

- State and Federal Unemployment Insurance
- Workers' Compensation
- Social Security
- State Temporary Disability Insurance (New Jersey, New York, Hawaii, Rhode Island, California)

Income Protection Programs (Non-Mandatory)

Health Care Benefits
- Medical Plans (Indemnity Plans and Managed Care Plans, such as HMOs, PPOs, and POS)
- Prescription Drug Coverage
- Dental Plans
- Vision Plans
- Hearing Plans

Welfare Benefits
- Employee Term Life Insurance
- Dependent Term Life Insurance
- Accidental Death and Dismemberment
- Sick Pay (Salary Continuation)
- Short-Term Disability
- Long-Term Disability
- Long-Term Care Insurance

Flexible Benefits
- Premium Conversion
- Flexible Spending Accounts (Health Care and Dependent Care)
- Full Flexible Benefits Plans

Retirement and Investment Plans
- Defined Benefit Plans
- Defined Contribution Plans (Savings/Thrift Plans, Profit-Sharing Plans, SIMPLE Plans, Money Purchase Plans, Employee Stock Ownership Plans)
- Hybrid Plans (Cash Balance Plans, Pension Equity Plans)

Executive Benefits
- Supplemental Executive Retirement Plans
- Supplemental Health Plans
- Supplemental Life Insurance Plans
- Supplemental Disability Plans

Pay for Time Not Worked (Non-Mandatory)

At Work
- Rest Periods
- Lunch Periods

- Wash-Up Time
- Clothes Change Time

Not at Work

- Vacations
- Holidays
- Personal Leave
- Jury Duty
- Military Duty

Income Protection Programs

Income protection programs are designed to protect the standard of living of the employee and his or her family. The programs include mandatory and nonmandatory or voluntary coverage.

Mandatory plans are required by federal or state law to cover employees for:

- Social Security.
- Workers' compensation.
- Unemployment.
- Nonoccupational disability (five states only).

Nonmandatory or voluntary plans are provided at the discretion of the employer and include:

- Medical.
- Prescription drug.
- Mental/behavioral health.
- Dental.
- Vision.
- Disability income.
- Survivor benefits.
- Flexible spending accounts.
- Retirement plans.

Pay for Time Not Worked Programs

Pay for time not worked programs are designed to protect the employee's income flow during certain periods, both at work and not at work, when the employee is not working.

For example, common paid time off benefits would include vacation, holidays, sick-pay, and leaves of absence including time off for jury duty, voting, military duty, and medical or bereavement leaves.

BENEFITS PLAN OBJECTIVES

Employers and employees value benefits differently. They will rarely agree on the level of benefits that plans should provide. Employers seek to balance the employees' needs and the cost to the organization. Employees wish to maximize the value of benefits received and minimize out-of-pocket expenses.

Employer Objectives

The employer objectives for benefits plans are influenced by:

- Meeting corporate, business, and compensation objectives.
- Actual dollar cost and percentage of payroll.
- Administration complexity and cost.
- Tax and accounting issues.
- The role benefits play in the total rewards objectives of the organization.

Employee Objectives

Employee objectives for benefits plans include income protection for:

- *Cash flow:* ensuring cash flow is not compromised due to large medical and/or dental claims.
- *Income replacement:* replacing income if employee becomes disabled.
- *Income for surviving dependents:* providing income for surviving dependents in the event of death.
- *Adequate retirement income:* providing adequate income upon retirement.

In order to design a benefits program, an organization should define its program objectives. Additionally, program objectives need to be aligned with the organization's and HR's philosophy and strategy. Because company philosophies and strategies differ, no two companies will share the same objectives for employee benefits plans.

Review the objectives listed in Figure 17.3 and rank the three to five objectives that are most important to your company regarding employee benefits.

FIGURE 17.3 Employee benefits plan objectives.

Please prioritize the top three to five objectives for employee benefits in your organization.

Objectives	Rank
Increase employee morale	_____
Motivate action	_____
Attract good employees	_____
Reduce turnover	_____
Keep unions out	_____
Better use compensation dollars	_____
Enhance employee security	_____
Maintain favorable competitive position	_____
Enhance organization's image among employees	_____
Increase employee productivity	_____

GOVERNMENT REGULATION OF BENEFITS PLANS

Management of employee benefits includes compliance with numerous federal and state laws and regulations. Sanctions and penalties for noncompliance can be severe, including plan "disqualification" under the Internal Revenue Code. Disqualification can cause employees to lose tax exemption or tax deferral of benefits values, and employers to lose the advantage of tax deductibility of plan expenditures.

Figure 17.4 highlights major laws affecting benefits plans and identifies principal agencies that issue regulations and monitor compliance. At least one new law each year affects some aspect of employee benefits. It is important to know that benefits continue to change due to legislation.

Federal regulations with the most significant influences include:

- *Internal Revenue Code (IRC).*
  - Refers to tax laws passed by Congress and administered by the IRS.
  - Early statute governing private pension plans.

FIGURE 17.4 Regulations of employee benefits.

Laws/Regulations	Scope/Provisions	Enforcing Agency
Family and Medical Leave Act of 1993 (FMLA)	Group health plans—requirement to continue regular coverage during periods of qualifying leaves (as many as 12 weeks per year).	U.S. Department of Labor (DOL)
Civil Rights Act of 1964	All benefits plans—regulations prohibiting discrimination against women and other protected classes in benefits plan "terms and conditions."	Equal Employment Opportunity Commission (EEOC)
Consolidated Omnibus Budget Reconciliation Act of 1985 (COBRA)	Group health plans—requirements for continuation of coverage following termination of employment and other "qualifying events."	U.S. Department of Labor (DOL) Internal Revenue Service (IRS) U.S. Public Health Service (for state and local employee plans)
Health Insurance Portability and Accountability Act of 1996 (HIPAA)	Group health plans—requires employers to provide terminated employees with a certificate of group health plan coverage, when requested.	U.S. Department of Labor (DOL)

(continued)

FIGURE 17.4 *(Continued)*

Securities and Exchange Commission (SEC) Regulations	Plans that provide employer stock to participants—information requirements	Securities and Exchange Commission (SEC)
State insurance regulation	Insured benefits plans—standards for coverage, conversion and coordination of benefits.	State insurance commissioners
Health Savings Accounts (Part of Medicare Prescription Drug Improvement & Modernization Act of 2003)	Provide tax incentives to lower health care costs. Includes "high deductibles." Must be under age 65 to participate.	Department of the Treasury

- *Title VII of the Civil Rights Act of 1964.*
  - Employers can never legally base benefits decisions on race, color, religion, sex, or national origin.
- *Age Discrimination in Employment Act of 1967 (ADEA).*
  - If an employer provides benefits to its employees, it generally must do so without regard to an employee's age. ADEA does permit employers to provide different benefits to older employees only under certain circumstances.
- *The Employee Retirement Income Security Act of 1974 (ERISA).*
  - ERISA introduced federal government involvement in the employee benefits arena.
  - ERISA establishes minimum standards to provide protection for participants and beneficiaries in employee benefits plans (participant rights). Among other things, ERISA standards cover access to plan information and fiduciary responsibility.
  - ERISA covers most private sector health and pension plans but does not apply to public-sector benefits.
  - Those individuals who manage plans (and other fiduciaries) must meet certain standards of conduct under the fiduciary responsibilities specified by law.

(For a more in-depth look at ERISA and other federal laws, see Chapter 18.)

For many years, the federal government has encouraged the development of employee benefits plans because of their social value. One way this has occurred is through changes in the tax code. In recent years, however, increasing controls and regulations have offset some tax advantages. These include:

- Federal tax advantages for *both* employers and employees.
- "Qualified plans" that meet IRS requirements and receive allowable offsets for statutory coverage.

The Pension Protection Act's Impact on Total Rewards Professionals

The Pension Protection Act (PPA) of 2006 ushers in perhaps the most significant changes to impact retirement security in 20 years. Most of the provisions will not take effect until 2008, but the bill will have immediate and long-lasting effects on how employers provide retirement security to their employees.
Highlights of the Act include:

- The PPA requires plans to be 100 percent funded and tightens the actuarial assumptions that apply when employers calculate the accrued liability and the return on plan assets.
- The PPA amends section 409A of the Internal Revenue Code to provide a 20 percent excise tax penalty to certain executives if funds are set aside to pay nonqualified deferred compensation if the employer or a member of its controlled group is bankrupt, has an at-risk plan, or a plan that has terminated with insufficient assets to cover all liabilities. In addition, the PPA blocks the employer from taking a deduction for tax gross-up payments intended to cover the penalties triggered by funding nonqualified deferred compensation.
- The PPA restricts payments from plans that are less than 60 percent funded and prohibits benefit increases for plans that are less than 80 percent funded, using a special liability measure, and limits lump-sum payments.
- The PPA permits employees who reach age 62 to continue working and to receive pension payments without being penalized under tax law or the Employee Retirement Income Security Act (ERISA).
- The PPA sets a single age discrimination standard for all defined benefit (DB) plans under ERISA. It clarifies that hybrid plans such as cash balance or pension equity plans do not violate the age discrimination provisions in ERISA, the Code or the Age Discrimination in Employment Act (ADEA) if the individual's accrued benefit would be equal to or greater than any similarly situated younger individual who could be a participant.
- The PPA places restrictions on conversions from traditional DB to hybrid plans. It requires employers to start benefit accruals under the new plan immediately after a conversion takes effect.
- The PPA makes it easier for employers to encourage employee participation in 401(k) plans by creating a safe harbor from fiduciary liability and state garnishment laws for automatic enrollment programs.
- The PPA provides for the purchase of long-term care from annuity and life insurance products, making these products more flexible.
- The PPA allows employees to diversify at any time out of employer stock purchased with employee contributions. It requires employers to allow diversification out of employer contributions after the employee has been in the plan for three years and may be phased in over three years.

(continued)

(Continued)

- The PPA requires all employer contributions, whether matching or non-elective, to vest entirely after three years or phased in 20 percent per year starting in the second year the employee participates in a plan.

The PPA of 2006 contains many complex provisions and the true implications will not be fully understood for some time to come. However, as the concept of retirement security continues to change, the measure provides new opportunities for total rewards professionals to add value for their employees and companies.

The role of government in addressing the social needs of the nation underwent a dramatic and controversial change in the 1980s and 1990s. Federal budget deficits forced Congress to:

- View with caution any proposals for new programs that would require increased federal spending.
- Look for additional methods of increasing revenues by taxing items that had not been taxed before.

Federal governing agencies that influence employee benefits plans include:

Equal Employment Opportunity Commission (EEOC)

Established by Title VII of the Civil Rights Act of 1964, the EEOC began operating on July 2, 1965. It enforces the following federal statutes:

- Title VII of the Civil Rights Act of 1964.
- The Age Discrimination in Employment Act of 1967 (ADEA).
- The Equal Pay Act of 1963 (EPA).
- Title I and Title V of the Americans with Disabilities Act of 1990 (ADA).

Department of Labor (DOL)

The Employee Benefits Security Administration (EBSA), formerly known as the Pension and Welfare Benefits Administration (PWBA), of the U.S. Department of Labor (DOL) is responsible for administering and enforcing provisions of ERISA.

Securities and Exchange Commission (SEC)

The SEC is responsible for ensuring that employees as investors receive financial and other significant information concerning securities being offered for public sale (e.g., company stock, 401(k), and employee stock ownership plans).

Pension Benefit Guaranty Corporation (PBGC)

The PBGC, an agency under the EBSA, guarantees vested defined benefit pensions up to a maximum amount established annually. Employers offering covered pension plans pay insurance premiums.

STATUTORY BENEFITS

Federal and state laws require all companies to offer the following "core" benefits: (1) Social Security (federal); (2) Workers' compensation (state); (3) Unemployment compensation (state); and (4) Nonoccupational disability (five states).

Social Security

Since its creation in the 1930s, Social Security has been at the center of national public policy debates. In 1945, there were 20 workers for every retiree and few sources of retirement income security outside the extended family. Today, there are only three active workers to support each retiree, and extended families provide minimal support.[1]

The Social Security system has four distinct types of benefits:

- OA—retirement income in "old age."
- S—survivor income.
- D—disability income.
- HI—health insurance benefits (Medicare).

The federal Old Age, Survivors, Disability, and Health Insurance Program (OASDHI) emerged as a result of the Social Security Act of 1935. The federal budget now includes almost $500 billion in spending toward Social Security; less than half of that amount goes toward retirement.

Old Age (OA): Retirement Benefits

Presently, the earliest age at which one can start receiving Social Security retirement benefits is 62. Those born prior to 1938 are eligible to receive full benefits beginning at age 65. Those born after 1959 cannot receive full benefits until age 67. Those born between 1938 and 1959 are on a graduated scale. An individual who wishes to retire early may do so but is subject to a reduction in benefits as follows:

- 5/9 of 1 percent for each month (up to 36 months)[2] that the benefit is paid prior to full retirement age (FRA), plus 5/12 of 1 percent for each month that the benefit is paid earlier than 36 months prior to full retirement age.

Individuals also are eligible for increased benefits beyond full retirement age (between 5 percent and 8 percent per year depending on the year of birth).

Floor of Protection

Monthly Social Security benefits provide a minimal standard of living. Compensation is taxed and benefits are calculated based upon the employee's covered compensation up to each year's taxable wage base. Social Security, however, was never intended to be a sole source of retirement income.

Previously, some retirement benefits were withheld from workers ages 65 through 69 when they reached a certain earnings level. In 2000, the "Freedom to Work Act" was passed, allowing older workers who reached full retirement age to work and receive their full Social Security retirement benefits. There continues to be an earnings limitation for Social Security retirees under the age of full retirement whose employment earnings exceed a certain level.

Social Security Survivor (S) Benefits Key Characteristics

- $255 lump sum death benefit payment.
- Benefit has not been indexed.
- Was originally intended to cover funeral costs.
- Widows and widowers.
- Survivors age 60 and older.
- Survivors ages 50 to 59 if disabled.
- Any survivor age if caring for dependent children (under age 16).
- Dependent children to age 18 (19 if a full-time student).
- Dependent parents (age 62 and older) who had been receiving at least half of their support from the beneficiary at the time of death.

Medicare Part B: Supplementary Medical Insurance Key Characteristics

- Cost.
  - Individuals who choose to participate in Part B: Supplementary Medical Insurance are required to pay a premium that is adjusted annually by the government. If a person does not enroll upon initial eligibility, he or she remains eligible to enroll during a future enrollment period but will pay a higher premium.
- Annual deductible.
  - After deductible, covered individuals pay 20 percent and Medicare pays 80 percent.
- Basic list of covered services.
  - Physicians' services.
  - Physical and occupational therapists.
  - Diagnostic X-ray, laboratory, and other tests.
- Prescriptions.
  - In December 2003, President George W. Bush signed into law the Medicare Prescription Drug, Improvement, and Modernization Act (H.R.1). This act created a prescription drug benefit for the first time in Medicare history. (See Sidebar 17.1.)

Social Security Health Insurance (HI)

Medicare is the most expensive component of Social Security. It covers persons aged 65 and over and persons who are disabled and have been receiving disability benefits from Social Security for two years.

Covered individuals pay the deductible for each confinement. The deductible is the amount that covered individuals pay for hospital charges, as determined each

Sidebar 17.1: The Impact of Medicare Reform

H.R. 1, the Medicare Prescription Drug, Improvement, and Modernization Act of 2003, has had—and will continue to have—a major impact on employer-provided benefits. A good start to understanding the Act's implications would be to examine the key provisions that affect employers in this new era of consumer-driven health care.

H.R. 1, commonly referred to as the Medicare Modernization Act (MMA), ushered in some important changes by creating health savings accounts (HSAs), which greatly alter the landscape of employer-provided health care arrangements.

An HSA is a trust created for an individual that is established to pay the qualified medical expenses of the individual (or the individual's dependents). The trustee of the trust typically is a bank, an insurance company, or a third-party administrator. HSAs are not taxed on any earnings accrued while the assets are held in trust.

HSAs, which took effect at the beginning of 2004, are portable (meaning rollovers are permitted from other HSAs) and may be funded on a pre-tax basis and through a cafeteria plan. Additionally, an individual's HSA can be transferred tax-free upon divorce or separation to another individual or to the individual's spouse upon death. If the HSA is transferred to someone other than the individual's spouse upon death, the account ceases to be an HSA and the HSA assets become taxable income at the fair market value to the individual or the individual's estate.

The Tax Relief and Health Care Act of 2006, which was passed before Congress adjourned in December 2006, includes important changes for HSAs. The new law, according to the Employee Benefits Institute of America Inc., affects HSA eligibility for certain individuals who are covered by health flexible spending arrangements (health FSAs) during a grace period, changes the limits for allowable HSA contributions, and allows a rollover from an IRA, health reimbursement arrangement (HRA), or health FSA to an HSA under certain conditions.

Medicare Part D

Under MMA, Medicare Part D provides a limited, voluntary benefit for outpatient prescription drugs. Although the number of employers offering post-retirement health benefits has declined significantly in recent years, Medicare's new drug benefit has revitalized discussions about whether and how to provide retiree health care.

The Medicare prescription drug benefit (Part D) is delivered to beneficiaries either through a private prescription drug plan (PDP) or Medicare Advantage plans (either Medicare HMOs or PPOs).

Medicare prescription drug plans must, at a minimum, provide a standard level of coverage. According to the Centers for Medicare and Medicaid Services (CMS), for the standard level of Medicare prescription drug coverage in 2007, participants pay a $265 yearly deductible, then 25 percent of the yearly

(continued)

Sidebar 17.1 *(Continued)*

drug costs from $265 to $2,400 (the plan pays the other 75 percent of these costs). Once a participant reaches $2,400 in total drug costs (not including premiums), there is a gap in Medicare's coverage. While participants are in this coverage gap, the plan will pay nothing toward the drug costs. But they will have access to the drug plan's discounted rate for their drugs during this time. After they reach $5,451.25 in total drug costs for the year, they will only have to pay 5 percent of the discounted cost of each prescription.

Those who qualify for extra help because of limited income and assets, receive help that pays for all or part of the monthly premiums, deductible, and fills in the coverage gap and lowers the prescription copayments.

According to the Medicare RX Education Network, as of December 2006, roughly a third of Medicare beneficiaries get drug coverage from their former employer. If a beneficiary's employer continues to offer prescription drug coverage, he or she can decide whether to keep the existing coverage or switch to another plan. Note: Those who drop their employer-sponsored drug coverage may not be able to re-enroll.

As of this writing, employer-sponsored plans that provide an "actuarially equivalent" prescription drug benefit to Medicare beneficiaries are eligible to receive a financial subsidy to help offset their costs. For up-to-date information, go online and visit www.medicare.gov.

---

year by the government, prior to Medicare paying. Medicare pays the full cost of remaining charges for the first 60 days per occurrence of illness.

Other limited hospital insurance benefits include skilled nursing facilities, home health services, and hospice care. Custodial care is not covered.

Social Security FICA Tax

Federal Insurance Contributions Act (FICA) taxes are the taxes for Social Security. Employers and employees equally share the tax, which was separated into two components in 1991. As coverage has become more comprehensive and more people have become eligible, the tax rate and wage base (indexed each year) have increased steadily. For the health insurance component, 1994 was the first year that no maximum tax applied.

Workers' Compensation

Workers' compensation is employer-paid and offered by all states. The employee receives income and the employer pays for medical and rehabilitation costs associated with a work-related incident resulting in an injury or illness.

Unemployment

Like workers' compensation, unemployment compensation is employer-paid and offered by all states. Unemployment compensation provides income (for a period of time) to an employee who loses employment and is willing and able to work.

Nonoccupational Disability

Five states (New York, New Jersey, Rhode Island, California, and Hawaii) offer a nonoccupational disability benefit. The benefit provides temporary or short-term income due to a nonoccupational incident resulting in a disability.

HEALTH AND WELFARE PLANS

Health and welfare plans are critical components of the employee benefits package. These plans have been affected by significant changes over the years, including the introduction of managed care in the 1990s. However, escalating health costs, particularly for prescription drugs, have placed increasing pressure on benefits professionals attempting to continue to offer competitive benefits while maintaining fiscal responsibility for their employers' benefits budgets. As a result of these challenges and changes in the tax code, programs such as consumer-driven health plans have emerged, offering employees greater benefits choices with certain tax incentives.

Health and Welfare: A Brief History

When Social Security first surfaced in the 1930s, it excluded health insurance, causing the private sector to take the lead in sponsoring health insurance coverage. Blue Cross/Blue Shield developed private plans, soon to be followed by commercial insurers.

The wage freezes of the post-WWII era prompted companies to offer noncash rewards in the form of health care. This is where the entitlement mentality began, with employees feeling entitled to health care insurance. Soon after, the Taft Hartley Act mandated the inclusion of benefits in collective bargaining. This era also saw the first major medical benefits introduced, supplementing the hospital and surgical coverage previously offered.

Over time, more companies began offering health insurance and other options, such as dental. However, health care costs began rising faster than the consumer price index. U.S. workers began to retire as they reached age 65 and found no viable health care insurance available. The federal government responded by instituting programs such as Medicare and Medicaid.

The lack of cost-cutting initiatives soon led to rising health care costs and the emergence of health maintenance organizations (HMOs) to curb these costs. Congress then enacted ERISA to protect qualified benefits plans, and the introduction of diagnostic related groups of service (DRGs) helped curb Medicare costs.

Soon, unions began to reduce bargained benefits due to most companies' inability/unwillingness to sustain current levels of coverage. Larger numbers of employers self-insured, finding they had more control over benefits offered and associated costs.

Although HMOs did help to control costs, quality of care and choice of providers became a prevailing issue with employees. Enter the era of preferred provider organizations (PPOs) with negotiated-fee contracts and a larger choice of providers.

Now, as health care costs again rise, many employers are opting to embrace a strategic approach to consumerism.

Health and Welfare Plan Elements

Health and welfare plans are primarily categorized as follows:

- Health care.
  - Medical.
  - Prescription drug.
  - Behavioral health.
  - Dental.
  - Vision.
  - Long-term care.
- Disability income.
  - Sick leave.
  - Short-term disability and/or salary continuation.
  - Long-term disability.
- Survivor benefits.
  - Term life.
  - Accidental death and dismemberment.
  - Dependent life.
  - Business travel accident.

HEALTH CARE

Health care programs, in particular medical care, are generally the most popular and most expensive component of a company's employee benefits program. *Managed care* plans, the most prevalent medical care programs, attempt to control cost and ensure quality of care by encouraging the utilization of network providers who have agreed to accept discounted fee payments. These models include health maintenance organizations (HMO), preferred provider organizations (PPO), point of service (POS), and other hybrid arrangements. *Indemnity* plans, now rare, are traditional plans that provide specific cash reimbursement for covered services.

Health Maintenance Organization (HMO)

An HMO provides a network of physicians and hospitals for employees and their dependents to receive comprehensive care, including preventive care. The traditional HMO model requires receiving a referral from the primary physician or "gatekeeper" to receive care from a specialist. Otherwise, the employee could be liable to pay the total cost to see the specialist.

Preferred Provider Organization (PPO)

Unlike HMOs, the PPO model does not include a primary physician or gatekeeper. PPOs include two levels: *in-network* providers (physicians and hospitals) and *out-of-network* providers. By using the in-network providers, employees receive a higher level of reimbursement for care. The PPO provider should not bill the employee for any differences between the discounted contracted rate and the

---

Health Maintenance Organization (HMO) Key Characteristics

HMOs are managed care plans that attempt to control the cost and ensure quality of care by encouraging preventive care. They provide both the financing and delivery of comprehensive medical coverage. Key features include:

- Primary care physician (PCP).
  - Employee-selected physician that provides all routine medical care.
  - Serves as gatekeeper by controlling specialist referral, therefore curbing unnecessary medical expenses.
- Preventive/routine care typically includes:
  - Well-woman, well-man, well-baby care.
  - Routine physicals.
  - Immunizations.
- Copayments eliminate deductibles and coinsurance.
- Provider pay is sometimes on a capitation or discounted fee-for-service basis; physicians are sometimes salaried.
- HMO models.
  - Independent Practice Association (IPA).
  - Group Practice Association (GPA).
  - Staff.
  - Combinations.

---

provider's normal fee. In contrast, out-of-network providers could charge more for services rendered.

Point of Service (POS)

A typical POS is a combination of HMO and PPO. The employee would need a referral to see an in-network specialist (similar to an HMO). However, the cost for seeing an out-of network specialist would be higher than an in-network provider (similar to a PPO).

Point of Service (POS) Key Characteristics

Point of service (POS) evolved as a response to a market force. It addressed the concerns employees had about being locked into the narrow network of an HMO plan. POS combines discounted fee agreements for cost savings with employee choice. Key features include:

- A hybrid between traditional indemnity, HMOs, and PPOs.
- A coordinated delivery system aimed at managing utilization and cost by means of:
  - Eliminating excessive utilization.
  - Reducing costs through negotiated discount payments and capitation.
  - Aligning the interests of all payers.

Preferred Provider Organization (PPO) Key Characteristics

PPOs are arrangements where providers agree to discount their normal fees. They continue to have the highest enrollment on a national basis. Key features include:

- Discounted fee for service.
  - To achieve greater volume.
  - No capitation.
  - Fees subject to a schedule.
- Broader choice of providers.
  - Choice of provider usually made at time medical care is needed.
- Incentives to use preferred providers.
  - Lower or reduced deductibles and coinsurance.
  - Increased coverage, such as preventive care.
- In-network/out-of-network.
  - Patient may access in-network specialty care without primary care physician gatekeeper coordination.
  - If patient chooses out-of-network care, financial incentives do not apply.
- Utilization reviews.
  - Assessment of medical necessity.
  - Curbs unnecessary procedures and monitors hospital stays.

- Choice of providers.
  - Selected at time of treatment.
  - Primary care physician gatekeeper coordinates in-network specialty care.
- In network/out-of-network benefits.
  - Out-of-network provider, deductibles, and copayments tend to be higher. Meaningful coinsurance differential provides incentives to use in-network care.
  - Patient retains some coverage for services even if not authorized by primary care physician.
- Models.
  - Open-ended.
  - Gatekeeper.

Indemnity Plans

Traditional indemnity medical plans (offered by Blue Cross/Blue Shield) are still available, but at a rapidly decreasing rate. The first health insurance plan in existence, an indemnity plan is designed where the employee pays a deductible after base benefits are exhausted. Indemnity plans offer greater "freedom of choice" in selecting providers because referrals are not needed, and the employee is free to visit any provider. However, the indemnity is now rare since it is the most expensive medical model.

Prescription Drug

Prescription/drug programs are growing in popularity and costs. These programs can be part of the medical program or carved out and managed by a Pharmacy Benefit Manager (PBM). Companies are now offering three or four tiers of coverage. Employee copayments also increase by tier. Examples include:

Tier 1: Generic drugs	$10–$15 copayment.
Tier 2: Brand drugs	$20–$25 copayment.
Tier 3: Lifestyle drugs	$30–$50 copayment.
Tier 4: Mail order	Three-month supply for "maintenance" drugs. Copayment can be equal to one or two months' copayments.

An emerging trend is for copayments to be a percentage of costs instead of a dollar amount.

Behavioral Health

Coverage includes mental health and chemical dependency services. Services can be provided on an inpatient or outpatient basis and are often integrated with an employee assistance program (EAP).

Dental Plans

Most dental plans have four components. They are:

1. Preventive and diagnostic.
2. Basic services.
3. Major services.
4. Orthodontia.

Dental plans often provide 100 percent reimbursement for preventive and diagnostic services; charges for these services usually are not subject to a deductible. The rationale is to encourage employees to have periodic dental visits because these exams can help prevent future dental services more costly to both the employer and employee.

Deductibles can apply to all other services. Because of costs, orthodontia (installation and adjustment of braces) is not included in all dental plans or only applies to dependent children. In addition, orthodontia services are usually subject to a per-person lifetime maximum ($1,000–$1,500).

The traditional dental model is the indemnity approach (similar to medical indemnity model). To control costs and expand services, companies provide managed care models called DMO (dental management organization—similar to medical HMO) or a DPPO (dental preferred provider organization—similar to medical PPO).

Vision

Vision care plans often provide a flat-dollar rate of reimbursement or a specific percentage reimbursement for an annual eye examination and a new pair of lenses per year. New frames are usually limited to one pair every two years.

Concern for eyewear and strain is growing due to use of computer monitors.

Long-Term Care

Long-term care is growing in importance as people live longer. Coverage commences when a person is unable to perform at least two of the five daily living activities—bathing, dressing, eating, walking, and using the bathroom.

DISABILITY INCOME

Disability income benefits are income replacement programs provided by employers or public agencies during the time an employee is unable to work due to a qualified disability.

Sick Leave

Key features:

- Specified number of days.
- Based on service.
- Continuation of full pay.
- May be carried from one year to the next.

Short-Term Disability (STD)

The STD benefit provides income when an employee is unable to work due to a short-term nonoccupational illness or injury. There is usually a seven-day calendar waiting period to qualify for benefit coverage that commences after the seventh day from the incident. Benefits can extend for up to six months. Payment is a percentage of pay, often 50 percent up to a weekly maximum.

Long-Term Disability (LTD)

The LTD benefit provides income due to a nonwork illness or injury; payments can be up to age 65. The waiting period to qualify for coverage ranges from three to six months from the date of incident. Payments range from 50 percent to 67 percent of wages up to a maximum monthly amount.

While an employee collects LTD, most employers will continue to accrue pension benefits for the employee at the predisability rate of pay.

If the employee pays the full cost of LTD coverage with post-tax dollars, then any benefits paid are nontaxable. If the employer pays the full cost of LTD coverage or the employee pays the premium with pretax dollars, then any benefits paid are subject to tax.

LTD plans typically have a split definition of disability eligibility. To be eligible, an employee must be unable to perform current job duties for the first two years when benefits are payable; and thereafter, unable to perform job duties of any occupation. This transition period is designed to help an employee prepare to change careers without a loss of income.

SURVIVOR BENEFITS

Term Life Insurance

The most typical form of survivor benefits is term life insurance. The insurance is paid to the employee's designated beneficiary (who can be anyone) in a lump sum. In contrast, under statutory programs such as Social Security and workers' compensation, payment of survivor benefits depends on whether the employee has a spouse or eligible dependents as outlined by applicable law.

The practice for lump sum payments for exempt (salaried) staff is usually multiples of annual salary. The norm for nonexempt (hourly) workers is a flat dollar amount (independent of annual wages) but in some companies is multiples of annual wages.

Term life insurance ends upon termination of employment. Employees have the right to convert within 30 days of termination to a whole life or universal life insurance policy. Rates per $1,000 of coverage are based on age. The benefit to employees is the waiving of passing a physical.

The Internal Revenue Code permits an employer to provide up to $50,000 of noncontributory group life insurance to an employee without any tax consequences, provided the plan does not discriminate in favor of higher-paid employees. Employees who receive more than $50,000 of employer-paid group life insurance are subject to additional taxes depending on an employee's age and amount of coverage in excess of $50,000. This additional tax is called imputed income tax.

Accidental Death and Dismemberment (AD&D)

AD&D provides a benefit to the employee in the event of dismemberment or the beneficiary in the event of accidental death. It often duplicates the term life amount and has two components: company-paid portion and supplemental (employee-paid) portion.

Supplemental Life Insurance

It's common for employers to provide employees with opportunities to purchase additional term life insurance. Rates vary by employees' ages. Older workers pay more per $1,000 of coverage than younger workers.

Dependent Life Insurance

Employees can purchase life insurance for a spouse and dependent children. This benefit is often called "burial insurance." The monthly premium is usually very low and the benefit is a set dollar amount.

FLEXIBLE BENEFITS

Flexible benefits provide employees with choices that allow them to select between cash and one or more qualified (nontaxable) benefits (e.g., health, life, disability insurance). Made possible by Section 125 of the Internal Revenue Code (IRC), flexible benefits plans are also referred to as "cafeteria plans."

Employees have a chance to change elections to their flexible benefits plan during an annual open enrollment period held by the employer. Changes during a plan year are only allowed in the event of a "qualified status change" as defined by the IRS. Qualified status changes include the birth or adoption of a child, the death of a dependent, open enrollment at a spouse's place of employment, marriage, or divorce.

Flexible benefits allow employers to:

- Manage rising costs.
- Maximize employee perceptions of benefits.
- Facilitate program design.
- Readily adapt to change in laws, benefits, and business conditions.
- Reap advantage of tax savings.
- Support a total rewards focus.
- Meet competitive pressures.
- Maintain progressive company image.

See Chapter 21 for a more in-depth look at flexible benefits.

RETIREMENT PLANS

Under the Employee Retirement Income Security Act of 1974 (ERISA), and the Internal Revenue Code (IRC), employer-provided pension plans are classified as either:

- Defined benefit (DB) plans, or
- Defined contribution (DC) plans.

Key differences between these two types of plans are highlighted in Figure 17.5.

Defined Benefit (DB) Plans

A defined benefit plan promises an employee a specific future benefit if certain age, tenure, and income projections are achieved. The actual plan formula and the definition of earnings in the formula have a significant impact on the level of benefits an employee will receive. Many DB plans use the average of an employee's highest 5 consecutive calendar years of earnings during the employee's last 10 years of service to calculate benefits. This "high" 5 of past "10" method frequently is referred to as FAP or final average pay.

An example of a DB plan is found in Figure 17.6.

Cash-balance plans, also categorized under hybrid pension plans, are DB plans. Companies are switching from traditional pension plans to cash-balance plans since they are less costly to the employer and provide a guaranteed pension to workers. An employee's vested balance is portable upon termination.

FIGURE 17.5 Primary differences between defined benefit and defined contribution plans.

Defined Benefit Plans	Defined Contribution Plans
Benefit is known	Benefit is unknown
Cost is unknown	Cost is known
Employer bears financial risk	Employee bears financial risk
Generally provides higher benefits for long-service employees	Can provide substantial benefits to short-service employees
Separate account for each employee is not required	Separate account for each employee is required
Requires sign-off by an enrolled actuary	Actuary not required. However, record keeper is required.
Subject to PBGC premiums	Not subject to PBGC premiums

In DB pension plans, employers typically fund the plan 100 percent. Employees make no contributions and become vested (entitled to pension) upon being vested. However, even after becoming vested, an employee may have to wait to receive the pension. Normal retirement is age 65 with early retirement at age 55. Plans can have lower age limits.

Most companies use either "cliff" or "graded" vested schedules. Cliff means the employee becomes fully vested after five years of qualified service. With graded, an employee becomes partially vested after two years and increases a percentage of vesting for each year after two, but must be fully vested after seven years. These vesting schedules are used for "qualified plans" as defined by ERISA. Qualified plans mean both the employer and employee receive favorable tax treatments on pension monies.

Most DB pension plans provide a variety of payout options. A key consideration is whether anyone is financially dependent on the employee. Generally, a single life annuity option will provide the largest monthly premium. Following are the most prevalent:

- *Single life annuity:* Benefits are payable only to the employee. There is no survivor benefit. When the employee dies, all payment ceases. This is the default option for single employees. This means if the single employee dies before selecting an option, the plan automatically selects single life annuity.
- *Joint and survivor option:* The employee is the "joint" and the spouse is the "survivor." This is the default option for a married employee who dies before electing an option. If a married employee wishes an option other than joint and survivor, then the employee's spouse must sign a form agreeing to permit the employee to do so. Otherwise, the employee must use the joint and survivor option.

  If the employee (joint) dies first, then the spouse (survivor), depending on the percentage for this option, will receive 100 percent, 75 percent, or 50 percent of the employee's monthly pension. Payment will stop once the survivor

FIGURE 17.6 Sample defined benefit plan.

Eligibility
Date of employment
Formula
1.75 percent × final average pay × years of service
Final Average Pay
An employee's highest five consecutive calendar years of earning during his or her last 10 years of service
Normal Retirement
Age 65
Early Retirement
At least age 55 and 10 or more years of service
Vested Benefit
100 percent vested after five years of credited service
Payment Option
Lump sum or 50 percent joint and survivor annuity or 100 percent joint and survivor annuity

dies. If the survivor dies before the employee, then payments will stop once the employee dies.

- *Lump sum:* The employer provides the employee with a lump sum amount that is calculated by determining the present value of the future annuity payments the employee could have received. Most plans give employees a lump sum payout if total payment is less than $5,000.
- *Period certain:* The employee receives a monthly amount for either three years (36 months) or 10 years (120 months). If the employee dies before receiving total months eligible, then the employee's beneficiary will receive the remaining number of monthly payments based on option selected.

Defined Contribution (DC) Plans

DC plans are increasing in popularity since companies can control costs by adjusting employer contributions and many employees like the possibility of managing their own pension monies. DC plans are also easier for employees to understand and, in many cases, provide short-service employees with higher benefits than DB plans. With DB plans, the company makes all decisions, including selection of investment vehicles. In contrast, with DC plans, employees have greater say on investment options and amounts to invest.

The most prevalent DC plan is a "savings/thrift" plan, with a 401(k) feature. Sometimes these 401(k) plans are called "capital accumulation" plans. An attractive feature is that employee contributions are tax deferred. Many plans have "matching" employer contributions that can be viewed by employees as "free money." The match amount varies by company. While in the plan, all monies compound tax-free. This means that an employee pays federal and state withholding tax upon redeeming funds, preferably upon retirement when the individual tax rate is usually lower than while working. An example of a 401(k) plan is found in Figure 17.7.

FIGURE 17.7 Sample 401(k) plan.

Eligibility
First of the month coinciding with or next following date of employment
Employee Contributions
2 percent to 15 percent of an employee's earnings
- Pretax basis or
- After-tax basis or
- A combination of pretax and after-tax

Company Contributions
50 percent match on first 6 percent contributed by employee
Vesting of Company Contributions (Cliff)
100 percent vested after three years of credited service
Investment Choices
Employee contributions
- Common stock fund
- Company stock
- Bond fund
- Fixed-rate-of-return vehicle

Company contribution – company stock
Withdrawal Provisions
Age 59 ½ or older
Death or disability
Retirement or termination of employment
Loan Provision
Up to 50 percent of value of vested account balance or $50,000, whichever is less
Payment Options
Cash
Company stock

Employees can make withdrawals for specific reasons, but the withdrawals are generally subject to taxation. Therefore, many plans contain a loan provision that enables employees to borrow rather than withdraw funds when necessary. IRS regulations limit the size of a loan to 50 percent of the employee's vested account balance or $50,000, whichever is less.

Distribution options are available when an employee terminates employment. These include a lump sum payment, an annuity arrangement, installment payments, and a direct rollover to an IRA or another employer's qualified plan. By directly rolling over a lump sum distribution to an IRA or another qualified plan, an employee is able to avoid the 20 percent withholding tax required by government regulations.

Vesting for employer contributions in 401(k) plans are:

1. 100 percent vested after three years if "cliff option" is selected.
2. 100 percent vested after six years if "graded" option is selected.

An employee is 100 percent vested immediately for all monies the employee invests.

Other types of DC plans include:

- *Money-purchase pension plans* whereby the company contributes a specified percent of each employee's salary to purchase annuities.
- *Employee stock-ownership plans* whereby the employee receives an annual allocation of employer stock.
- *Deferred profit-sharing plans* whereby the company contributes an amount of profits each year, and each participant is credited with a share.

PAY FOR TIME NOT WORKED BENEFITS

Pay for time not worked benefits are generally not regulated by the government. Typically they are covered by company policy. The most frequently provided time-off benefits are:

1. Vacation.
2. Sick leave.
3. Legal holidays.
4. Bereavement leave.
5. Military leave.
6. Jury duty.
7. Personal holidays.
8. PTO (paid time off) banks.

Vacation

Vacation allowances are often based on service and position. Exempt staff usually receives more generous vacation time than nonexempt, especially during the earlier years of employment. Increases based on service can be as follows:

Years of Service Annual Vacation Allowance

3 months to 1 year	5 days
1 to 5 years	10 days
5 to 15 years	15 days
15 to 20 years	20 days
20 or more years	25 days

Sick Leave

Companies provide a set number of days per year for salary continuation in the event an employee is unable to work due to a personal illness.

Legal Holidays

Most companies provide employees with payment for not working on legal holidays. Holidays typically include:

- New Year's Day.
- Martin Luther King's Birthday.

- Memorial Day.
- July 4th.
- Labor Day.
- Thanksgiving Day.
- Christmas Day.

Companies often pay non-exempt employees "premium" time if they work on a legal holiday and grant another day off with pay as the legal holiday.

Bereavement Leave

Companies often grant time off to attend the funeral of an immediate family member. Typical number of days off with pay is three.

Military Leaves

According to the Uniformed Services Employment and Reemployment Rights Act, employees who serve in the armed forces are entitled to the continuation of their position, seniority, status, and pay rate as if there had not been a break in employment.

Jury Duty

Companies are required to grant employees time off for jury duty. The employee receives nominal payment for serving from the court. Additional compensation is based on company policy.

Personal Holidays

Companies frequently provide two to three paid personal days per year for an employee to use for any purpose. Some companies view these days as "emergency days."

PTO (Paid Time Off) Banks

Unscheduled absences are costly and can negatively affect a company's ability to meet customer demands. In response, companies are implementing paid time off (PTO) programs to control costs associated with unscheduled absences and give employees time off with pay to balance work and nonwork pressures.

With PTO programs, an employee receives a bank of time to use for time off activities regardless of reason. PTO replaces traditional separate accounts for vacation, personal time, sick time, and in some cases legal holidays. When designed properly, PTO can save company money and still provide a safety net of time off with pay for workers to meet nonwork pressures.

OTHER BENEFITS

Many "other benefits" are self-explanatory. However, it is important to note that a specific written company policy should be prepared and available for employees to use. Written policies help to ensure equity among all employees and resolve disputes if an employee questions the appropriateness of any procedures. Examples of "other benefits" include:

Adoption benefit. Some companies decided that because medical plans provide maternity coverage, it is appropriate to also provide some reimbursement to employees who elect to adopt a child. Reimbursements can range from $1,500 to $3,000 per adoption.

Commuting assistance. This benefit includes vans or vouchers used for public transportation.

Credit unions. These employee-run endeavors provide loans for employees and give interest on account balances.

Dependent care and health care reimbursement accounts (flexible spending accounts). Both accounts use pretax dollars to reimburse for eligible services and have a "use it or lose it" provision. This means any money left in the plan at the end of the plan year's grace period is forfeited back to the plan.

With a dependent care account, an employee uses the money to reimburse caregivers who provide covered services to an employee's dependent child or children. With the health care reimbursement account, an employee pays for services not covered by the company's health care plans. Also included are deductibles, copayments, and co-insurances.

Educational assistance plans. These plans are sometimes called "tuition reimbursement" plans. The plan provides for full or partial reimbursement of eligible educational expenses per year that are incurred by employees.

Employee assistance program (EAP). This program often features a toll-free telephone number employees can call to seek help to resolve personal matters, i.e., financial, marital, or substance abuse problems.

Employee health services. This benefit usually provides on-site medical care in the event an employee becomes ill at work or is injured on the job.

Financial counseling. This benefit provides financial advice to workers, especially for those enrolled in 401(k) plans.

Flextime. This policy allows employees to choose convenient starting and quitting times and under some plans, extended lunchtime, while still requiring the standard number of hours worked each day or week.

Product/service discounts. Employees use many companies' services and products. Therefore, it's common for companies to make their services or products available to workers at a reduced cost.

Relocation allowances. Companies often ask exempt staff to relocate to a different company facility. To assist with the move, companies underwrite the costs to help cushion any upset associated with relocation. Allowances are sometimes provided to new hires, but generally are less generous than for current employees.

Subsidized food service. Employers typically subsidize the cost of food served in employee cafeterias.

Job share. This is where two part-time workers end up doing the work of a full-time employee. The two employees share the workload. This arrangement is often effective when employees do not want to work full-time and can complement each other.

THE IMPORTANCE OF EFFECTIVE COMMUNICATION

Effective communication (both written and oral) is essential for employees to understand and appreciate the value of your company's total rewards program. Compared with wages and salaries, which are relatively easier to understand and highly visible, benefits tend to be complex, diverse, and, to some extent, hidden. You only use benefits when you need them. Therefore, nonused benefits tend to be invisible.

To be effective, a benefits communication program should:

- Meet legal requirements (ERISA) for reporting and disclosing critical information to employees and regulators.
- Have means for employees to express interests and concerns, and include a feedback mechanism to respond to workers' comments.
- Enable employees to clearly understand the provisions of their benefit package.
- Gain employee confidence that the information about their benefits is easily accessible and accurate, and that the benefit plans will deliver what they promise.
- Highlight value of benefits.
- Have employees realize the dollar investment made by employers for providing employees with benefits.

Legal Requirements

ERISA (Employee Retirement Income Security Act) requires plan sponsors (employers) to give participants (employees) various documents. Two basic ones are:

1. A summary plan description (SPD) is the benefits "handbook." This document should explain the benefit in a way an average worker would understand. The SPD must be given to each plan participant within 90 days of participation.
2. A summary annual report (SAR) includes key financial information about the benefit plan. The SAR must be given to participants within nine months following the end of each plan year.

In addition to satisfying ERISA reporting and disclosure provisions, benefits administrators need to comply with other federal and state requirements for distributing and posting various information affecting employees.

Cobraize Employees

Employees become eligible for COBRA (Consolidated Omnibus Budget Reconciliation Act of 1985) upon losing welfare benefits due to various qualifying events (e.g., loss of job). COBRA allows an eligible employee to continue receiving some benefits for themselves and their eligible dependents and spouse for up to 18 to 36 months by paying the *full* monthly premium, plus a 2% administrative fee.

Most workers are shocked with the high cost of medical coverage. The information causes many employees to appreciate what the company had done for them; unfortunately, this awareness occurs when most workers leave the company.

What is recommended is to "Cobraize" employees the first day of employment (in addition to meeting traditional COBRA requirements). This means informing employees what the employer is paying for benefits (in particular, medical) in addition to what workers pay. Numbers convey value, and perhaps the disclosure will cause employees to have a greater appreciation of what companies are doing for them.

Creating and Building Awareness of Benefits

In some instances, employees and their dependents become aware of benefits coverage only when needs become acute. For example, when someone becomes ill or disabled, when the day of retirement nears, or when a death occurs, there will be search for and inquiries about necessary application forms. However, workers may fail to use other company-provided benefits unless they receive periodic reminders. Examples, as described earlier, include educational assistance, employee assistance programs, long-term care, and adoption benefits.

Ways to inform employees about benefits include:

- Articles in company newsletters and company intranet site.
- Notices posted on bulletin boards.
- Information mailed to employees' homes.
- Payroll inserts.
- Benefits fairs.
- Special programs (e.g., a representative from the Social Security Administration makes a presentation and answers questions).

Permit employees to invite nonworkers to attend benefits information meetings held by the company. Often, benefit decision makers are not the workers. Allowing employees to bring a family member or friend will help foster better understanding and decision making.

Enhancing Confidence and Trust

Credibility is enhanced when employees have confidence in the accuracy of plan information and believe they can obtain information about benefits on a timely basis. Responding quickly and accurately is the key to building credibility. The delivery of benefits information to workers can be facilitated by the use of:

- Interactive voice response via touch-tone telephones.
- Touch-screen kiosks.
- Intranet.
- E-mail.

Involve Employees in Benefit Changes

Many companies find success by actively involving employees when changing benefits programs. This includes use of "employee task forces" or "focus groups" to review ideas and express opinions of planned changes. Other task forces are asked to review proposed communication pieces to ensure employee understandings. These interactions are similar to companies asking a group of paying customers to critique a new product or service before being marketed.

Marketing executives have learned the value of customer feedback to ensure new products or services meet customers' needs. The best way is to ask for comments rather than wait until after the product or service goes live. The same logic applies to asking employees for comments prior to finalizing a new benefits program or communication piece.

PROJECTED BENEFITS TRENDS

Employee benefits are an essential component of any company's total rewards program. Benefits have evolved from being fringe to significant, and the future portends even more changes to how benefits packages will be designed, paid for, selected, and managed.

The following are some projected benefits trends:

- Increased personal responsibility for selection, payment, and management of benefits programs.
- Revisions in Social Security coverage.
- Growth of employee self-service through technology (i.e., intranet).
- Continued growth of outsourcing of benefits administration.
- Greater emphasis on wellness/prevention.
- Extension of benefits coverage for nontraditional partners.
- Increased pressure to balance work and nonwork needs.
- Movement toward lifecycle benefits planning in response to demographic changes.

18 Benefits Compliance: An Overview for the HR Professional

The United States is unique among industrialized nations in the extent to which its citizens receive employment-based welfare and retirement security. More than 140 million workers are covered by employer-sponsored group health plans, and employer-based pension funds have trillions of dollars in assets. With numbers of this magnitude, regulatory complexity is inevitable.

Several significant federal laws exist that govern the design, maintenance, and operation of employee benefits plans, provide basic employment safeguards, and regulate the conduct of the collective bargaining process through which employee benefits are negotiated.

Significantly, states generally are prevented from enacting laws that regulate employee welfare and pension arrangements. Still other subjects, like health care portability and medical privacy (covered in chapter 19), are subject to regulation by the states but only to the extent that state-mandated protections exceed a federally established floor. States are free to regulate most other aspects of the employment relationship. While state laws are beyond the scope of this work, an understanding of the federal laws in this area will provide the HR and benefits professional with a good deal of what he or she needs to know in order to function effectively.

This chapter focuses on the impact of legislation directly affecting employee benefits, specifically the Employee Retirement Income Security Act of 1974, the Internal Revenue Code, and the Economic Growth and Tax Relief Reconciliation Act of 1991.

THE EMPLOYEE RETIREMENT INCOME SECURITY ACT OF 1974 (ERISA)

The cornerstone of federal regulations that govern employee benefit plans is the Employee Retirement Income Security Act of 1974 (ERISA). ERISA is organized into four separate titles. Title I, sometimes referred to as the "Labor Title," governs

FIGURE 18.1 ERISA's Title I requirements.

ERISA's Title I requirements include the following:
- Reporting and disclosure requirements
- Minimum participation standards
- Minimum vesting standards
- Benefits accrual requirements
- Form and payment of benefits requirements
- Minimum funding standards
- Fiduciary responsibility requirements
- Group health plan continuation coverage requirements

pension plans and welfare plans. Title II contains amendments conforming to the Internal Revenue Code. These essentially are the rules that govern tax-qualified retirement plans. Title III, titled "Jurisdiction, Administration, Enforcement: Joint Pension Task Force, Etc.," is important because it governs, among other things, the enrollment of actuaries who can certify pension-related calculations. Lastly, Title IV establishes the Pension Benefit Guaranty Corporation. Figure 18.1 shows the basic participant protections covered under ERISA Title I.

The Nature of the Pension Promise: Defined Benefit vs. Defined Contribution

A pension plan essentially is a set of promises made by an employer or other plan sponsor (e.g., a trade union) to provide retirement-type benefits to employees or members. There are two fundamentally different ways describing the pension promise: (1) specifying the amount to be deposited to the plan each year (defined contribution); or (2) specifying what the benefit will be at retirement (defined benefit). ERISA recognizes and regulates both approaches. ERISA §3(34) defines **defined contribution plan** or **individual account plan** to mean:

> [A] pension plan which provides for an individual account for each participant and for benefits based solely upon the amount contributed to the participant's account, and any income, expenses, gains and losses, and any forfeitures of accounts of other participants which may be allocated to such participant's account.

ERISA §3(35) defines the **defined benefit plan** to mean (with certain exceptions) a pension plan other than an individual account plan.

While perhaps at first puzzling, these definitions reflect the pre-ERISA distinction between savings and thrift plans, on the one hand, and traditional pension plans, on the other. Annual employer contributions fund a savings plan. Where employee contributions also are permitted or required, the plan sometimes is called a thrift plan. The key feature of these plans is that each participant has an account, and the participant's benefit under the plan (or accrued benefit in ERISA parlance) is the then-current value of the account. It is therefore the participant who bears the risk of investment loss.

A traditional pension plan, on the other hand, expressed the accrued benefit as something to which the participant is entitled at retirement, the normal form of which is usually expressed as an annuity for the life of the participant. A traditional defined benefit promise might provide a participant an annuity for life equal to some percentage of his or her final average compensation when he or she retires. Other benefits forms are permitted (and in some instances, such as certain spousal benefits, required), but in each case, they are calculated with reference to the actuarial equivalent value of the straight life annuity at normal retirement age. In a pension plan, it is the employer who bears the investment risk.

As described at length in Article II, the Internal Revenue Code imposes its own classifications on tax-favored retirement arrangements. Code Section 401(a) regulates "pension, profit sharing and stock bonus plans." Tax-qualified pension, profit sharing, and stock bonus plans usually are pension plans as defined in ERISA. See Figure 18.2 for a summary of common plan classifications under both ERISA and the Code.

The Scope of ERISA

ERISA Title I broadly defines pension plans to encompass all manner of retirement arrangements. Under ERISA, **employee pension benefit plan** and **pension plan** mean "any plan, fund, or program . . . to the extent that by its express terms or as a result of surrounding circumstances such plan, fund, or program—(i) provides retirement income to employees, or (ii) results in a deferral of income by employees for periods extending to the termination of covered employment or beyond, regardless of the method of calculating the contributions made to the plan, the method of calculating the benefits under the plan or the method of distributing benefits from the plan." This definition is sufficiently broad to encompass tax-qualified plans, nonqualified deferred compensation arrangements, and many other informal arrangements.

FIGURE 18.2 Plan classifications.

Internal Revenue Code Categories	ERISA Pension Plan Categories	
	Defined Benefit Plans	**Defined Contribution Plans**
Pension Plans	- Defined Benefit Pension Plans - Cash Balance Plans	- Money Purchase Plans - Target Benefit Plans
Profit-Sharing Plans		- Profit Sharing Plans - Age-Weighted Plans - New Comparability Plans - 401(k) Plans
Stock Bonus Plans		- Stock Bonus Plans - ESOPs - Leveraged ESOPs

Pension Protection Act of 2006

On August 17, 2006, President Bush signed into law the Pension Protection Act (H.R. 4), a comprehensive pension bill that was passed by the U.S. Senate on August 3 and by the House of Representatives on July 28.

The Pension Protection Act of 2006 tightens rules governing how companies fund their pension plans, in hopes of eliminating the need for rescue by the PBGC without forcing private sector plan sponsors to terminate their pension benefits. In addition, the law makes a number of significant changes in defined contribution rules to encourage automatic enrollment in 401(k) plans and to make it easier for 401(k) sponsors to offer investment advice to plan participants.

The new law also provides long-awaited clarity about the legal status of cash balance pension plan designs and new guidance about the requirements for future cash balance conversions. These changes are likely to be embraced by many employers and should lead to enhanced levels of participation in company-sponsored savings plans in the future. (See Chapter 17 for more information.)

Welfare benefits plans, on the other hand, are defined as "plans, funds, or programs, established or maintained by an employer or employee organization, or both, for the purpose of providing to participants or beneficiaries medical, health, accident, disability, death, unemployment, or vacation benefits, apprenticeship or other training programs, day-care centers, scholarship funds, prepaid legal services, or any benefit described in Section 302(c) of the Labor Management Relations Act of 1947 other than pensions on retirement or death and insurance to provide such pensions." While this definition is daunting, the most significant welfare benefits are group medical and dental plans, group term (and other) life insurance arrangements, most disability benefits programs, and employee assistance programs (EAPs), except for referral-only EAPs.

Group health plans (i.e., plans that provide for medical care) are common among U.S. employers. For federal income tax purposes, **medical care** is defined to include amounts paid for "(i) the diagnosis, cure, mitigation, treatment, or prevention of disease, or for the purpose of affecting any structure or function of the body; (ii) transportation, primarily for and essential to such medical care; and (iii) insurance (including Medicare part B premiums) covering medical care." Benefits commonly covered by employer-provided group health plans include hospital expenses, surgical expenses, physicians' services, nurses' services, prescription drugs, orthopedic appliances, and dental and vision care, among others. These plans also are ERISA-covered welfare plans unless an exception applies.

Certain plans are excluded from coverage under Title I of ERISA. They include governmental plans, certain church plans, unfunded excess benefits plans, plans maintained outside of the United States primarily for the benefit of persons substantially all of whom are nonresident aliens, and plans maintained solely for the purpose of complying with applicable workers' compensation, unemployment compensation, or disability insurance laws.

Governmental plans are employee benefits plans established or maintained by the federal government, by the government of any state or political subdivision thereof, or their agencies or instrumentalities. Church plans are plans established and maintained by churches or associations of churches that are exempt from taxation under the Internal Revenue Code. A workman's compensation plan is a plan that is maintained solely for the purpose of complying with applicable workers' compensation laws or unemployment compensation or disability insurance laws. Foreign plans are those that are maintained outside of the United States primarily for the benefit of persons substantially all of whom are nonresident aliens.

Regulatory Exemptions

There are some important regulatory exemptions described in regulations issued by the Department of Labor. The list of items *not* covered by ERISA includes the following:

- *Payroll practices.* Payroll practices excluded from Title I are divided into the following three groups by regulations: (1) payment of compensation by an employer on account of work performed by an employee, including compensation at a rate in excess of the normal rate of compensation, because of the performance of duties under other than ordinary circumstances; examples of such practices are overtime pay, shift premiums, holiday premiums, and weekend premiums; (2) payment of compensation from the employer's general assets for time periods during which the employee is physically or mentally unable to perform his or her duties, or is otherwise absent for medical reasons (such as pregnancy, a physical examination, or psychiatric treatment); and (3) Payment of compensation out of the employer's general assets for time periods in which an employee able to perform his or her duties and not absent for medical reasons performs no duties (such as paid vacation time).
- *Premises facilities.* The following two types of facilities are excluded by regulations:
  - Recreation, dining, or other facilities (other than day-care centers) maintained on the employer's premises for use by employees (or maintained on the premises of an employee organization for use by its members).
  - Facilities maintained on the employer's premises for the purpose of treating minor injuries or illnesses or rendering first aid for accidents occurring during working hours.
- *Holiday gifts.* Gifts distributed by employers on account of holidays, such as turkeys or hams, are excluded.
- *Sales to employees.* Sales to employees by employers of articles or commodities that the employer offers for sale in its regular course of business are excluded. This exclusion applies regardless of whether the sale is made at prevailing market prices.
- *Hiring halls.* Hiring hall facilities maintained by employee organizations (e.g., unions) are excluded.
- *Remembrance funds.* Remembrance programs such as flowers, the insertion of an obituary notice in a newspaper, or small gifts made in connection with deaths or illnesses are excluded.
- *Strike funds.* Strike funds maintained by employee organizations are excluded.

- *Industry advancement programs.* These are programs maintained by an employer or a group of employers, which do not have any employee participants and which do not provide benefits to employees or their dependents.
- *Certain group insurance programs.* Group insurance programs are excluded if they are offered to employees (or members of an employee organization) and if they meet the following criteria:
  - No contributions are made by the employer or by the employee organization.
  - Participation in the program by employees or organization members is voluntary.
  - The employer or the employee organization does not endorse the program, and their only functions are to permit the insurer to publicize the programs to employees or members and to collect premiums through payroll deductions or dues check offs and remit them to the insurer.
  - The only consideration the employer or employee organization receives in connection with the program is reasonable compensation (excluding any profit) for administrative services actually rendered in connection with payroll deductions.
- *Unfunded scholarship programs.* Scholarship programs, including tuition and education expense refund programs that are funded solely from the general assets of an employer or of an employee organization, are excluded.

Reporting and Disclosure

ERISA generally requires that the plan administrator of each pension benefits plan (including defined benefit pension plans, money purchase pension plans, profit-sharing plans, employee stock ownership plans, 401(k) plans, and other retirement plans) and welfare benefits plans (including health, dental, long-term disability, group life insurance, severance pay, and other welfare plans) file an annual report (on Form 5500), which includes detailed financial information about the plan and provides a summary of the annual report to each plan participant.

The plan administrator of either a pension plan or a welfare benefits plan also is required to satisfy numerous disclosure requirements, including furnishing plan participants with a summary plan description document (a plain-language explanation of how the plan works), making copies of the documents under which a plan is operating available for examination by plan participants (including the latest annual report, the collective bargaining agreement, the trust agreement, and the insurance contract, if applicable), and furnishing copies of such documents (for a reasonable charge) to plan participants upon written request.

The plan administrator of a pension plan also is required to furnish to a plan participant (not more than once a year and upon the participant's written request) an individualized benefits statement showing the participant's total accrued benefits and the vested portion of such benefits or the earliest date on which benefits will become vested.

While annual reporting and disclosure requirements under ERISA apply to most plans, there are some exceptions. Governmental plans, church plans, plans maintained for complying with workers' compensation, unemployment compensation, or disability insurance laws, and plans maintained outside the United States for nonresident aliens are exempt from ERISA reporting and disclosure requirements. Exemptions include (1) apprenticeship and training benefit programs; (2) unfunded or fully insured welfare benefit plans providing benefits for a select group of management or highly compensated employees (top-hat plans); (3) day-care centers; and (4) dues-financed welfare benefit plans maintained by employee organizations. Department of Labor (DOL) regulations provide exemptions for some reporting and disclosure requirements for unfunded or fully insured welfare benefit plans with fewer than 100 participants at the beginning of the plan year.

Plans also must furnish participants with a summary annual report. As the name implies, the summary annual report must contain certain financial and other information contained in the annual report. DOL regulations set forth the requirements of the summary annual report. Participants also may request copies of the written plan, annual report, and a participant's benefit statement showing, among other things, accrued benefits, percentage vesting, and, if not fully vested, the time at which vesting will occur.

The "Written Plan" and Claims Procedure Requirements

ERISA imposes certain formal plan requirements. Specifically, a plan must be described in a written instrument, which must contain a procedure for establishing and carrying out a funding policy and method, a procedure for amending the plan and identifying the persons who have authority to amend the plan, the basis on which payments are made to and from the plan, and, except for plans providing apprenticeship benefits, a reasonable claims procedure. The claims procedure must (1) be included in the summary plan description; (2) not contain any procedures that unduly hamper or inhibit the processing of claims; and (3) comply with standards set forth in regulations for filing claims and notifying participants of claims denials, and for review procedures.

The rules governing ERISA claims procedures on group health plans and disability plans have been overhauled. Final DOL regulations, issued in November 2000, set forth the benefits, medical provider, and other information that must be disclosed in a group health plan summary plan description, and significantly shorten the disability claim timeline. These rules provide for much shorter time frames for processing.

Group health plan summary plan descriptions must now include, among other information: (1) any cost-sharing arrangements for which participants and beneficiaries are responsible, including premiums, coinsurance, deductibles, and copays; (2) any annual or lifetime caps on benefits; (3) coverage for preventive services, existing and new drugs, medical tests, devices, and procedures; (4) conditions or limits on coverage for emergency care; (5) provider network information including the use of network providers, coverage for out-of-network services, and any conditions or limitations on the selection of primary or specialty care providers; (6) limitations or conditions on coverage for emergency care; (7) preauthorization and other utilization review requirements that are a condition to obtaining a benefit; and (8) circumstances that may result in the loss, forfeiture, suspension, offset, or reduction of any benefits that a participant might otherwise expect the plan to provide on the basis of the description of benefits in the summary plan description.

The summary plan description also must identify any health insurance issuer (for example, an administrative-services-only[ASO] provider) responsible for the financing and/or administration of the plan. Furthermore, it must describe the extent to which plan benefits are guaranteed under the issuer's contract or policy of insurance, if any, and the nature of any administrative services the issuer provides.

Standards also have been established for group health plans and disability plans, for the purpose of requiring more timely review of initial claims, improving participant access to information, and affording a full and fair review of denied claims. The regulations apply to health claims filed on or after the first day of the plan year commencing July 1, 2002, but not later than January 1, 2003. For disability claims and other ERISA claims, new claims procedures were effective for claims filed on or after January 1, 2002.

Where initial claims for benefits are concerned, the final regulations require health plans to make decisions within 72 hours for "urgent care" claims. **Urgent care claims** are defined as claims for medical care or treatment "that could seriously jeopardize the life or health of the claimant or in the opinion of a physician would subject the claimant to severe pain that could not be managed without the care or treatment the claimant is seeking." Claims that are not urgent, but require preauthorization (pre-service claims), must be decided in 15 days (with up to two 15-day extensions). Claims that do not require preauthorization (post-service claims) have a 30-day processing period (with up to two 15-day extensions). Claimants have 180 days to request an appeal, but rather than the minimum 60 days allowed for decisions on appeal under the prior summary-plan-description regulation, the decision now must be made no later than (1) 72 hours for urgent care claims; (2) 30 days for pre-service claims (or 15 days if plan provides two appeals); and (3) 60 days for post-service claims (or 30 days each if plan provides two levels of appeal).

When a claim is denied, the plan administrator must provide the claimant with written or electronic notification of an adverse benefit determination (including eligibility and benefit determinations) that includes (1) the specific reason(s) for the adverse determination; (2) reference to specific plan provisions; (3) a description of any additional materials or information needed from the claimant necessary to perfect the claim and why the information is necessary; (4) a description of the plan's review procedures and the applicable time limits, including a statement of the claimant's right to bring a civil action; and (5) the specific internal rule, guideline, protocol, or other criterion it relied upon (for group health plans and disability plans).

Did You Know?

Disability plans have their own distinct rules. Generally, initial claim determinations must be made no later than 45 days after the claim is filed, and the plan may have up to two 30-day extensions, if the extensions are based on reasons beyond the plan's control, and the participant is notified before the end of the initial period (or first extension, if applicable) of the need for the extension. In addition, the plan may have up to 45 additional days in special circumstances to make a determination on appeal.

If the claim is denied based on a medical necessity or experimental treatment provision (also for group health plans and disability plans), the notice must explain the scientific or clinical basis for the denial, and if the claim involves urgent care, it must include a description of the expedited review process applicable to the claim. For urgent care plans the information in the notice may be provided orally, but written notice must follow within three days thereafter. Similar rules apply with respect to notice of a decision on appeal.

The Summary Plan Description

ERISA requires that participants in an employee benefits plan be furnished with a summary of a plan's provisions and the participant's benefits, rights, and obligations by way of a summary plan description (SPD). Under the original DOL regulation, SPDs must be furnished to participants and beneficiaries no later than 90 days after becoming a participant or first receiving benefits, as the case may be, or within 120 days after the plan first becomes subject to ERISA's reporting and disclosure requirements. The Health Insurance Portability and Accountability Act of 1996 (HIPAA) added a new disclosure obligation in the case of a material reduction in benefits under a group health plan. A so-called "summary of material reductions" must be provided no later than 60 days after the adoption of such a modification at regular intervals of not more than 90 days (i.e., a benefits newsletter). Among other things, the SPD must contain the name of the plan, the name and address of the employer whose employees are covered by the plan, the employer identification number, plan number, and plan type. SPDs must be updated every 5 years (or once every 10 years if there are no modifications).

At one time, SPDs were required to be filed with the DOL, but this is no longer the case. A plan administrator must furnish a copy of any SPDs and summaries of material modifications within 30 days of a request by the DOL.

Although there is no separate penalty or sanction for failing to provide an SPD, there can be serious consequences. Where employers seek to reduce retiree medical benefits, for example, courts have held that the failure to reserve the right to amend or terminate the plan in an SPD can be fatal to the employer's efforts. Moreover, there are substantial protections that an employer can include in an SPD, such as a deferential standard of review, that are not available if no SPD is provided. Lastly, there are now specific items, such as notices of health care continuation rights, health care portability notices, and privacy rights, that need to be disclosed in an SPD (or some other document having the effect of an SPD), and that carry sanctions for noncompliance.

Plan Assets and the ERISA Trust Requirement

ERISA has been singularly successful in safeguarding benefit promises made to employees—particularly, though not exclusively, those relating to retirement. This success flows from the ERISA trust requirement, under which, with few exceptions, one or more trustees must hold plan assets in trust. This way, even if the plan sponsor becomes insolvent, the funds that are set aside to pay benefits are unaffected. The plan or trust instrument must name the trustee, or a named fiduciary must appoint the trustee. Insurance policies and plan assets held by insurance companies are not subject to this rule inasmuch as state insurance laws provide similar protections.

Since pension plans must be funded under the ERISA funding rules (described under the section, "Minimum Funding Standards"), the trust requirement rarely is an issue. The funding rules do not apply to welfare plans. But if an employer chooses to set aside assets to fulfill the plan's benefit obligations, then those assets likely will need to be held in trust. Employee contributions to the plan are plan assets for ERISA purposes. This rule poses some vexing problems for contributory, self-funded medical plans. Many of these plans do not hold assets in trust, relying on a 1992 DOL notice that suspended enforcement of the trust requirement for welfare plans with employee contributions under a cafeteria plan. It is not clear, however, that this non-enforcement policy is sufficiently broad to extend to self-insured plans.

While the trustee has the authority and discretion to manage and invest plan assets, ERISA does allow the trustee to elect to be subject to the direction of a named fiduciary who is not a trustee. Where this occurs, the trustee is relieved of the authority to manage, provided the trustee follows proper directions that are not contrary to the plan provisions or ERISA. Control over investments also can be ceded to plan participants, as with a self-directed 401(k) plan. The plan trustee in this case relinquishes the authority and discretion over assets in the individual participant accounts, but the participant is not a fiduciary even though he or she controls plan assets. The trustee or other plan fiduciary, however, retains residual liability for the selection and monitoring of the menu of investment options.

Minimum Participation Standards

ERISA provides that, in general, an employee's eligibility for plan participation may not be conditioned, with the exception of completing more than one year of service for the employer and reaching the age of 21. A pension plan that provides for the immediate vesting of all benefits may require that an employee complete two years of service and attain age 21. As amended by the Age Discrimination in Employment Act (ADEA), ERISA also mandates that a pension plan may not exclude an employee from participation by reason of the employee having attained a specific age. There are no similar requirements for welfare benefits plans.

Minimum Vesting Standards

ERISA requires that all pension plans must:

- Provide their participants with a fully vested (nonforfeitable) right to the benefits derived from their own contributions to the plan.
- Acquire a nonforfeitable right to the benefits derived from employer contributions to the plan upon attaining normal retirement age (the later of the date on which a participant attains age 65 or the fifth anniversary of the participant's commencement of participation in the plan, unless an earlier date is specified in the plan).
- Satisfy one of two alternative vesting schedules, for periods before normal retirement age, based on the participant's completed years of service. The first alternative vesting schedule provides that an employee who has completed at least five years of service has a nonforfeitable right to 100 percent of the benefits attributable to employer contributions. The second alternative vesting schedule is that a participant who has completed three years of service has

a nonforfeitable right to 20 percent of the benefits attributable to employer contributions and has a nonforfeitable right to an additional 20 percent of such benefits for each additional year of service. The alternatives are displayed in Figure 18.3.

Special vesting rules are provided by the Internal Revenue Code for so-called "top-heavy" pension plans that primarily benefit certain higher paid or "key" employees.

For plan eligibility and vesting purposes, years of service generally include all of an employee's years of employment with the employer, its subsidiaries, and

---

Did You Know?

The Economic Growth and Tax Relief and Recovery Act of 2001 (EGTRRA) shortened the vesting schedules for employer matching contributions in 401(k) plans. These contributions must now vest ratably over five years, or 100 percent after three years. The new matching contribution vesting schedules are displayed in Figure 18.3A.

FIGURE 18.3 Alternative vesting schedules.

First Alternative
- **Years of Service**   • **Nonforfeitable Percentage**

Years of Service	Nonforfeitable Percentage
Fewer than five	0
Five or more	100

Second Alternative
- **Years of Service**   • **Nonforfeitable Percentage**

Years of Service	Nonforfeitable Percentage
Three	20
Four	40
Five	60
Six	80
Seven or more	100

FIGURE 18.3A Alternative vesting schedules for matching contributions.

First Alternative
- **Years of Service**   • **Nonforfeitable Percentage**

Years of Service	Nonforfeitable Percentage
Fewer than three	0
Three or more	100

Second Alternative
- **Years of Service**   • **Nonforfeitable Percentage**

Years of Service	Nonforfeitable Percentage
Two	20
Three	40
Four	60
Five	80
Six or more	100

affiliated entities, and require completion of a specific number of hours of service in each year.

Benefits Accrual Requirements

ERISA requires that defined benefit pension plans meet certain minimum benefits accrual requirements intended to preclude excessive "back loading" of plan benefits to a participant's final years of employment. As amended by the ADEA, ERISA also prohibits pension plans from stopping benefits accruals (allocations of employer contributions in a defined contribution plan) or reducing the rate of benefits accrual (or allocations) because of the participant's attainment of a specified age.

Form of Payment of Benefits Requirements

ERISA requires that benefits under certain pension plans (defined benefit pension plans and money purchase pension plans) be paid in the form of a qualified joint and survivor annuity. If the plan participant is unmarried, this annuity is a monthly annuity for the life of the participant. In the case of a married participant, the annuity is a monthly annuity for the life of the participant with a survivor annuity payable to the participant's spouse equal to at least 50 percent of the amount payable to the participant. The qualified joint and survivor annuity form of payment may be waived in favor of a different form of payment. For such a waiver to be effective, the participant must first be provided with a written explanation of the qualified joint and survivor annuity form of payment and the effect of the waiver of such form of benefit on the participant's and beneficiary's rights, and the waiver must be made within the 90-day period before benefits payments begin. In addition, the participant's spouse must consent in writing to the waiver of the qualified joint and survivor annuity by a married participant, and either a notary public or plan representative must witness the consent.

Pension plans that are subject to the qualified joint and survivor annuity rules also are required to provide a pre-retirement survivor annuity in the case of married participants. This annuity is intended to provide a participant's surviving spouse with the same benefits the spouse would have received if the participant had separated from service on the date of death, survived to the earliest retirement age under the plan, retired with an immediate qualified joint and survivor annuity at such earliest retirement age, and died after the first payment of such annuity had been made. A participant may waive the pre-retirement survivor annuity with spousal consent.

A plan may effectively charge participants for providing survivor benefits under qualified joint and survivor annuities and pre-retirement survivor annuities by reducing the participants' benefits for the actuarial cost of survivor protection. Alternatively, the plan may fully subsidize the cost of providing one or both of these benefits. Participants need not be given an opportunity to waive a survivor benefit that is fully subsidized by the plan.

The qualified joint and survivor and pre-retirement survivor annuity requirements do not apply to a defined contribution plan that is not a money purchase pension plan if the plan provides that, upon the death of a participant, the participant's vested benefits will be paid in full to the participant's surviving spouse (unless the spouse consents to the designation of another beneficiary).

Unless a participant agrees to a later date, benefits under a pension plan must begin by the 60th day after the close of the plan year in which the latest of the following conditions is met:

- The participant attains the earlier of age 65 or the normal retirement age specified in the plan.
- The 10th anniversary of the year in which the participant commenced participation in the plan occurs.
- The participant terminates service with the employer.

ERISA also requires that a pension plan provide that benefits under the plan are not subject to assignment or alienation, except pursuant to a qualified domestic relations order (a court order requiring the payment of benefits to a participant's spouse, former spouse, child, or other dependent) or to pay certain federal tax obligations.

Minimum Funding Standards

ERISA contains detailed rules prescribing minimum funding requirements for defined benefit and money purchase pension plans. Such requirements offer many alternative actuarial funding methods for defined benefit pension plans. Required yearly contributions to a defined benefit plan usually must be made in quarterly installments. If required contributions are not made, the employer and all affiliated entities are jointly and severally liable for the amount of the contributions.

Fiduciary Duties

ERISA prescribes fiduciary responsibility rules that apply to all pension plans and welfare benefits plans, including the requirement that each plan be maintained pursuant to a written instrument and that all assets of a plan be held in trust. Usually, the trust requirement is waived in the case of certain insured arrangements and for welfare benefits paid from the general assets of the employer.

Plan fiduciaries are required to exercise their fiduciary duties according to specified standards. In general, a person is a fiduciary with respect to a plan to the extent that the person does any one of the following: (1) exercises any discretionary authority or control over the management of the plan or the management or disposition of its assets; (2) renders investment advice for compensation; or (3) has any discretionary authority or responsibility in administration of the plan.

Plan fiduciaries are required to exercise their duties in the following manner:

- For the exclusive purpose of providing benefits to participants and their beneficiaries.
- With the "care, skill, prudence and diligence under the circumstances then prevailing that a prudent person acting in a like capacity and familiar with such matters would use in the conduct of an enterprise of a like character and with the like aims."
- By diversifying plan investments to minimize the risk of large losses.

FIGURE 18.4 Transactions prohibited by ERISA.

Transactions that are expressly prohibited include the following:
- Sale, exchange, or leasing of property
- Lending of money or other extension of credit
- Furnishing of goods or services
- Use of plan assets by or for the benefit of the party in interest
- Investment of plan assets in employer securities or employer real property (except as provided in specific exemptions for certain transactions in employer securities and employer real property)

- In accordance with the documents and instruments governing the plan, insofar as such documents and instruments are consistent with the provisions of ERISA.

Fiduciaries may be liable, not only for their own breaches of duty, but also for a breach of fiduciary duty by another plan fiduciary. They are liable if they have knowledge of a breach by another fiduciary, unless they make reasonable efforts to remedy the breach.

ERISA also prohibits certain transactions between a plan and a "party in interest" with respect to the plan. Figure 18.4 lists the transactions that are expressly prohibited. A party in interest includes a plan fiduciary, anyone providing services to the plan, an employer whose employees are covered by the plan, a union whose members are covered by the plan, an employee who participates in the plan, and related entities.

There are specific exemptions from the prohibited transaction provisions of ERISA, including a general exemption that enables a plan to pay reasonable compensation to a party in interest for office space or necessary services concerning the administration of the plan. With certain exceptions, all plan fiduciaries and every person who handles the funds or other property of a plan is required to be bonded.

COBRA Group Health Plan Continuation Coverage Requirements

The Consolidated Omnibus Budget Reconciliation Act of 1985 (COBRA) added provisions to ERISA that govern certain group health plans (including insured plans, self-insured plans, and special arrangements such as health care flexible spending accounts). Specifically, COBRA mandates that employers with at least 20 employees must offer each "qualified beneficiary" an opportunity to continue coverage, although the beneficiary would otherwise lose coverage under the plan due to a "qualifying event." Such qualifying events may include the employee's death or other termination of employment, the employee's transfer to part-time status, the qualified beneficiary's divorce, Medicare entitlement, or termination of status as a dependent child.

In theory, COBRA continuation coverage should not cost an employer anything, because the plan may charge a premium for COBRA coverage equal to 102 percent of the cost to the plan of covering similarly situated persons who have not had a qualifying event. In practice, however, there is usually a significant cost to the employer due to adverse selection and the fact that the COBRA premium may not consider an individual's health, age, or sex.

The COBRA continuation coverage period depends on the type of qualifying event that entitles a qualified beneficiary to COBRA coverage. COBRA continuation coverage generally extends for 36 months after the date of the qualifying event. However, COBRA coverage continues for only 18 months (29 months if the qualified beneficiary is disabled under the Social Security Act of 1935 at any time during the first 60 days of COBRA continuation coverage) in the case of the termination or reduction of hours of an employee's employment. HIPAA made it clear that the disability extension of continuation coverage also is available to the spouse and dependent children of the disabled beneficiary, and it also ensured that children born or adopted during the continuation coverage period are treated as qualified beneficiaries.

In general, the administrator of a group health plan must give a qualified beneficiary notice of the individual's rights under COBRA at the time the individual first becomes covered by the plan and of the individual's ability to elect COBRA coverage within a short period after a qualifying event occurs. COBRA continuation coverage is lost if not elected or if premium payments are not made in a timely manner.

Pension Plan Termination Insurance

Title IV of ERISA created the Pension Benefit Guaranty Corporation (PBGC) and calls for a comprehensive system to insure pension benefits under most private sector defined benefit plans.

The PBGC is a separate corporation established within the DOL. The PBGC has jurisdiction over the termination of defined benefit plans, and it insures, subject to certain limits, the pension benefits payable under defined benefit plans. The PBGC also has certain powers to enforce the claims of a defined benefit plan for unpaid employer contributions. PBGC insurance is funded by mandatory premium payments that are based, in part, on the financial condition of a defined benefit plan. The PBGC also has the power to bring proceedings in federal court to terminate an inadequately funded defined benefit plan and has a claim against the sponsor of a defined benefit plan (and its related entities) for the full amount of unfunded liabilities upon plan termination.

Title IV of ERISA, as amended by the Multi-Employer Pension Plan Amendments Act of 1980, also establishes a system to protect the financial condition of union-sponsored multi-employer pension plans. The principal mechanism to protect the finances of multi-employer pension plans is the collection of withdrawal liability payments from employers that partially or wholly withdraw from, or stop contributing to, a union-sponsored multi-employer pension plan. Withdrawal liability also may be triggered by the sale of a contributing employer's assets. ERISA prescribes rules to calculate the amount of an employer's withdrawal liability and provides plans with remedies to collect the amount of unpaid withdrawal liabilities.

Multiple Employer Welfare Arrangements

ERISA §3(40)(A) defines **Multiple Employer Welfare Arrangement (MEWA)** to mean "an employee welfare benefit plan . . . which is established or maintained for the purpose of offering or providing any [welfare] benefit . . . to the employees of two or more employers," except that a plan or arrangement is not a MEWA if it "is established or maintained . . . under or pursuant to one or more agreements which the Secretary finds to be collective bargaining agreements, or by a rural electric cooperative or a rural telephone association." As the definition suggests, MEWAs afford groups of unrelated employers the opportunity to collectively purchase welfare benefits. By banding together for this purpose, employers—small employers in particular—can negotiate lower premiums and obtain better coverage, and they can take advantage of centralized claims processing and other administrative functions. An example of a typical MEWA is a trade association-sponsored master health plan under which member companies can purchase medical coverage at a discount for their employees.

MEWAs, which are not collectively bargained, differ from multi-employer plans, which are collectively bargained industry plans. Unlike employers participating in collectively bargained plans, employers participating in most MEWAs are able to enter or leave essentially at will. As a result, it can sometimes be difficult for a MEWA to predict claims experience, and there is a risk that reserves may prove to be insufficient to cover claims. While MEWAs promise cost savings and administrative efficiencies, they have historically been plagued with some serious, practical problems. Unsavory or incompetent MEWA operators have promoted MEWA schemes that promised competitive premium rates and benefits only to run out of money as a result of fraud or poor management or both. When these schemes collapsed, plan participants were left without promised coverage and claims were left unpaid.

When a MEWA is self-funded, in whole or in part, the plan's assets typically are held in a trust, which is referred to as a multiple employer trust (MET). State insurance regulators early on took the position that METs act as unregulated insurance companies and must therefore comply with state insurance laws (including those prescribing minimum reserves). MET sponsors responded that the ERISA preemption rules exempted them from state insurance regulation. A number of courts rejected these assertions in the years following ERISA's enactment on the grounds that METs were not "plans" principally because they were not sponsored by either an employer or an employer organization. Because of the inherently fact-driven nature of deciding whether a MET is a plan, and because METs could continue to collect premiums during protracted litigation over ERISA coverage and then relocate to new jurisdictions when they lost, litigation did not lead to effective state regulation.

Congress sought to clarify the matter in 1983 by providing a specific exception to ERISA preemption respecting MEWAs. As a result of these changes, if a MEWA is self-insured, then a state can subject the MEWA to all of its insurance licensing requirements (unless they conflict with any of the protections otherwise afforded by ERISA) including laws directed to licensing, registration, certification, and financial reporting, among others. If a MEWA is fully insured, then a state can apply its insurance laws to the MEWA, but only to the extent of requiring the maintenance of specific levels of reserves and specified levels of contributions and provision to enforce the same. A MEWA is fully insured only if the secretary of labor determines that all of its benefits are guaranteed under a contract or policy of insurance issued by an insurance company qualified to conduct business in a state.

The ERISA reporting and disclosure obligations of a MEWA turn in large part on whether the MEWA is itself a welfare benefit plan. If it is, then the MEWA must annually file a single annual report (Form 5500). If the MEWA is not itself a welfare plan (e.g., it is not maintained by an employer or employer organization), then each employer that participates in the plan will need to file its own annual report.

Except in certain instances where a MEWA is established under a state law, MEWA administrators must file Form M-1 if the MEWA offers or provides medical care benefits. This rule also extends to arrangements that are established or maintained pursuant to a collective bargaining agreement. These arrangements, referred to as entities claiming exception (ECEs), are required only to file annually for the first three years following startup or "origination." In addition to federally mandated filing requirements, state statutes that regulate MEWAs almost universally impose their own filing requirements.

Professional employer organizations (PEOs)—organizations that outsource the entire human resources function of a recipient employer—routinely claim to be the common law employer of workers placed by the PEO with client companies. PEOs typically maintain their own employee benefit plans that include medical coverage. But if sufficient control and other indicia of employee status reside with the recipient company (as is often the case), the workers may be the common law employees of the recipient and not the PEO. If so, the PEO medical plan likely will be a MEWA since it furnishes benefits to employees of more than one employer.

THE INTERNAL REVENUE CODE

Tax Advantages of Qualified Retirement Plans

The Internal Revenue Code (the Code) confers significant tax advantages on "tax-qualified pension, profit-sharing and stock bonus plans." These advantages include the following:

- The employer/plan sponsor receives a current income tax deduction for contributions to the plan.
- A plan participant need not include in gross income his or her interest in employer contribution or earnings until the participant, or his or her beneficiary in the case of death, actually receives the funds.
- The earnings of the trust that funds the plan are exempt from tax while in the trust.
- Distributions are in certain instances eligible for special income tax treatment.

To reap the substantial benefits associated with tax qualification, a plan's terms and operation must meet a long list of the Code's qualification requirements. These qualification requirements reflect the congressional desire to use the tax system as a means to encourage expanded retirement plan coverage. These provisions are designed to prevent prohibited group employees (i.e., officers, owners, and highly compensated employees) from unduly benefiting under a plan at the expense of rank-and-file employees. The qualification rules include:

- Participation rules that specify the maximum age and number of years of service that can be required for eligibility.
- Vesting rules that specify the maximum number of years of service that can be required before an employee is fully vested in his or her benefits.
- Nondiscrimination rules, which ensure that the plan does not impermissibly discriminate in favor of prohibited group employees.

When a plan intended to be tax-qualified loses its tax-qualified status, there are substantial adverse tax consequences to the plan sponsor, plan participants, and the trust (or other funding vehicle) that holds plan assets.

Pension, Profit-Sharing, and Stock Bonus Plans

The tax-qualification rules of the Internal Revenue Code operate on pension, profit-sharing, and stock bonus plans. Treasury Regulation §1.401–1(b)(i) defines **pension plan** to mean (in relevant part) a plan that is:

> established and maintained by an employer primarily to provide systematically for the payment of definitely determinable benefits to his employees over a period of years, usually for life, after retirement. Retirement benefits generally are measured by, and based on, such factors as years of service and compensation received by the employees. The determination of the amount of retirement benefits and the contributions to provide such benefits are not dependent upon profits. . .

This, essentially, is a defined benefit plan. The retirement promise is stated in terms of what the participant is entitled to once he or she retires. There is no need for an individual account because the employer's promise, vis-à-vis retirement benefits, does not depend on it.

Treasury Regulation §1.401–1(b)(ii) defines **profit-sharing plan** to mean (again in relevant part) a plan that is:

> established and maintained by an employer to provide for the participation in his profits by his employees or their beneficiaries. The plan must provide a definite predetermined formula for allocating the contributions made to the plan among the participants and for distributing the funds accumulated under the plan after a fixed number of years, the attainment of a stated age, or upon the prior occurrence of some event such as layoff, illness, disability, retirement, death or severance of employment. A formula for allocating the contributions among the participants is definite if, for example, it provides for an allocation in proportion to the basic compensation of each participant.

Perhaps the most commonly encountered profit-sharing plan is that coupled with a so-called cash or deferred arrangement (CODA), which is better known as

---

Did You Know?

Unlike pension plans, profit-sharing plans must have a predetermined formula for allocating contributions, which once identified are allocated to an individual account. While this regulation refers to "participation in an employer's profits," the requirement that contributions to a profit-sharing plan be made out of current profits or retained earnings has since been eliminated.

the 401(k) plan. More specifically, Code §401(k)(2) describes a qualified CODA as an arrangement that is part of a qualified profit-sharing or stock bonus plan. As a result, elective plan contributions under the CODA need not be the only contributions under the plan. Often, they are combined with matching and other employer contributions.

Impact of EGTRRA on Money Purchase Pension Plans

A close cousin to the profit-sharing plan was the money purchase pension plan, which was an individual account plan with a fixed funding obligation. A typical money purchase allocation formula might have provided for an annual contribution of 10 percent of compensation for all participants without regard for the employer's profits. By making the promise of a fixed annual contribution, the money purchase plan was subject to a funding obligation, which is a key requirement of a pension plan for Code purposes. But because the money purchase plan also was an individual account plan, it was a defined contribution rather than a defined benefit plan.

Prior to the Economic Growth and Tax Relief Reconciliation Act of 2001 (EGTRRA), money purchase pension plans were permitted deduction of up to 25 percent of covered compensation while the deduction limit was only 15 percent for profit-sharing plans. This led many employers to adopt both a mandatory 10 percent money purchase plan plus a profit-sharing plan with a discretionary contribution of up to 15 percent, thereby getting to the maximum deduction limit. Under EGTRRA, the profit-sharing deduction limit was increased to 25 percent, thereby making money purchase plans unnecessary.

Stock bonus plans are similar to profit-sharing plans, except that benefits are paid in the stock of the employer. Alternatively, in certain circumstances a stock bonus plan may pay benefits in cash, subject to the participant's right to demand stock. According to Treasury Regulation §1.401–1(b)(iii), "A **stock bonus plan** is a plan established and maintained by an employer to provide benefits similar to those of a profit-sharing plan, except that . . . benefits are distributable in stock of the employer company."

Employee stock ownership plans (ESOPs) are stock bonus plans designed to invest primarily in stock of the employer/plan sponsor or members of the controlled group of corporations that include the employer/plan sponsor. There also are leveraged ESOPs that are allowed to borrow money for the purpose of purchasing employer stock. This allows the ESOP to create a market for closely held stock, and it permits publicly held companies to raise money at favorable interest rates.

It also is possible to design so-called hybrid plans. A defined benefit plan, for example, can be modified by relating the benefit formula to investment experience, thereby giving the plan some of the attributes of a defined contribution plan. This is called a target benefit plan. Or the plan benefit formula can be linked to some standard price index, thereby adjusting for the effect of inflation. This approach results in a cash-balance plan. Cash balance plans have the "look and feel" of a garden-variety profit-sharing or money purchase plan except that the plan benefit is established by plan formula and not by the amount of money in a participant's account. That is why cash balance accounts are referred to as notional or hypothetical accounts. Cash balance contributions often are stated in terms of a fixed percentage of salary, but rather than investment earnings, notional accounts are increased by annual interest credits that are to some usually fixed investment benchmark.

Two other common hybrid plans are referred to as age-weighted plans and new comparability plans, each of which allocate contributions based not on some percentage of compensation but rather on the amount necessary to produce a particular benefits at retirement.

In an age-weighted profit-sharing plan, the contribution takes into account the amount of time that a plan contribution has before the plan's normal retirement date. By way of example, if a company has two employees, one age 50 and the other age 25, and if each employee makes $50,000 annually, the contribution for the 25-year-old would be much less than that for the 50-year-old. This is so because the contribution for the 25-year-old has 40 years to grow before being distributed at age 65, while the contribution for the 50-year-old has only 15 years to grow. Even though the dollar amounts differ, the benefit at the plan's normal retirement date (i.e., age 65 in this example) is identical.

This approach works because the basic nondiscrimination rule of Code §401(a)(4) requires that plans not discriminate as to either contributions or benefits. There is nothing in the statute that requires profit-sharing plans to demonstrate compliance on the amount of contributions and pension plans to demonstrate compliance on the basis of benefits.

New comparability plans take a different tack to nondiscrimination by exploiting the permitted numerical tolerances built into the final nondiscrimination regulations. One way to establish compliance is to show that the average contributions made for rank-and-file employees are, in the aggregate, a designated percentage of the average contributions made on behalf of prohibited group employees. The test in issue is referred to as the average benefits test, and its mechanics are fairly complicated. But it allows a plan to separate its prohibited group and nonprohibited group employees into different allocation classes with a significantly higher contribution being made to the owners. While IRS guidance has narrowed the gap in the allocation rates somewhat, new compatibility plans still are prized by small business owners for their ability to slant contributions in their favor.

The ERISA classifications (i.e., defined contribution plan and defined benefit plan) are carried over into the Code. Code §414(i) defines **defined contribution plan** to mean "a plan which provides for an individual account for each participant and for benefits based solely on the amount contributed to the participant's account, and any income, expenses, gains and losses, and any forfeitures of accounts of other participants which may be allocated to such participant's account." And Code §414(j) defines **defined benefit plan** to mean "any plan which is not a defined contribution plan." The table in Figure 18.2 juxtaposes the ERISA and Code plan classifications and shows how most of the common plan designs fit into the larger regulatory scheme.

The Income Taxation of Fringe Benefit Plans

The Code also regulates a class of benefits known as "fringe benefits" that includes many ERISA-covered welfare benefits plans. The universe of fringe benefits plans is set out in Code §6039D, which covers the following arrangements: (1) group-term life insurance purchased for employees (Code §79); (2) amounts received under accident and health plans (Code §§104, 105 and 106); (3) cafeteria plans (Code

§125); (4) educational assistance programs (Code §127); (5) dependent care assistance programs (Code §129); and (6) adoption assistance programs (Code §137). These arrangements are discussed below.

Group-Term Life Insurance (Code §79)

Code §79 allows employers to provide employees with group term life insurance coverage on a tax-advantaged basis. Under a properly structured group-term life plan, an employer can provide each employee up to $50,000 of group-term life insurance coverage without the employee having to recognize income on the cost of the insurance. The employer is provided with a deduction for the cost of providing coverage. Coverage in excess of $50,000 of death benefit is included in the employee's taxable income. Self-employed individuals, including partners, are not eligible, nor are S corporation employees who own more than 2 percent of the outstanding stock or total voting power of the S corporation.

Code §79(d) bars "key employees" from receiving the exclusion from income under §79(a) unless the plan under which the coverage is provided does not discriminate in favor of key employees with regard to eligibility and the type and amount of benefits available to participants. Post-EGTRRA, key employee means and includes (1) an officer with compensation in excess of $130,000 (adjusted for inflation in $5,000 increments); (2) a 5 percent owner; or (3) a 1 percent owner with compensation in excess of $150,000.

Accident and Health Plans (Code §§104, 105, and 106)

The taxation of medical benefits is governed by three interrelated sections of the Code. Code §104 provides exclusions from an individual's gross income for amounts received from workers' compensation, as damages for personal injuries, and from accident and health benefit coverage not financed by an employer. Thus, an individual can receive benefits under a disability or medical insurance plan tax-free, but only if he or she has paid the premiums with after-tax dollars. Without the exclusions provided by Code §105(b), benefits payments would be included in taxable income under Code §61. A corresponding deduction would be available

---

Did You Know?

Life insurance provided to employees under a group term life insurance plan cannot qualify for favorable tax treatment unless it covers at least 10 full-time employees, or all of the employer's full-time employees if the employer employs less than 10 full-time employees. There also is an exception to the 10-employee rule that affects plans maintained by unrelated employers. In applying either exception, the following employees are excluded: (1) employees who are 65 or older; (2) employees who customarily work 20 hours or less a week or five months in a calendar year; and (3) employees who have not satisfied a waiting period that does not exceed six months

either under §213(a) (with respect to medical expenses) but only to the extent that it exceeds 7.5 percent of adjusted gross income.

Under Code §105(a) amounts received by an employee through accident or health insurance for personal injuries or sickness are taxable to the extent the amounts are attributable to contributions by the employer that were not includible in the gross income of the employee or are paid by the employer. Section 105(b) contains the exceptions to the general rule of Code §105(a). The exceptions are for amounts expended for medical care (i.e., medical expense reimbursements) and permanent injury payments. Medical care means amounts paid for the diagnosis, cure, mitigation, treatment, or prevention of disease, or for the purpose of affecting any structure or function of the body; for transportation primarily for and essential to medical care; for certain qualified long-term care services; or for supplementary medical insurance for the aged (i.e., Social Security).

Under Code §106, employer-paid coverage under an accident or health plan is not taxable to the employee. Employee contributions toward medical plan premiums or costs would, in the absence of Code §125, be taxable under Code §106, which deals only with employer contributions.

For reasons that are largely historical, no benefits-related, nondiscrimination rules apply in the case of an insured accident and health plan. But unlike their insured counterparts, self-insured medical expense reimbursement plans are subject to the nondiscrimination requirements set out in Code §105(h). The exclusion from income provided under Code §105(b) is totally or partially denied to "highly compensated individuals" who are covered under a self-insured medical reimbursement plan that discriminates as to either eligibility or benefits. When a self-insured medical reimbursement plan fails a nondiscrimination requirement, benefits paid to highly compensated individuals become taxable in whole or in part.

Cafeteria Plans (Code §125)

When an employer pays for medical benefits on behalf of its employees, its payments are excluded from the gross income of employees under Code §105(b). Also, accident and health benefits attributable to after-tax employee contributions generally are excludible from income under Code §104(a)(3). Code §106 first appeared in 1954 when the vast majority of employer-sponsored accident and health plans were fully employer paid. Plans requiring employees to contribute to the costs of coverage came in 1978 with the enactment of Code §125, which made employee contributions to accident and health plans deductible.

Code §125 defines **cafeteria plan** to mean "a written plan under which (1) all participants are employees, and (2) the participants may choose among two or more benefits consisting of cash and qualified benefits." A cafeteria plan cannot discriminate in favor of highly compensated individuals as to eligibility to participate or highly compensated participants as to contributions and benefits. Highly compensated participant and highly compensated individual refer to individuals and participants who are (1) officers; (2) shareholders owning more than 5 percent of the voting power or value of all classes of stock in the employer; or (3) highly compensated. Moreover, key employees may not receive more than 25 percent of all of the qualified benefits (i.e., tax-advantaged benefits) under the plan.

Cafeteria plans also may include medical and dependent care flexible spending accounts. To exhibit insurance-like, risk-shifting characteristics, amounts selected under a medical flexible spending account must be fully available during the period of coverage, which usually is the plan year. This means that if a participant elects to defer $100 per month, he or she could submit—and the employer would be required to honor—a $1,200 reimbursement request in January. While dependent care accounts are not subject to this rule, both medical flexible spending accounts and dependent care accounts are subject to a "use-it-or-lose-it" rule under which amounts not used during the period of coverage are forfeited.

Educational Assistance Programs (Code §127)

Code §127 provides that the gross income of an employee does not include amounts paid or expenses incurred by the employer for educational assistance to the employee if the assistance is furnished pursuant to a program that benefits employees who qualify under a nondiscriminatory classification. The exclusion from income is generally limited to $5,250. **Educational assistance** means amounts paid or incurred for an employee's educational expenses, including books, equipment, fees, and tuition. Expenses for graduate-level courses of a kind normally taken by a person pursuing a program leading to an advanced academic or professional degree may not be covered, nor may costs of courses involving sports, games, or hobbies unless the education has a reasonable relationship to the employer's business or is required as a part of a degree program.

Dependent Care Assistance (Code §129)

Code §129 provides an exclusion from gross income of the employee for amounts paid or incurred by the employer for dependent care assistance provided to the employee if the assistance is furnished pursuant to a dependent care assistance program. Specifically, an employee may exclude (1) the value of services provided to the employee; (2) the amount paid directly to the provider of dependent care assistance; or (3) the amount reimbursed to the employee for expenses incurred for dependent care assistance under a dependent care assistance program. The exclusion cannot exceed $5,000, or $2,500 for married individuals filing separately, nor can the exclusion be more than the earned income of the employee or the employee's spouse. The exclusion may be further reduced because of the earned income limitation found in Code §129(b). Also, Code §129(c) prohibits certain payments to related individuals.

Code §129(e)(1) defines **dependent care assistance** as the payment of, or provision of, those services, which if paid for by the employee would be considered employment-related expenses under Code §21(b)(2) relating to the dependent care credit. Services may be incurred either inside or outside the employee's home, but if they are incurred for services outside the home, then the services must be provided to either a dependent of the employee under age 13 or a spouse or dependent of an employee who is physically or mentally incapable of caring for himself or herself who spends at least eight hours a day in the employee's household.

Code §129(d)(1) requires that a dependent care assistance program must be a separate written plan of the employer for the exclusive benefit of the employees. Contributions or benefits provided under the plan may not discriminate in favor of highly compensated employees within the meaning of Code §414(q) or their dependents. The eligibility test of Code §129(d)(3) requires that the program benefit employees who qualify under a nondiscriminatory classification of employees.

Under Code §129(d)(4), not more than 25 percent of the amounts paid or incurred by the employer for dependent care assistance during the year may be provided for the class of individuals who are shareholders or owners (or their spouses or dependents). Code §129(d)(8)(A) requires that the average benefits provided for dependent care assistance to all non-highly compensated employees be at least 55 percent of the average benefits provided to all highly compensated employees. If a program qualifies as a dependent care assistance program but fails to meet these requirements in operation, then the benefits are taxable to highly compensated employees.

Adoption Assistance Programs (Code §137)

Under Code §23 and 137, gross income of an employee does not include amounts paid or expenses incurred by the employer for qualified adoption expenses in connection with the adoption of a child by an employee provided such amounts are furnished pursuant to an adoption assistance program. An **adoption assistance program** is defined as a separate written plan of an employer for the exclusive benefit of its employees that provides for adoption assistance and meets certain other requirements. Qualified adoption expenses are defined in Code §23(d) to mean, subject to certain limits, reasonable and necessary adoption fees, court costs, attorney fees, and other expenses directly related to (and the principal purpose is) the legal adoption of an eligible child by the employee. Eligible child means a child who is under age 18 or physically or mentally incapable of self-care when the expense is paid or incurred.

The aggregate amount of adoption assistance expenses paid to or incurred by a taxpayer that may be taken into account for all taxable years with respect to the adoption of a child by the taxpayer may not exceed $10,000. The exclusion is phased out for taxpayers whose adjusted gross income exceeds $150,000 for plan years commencing after 2001, and it is eliminated once adjusted gross income exceeds $190,000.

THE ECONOMIC GROWTH AND TAX RELIEF RECONCILIATION ACT OF 2001 (EGTRRA)

The Economic Growth and Tax Relief Reconciliation Act of 2001 ("EGTRRA") was a massive piece of federal tax legislation that:

- Enacted substantial changes in the income and estate tax rate structures.
- Made major changes in the alternative minimum tax rules.
- Established qualified tuition programs and college savings accounts.
- Created a new tax credit for low-income savers.
- Liberalized estate and gift tax rules.
- Adopted a broad range of enhancements affecting tax-qualified retirement plans.

The changes affecting qualified retirement plan represent a major retirement-policy turning point. Prior to EGTRRA, the trend in tax and benefits policy was to generally constrict the amounts that could be contributed to, and benefits that could accrue under, tax-qualified retirement plans. While it is true that the deferral limits for 401(k) plans were rising modestly over time with increases in the cost of living, the overall contributions limits under Code §415, among others, were

---

Did You Know?

Employees who are 50 years of age are older can also make additional catch-up contributions. Catch-up contributions are not subject to other contribution limitations and are not taken into account in computing other testing limits, but they are subject to a universal availability requirement under which an employer must offer the catch-up in all or none its 401(k) plans.

---

cut substantially. EGTRRA represents an abrupt departure from this trend, and it opens up significant new planning opportunities, especially for small, closely held businesses. With the passage of EGTRRA—as supplemented by certain technical corrections made in the Jobs Creation and Worker Assistance Act of 2002 (JCWAA), Congress has both liberalized and rationalized the rules that govern the design, adoption, and operation of qualified plans.

Increases in Annual Employee Deferral Limits

EGTRRA increased the annual amount that participants can defer under 401(k) plans, tax-sheltered annuity plans, and Section 457 plans in annual increments of $1,000 beginning in 2002 ($11,000) and ending in 2006 ($15,000). For the years beginning with 2007, these limits increase in $500 increments with changes in the cost of living. The amount of compensation that can be taken into account for purposes of determining the allowable contribution increases to $200,000, also indexed for inflation.

The catch-up contribution amount is $5,000 as of 2006. As is the case with the basic deferral limits, these limits will increase with changes in the cost of living in $500 increments after 2006. Catch-up contributions may not be made to Savings Incentive Match Plan for Employees of Small Employers (SIMPLE) 401(k) plans, or individual retirement accounts (IRAs).

Under interpretive regulations issued by the Internal Revenue Service (IRS), an individual is treated as being 50 or older as of Jan. 1 of the year in which he or she attains age 50 (even if the employee dies or is terminated before his or her 50th birthday). The proposed regulations clarify that catch-up contributions are calculated on a calendar year, rather than on a plan year. Catch-up contributions can come from contributions that exceed the applicable dollar limitation, a plan-imposed limitation (e.g., 10 percent of pay), or the Section 401(k) nondiscrimination test.

Increases in the Overall Code §415 Contribution Limitation

Code §415 governs the amounts that can be contributed to a tax-qualified retirement plan on behalf of an individual participant in any year. The precise measuring period for §415 purposes is called the limitation year, which often is but not necessarily the plan year. This limitation stands in marked contrast to the deduction limits, which are based on the aggregate compensation of all participants in the plan. Where defined contribution plans are concerned, the Code §415 limits take into account both employee deferrals and employer contributions. In contrast, the Code §402(g) limit, as well as the parallel limits for tax-sheltered annuity and 457(b) plans, take into account only employee elective deferrals.

The contribution limits that apply to defined contribution plans are set out in Code §415(c). EGTRRA increased the Code §415(c) limit to the lesser of $40,000 or 100 percent of compensation. The pre-EGTRRA limit was the lesser of $35,000 (in 2001) or 25 percent of compensation.

The contribution limits that apply to defined benefit plans are recorded in Code §415(b). Code §415(b) limits the annual benefit that can be provided under a defined benefit plan to the lesser of (1) the defined benefit dollar limitation under Code §415(b)(1)(A) or (2) the defined benefit compensation limit of Code §415(b)(1)(B). Both of these limits are adjusted from time to time to reflect cost-of-living increases. The pre-EGTRRA defined benefit dollar limitation of $90,000 had increased to $140,000 as a result of cost-of-living increases. This limit was adjusted (i.e., reduced or increased) where benefits commenced before or after the participant's Social Security normal retirement age. A further reduction was required under Code §415(b)(5)(A) where a participant had less than 10 years of plan participation.

EGTRRA increased the defined benefit dollar limitation under Code §415(b)(1)(A) to $160,000, and it also modified Code §415(b)(2)(C) to require that the defined benefit dollar limitation be reduced or increased when payment of a participant's benefit starts before age 62 or after age 65 (as opposed to before or after a participant's Social Security retirement age). This means that the nonforfeitability requirement under Code §411 must be coordinated with the new Code §415 limits. By reducing the age at which reductions commence, the net result is an increase in the effective 415 limit. The maximum amount of compensation that can be taken into account for computing benefits under a qualified plan increased to $200,000 under EGTRRA.

EGTRRA also made changes affecting tax-sheltered annuity plans under Code §403(b). In addition to being subject to Code §415, tax-sheltered annuities for years have been subject to a limit referred to as the maximum exclusion allowance (MEA). The MEA equaled 20 percent of so-called includible compensation multiplied by years of service, minus prior contributions. The MEA limit proved nearly impossible to apply and was routinely violated. Recognizing this, Congress took the opportunity in EGTRRA to eliminate it.

Deferred Compensation Plans Under Code §457

While the provisions of Code §457 apply to plans of state and local governments *and* to certain tax-exempt entities, the rules that apply to each type began to diverge with the enactment of the Small Business Job Protection Act of 1996. This change was in response to the financial difficulties experienced in the mid-1980s by Orange County, California, in which the retirement benefits of municipal employees were put at risk as a result of investments in derivatives. Congress responded by mandating that Code §457 plans maintained by state and local governments be funded (i.e., that plan assets be held in trust).

With the passage of EGTRRA, the rules that apply to governmental and tax-exempt employer 457 plans diverge even further. Code §457 plans of state and local governments are now being treated more like broad-based tax qualified plans, while

§457 plans maintained by tax-exempts are treated more like unfunded, executive deferred compensation plans. Some of the key provisions that apply to governmental 457 plans but not to tax-exempt employer 457 plans are the following:

- Catch-up contributions under Code §414(v).
- The direct rollover provisions of Code §401(a)(31).
- The withholding and reporting rules under Code §3504(a) (eligible rollover distributions are reportable on IRS Form 1099-R and subject to 20 percent withholding unless rolled over in a direct rollover).
- Taxation of benefits only on payment under Code §457(a)(1)(A); i.e., the repeal of the constructive rules under EGTRRA §649(a) amending Code §457(d)(2), (3) and Code §457(e)(9).
- Deemed IRA availability under Code §408(q).

EGTRAA made another significant change affecting Code §457 plans. Prior to EGTRRA, the limit on elective deferrals was aggregated for 401(k), 403(b), and 457 plans. This meant that a participant's deferrals into a tax-sheltered annuity plan reduced dollar-for-dollar the amount that the participant could defer into a Code §457 plan. EGTRRA eliminated this offset. This means that eligible employees can now contribute to both a 403(b) plan and a 457 plan.

Rollovers

Before EGTRRA, retirement accounts could not be freely moved from one type of plan to another or from an IRA to a plan and vice versa. EGTRRA changes this. Under EGTRRA, if an individual moves from one employer to another who maintains a different type of plan, the old account can be rolled over into the new plan of a different type (but only if the receiving plan is amended to allow it to receive the rollover). Rollovers may be made among qualified retirement plans, tax-sheltered annuity plans, and governmental 457 plans. Nongovernmental Section 457 plans are not covered. As a result of EGTRRA's changes to the rollover rules, workers who move from job to job now have more flexibility when it comes to investing their retirement plan funds.

The Roth 401(k) Plan Option

EGTRRA permits the addition of a Roth IRA feature to a 401(k) plan. Employees will be able to designate part of their elective deferrals as Roth contributions that

---

Did You Know?

Surviving spouses also have more rollover options under EGTRRA. A surviving spouse may roll over a decedent's distribution from a qualified plan or IRA into an IRA or into a qualified plan, 403(b) annuity, or 457 plan in which the surviving spouse participates. Before 2002, a payout to the surviving spouse from the decedent's qualified plan or IRA could only be rolled over into another IRA.

would not be tax-deductible currently. Rather, they (along with subsequent earnings) will escape tax when distributed. Roth IRA contributions would be subject to all of the other rules pertaining to qualified plan distributions.

Deduction Limits

Code §404 contains limits on the amount that an employer can deduct each year to a tax-qualified retirement plan. Pre-EGTRRA, the deduction for employer contributions to defined contribution plans generally was limited to 15 percent of the aggregate plan year compensation of all active participants. For this purpose, the term "compensation" excluded participant elective deferrals. Under EGTRRA, the deduction limit increased to 25 percent of compensation, and the definition of compensation has been revised to include participants' pretax contributions to employer-provided retirement plans, cafeteria plans, and qualified transportation fringe benefits. Moreover, participant elective deferrals are no longer subject to the deduction limit.

Prior to EGTRRA, the employer's deduction for employer contributions to qualified defined benefit plans generally was limited to an amount required to satisfy the minimum funding standard for the plan year. Prior law also contained a special rule that applied to sponsors of qualified defined benefit plans (other than multi-employer plans) with more than 100 participants. These employers were permitted to deduct a maximum amount that is not less than the plan's unfunded current liability. EGTRRA expanded this special rule to all defined benefit plans but with some limitations affecting plan amendments that enhance benefits for highly compensated employees. Also, for plans subject to PBGC coverage, the deductible limit for the year in which a plan terminates is increased to the amount required to satisfy all benefit liabilities.

EGTRRA also made changes to the "full funding" limit. This is a limit that originally was intended to prevent employers from taking excessive deductions, but in practice has resulted in lower overall funding of pension promises. This means that, even if a plan was significantly underfunded—as a result of substandard investment returns, for example—the employer is limited to the amount that it could contribute. EGTRRA increased the full funding percentage limitation incrementally beginning in 2002 and eliminated it in its entirety in 2005.

Notice Requirement for Pension Plan Benefit Accruals Reduction

ERISA §204(h) imposes on plan sponsors the obligation to provide advanced notice to plan participants and others of any plan amendment that reduces future benefit accruals. Prior to EGTRRA, the employer was required to provide this so-called 204(h) notice at least 15 days prior to its effective date, and the notice had to summarize the amendment in a manner calculated to be understood by the average participant. Particularly as a result of concerns raised by defined benefit/cash balance plan conversions, Congress modified ERISA §204(h) and added parallel provisions to the Code that changed the applicable notice period and expanded upon the types of information that the notice must contain. EGTRRA also added tax penalties for noncompliance. New Code §4980F generally imposes a $100 per participant, per day excise tax for failure to provide timely notice of plan amendments that would result in a significant reduction in the rate of future benefit accrual.

The IRS issued a proposed rule in April 2002 interpreting the changes to the 204(h) notice requirements that clarified when pension plan administrators are required to notify plan participants and what needs to be included in the notice. The proposed rules would require notification of a plan change at least 45 days prior to the change; 30 days prior to a change made in connection with a business merger or acquisition and that only affects an early retirement program or retirement-type subsidy; and 15 days prior to another change made in connection with a business merger or acquisition or a change to a small pension plan.

Top-Heavy Rules

Under prior law, a **key employee** was defined as an employee who, at any time during the plan year or any of the four preceding plan years, was:

- An officer of the employer having an annual compensation greater than 50 percent of the amount in effect under §415(b)(1)(A) for any such plan year.
- One of the 10 employees having annual compensation from the employer of more than the limitation in effect under §415(c)(1)(A) and owning (or considered as owning within the meaning of §318) the largest interests in the employer.
- A 5-percent owner of the employer.
- A 1-percent owner of the employer having an annual compensation from the employer of more than $150,000.

EGTRRA made some important changes to the top-heavy rules, which were intended to ease compliance burdens. Specifically, EGTRRA changed the definition of key employee to (1) delete the "top 10 employees" rule; (2) provide that an officer will be treated as a key employee only if he or she earns more than $130,000 in the year (which will be indexed in $5,000 increments); and (3) in most instances, eliminate the four-year "look-back rule" for identifying key employees. Matching contributions previously could not be used to satisfy the minimum contribution amount required when a plan was top heavy, but EGTRRA now allows matching contributions to count toward the top-heavy minimum contribution.

Prior to EGTRRA, when determining the benefits of a key employee for top-heavy purposes, any distribution occurring during the five-year period ending on the determination date had to be included for top-heavy testing purposes. EGTRRA shortened the determination period to one year, except that the five-year determination period continues to apply to distributions made for reasons other than separation from service, death, or disability. While EGTRRA modified the rules governing elective deferrals under 401(k) plans to allow for distributions upon "severance from employment" rather than upon "separation from service," the phrase "separation from service" was used to describe distributions not subject to the five-year, top-heavy look-back rule. JCWAA substituted the phrase "severance from employment" for "separation from service" for top-heavy purposes. As a result of this change, a distribution made in connection with a key employee's "severance from employment" is not subject to the five-year look back.

Multiple-Use Test Repealed

Elective deferrals under 401(k) plans are subject to three special nondiscrimination tests. The first, referred to as the actual deferral percentage (ADP) test, measures the percentage of elective deferrals made by highly compensated employees against the percentage of elective deferrals made by nonhighly compensated employees. To pass the ADP test, the percentages must fit with tolerances prescribed by regulation. A similar test, referred to as the actual contribution percentage (ACP) test, applies to matching and after-tax contributions. A third test, referred to as the multiple-use test places an overall, combined limit on the ADP and ACP tests. For years, plan sponsors have complained about the complexity of the multiple-use test, arguing that it is unnecessary. Congress apparently heard the call: EGTRRA repealed the multiple-use test for plan years beginning after December 31, 2001.

Same Desk Rule Eliminated

Prior to EGTRRA, distributions could not be made from a 401(k) plan to a participant working at the "same desk" and completing essentially the same job for a new employer after certain sales of a subsidiary or business divisions until the employee terminated employment with the successor employer or until another distributable event occurs. This rule, known as the "same desk rule," originally was intended to prevent plan participants from manipulating their termination of employment to take advantage of income tax averaging rules that are, for the most part, no longer available. The same desk rule, which became a problem particularly for employers engaged in mergers and acquisitions, resulted in the premature termination of many 401(k) plans. Congress was concerned that the same desk rule was causing premature termination of 401(k) plans and unnecessary "leakage" of retirement assets. EGTRRA repealed the same desk rule for all distributions after December 31, 2001.

Safe Harbor Hardship Withdrawal Rules Modified

To allow participants early access to some of their deferrals in certain circumstances, 401(k) plans may provide for hardship withdrawals. Generally, hardship withdrawals only may be made out of salary deferral contributions (i.e., employee contributions as opposed to employer contributions), but they may not include earnings. Prior to EGTRRA, IRS regulations required that a participant's contributions to all employer plans be suspended for at least 12 months after a hardship withdrawal.

Under IRS Notice 2001–56, EGTRRA directed the IRS to modify the Section 401(k) safe harbor hardship withdrawal regulations to reduce the suspension period from 12 months to 6 months. However, plan sponsors, other than those with a safe harbor Section 401(k) plan, may retain the 12-month suspension periods for all hardship distributions.

19

Worker Privacy, Unpaid Leave, and Other Benefit-Related Laws That Protect the Individual

A complex web of overlapping and sometimes conflicting federal and state laws create an ongoing challenge for human resource professionals. Government regulation of benefits plans:

- Mandate certain benefits and basic protections (e.g., the Fair Labor Standards Act, the Family and Medical Leave Act, the Occupational Safety and Health Act, and the Worker Notification and Retraining Notification Act).
- Prohibit discrimination (e.g., Title VII of the Civil Rights Act).
- Protect worker privacy (e.g., the Employee Polygraph Protection Act and the Health Insurance Portability and Accountability Act) and even whistleblowers (e.g., the Whistleblower Protection Act).
- Impose constraints on the conduct of collective bargaining (e.g., the National Labor Relations Act).

The following discussion emphasizes the legal requirements of employers pertaining specifically to worker privacy (HIPAA), unpaid leave (FMLA), and other legislation that protects the rights of the individual.

THE HEALTH INSURANCE PORTABILITY AND ACCOUNTABILITY ACT OF 1996 (HIPAA)

Title I: Group Health Plan Portability

Title I of the Health Insurance Portability and Accountability Act of 1996 (HIPAA) amended Title I of ERISA, the Internal Revenue Code, and the Public Health Service Act (PHSA) to impose new requirements on employer-sponsored group health plans, insurance companies, and health maintenance organizations (HMOs). These

---

Did You Know?

Under HIPAA, pre-existing condition exclusions cannot be applied to pregnancy, regardless of whether the woman had previous coverage. Nor can the pre-existing condition exclusion be applied to a newborn or adopted child under age 18 as long as the child became covered under the health plan within 30 days of birth or adoption (provided they do not incur a subsequent 63-day or longer break in coverage).

---

rules include provisions that limit exclusions for pre-existing conditions, prohibit discrimination against employees and dependents based on their health status, and guarantee renewability and availability of health coverage to certain employers and individuals.

While these protections are often referred to as the "health care portability" rules, they do not provide for true portability in that a person transferring from one plan to another is provided with and entitled to only the benefits under the new plan. Coverage under the new plan could be less or could be greater. Moreover, employers and insurance companies may continue to establish waiting periods before enrollees become eligible for benefits under the plan, and HMOs may have "affiliation periods" during which an enrollee does not receive benefits and is not charged premiums. Affiliation periods may not last for more than two months, however, and they only are allowed for HMOs that do not use pre-existing condition exclusions. Even after HIPAA, the provision of health coverage by an employer is still voluntary.

Pre-existing Condition Limitations

HIPAA limits the extent to which group health plans can limit coverage of pre-existing medical conditions, by requiring plans to cover an individual's pre-existing condition after 12 months (or 18 months in the case of a late enrollee). Moreover, for purposes of determining the pre-existing exclusion period, employees must be given credit for previous coverage that occurred without a "break in coverage" of 63 days or more. This is referred to as "creditable coverage." Any coverage occurring prior to a break in coverage of 63 days or more would not be credited against an exclusion period. Significantly, COBRA coverage counts as creditable coverage.

Pre-existing Conditions

Under HIPAA, a "pre-existing condition" is a condition for which medical advice, diagnosis, care, or treatment was recommended or received within the six-month period ending on the enrollment date in any new health plan. Thus, if an employee had a medical condition in the past, but he or she received no medical advice, diagnosis,

---

Sidebar 19.1: HIPAA Nondiscrimination and Wellness Program Regulations

On December 12, 2006, the U.S. Departments of Labor and Health and Human Services and the Internal Revenue Service jointly issued final regulations governing the nondiscrimination provisions of the Health Insurance Portability and Accountability Act (HIPAA). These provisions prohibit discrimination in group health coverage based on a health factor of a participant or beneficiary. The final regulations, which also include requirements for wellness programs, become effective on February 12, 2007 and apply to plan years beginning on or after July 1, 2007.

Although the final regulations generally adopt the requirements of the interim HIPAA rules or the proposed rules on wellness programs released in January 2001, they do include some important changes and clarifications. According to the American Benefits Council, the final regulations make clear that:

- Compliance with the HIPAA nondiscrimination rules is not determinative of compliance with other federal laws, such as the Americans with Disabilities Act (ADA) or state laws;
- Carryover of unused health reimbursement arrangement (HRA) amounts do not violate the HIPAA nondiscrimination rules; and
- Benefits may not be denied for injuries resulting from a medical condition, even if the medical condition was not diagnosed before the injury occurred.

The final regulations on wellness programs establish the maximum amount of an award under a wellness program may not exceed 20 percent of the cost of coverage. The wellness program final regulations also clarify some ambiguities in the proposed rules, make some changes in terminology (eliminates reference to "bona fide" in connection with wellness programs) and organization, and add a description of wellness programs that are not required to satisfy additional standards in order to comply with nondiscrimination programs.

---

care, or treatment within the six months prior to enrolling in the plan, the old condition is not a pre-existing condition for which the exclusion can be applied.

Certificates of Creditable Coverage

HIPAA requires insurers and group health plans to provide documentation (referred to as "certificates of creditable coverage") to individuals that certify their creditable coverage. Insurers and group health plans that fail or refuse to provide certificates of creditable coverage in a timely manner are subject to monetary penalties. HIPAA also requires that a process be established that will allow individuals to show they are entitled to creditable coverage in situations where they cannot obtain a certification from an insurer or group health plan.

Nondiscrimination

Group health plans and insurers may not establish eligibility for enrollment based on an employee's health status, medical condition (physical or mental), claims experience, receipt of health care, medical history, genetic information, evidence of insurability, or disability. For example, an employee cannot be excluded or dropped from coverage just because he or she has a particular illness. Employers may establish limits or restrictions on benefits or coverage for similarly situated individuals under a plan, but they may not require an individual to pay a premium or contribution that is greater than that for a similarly situated individual based on health status. HIPAA does not require specific benefits nor does it prohibit a plan from restricting the amount or nature of benefits for similarly situated individuals.

Special Enrollment Rights

HIPAA provides for two types of "special enrollment periods." The first covers individuals who did not enroll in an employer's group health plan when they first were eligible due to the existence of alternative coverage, and the second applies where an individual acquires a new dependent (e.g., marries or has a child).

A group health plan must permit an employee (or dependent) who is eligible but not enrolled to enroll in the plan at a date later than the initial enrollment period if (1) the employee was covered under a group health plan when coverage was initially offered; (2) the employee stated in writing that the other coverage was the reason for declining enrollment (but only if the plan sponsor required such a statement and provided the employee with a notice and the consequences of such requirement); (3) the other coverage was either COBRA coverage that was exhausted or other health plan coverage that was terminated due to loss of eligibility or termination; and (4) the employee requests enrollment within 30 days of exhaustion or termination of coverage.

If a group health plan offers dependent coverage, it also must offer dependents a special enrollment period of at least 30 days if they become dependents through marriage, birth, adoption, or placement for adoption. These individuals can become covered dependents of the employee during that special enrollment period. If the employee (or spouse, in the case of birth or adoption) is otherwise eligible for plan enrollment at that time, but he or she has not enrolled, the employee (or spouse) also is allowed to enroll at this time (presumably to allow for the dependent coverage). Coverage through this special enrollment period is retroactive to the date of birth or adoption.

Guaranteed Access Individual Market Coverage

HIPAA also ensures individual access to insurance for those who:

- Have had group coverage for at least 18 months.
- Did not have their group coverage terminated because of fraud or nonpayment of premiums.
- Are ineligible for COBRA or have exhausted their COBRA benefits.
- Are not eligible for coverage under another group health plan.

The opportunity to buy an individual insurance policy is the same whether the individual is laid off, fired, or quits his or her job.

Title II, Subpart F: Administrative Simplification

HIPAA Title II is titled "Preventing Health Care Fraud and Abuse, Administrative Simplification and Medical Liability Reform." Although adopted in 1996, the "administrative simplification" provisions of HIPAA had a delayed effective date, so employers and benefits practitioners alike lost sight of them at the time. Under the heading of administrative simplification, Congress created national standards for electronic transmission of health care data, mandated the establishment of unique health care identification standards and security standards, and also directed the U.S. Department of Health and Human Services ("HHS") to issue a whole new set of medical privacy rules if Congress failed to do so within three years (i.e., by August 21, 1999). Congress failed to meet this self-imposed deadline, so HHS, acting under its statutory mandate, published a privacy rule, which will have far-reaching consequences for employer-sponsored health plans.

National Standards for Electronic Transmission of Health Care Data

Congress sought to improve the efficiency and effectiveness of the U.S. health care system in general, and the Medicare and Medicaid programs in particular, by requiring the establishment of standards to enable entities within the health care system to exchange medical, billing, and other information, and to process health care transactions in a cost-effective manner. To do this, Congress has mandated that the electronic transfer of health care information be accomplished in a standard format that is commonly known as electronic data interchange (EDI). In undertaking this endeavor, Congress focused on the existing lack of standardization with respect to EDI. Moreover, it was concerned that more than 400 formats were being used for the processing of electronic health care claims in the United States.

Final regulations issued by HHS on August 17, 2002, titled "National Standards for Electronic Transmission of Health Care Data," mandate the use of EDI in the health care industry by adopting industry-wide standards for eight electronic transactions and for code sets to be used in those transactions. The covered transactions are as follows:

- Health claims and encounter information.
- Enrollment/disenrollment in a health plan.
- Eligibility for a health plan.
- Health care payment and remittance advice.
- Health plan premium payments.
- Health claim status.
- Referral certification and authorization.
- Coordination of benefits.

Under the final transaction rule, the U.S. Department of Health and Human Services also specifies what "code sets" must be used with each transaction standard. While most organizations already use these code sets, HIPAA ultimately will prohibit the use of additional, local codes. The final transaction rule mandates the use of the following code sets (many of which already are familiar to anyone who works with group health plans):

- ICD-9-CM, Volumes 1 and 2 for diseases, injuries, impairments, or other health-related problems and causes.
- ICD-9-CM, Volume 3 for prevention, diagnosis, treatment, and management for hospital inpatients.
- Combination of HCPCS and CPT-4 for physician services and other health-related services.
- HCPCS for all other substances, equipment, supplies, or other items.
- National Drug Codes (NDC) for prescription drugs.
- CDT-2 for dental services.

Unique Health Identifiers

HIPAA requires HHS to establish unique identifiers for employers, individuals, providers, and health sponsors. Congress believed that uniformity for those identified as entitled would facilitate the workings of the health care system. Final rules establish the taxpayer identification number as the standard employer identifier, and under a proposed rule, providers will use an 8-digit alphanumeric NPI code that will be assigned to hospitals, physicians, laboratories, ambulance companies, HMOs, and pharmacies. No identifiers have yet been proposed for health plans.

Individuals by far are the most daunting to identify from the regulatory perspective. The Centers for Medicare & Medicaid Services (CMS), previously called the Health Care Financing Administration, is charged with this task. For obvious reasons, an individual's Social Security number seems to be the most obvious candidate, but the fear is that Social Security numbers might be too easily linked to credit and financial data. The matter has become politically charged, and Congress has refused to allocate any further monies to fund the development of an individual identifier.

Privacy of Individually Identifiable Health Information

A basic statement of the HIPAA medical privacy rule is as follows:

> A *covered entity* may not use or disclose *protected health information* except as authorized by the individual who is the subject of the information or is explicitly required or permitted by the rule.

Covered entity refers to health plans, health care clearinghouses, and health care providers. Employers and third party administrators, among others, are *not* covered entities. Congress' failure to include employers among the list of covered entities has resulted in a rule that is far more complicated than perhaps it needs to be.

Covered entities are permitted to use and disclose protected health information for purposes of *treatment, payment,* and *operations. Protected health information* means individually identifiable health information that relates to an individual's past, present, or future physical or mental health. Health information is individually identifiable if it reasonably identifies an individual. *Treatment* means the provision, coordination, or management of health care and health care related services; *payment* means and includes activities undertaken to provide or obtain reimbursements, and it includes termination eligibility; and *health care operations* mean activities necessary to carry out covered functions. For protected health information to flow from a covered entity to a noncovered entity (such as an employer/plan sponsor) certain procedural safeguards must be observed.

Employers that require protected health information must:

- Adopt plan amendments that conform to the privacy rule.
- Identify employees or classes of employees that have access to protected health information (PHI).
- Establish mechanisms for resolving noncompliance.
- Certify compliance with the HIPAA privacy rule to the group health plan.

Where a group health plan depends on an outside entity to assist with plan administration, such as a third party administrator, accountant, consultant, or attorney, the plan must enter into a so-called business associate agreement with that third party. The business associate agreement is a written agreement that sets out the permitted uses and disclosures of PHI. The agreement also must provide that the business associate will not further use or disclose PHI, will adopt appropriate safeguards, report unauthorized uses of PHI to the covered entity, ensure that employees and agents will comply with the requirements, and permit the Secretary of HHS and representatives of the covered entity to audit the business associate's books.

The final privacy requires that a covered entity obtain a participant's authorization for any nonroutine disclosures.

Where a covered entity is permitted to use or disclose PHI, it must limit the use or disclosure to the minimum amount necessary to accomplish the intended purpose. An Explanation of Benefits Form, for example, may contain only the health information that is the subject of the explanation.

Health plan is defined broadly to include any ERISA-covered group health plan, as well as all health insurance issuers (insurance companies, HMOs, etc.) and all government programs such as Medicare, Medicaid, and state high-risk pools, among others.

In addition to regulating the conduct of plan sponsors, the HIPAA privacy rule imposes a series of substantive requirements on covered entities. Covered entities must:

- Issue a privacy notice.
- Designate a "privacy official."
- Develop a privacy training program.
- Implement safeguards to protect PHI.
- Provide a complaint resolution program.
- Develop sanctions for violations.
- Mitigate harm from improper disclosures.
- Not require any waiver of privacy rights.
- Maintain documentation of policies.

There are three significant exceptions to these requirements. First, a self-administered group health plan with fewer than 50 participants is not subject to the privacy rule. The principal application of this rule is to medical flexible spending accounts maintained by small employers. Second, not all PHI is individually identifiable. Information that is "de-identified" is not subject to the rule. To be de-identified, health information must be stripped of all identifying data, or that information that would enable someone to recognize the individual who is the subject of the inquiry. The rule contains a safe harbor that describes a series of specific items that must be deleted for the information to be de-identified, and it also allows for other statistically valid methods that are properly certified. Last, and perhaps of most importance to fully insured group health plans, is an exception under which plans are exempt from the privacy rule to the extent that they receive only summary health information and only for the purpose of establishing renewal premiums and amending or terminating the plan.

The scope of the HIPAA privacy rule is narrowly proscribed. Covered entities are the only entities that are regulated. Arrangements such as workers' compensation programs, group life insurance plans, and disability plans, among others, are not subject to the rule. This poses a problem for any arrangement that relies on health plan data or otherwise operates in tandem with an employer's group health plan. It also imperils many disease management programs that require health information from a number of sources.

Security

The HIPAA administrative simplification provisions also mandate certain security measures. The terms "privacy" and "security" are sometimes confused. In the context of HIPAA, *privacy* determines who should have access, what constitutes the patients' rights to confidentiality, and what constitutes inappropriate access to health records. *Security,* on the other hand, establishes how the records should be protected from inappropriate access (i.e., electronic or cyber-security). HIPAA directs the Secretary of HHS to develop security standards that, among other things, "ensure the integrity and confidentiality of [health] information," and protect against unauthorized uses and disclosures.

HHS issued proposed security rules in August 1998 that are designed to help protect the privacy of both medical and financial information from improper access and interception. The rules require that business processes be implemented to protect the operational security of health information and that technical safeguards be developed and adopted to secure the information's physical safety. The proposed security rule attempts to strike a balance between impenetrable security and no security at all by requiring "prudent" protections in light of a company's business. Systems must be established to protect information against foreseeable threats, especially from employees who may be accessing the health information of other employees.

Recognizing that employers of differing sizes might be impacted in very different ways, HHS described its standards as "scaleable," which means that they are intended to be general and flexible enough to be used in varying degrees according to covered entity size, sophistication, and financial ability. The requirements include administrative procedures, physical safeguards, technical security services, and technical security mechanisms. The security standards also place a significant emphasis on initial and ongoing training and certification, formal records processing mechanisms, access controls, and internal audits, and they also require chain of trust partner agreements where data is processed through a third party.

THE NEWBORNS' AND MOTHERS' HEALTH PROTECTION ACT

The Newborns' and Mothers' Health Protection Act (NMHPA) became effective for plan years beginning on or after January 1, 1998. It governs the amount of time a mother and newborn child can spend in the hospital in connection with the birth of a child. Under NMHPA, group health plans, insurance companies, and health maintenance organizations offering health coverage for hospital stays in connection with the birth of a child must provide health coverage for a minimum period of time. NMHPA provides that coverage for a hospital stay following a normal vaginal delivery generally may not be limited to fewer than 48 hours for both the mother and newborn child. Health coverage for a hospital stay in connection with childbirth following a cesarean section generally may not be limited to fewer than 96 hours for both the mother and newborn child. Employers (including small employers) with group health plans that fail to comply with maternity length-of-stay rules are subject to a $100 per day penalty for each day a failure occurs.

NMHPA's requirements only apply to group health plans, insurance companies, and HMOs that choose to provide insurance coverage for a hospital stay in connection with childbirth. NMHPA does not require that such coverage be provided. Moreover, NMHPA does not prevent a group health plan, insurance company, or HMO from imposing deductibles, co-insurance, or other cost-sharing measures for health benefits relating to hospital stays in connection with childbirth as long as such cost-sharing measures are not greater than those imposed on any preceding portion of the hospital stay.

NMHPA requires the notice of the act's provisions be included in the plan's summary plan description. New employees must be provided with notice of the act's provisions at the time of hire, and all employees must be provided with an annual notice.

THE MENTAL HEALTH PARITY ACT OF 1996

The Mental Health Parity Act (MHPA) provides for parity in the application of limits to certain mental health benefits. The law was subject to a sunset provision that has since been extended. The mental health parity requirements do not apply to small employers of 2 to 50 employees or to any group health plan whose costs increase 1 percent or more because of the application of these requirements.

Under MHPA, group health plans, insurance companies, and HMOs offering mental health benefits may not set annual or lifetime limits on mental health benefits that are lower than the plan's limits for medical and surgical benefits. A plan that does not impose an annual or lifetime limit on medical and surgical benefits may not impose such a limit on mental health benefits. Plans can still set the terms and conditions (such as cost-sharing and limits on the number of visits or days of coverage) for the amount, duration, and scope of mental health benefits.

Did You Know?

Group health plans are not required to include mental health in their benefits package. The Mental Health Parity Act (MHPA) applies only to plans offering mental health benefits. MHPA's provisions do not apply to benefits for substance abuse or chemical dependency.

The MHPA was originally subject to a sunset provision on September 30, 2001. But the Appropriations Act for the Departments of Labor, Health and Human Services, Education and Related Services, 2002 (for the Job Creation and Worker Assistance Act of 2002), extended the MHPA sunset date to the end of 2003. As a result of a technical glitch, the 2002 appropriations bill amended ERISA but failed to amend the Code. While the later bill addressed this oversight, there was a brief period of time during which compliance failures were not subject to tax penalties. Every year this continues to be extended by an additional 12 months. So it is fair to say that at the time of this writing, it has been extended through December 31, 2007.

THE WOMEN'S HEALTH AND CANCER RIGHTS ACT OF 1998

In the Women's Health and Cancer Rights Act (WHCRA), Congress amended ERISA and the Public Health Service Act to add some limited but nonetheless important protections for mastectomy patients who elect breast reconstruction. Among other things, WHCRA requires that group health plans and health insurance issuers, including insurance companies and HMOs, notify individuals regarding the coverage required by WHCRA. All group health plans, and their health insurance issuers, that offer coverage for medical and surgical benefits with respect to a mastectomy are subject to the notice requirements under WHCRA.

WHCRA contains three separate notice requirements. The first notice is a one-time requirement under which group health plans, and their insurance companies or HMOs, must have furnished a written description of the benefits that WHCRA requires to participants and beneficiaries no later than January 1, 1999. The second notice must also describe the benefits required under WHCRA, but it must be provided to participants upon enrollment in the plan. The third notice is required to be furnished annually to participants under the plan. But if a plan or health insurance issuer provides appropriate enrollment notice to a participant upon enrollment in the plan, then the plan or issuer does not have to provide that participant with an annual notice for the plan year during which that participant enrolled.

The plan or health insurance issuer must use measures reasonably calculated to ensure actual receipt of the annual notice by plan participants. The notice may be provided by first-class mail, via e-mail, or by any other means of delivery prescribed in the regulation. The annual notice may be sent separately or may be included in a summary plan description (SPD), a summary of material modifications (SMM), an employee newsletter, with open enrollment materials, or with any other written communication by the plan.

FIGURE 19.1 Women's Health and Cancer Rights Act of 1998—model annual notice.

Did you know that your plan, as required by the Women's Health and Cancer Rights Act of 1998, provides benefits for mastectomy-related services including reconstruction and surgery to achieve symmetry between the breasts, prostheses, and complications resulting from a mastectomy (including lymph edema)? Call your Plan Administrator [insert phone number] for more information.

FIGURE 19.2 FMLA Eligibility.

To be eligible for FMLA benefits, an employee must meet the following conditions:
- Work for a covered employer
- Have worked for the employer for at least a total of 12 months
- Have worked at least 1,250 hours during the past 12 months
- Work at a location where the employer within a 75-mile radius employs at least 50 employees.

Note: An employee also is eligible if he or she has worked at least 12 months for a covered employer that has failed to keep records regarding service time.

A covered employer must grant an eligible employee as many as 12 work weeks of unpaid leave during any 12-month period for one or more of the following reasons:
- Birth of a child or placement of a child for adoption or foster care
- To care for an immediate family member (spouse, child or parent) with a "serious health condition"
- To take medical leave when the employee is unable to work because of a "serious health condition."

The benefits required by WHCRA and covered under the group health plan, and its insurance companies or HMO, must be in the enrollment notice. The notice also must indicate that, in the case of a participant or beneficiary who is receiving benefits in connection with a mastectomy, coverage will be provided in a manner determined in consultation with the attending physician and the patient, for the following: (1) all stages of reconstruction of the breast on which the mastectomy was performed; (2) surgery and reconstruction of the other breast to produce a symmetrical appearance; and (3) prostheses and treatment of physical complications of the mastectomy, including lymph edema. The enrollment notice also must describe any deductibles and co-insurance limitations applicable to such coverage. Coverage of breast reconstruction benefits may be subject only to deductibles and co-insurance limitations consistent with those established for other benefits under the plan or coverage. A model notice prescribed by the U.S. Department of Labor is set out in Figure 19.1.

FAMILY AND MEDICAL LEAVE ACT OF 1993 (FMLA)

FMLA entitles employees to take as many as 12 weeks of unpaid, job-protected leave each year for specified family and medical reasons. FMLA is intended to allow employees to balance their work and family lives by taking reasonable unpaid leave under limited circumstances.

Employer Coverage, Employee Eligibility, and Leave Entitlement

FMLA applies to public agencies, including state, local, and federal employers and local education agencies (schools), and it applies to private sector employers with at

FIGURE 19.3 Serious health condition.

"Serious health condition" means an illness, injury, impairment, or physical or mental condition that involves one of the following:

- Inpatient care (i.e., overnight stay) in a hospital, hospice, or residential medical care facility, including any period of incapacity (i.e., inability to work, attend school, or perform other regular daily activities due to the serious health condition, treatment therefore or recovery therefrom), or any subsequent treatment concerning such inpatient care.
- Continuing treatment by a health care provider. A serious health condition involving continuing treatment by a health care provider includes any one or more of the following:
  - A period of incapacity of more than three consecutive calendar days and any subsequent treatment or period of incapacity relating to the same condition, which also involves:
- Treatment two or more times by a health care provider, by a nurse or physician's assistant under direct supervision of a health care provider, or by a provider of health care services (e.g., physical therapist) under orders or on referral by a health care provider
- Treatment by a health care provider on at least one occasion that results in a regimen of continuing treatment under the supervision of the health care provider.
  - Pregnancy or prenatal care. A visit to the health care provider is not necessary for each absence.
  - A chronic serious health condition that continues over an extended period, requires periodic visits to a health care provider, and may involve occasional episodes of incapacity (e.g., asthma, diabetes). A visit to a health care provider is not necessary for each absence.
  - A permanent or long-term condition for which treatment may not be effective (e.g., Alzheimer's, a severe stroke, terminal cancer). Only supervision by a health care provider is required rather than active treatment.
  - Any absences to receive multiple treatments for restorative surgery or for a condition that would likely result in a period of incapacity of more than three days if not treated (e.g., chemotherapy or radiation treatments for cancer).

Note: According to the law, an employee is unable to perform the functions of the position if the health care provider finds that the employee is unable to work at all or is unable to perform any essential function of the employee's position within the meaning of ADA.

least 50 employees. Figure 19.2 shows conditions an employee must meet to be eligible for FMLA benefits and the reasons he or she must use for taking FMLA leave.

Spouses employed by the same employer are jointly entitled to a combined total of 12 work weeks of family leave for the birth of a child or for placement of a child for adoption or foster care, and to care for a parent (but not a parent "in-law") who has a serious health condition. Leave for birth or adoption (including foster care placement) must conclude within 12 months of the birth or placement.

Intermittent Leave

Under certain circumstances, employees may take FMLA leave intermittently. This means that an employee may take leave in blocks of time or by reducing his or her normal weekly or daily work schedule.

If FMLA leave is to care for a child following the birth of the child or the placement of a child with the employee for adoption or foster care, use of intermittent leave is subject to the employer's approval.

FMLA leave may be taken intermittently when medically necessary for planned and/or unanticipated medical treatment or a related serious health condition by or under the supervision of a health care provider or for recovery from treatment or recovery from a serious health condition. It also may be taken to provide care or psychological comfort to an immediate family member with a serious health condition. Figure 19.3 shows the conditions that must be met to qualify as a "serious health condition."

Substitution of Paid Leave

In most cases, FMLA leave is unpaid. However, under certain circumstances, FMLA permits an eligible employee to choose to substitute paid leave for FMLA leave. If an employee does not choose to substitute accrued paid leave, the employer may require the employee to substitute accrued paid leave for FMLA leave. If an employee has earned or accrued paid vacation or personal or family leave, that paid leave may be substituted for all or part of any unpaid FMLA leave.

However, an employer may not override an employee's initial election to substitute paid leave for FMLA leave, nor place limitations on its use. Therefore, an employer may not require that an employee take a minimum period of leave time, such as one full day, for the time to qualify as FMLA leave.

An employee who is injured on the job must elect either workers' compensation insurance benefits or paid leave. As such, if an employee is receiving workers' compensation benefits, the employer cannot require substitution of vacation or other leave. However, the workers' compensation absence can count against the employee's FMLA entitlement if the employer properly designates the leave as FMLA leave. Subject to certain conditions, employees or employers may choose to use or require the use of accrued paid leave (such as sick or vacation leave) to cover some or all of the otherwise unpaid FMLA leave.

Once the employer has learned that the leave is being taken for an FMLA-required reason, the employer must notify the employee within two business days that the paid leave is designated and will be counted as FMLA leave.

Did You Know?

The employer is responsible for designating if paid leave used by an employee counts as FMLA leave, based on information provided by the employee. In no case can an employee's paid leave be credited as FMLA leave after the leave has been completed.

Health Care Providers

Health care providers that qualify under the regulations to provide certification of a serious health condition for an employee or an immediate family member include the following:

- Doctors of medicine or osteopathy authorized to practice medicine or surgery (as appropriate) by the state in which the doctor practices.
- Podiatrists, dentists, clinical psychologists, optometrists, and chiropractors (limited to treatment consisting of manual manipulation of the spine to correct a subluxation as proved by x-ray to exist) authorized to practice in the state and performing within the scope of their practice under state law.
- Nurse practitioners and nurse-midwives authorized to practice under state law and performing within the scope of their practice as defined under state law.
- Christian Science practitioners listed with the First Church of Christ in Boston.
- Any health care provider recognized by the employer or the employer's group health plan benefits manager.

Maintenance of Health Benefits

A covered employer is required to maintain group health insurance coverage for an employee on FMLA leave whenever such insurance was provided before the leave was taken and on the same terms as if the employee had continued to work.

Where appropriate, arrangements will need to be made for employees taking unpaid FMLA leave to pay their share of health insurance premiums while on leave. For example, if the group health plan involves deductions by the employer and the employee, an employee on FMLA leave must continue making his or her portion of the insurance premium payments to maintain insurance coverage, as must the employer. The employee and employer need to devise a method for the employee to pay his or her share of health insurance premiums while on unpaid FMLA leave.

Continued health insurance coverage during FMLA leave must be at the same deduction rates as for active employees. Higher COBRA premiums may be required only after FMLA leave ends.

An employer's obligation to maintain health benefits under FMLA ends if an employee informs the employer that he or she does not intend to return to work at the end of the leave period, or if the employee fails to return to work when the FMLA entitlement is completed. In certain instances, the employer may recover premiums it paid to maintain health insurance coverage for an employee who fails to return to work from FMLA leave. However, an employer cannot recover premiums paid to maintain group health coverage if the employee does not return to work for reasons "beyond the employee's control."

In addition, an employer's obligation to maintain health insurance coverage generally ceases under FMLA if an employee's premium payment is more than 30 days late. To stop coverage for an employee whose premium payment is late, the employer must provide written notice to the employee that payment has not been received. Such notice must be mailed to the employee at least 15 days before coverage is to cease, advising that coverage will stop on a specified date unless payment has been received by that date.

Did You Know?

Certain types of earned benefits, such as seniority, need not continue to accrue during periods of unpaid FMLA leave. For other benefits, such as elected life insurance coverage, the employer and the employee need to make arrangements so that the benefits may be maintained during periods of unpaid FMLA leave. Except for accrued or earned benefits, the employee must be restored to the same benefits upon return from FMLA leave as if the employee had continued to work the entire FMLA leave period. Use of FMLA leave cannot result in the loss of any benefits that accrued before the employee's leave began. Accordingly, an FMLA leave period cannot be counted as a break in service for purposes of vesting or eligibility to participate in benefits programs.

Job Restoration

Upon return from FMLA leave, an employee must be restored to his or her original job, or to an equivalent job with equivalent pay, benefits, and other employment terms and conditions.

Employee Notice and Certification

An employee seeking to use FMLA leave may be required to provide several notices, documents, and reports. Figure 19.4 shows what an employer may require of an employee.

When leave is needed to care for an immediate family member or for the employee's own illness and is taken for planned medical treatment, the employee must attempt to schedule treatment so that it will not unduly disrupt the employer's operation.

FIGURE 19.4 Items an employee may be required to produce.

An employee seeking to use FMLA leave may be required to provide the following notices, documents, and reports.

- Thirty-day notice of the need to take FMLA leave when the need is foreseeable—if it is not foreseeable, then as soon as practical, typically no more than one or two days after the employee learned of his or her need for leave.
- Medical certifications supporting the need for leave due to a serious health condition affecting the employee or an immediate family member.
- Second or third medical opinions and periodic recertification, at the employer's expense.
- Periodic reports during FMLA leave on the employee's status and intent to return to work.
- A "fitness-for-duty" certification to return to work.
- A schedule of any planned medical treatment generally before scheduling such treatment so as to not disrupt the employer's operations.

An employee is required to advise the employer if FMLA leave needs to be extended. If an employer requires an employee to provide written notice of leave, and the employee fails to do so, the employer may not delay or deny FMLA leave, but may take appropriate disciplinary action. At least verbal notice by an employee is required. However, it is not necessary that the employee state that he or she is asserting any rights under FMLA.

Employer Notice and Certification

Covered employers must post a notice approved by the secretary of labor explaining rights and responsibilities under FMLA. In addition, covered employers are obligated to provide written notice to their employees about their rights and responsibilities under FMLA, what will be required of the employee, and what might happen in certain circumstances, such as if the employee fails to return to work from FMLA leave. Figure 19.5 illustrates what items such notices must include.

The notice must be given to the employee within a reasonable time (preferably in one or two business days) after the employee has given notice to the employer of the employee's intention to take an FMLA leave. If leave already has commenced, the employer should mail the notification to the employee's address of record.

If an employer has any written guidance to employees concerning employee benefits or leave rights, such as an employee handbook, information concerning FMLA entitlements and employee obligations must be included in the handbook.

If an employer does not have any written policies, the employer must provide written guidance to an employee concerning all of the employee's rights and obligations under FMLA. This notice must be given each time the employee requests leave under FMLA.

Employers also are expected to answer questions from employees concerning their rights and responsibilities under federal and state law. If an employer does not comply with the notification requirements, the employer cannot take action against an employee who also fails to comply.

FIGURE 19.5 Legal notification of FMLA.

The law requires covered employers to post a notice explaining FMLA. The notice must include the following:
- That the leave will be counted against the employee's annual FMLA leave entitlement.
- Any requirements for the employee to furnish medical certifications and the consequences for failure to do so.
- The employee's rights concerning substitution of paid leave.
- Requirements of premium payments.
- Requirements relating to fitness for duty certifications.
- The employee's right to return to the same or similar job.
- The employer's right to be refunded for any premium payments if the employee fails to return to work after taking FMLA leave.

NONDISCRIMINATION LAWS

The four most significant pieces of legislation concerning employee discrimination include Title VII of the Civil Rights Act of 1964, the Age Discrimination in Employment Act of 1967 (ADEA), Title I of the Americans with Disabilities Act of 1990 (ADA), and the Equal Pay Act of 1963 (EPA).

Title VII of the Civil Rights Act of 1964

Title VII prohibits discrimination in terms and conditions of employment (including fringe benefits) based upon a person's race, color, religion, sex (including pregnancy), or national origin. In the context of employee benefits, Title VII has been invoked largely to challenge distinctions in employee benefits plans as unlawful "sex" discrimination.

The Equal Employment Opportunity Commission (EEOC) has issued guidelines broadly defining "fringe benefits" as including medical, hospital, accident and life insurance, profit sharing, bonuses, leave policies, and retirement benefits. The EEOC further holds that the cost of such benefits for members of one sex shall not be a defense to an employer who fails to provide benefits equally to members of both sexes.

Retirement Plans: Contributions and Benefits

The law in the area of sex-based distinctions in pension plans is relatively settled. Historically, insurance companies have maintained separate statistics on males and females, because they presumed women out-lived men. As a result, women covered by hybrid pension plans often were required to contribute greater premiums than men for the same benefits or they received lesser benefits than men although they paid the same premiums as men.

However, in 1978 the Supreme Court held that an employer violated Title VII's proscription against sex discrimination by requiring females to make larger contributions to a hybrid pension plan than required of males. And in 1983, the Supreme Court held that Title VII also is violated when an employer provides lower retirement benefits to females than to males, when both males and females have made equal contributions to a pension plan.

Retirement Plans: Eligibility

It used to be common for pension plans to permit women to retire with full pensions at an earlier age than men or to have sex-based differences in compulsory or voluntary retirement ages. Similarly, it was not uncommon for profit-sharing plans to allow the interest of one sex to vest after fewer years of service than were required of the opposite sex. It is now clear that such sex-based distinctions in retirement or other compensation plans violate Title VII as unlawful sex discrimination in terms and conditions of employment.

Death Benefits

To avoid transgressing Title VII's bar against sex discrimination, the surviving spouse of an employee of one sex must have the same rights under a death benefit plan as the surviving spouse of an employee of the opposite sex.

Health and Disability Insurance

Title VII requires that health insurance and disability insurance be provided without sex-based distinctions. Thus, plans that exclude the dependents and/or spouse of female employees while covering those of male employees are unlawful.

The "head of household" eligibility requirements (i.e., an employee is eligible for benefits only if he or she first establishes that he or she is the "head of the household") have been challenged as impacting women disparately. The argument is that, statistically, fewer women are primary household breadwinners, and the ostensibly neutral rule has the effect of disproportionately denying benefits to women. At this writing, the courts have not adopted a uniform approach to this question, and the "head of household" eligibility criterion remains an open issue.

Age Discrimination in Employment Act of 1967 (ADEA)

The ADEA generally prohibits discrimination in employment against individuals who are age 40 or older. Among other things, the ADEA generally prohibits mandatory retirements. However, the ADEA contains some qualifications and exceptions to its general bar against age discrimination.

Section 4(f)(2)(B)

Section 4(f)(2)(B) of the ADEA permits employers to observe the terms of a bona fide employee benefits plan, even if the plan contains age-based distinctions. To qualify as a bona fide plan, the plan must provide that, for each benefit or benefits package, the actual amount of payment made or cost incurred on behalf of an older worker is no less than that made or incurred on behalf of a younger worker. In addition, Sec. 4(f)(2)(B) permits voluntary early retirement incentive plans that are not a subterfuge for age discrimination.

Section 4(i)

Section 4(i)(1) of the ADEA generally prohibits an employer from establishing or maintaining an employee pension plan that requires or permits either of the following:

- In the case of a defined benefit plan, the cessation of an employee's benefits accrual or the reduction of the rate of an employee's benefits accrual, because of age.
- In the case of a defined contribution plan, the cessation of allocations to an employee's account or the reduction of the rate at which amounts are allocated to an employee's account, because of age.

However, Sec. 4(i)(2) makes it clear that an employee pension plan may impose (without regard to age) a limitation on the amount of benefits that the plan provides or a limitation on the number of years of service or years of participation, which are considered for the purpose of determining benefits accrual under the plan.

Section 4(l)

Section 4(l) of the ADEA addresses certain minimum age requirements, early retirement benefits, and waivers of rights. Generally, it is permissible under the ADEA to require that an employee attain a minimum age as a condition of eligibility for normal or early retirement benefits under an ERISA plan.

This section also sets forth the circumstances under which an individual's right to Social Security or disability payments may be considered to determine benefits under an employee benefits plan. In addition, this section addresses the use of age as a component in establishing and maintaining a retiree health benefits plan.

Of growing importance are the provisions of the section that deal with securing waivers of rights. The Older Workers Benefit Protection Act of 1990 (OWBPA) amended this section by adding explicit requirements governing the validity of waivers under the ADEA. To make effective a valid waiver of an individual's rights with respect to his or her termination that is unrelated to any reduction in force, an employer must provide the individual with at least 21 days to consider the agreement that contains the waiver and, after the individual executes the agreement, the employer must provide the individual with an additional seven days within which the individual may revoke the waiver unilaterally.

In cases involving an exit incentive or other employment termination program that is offered to a group or class of employees, the employer similarly must provide the individual(s) affected with at least 45 days to consider the agreement that contains the waiver and, after execution of the agreement, an additional seven days within which the individual may revoke the waiver unilaterally. Further, the employer must make available to all such individuals information regarding the class, unit, or group of individuals eligible for the program; the program's eligibility criteria and any applicable time limits; and the job titles and ages of all individuals eligible or selected for the program, as well as the ages of all individuals in the same job classification or organizational unit who are not eligible or selected for the program. In all cases (individual and group), the employer must advise the employees in writing to consult with legal counsel regarding the terms of the waiver, and the waiver itself must refer expressly to the ADEA.

Americans with Disabilities Act of 1990 (ADA)

Title I of the ADA prohibits discrimination in employment because of an individual's disability, if the individual is qualified for the job in question or, with a reasonable accommodation, would be qualified. The ADA likewise prohibits disability-based discrimination in the terms and conditions of employment, including the provisions and administration of employee benefits plans.

Thus, if an employer provides insurance or other benefits plans to its employees, it must provide the same coverage to its employees with disabilities.

An employer cannot deny insurance to an individual with a disability or subject an individual with a disability to different terms or conditions of insurance, based upon disability alone, if the disability does not pose increased insurance risks. Similarly, an employer may not enter into a contract or agreement with an insurance carrier or other entity that has such an effect.

Did You Know?

Self-insured plans that are not subject to state insurance laws may provide coverage that is consistent with basic accepted principles of insurance risk classification, even if this results in limitations in coverage for individuals with disabilities.

Health Insurance

The ADA most dramatically impacts employer-provided health insurance. The ADA and its implementing regulations do not fully resolve the host of questions raised by the ADA's application to health insurance plans, but some parameters are clear.

An employer may not fire or refuse to hire an individual with a disability because the employer's current health insurance plan does not cover the individual's disability or because the individual may increase the employer's future health care costs. Nor can an employer fire or refuse to hire an individual (regardless of whether that individual has a disability) because the individual has a family member or dependent with a disability that is not covered by the employer's current health insurance plan or that may increase the employer's future health care costs.

On the other hand, the ADA permits employers to provide insurance plans that comply with existing federal and state insurance requirements, even if provisions of these plans have an adverse impact on people with disabilities, if the provisions are not used as a subterfuge to evade the ADA's purpose. For example, if an employer provides health insurance through an insurance carrier that is regulated by state insurance laws, it may provide coverage following accepted principles of risk assessment and/or risk classification, as required or permitted by such law, even if this causes limitations in coverage for individuals with disabilities.

Thus, an employer may continue to offer health plans that contain pre-existing condition exclusions, even if this adversely affects individuals with disabilities. Further, an employer also may continue to offer health plans that limit coverage for certain procedures and/or limit particular treatments to a specified number per year, even if these restrictions adversely affect individuals with disabilities, as long as the restrictions are uniformly applied to all covered individuals, regardless of disability. In each case, such conditions and restrictions are permitted only if they are not being used as a subterfuge to discriminate against individuals with disabilities.

At this writing, the EEOC has announced its intention to issue guidelines on the ADA's application to employer-provided health plans. These guidelines are expected to address in greater detail the issues arising over the interplay between the ADA and employer-provided health plans, including the ADA's application to corporate "wellness" programs and to disability-based distinctions in employer-provided health insurance plans.

Disability Retirement Plans and Service Retirement Plans

Following passage of the ADA, many employers sought clarification from the EEOC over the ADA's application to disability retirement plans and to service retirement plans. In general terms, a disability retirement plan provides a lifetime income for an employee who becomes unable to work because of illness or injury, without regard to the employee's age. A service retirement plan provides a lifetime income to employees who have reached a minimum age stated in the plan and/or who have completed a specified number of years of service with the employer. On May 11, 1995, the EEOC issued guidance on the ADA's application to these types of employee benefits plans.

The EEOC acknowledged that nothing in the ADA requires an employer to provide a disability retirement plan if an employer offers a service retirement plan. Further, if an employer offers only a service retirement plan, there is no ADA violation, provided the service retirement plan treats employees with disabilities the same as other employees.

In its guidance, the EEOC listed the following examples where disability retirement benefits or service retirement benefits would be considered an ADA violation, because qualified individuals with disabilities were treated less favorably under, or denied access to, a plan:

- An employer excludes from participation in a disability retirement plan an employee who has a particular disability but otherwise meets the plan's criteria.
- ADA-covered individuals are qualified for both service and disability retirement plans, but are required to take less-advantageous disability benefits.
- ADA-covered employees are required to serve a longer period of employment as compared to other employees before obtaining service retirement benefits or are given a longer eligibility requirement before being covered for disability retirement protection.

In these situations, the EEOC assumes that the employer has violated the ADA unless the employer demonstrates that it did not act on the basis of disability or proves that the plan is otherwise exempt from the ADA's prohibition against disability-based discrimination.

UNIFORMED SERVICES EMPLOYMENT AND RE-EMPLOYMENT RIGHTS ACT OF 1994 (USERRA)

The most significant law concerning the employment rights of military veterans is the Uniformed Services Employment and Re-employment Rights Act of 1994 (USERRA).

USERRA expands job protections for veterans returning to civilian employment and the obligations of employers both during and after the veterans' military

FIGURE 19.6 Goals of USERRA.

USERRA has three primary goals:
- Encourage noncareer service in the armed forces by eliminating or reducing the disadvantages to the civilian careers of veterans that can result from their military service.
- Reduce the disruption to the lives of veterans by providing for their prompt re-employment upon completion of military service.
- Prohibit discrimination against veterans because of their service in the armed forces.

service. USERRA covers veterans who are re-employed on or after December 12, 1994, (60 days after the date of enactment) and employees who leave employment to serve in the armed forces on or after the same date. However, an individual who separates from the armed forces because of a dishonorable discharge will not be protected or entitled to any rights under the act. Figure 19.6 details the primary goals of USERRA.

Both voluntary and involuntary service in the armed forces qualify a veteran for the protections afforded by USERRA, including active duty, active or inactive duty for training, full-time National Guard duty, and any absence from employment because of an examination to determine the fitness of the person to perform military duty.

Profit-Sharing Contributions Required

USERRA supersedes the Veterans' Re-employment Rights law that was enacted in 1940 and was loaded with loopholes and unclear employer obligations. The most contentious of these ambiguities was whether employers were required to make up contributions to a profit-sharing plan in the same manner that they are required to make up lost benefits under a defined benefit plan for the time during which an employee was on military leave.

Congress has made it clear in USERRA that employers must make returning veterans whole under both pension and profit-sharing plans for periods of military leave. Veterans are to be treated as if they did not incur a break in service for purposes of vesting and accrual of benefits. Employers must make up missing contributions to profit-sharing plans in the same manner and to the same extent as contributions were made on behalf of continuing employees. No contribution is required, however, to make up for lost investment income or allocations of for feitures.

401(k) Contributions

Upon their return from military service, veterans must be permitted to make up elective contributions (whether before-tax or after-tax) to 401(k) plans within a period that is three times the duration of their military leave, not to exceed five years. Veterans who make up such elective contributions must receive allocations of any employer-matching contributions that would have been contributed with respect to such elective contributions. Under the prior law, employers were not required to permit veterans to make up elective contributions.

Re-employment Rights

Employers are prohibited from denying employment, re-employment, promotions, and benefits to veterans who are absent from work due to military service as long as the veteran's lifetime military service does not cumulatively exceed five years. Before active military duty, an individual must provide his or her employer with advance written or verbal notice of military duty, unless advance notice is impossible or unreasonable. Upon discharge from military duty, the veteran must submit an application for re-employment to the employer. USERRA contains various time limits on the filing of the re-employment application. The limits are determined by the duration of the military duty.

The re-employment rights of veterans may be extinguished under certain circumstances. This may happen when employment conditions change or when the employer would suffer undue hardship from reinstating the returning veteran. The re-employment rights under the act are the same as those found under the prior law.

Benefits Entitlement

Veterans are entitled to reinstatement of seniority, and other rights and benefits that are determined by seniority, as if their service with the employer had not been interrupted. Veterans are entitled to those rights and benefits that are not based on seniority as if they were on a leave of absence for any other reason. USERRA's benefits entitlement provisions are the same as those under the prior law. Health benefits and pension plans are protected by USERRA for 24 months.

Military COBRA Rights Required

Unlike the prior law, USERRA contains special health care continuation provisions for veterans and their families that are similar to the COBRA provisions in ERISA and the Internal Revenue Code for terminated employees. As under COBRA, veterans may be required to pay a premium of as much as 102 percent of the cost of coverage. In some cases, USERRA's requirements overlap COBRA, but the act is more extensive in some respects (e.g., it applies to employers with fewer than 20 employees).

If a veteran's medical coverage terminates for any reason while on military duty, USERRA prohibits the plan from imposing a waiting period on pre-existing conditions upon his or her return to employment if the plan would not have imposed the same waiting period for a newly hired employee.

WORKER ADJUSTMENT AND RETRAINING NOTIFICATION ACT OF 1988 (WARNA)

WARNA generally requires that employers of 100 or more employees give at least 60-day advance notice of a plant closing or mass layoff to affected employees or their representatives, the chief elected official of the appropriate local government, and the state dislocated worker unit.

Plant Closing

Plant closing is defined as the permanent or temporary shutdown of a single site of employment or one or more facilities or operating units within a single site of employment, if the shutdown results in an "employment loss" at the single site during any 30-day period for at least 50 full-time employees. A shutdown includes any employment action that results in the effective cessation of production or work performed by a unit, even if a few employees remain. A temporary shutdown is deemed to be a plant closing only if there are a sufficient number of terminations, layoffs in excess of six months, or a 50-percent reduction in hours of work of individual employees during each month of any six-month period.

Mass Layoff

Mass layoff is defined as a reduction in force that is not the result of a plant closing and results in an "employment loss" at a single site of employment during any 30-day period for either at least 33 percent of the full-time employees and at least 50 full-time employees or 500 part-time employees.

Impact on Employee Benefits

Practically speaking, WARNA has no impact on employee benefits unless the requisite 60-day notice is not given. In such a case, the affected employees may recover the compensation they would have earned had they received the full 60 days notice. This compensation includes any payment they would have received and any other rights that would have accrued under the benefits plans, had they been employed during the 60-day notice period.

IN CLOSING

From time to time, our elected representatives complain publicly about the complexity of our employee benefits laws, and they announce, usually with some fanfare, their proposals for simplification. But the promise of simplification never seems to materialize. Sponsors of employee benefit plans and their advisors instead face an increasingly high compliance bar. This phenomenon can be attributed at least in part to the existence of a permanent lobbying infrastructure that exerts a profound influence on the legislative and regulatory process. Which proposals make it into a benefits reform bill—and which do not—are hotly contested long before they surface in a congressional committee. Phalanxes of lobbyists, trade association staff members, and interest groups representatives clash over items ranging from the fundamental contours of benefits regulation to the wording of a final agency rule on the most esoteric of subjects. This environment fosters incremental complexity and smothers simplification.

While simplification may not be in the cards, wholesale change may be. Two nascent trends—one relating to welfare plans and the other to pension plans—could markedly affect the benefits landscape sooner rather than later:

1. Rapidly increasing health care costs are straining employers' ability to conduct business as usual where medical plans are concerned. A decade ago, a legislative proposal to establish regional medical buying associations was soundly defeated, and the idea of a "single-payer" system was for the most part ridiculed. These concepts have reemerged, and they are being given serious consideration. Whatever the outcome, this is an issue that will not go away. Health reimbursement arrangements are only the opening salvo. No one should be surprised if Congress adopts major structural changes regarding group medical benefits in particular.
2. The traditional defined benefit plan has been largely replaced by the 401(k) plan, principally if not exclusively because of cost. But recent market down-

turns coupled with concerns over corporate governance have exposed some basic fault lines in the 401(k) model, which transfers both investment risk and investment selection to the participant. It is beginning to dawn on baby boomers in particular that their 401(k) plans might not provide them with the retirement income that they had hoped. Absent a significant expansion of private nonemployer-based retirement arrangements or a radical overhaul of our public retirement system, cash-balance plans could perhaps fill the void, but these plans are under withering assault from detractors who claim that they shortchange older workers. It's safe to say that we have not heard the last of this issue.

It is a daunting challenge for plan sponsors and their advisors to keep pace with the laws that regulate employee benefit plans. This book provides an overview of the major highlights, but it does not and cannot in the space available provide an understanding of the practical nuances of these laws or the many and varied ways that they apply in the workplace. Such an understanding can occur only with a long-term commitment to study and experience.

20 Planning Benefits Strategically

While many people are familiar with the concept of "strategy," fewer might associate this concept with human resources. *Webster's Dictionary* provides a first definition of strategy as "the science of planning and directing large-scale military operations, specifically (as distinguished from tactics) of maneuvering forces into the most advantageous position prior to actual engagement with the enemy." If strategy is crucial to warfare, it is also crucial to business.

Numerous internal and external forces are having an impact on today's organizations, and these forces demand corporate strategies that help organize, plan, and direct the organization's efforts to:

- Produce high-quality products and services.
- Position itself favorably with competitive prices and sensible costs, including human resources programs that provide a good return on investment.
- Engage domestic and global competitors successfully.

Benefits strategy is the one definable link in a strategic chain that starts with an organization's overall business objectives. Once the overriding business objectives are set by senior management, they cascade down throughout the organization, supported by strategic plans at the division, business unit, department, work group, team, and, possibly, even the individual level. The human resources function is not exempt from this process; in fact, HR strategies in general and benefits strategies in particular must support overall business objectives. This chapter reviews how the benefits strategy planning process can provide an organization with maximum competitive advantage and which steps can lead to successful strategy formulation.

INTERNAL AND EXTERNAL INFLUENCES ON STRATEGY

During the past three decades, many influences have significantly changed the design, administration, and perceived importance of employee benefits programs.

Today, employee benefits programs are highly visible to both employees and management. Benefits executives are frequently described as "corporate firefighters." Their successes and failures directly affect corporate profitability.

Internal and external forces to the organization influence the bottom-line impact of employee benefits. (See Figure 20.1.) Internal forces originate from changes in business practices and the human resources function that define attraction, motivation, retention, and engagement strategies. These forces include the following:

- *Corporate restructuring.* Mergers, acquisitions, divestitures, and corporate restructuring efforts can lead to profit centers that are more centralized or more decentralized. Under these circumstances, a successful benefits package must adapt constantly to evolving corporate configurations.
- *Business reengineering and the quality movement.* Process improvement initiatives such as reengineering and total quality are increasingly being applied to the HR function. As a result, benefits departments need to:
  - Provide service to various customer groups and constituencies.
  - Streamline work processes.
  - Provide improved, cost-effective services to their customers.

These objectives need to be accomplished even as benefits staff sizes are frozen or reduced.

- *New corporate cultures.* In the "good old days," the corporation functioned largely as a parent. Employees felt a sense of entitlement because their career and benefits were perceived as the responsibility and domain of management. Today, organizations are replacing the traditional parental employer-employee relationships with partnerships. Career employment, where employees work 20–25 years with the same organization, is no longer the norm. In this new culture, employees assume greater personal responsibility for their benefits. They are, for example, paying a greater percentage of benefits costs (e.g., copayments and higher deductibles under health care plans). Additionally, employees increasingly are planning for their retirement and long-term financial security through personal savings and defined contribution plans. Today's partnership requires employees to use

FIGURE 20.1 Forces that influence benefits strategy.

Internal
- Corporate restructuring
- Business reengineering and the quality movement
- New corporate cultures
- Unions
- Cost management
- Total rewards philosophy

External
- Global economy and labor market
- U.S. political and legal environment
- The Information Revolution

employer-sponsored benefits programs effectively and to assume responsibility for the implications of their choices.

- *Unions.* Depending on industry and geographic region, the development, design, and redesign of benefits programs is influenced heavily by organized labor, which helps shape employee expectations. The most visible arena has been in "smokestack" industries, where active employee and retiree medical benefits have been the focal point of labor negotiations.

- *Cost management.* Despite an apparent stabilization of benefits costs, corporate executives remember the past decade of rapidly escalating and seemingly uncontrollable health benefits costs that prompted intense interest and scrutiny from corporate boardrooms, the media, and the federal and state governments. A well-planned strategy can improve overall benefits cost management as well as cost management on a per-plan basis.

- *Total rewards philosophy.* Total rewards can be defined as "all of the tools available to the employer that may be used to attract, motivate, and retain employees." The concept of total rewards is an effective way to illustrate an organization's total investment in human capital and to demonstrate the significant investment that organizations make in employee benefits plans. Employees might not always appreciate the costs involved in benefits, but organizations have no choice but to recognize what they are spending and to evaluate whether the investment is worthwhile.

In general terms, external forces—domestic and global—demand that corporations develop coherent strategies to ensure their competitiveness and profitability. While many external forces can be anticipated, their specific impact is not easily predicted. External forces include the following:

- *Global economy and labor market.* Country-specific government mandates and regional precedents or cultural norms can define benefits expectations. It is an ongoing challenge in today's global environment, where new markets are constantly being created, to design and manage a benefits package that balances corporate business objectives with each country's particular regulations and customs.

- *U.S. political and legal environment.* Government rules, regulations, and court decisions add complexity to the benefits environment. The constraints placed upon organizations by government can increase the difficulty of day-to-day benefits administration, and it complicates corporate policymaking and program design. For example, the U.S. federal government might decide to reduce its deficit by taxing benefits—a move that would have profound implications for employee benefits plans. Or state-specific legislation might promote health care reform in scattered regions throughout the country, creating difficulties for employers with operations that cross state boundaries. Unclear court decisions can promote legal challenges to longstanding corporate policies. When legal decisions and/or regulations contradict, complexity evolves quickly into confusion.

- *The Information Revolution.* The so-called Information Revolution is continually redefining business operations, success, and productivity. Sales in new micromarkets, customer satisfaction, and reduced cycle times are among the new performance measures being developed and refined. The Information Revolution is redefining corporate culture and employee expectations. Employees expect newer, better, and faster services, products, and information from the human resources function.

THE STRATEGIC PLANNING PROCESS

From a strategic standpoint, benefits should not be viewed as individual plans or programs but instead as integrated sets of plans to be managed as any other business function. They should be viewed as an integral component of a total rewards package and as part of an investment in human capital. In addition, benefits should be viewed not as a "fringe" cost but instead as a business tool to reinforce and support an organization's goals.

In this context, benefits programs cannot be defined in terms of narrowly defined, program-specific goals. Each benefits program—health, welfare, retirement, or work-life—should be evaluated in relation to other benefits programs as well as in relation to all other compensation and human resources initiatives. Strategic benefits planning is a process that facilitates those efforts.

Strategic benefits planning combines a way of thinking that is specific to each organization with an ongoing process. Because of this, there needs to be an ongoing process of realignment between organization-sponsored benefits programs and the strategic business direction.

Strategic benefits planning is not a one-time event but a continuous effort to provide corporations with a return on their investment in employees. The process includes an evaluation of existing benefits programs and concludes with a definition of the direction for future employer-sponsored programs and policies. In essence, strategic benefits planning addresses the following question: How can the organization's benefits plans better support the business direction?

Strategic benefits plans are not static documents developed in a vacuum. Instead, they are dynamic blueprints that reflect and balance an organization's business mission and strategic business direction with the human resources mission. Successful strategic planning efforts consist of several defined characteristics. The following elements characterize organizations that are engaged in strategic benefits planning:

- *Long-term perspective.* While most strategic benefits planning is seen as an ongoing process tied to an overriding business strategic plan and culture, many organizations adopt concrete time frames (e.g., three to five years) within which an organization can identify, achieve, and sometimes evaluate clearly defined and measurable goals. Strategic benefits plans should not generate knee-jerk reactions.
- *Consideration of scenarios that might reasonably affect the organization.* Strategic plans should relate benefits to the business function(s). Because strategic benefits planning generally is not intended to be an academic exercise, the process should reflect the current business realities as well as situations that may affect the organization in an identified time frame. Specifically, the strategic planning process and plans need to reflect the corporate structure.

   For example, centralized and decentralized organizations likely will produce strategic plans that are significantly different. This is partially the result of different decision-making structures. For another example, organizations that expect a tremendous increase in domestic sales and domestic employees are likely to articulate a strategic benefits plan that is far different from the plan by an organization whose projected sales may be similar in volume but are the result of global expansion. Organizations in mature or declining industries, or organizations that expect to divest or close operations, likely will develop distinctly different plans from those in growth industries.

FIGURE 20.2 An expanded view of benefits.

Following are four key ways in which the definition of benefits and benefits management might be expanded during the strategic benefits planning process:
1. *By including benefits as an integral part of a total rewards package.* Whether or not benefits are communicated to employees as part of their total rewards, benefits, compensation, and other elements should be combined when identifying and managing employment costs and when assessing and communicating the return of these costs. A total rewards approach answers the universal employee question: What's in it for me?
2. *By redefining benefits to include new programs and initiatives.* Benefits may be defined to include initiatives not included among traditional health, welfare, and retirement programs. These other initiatives can include items such as personal financial planning or work-life programs.
3. *By evaluating benefits management, communication, and administration.* By assessing the corporation's culture, capabilities, and operations, the strategic benefits planning process can include a review of benefits administration and delivery systems. This review can provide insight into how to best deploy resources to administer benefits programs or into how to educate employees about benefits.
4. *By relating benefits to the broader corporate business philosophy/mission.* Benefits planning enables the benefits function at least to support the human resources function and, ideally, the overall business. Developing a strategic plan and articulating the linkage through a benefits philosophy are parts of the process.

- *Expansion of the traditional definition of benefits and benefits management.* In addition to looking at benefits and benefits design as an integrated whole, strategic benefits planning provides a broader definition of benefits and benefits management. This occurs in at least four ways. (See Figure 20.2.)

APPROACHES TO STRATEGIC BENEFITS PLANNING

A simple conceptual model can help managers understand the strategic benefits planning process. This model is predicated upon an organization's overarching human resources vision and philosophy that links benefits to business strategy.

For example, a hypothetical organization called Management Group might have as its mission to be a national outsource vendor that provides the highest-quality customer-driven and computer-based training/development and services. Management Group's human resources philosophy would include providing employees with the opportunity to earn a total rewards package that is in the top quartile.

Management Group's benefits philosophy would be to provide a competitive benefits package that is affordable to both the company and employees, and that contains innovative benefits.

Following are the key elements of the conceptual model for the strategic benefits planning process:

- A *philosophy* articulates what an organization believes in and what it values. It incorporates the organization's overall view and vision of how it must operate to achieve its business objectives.
- A *mission* answers three fundamental questions: who we are, why we are here, and what we are doing. A mission encompasses the goals of the overall benefits package and specific program benefits, and it provides insight into how benefits programs interrelate with each other and other human resources initiatives.
- *Strategies* are detailed statements that contain quantifiable objectives (e.g., time frames, financial goals, organizational intent). They provide a framework to align and/or refine benefits programs to support the organization's mission.
- *Tactics* are the detailed methods that will be used to achieve desired change or changes. Tactics might include steps to design new programs or to redesign existing programs.
- *Assessment* incorporates a review of how the planning process worked. It covers factors such as whether goals and objectives were met.

This simple model provides an overview of the strategic planning process. To implement the model, there are two possible approaches that represent two ends of a continuum: the "top-down" approach and the "backing-in" approach. Most organizations employ various aspects of the two approaches when organizing the benefits planning process and/or educating managers about the value of strategic benefits planning.

Top-Down Approach

The top-down approach to strategic benefits planning allows for a balancing of corporate business goals with organization-sponsored human resources and benefits programs. After longer-term, strategic goals are set for specific program groups (e.g., health, welfare, retirement) or administrative/management functions (e.g., outsourcing, financing), shorter-term, tactical objectives for specific plans are articulated. The approach is somewhat analogous to a plumbing system consisting of a series of valves that can be opened or closed while responding to changing business objectives.

For example, suppose that an organization with a top-down strategic benefits plan begins a three-year initiative. During the first year, it evaluates all health and welfare plans. During the second year, it completes a strategic analysis of its retirement programs. The third year results in a transition to a credit-based full flex plan that integrates the organization's compensation, benefits, and work-life elements into a total rewards package.

A top-down strategic benefits plan is contextual. It is driven purely by business needs, which are identified and communicated by senior management. The business mission and strategic plan from which benefits philosophies are derived provide a structure for developing the overall benefits package along with specific programs.

The top-down approach is especially useful when a full review of all programs is necessary. It forces a critical examination of the benefits package that is both programmatic and administrative. In other words, the top-down approach is especially useful when previously employed "quick fixes" prove to be too expensive or unwieldy to administer. The model also can be quite valuable in decentralized organizations where, at a minimum, it can facilitate benefits decisions that balance corporate requirements with the needs of diverse subsidiaries. In some environments, the model can force corporate leadership to make difficult or unpopular decisions.

Backing-in Approach

The backing-in approach is appropriate for organizations where the benefits package has recently evolved or where decision making is fractured, problem-based, or crisis-oriented. An event—such as a significant cost increase or the need to bring the organization into legal compliance—provides the opportunity to introduce or force a refocusing of benefits through the strategic planning process. Using the problem as a vehicle to create interest, the backing-in approach starts with the problem at a tactical level and ends with a broader framework of organizational strategy.

The backing-in approach can leverage an unanticipated situation into a successful outcome. A series of questions that reflect key issues can help address the problem. (See Figure 20.3.) While addressing these questions, senior management becomes educated about the broader benefits issues as well as the overall context in which they are raised. Through this process, previously applied benefits solutions that were not based on a specific strategy are likely to be recognized as ineffective and potentially more costly over the long term.

FIGURE 20.3 Questions to ask—from tactical to strategic.

From Tactical →

- How should our health plan be changed to control employer health care costs?
- Which health care costs are increasing most rapidly?
- What programs, such as EAPs, wellness, and communications, can be used to ensure cost-effective utilization?
- Which health care benefit designs, such as managed care, or management procedures, such as utilization review, will provide the greatest return on investment?
- How do workers' compensation and short- and long-term disability programs affect health benefit costs?

→ To Strategic

- What is our commitment to retiree health care?
- What is our corporate approach to all health-related benefits?
- Do our health, welfare, and retirement plans form an integrated benefits program?
- What is our mission regarding employee benefits?
- What is the relationship of benefits to compensation and other total rewards programs?
- How do benefits support the corporate business mission?

SOURCE: The Conference Board.

WHO'S MANAGING THE STRATEGIC BENEFITS PLANNING PROCESS?

Rightsizing and reengineering efforts have resulted in most managers assuming additional responsibilities with streamlined staffs. Who manages the strategic benefits planning process usually depends on an organization's size and its access to internal and external resources. The most common positions and roles include the following:

- *Benefits planner.* Usually found in large organizations, the benefits planner assumes responsibility for the strategic benefits planning process. The planner's responsibilities are clearly delineated from those of the operations manager, whose focus is on plan administration.
- *Internal consultant.* Frequently, highly decentralized organizations retain an internal consultant whose responsibilities include strategic benefits planning. The consultant often works with individual business units to ensure an overall balance between corporate goals/culture and business unit requirements.
- *Administrator/planner.* Wearing two hats, the administrator/planner usually juggles long-term goals with day-to-day operations. While not ideal, this often is the role of the senior benefits/human resources executive in smaller organizations. Successful benefits administrators or planners find themselves able to access additional outside resources and/or to compartmentalize responsibilities for some period of time.
- *Outside advisers.* Outside advisers—usually benefits or human resources consultants—are sometimes asked to help manage the strategic planning process. Generally, the role of outside advisers is limited to providing focused expertise during specific phases. There is an implicit assumption that the outside adviser brings a level of impartiality and objectivity to the process. While this is often correct, internal managers still need to preclude any loss of understanding about the corporate culture and organization history. Managers also need to ensure that the organization's needs remain the primary focus and are not compromised during the process.

Regardless of how the process is managed or what job title you give it, other key resources central to the planning process's success are listed in Figure 20.4.

FIGURE 20.4 Key resources in the strategic benefits planning process.

- Executive management
- Other HR departments (especially compensation)
- Finance department, including payroll and accounting
- Information systems
- Strategic business units
- Employees
- Actuaries and other consulting resources
- Tax department
- General counsel
- Organized labor
- Public relations and legislative affairs

DESIGN AND IMPLEMENTATION

Regardless of the model used to obtain organization buy-in for a strategic benefits planning initiative, implementation necessitates careful planning, execution, and management. Following is a description of key steps to designing and implementing a benefits strategy.

Step 1: Developing a General Philosophy

A well-constructed benefits philosophy has three primary characteristics: It is contextually appropriate, internally consistent, and clear. Regardless of whether a top-down approach or backing-in approach has been adopted, the benefits philosophy is central to evaluating existing programs. The benefits philosophy ideally is derived from and represents a broader human resources and business mission or philosophy. It also serves as the basis or touchstone for testing any potential plan redesigns.

A benefits philosophy should be inclusive and consistent. The same decision-making criteria should be applicable to all benefits-related programs. The philosophy requires consistency, whether the programs are health and welfare, retirement, or non-ERISA plans. ("ERISA" refers to those benefits plans subject to regulation under the Employee Retirement Income Security Act of 1974.) The philosophy should be communicated throughout the organization.

The benefits philosophy represents a longer-term organizational commitment. It is the foundation for benefits-specific strategies and tactics. An effectively designed and communicated benefits philosophy supports a continuum of issues on a per-plan basis. These include:

- The relationship between compensation and benefits as part of total rewards, as well as the role of total rewards as part of a greater human resources philosophy.
- The allocation of spending for retirement, health and welfare, or other benefits.
- Benefits levels compared to the open market (e.g., above average, average, below average).
- Levels of choice given to the employee (i.e., the continuum from totally flexible benefits to a one-size-fits-all package).
- Distribution of risk (e.g., individual employee vs. plan sponsor, plan sponsor vs. insurer).
- Levels of employee/employer cost sharing.
- Employee benefits as a community relations and/or recruitment tool.

Step 2: Understanding the Environment

Understanding the environment entails collecting and organizing information that articulates organizational opportunities and constraints that may be either internal or external. Once collected, these data provide some working parameters for the actual benefits planning process.

When effectively used, these parameters not only define the constraints but also become the basis for developing creative design options and effective communication for all levels in the organization. Depending upon the breadth of

FIGURE 20.5 Data to collect during strategic benefits planning.

Internal
- Corporate business goals
- Human resources objectives
- Work-force demographics (e.g., age, sex, education, exempt/nonexempt, full-/part-time)
- Benefits plan description (e.g., eligibility criteria)
- Detailed cost data
- Vendor analyses
- Geographic distribution of employees
- Technological and administrative capabilities
- Labor agreement

External
- Labor-force demographics
- Legal, regulatory, and cultural requirements
- Available services (e.g., technological, administrative, brokerage/consulting, insurance)
- Normative practices
- The organization's current and projected competitive position

data and whether it is kept current, the information gathered during this step can be an invaluable resource for other human resources planning projects. (See Figure 20.5.)

Once the internal information (i.e., specifics about the organization) is gathered, the following questions can be addressed:

- Given major employee groupings, is it appropriate (e.g., financially, administratively) to design or offer different plans? Or do the differences among employees raise the possibility of unionization?
- How much flexibility or employee choice in plan design is desired?
- Are there pockets of employees who for business reasons (e.g., technical skills, competitive advantage, labor force availability) require special treatment?
- How well do employees understand and use organization-sponsored benefits programs?
- Is there significant overlap among various plan designs/vendors (especially prevalent among health benefits plans)?
- Are the existing plans in legal compliance?

Step 3: Creating the Design Blueprint

The top-down approach provides a blueprint to organize groupings of benefits programs into a package. In other words, program integration or a priori definition of interrelationships among plans clarifies later plan objectives, design options, and/ or the requisite trade-off decisions. Poorly integrated benefits packages likely result in cost-ineffective designs (e.g., duplicative services) or inconsistent messages sent to employees. For example, an organization desiring high turnover rates probably would not implement a traditional defined benefit pension plan with rich retirement benefits that are accessible after a long tenure.

A similar outcome could result from a backing-in approach. For example, under this approach, an organization would examine various types of retirement programs to determine whether they facilitate the desired turnover rates.

In addition to setting broad objectives, the design blueprint needs to reflect the organization's desire for program breadth. Depending on philosophy and goals, benefits programs can retain a narrow focus such as only traditional health, welfare, and retirement, or a program can assume a broader focus, including a full range of ERISA and non-ERISA initiatives (e.g., work-life benefits, time off, education).

Once the breadth of programs is defined, plan sponsors are still able to include significant levels of choice within each plan. Examples include health plans that contain a variety of deductibles and/or plan design features, or life insurance vehicles (e.g., group universal life, whole life) that allow plan participants to increase their personal wealth.

Justifying Costs

Regardless of who authorizes changes in an organization's benefits plans, these changes will lead to additional costs. Identifying and planning for these costs should be part of any strategic benefits plan.

Examples of direct and indirect costs may include:

- Impact on existing staff.
- Extra contract employees.
- Professional advisers (e.g., legal and benefits consultants).
- Benchmarking studies.
- Communication/education materials.

While the costs are real, they can be considered investments. For example, return on investment and cost/benefits analyses can be derived by compiling potential and actual savings, increased profitability, and performance against established productivity measures. The potential benefits can be demonstrated further when these quantitative assessments are combined with qualitative measures such as anecdotal reports and focus group analyses.

Step 4: Testing and Finalizing the Design

Before finalizing any plan designs, it is important to create some "what if" scenarios. Thinking through these scenarios can allow designers to fine-tune the strategic benefits plan and facilitate the plan's rollout.

Major areas that usually are considered during this step include competitive or benchmark analyses. (See Sidebar 20.1.) Other critical areas include financial management, including cost estimates and projections, and regulatory requirements. Depending upon the breadth of projected plan changes and the organization's role within a given community, the impact of proposed changes upon corporate culture, as well as labor and community relations, also may be considered.

Sidebar 20.1: The Role of Benchmarking

Benchmarking can provide an objective review and assess the competitiveness of organization-sponsored benefits plans. Benchmarks rarely are absolutes. They are best understood when an organization's plans are assigned some relative value on a predetermined continuum. In this context, benchmarks serve as tools that can:

- Provide a business rationale and support proposed plan changes.
- Ensure that the changes support business (i.e., corporate, subsidiary) objectives.
- Realize the best value for dollars spent.

When they are organized effectively, benchmarks can demonstrate how the suggested changes will "connect" the "disconnects" among existing plans. They also can serve as educational tools to help ensure education, buy-in, and ownership among affected constituencies.

In broad terms, benchmarking evaluations can add a variety of cost, service, and quality measures to the process. Benchmark criteria for health benefits plans can include:

- Total cost per employee or family.
- Employer and employee contributions.
- Cost increases.
- Levels of medical management.
- Deductible levels.
- Cost per employee.
- Out-of-pocket costs.
- Utilization rates such as inpatient, outpatient, emergency room, mental health, and substance abuse.

Benchmarks can be industry-specific, geographic, and/or best practices. Industry-specific analyses compare one company's benefits programs to other companies within the same industry. Geographic benchmarks are especially valuable when most of the organization's work force works or resides in a specific area, or when benefits are a key element in recruitment and retention in a tight labor market. Best-practice analyses—probably the broadest type of benchmarking—can help companies look beyond their own industry and geographic presence. They can translate benefits into specific business practices and ensure that they provide the best value to the business.

Financial Management

Benefits designs for many companies are driven by the financials. In earlier decades, when current and projected benefits costs were considerably lower, decision making was far simpler. Prior to and during the finalization process, cost issues need to be detailed explicitly. Cost-sharing implications (i.e., employer contributions vs. the organization's overall cost) are usually the most visible. However, other financial management decisions can include projected costs over time, cash flow, investment of plan assets, and costs to operating units (especially a concern in highly decentralized organizations and/or organizations where the profit margin is much greater in one operating unit than another).

Ensuring legal compliance is a critical and often overlooked element in the actual testing and finalization of plan designs. While counsel should be included in all planning phases, outside legal advisers play a critical role in making sure that the appropriate plan filings occur, drafting appropriate plan documents, and providing timely notification to appropriate groups of employees and/or agencies such as the Department of Labor (DOL), Internal Revenue Service (IRS), and Pension Benefit Guaranty Corp. (PBGC).

Administration and Systems Support

Strategic benefits planning often can address questions about plan administration and systems. Greater time is needed to effect changes at organizations where administration is highly manual and existing systems are fractured. Even when the decision is to outsource benefits administration, significant time may be required to ensure that the existing data and information shared with the outsource vendor are accurate and that there are systems/procedures in place to update the vendor on a timely basis.

Similarly, adequate time is required for implementation and testing if the imperative is to retain plan administration and/or upgrade existing computer systems. A less-frequently considered option is an initial strategy of outsourcing with the long-term goal of returning the administration to the plan sponsor.

Outsourcing allows the plan sponsor to assume ongoing management once effective systems and procedures are both documented and implemented.

Step 5: Implementing the Rollout

The length of time from finalizing plan designs to rollout is largely a function of how much the new plan deviates from the existing package and programs. The greater the change, the longer the time frame.

With minimal plan redesign, the period from the actual decision to design implementation may range from three months to one year. If there has been an overhaul in the benefits package, some organizations implement incremental changes over a time period of two or three years.

Effective strategic benefits planning requires the planning team and management to retain the bigger picture. In other words, management needs to be able to discuss the process and trade-offs with affected employees or sites who perceive some potential or actual loss of benefits.

Ideally, plan design changes should be keyed to plan years and/or re-enrollment. Pairing the transition to established plan dates can minimize the potential disruption to ongoing administration, systems, employee relations, and communication.

During the entire strategic planning process, ongoing communication plays a key role in ensuring success. In this last phase, however, the role is heightened. Without a carefully developed communication plan, the investment in the benefits planning process is at risk. Focused communication helps shape and carry the actual and underlying messages. Specific audiences—at all levels within the organization—should be paired with the appropriate messages. For example, communication targeted to employees will help ensure that they receive the maximum benefits from any plan changes. Communication also provides management with the tools to understand the various trade-offs and to carry messages to various constituencies.

OUTCOMES OF STRATEGIC BENEFITS PLANNING

Strategic benefits planning is not an end product but a process that improves decision making and results in specific initiatives and outcomes. Outcomes of successfully completed strategic benefits planning initiatives include the following. (See Figure 20.6.):

- *Documentation of existing programs.* Strategic benefits planning likely will force documentation of all existing benefits programs. This can enable the organization to conduct a full compliance review or audit of company-sponsored benefits programs. More specifically, it allows for careful reviews of summary plan documents (SPDs), Form 5500s, summary annual reports (SARs), and other forms of employee communication, and it also provides a vehicle to ensure that plan features and financing comply with current regulations.
- *A tool to evaluate the balance among different plans.* Strategic benefits planning provides an opportunity to assess objectively if the organization's benefits resource allocation (e.g., dollars) is appropriate and/or aligned with the organization's intent.

    For example, it evaluates whether benefits programs align with work-force demographics as well as recruitment, retention, and retirement goals.
- *A framework to redesign existing benefits programs.* At minimum, strategic benefits planning will identify contradictions among existing plan designs. More frequently, organizations use a strategic review to evaluate how well existing programs fit the desired business goals and/or to assess the availability of a better program or set of programs. For example, the process might result in the decision to shift from a defined health care benefit, in which the employer provides and subsidizes one or more health plans, to a consumer-directed health plan (CDHP), in which the employer provides a defined payment linked to one plan option, and the employee selects a health plan, either paying any incremental

FIGURE 20.6 Outcomes of strategic benefits planning.

1. Documentation of existing programs
2. A tool to evaluate the balance among different plans
3. A framework to redesign existing benefits programs
4. The impetus to design and implement new benefits initiatives
5. A decision to change benefits administration
6. A review of plan financing vehicles
7. Articulation of the relationship between benefits and other human resources functions
8. Education of management and employees

premium difference or receiving credit for a lower-priced option (Bureau of National Affairs 2001). In theory, a CDHP model of health benefits encourages greater employee accountability, offers more flexibility in plan design options, and gives employees greater choice (Employee Benefit Research Institute 2003). It may also reduce cost growth (Fowles 2004; Nichols 2002). Another decision might be to increase the number of 401(k) plan investment choices in an organization where there is a significant percentage of financially sophisticated employees. In contrast, an organization with comparatively less sophisticated employees would not be likely to reduce the number of investment options; however, it might consider introducing financial education initiatives.

- *The impetus to design and implement new benefits initiatives.* Frequently, strategic benefits programs allow an organization to identify new benefits programs that add value from an employee's and manager's perspective. While some programs may have some relatively significant costs, many innovative programs such as long-term care and auto insurance are usually cost-neutral to the employer (e.g., employee-pay-all programs and programs paid for with flex dollars).

- *A decision to change benefits administration.* Despite the increased visibility of outsourcing and its popularity, the wholesale movement of benefits administration to a third party may not always be in the employer's best interest. Strategic benefits planning allows an organization to define those benefits programs that should remain in-house and those that should be outsourced based on its unique corporate culture, business goals, organization structure, and staff capabilities. Similarly, the outcome may be a reorganization that results in an internally managed benefits service center. Strategic planning clearly sets the stage to evaluate the effectiveness of information systems that are used for benefits planning and management.

- *A review of plan financing vehicles.* In conjunction with the review of plan design and administration, strategic benefits planning forces an organization to revisit its benefits financing options. The strategic review allows management to evaluate various funding and financing options for each plan. Depending on the plan, these options may include individual and aggregate stop-loss levels, or they may include fully, partially, or self-insured health plans.

- *Articulation of the relationship between benefits and other human resources functions.* Strategic planning can enable management to identify redundancies and/or gaps among benefits and compensation programs as well as the relationships of benefits to other HR programs. This analysis also can shed light on where benefits are best housed—as part of human resources, finance, or risk management.

- *Education of management and employees.* Effective strategic benefits planning forces decision making based on an understanding of business and benefits realities. It provides an opportunity to educate all management levels from line managers to senior executives. In addition, it can create an environment within which benefits and human resources managers can educate employees/management about the value, cost, and investment that organizations make in benefits programs.

EVALUATION

Strategic benefits planning initiatives represent a corporate investment in human assets. In addition to helping organizations take the proverbial step back and examine their policies, well-executed initiatives result in redesigned benefits plans and packages that may help companies achieve business goals through their employees. (See Figure 20.7.) Success, however, requires both evaluation and the ability to relate the planning process to broader organization and business requirements.

The Role of Evaluation

Historically, qualitative (e.g., anecdotal) reports have been used to demonstrate the success of many human resources efforts. While rigorous qualitative techniques (e.g., focus group and structured interviews) provide opportunities to assess outcomes, there is a growing corporate emphasis on quantitative measures or metrics. The challenge of benefits professionals is to develop meaningful measures.

Quantitative measures require an assessment of the impact of program changes or benefits redesigns on benefits-specific concerns such as cost, efficiency, operations, employee satisfaction, and corporate culture. These concerns reflect HR goals as well as overall business objectives. Other outcomes that can be defined both qualitatively and quantitatively include reducing management exposure or potential liabilities.

For qualitative and quantitative measures, it is crucial to set appropriate time frames and expectations for when success is to be achieved.

For example, changes in a health care benefits plan may result in desired migrations within one re-enrollment period. Meaningful cost savings due to a transition from a preferred provider organization (PPO) to a point-of-service (POS) plan may be seen within one year. In contrast, assessing the return on investment (ROI) derived from the implementation of a full flexible benefits package, which is part of a corporate cultural shift, may only be realized in four to six years.

FIGURE 20.7 Ground rules for strategic benefits planning.

- *Ensure that commitments are real.* Without senior management's explicit and on-going support, success is impossible.
- *Develop and apply benchmarks.* Know where you are, and know where you want to be. It is also important to know why you want to be there.
- *Be flexible.* Define priorities and be prepared, as necessary, to re-evaluate and revise them during the process.
- *Recognize the requisite time requirements.* Avoid underestimating the time needed to do things the right way.
- *Make some quick wins.* Waiting until the end may be too far away.
- Consider the gains. Look at accomplishments in absolute terms as well as relative to where you started.
- Simplify the process. Write the plan, and keep it simple and understandable to management.
- Communicate. Manage communication effectively, trumpet program successes, and continually educate staff at all levels.
- Define roles and responsibilities. Know who is doing what and why.

BEYOND THE STRATEGIC PLAN

In rightsized organizations, the ever-increasing complexities of benefits combined with ongoing operational staff requirements can create unintended myopia. In other words, employee benefits are seen as a cost center, not as a means to provide value-added business services.

To make the transition, organizations need to benefit from the opportunities that are available to them. These opportunities can be defined both narrowly and broadly.

At the narrowest end, demonstrating and communicating how benefits contribute to a total rewards package represents a significant change for many organizations.

Similarly, identifying how the benefits package supports an organization's investment in human capital provides a fairly narrow approach.

At the other end of the spectrum, the expanding emphasis on improved management techniques represents opportunities where the strategic benefits plan can make a difference. For example, the benefits function and package can be reviewed and/or reconfigured to support many current approaches, such as the learning organization, redefined employer/employee relationship, change management, and quality improvement/reengineering. In essence, benefits departments with a strategic plan have the opportunity to be more active players in the dynamic and changing business environment.

REFERENCES

Bureau of National Affairs. 2001. "Employee Benefits Defined Contribution Health Plans Face Many Obstacles, Panelists Say." *Health Care Policy Report,* 9(9): 359.

Employee Benefit Research Institute. 2003. *Consumer-Driven Health Benefits: A Continuing Evolution?* Washington, DC: Employee Benefits Research Institute.

Fowles, Jinnet Briggs. 2004. Early Experience with Employee Choice of Consumer-Directed Health Plans and Satisfaction with Enrollment. *Health Services Research* (August).

Nichols, L. M. 2002. "Can Defined Contribution Health Insurance Reduce Cost Growth?" *EBRI Issue Brief* 246: 1–15.

21 Implementing Flexible Benefits

Flexible benefits plans can be used as a valuable tool to help employers meet the unique needs of an increasingly diverse work force through greater choice and flexibility in benefits options, while effectively managing plan costs.

The number of flexible benefits plans has increased so dramatically since the early 1980s that "flex plans" have become an industry standard. These programs tend to have two common links: employee choice and tax advantages, as allowed by Section 125 of the Internal Revenue Code.

Section 125 refers to flexible benefits plans as "cafeteria plans" and defines them as plans that allow a choice of at least one nontaxable benefit, such as life insurance, disability insurance, and health care, and at least one taxable benefit, such as cash.

Implementing a flexible benefits plan typically involves action in the following areas:

- Benefits plan design.
- The pricing of benefits (or cost to both employer and employees).
- Employee communication.
- Internal or external benefits administration.
- Internal legal/accounting issues.

These implementation factors will vary depending on the type of flexible benefits plan involved.

TYPES OF FLEXIBLE BENEFITS PLANS

There are four basic types of flexible benefits plans:

1. Pretax premium plans (aka premium conversion or premium-only plans).
2. Flexible spending accounts.

3 Simple choice plans (aka modular plans).

4. Comprehensive flexible benefits plans (aka full flexible).

Pretax Premium Plans

This most elementary type of flexible benefits plan involves redefining employee contributions so that, under Section 125, they may be paid with pretax rather than after-tax dollars. These premium conversion or premium-only plans may involve nothing more than allowing employees the "choice" to pay for certain benefits with pretax dollars. Implementing these plans requires:

- A Section 125 plan document and Form 5500 filing.
- Some type of employee consent or agreement.
- A payroll system equipped to calculate and maintain pretax contributions.

A variation would be for an employer to specify that the "choice" involves pretax contributions for benefits or no coverage. Increasingly, employers are moving away from allowing employees the choice of pretax or after tax. The reason behind this approach is that few employees choose after tax, and for those that do, it becomes an administrative complexity.

Flexible Spending Accounts

Under Section 125, Section 105, and Section 129, employees may be allowed to set aside an amount of money using pretax dollars to pay for health care or dependent care expenses not otherwise covered by the benefits plan. While there are certain limitations, rules, and restrictions surrounding these plans, implementing them requires:

- A separate written plan document (which may be part of a Section 125 plan) and Form 5500 filing.
- Some form of employee communication.
- Enrollment materials (that include the "pretax" consent).
- A payroll system equipped to calculate and maintain account contributions.
- An administrator or system to manage spending account claims processing.
- An accounting system that can track collections and disbursements.

Simple Choice Plans

Both pretax plans and spending accounts may be added to a benefits program with no change in underlying benefits choices. A simple choice or modular plan typically involves additional options to existing benefits. While the choices may involve different levels of coverage in life, disability, or health benefits, they are characterized by a difference in employee cost, depending on the option selected.

These employee contributions tend to be expressed as weekly, biweekly, or monthly payroll deductions. From an employee perspective, the cost is equal to the portion they are required to pay. The portion paid by the employer generally remains unknown to the employee.

Implementing a simple choice plan requires:

- A Section 125 document, with appropriate separate plan documentation for the spending account plans, and Form 5500 filing.
- Employee communication explaining the different choices.
- Enrollment materials (that include the "pretax" consent).
- A payroll system that can account for each choice being offered.
- An administrator or system that can manage the enrollment process of each choice.
- An accounting system that can track the multiple combinations of choices that are available.

While pretax plans and spending accounts involve adding one, two, or three new choices, simple choice plans may involve many more choices, including multiple choices for life insurance, disability, dental, or medical coverage. As a result, the payroll, administration, and accounting functions are substantially more complex.

Full Flexible Benefits Plans

Most complex of all, these rarely used comprehensive flexible benefits plans involve not only a wide range of choices in traditional life, disability, and health benefits but also potential choices in vacation and 401(k) benefits.

The dividing line between a simple choice and a comprehensive plan is difficult to identify; however, comprehensive plans tend to approach employee costs differently. These plans often characterize employer costs in terms of a defined contribution of "flex dollars" or "flex credits" that can be more easily controlled by employers.

Rather than hiding an employer subsidy of the plans, these "flex dollars" represent an employer's contribution to the plan, whether an employee chooses to buy a benefit or not. In this process, employees' benefits choices often are priced at the full cost of each benefit, with "flex credits" available to offset these costs.

Implementing comprehensive plans requires the same elements as simple choice plans. However, by definition, communication, enrollment, payroll, administration, and accounting requirements are more demanding and complex.

FLEXIBLE BENEFITS PLAN DESIGN

All flexible benefits plans address four key areas of plan design:

1. Eligibility.
2. Enrollment choices.
3. Family and employment status changes.
4. Special classes of employees.

Eligibility

For many employers, eligibility provisions vary from benefit to benefit. In some instances, coverage is effective immediately, while in others there may be a 30-, 60-, or 90-day waiting period.

For ease of communication and administration, many employers seek to have eligibility provisions as uniform as possible. However, even with this goal in mind, benefits such as long-term disability (LTD) generally require a 3- to 12-month waiting period.

There are three approaches used by flexible benefits plans to address multiple eligibility dates:

- Require employees to make all their coverage elections during the enrollment process, even though certain elections such as LTD will not be effective for some time.
- Allow employees to enroll for benefits as they become eligible.
- Schedule periodic "interim" enrollment periods, at mid-year, for example, to allow enrollment "windows" for benefits of which employees are now eligible.

The second approach involves greater day-to-day administration because employees may enroll throughout the year, although increasing sophistication in technology and systems makes this less of an issue than in the past. The more common approach is a blend of the first and third approaches. The third approach may be used exclusively for benefits such as LTD or 401(k) while the first approach would be used for all other benefits.

Interim Core Plan

In certain circumstances, an employer might require a waiting period of 30, 60, or 90 days for the benefits available through the flexible benefit plan. In these cases, employees may have an interim, or temporary, "core plan" available to provide a "safety net" level of coverage. These might include a modest amount of life insurance, disability coverage, or medical benefits that require fairly high deductibles or low plan maximums.

This approach has largely fallen out of favor in recent years. The drawbacks to an interim core plan are the time and expense associated with additional communication, plan documentation, and administration of an additional set of benefits.

Deduction Effective Dates

There are three ways that employers may deal with the timing of coverage relative to the effective date of deductions. These are:

- Begin and end coverage exactly on the date employment commences or terminates. This approach is the most precise, but it often requires manual intervention to adjust payroll and benefit administration processes.
- Begin and end coverage as soon as "reasonably possible"—30 days or first/end of month, for example. Given that there is a time lag in setting up a new employee or terminating an old one from the various administrative systems that track eligibility, employees may receive a short period of "free" coverage in the interest of administrative simplicity.
- Establish benefit administration and payroll rules that automatically take full pay period deduction during the first period of coverage or the last pay period of coverage, regardless of whether the employee was covered for the entire period. While this approach can cause employee relations concerns, it often eliminates or reduced manual intervention.

Enrollment Choices

While flexible benefits plans seek to increase employee choice, certain limitations may be needed. These limitations allow an employer to control adverse selection—the ability of employees to intentionally select and use benefits in a way that will be "most costly" to an employer. The degree to which an employer will exercise any of these techniques will be influenced by:

- *Plan costs.* Plans experiencing good financial results may tend to be less restrictive.
- *Administrative capabilities.* The administrator(s) must have the ability to manage the data required to enforce these procedures.
- *Employee attitude/morale.* Too many restrictions may impact employee perception of the plan.

Adverse selection has become much less of a concern as flexible benefit plans have become more prevalent and the percent of employees with benefits coverage grows. To the extent select employees did adversely select against a plan, it tends to flow through the claims experience and become self-adjusting over the course of time.

Changes in legislation, such as HIPAA, have restricted the use of medical evidence to manage potential adverse selection.

Techniques that are used to address adverse selection might include:

- Limiting some of the options that are available to new hires.
- Requiring a two-year minimum election period for coverages such as dental care, where it is often easier for an employee to plan their treatment around their coverage period. The two-year provision essentially spreads the risk.
- The use of medical evidence at certain levels of optional life or disability coverage.

In general, adverse selection is no longer a significant concern with flexible benefit programs. The employee population receiving such benefits has typically had some type of comprehensive benefits coverage available in the past. Adverse selection would be a much bigger issue if a flexible benefits program was being extended to a group of employees who had previously had limited or no benefits coverage.

Annual Re-enrollment

Employees have the right to change their elections during annual re-enrollment. To minimize the effect of employees selecting richer benefits because of a known illness or injury, certain controls are available:

- First, the plan may limit employees to selecting no more than one benefit option higher than current coverage.
- Second, if employees wish to go beyond one option higher, medical evidence of insurability would be required for certain benefits.
- Third, medical evidence of insurability also may be required if employees add coverage for themselves or dependents after they initially chose not to be covered by the medical plan.

Default Elections

During an initial enrollment, a core level of coverage typically will be defined for those employees who do not turn in an enrollment form. This core might involve a basic amount of life insurance and a low to intermediate level of medical coverage. The rationale behind the default is to require a minimal level of coverage for employees who neglect to enroll and to limit the coverage to discourage employees from ignoring their enrollment responsibilities.

For subsequent annual enrollments, the default election is generally defined as the level of coverage an employee had in place before the enrollment period. This practice is not available to spending accounts that generally require an active election every year. Because spending accounts are funded with employee pretax contributions and are subject to forfeiture if unused, it is important that employees actively elect to continue participation.

Family and Employment Status Changes

IRS regulations permit an employer to allow employees to change benefits elections due to a family or employment status change, provided the election change *is resulting from* and consistent with the status change.

The status changes most frequently included in the plan are:

- Marriage.
- Divorce or legal separation.
- Death of an employee's spouse or dependent.
- Birth or adoption of a child.
- Commencement or termination of the employment of an employee's spouse.
- Change from part-time to full-time or from full-time to part-time employment status by an employee or an employee's spouse.
- Commencement of an unpaid leave of absence from employment by an employee or an employee's spouse.
- Significant change in the health coverage of an employee or an employee's spouse attributable to the employment of an employee's spouse.

While this list is not comprehensive, it provides some insight into the flexibility available to employers in establishing eligibility status. In fact, employers may permit a change to benefit elections for any event determined to be in accordance with the rulings and regulations of Section 125. Examples of such events include:

- The involuntary transfer of an employee that significantly changes benefits coverage (e.g., an employee moves out of an HMO's service area).
- An eligible plan dependent reaching the limiting age and becoming ineligible for coverage (e.g., the dependent qualifies for coverage under provisions of the Consolidated Omnibus Reconciliation Act of 1985 [COBRA]).

Employers use certain guidelines to determine appropriate status changes. For example:

- Events are allowed that are not administrative or cost burdens to employers.
- The distinction is recognized between "changing a level of coverage" and a "change in benefits plans." An employee may have a legitimate qualifying event, such as a birth or marriage, that would warrant adding a dependent

under the existing medical plan. Because the risk of adverse selection is greater if an employee also has the option to change to a richer medical plan option, some employers only would allow this employee to change levels of dependent coverage within the elected medical plan option.

- An effective date is used for changes that pose the least administrative burden. Employers may require a 30-day notice or make the change effective on the first of the upcoming month. The exception to this approach tends to be the addition of a new dependent, which usually is effective immediately.

- The financial impact of status changes is evaluated, including compliance with insurance company underwriting requirements. The loss of a spouse's employment is regrettable, but allowing that spouse to enroll in one's own plan may have a significant financial impact, depending on the size of the employer and the health of the spouse. To limit exposure, an employer may limit coverage to the lowest-level medical plan.

Special Classes of Employees

One of the challenges addressed by most flexible benefits plans involves the treatment of employees who are:

- Part-time.
- On a leave of absence.
- Former employees who choose to participate in the plan as allowed by COBRA.
- Retired.

Part-Time Employees

The strategies that employers tend to have in place for part-time employees before the introduction of flexible benefits can be preserved or modified in the design of a flexible benefits plan. The alternatives range from providing no coverage to providing a different, more modest type of flexible benefits plan to providing the same flexible benefits plan as full-time employees (typically with significantly increased cost-sharing for part-time participants).

One administrative difficulty is the movement of employees from part-time to full-time status and the reverse. Administrative procedures must be in place to allow for the smooth transition of benefits changes and the resulting payroll impact.

Leave of Absence

There are several types of leave to be considered:

- *Disability.* Generally, disabled employees are not allowed to increase their benefits once disabled.
- *Not "actively at work."* In certain cases, an active employee enrolls for coverages under the flexible benefits plan but is not actively at work on the day coverage becomes effective. Generally, an employee must return to work before those coverages can go into effect.

- *Paid vs. unpaid leave.* Typically, the policies in place before the flexible benefits plan will remain in force. Generally, for enrollment changes to increase coverage, the actively-at-work limitation would apply.
- *Family and Medical Leave Act.* There is no flexibility with leave under the Family and Medical Leave Act of 1993 (FMLA). In an FMLA-related leave, federal law is reasonably clear that an employee must be provided the same election rights as an active employee and would override other plan limits on election changes.
- *COBRA participants.* These former employees are entitled to select any of the health benefits options they had in place before their termination. The law requires that these former employees be treated the same as any similarly situated active employee. This extends to health care spending account elections, which, if elected in a COBRA environment, must be funded with after-tax dollars—essentially voiding the inherent value of the spending account.

At the time of annual re-enrollment, COBRA participants again are afforded the rights of an active employee and may enroll for health care options available to the active employee at the higher COBRA rates. This includes benefits the employees chose not to continue immediately following their COBRA qualifying event.

- *Retirees.* Flexible benefits plans for retirees introduce a number of complexities that may negate any advantages. These factors include the mobility and geographic disbursement of retirees and the associated difficulty of communicating and administering an enrollment, particularly if media such as voice enrollment are utilized. The financial impact of FAS 106 has, however, encouraged many employers to significantly increase the choices retirees have for medical care, in those instances where lower cost choices (e.g., Medicare HMOs) will reduce the FAS 106 liabilities. However, even in those instances, the plans are seldom characterized as "retiree flexible benefits plans."

PRICING FLEXIBLE BENEFITS OPTIONS

Finalizing the approach to be used in pricing flexible benefits plan options involves many factors, including:

- *An employer's HR and financial objectives.* The way costs are passed on to employees will be a direct function of these objectives.
- *Sophistication of the work force.* A more highly educated work force will tend to understand more complex plans and pricing.
- *Complexity of the plan design.* A simpler design typically avoids complex credit formulas.
- *Communication needs.* If the pricing method being implemented is significantly different from the past, extra time and care will be needed to communicate the new approach to employees.
- *Time frame for implementation.* More complex plan design and pricing require a longer time frame for the planning and coordination needed by all affected parties.
- *In-house administration capabilities.* Internal payroll human resources systems will need to be equipped to handle the pricing techniques.

- *External administration capabilities.* Coordination with claims administrators and insurers may be required depending on the complexity of the approach.
- *Financial issues.* The costs associated with communicating and administering more complex designs and cost strategies can have a bearing on ultimate design.

There are three basic models used for pricing flexible benefits options:

- Market-based pricing and credits.
- Incentive-based pricing and credits.
- Net cost pricing without credits.

Market-Based Pricing and Credits

With market-based pricing, the full cost of each benefit option is based upon an estimate of its true "marketplace" cost. In other words, while the cost of any given benefit option may be actuarially adjusted for factors such as future trend and adverse selection, there is no effort to "subsidize" or artificially distort the cost beyond what it is truly believed to be.

This approach provides an employer with the most control over future costs because the flexible benefits credits represent the employer's total cost. The employer defines its contribution annually by adjusting flexible benefits credits in line with its budget, allowing benefits prices to increase based on market.

Typically, employee communications identify the full market-based price of each option. Each employee is provided a certain number of "flex credits" to spend against these full market prices.

Incentive-Based Pricing and Credits

With incentive-based pricing, the full cost of each benefit option communicated to employees is set artificially to send a certain message about the relative value of the different choices and, typically, to help encourage employees to spend their supply of credits on those options that best meet the employer's cost objectives.

This approach gives employers more control over benefits selections but perhaps less control over cost. To the extent that an employer subsidizes benefits prices based on incentive pricing, the employer is assuming the market inflation built into the subsidized price. In other words, this approach allows employers to artificially price options to influence employee selection or to save employer costs.

Net Cost Pricing without Credits

With net cost pricing without credits, no effort is made to communicate any form of "full cost" to employees. Rather, employees are advised of the payroll deduction that applies to each benefit option. Those employee contributions (deducted weekly, biweekly, or monthly) are the only cost figures conveyed to employees. As such, there are no "flexible benefits credits" to be spent on each choice.

This approach can be the simplest to communicate and administer, but it provides the least control over employer cost. The employer is assuming the inherent inflation in the cost of each benefit and must justify any increase in net cost annually to employees.

To help identify the appropriate pricing strategies, employers should follow certain guidelines:

- *Use the pricing approach that best meets your objectives.* If the flexible benefits design is relatively simple, cost issues are not significant, and the communication budget is limited, then the net-cost approach may be the most effective approach. If the primary goal is controlling adverse selection and "steering" employees toward certain options, incentive-based pricing is considerably more effective than market-based pricing. If overall employer cost control and employee understanding of true costs are the goal, market-based pricing is the recommended approach.
- *Use different pricing methods for different types of benefits.* Frequently, employers prefer the incentive or market-based pricing for medical benefits. These approaches allow the employer to underscore the high cost of coverage and to set prices that encourage enrollment in certain options. The same employer might use the net-cost approach for dental or disability benefits, for simpler communications, and for controlling dollars available to employees who opt out of coverage.
- *Use a "cash out" option that allows an employee to decline coverage in exchange for cash.* With incentive and market-based pricing, the credit for the "cash out" option will not equal the full cost of coverage nor the full value of credits given to purchase coverage. Rather, the value of "cashing out" will be set at a significantly lower, fixed-dollar amount to allow for the impact of adverse selection.

In addition to deciding upon appropriate pricing models and strategies, most flexible benefits plans address certain other pricing issues.

TAX ISSUES AND EMPLOYER OBJECTIVES

Section 125 allows certain benefits to be paid for by employees with pretax dollars. By choosing this approach, employees technically reduce their salary to allow the employer to pay for the designated benefits. As a result, those pretax dollars become characterized as an employer-provided benefit.

Pretax Benefits

Medical and dental coverage are the most common pretax benefits. The advantage to an employee is lower taxes. The advantage to the employer is a reduced wage base—due to the salary reductions—and, as a result, lower FICA taxes. In addition, insured medical and dental benefits are not subject to taxation when received by employees, regardless of how they are purchased.

Pretax or After-Tax Benefits

Certain benefits are treated differently from medical and dental plans. LTD, for example, may be purchased on a pretax basis, but then the benefits will be subject to taxation if and when received. However, if LTD is paid for with after-tax dollars, the benefits would be received tax-free.

Supplemental group-term life benefits are received tax-free, regardless of how they are purchased. However, the premiums for coverage in excess of $50,000 are subject to a type of taxable, imputed income based on IRS regulations under Section 79.

After-Tax Benefits

Certain benefits, such as dependent group life and long-term care, do not have the tax-favored treatment of medical and dental plans. These benefits may be offered on an after-tax basis only and cannot be included in a cafeteria plan. However, these benefits can be offered coincident with the flexible benefits plan enrollment process.

For administrative simplicity, most plans will include all options (whether pretax or after-tax) as part of the same enrollment process and will discuss both in enrollment materials. To some extent, the real challenge is one of clear, effective communication to ensure employee understanding.

"Freezing" Pay for Pricing Purposes

Certain benefits, such as life insurance and LTD coverage, are based upon an employee's earnings. In establishing flexible benefits plan prices and credits for these wage-based benefits, most plans use an employee's earnings as of a certain date. While an employee's earnings may change over the course of the plan year, the prices and credits (and often the coverage amount) typically remain based upon the "frozen" amount, primarily for reasons of administrative simplicity.

Adjusting Prices from Insured Rates

In those instances where an employee has the opportunity to reduce coverage, there may be a need to move away from rates quoted by the insurer. This approach would involve providing less of a credit to reduce coverage than true market pricing might indicate as a way to offset the impact of adverse selection by those employees who elect higher levels of coverage. For example, even if the life insurance company provides one composite rate, employers frequently use age-weighted rates to provide appropriate incentives to employees in the election process. In this way, the age rates more accurately reflect the risk of the different age groups.

Figure 21.1 shows an example of a corporation that had the following objectives in the pricing of its flexible benefits for its employees:

- Include incentives to encourage employee wellness.
- Achieve maximum control over future employer costs. Credits would increase in the future based on employer profitability, separate from benefit costs that would increase based on the market.
- Encourage employee appreciation of actual costs of benefits.
- Provide limited credits to employees who opt out of medical coverage (employees already contributed to the cost for employee-only medical benefits).
- Net employee contributions to keep current benefits would increase. Offering lower benefit options would be used to offset expected employee concerns with higher contributions for current benefits.

The most carefully designed and priced flexible benefits plan has the potential to fail unless it is communicated properly. Given the diversity of flexible benefit plans, there is no one set of communication strategies that meets the needs of all employers. There are, however, certain common elements:

- *Precommunication planning.* Set communication objectives carefully to allow for a clear series of intended messages using communication media that fit the available budget.

FIGURE 21.1 Sample credit formula.

This sample credit formula is based on the level of family medical coverage elected by an employee:

No medical coverage	$15/month
Single	$150/month
Employee + 1	$200/month
Family	$250/month

Employees also were provided credits for the following wellness activities (appraisal ratings were kept confidential from the employer):

Participation in wellness risk appraisals	$5 per month
Achieving "good" or "excellent" rating in risk appraisal	$5 per month

Employees also were provided the following credits:

One-times-pay life insurance (based on "frozen" pay as of Oct. 1)

60-percent-of-pay long-term disability coverage (based on "frozen" pay as of Oct. 1)

- *Employee input.* Use surveys, focus groups, or mock enrollments to collect employee comments. This process allows an employer to identify concerns and issues to be addressed in the communication campaign.
- *Announcement.* The initial announcement of the flexible benefits plan often is viewed as a "declaration" from senior management about the value and need for the new program or the changes being introduced.
- *Progressive disclosure.* This practice involves gradually and progressively educating employees about the flexible benefits plan changes being introduced. The goal is to avoid overloading employees with information. Instead, they are given the opportunity to be informed about different changes over a number of weeks or months, depending on the complexity of the message.
- *Enrollment.* In recent years, there has been a clear trend toward personalized enrollment materials and the use of voice-response systems to streamline the process, minimize errors, and increase employee understanding. Typically, the process involves an enrollment kit to guide employees.
- *Post-enrollment.* Once enrollment is complete, ongoing reinforcement can be achieved through confirmation statements, follow-up newsletter announcements, and updates.

COMMUNICATION APPROACHES

Typically, flexible benefits plan communication incorporates the following approaches:

- Involve management in the communication plan.
- Listen to rank-and-file employees for benefit and information needs.
- Anticipate emotional reactions.

- Carefully weigh demographic considerations, such as diversity of the work force.
- Define key messages and concepts.
- Select communication media that will carry the message most effectively.
- Test the media and the message with representative groups of employees.
- Formalize a plan that involves a clearly defined timetable, responsibilities, and budget.

Communication Timing

While the timing of the communication process can be as short as 2 to 3 months or as long as 9 to 12 months, the communication timetable must be coordinated closely with the administration timetable. In many respects, flexible benefits plan communication and flexible benefits plan administration are two sides of the same coin.

Before the design of a flexible benefits plan is complete, most employers evaluate how to administer the plan. Employers typically allow a minimum of six months to prepare for and process the first annual enrollment, using one or a combination of the following options:

- *Internal development.* Most organizations find it difficult to allocate data-processing staff and resources for benefits projects. Allocating the resources necessary to develop an in-house enrollment system is the key to this option. If resources are available, the level of benefits expertise required to develop this software must be available. Many employers have used an outside consultant to assist with this development. Internal development may add four to six months to implementation.
- *Purchased software and internal administration.* A minimum of two months generally is necessary to evaluate available software packages and their capabilities, flexibility, and ease of use. Above all, the system selected must be flexible enough to meet the plan's needs. After investing much time and energy on plan design, most organizations do not want to redesign the plan because administration software is limited.
- *External administrator.* When evaluating outside enrollment administrators, two key issues are expertise and flexibility. An administrator with flexible benefits knowledge and experience will be able to administer the plan properly based on complex federal tax and labor law and applicable state regulations. Again, administrative flexibility is a key factor to evaluate to ensure that careful objective setting and plan design are not forced to change because of administrative limitations.

Administrative planning involves:

- Developing administrative procedures and forms.
- Coordinating activities with payroll or human resources systems and personnel.
- Verifying computation of data items by benefit option.
- Developing an implementation schedule.

ANNUAL ENROLLMENT PROCESS

Regardless of the enrollment administration option selected, six phases typically constitute the annual enrollment process.

Phase I: Data Setup

The first phase is to determine the information that needs to go into the enrollment system. This information includes the demographic and financial information necessary to determine eligibility as well as the coverage and cost for each benefit per pay period.

Most often, this information will be extracted from the payroll or human resources system. The number of payroll systems increases the implementation time required during this phase. Payroll or human resources system staff should be included as early and often as possible in the design phase.

Phase II: Individualized Worksheets

Depending on complexity, individualized benefit option worksheets may be needed by employees to ease the election process. These worksheets detail each employee's current coverage, available benefit options, level of coverage, cost of each option, and credits, if available, to purchase benefits.

Phase III: Distribution of Information

During Phase III, employees receive the individualized benefit options worksheet along with an enrollment form. Other communication materials may be distributed at the same time, either at meetings or by mail to employees' homes. Employees make their enrollment elections at this point.

Other information that may need to be collected and/or processed during this phase includes dependent information, primary care physicians, beneficiary designation forms, and evidence of insurability forms.

Phase IV: Confirmation

Once all employee elections have been entered into the enrollment system, a confirmation statement is produced and distributed to each employee. This statement communicates in detail the results of each employee's elections. Default or assigned coverages should be noted as such.

The confirmation statement gives employees an opportunity to verify or modify elections before the beginning of the plan year.

Phase V: Integration of Information

After all the election information has been assimilated, this information must be dispersed to the appropriate individuals and systems. Eligibility information is provided to insurance carriers; deduction and income information is provided to the payroll system.

Phase VI: Review

Management reports that summarize the election results will help determine how well communication and plan design objectives were met. The planning process for the next annual enrollment begins by reviewing these results and considering what changes need to be made to achieve goals and fine-tune the process.

ONGOING ENROLLMENT

Before the annual enrollment is complete, procedures must be determined for enrolling new and newly eligible employees and handling *changes in status*. Depending on employee turnover and eligibility waiting periods, ongoing enrollment can present interesting challenges. The task of enrolling an employee and submitting those elections to the payroll system requires coordination. If there is a short waiting period for eligibility and high employee turnover, ongoing enrollment can be time-consuming. Frequent *employment status changes* (part-time to full-time, for example) also can increase the administrative support for enrollment. In ongoing enrollment, all phases of annual enrollment are compressed into a shorter time frame but with a lower volume of transactions. Election changes resulting from family-status changes also must be monitored during this process for consistency.

ANNUAL RE-ENROLLMENT

After the implementation of the flexible benefits plan is accomplished, employees are allowed to change elections annually during a re-enrollment phase. Similar processes are involved, but re-enrollment requires much less commitment of resources, unless there are significant plan changes. Many employers use a passive enrollment, where employees keep current coverages if they do not turn in an enrollment form. Typically, an employee is required to re-elect the spending account contribution rather than automatically carrying over the spending account election to the following year.

Some of the trends in enrollment administration are targeted to manage or reduce the volume of paper generated in the process. Interactive systems generally have replaced bar-coding and scanning as ways to improve enrollment efficiency. These interactive trends include:

- *Interactive voice.* Interactive voice allows employees to enter elections by using a touch-tone telephone connected to a computer system. The interactive script talks employees through each benefit selection, allowing each employee to enter or modify each election. Even dependents can be enrolled via the phone, through the keypad or by accessing an employee benefits specialist. Because the elections are transferred to the computer enrollment system automatically, this process eliminates the need for an enrollment form to be keyed.
- *Interactive video.* Interactive video works on the same principle as interactive voice. Benefits options are displayed on a computer screen but instead of using a telephone, the employee uses a "touch screen." The employee is instructed to touch a specific plan on the screen to select the desired benefits coverage. These elections are then transferred to the enrollment system.
- *Personal computer web-based enrollment systems.* Personal computer enrollment systems allow employees to sit at a kiosk or private work station to go through the enrollment process, typically using the keyboard instead of "touch screens." These systems vary from simply electronically capturing enrollment selections to more complex "what-if" programs that perform tax computations or model election results based on varying scenarios of benefits elections. This information

then is transferred to the enrollment system. Many insurance carriers are developing Internet and intranet enrollment tools for use by employers.

SPENDING ACCOUNT ADMINISTRATION

Typically, spending account administration is performed by an employer's medical claims administrator, flexible benefits enrollment administrator, or internally on purchased software. The medical claims administrator may offer an automatic "rollover" of unpaid medical claims to the spending account while the enrollment administrator offers a direct tie to employee election data already on the system. Most employers set up a separate bank account for claims payments.

A major administrative challenge is determining whether a submitted health or day-care expense is an allowable claim based on IRS guidelines. Keeping track of the impact of family status changes under the employer at-risk rules for the health spending account is an issue that many claims systems do not handle well.

LEGAL ISSUES

Section 125 requires that a written plan document describe the flexible benefits plan, although there is currently no procedure for IRS review of the document or for issuance of a determination letter.

Summary Plan Description

A *written plan document* and Summary Plan Description (SPD) is required for the health and welfare plans that are included in the flexible benefits program, assuming the employer is subject to the Employee Retirement Income Security Act of 1974 (ERISA). A dependent care spending account is not covered by ERISA, and therefore an SPD is not required. An SPD should be provided for the health care flexible account and must be filed with the Department of Labor if the plan covers 100 or more employees. *A written plan document is also required.*

Form 5500

A Form 5500 must be filed for the flexible benefits plan, even if the number of participants is fewer than 100, even if the plan covers fewer than 100 employees, and even if the plan sponsor is not covered by ERISA. Many employers combine the flexible benefits plan Form 5500 with the spending account Form 5500, assuming both plans are contained in the same plan document. Some employers file one overall Form 5500 that incorporates all employee benefits programs included within the flexible benefits plan, *but the document must be drafted in a way that allows such an approach.*

Nondiscrimination Rules

There are several nondiscrimination rules related to a Section 125 flexible benefits plan, which may require annual calculations to prove nondiscrimination, including:

- No more than 25 percent of tax-free benefits in the cafeteria plan can be provided to "key employees."

Definition of highly compensated employee (HCE) as defined by IRC Section 414 (q):

- Owns 5 percent or more of the company in the current or prior year.
- Earns more than the HCE limit in the preceding plan year.
- At the employer's election is in the top 20 percent of the organization's employees in terms of pay.

Definition of key employee:

- An officer with compensation that exceeds annual indexed limits.
- A 5 percent owner, or a 1 percent owner with compensation that exceeds annual indexed limits.
- Families and beneficiaries of key employees.
- An employee is considered a key employee based on the prior year's annual compensation.

- For dependent care spending accounts, the average pretax benefit (including salary reduction) for non-highly compensated employees must equal at least 55 percent of the average pretax day care benefit of highly compensated employees. Depending on how many highly compensated employees participate, the 55-percent test can prove to be difficult to pass. The test should be done before the end of the year, so pretax benefits for the highly compensated can be adjusted, thereby avoiding complete taxation of all day-care benefits to the highly compensated.

Figure 21.2 describes the various tax issues that need to be considered when establishing a flexible benefits plan.

FIGURE 21.2 Tax issues.

State income tax. With the exception of Pennsylvania and New Jersey, all states currently follow Internal Revenue Code (IRC) Section 125 for pretax treatment of cafeteria plan salary reduction and credit amounts.

Local income tax and state unemployment tax. The exclusion from these taxes will vary from location to location. The best source for up-to-date information on these tax issues is a payroll service or a benefits consulting firm.

Social Security. Employees' pretax contributions are not subject to Social Security tax. Therefore, Social Security benefits are reduced as a result of flex salary reductions, typically from 1 to 5 percent. However, employees receive current tax savings for income taxes and Social Security taxes, which, except in a few cases, more than offset the Social Security benefits received at retirement.

Spending accounts. In virtually all cases, an employee is better off taking advantage of the health care spending account instead of having the same dollars available for an individual tax deduction, because the threshold for an individual tax deduction is 7.5 percent of adjusted gross income. However, the advantage of the dependent care spending account over the individual income tax credit varies based on the amount of day-care expenses, the employee's family income, and state income tax provisions for day-care expenses. In general, employees with family income greater than $24,000 per year are better off with the dependent care spending account, and employees with family income under $24,000 per year are better off taking the individual tax credit on their tax returns.

This chapter identifies the many roles played by flexible benefits plans in an environment where employers are redefining themselves as "facilitators" rather than providers. The success of any strategy using flexible benefits will require an employer to carefully define their objectives and select those approaches that will meet those goals.

The process involves balancing:

- Plan design needs.
- Pricing strategies.
- Communication capabilities and budget.
- Administrative capabilities.
- Tax and legal issues.

Figure 21.3 lists pitfalls to avoid in designing and administering a flexible benefits plan.

Above all, this process must recognize each employer's unique culture and organizational needs for flexible benefits plans to achieve their goals.

FIGURE 21.3 Pitfalls to avoid.

Lack of management commitment. Management's attitude toward and participation in the flexible benefits plan will influence employees directly. In many instances, several layers of management are involved throughout the entire planning and implementation process.

Allowing too little time/funds for communication. Much of an employee's perception of a "successful" plan will depend on the amount of time and money spent on careful and focused communications. Many well-designed plans have failed due to inadequate communication.

Feeling pressure to "do it all" the first year. A flexible benefit program is a process that can be implemented over a number of years. In some instances, multiyear implementation simplifies communication and administration.

Expecting employees to read. Experience has proven that many employees do not read printed material but will rely on other media, such as video, posters, audio tapes, etc., to learn about the plan.

Underestimating employees' ability to choose. The widespread acceptance and availability of flexible benefits plans underscores the fact that employees are capable of making benefits choices.

Expecting employees to calculate correctly. Frustration and errors result when employees are required to perform specific calculations as part of the enrollment process. Personalized enrollment materials help avoid this problem.

Failing to follow up after implementation. Because flex is an ongoing process, employers should provide ongoing information and reinforcement about the benefits.

Forgetting objectives in ongoing design. By staying focused on the initial strategic objective throughout planning and implementation, the ultimate plan design and pricing will reflect those goals.

22 Work-Life Effectiveness

It has been said that the only thing we can be certain of is change. That's certainly true in today's business environment. In addition to constant change in the way companies do business, employees' personal lives continue to change and have become far more complex than ever before. Dramatic change in the world of work and in peoples' lives has accompanied us into the twenty-first century. The focus on a competitive, fast-paced global economy, the ever-changing challenges of personal and family life, and the dramatic impact of technology have forced profound changes in how we define the workplace, the workforce, work, and our personal lives.

Companies have long said that employees are their most valuable assets, and today they face a human capital crisis. More than ever before, organizations are realizing that—if they want to remain competitive—they must find innovative ways of engaging employees that encourage and support their commitment and improve their performance. Companies today actually compete to become the employer of choice, the best place to work, the best work environment, and so forth, in order to attract and retain employees and to improve productivity.

In response to these dramatic changes, companies now view implementing effective work-life initiatives as a business imperative. Companies need to distinguish themselves from their competition by "connecting the dots" between issues such as overwork, stress, and increased health care costs and the advantage they can gain by implementing preventative approaches, such as work-life effectiveness. In a knowledge economy, more than ever before, employers are realizing that they must understand and address the diverse needs of their workforce in order to survive and thrive. Effective work-life practices—which include programs, policies, benefits, and practices—are a critical way to "walk the talk" when it comes to corporate values and to create a culture that "puts its money where its mouth is" when it comes to human capital assets.

518

CHANGING DEMOGRAPHICS

In most countries, companies and their workforce do not look very much like their counterparts of just 10 years ago, and the impact of these changes has given birth to the phenomenon we generally refer to today as "work-life." The dramatic increase of women in the workforce, resulting in the rise of the dual-focus worker—workers focused on work *and* family, rather than on work *or* family—and the aging of the workforce are among the most critical factors shaping today's workplace and affecting the way people live and work.

Let's take a look at demographics, the workforce, and the family. As Sandy Burud and Marie Tumolo describe in their book, *Leveraging the New Human Capital* (2004), the change in the old "breadwinner" profile of worker—56 percent of employees in 1950, and as of 2000, only 21 percent of employees—is driven by the fact that, today, primarily for economic need and personal satisfaction, large numbers of women are working outside the home.

Consider these facts, according to Burud:

- In 55 percent of families, women earn more than half the household income.
- In one in five families, since no male is present, women are the sole support.
- Most married women are now employed, an increase from 37 percent in 1967 to 61 percent in 2000.

And, according to the Bureau of Labor Statistics:

- As of 2002, the workforce was almost even—53 percent men to 47 percent women—and almost half of all graduates from professional programs today are women.
- As of 2003, the majority of mothers of young children worked outside the home—51 percent of mothers of infants under one year, and 56 percent of mothers of children under six.
- In 2001, more women with children under 18 were employed (73 percent— the same as the percentage of all men employed) than were women without children (55 percent).

In addition to child care, with the aging of the population and the aging workforce, employees also have to deal with elder-care issues. As a result, the majority of today's employees (53 percent) have either children or elders whom they care for. These demographic changes have resulted in changing employee needs. In a 2001 Radcliffe Public Policy Center survey, 82 percent of men surveyed and 85 percent of women ages 20 to 39 placed family time at the top of their work-life priorities. In a Rutgers University and University of Connecticut study of that same year, 90 percent of working adults said they were concerned that they do not spend enough time with their families. Caregiving responsibilities are impacting the way employees feel about their work.

Work-life has also become a recruitment issue, because new entrants into the workforce are asking how they are going to manage both their work and their personal lives. Headhunters often report that candidates now ask, "How flexible is the work environment?" and "What kind of work-life programs does the company offer?" These questions are even being asked globally.

Managing a workforce with diverse needs has grown to a position of paramount importance as knowledge workers have taken their place in the majority of organizations as their companies' most precious asset. These organizations must find new ways to accept, incorporate, empower, and engage the vast array of human talent available. Companies must do whatever is necessary to help each and every employee work up to his or her full potential, no matter what their personal or family responsibilities. In other words, companies simply must create work-life effectiveness for individuals and organizations or lose their competitive advantage.

THE EVOLUTION OF WORK-LIFE INITIATIVES

The work-life field has evolved along with the workforce itself. The work-life field first emerged on a wide scale in the United States in the early 1980s in order to address the child-care needs of working mothers who entered the paid workforce in record numbers. In the mid-1980s elder care was recognized as another area that impacted women's ability to participate fully in the workforce, and dependent care information and resources and child-care centers were seen as the "solution" to what was then called "work-family" issues. Most of the responses to these needs were designed primarily to make it possible for the employee to be able to work, not to change the workplace, or necessarily to change the way work was done or to accommodate personal needs.

In the early 1990s, with the advance of technology and increased work demands, the issue of "time" became a major focus as women and men realized that multitasking could only stretch the day so far. At that point, organizations began to implement flexible work arrangements to address the need for more options for where and when to work. In the late 1990s and today, these issues continue to exist, along with an effort to "connect the dots" and change the culture of the organization by redesigning work, address escalating health care costs because of stress and overwork, and redefine benefits and total rewards—all to attract, energize, and engage employees. While the focus in many organizations is still on responding to real or perceived employee needs, progressive companies see real advantages in taking a preventive, proactive approach to work-life issues and linking the effort directly to business goals.

WORK-LIFE EFFECTIVENESS: A DEFINITION

Today, companies are thinking more strategically about the words they use to describe their work-life initiatives. This is more than semantics; it's a critical, as well as a philosophical and organizational, issue. Vocabulary is very important, as are labels, especially in an evolving field. The words we use shape our thoughts, and there are many opportunities for misunderstanding when we're talking about "work-life."

Still, work-life means different things to different people depending on where they are in their lives and career cycles. For many employees, work-life effectiveness means being able to take care of child-care or elder-care needs while working; for some, it's having the time to take care of their own or a family member's medical needs; for others, it's the ability to go to the gym when they want to, or to learn a new skill; and for still others, it's being able to avoid commuting during peak traffic periods. Whatever the need, what is clear is that many of the policies, programs, benefits, and practices in organizations today were designed for the needs of the "traditional family" (i.e., stay-at-home mom, working dad), which, according to the Bureau of Labor Statistics, now represents less than 20 percent of the workforce.

Work-life has become part of the culture change process that is taking place in the most progressive companies as they work to engage employees, create a more results-oriented organization, foster productivity, and compete more effectively for talent. Organizations are beginning to move from the notion of "work-life balance"—which no employee seems to have and most employers don't want, since it implies a win/lose situation—to work-life effectiveness, where the goal is for both the organization and the employee to work together for effective management of personal life and work. While that may be common sense, it hasn't always led to common practice. Today, employers of choice and the best places to work are trying hard to make common sense be the common practice. In these companies, work-life has become a package of total rewards—a combination of programs, policies, benefits, and practices designed to address both changing business and employee needs.

Some other labels that are still being applied to the field include work-life balance, integration, and harmony. Of course, each organization must select the best terms for its purpose. However, it is important to think about the message behind the label. In the case of "balance," balance has been shown to imply a zero-sum game, where if one side wins (the employee), then the other side loses (the company). This makes it more difficult to "sell" or overcome management's resistance to work-life. The terms "harmony" and "integration" both seem to imply that employees and the organization can just mix everything together and it will come out all right. However, increases in stress-related illness and depression, as well as reduced engagement, loyalty, and commitment, show that this is not the case.

How an organization defines work-life depends on its culture, leadership, and in some cases, the length of time the company has had a work-life initiative in place. For some organizations, work-life is simply a collection of programs, policies, and benefits. In the most progressive companies, work-life has come to represent culture change efforts or practices that include changing work, the way employees are managed, and how productivity is measured. Some of these companies are beginning to "connect the dots" between traditional benefits and "nontraditional" work-life efforts. In some cases, this means including a broad definition of health and wellness as part of the work-life effort with the goal of reducing stress and health care costs. It can also involve an ongoing examination of the way work is actually done with the goal of reducing "low value" work and inefficiencies. Work-life effectiveness, because of the uniqueness of each person's personal work and personal life cycle, also relates to diversity. And it often involves assessing how well the process and methods of communication and the messages and branding for work-life meet the goal of ensuring a focus on a broad range of life cycle and career cycle issues.

According to the Alliance for Work-Life Progress (AWLP), work-life effectiveness is a specific set of organizational practices, policies, and programs along with a philosophy that recommends aggressive support for the efforts of everyone who works to achieve success both at work and at home. The organization also includes those efforts initiated by employers to create a supportive work environment that acknowledges the personal and family commitments of their employees, supports them in fulfilling those commitments, and improves work and personal effectiveness in the process. Clearly, work-life is not an easy concept to get one's arms around, and that may be why responsibility for work-life can be found in almost any area of a company that deals with people strategy—including benefits, personnel, human resources, employee relations, training, diversity, and health and wellness.

WHY COMPANIES ADDRESS WORK-LIFE ISSUES

There are at least eight very important interrelated business-related reasons why a company should have a comprehensive work-life initiative.

To Attract and Retain Talent

For many companies, the main reason for work-life initiatives is to attract and hold on to talented people. Even in a difficult economy, good people are hard to find and keep. Studies indicate that as the job market improves, many employees who have been frustrated and dissatisfied in their current situations will begin to look for other opportunities. In surveys and focus groups, employees frequently report they have considered looking for other jobs because their companies are not supportive of their work and personal needs.

Work-life initiatives have given corporations a human face that can help prospective employees tell one corporate face from another. When companies set out to recruit today's stars, they're not only offering a job and benefits; they're also selling an identity. This message is especially significant in an era of corporate scandal and mistrust.

Companies are also using their work-life initiatives to bring people who wouldn't otherwise be available to do the job into the workforce. These new workers may include new mothers who want to spend time with their babies, other parents or caregivers who will work as long as their schedule allows them to care for family members, young people who want to continue their education while working, older workers looking for more flexibility, the disabled who can work from home or from an office with accommodation, and workers, otherwise unavailable, who can participate remotely across the globe with vital skills.

Forward-thinking companies are doing their best to let prospective employees know that they respect the importance of their lives, their involvement in the community, their families, and their ability to manage multiple demands simultaneously. They want employees to know how valued they are as "whole people." Post–9/11, these issues have become even more salient.

Many research studies show that when companies offer staff resources to help them manage work-life priorities, including flexible schedules, there is a lower rate of job turnover and higher job and customer satisfaction. Lower turnover saves money. According to a 2005 survey by Managing Work/Life Balance, 29 percent of "best practices organizations" say they have data that shows their work-life strategies have contributed to a reduction in staff turnover, and 35 percent say that the strategies have helped increase employee motivation and satisfaction.

Merck and the Saratoga Institute, among others, have documented the cost of turnover. Typically they find that it costs 150 percent to 200 percent of an exempt person's yearly salary to lose them, and 75 percent of a nonexempt person's salary. Deloitte has quantified the cost savings that can be attributed to flexibility by calculating the cost of turnover for those professionals who say they would have left the firm had they not had a flexible arrangement. Based on this calculation, the firm determines that it saved an estimated $41.5 million in turnover-related costs in 2003 alone.

A professional services firm recently documented its losses at two times salary. When the people leaving are not ones the organization wants to lose—undesirable losses—this is clearly not good for the bottom line. These are numbers senior management should be paying attention to.

Figure 22.1 provides an example of a way to quantify the potential cost to a company from turnover related to work-life issues based on a hypothetical company survey.

Employee satisfaction or lack thereof is directly linked to turnover. While many companies have not calculated the cost of turnover, they ignore this expense at the risk of losing competitive advantage. Companies can maximize the investment in their human capital by being more responsive to employees' needs.

Companies Want to Retain Women

Many companies are becoming more sensitive to the proportion of women they recruit and retain, especially now that women graduates represent more than half of all professional programs (e.g., accounting, law, MBAs, etc.). Often work-life issues are the underlying cause for women leaving an organization. In fact, recent company studies have shown that frequently it is the women the organization has a significant investment in—those with five to seven years of experience—who are leaving in large numbers. Typically, these highly competent women, who are in demand elsewhere, are looking for more supportive work environments, and specifically, more flexibility to manage their work and personal lives. Now that half the workforce is female, and more women are taking critical roles in their organizations, it has become even more important to find ways to retain and develop them.

FIGURE 22.1 Annual cost—work-life related turnover.

Of 2,727 survey respondents, 42.4 percent report actively looking or considering looking for a more flexible job at a different company to better manage their work and personal life.

Assuming one-third of those looking or considering looking actually leave, the estimated annual replacement cost of work-life related turnover at Company X is $22,440,000.

Calculation:
- Assumption: Average salary (exempt) = $50,000
- Assumption: Average salary (nonexempt) = $28,000
- Assumption: 70 percent of the population is exempt, 30% nonexempt
- 42.4% of 2,727 employees = 1,156 employees
- Assuming 33 percent of the 1,156 employees looking to leave actually leave = 382 employees leave. Replacement cost* per exempt employee = ($50,000 × 1.5) = $75,000
- Replacement cost* per nonexempt employee ($50,000 × .75) = $21,000
- 267 separated exempt employees × $75,000 = $20,025,000
- 115 separated nonexempt employees × $21,000 = $2,415,000

*Using assumptions that employee turnover costs a company roughly 150 percent of an exempt employee's annual salary (finding a replacement, getting that person up to speed, etc.) and 75 percent of a nonexempt salary as a guideline.

To Raise Morale and Job Satisfaction

The second reason to actively support work-life effectiveness is to raise morale and job satisfaction. Wilson Learning Corporation studied 25,000 workers and concluded that the single most important thing a company could do to improve its performance and bottom line is to increase employee morale. Sears, MCI, and Northern Telecom all conducted studies that found that when employees are satisfied, both customer retention and financial returns go up. Work & Family Connection, Inc. surveyed 153 companies for *Working Mother* magazine, querying them about their work-life programs, how they had evaluated them and what they had found. Out of 40 different work-life initiatives, all but 5 had been found to increase employee satisfaction and morale. The Family and Work Institute's *National Study of the Changing Workforce* also found job satisfaction improved when the work environment was supportive.

In the *2004 Overwork in America Study*, findings show that employees are less likely to feel overworked if they have:

- Jobs that provide more opportunities to continue to learn.
- Supervisors who support them in succeeding on the job.
- The flexibility they need to manage their job and their personal and family life.
- Input into management decision making.

This holds true even when these employees work long hours and have very demanding jobs.

Survey findings from AstraZeneca, the pharmaceutical company, show that commitment scores are 28 percent higher for employees who say they have the flexibility they need compared to employees who do not have the flexibility they need. And, according to *Business Impacts of Flexibility: An Imperative for Expansion* by Corporate Voices for Working Families (November 2005), at Bristol-Myers Squibb, commitment scores of users of flexible work arrangements were higher than that of nonusers, especially in relation to the effective elements of commitment associated with loyalty, job satisfaction, and recommending the company as a good place to work.

To Increase Productivity

The third reason to implement a work-life initiative is to make the people you have more productive. Companies that have studied the results of their work-life programs have found that they reduced absenteeism and increased productivity, which makes sense. People who feel they have more control over how they manage their work and personal lives can focus more intensely on their work. More than half the companies surveyed by Work & Family Connection found that work-life programs increased productivity. Many other companies have reported increases in productivity after initiating a work-life effort. Scott Paper Co., for instance, said its work-life programs increased production by 35 percent. In the case of telecommuting, many studies have found productivity eventually rises when employees can work from home or a more convenient location, even for only a few days a month.

According to the *Way Ahead Report on the Year 2005 Survey* (Managing Work Life Balance International, Australia), 24 percent in best practices organizations, compared with 2 percent in lower-ranked groups, say they have reliable data that shows their work-life strategies have contributed to a positive impact on productivity.

Reducing absenteeism means increasing productivity. The *2004 Unscheduled Absence Survey* by CCH, Inc., a provider of human resources and employment-law information, revealed the hidden costs of unscheduled absences because of work-life issues, ranged from an average of $60,000 for small firms to more than $1 million for large companies.

To Increase Commitment and Engagement

Increased productivity doesn't tell the whole story. Employee commitment and engagement are becoming more important with the increase in knowledge and service workers who can take their knowledge and expertise with them if they leave the job, and whose emotions—how they feel—impact how they do their jobs on a daily basis. Engagement could be defined as when employees:

- Notice when little mistakes are made.
- Try to make sure they're putting out quality work.
- Spend some time thinking about how to do a better job.
- Use time more wisely.
- Don't listen when others put down management or coworkers.
- Give their discretionary effort to the job at hand.

Among employees in effective workplaces, more than twice as many (82 percent) express high levels of job engagement and commitment as employees in ineffective workplaces (36 percent), according to *When Work Works,* a summary of findings from the national *Study of the Changing Workforce* (Families and Work Institute, 2002).

To Reduce Health Care Costs

The fifth reason to implement a work-life initiative is to cut the rise in health care costs. Duke University Medical Center reported in a 1997 study that workplace stress, especially in tandem with a lack of job autonomy, heightens the incidence of depression, anxiety, anger. and a whole range of physical health problems. According to the Stress Institute of America's latest figures, stress is costing U.S. employers about $300 billion per year in lost productivity, health care, and replacement costs. The National Institute for Occupational Safety and Health (NIOSH) reported in 1999 that because the nature of work is changing at whirlwind speed, job stress poses a threat to the health of workers, and in turn, to the health of the organization. In 2000, the World Health Organization reported that by 2020, clinical depression was expected to outrank cancer and follow only heart disease to become the second greatest cause of death and disability worldwide.

It is widely believed that lack of control over one's job can lead to major health problems. *The New York Times* (June 1, 1999) reported on a large-scale study of civil servants in which employees were asked to rate the amount of control they felt over their jobs. Managers also rated the amount of control employees actually had. Job control, the researchers found, varied inversely with employment grade: the higher the grade, the more control. The less control employees had, as defined either by their own or their managers' ratings, the higher the employees' risk of developing coronary disease. Job control, in fact, accounted for about half the gradient in deaths from pay grade to pay grade.

Another study in 2000 by the Health Enhancement Research Organization found the health care bills of employees who suffer from (clinical) depression are 70 percent higher than those of other workers. The study tracked the medical bills of 46,000 employees from several major U.S. companies for up to three years. When several risk factors associated with heart disease were combined—smoking, high blood glucose levels, cholesterol, blood pressure, body weight, and poor exercise habits—medical costs were more than three times those of low-risk workers, and combining stress and depression led to costs nearly 2.5 times higher. The findings come at a time when downsized workforces are being pressured to be productive. The cost of such pressure could be more significant than has been previously acknowledged.

Employers are realizing that to get to the root of the health care cost problem, they must take a more active role in managing the health of their employees. Programs that focus on managing specific diseases and help workers make lifestyle behavior changes aimed at weight management, exercise, and smoking cessation can go a long way toward slowing rising costs over the long term.

Nearly 7 of 10 respondents (69 percent) are using disease management programs through a health plan this year, a 50 percent increase over last year, according to the 2005 Watson Wyatt *Health Survey of Large Employers*. Similarly, the number of employers adopting lifestyle behavior change through a health plan doubled to 40 percent this year. Additionally, 32 percent offer obesity-reduction programs, compared with just 14 percent in 2004.

To Combat Burnout

"Burnout" may be hard to define, but both employees and their employers feel its effects. Employees who feel "burned out" tend to leave the organization, have less commitment and focus, be depressed, and have a host of stress-related illnesses that include heart disease and cancer as well as headaches and other minor but debilitating ailments.

One study that found burnout and stress were very closely related, and 4 out of every 10 workers told researchers they thought about quitting because of it. While most companies think stress is too "soft" an issue to demand their attention, 50 percent of workers surveyed said job stress and burnout had reduced their productivity. Of those who reported having "severe" stress, 59 percent wanted to quit, and 55 percent said they became ill more frequently.

Sixty-one percent of workers say their workloads increased over the last six months of 2005, contributing to increased stress levels and dissatisfaction with work-life balance, according to the results of the CareerBuilder.com annual survey that projects recruitment and job search activities for the coming year. Thirty-one percent of those same workers say they are struggling to balance both professional and personal commitments.

A 2001 study by the Families and Work Institute (FWI) found that one in three U.S. employees experienced feeling overworked as a chronic condition. In a follow-up 2004 study, FWI found that 26 percent of employees were overworked often or very often in the last month, 27 percent were overwhelmed by how much work they had to do often or very often in the last month, and 29 percent often or very often didn't have time to step back and process or reflect on the work they were doing during the last month. This study also found that 44 percent of U.S. employees were overworked often or very often according to these measures. The more overworked employees are, the more likely they are to make mistakes at work and to feel angry with their employers for expecting them to do so much.

AON Consulting's 1999 America@Work study found more than half of the 1,800 workers surveyed said they were burned out by job stress. A 2005 study showed that employees at Bristol-Myers Squibb who use flexible work arrangements are significantly less likely to report feeling stressed and burned out. Those on flexible arrangements scored, on average, 30 percent lower in stress and burnout (Corporate Voices for Working Families, 2005). A New England-based financial services company found that employees who say they have the control they need over their work schedules have burnout index scores less than half that of employees who do not have control over their work schedules. And WFD Consulting found that employees who have control over their work schedules are more committed to their employers and are less likely to suffer from burnout.

To Attract Investors

The seventh reason is that shareholders increasingly value companies that are good citizens, are good to their employees, and are active in their communities. There are a number of new studies that show such supportive companies are more profitable, including one from Cornell University. That study concluded that the way a firm treats its employees may be a window on both its stock price and survival rate. When companies treated their workers well—offering stock options and profit sharing, providing training, emphasizing employee relations—they would be more likely than other new companies to still be doing business five years down the road.

The Cornell study tracked the 136 nonfinance companies that went public in 1988 and found personnel policies were an important factor for the 60 percent that survived five years later. Study author professor Theresa Welbourne concluded, "In the long run, employee rewards get you the performance you need in an organization." And according to Harvard Business School professor Rosabeth Moss Kanter, a comparison of the 20-year performance of progressive companies (those with a variety of human resource programs) and nonprogressive companies found that the former had significantly higher long-term profitability and financial growth.

Watson Wyatt's Human Capital Index found that firms with high employee satisfaction have decidedly higher market value—and that a flexible work place is associated with a 9 percent change in market value.

First Tennessee Bank also used flexibility as a centerpiece in putting the service profit chain theory into practice. In several branches, the bank trained managers on flexibility practices and focused on creating a work environment in those branches that was supportive of flexibility and people's personal lives. The result was that employee retention in these branches proved to be 50 percent higher than in other branches, and this contributed to a greater retention rate of customers at these branches. The bank demonstrated that as employee satisfaction increased, customer retention increased by 7 percent, which translated into $106 million profit increment in two years' time.

In an analysis of its employee survey results, Ernst and Young found that individuals' perceptions of their own flexibility are highly predictive of level of commitment, which in turn was found to be highly predictive of revenue per person as well as retention. The firm found that business units in the top quartile of people commitment scores had revenue per person that was 7 percentage points better than business units in the middle half, and 20 percentage points better than business units in the lowest quartile of people commitment scores. This led the firm to conclude that having flexibility is an important driver of performance and, ultimately, of financial results.

To Be a Good Corporate Citizen

The eighth reason is simply that it's the right thing to do and it can demonstrate support for the community from which both clients and the workforce are drawn. Companies are becoming more aware of the connection between their employees, their customers, and the larger community. Some companies, such as Prudential, are beginning to examine ways to link their volunteer initiatives with employees' career development—benefiting employees, the company, and the community. Today, the most progressive companies focus not only on their employees' needs, but also on the larger community in which they live and work. In some cases, companies leverage their corporate contributions and community relations resources to support this win-win effort.

WAYS TO ADDRESS WORK-LIFE ISSUES

One way to describe work-life efforts is to separate them into categories according to programs, policies and benefits, and practices. While the following is not an exhaustive list, it does provide some examples of each category.

Programs

Often the intent is to offer "something for everyone" in terms of work-life programs. While every employee won't use every program, over their careers, most employees will make use of some of the following offerings:

- Adoption assistance.
- Car maintenance or repair services.
- Career planning.
- Child-care assistance to find and manage care.
- Company cafeteria or store.
- Corporate discounts, reserved spaces, and preferred customer status at child-care centers.
- Child-care centers on-site or nearby.
- Educational scholarships or tuition reimbursement for employees and/or their children.
- Dependent care reimbursement accounts.
- Educational seminars for employees to help them handle personal responsibilities.
- Elder-care case management and other elder-care support services.
- Emergency or back-up care subsidy or on-site emergency care centers.

- Fitness centers, on- or near-site, and/or local centers (subsidized).
- Housing assistance (either financial aid or help in locating housing).
- Information and support for both elder-care and child-care needs.
- Literacy and remedial education mentoring.
- Nursing room and lactation assistance.
- Overnight travel child-care expense subsidies.
- Pagers for expectant fathers.
- Peer support groups.
- Recreation site for family use.
- Relocating assistance for families.
- Reserved parking for pregnant employees.
- Summer camp or other summer care; summers off.
- Warm line for after-school phone calls.
- Wellness and prevention programs.

Policies and Benefits

The trend among leading companies is to reexamine and redesign policies and benefits to ensure that they reflect the company's commitment to mutual trust and respect, to treating employees like responsible adults, and to reducing health care costs while focusing on outcomes and results. In some cases, companies are examining their time-off practices and are allowing employees to take all their paid leave days—personal or emergency days, vacation, and sick days—for whatever purpose they want without having to present their need, make the case, and secure permission. This type of "paid leave bank" has grown in use and is being found not only to raise morale and save money, but to give employees more control over their time. This helps make employees feel as if they're being treated like adults instead of children who have to ask permission for every day off and present the reasons to someone for approval. Companies are also realizing that employees need true time off, time away from work, to regenerate, which can help reduce health care costs while improving productivity.

Many companies are examining their benefits to determine if a life-cycle approach is more appropriate to meet increasingly diverse employee needs. Some companies have instituted flexible (cafeteria) benefits that allow employees to select from a menu of options and make choices based on individual career and life stage. While most cafeteria plans primarily focus on traditional benefits, in some cases companies are experimenting with including work-life related benefits as well. For example, Xerox implemented a life-cycle benefit that allowed employees to use a $10,000 lifetime account to help pay for child care, buy a home, and finance other work-life related needs.

Other work-life related polices and benefits might include the following:

- Gradual return to work after parental, family, or disability leave.
- Flexible work arrangements.
- Phased retirement.
- Time off to volunteer or for community service.
- Sabbaticals.
- Family sick days.
- Subsidies to pay for child- or elder-care services.
- Convenience services.

- Financial assistance to equip a home office.
- Group insurance policies for life, home, car.
- Subsidies for health/fitness classes, gyms, and so forth.

Innovative companies are taking a strategic approach by analyzing their existing policies and benefits, examining employee needs, and identifying gaps in services. It is important that such an analysis include a review of those policies and benefits based on usage, value, and cost.

Practices

Workplace practices and culture are inextricably tied together; it is impossible to view one without the other. Enlightened companies are changing the way work is done in order to become more efficient and to alter their company cultures. Flexibility is the work-life practice most frequently requested by employees, and most major companies claim to offer it. But for most companies that means a policy that says, "If it's okay with your manager, it's okay to be flexible." *Fortune* Magazine's annual "Best Companies To Work For" issue includes criteria such as whether a company surveys its employees. Great Places To Work Institute conducted the research for *Fortune* and found that employee answers and company executives' answers about company flexibility were often different.

The goal for leading-edge companies now is to treat employees as trusted, responsible adults with unique personal and career needs. Rather than focusing on obeying rules, their focus is on outcomes and results. The flexible scheduling tools that facilitate this change include job sharing, telecommuting, compressed workweeks, part-time work, temporary part-time work, and informal flexibility—which allows employees to leave work when necessary and make up the time and/or work later.

SUPPORTIVE WORK ENVIRONMENT

The impact of a supportive work environment cannot be overestimated. A study by Stewart Friedman, of the University of Pennsylvania's Wharton School of Management, and Jeff Greenhause, Drexel University, shed new light on ways that a supportive work environment impacts the workplace, its workers, and their home lives. The researchers reported in March of 1999 that they had tracked 861 graduates of Wharton and Drexel, questioning them several years after they graduated about their work, their families, and the impact each had on the other. In every case where the organization was perceived as supportive (family-friendly), flexibility and self-control were present. Those in a supportive work environment felt better about their performance at home, took more time for personal relaxation, worried less about work when they did, and reported no difference in work performance. Their families interfered less with work, and they experienced fewer work-life conflicts. They were more satisfied with their jobs and their careers. They were more likely to align their future career plans with the future direction of the firm. They were more committed to the long-term interests of the organization. Working parents rated themselves more highly as parents.

The study drew a clear picture that, in truth, summarizes 10 years of learning about work-life. It indicates that work and life are irrevocably connected. Work and personal life have a circular impact; one cannot be experienced without a reaction from the other. Friedman has since extended that work by creating a process for improving leadership skills that involves aligning personal goals for family and community along with business objectives. Implemented at Ford Motor Company, these tools are beginning to be used by other companies and organizations.

COMPANY CULTURE

Each corporation has a unique company culture, its own way of doing business. Factors that influence a company's culture include:

- Company's leaders and values.
- Type of industry.
- Age and size of the company.
- Geographic location.
- Union or nonunion.
- Centralized or decentralized.
- Private or public institution.
- Structure of the company (pyramid organizational structure or flatter organizational structure).
- Workforce demographics.

All of these factors combined create a unique workplace—one that has different cultural norms, different resources and restrictions, and unique ways of addressing workplace issues. Each corporate culture dictates the way business is conducted. If the corporate environment is extremely conservative, a strong "code of conduct" may exist that discourages alterations to the traditional office-based, 40-hour, 9-to-5, and 5 days-a-week schedules.

But studies increasingly point to the need to change the way work is done. The Ford Foundation sponsored a three-year study (1993–1996) at Xerox, Tandem Computers, and Corning to see if taking steps to integrate work and personal life would improve business performance, work-life effectiveness, and gender equity. The study found that traditional assumptions should be reexamined and work tasks reengineered. It showed that business concerns are inextricably tied to work-life issues and that the same innovative, systemic changes that ease work-life dilemmas will also help to achieve business goals.

Academics from Radcliffe Public Policy Institute, working with New England-based Fleet Financial Group (now part of Bank of America), quantitatively measured the impact of work redesign on both home life and work. The study posed three questions to workers: How is work organized and what are the business measures for success? How does the way work is organized affect employees' personal lives? How can changes in the way work is done positively affect both business outcomes and employees' lives?

Researchers heard from staff about sleepless nights, neglected families, too much work, and a sense of frenzy about getting everything done. Employees began to brainstorm in order to come up with suggestions for how their work might be redesigned. The changes they chose seem simple at first glance: a shifting of administrative tasks, a new way to assign credit applications, a new form designed to yield more complete information, and, of course, new flexibility—flextime at one site and telecommuting at both sites.

With strong leadership, a company culture can change rapidly. For work-life efforts to succeed, champions must make every effort to obtain resolute support from top management, to set clear, measurable goals, and to assess progress and reward managers who demonstrate supportive behavior. As companies move from implementing work-life programs toward work redesign and culture change, many new challenges and rewards will surface.

WORK-LIFE STRATEGY

Just as with other business undertakings, in order to successfully develop, implement, and manage a work-life initiative there must be a strategy that is aligned with the overall business strategy. The Boston College Work & Family Roundtable for Employers recommends the following guiding principles to help shape a work-life strategy. These guiding principles can be used by organizations of any size as a guide for a self-assessment process.

The guiding principles are:

1. The employer recognizes the strategic value of addressing work and personal life issues.
   - Business is practiced with sensitivity to employees' personal life needs.
   - Work and personal life solutions are aligned with business goals.
   - The employer's commitment to addressing work and personal life issues is viewed as a long-term investment.
   - Work and personal life strategies are flexible enough to meet changing transitional and employee needs.
2. The work environment supports individual work and personal life effectiveness.
   - The employer's informal culture supports healthy work and personal life management.
   - The employer provides meaningful work and personal life programs and policies.
   - The employer is committed to ongoing education of key stakeholders: employees, management, and the community.
   - The employer strives for continuous improvement through ongoing evaluation and assessment.
3. The management of work and personal life effectiveness is a responsibility shared by employer and employee.
   - Managers and employees are empowered to develop solutions that address both business and personal objectives.
   - Managers and employees are held accountable for their behavior in support of these objectives.
4. The employer develops relationships to enhance external work and personal life resources.
   - Partnerships are formed to maximize the value of employer and community resources available to employees and community members.
   - The employer serves as an active role model.
   - The employer is open to working with the public sector to strengthen policies that benefit both employers and individuals.

Developing a Work-Life Vision

A work-life vision can help shape your strategic plan. In many cases, organizations have developed mission or vision statements that, while they may not state it explicitly, may have elements related to work-life issues. For example, if the organization's mission statement includes concepts related to people, the community, respect, excellence, customer service, and so forth, these can all be linked to work-life.

To develop a work-life vision statement, it is helpful to start with a "straw man" or sample statement and ask key people in the organization to react to it. The process of developing a work-life vision encourages the company to recognize the connection between the work-life initiatives and the organization's purpose. It provides a roadmap for current and future decision making regarding programs, policies, benefits, and practices.

Marketing Work-Life Initiatives

As work-life programs, policies, benefits, and practices are developed, marketing becomes critical. The process of internally marketing work-life programs requires creativity and perseverance on the part of all those involved. It also requires considerable knowledge about the organization, its culture, and the relevance of work-life issues to the company's goals and concerns. In terms of marketing the work-life agenda, it is important to know whom to target and the likely obstacles or resistances that will be encountered.

Effective marketing is necessary if any new concept or product is to survive. Marketing new products and/or services and dealing with new ideas is very difficult and challenging. In many ways, marketing work-life programs and policies is similar to marketing any other human resource program. The key to getting a company to adopt work-life programs and to making them successful is to take a basic marketing approach and sell the ideas as part of an overall business strategy that meets corporate objectives. Promoting work-life is an ongoing process that must include constant feedback and communication. Packaging the work-life message, customizing communication for different target audiences, and involving employees all contribute to the long-term success of a work-life agenda.

Marketing can be defined as the performance of business activities that direct the flow of goods and services from producer to consumer or user. Some basic principles that apply to marketing work-life are:

- *Know your customer(s) and assess needs.* Conduct an informal or formal work-life needs assessment. Identify the key audience(s) and separate those groups in terms of their different needs. For example, identify the employee segments that a new program is most likely to benefit. Then estimate the size of the segment and project the benefits to the company that are expected from the program. Quantify the benefits as much as possible. Always include ongoing market research—ask customers what they like, dislike, want, don't want, and so on.
- *Know your culture.* What works in one corporate culture may not work in another. Companies are like families; in some ways they are very similar, and in many ways they are very different. Consider what has been effective in your organization in the past and why. Develop a work-life marketing plan that takes into account the "personality" of your organization. Know current "hot" issues

in the company, where the "pain" is (recruitment, retention, absenteeism, etc.). Involve someone in the process who really understands the corporate culture. Be aware of the image the company wants to project. Know if there is a new division, product, or market niche that is being developed.

- *Attach work-life agenda to business needs.* Establish a positioning strategy that defines the work-life program in terms of its benefits to the target audience(s) and to the organization's short-term and long- term goals. Find out if the company is concerned about quality, diversity, productivity, morale, cost savings, downsizing, and so forth, and use this to promote the work-life agenda.

- *Check out the competition.* Benchmark the activities of your competition. This competition can be from different companies or within the company or division. Sibling rivalry, which is in keeping with the work-life tradition, can be useful in getting senior management's attention. Consider ways work-life programs and policies can help define your organization as different/better than the competition. Find ways to keep people informed about what the competition is doing on work-life issues. Also assess competing issues or products that may draw needed resources and attention away from the work-life agenda.

- *Identify key decision makers and their preferred influence style.* Know who has to be convinced and find out how she or he prefers to be influenced. Consider visual, verbal, written, face-to-face, and phone, as well as formal presentations. Anticipate objections that will be raised and develop tactics to overcome those objections.

- *Position work-life in its broadest context.* Develop a sequential or staged approach for focusing on different audiences and/or objectives. Try not to compartmentalize each work-life initiative as a separate item; package the whole "product" instead. Work-life is not one thing (for example, child care), but a combination of many policies, benefits, and programs. Consider the life cycle of employees and include the needs of singles, retirees, and so forth in your plans.

- *Use internal and external resources.* Explore a wide range of methods and approaches to communicate about work-life programs and policies. Internal resources might include newsletters, posters, e-mail messages, and so on. External resources might be the local press, community organizations, and so forth. Also involve a wide range of resources in your information gathering and evaluation process, including consultants, professional organizations, and publications and conferences.

HOW TO BEGIN

Marketing involves understanding and addressing your customer's needs and wants and getting feedback. It is important not to assume that the customer's needs/wants are known. Programs have failed when they were implemented for the wrong audience and/or the wrong reason. In many companies, the decision maker for work-life issues is senior management. The person who is often responsible for selling programs to senior management may be the head of human resources or benefits. Each person has his or her own agenda. The work-life strategy must take into account the interim decision makers as well as the final decision maker.

Getting to know your customer is critical to planning a successful work-life program. As it was said about Alice in Wonderland, "If you don't know where you're going, how will you know when you get there?" A work-life strategy must be carefully thought out and developed. The word "strategy" is taken from the Latin word meaning "battle plan," and that is what is required. Too often, work-life initiatives are undertaken because someone thinks they are "nice to do." Work-life programs can be implemented for many reasons—to keep up with the competition, to recruit and retain the desired workforce, to improve morale and/or productivity, and so forth—but how work-life programs and policies will serve the needs of the intended audience must always be clear.

In developing a marketing plan, it is important to determine where support will come from and where there might be a restraining factor. In some cases, the support or restraint will be a person, and in other cases it might be an organizational issue or resource. Whatever the case, successful marketing requires that you make the best use of supportive forces while you cope with or minimize the restraining forces.

In the best of all possible worlds, the organization's values dictate its mission. Strategies evolve from the mission and indicate tasks that need to be accomplished. When this kind of organizational structure is in place, the marketing strategies for work-life initiatives can be clearly determined. However, in most organizations, there is not such a clear definition of purpose or direction. This makes it somewhat more difficult to determine the appropriate strategy for creating and marketing work-life programs. Deciding the appropriate course for marketing work-life programs and policies involves research, advertisement, public relations, and communication.

SOURCE OF COMMITMENT

It's clear that the more senior management support there is for work-life issues, the better. The reasons why a company begins to address the work-life needs of employees vary greatly. The reasons might be organizational, personal, or those that result from some external influence. In some companies, unions are influential in getting work-life on the agenda. In other organizations, there is an informal network, often of mothers, that may work for years trying to determine the needs and then presenting ideas to management. In some cases, the work-life agenda surfaces when the company realizes it is having recruitment and/or retention difficulties with a particular segment of the workforce.

Some companies respond to their competition's activities and initiate programs and/or policies in an attempt to "keep up with the Joneses," especially when another company's initiative receives positive press. In some companies, work-life programs are implemented because they are consistent with the organization's philosophy or culture. In some organizations, if the CEO or other senior leader experiences a work-life problem personally, that is when the organization develops a response. Whatever the originating cause for implementing work-life programs initially, once started, they tend to continue and expand.

It is important to note that there is no guarantee for successful marketing of work-life programs. One might assume that with top management's involvement, support from all levels within the organization will be forthcoming. However, that is not necessarily the case. Senior management may have indicated support for work-life initiatives, but to sustain work-life programs, this support needs to be continuously nurtured and expanded to middle managers.

ANTICIPATING PROBLEMS

Be prepared to respond appropriately to obstacles. There will always be resistance to implementing work-life initiatives. One thing to check is the vocabulary that is used to describe the work-life initiatives and how they are communicated and marketed to the various stakeholders. There are many "messages" that are heard within organizations that may or may not be accurate but are often given as the reason why a particular work-life initiative cannot be undertaken. In many cases, these obstacles can be counteracted with timely, accurate information. What is important is to identify the obstacle, to understand what it means, especially taking into consideration its source, and then to prepare to counteract it.

DEVELOPING AN APPROPRIATE MARKETING STRATEGY

The appropriate marketing strategy depends on where the company is in the process of developing a work-life initiative. The strategy will be somewhat different for a company that is at the beginning stages of developing a work-life agenda versus a company that wants to expand an existing program or a company that is involved in changing its corporate culture.

A needs assessment can be conducted to find out what kind of work-life initiatives are appropriate and what the priorities might be. The involvement of an experienced work-life consultant can be invaluable when conducting a needs assessment. The assessment might be formal or informal. A formal needs assessment could involve focus groups, questionnaires, and/or an attitude survey. It might be done to investigate the company's goals, employee needs, and/or community resources. A task force, steering committee, or other interested group can conduct an informal assessment.

For a company at the beginning of the process of developing a work-life agenda, one of the first steps might be just to get official permission to study the issue or to gather information. A work-life task force can be an effective method of collecting information and making recommendations. If a task force is formed, it is important to include members representing diverse groups or positions within the company. If possible, a high-level champion should function as the leader or spokesperson of the group. The goal of the task force is to define a direction for the company regarding work-life issues. Individual issues must be handled in such a way that they can be easily explained and related to the overall business strategy of the organization.

In some companies, the first job of a work-life task force is not to solve a particular problem but to position work-life as part of a larger effort to improve productivity. In this way, the value of work-life to the organization is clear, and the mission of the work-life task force is seen as relevant to the organization's success. The task force should go about obtaining the necessary information on work-life issues just as it would for any other business issue it might be investigating. If necessary, contact other companies to find out how they have handled particular situations. It is not necessary to reinvent the wheel!

PUTTING IT ALL TOGETHER: CHECKLIST

You may find that employees may rate individual work-life programs as marginally important or unimportant when they are considered separately. However, when presented and described as a group under one umbrella, employees will most likely rate them as very or extremely important. It all depends on how these initiatives are developed, implemented, and communicated.

Consider the following when planning your overall work-life strategy:

- *Know your customers.* This may include management, employees, those within the organization, representatives from the community, and so forth.
- *Package the product.* Create a look, a logo that communicates the message you want to convey about work-life initiatives.
- *Deliver a consistent product over time.* This helps build awareness and manage employee expectations.
- *Develop linkages/connections to other work-life related programs, policies, and practices.*
- *Think long term, but propose in stages/phases/segments.* Be aware of what you want to accomplish over the long term, but if it helps sell the program or policy, present it in smaller segments. Once that part is proven successful, then you can return and ask for approval for another part of the program.
- *Pilot, pilot, pilot.* It may be easier to sell a program or policy to senior management if they know it is a test. This is also helpful because it allows you to experiment and modify as you go along. Letting employees know that the program is a pilot is also useful because they can understand if something has to be changed to make the service more effective.
- *Live by "just enough" or "just manageable difficulty" motto.* It helps to give senior management the information that they need to know to make a decision, but no more. Too much information can be overwhelming, especially when you are not familiar with the subject. There have been situations where a work-life task force or committee has worked for long periods of time to research the topic and when they finally present to senior management, they try to review everything they have learned and recommend everything they want to accomplish for the next five years. This is too much. Determine what the goal is for senior management. Is it to get buy-in, to make a commitment to begin, to adopt a work-life strategy, or to implement a particular program or policy? Chunk down—overkill usually does not work.
- *Evaluate and report progress.* Emphasize the *process*, not just the product. Track the number of employees who use a particular program or policy. Count those who sign up for a program, as well as those who show up. That way, you can choose to report both numbers (usually sign ups exceed show ups). Be creative with cost/benefit analysis information. It may be difficult to obtain hard data to document the cost/benefit of all work-life programs.
- *Watch for "smoke screens" of resistance.* Some companies have conducted extensive research on work-life options, and when they were finally presented to the president, they were not approved. In some cases, the reasons given had to do with liability and insurance. In reality, these were not real problems, but management could not be convinced at that time. The same kind of argument is sometimes given for not implementing flexible scheduling—that everyone will want to work part-time, or that there will be no way to know that people are really working if they work from home. In these cases, providing examples of other companies' experience can often alleviate these fears. In other cases, proposing a pilot project over a specific period of time can be a way to get started.

- *Consider the message and the medium.* Effective marketing requires that you think about both the content and the media that can be used. There are many ways to "cross market" work-life programs.
- *Use a variety of vehicles/tools for marketing work-life programs.* A good marketing strategy does not depend on one kind of media to convey its message. Try to use a variety, including e-mail, newsletters, activities like an expo, videos, speeches or talks, brochures, and so forth. Even meetings that promote the work-life agenda can be considered marketing. Sometimes just including an influential person on the distribution list of relevant material can be part of a marketing strategy. A good marketing strategy might tie a program or activity to a "theme" to help employees remember to use it.
- *Consider internal and external marketing activities.* Some of the most effective marketing efforts within companies have begun with an article in the local press. The article might even be talking about your competition.
- *Promote your success stories.* You must be your own best advocate. Be sure the internal newsletter covers work-life activities and programs. If there is an example of job sharing, perhaps the partners can be interviewed. If an employee writes a letter praising a particular service, find a way to share that praise, if only with senior management. Keep track of employee contacts about programs and requests for additional services. Document any contacts from the press or media. When there are articles about your work-life programs and policies, be sure that they are copied to all those involved. Keep your communication network very active.
- *Collect other companies' materials.* Share your materials (brochures, flyers, booklets, web sites, etc.) with others and ask them to do the same. A great deal of information and many good ideas can be gathered from examining these materials. Even if you are not ready to implement a marketing idea today, keep a file of these materials so that when you are ready for the next step, the material will be at your fingertips.

CALCULATING THE RETURN ON INVESTMENT

For the success of work-life initiatives, it is important to strategically determine the most appropriate programs, policies, benefits, and practices for each organization. In order to accomplish that goal, an analysis of current and future programs, policies, and practices is critical. The process includes documenting all work-life related initiatives and determining their real and perceived value to employees.

These findings can then be used to determine the most highly valued and cost effective programs, policies, and practices, as shown in Figure 22.2.

Cost and Value

By analyzing existing polices and benefits according to business or employee value (real and perceived) as well as cost, it is possible to see where the greatest return on investment (ROI) exists. Clearly, those initiatives that are low in cost and highly valued, as well as possibly those that are high in cost yet have high value, are the ones the organization most likely should retain and support. Those with high cost and low value, or low cost and low value, might be modified or eliminated.

FIGURE 22.2 Documenting work-life initiatives using the quadrant approach.

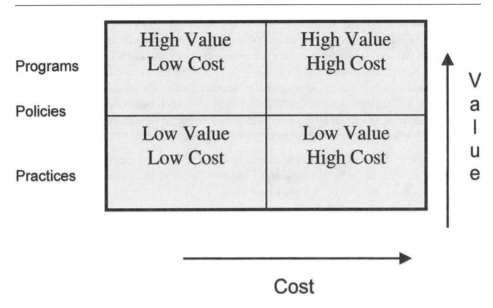

Developing the most appropriate combination of work-life effectiveness programs, policies, and practices will lead to improved prevention, increased productivity, and "presenteeism" as well as employee passion. These are all necessary for bottom-line success, that is, improved profitability.

THE FUTURE OF WORK-LIFE EFFECTIVENESS

The Society for Human Resource Management (SHRM) asked a panel of HR experts to make predictions for the future of HR. The top 10 predictions for work and society point to the importance of work-life initiatives for the future. Their predictions, presented in the order of importance, were:

1. Family and life interests will play a more prominent role in people's lives and will be a greater factor in people's choices about work—there will be more of a "work to live" than a "live to work" mentality.
2. Employees will demand increases in workplace flexibility in order to pursue life interests.
3. Dual-career couples will refuse to make the sacrifices required today in their family lives, and more people (not just women) will opt out of traditional careers.
4. Families will return to the center of society; work will serve as a source of cultural connections and peripheral friendships.
5. Workers will continue to struggle with their need for work-life effectiveness, and it will get worse.

6. Integration of work with quality-of-life initiatives will create solutions to problems formerly seen as the responsibility of government.

7. Community involvement and social responsibility will become part of an organization's business vision.

8. "Cocooning" will become more popular as workers look to their homes for refuge from the pressures of a more competitive workplace and depersonalized society.

9. Companies will take on increasing responsibility for elder care, long-term care, and other social needs through cafeteria-style benefits programs.

10. Those people who refuse or are unable to adapt to new technologies will find they're working harder and accomplishing less.

Only time will tell if these predictions will come true, but one thing we do know: The issue of work-life effectiveness will continue to grow in importance as long as work depends on people to get the job done.

23 Caring for Dependents

The first work-life conundrum encountered by employers centered on options for child care because of a huge influx of women entering the workforce following WWII. In light of today's aging population, a growing number of employees now contend with unprecedented elder-care issues as well.

The emergence of the "sandwich generation"—a growing contingent of working parents who must also cope with the primary responsibility of caring for their own aging parents—has caused some employers to consider implementing dependent care programs.

Although not considered a traditional benefit, or a clearly defined type of compensation, the fact is that organizational support for dependent care *does* effectively put money in the pockets of employees, and it has come to be considered so important to the effectiveness of working parents that companies are now given tax relief for providing it. It is also a source of competitive advantage, since parents and the many employees who become parents during their careers are more likely to choose to join such family-friendly employers and to stay with them longer once hired.

CHILD-CARE ISSUES

Employers today realize that issues related to child care pose many challenges for working parents and the companies themselves. Child care is an infrastructure in our society—it is necessary for working parents to have child care in order to work. According to the Economic Policy Institute, as of 2002, nearly one-half (45 percent) of employed people were raising children while all the adults in the household were working. In 2001, according to the Federal Interagency Forum on Child and Family Statistics, 61 percent of children from birth through age 6 (and not in kindergarten) spent time in some form of child care; the majority were in child care from infancy onward, often for more hours than their parents spent at work. Despite the importance of child care for working parents, there are many difficulties with the child-care delivery system in the United States in terms of its quality, convenience, and affordability.

Regardless of the age of the child, care can be difficult to find and manage, and in most cases is made up of a patchwork of services that parents have to put together for each child. Typically, young (infant-preschool) children are cared for in their own homes, someone else's home (called family child care), in a child-care center, or in some combination of these arrangements. For parents of school-age children, the difficulties don't necessarily disappear. Most school hours don't coincide with parents' work schedules, leaving portions of the day (before and after school), and portions of the year when children must attend another program or take care of themselves while their parents work.

Everyone should be concerned about the lack of quality, affordable child care in our country. Quality of care is directly correlated with a parent's ability to work. When good quality, reliable child care is not available and parents must work, the result is increased anxiety and absenteeism. A potentially larger concern for employers should be the quality of the future workforce. Recent research has emphasized the importance of the experiences in the early years in terms of brain development. As a nation, we cannot afford the long-term cost of poor-quality child care. Companies can play an important role in educating employees and in reinforcing and enhancing the quality of child care in their communities—not only for their employees, but for their customers as well.

Employers first became aware of the connection between the child-care needs of employees and their ability to work in the late 1970s and early 1980s with the influx of women into the workforce. At that time, the primary response to employees' child-care needs was usually thought to be an on- or near-site corporate child-care center. Although some companies were addressing employees' needs in other ways—typically by providing information through resource and referral services and workshops—in the early 1980s (and now as well, to some extent) the media coverage focused primarily on companies that developed child-care centers.

Today, both employees and management are more aware of the range of issues and options related to supporting the needs of working families. It is now clear that child-care centers are not the only option and may not even be the best way to respond. However, in cases when the development of a new child-care program is appropriate, a child-care center can be a wonderful way to respond to working family challenges while at the same time meeting business objectives. Such a center should be considered only after careful examination of employees' needs, the company's goals, and the community's resources. Companies with child-care centers report an increased ability to recruit and retain employees, a reduction in absenteeism related to child-care issues, increases in productivity, improved morale and loyalty (even among childless employees), and an enhanced public image. However, according to a study by the Families and Work Institute, 2 percent of U.S. companies that offered workers access to day care in 2000 had off-site child care, and 3 percent had on-site child care. Among companies that offered child-care benefits, 24 percent perceive negative return on investment, 36 percent think benefits of the program outweigh its cost, and 40 percent perceive child-care programs to be cost-neutral.

When developing a child-care initiative, it's important to consider the broad range of child-care options. These include supporting family child care and/or consortium networks; before- and after-school programs; care for sick children; emergency or back-up care; providing information and support through workshops and counseling and referral services; financial support, including subsidizing the cost of care; a strategic investment in community programs and services; and the option requested most frequently—flexibility and control over time.

A Hewitt *United States Salaried Work-Life Benefits 2003–2004 Survey* of 975 employers found that 95 percent are offering some kind of child-care assistance to employees. The following are the top six types of child-care benefits offered by these companies.

- Dependent care spending accounts—Allow employees to pay for child care out of their salaries on a pretax basis (94 percent).
- Resource and referral services (42 percent).
- Emergency child-care program (13 percent).
- Child-care centers (13 percent).
- Nursing mother's room; lactation consultant (11 percent).
- Employer-arranged discounts with child-care providers (9 percent).

DIRECT CHILD-CARE SERVICES

The three main types of child care for young children (infants–preschool) are:

- *Child-care centers:* care in a facility.
- *Family child-care homes:* care in someone else's home.
- *In-home care:* care in the child's own home.

Any of the three main types of child care might provide the following:

- *Full-time child care:* care during working hours.
- *Back-up/emergency care:* care when a child's current child care is not available, for example, the caregiver is sick or schools are closed.
- *School-age care:* care for a school-age child during school holidays, the summer months, or before and after school.
- *Sick care:* care for mildly ill children.

The need for affordable, convenient, accessible quality child care for working parents is obvious. However, an employer's decision to provide child care requires careful consideration. Any child-care option an employer might support will have advantages and disadvantages that must be carefully weighed in light of specific business, employee, and community needs. Care should be taken to not duplicate existing community services. Employers should consider enhancing existing services by improving their quality and increasing the supply of much-needed care for various groups of children, including infants.

While in most cases licensing, quality control, location, possible vendor selection, and cost will be factors to consider if the company is interested in developing child care, there are many other issues to consider. Figure 23.1 is an outline of some of the advantages and disadvantages of various corporate child-care options.

FIGURE 23.1 Advantages and disadvantages of various corporate child-care options.

Direct Care Program/Description	Advantages	Disadvantages	Other Issues to Consider
On- or Near-site Child-Care Center Sponsored by an employer or union at the worksite or at another location and operated by the employer or by a nonprofit or for-profit child-care provider. Usually employers subsidize the cost, while cost to users is comparable to community rates.	• Often higher quality than most community programs. • Can meet business needs. • Visible support and recruitment tool. • Reduces absenteeism related to child care. • Increases productivity. • Improves morale and loyalty (even among childless employees). • Enhances public image.	• Serves limited population of employees and age group of children. • Start-up is often expensive, and ongoing financial support is required to ensure quality and affordability. • Equity issues, as use is often limited by tuition, space constraints, commuting patterns, etc. • Not always accessible to all employees, particularly those working for multisite companies. • May be open to community children to fill vacancies.	• Well-designed needs assessment should be conducted to determine business, community, and employee needs/interests. • Consideration of type, size, and location of facility as they relate to cost, accessibility, etc. • Extent of quality control desired by the employer and how this relates to liability issues. • Start-up and ongoing management issues. • Possible tax advantages.
Consortium Center Groups of employers share the cost and benefits of establishing and operating an on- or near-site child care center that may be run by community group or vendor.	• Resources, liability, and costs are shared. • Small employers can participate. • Large size of the combined labor force protects the center from long-term under-enrollment.	• May involve complicated negotiations among firms regarding structure, costs, policies, and decision making. • Center may be able to serve only a limited number of employees from each participating.	• Well-designed needs assessment should be conducted to determine business, community, and employee needs/interests. • Amount of employer control over the program has implications for corporate liability.

Program	Advantages	Disadvantages	Considerations
• Community children may be included to fill vacancies.	• Recruitment/public relations value for individual companies may be reduced. • As needs change, some companies may choose to discontinue participation.	firm, thus diluting the value for individual companies.	• Employers often receive tax advantages. • Ongoing subsidy may be necessary to ensure that fees remain affordable for all employees.
Sick Child Care-Program Provides care for children who are mildly ill or recovering from a health problem. Care can be provided in a "sick bay" of a child-care center, in a hospital, or by in-home services such as visiting nurses.	• Improves recruitment, employee morale, and workflow. • Reduces absenteeism. • Relieves stress on parents. • Enhances company image.	• Monitoring quality control may be difficult in a visiting nurse program. • Parents may be reluctant to use caregiver or program that is unfamiliar to the child. • Usage may be low due to unfamiliarity with the concept or cost. • Employers usually subsidize some of the cost of sick child-care programs.	• Well-designed needs assessment should be conducted to determine business, community, and employee needs/interests. • Licensing restrictions might preclude employers from providing sick children services in some states. • Sick children represent a significant cause of absenteeism related to child care among employees. • Hospital-based and visiting nurses are the least expensive to start up.
Back-Up/Emergency Child-Care Program Offers care for employees' children when their regular care is not available, when employees are needed for holiday or weekend work, or	• Provides a relief and timely help for employees. • Can meet emergency child-care needs of large number of employees.	• Usage tends to be higher for single-company on-site facility. • Puchase of slots in consortium center may not meet demand. • Care must be taken to assure parents understand program's "emergency" purpose.	• Well-designed needs assessment should be conducted to determine business, community, and employee needs/interests. • For on-site service, consider what ages and child-care needs will be covered.

(continued)

FIGURE 23.1 (*Continued*)

when schools are closed. Usually vendor-operated for one company or consortium on- or near-site.	• Can provide temporary care for infants as parent transitions back to work from parental leave. • Easy to calculate return on investment. • Relatively small space and small staff required. • Increased productivity. • Reduced absenteeism. • Enhances company image.	• Employers usually subsidize the tuition. • Curriculum and staffing are different from regular child-care program. • Often provides example of "quality" child care. • The cost will vary depending on whether the program is on-site or offsite, its size, type of facility, etc.
Family Child-Care Network A network of individual family child-care home providers who are connected through a child-care center, agency or association. The network provides support services such as training, equipment, lending libraries, and licensing assistance.	• Children can be cared for close to where they live. • Family child-care homes are often more conducive to caring for multi-age groups and siblings. • Can provide infant care, one of the most difficult types of child care to find.	• Much coordination and support needed to be effective. • Home-care providers may be difficult to recruit and retain; quality control is difficult to ensure. • Critical to provide incentives/benefits/training for providers. • Insurance can be an issue; structure of the network may raise tax questions. • Well-designed needs assessment should be conducted to determine business, community, and employee needs/interests. • Networks are less expensive to start up than on-site or consortium centers. • Ongoing financial support is generally advisable. • Quality is closely akin to the availability of support services.

Program			
	• Networks stimulate the supply of community home providers, often the most cost-effective and convenient care for employees.		
School-Age Child-Care Program Provides care for children aged 5-14 before and after school, during school holidays and/or during the summer.	• Addresses one of the most critical child-care shortages. • Provides comfort to children and reduces their anxiety. • Improves morale and reduces parent stress. • Contributes to lower absenteeism and higher productivity.	• Requires transportation if the program is not housed at the child's school. • Programs for older children may be hard to develop, because these children may feel that they are too old for child care.	• Well-designed needs assessment should be conducted to determine business, community, and employee needs/interests. • Location is critical because employees' children are likely to come from a variety of locations. • Availability of organizations and/or sites for the development of such programs can be an issue.

ASSESSING CHILD-CARE NEEDS

The decision to implement child-care options requires a fairly simple needs assessment. Clearly, the most visible work-life option for an employer to support is the development of a child-care center at or near the worksite. Because they are so visible, on- or near-site centers are considered more useful in recruiting and retaining employees than other options. However, the decision to develop a child-care center should not be made lightly. Careful analysis is critical to the success of a company-sponsored child-care center. A decision about whether to implement a child-care program should take into account three important factors:

- Professional investigation of employees' child-care needs and preferences.
- Clarity about employer's goals and resources.
- Knowledge about the supply of and demand for child-care services that already exist in the community.

A child-care center will not meet the needs of all employees, so it's important to simultaneously consider what other programs related to child care that the organization might implement in addition to or instead of a center. These options might include assisting employees with the cost of child care (through a flexible-spending account or subsidies, for example), providing information about community child-care services and educational seminars, or partnering with community agencies to help improve the quality and accessibility of existing child-care services.

A good needs assessment will reveal:

- The kinds of child-care needs employees have (or expect to have).
- The groups of employees having the most needs.
- The impact of employee needs on their work.
- The types of child-care programs that would most effectively address employee needs.

Methods for collecting data include an employee survey and one-on-one interviews with senior management, employee focus groups, human resource focus groups, and so forth.

The decision-making and planning process is considerably more complex for building a child-care facility than for other work-life benefits; therefore, working with an expert is critical. Child care is a regulated industry, and the consultant can help you conduct a feasibility study and develop a request for proposals (RFP) when you are ready to select a company to develop and manage the child-care center.

Some of the things to consider in terms of feasibility are the availability of a site and the financial resources that will be required. Is an appropriate location for a child-care center available? Is it zoned for child-care use? Do you have the financial resources to develop and *maintain* a high-quality center? Also, it is important to have a realistic projection of utilization. As a rough guideline, a majority of experts predict that between 2 percent and 4 percent of the employee population is likely to enroll their children in an employer-sponsored child-care center. If you are using an employee survey to predict utilization, the survey should have a high return rate (50 to 70 percent of employees with children) in order to increase accuracy. Results of employee surveys must be carefully interpreted; typically, only about 50 percent of those parents who *say* they will enroll their children in a corporate-based center actually do so. Accurate prediction of utilization numbers is critical, because centers have closed because of miscalculations about utilization.

When conducting a child-care feasibility study, care should be taken to determine current child-care difficulties experienced by employees, including cost, location, quality, convenience of hours, and so forth. It is extremely important when a company considers developing its own child care to have the feasibility study conducted by an objective third party. Child-care center developers often conduct such studies, but they have a vested interest in the outcome. A child-care counseling and referral service vendor may also provide consulting services or may be able to refer you to an independent consultant who can conduct an objective assessment.

ON-SITE AND NEAR-SITE CHILD-CARE CENTERS

On-site or near-site centers can be for primary care—the ongoing daily care of a child—or for back-up care that is provided on a temporary basis when primary-care arrangements are unavailable. Some centers provide both types of care, but many do not. Back-up care has grown in popularity over the past five years, particularly in urban areas where transporting a child to the work site on a regular basis is impractical for parents. Employees who are able to use an on-site or near-site child-care center usually appreciate the high quality and convenient location.

Additional *advantages* of on-site or near-site centers include the following:

- Absenteeism and lateness related to child-care issues is reduced because of the reliability of the child-care arrangement.
- Morale is improved because employees appreciate the convenience of having child care at or near the worksite.
- A parent is close by to handle unusual upsets and respond in case of an emergency.
- The company can closely monitor the quality of the child-care program.
- The hours of operation can be adjusted to meet the needs of the company and the employees.
- The visibility of a child-care center can help attract and retain employees, can heighten the morale and loyalty of employees who use the center, and can offer positive employee relations opportunities.
- Greater parental involvement in the center's activities is encouraged. Frequent contact between parents and a center can result in better center-parent relationships.
- Employees are able to enjoy a higher quality of child care at a fee typically comparable to fees associated with community-provided child care.
- Employers are eligible for tax incentives.

Disadvantages of on-site or near-site centers include the following:

- The start-up and operating costs can be high, and there is usually a need to subsidize the ongoing operating costs of the center.
- The number of employees who indicate interest will likely be greater than the number who actually sign up once the center is open.
- If the center is not fully enrolled, staff and space may be underutilized.
- There may be equity issues as out-of-office workers, including sales and those working at other locations, may find an on-site center less convenient than other forms of care.
- Waiting lists for a center may cause friction among employees.

- A full-time on-site child-care center may not be practical for employees who travel long distances or use public transportation.
- A child-care center is highly visible and may contribute to a sense of inequity in a multisite company if the center does not serve all locations.

CONSORTIUM CHILD-CARE CENTERS

Consortium child-care centers are developed for several employers who want to function as partners with one another and share resources, liability, and the cost of the facility. They offer a way for smaller companies to provide child care while not taking on all the responsibility, and they also offer a way for multisite companies to possibly address the child-care needs of employees in a variety of locations. A consortium center can be developed to serve employers in the same industry or to serve different industries that are in the same geographic area.

Developing a consortium center requires that the companies involved be able to cooperate in planning and operating the center. They must trust each other and share similar points of view in order for the collaboration to be successful. Often a child-care vendor develops a consortium center and solicits companies to participate. Some possible prerequisites for gaining cooperation among members of a consortium include:

- After a proposal has been initiated, a period of time ("stew time") must be built in to the process to allow the potential members to carefully consider how great their commitment to the center is.
- Vendors can provide information on the general benefits of employer-supported child care and those benefits that are specific to consortium ventures.
- Probable costs, potential problems, and consortium participation should be discussed during stew time.
- Most company officials will need to be educated about the requirements for quality child care and about how a consortium operates.
- Vendors should assist participants in clarifying both individual company and joint consortium goals, and they should point out contradictory or conflicting goals.
- When the financial and contractual commitments for each company are large, prospective members must determine whether or not the costs to their individual organizations are outweighed by the benefits expected from consortium participation.
- Cooperation is influenced by the shared history of the participants; a history of competition can adversely affect the ability of participants to work together.

The interests of the various corporate members of a child-care center consortium may not be equal. This may be the case when a small company with limited child-care needs enters into a consortium with larger companies that have substantial child-care needs. Spaces for children are usually divided according to the employer's estimated percentage of participation in the consortium. To avoid misunderstandings, partners should work out agreements at the outset that deal with procedures for handling management, liability, and withdrawal from the consortium. A consortium can be initiated by a community group or a private developer, or by a group of companies. In case of a vendor, the service is usually marketed to corporations on a per slot basis.

Advantages of a consortium center include the following:

- Because the costs are divided among partners, they may be lower than comparable costs per participant employee in a center sponsored by a single company. When a developer assumes the cost of creating the center, the costs may be even further reduced.
- Liability is shared. Because the consortium is often established as an independent entity, participating companies may be legally distanced from claims that may arise out of a damage or injury suit.
- Community relations and intercompany employee relations can be strengthened.
- A decline in use by one company can be offset by use by other participating companies.
- Multisite companies have the possibility of replicating the consortium model in other locations.

Disadvantages of a consortium center include the following:

- The financial stability of the consortium depends on the financial stability of all of the partners.
- The demand for spaces in the center may be greater than the supply, and the consortium may not have the flexibility to expand.
- Rules for who may use the center and how much they must pay (or how much employees must copay) may differ widely among the partners in the consortium. Policy setting, paperwork, and procedures for handling problems may become complex and difficult for staff to manage.
- Public relations advantages, although still significant, may be somewhat diluted, because no single company gets full credit for the center.

In addition to regular, full-time care, consortium centers are a popular way to provide back-up care and emergency child care.

BACK-UP (EMERGENCY) CHILD CARE

Parents must have some form of child care in place so that it's possible for them to go work. But, because of the nature of the child-care delivery system in this country, parents must often rely on a patchwork of arrangements. And it is not unusual for something to go wrong—a caregiver gets sick or takes time off, a center or school is closed, and so on. When care breaks down, parents often have no alternative but to take time off and stay home with the child, which is estimated to cost American businesses more than $3 billion a year in lost productivity. Realizing the stress involved and the enormous cost in lost productivity, employers are addressing the need for back-up or emergency care in a variety of ways. Employers can establish or reserve slots in an on-site or near-site back-up child-care center, or they can contract with a service that provides in-home care. Typically, employee use of these services is fully or partially subsidized by the employer.

Hewitt's *2004–2005 U.S. Salaried Work/Life Benefits Report* shows that of 936 employers surveyed, 97 percent offer some type of child-care benefit and 12 percent offer sick/emergency child care. State regulations, or the lack of them, don't seem to be a barrier to growth. Back-up care allows companies to provide services to a larger number of employees than a full-time child-care center can, and back-up child care's clear-cut effect on productivity (through reduced absenteeism) makes it easy to quantify savings. Back-up care, which is used occasionally, also makes a lot of sense in urban areas where it may be impractical for employees to bring their children to a worksite child-care center on a daily basis. Most back-up centers are facilities built specifically to care for children when their regular care is not available, although some permanent child-care centers also provide back-up care. Some companies offer back-up care in addition to permanent or full-time care; others offer only back-up care. Back-up care requires less space and a different staffing pattern that full-time child care. The registration and reservation processes must be carefully established and handled so that when there's a need, employees can use the facility.

CARE FOR SICK CHILDREN

For all working parents and their employers, care for a sick child is another major problem. The overwhelming majority of employees must change their child-care arrangements when their children become ill. The American Medical Association estimates that children become sick between 6 and 10 times a year, and studies indicate the rate of absenteeism because of sick children ranges from four and a half to eight days per year.

Sick child day care is a complex problem for employers. Even if parents are able to attend work when their children are sick, they are often stressed and less productive. Most prefer to stay home at the beginning of an illness or if their child is very sick and to use their paid sick leave to care for a sick child. In worksite focus groups, parents frequently talk about how torn they feel when they have to choose between staying home and leaving a sick child. Often they feel forced to lie to their employers, calling in to say they are sick in order to get a paid sick day off, when it is really their child who is ill. It is a no-win situation for most parents. In using sick days for their child's illness, employees may not have any leave left for their own illness. They often go to work even when they're not well themselves, because they're afraid they will not have any sick days left if and when their child becomes sick. In some cases, new technology has allowed employees to work from home when their child is sick, and some companies are changing their sick leave policies by creating time-off "banks" to help employees avoid this problem.

Most child-care programs do not now permit enrollment of sick children. However, regulations are being developed in most states to allow child care for sick children. Options for care generally include freestanding centers dedicated to the care of sick children, hospital-based centers, "sick bays" attached to regular centers, Family Child Care homes, and in-home care. Although pediatricians have traditionally been opposed to child care for sick children, in the last few years pediatricians have changed their position and are now becoming involved in child care for sick children in a variety of ways—from providing advice to actually running centers. At an average cost of $40 to $50 per day (in addition to the cost of regular child care), most child care for sick children cannot exist without employer subsidies. Many companies are becoming more comfortable with the concept of child care for sick children and are accepting the cost because they recognize that what they save by reducing absenteeism more than offsets the cost.

Hospital-based child-care centers for sick children have historically had the longest lives. Freestanding centers have difficulty surviving financially but have been known to work, especially when they have enough corporate support. Some full-time child-care centers are adding "sick bays" where specially trained care-givers provide care to mildly ill children in specifically allocated and designed space.

SCHOOL-AGE CHILD CARE

There are many times during the year when schools are closed and school-age children require additional care. This can include daily before- and after-school care, summers, and school holidays. There are approximately 1,000 hours in the year when school-age children are not at school or with their parents. Employees whose children care for themselves before and after school miss an average of 13 days of work.

Research has documented the fear, loneliness, and boredom children who are left home alone ("latchkey kids") feel and the stress this causes their working parents. Research indicates that there are other reasons to help employees who need school-age child care. School-age programs might be located in the child's school, in a Family Child Care home, a child-care center, a church or synagogue, a recreation center, or a community center. The key point is that these programs must supplement the normal school schedule in order to meet the working parent's schedule.

Corporate support for the care of school-age children can take many forms, including training in self-help skills. Employer-supported programs for school-age children generally fall into one of the following categories:

- On- or near-site programs for employees' school-age children, including before- and after-school programs and vacation/holiday activities.
- Information and resources for employees who have school-age children, including resource and referral services, a homework helpline, tax-free salary set-asides for dependent care, and flexible work arrangements.
- Support for community programs that serve school-age children, including financial contributions and participation in community partnerships.

24-HOUR (ODD-HOUR) CARE

It is difficult for most working parents to find affordable and high-quality child care, but the problem becomes even greater when care is required during nonstandard hours. The issue of 24-hour or odd-hour child care is growing because of the following trends:

- More employers operate around the clock. The long-term trend toward a service-based economy has led to the operation of more businesses during early mornings, evenings, nights, and weekends.
- The global nature of the economy, which has people doing business with people all over the world at all hours of the day and night, has also contributed to this 24-hour trend.
- Employers in all sectors are changing their schedules for reasons ranging from increased flexibility to enhanced customer satisfaction to reduced air pollution.

Shift workers have been found to struggle with huge obstacles in fulfilling family responsibilities. These obstacles often severely impact shift workers and are costly to their employers in terms of absenteeism, tardiness, safety infractions, and—ultimately—productivity. Because of the lack of regular child care that fits their schedules, these workers are more likely to rely on relatives, neighbors, or friends for child care. They often have a hard time finding care, and their children are frequently left alone before and after school.

OTHER CHILD-CARE OPTIONS

Providing Information and Support

Working parents are often unaware or unsure of where to turn for answers to questions about child care and parenting. To help employees become more effective and educated consumers, employers can provide information to their employees using a resource and referral service through a vendor and/or conducting workshops on topics of interest. Resource and referral services typically provide employees with information and counseling on child-care issues and help employees find and manage child-care arrangements. The service often includes education (telephone counseling, print material, online information, and/or workshops) about a broad range of child-care issues, including quality care, adoption, information and support for nursing mothers, finding colleges, and so forth.

Policies and Customized Work Arrangements

In trying to manage work and family responsibilities, time and scheduling problems often arise. Parents' work schedules may be frequently interrupted by breakdowns in child care, illnesses, and other family needs that cost employers in lost work time. The ability to customize a work schedule to fit with personal needs is one of the most cost-effective supports an employer can offer. Companies typically have policies regarding scheduling options such as flextime, part-time, compressed schedules, job sharing, flex place or telecommuting, and sabbaticals. Both employers and employees benefit when these options are made available—and when employees and managers are educated about them, encouraged to use them, and suffer no penalty for using them.

Many companies offer parental leave for fathers and mothers for birth and adoption, with some portion paid. Allowing new parents time to bond with their child and establish comfortable routines helps avoid absenteeism and unnecessary stress. In addition, leave policies that allow employees a specified number of days (with or without pay) to care for a sick child assure parents that they won't need to choose between a sick child and their jobs. Many employers also realize that providing support for nursing mothers can be an advantage for both the employee and the employer in terms of reduced absenteeism and stress. Providing a lactation room for nursing mothers is another way to demonstrate that support.

Providing Financial Assistance

Child-care expenses can place severe financial stress on a family. The cost for child care can range from $1,500 to $15,000 per year depending on the child-care fees and the number of children in the family. Many families spend at least 10 percent of their income on child-care services, with lower-income families paying a larger percentage, sometimes as much as 25 percent. The cost of care prevents some families from choosing the highest quality of care. As a result, they may select less stable and less expensive care, which creates even greater stress and reduces effectiveness at work. Employers can help by offering a Dependent Care Spending Assistance Plan (DCAP) that allows employees to use pretax dollars to pay for care, by offering a flexible benefit plan or "cafeteria plan" that allows employees to choose from a range of benefits and customize their benefit package, by providing a subsidy through vouchers or reimbursement for a portion of the cost of care, and by financially supporting local child-care programs through grants and/or in-kind services.

Companies can support community child-care programs by underwriting training, by providing equipment and supplies, and/or by offering volunteers to help with purchasing, bookkeeping, marketing, and so forth. This type of support can be a valuable way of connecting with the community and customers while effectively addressing employees' needs. In some cases, companies are leveraging their corporate contributions to focus on early child-care needs in communities in which the companies have operating units and/or residing employees. Even a small contribution can often go a long way in the child-care industry. In some communities, companies are joining forces to improve the quality, quantity, and accessibility of child care. By combining corporate volunteer efforts with services that meet the child-care needs of employees and the community, employers can make a dramatic difference in the lives of their employees, their customers, and their future work force.

Child care is a complex issue, but there are many ways an employer can help. Companies that address the child-care needs of their employees find that the investment can have enormous benefits.

ELDER-CARE ISSUES

Over the last decade and primarily because of the aging population and the dual-focus workforce, the time one adult spends caring for another adult has emerged as a workplace issue. Finding and coordinating elder-care services is no easy task, especially for an employed caregiver. It requires an in-depth knowledge of complicated systems such as health care, insurance, and housing options.

Holding a job and providing elder care at the same time frequently causes stress, depression, and burnout that can lead to increased absenteeism and turnover. The study *Overwork in America: When the Way We Work Becomes Too Much* (Families and Work Institute, 2004) found that employees with elder-care responsibilities tend to be more overworked than employees without these responsibilities. And, the study reports, only 25 percent of organizations offer elder-care benefits.

In addition, elder caregivers who are working may also be dealing with the stress of long-distance caregiving and financial hardship. Though concentrated among older employees, a surprisingly large percentage of younger employees are reporting elder-care responsibilities. The number of employees with both child-care and elder-care responsibilities, the so-called "sandwich generation," is evolving into a rather large "club sandwich."

According to a 2003 study by ComPsych Corporation, workers who care for both children and elderly relatives put in enough caregiving hours to make it a second job. Of the employees polled, 8 percent are part of the sandwich generation. These individuals reported spending an average of 36 hours per week on caregiving duties, as follows:

- 10.4 hours per week on child-care tasks such as bathing, feeding, or making care arrangements.
- 9.6 hours per week on extracurricular activities for children.
- 4.5 hours per week driving children to school.
- 4.1 hours per week on caregiving tasks for an elderly relative.
- 2.6 hours per week traveling to the elder's residence.
- 4.7 hours per week on making arrangements (financial, legal, social, or health-related) for the elder.

These caregivers reported getting only six hours of sleep per night and needing to take off 18.9 vacation and sick days per year to deal with personal and caregiving issues. Although elder care should not be considered a woman's issue, the role of women as traditional caregivers and the increase in their participation in the labor force have become major factors in the evolution of the need for elder-care support.

Several other studies have also documented how widespread elder-care responsibilities are among the American workforce. According to the *National Study of the Changing Workforce,* published by the Families and Work Institute, 25 percent of the U.S. labor force has elder-care responsibilities. *The Wall Street Journal* reported in 2001 that elder care was becoming as big an issue in the United States as child care, and that quite possibly it would loom even larger in the near future, with almost two-thirds of employees under age 60 believing they'll have elder-care responsibilities in the next 10 years. The *Journal* cited a survey sponsored by Metropolitan Life Insurance Co. that found that as the nation's workforce ages, employers can expect to lose between $11 billion and $29 billion annually because of work-schedule conflicts traced to elder care.

The *Journal* report noted that by 2006, nearly 40 percent of the population will be older than age 45, and many will face elder-care situations. In company-sponsored surveys, in addition to those currently providing elder care, another 20 percent frequently predict they will have elder-care responsibilities in the next one to five years. In fact, the National Council on Aging estimated that between 30 percent and 40 percent of all employees will assist their elderly parents in 2020, compared with 12 percent today.

Employers have begun to offer a variety of programs to help their employed caregivers, but in many cases that support has not reached the same level of assistance offered for child care. According to a July 30, 2001, *USA Today* report, many employers don't know whom elder-care issues affect. Citing a survey by the Human Resource Institute and Boomerang of 150 large employers, *USA Today* reported that most companies don't have accurate data on the number of caregivers among employees. Additionally, 80 percent of the survey respondents either didn't know or had to guess at the percentage of caregivers in their workplace.

With greater numbers of workers expected to be caring for elderly relatives in the future, it's critical for employers to find ways to help employees cope with those demands. Recommended employer actions cited in the report were:

- Support the caregiver by providing counselors who are ready to let the employee talk about what is going on.
- Educate the workforce so they know what they may face in the near future. Let them know that the average duration of caregiving is about four years but that the time period is likely to increase as medical advances prolong life.

- Ensure that supervisors understand what caregivers experience and how to help them manage the stress.

DESCRIPTION OF ELDER CARE

Unlike child care, which typically involves finding services primarily for healthy children who live with the employee, elder care requires a set of services to respond to a wide range of often unpredictable medical, emotional, physical, and financial possibilities. These services are frequently required to be delivered some distance from the employee. Elder care takes many forms, including providing meals, transportation to medical appointments, food shopping, financial assistance, assisting with housework, or providing emotional support. When elder-care needs occur, they tend to be unpredictable and involve many unknowns. These needs often cause anxiety about such things as the ability to find and pay for immediate care or ways to take preventative measures like withholding car keys away from an elderly parent. Employees with elder-care responsibility are often called upon to assist in making costly financial decisions around issues of long-term care. In many cases they have very little information and little confidence in their ability to get comprehensive information on public and private benefits, service and financial options, and risks of needing extensive care over time. Adult children usually want to respect the autonomy and decision-making capability of their older adult relatives; however, most people are not pro-active when it comes to elder care, and critically important discussions about "what to do if" rarely take place in advance.

COST OF ELDER CARE AND THE NEEDS OF WORKING CAREGIVERS

Elder care is estimated to cost employers $1,141 per employee per year in absenteeism, turnover, and lost productivity, according to a 1997 study by MetLife. Based on this data, the cost for a company with 10,000 employees, of which 20 percent (2,000) have caregiving responsibility, would be about $2,282,000 ($1,141 × 2,000) per year.

Employed caregivers need help obtaining the comprehensive information, guidance, and support required to make complex financial, service, and care management decisions. The needs of working elder caregivers typically fall into the following categories:

- *Time:* Flexibility to schedule work and caregiving activities in ways that allow effective management of the two sets of responsibilities along with respite time that offers time away from both work and caregiving responsibilities.
- *Information:* Access to accurate, up-to-date information about community-based services, community-based resources, and legal and financial issues.
- *Financial Assistance:* The ability to pay for services needed to appropriately care for an older adult relative. Payment may require combining the financial resources of the elder, the working caregiver, other family members, and government or private-sector programs.
- *Emotional Support:* An understanding and caring support network that includes family members, friends, coworkers, supervisors, and perhaps advisory professionals.

EMPLOYERS' RESPONSES TO EMPLOYEES' ELDER-CARE NEEDS

The National Study of the Changing Workforce (Families and Work Institute, 2002) shows that 24 percent of employees have access to elder-care resources and referral services, as compared to only 11 percent in 1992.

In 1998, a Mercer and Bright Horizons Family Solutions study found that the elder-care services most frequently offered by companies were:

- Consultation and referral (81 percent).
- Long-term care insurance (35 percent).

FIGURE 23.2 Potential employer-sponsored elder-care supports.

Flexible or Customized Work Arrangements
  Informal or occasional flexibility
  Part-time and job sharing
  Voluntary reduced time
  Phased retirement
  Compressed schedule
  Flex time
  Telecommuting or flex place

Paid or Unpaid Time Off
  Family leave
  Medical or emergency leave
  Personal leave
  Bereavement leave

Insurance Coverage
  Health insurance
  Dental insurance
  Life Insurance
  Unemployment insurance
  Workers' compensation insurance
  Long-term care insurance

Access to Information
  Distributing educational materials
  Resource library, possibly online
  Workplace caregiver fairs
  Workplace caregiver workshops and
  support groups
  Elder care counseling and referral
  Promote elder-care locator
  Elder-care counseling through
  employee assistance program

Paid Time Off
  Sick days
  Vacation
  Sabbatical
  Personal days
  Paid time off bank

Policies
  Time off
  elocation policies

Financial Assistance
  Publicizing federal or state tax
  credits
  Dependent-care reimbursement
  plan
  Subsidized dependent-care
  reimbursement plan
  Subsidized care or vouchers
  Discounts for care

Direct Service Programs
  Geriatric case or care management
  On-site adult care center
  Near-site adult care center
  Intergenerational program
  Community resource development

- Counseling (14 percent).
- Financial support/other (4 percent).

Companies providing elder-care benefits report that employee utilization of these programs is growing but is still relatively low, usually for the following reasons:

- General discomfort on the part of workers when discussing issues related to elder care, perhaps rooted in the feeling that addressing such an issue is a private family matter.
- Corporate cultures where it's still not acceptable for employees to admit they have outside family demands that impact their work time and priorities.
- Ineffective communication techniques for reaching workers who need the information and assistance most (i.e., the working caregiver in a crisis situation) and a lack of awareness on the part of employees as to the actual range of elder-care benefits provided.
- The demographic bulge in the number of working elder caregivers that is just beginning to be felt as baby boomers enter their 60s.

Elder-care experts agree that the objective of any company elder-care initiative should be to help employees plan ahead. Continual marketing is necessary to make sure employees know about available resources and to increase utilization of elder-care services. Communication should stress a positive, long-range planning approach. Human resources, benefits, wellness, and work-life areas can all share responsibility for the elder-care initiative and find ways to publicize the issue and resources. When employees are able to plan ahead and prepare for elder-care responsibilities, their employers also benefit.

See Figure 23.2 for a comprehensive list of potential employer-sponsored elder-care supports.

INFORMATION AND SUPPORT

According to a September 23, 2003, report by the U.S. Department of Health and Human Services' Administration on Aging, family and friends informally provide 80 percent of the care needed by elders. These caregivers, many of whom are working, need a great deal of information and support to be most effective. The programs that most companies offer include resource and referral services, elder caregiver fairs or expos, elder-care material in a resource area or online, and workshops and support groups on elder-care issues. According to the *National Study of the Changing Workforce,* elder-care resource and referral services are one work-life program that has increased significantly. In 1992, only 11 percent of employees had access to this service, while nearly a quarter (24 percent) have access today. More employees also need elder-care services as the population ages: 35 percent of workers, men and women alike, say they have provided care for a relative or in-law who is 65 years old or older in the past year. The purpose of providing information and support is to offer accurate, time-saving access to information so that the best care available can be provided. Knowing they have access to this information can help those employees interested in planning ahead and can relieve stress levels in those individuals who would not know where to start without this assistance.

Elder-Care Consultation and Referral

About 7.7 million employees working today for employers of all sizes have access through their employers to elder-care resource (or consultation) and referral services. Approximately 3 million employees receive the services in-house and 4.8 million receive them through a third-party vendor. IBM was the first U.S. company to provide such services.

Many companies offering elder-care consultation and referral services find the utilization rate typically ranges between 5 and 10 percent annually. However, once employees use the elder-care consultation and referral service and are more knowledgeable about the range of services provided, they are likely to be repeat users. The company typically pays for employees' use of the service. In a recent focus group, a senior manager shared her anxiety over the need to move her elderly mother with Alzheimer's disease into a facility. The manager was not aware that her company offered a service to help find and manage this type of care. Upon hearing this, the manager began to cry, saying how relieved she was to know help was available; it would not only save time away from work, but would give her peace of mind.

The purpose of contracting for elder-care consultation and referral typically is to:

- Relieve stress and anxiety by providing employees with access to expert counseling that can help them identify concerns and make informed decisions based on detailed knowledge of local community and national resources.
- Provide consumer education through counseling and written materials to help employees select appropriate care.
- Provide individually researched referrals for a broad range of providers and help employees manage their elder-care needs.

Such a service can save employees a great deal of time and aggravation, and thus the company reduces lost productivity. For example, if an employee's parent needs frequent transportation to and from the doctor's office to receive treatment for a chronic illness and the doctor's office hours conflict with the employee's work hours, the employee will either have to take several hours off every week, eating up precious vacation time, or take unpaid time off to accommodate this need. However, by calling the consultation and referral service, the employee can get access to community-based resources that could provide the necessary transportation.

Most elder-care consultation and referral services include the following:

- A toll-free number for employees to call. A professional takes each employee through a screening process to clarify the reason for the call.
- A variety of print, video, audio, and online educational materials. Regardless of the format, educational materials cover relevant elder-care topics and can be sent to the employee directly, or to the older adult dependent.
- Referrals to appropriate resources in specific communities, often cited as the greatest time-saving aspect of the service. After identifying the reason for the employee's call, a list of resources that meet the criteria is sent to the employee.
- Access to the service through the Internet. Many employers link their intranet benefit sites to a national vendor's online version of the consultation and referral services. In general, employees can access and download educational materials, can e-mail elder-care specialists or consultants a question, can order additional elder-care materials, and can perform their own searches within the vendor's database.

- On-site seminars on elder-care topics and follow-up customer satisfaction phone calls and/or surveys.

Companies are increasingly adding new specialized services to enhance their offerings.

Elder-Care Workshops/Support Groups

Networking is one of the best ways to discover resources that address elder-care concerns. Many employees caring for older adult relatives build support systems that include their older adult's neighbors, clergy, friends, doctors, accountants, and other advisors. Employed elder caregivers can expand their networks to include their co-workers at various company workshops that may be offered throughout the year. These workshops tend to focus on health, medical, financial, legal, and emotional issues specific to elder care. Such issues include wills and trusts, Medicare and Medicaid, housing options, long-term care choices, communication with older relatives, and understanding the normal aging process. These sessions, usually facilitated by an elder-care expert, can be an important component of a company's support.

Since elder care is frequently a long-term commitment, elder-care support groups may evolve out of the workshops or be established independently by employees themselves. The main purpose of a support group is to give elder caregivers a chance to share experiences and to know that they are not alone in facing the challenges and dilemmas of caring for an older relative. Support groups are usually small groups of employees that meet regularly to deal with one issue. The success of support groups relies heavily on the commitment of its members and having access to resources to help manage the process. In some cases, resource and consultation or employee assistance services may provide occasional facilitators for support groups. Such support can make the difference between an employee who is able to cope with work and family during an emotional time and an employee who is not able to function effectively.

Elder-Care Resource Expo

An expo or fair can highlight community resources that deal with elder-care issues. Local and national organizations involved in elder care might come to the worksite during an expo to publicize the services they offer. At such an event, which may be part of a larger health care or benefits fair, employees are able to obtain literature on topics of interest and to talk directly to a representative of the organization. Some companies ask employees who attend the expo to fill out a short survey so they can gather more specific information about the elder-care needs of their employee population. An expo can be an effective way to encourage employees to be more proactive regarding elder-care issues.

Work-Life Resource Area

Material on elder-care issues can easily be included in a work-life resource area. Providing books, magazine articles, newsletters, and visual media on issues of concern to employees dealing with elder care extends the potential audience for the resource area. Some companies sell products or services that are directed to the older population—medications, health aids, vacation packages, and so forth that might be included in the employee resource area.

Another way to provide employees with information on elder-care issues is to produce a booklet on the subject. The guide can contain information about the normal aging process, physical and mental health, and how to find help with elder-care issues.

End-of-Life Supports

End of life care may occur in three phases:

- Providing care in advance of the death of a loved one.
- Dealing with the practical and emotional issues surrounding the death itself.
- Mourning and recovery.

In many cases, the workplace doesn't know how to respond to these events. Program policies or services specifically targeted to mourning and recovery (which may take an extended period of time) seem to be less common than those targeting the practical and emotional issues surrounding the death itself. Possible workplace responses for employees dealing with end-of-life issues include the use of flexible work arrangement policies, taking personal and bereavement leaves, and using consultation and referral services, geriatric case management services, seminars, support groups, or resource libraries.

POLICIES

Employees dealing with elder-care issues will probably encounter difficult personal situations that will impact, temporarily or permanently, the way they work. They may need a respite from work. Some companies let employees use sick time, vacation, and personal days with or without pay. If caregivers don't rest, they will burn out at some point, and the company will also lose. Sometimes, because the person who's ill gets so much attention, we forget that the caregiver needs help to maintain health, handle stress, and battle exhaustion.

Elder-care needs are often sudden and unpredictable and require flexibility and responsiveness from the employee caregiver. Working for a company that understands the unpredictable nature of the elder-care challenges facing employees allows employees to feel dedicated to both their jobs and their families. Employed elder caregivers can benefit greatly from having flexible, customized work arrangements. Some companies recognize that employees often need more than personal or vacation time to deal with family-related crises, especially those related to elder care. In response, some employers include policy language allowing employees to use sick leave to care for sick children and other family members. Many companies combine personal sick days with family sick days, giving employees a certain number of days off each year that can be used for either personal sick time, when a family member is sick, or some combination of both. However, there is typically no increase given in actual number of days off, with the majority of companies allowing 3 to 12 days off per year for family illness.

FINANCIAL ASSISTANCE/FINANCIAL PLANNING

Subsidized Emergency or Respite In-Home Elder-Care Services

Elderly relatives occasionally need emergency care in their homes or in employees' homes, either because of illness or accident or because of some other disruption in their regular schedules. A few companies offer employees help in finding and paying for emergency in-home elder care. Emergency elder-care services are usually subsidized by employers as a way of ensuring that employees will be able to use the program, resulting in reduced absenteeism. Employers often place limits or a maximum number of days or hours that an employee can use this service during a year or some other specified period of time.

In rare instances, an employer, or a consortium of employers, may subsidize full-time in-home elder-care services. This has occurred because employees frequently rely on community-based services, like a home health aide, to care for their older adult relative during the hours they are at work. Without this care option, many employed elder caregivers would not be able to work. Unfortunately, home health aides are typically underpaid and many have no certification, which creates care arrangements that at best may be unpredictable. In response to this need, some employers are subsidizing employees' home health aide expenses.

DIRECT ELDER-CARE SERVICES

Although still relatively rare, some companies have established breakthrough direct service programs to meet the elder-care needs of their employees. Currently not used by large numbers of employees, these programs are charting new ground and will likely become more common in the future. They could include geriatric care managers, support for community-based services, adult care centers, intergenerational care programs, and Life Design.

Geriatric Care Managers

Geriatric care managers are doing the job families used to do, helping move their elders through a system that is increasingly complex. Geriatric care managers specialize in understanding the complex maze of services available to older adults. These professionals assess an older adult's specific needs, link the older adult to resources that will address their needs, and follow up to make sure the older adult is getting the best possible care available. By using a geriatric care manager to connect to the most appropriate resources specific to an elder's need, long-distance caregivers can extend their reach into the older relative's community. This also gives the older relative a local advocate and the family an educator on a variety of geriatric issues. The services of a geriatric care manager may be subsidized by the employer, and in some cases are offered through the resource and referral vendor.

Supports for Community-Based Services

Some companies are investing in community programs that provide services for older adults as a way to expand the supply and improve the quality of elder care around the country and in areas where employees work and live.

Adult Care Centers

Some older adults need care during the day but are otherwise healthy enough to stay in their own homes. These centers are typically staffed by physical therapists, nurses, occupational therapists, geriatric aides, and support workers. Adult day-care centers can meet the needs of employees and their elderly relatives and are an option a few companies have chosen to develop.

Intergenerational Care Programs

In some cases, companies that are presently supporting on-site or near-site child care may consider adult or intergenerational day care as appropriate add-ons. There are a few state governments that encourage the development of elder-care facilities. Michigan has provided tax incentives to companies developing intergenerational day care.

The goal of intergenerational programming is typically to:

- Provide children with accurate information and knowledge about the elderly that will enable them to form positive, realistic concepts of and attitudes toward the elderly.
- Expose children to an unbiased look at the diversity of older people, teaching them to value the many and varied characteristics, attributes, and qualities of the elderly.
- Enable children to feel positively about their own aging and about the elderly, and offer the elders planned interaction with young children.

IMPLEMENTING A NEW ELDER-CARE PROGRAM

There is no one way to proceed when developing a corporate elder-care program, and there are many opportunities to experiment. In order to plan effectively, the organization should consider:

- Who will be covered or eligible under the program/policy—usually the parent, in-law, or spouse of an active employee.
- What types of programs and policies to offer.
- Where to provide services—near the workplace, where employees live, or where elders live.
- Frequency of services—an ongoing program or an intermittent program.

Before approaching the development of new programs, the company should assess existing programs and policies. Most companies have some programs and policies in place that would be helpful to employees with elder-care concerns. However, in many cases, the programs and policies have not been packaged to reflect the assistance they provide for elder care. The first step in creating an elder-care program is to take a look at existing programs and policies and see how they might be organized as part of an elder-care program. Some programs and policies might not currently have an elder-care component but could easily be adapted. For example, if the company currently conducts wellness seminars that focus on medical issues, the topics might be extended to include issues of concern to employees dealing with elder care.

The methods used to determine elder-care needs can be similar to those used to assess child care or other work-life needs. Some companies choose to undertake an employee survey just to assess elder-care concerns. The assessment can be useful when companies are determining the most pressing needs of working caregivers; analyzing the company's current policies, benefits, and services; and identifying the gap between employees' needs and existing policies. An assessment will make it easier to identify and create a list of recommendations for new programs or policies that will address specific employee caregiver needs.

It can be extremely beneficial to involve an expert on elder-care issues in the assessment and planning process. The elder-care expert should understand both the viable options for support and the special issues of employed caregivers and corporate involvement.

EVALUATING AN ELDER-CARE PROGRAM

Some companies run into difficulty when evaluating the effectiveness of elder-care programs. One of the first questions usually asked is, "How many employees use the program or policy?" Although this question provides an interesting measure, answers to the following additional questions may produce a more accurate evaluation of the impact of the program than can utilization figures alone:

- Did the program or policy address employees' need? If not, why not?
- What is the overall objective of the program?
- How well does the program or policy meet its objectives?
- How well was it communicated?
- How would employee caregivers change the program or policy to make it more helpful?
- What other kind of support do employee caregivers report needing?

Such questions provide qualitative data that can be most helpful in determining if a program has met its objectives and how best to modify it in the future. Programs might be evaluated by tracking utilization using a questionnaire, an evaluation or feedback form, focus groups, and individual interviews.

THE FUTURE OF CORPORATE ELDER CARE

Based on the demographics, elder care will be an issue of increasing importance to workers in the future. Additional research is needed. Centers such as the Boston College Center on Aging & Work, which was created with a $3 million grant from the Sloan Foundation, will help to explore the impact of elder caregiving on the workplace and will help shape the corporate response to the issue.

It seems clear, given the magnitude of elder-care concerns, that responsibility for addressing employees' elder-care issues cannot be handled by individual corporations by themselves. This responsibility must be a cooperative effort on the part of government, employers, local colleges, advocacy organizations, senior centers, adult day-care programs, and other organizations. Companies can play an important role in actively encouraging public-private partnerships. Collaborative partnerships perhaps offer the most promise for innovation and new resource development.

24 Culture at Work

Creating the right culture for employees is a major challenge for organizations and their leaders. However, the reward for developing a culture that employees and other key stakeholders can embrace pays big dividends for the organization. These dividends include lower job vacancy rates, reduced employee turnover, higher employee morale, enhanced public image, and increased customer loyalty.

Culture is the one component often taken for granted in an organization's rewards program. Yet, culture provides leaders with a valuable tool to get employees and key stakeholders actively involved in the organization's success.

Culture is also a key component of the WorldatWork Total Rewards model. Culture is an integral part of the "work-life" component that focuses on the individual needs of the employee. As part of the work-life component, culture is an important initiative in creating support for work-life programs. Culture is also a determinant of how well unique programs, such as diversity education, women's advancement, and mentoring, will be received.

Organizational culture is also one of the three key drivers of the total rewards strategy. As a key driver, organizational culture impacts how new total rewards programs will be received and integrated into the organization. When crafting a total rewards strategy, it is imperative that organizational culture be addressed before deciding what total rewards programs to offer.

Culture also has a major impact on all of the other elements of the total rewards model. It impacts how we design programs for compensation, benefits, performance and recognition, and development and career opportunities. Culture is a major resource for determining what the employees expect and what the organization is willing and able to provide in all of the total rewards elements. As we delve into this important topic, remember that culture establishes the expectations and norms of behavior that employees have formed and value. These expectations and norms of behavior ultimately impact the success or failure of the total rewards strategy.

DEFINING CULTURE

Culture is an elusive concept for many organizations and its leaders. It seems that everyone has his or her own definition of this concept. Steven McShane and Mary Ann Von Glinow in *Organizational Behavior* provide a comprehensive definition of organizational culture:

> It is the basic pattern of shared assumptions, values and beliefs governing the way employees within an organization think about and act on problems and opportunities . . . It (culture) defines what is important and unimportant in the company. You might think of it as the organization's DNA—invisible to the naked eye, yet a powerful template that shapes what happens in the workplace.

The definition helps frame the importance of culture. We often cannot see or sometimes totally describe all of the aspects of culture. Many of us take a simplistic approach and describe culture "as the way things are done around here." To help answer the burning question of "What is Culture?" Figure 24.1 identifies elements and behavioral aspects that we often attach to culture. These attributes help us understand how culture dramatically impacts an organization.

Values are at the top of the list in Figure 24.1 because it is easy for an organization to publish values that do not necessarily represent the culture. Espoused values are those publicly announced values that were mentioned in the introduction. The real values are harder to define and must be shared by all members of the organization. A good example of a shared value is to place a high value on learning. In looking closer, this value encourages the development of all staff members and indicates a "learning culture." This learning culture must be reinforced with programs and actions that in fact support this shared value. Some total rewards programs that would support a learning culture include tuition reimbursement programs for all employees, generous continuing education programs, on-site corporate universities, and pay-for-knowledge incentives. Shared values are a critical cultural driver because they help give meaning and shape to the organization. When an organization begins building its long-term strategy, it is the shared values that will help develop a successful strategy. Many leaders forget about culture as an important element in helping define an organization's strategy.

FIGURE 24.1 Components of culture.

- *Values:* Espoused vs. Shared
- *Norms:* Organizational vs. Group
- *Leadership:* Formal vs. Informal
- *Patterns of Behavior:* Individual vs. Group
- *Communication Style:* Open vs. Closed
- *Beliefs and Rituals:* Defined vs. Hidden
- *Mission:* Espoused vs. Enacted
- *Cultural Sensitivity:* High vs. Low Level of Awareness
- *Diversity:* Representative vs. Controlled
- *Formality:* Formal vs. Informal
- *Innovation:* Encouraged vs. Discouraged
- *Trust:* High Level vs. A Trust Gap

This explains in part some of the devastating outcomes that have befallen large organizations in the past five years. Norms help frame the organization's culture. There are two types of norms: organizational and group norms. The organizational norms are those behaviors either formally defined or strongly encouraged by the organization. Some of these defined or highly encouraged norms can lead to negative consequences for the organization's culture. For example, even though an organization has a published attendance policy, if it is not uniformly administered, the culture will soon accept poor attendance as the norm. Group norms also impact the culture. This is a norm followed by the work team in the daily operations of the organization. Group A, for example, may have a norm that all group members must contribute equally in the workload. Being ostracized by the rest of the group members is the result for those who fail to contribute their fair share.

Group norms can produce "cultural shock" for new employees. The group norms may be different than what the employee understood about the organization when they accepted the job. Figure 24.2 provides some examples of positive and negative norms. It is interesting to note that if left alone, negative norms will develop and become the basis for the culture.

Leadership is defined by culture. For example, if the culture values employees, leaders will generally value their employees. Leadership is the cultural driver that helps establish what direction the culture will follow. This direction may have positive or negative outcomes for the organization. Some organizational cultures do not

FIGURE 24.2 Positive vs. negative norms.

Positive Norms
- The organization rewards employees for providing excellent customer service.
  - —Note: Customer service is a major component of the performance evaluation system.
- Employees are encouraged to participate in developing new ideas and programs.
  - —Note: A well-designed suggestion program reinforces this.
- Employees are expected to keep their skill levels at a high level.
  - —Note: This is supported by a performance incentive plan.
- All employees will be free from harassment of any kind.
  - —Note: The organization has adopted a code of conduct for all employees.

Negative Norms
- It doesn't matter what you do around here; nobody cares anyway.
  - —Note: There is an absence of any formal employee recognition program or informal recognition approaches.
- The bottom line is more important than quality or service.
  - —Note: Leadership of the organization places very little value on quality or service.
- Leaders are not held to the same level of performance standards as regular employees.
  - —Note: Individuals in leadership roles are conspicuously absent or unavailable to their employees. Feeling of trust and fairness is violated; leaders' "Talk and Walk" not the same.

Reader Action Point

Figure 24.2 provides examples of how to reinforce positive norms. What happens if leaders have no desire to provide total rewards programs to create positive work norms? The role of the HR practitioner is to make the "business case" for offering new total rewards programs. One of the cultural drivers is return on investment. This is part of the business case. The HR practitioner (i.e., *you*) must show how offering new "culturally fit" programs will positively impact the bottom line and the success of the organization. This business case must show in dollars and cents how the new program reduces turnover, improves morale, or improves productivity. Few managers are wedded to providing new programs to build a positive culture unless it can be proved that it will somehow help the organization financially grow or survive. This is a real challenge that HR practitioners face when introducing a new "culture friendly" program. The business case is enhanced if we can use benchmark data or "success stories" to illustrate how cultural enhancements have been successful in other organizations. A major resource is *Fortune*'s annual "100 Best Companies to Work For."

have the benefit of having one leader to provide this direction. There is a big gap between managers and leaders. Figure 24.3 provides a comparison between what managers typically do and what leaders provide. The list provided in Figure 24.3 can be argued by management practitioners. It is meant as a tool to help differentiate the importance of looking at the difference between managers and leaders. The emphasis for the manager is on doing, while the leader seeks to provide "shared vision." Leaders know the importance of involving their followers in establishing the organization's vision and shaping its culture. For example, managers rely on their position's power to make decisions. Leaders *empower* employees to come up with a better decision.

FIGURE 24.3 A leader vs. a manager.

A Leader
- Shapes culture
- Aligns people to the culture
- Empowers others
- Creates shared vision
- Is future oriented
- Is proactive
- Seeks consensus
- Serves or stewards followers
- Focuses on *what* decisions mean to others
- Motivates and inspires
- Creates shared solutions

A Manager
- Reacts to the culture
- Seeks to protect the existing culture
- Uses position's power
- Provides limited options
- Is oriented to the present
- Is reactive
- Seeks compliance
- Directs others
- Focuses on *how* to get things done
- Controls and monitors results
- Fixes problems

Tips for Contending with Resistance

What happens when a manager refuses to let employees be involved in shaping the culture? This is often a reality that HR practitioners must face. Some potential tips for dealing with this issue are:

1. *Utilize the subcultures within the organization.* According to McShane and Von Glinow, "subcultures are located throughout {an organization's} divisions, geographic locations and occupational groups." HR can tap these subcultures to help improve morale and obtain the benefits of having a unified culture. By focusing on each subculture, HR can focus its resources on the employees contained within the subculture.

2. *Present feedback from cultural audits and surveys to top management.* This at least gives top management some data on what is really important to employees. What they choose to do with this information can not always be predicted. It is HR's role to be an employee advocate and provide feedback so management is kept informed.

3. *Provide "best practices" information about culture to management.* Again, this can take many forms and must be carefully communicated. Still, it keeps culture in front of top management as an issue to consider.

4. *Integrate culture within the human resources strategy.* Culture should be part of the HR strategy that is communicated to top management and to employees. It tells executive leadership that HR views culture as important to the organization's success.

5. *Conduct training or information sessions with all levels of management about the importance of culture.* HR should make a concerted effort to discuss the importance of culture with all management levels. The sessions can be 20 to 30 minutes initially. The trick is to get management involved with culture as a topic.

6. *Seek out an executive champion.* Identify an individual on the executive team who will be a spokesperson for the importance of culture to the organization. Finding someone on the executive team to do this takes patience and a willingness to teach this individual all about culture as an important organizational component.

Leaders energize, motivate, and inspire their followers. Managers monitor results, plan for and prioritize problems, and ensure proper staffing. An organization needs leaders and managers. Some individuals are good at being leaders and some at being daily operational managers. However, if there is an absence of one or the other, the culture will be dramatically impacted. Leaders *align* people so the culture can be allowed to develop. Managers, however, *protect* the existing culture and ensure it can survive and be successful. This seems straightforward for the formal side of leadership. But the informal leader can have just as big of an impact on the culture. Who are these informal leaders? Informal leaders are those individuals that employees look to for support and approval.

Informal leaders do not have the title of manager or supervisor, but still employees see them as important to the culture. Smart organizations know the importance of the informal leader and will voluntarily involve them in the decision-making process.

Informal leaders help feed the grapevine by giving employees information—negative and positive—about the organization. The result can be devastating when making change or merging cultures. Without accurate information, informal leaders may fill in the blanks based on their perceptions, personal values, and needs of their work group. An informal leader can be a friend or mighty foe to how the culture develops and how it continues to be communicated. Bottom line: Identify these leaders and involve them as much as possible.

Patterns of behavior also determine how the culture develops. Do we strive for an organization based on individual accomplishments and contributions? Or do we seek a culture based on group behavior and group achievements? There really is no right answer. The reality is that most organizations are driven by individual and group behavior. In fact, we reward employees for their individual and team accomplishments. Patterns of behavior can be extremely negative on a team basis. Teams may have difficulties working together and sharing the workload. "Social loafing" can be the consequence when all team members do not contribute equally. The social loafer piggybacks on the accomplishments of the team. The reaction can be outrage by the rest of the team and can force negative patterns of behavior. Some individuals are committed to the organization's success. This individual pattern of behavior can be contagious, particularly if this individual is rewarded for her/his contributions. Conversely, "one bad apple" does seem to spoil the whole bunch, but individuals who display negative patterns of behavior, if left unchecked, can erode a positive organizational structure.

The big takeaway is to harness positive patterns of work behavior and incorporate them into the culture and work environment. The communication style of an organization may be open or closed. Figure 24.4 provides a graphic of how the two styles work. Communication flows two ways in an open communication culture. If you look closer, it resembles an endless circle with continuous feedback and communication.

Reader Discussion Point

In many instances, the informal leader is the "keeper" of the subculture. The informal leader may have defined or helped form the subculture for the individual department, unit, or division. This individual is key to determining what employees really view as valuable and important to their world. Informal leaders should have as much information as possible about changes that will impact the organization. This is not a move to manipulate the informal leader but a proactive step in developing an overall culture that more accurately reflects the needs of the employee. Feedback from informal leaders should be scrutinized and shared with executive leadership unless the informal leader does not want her/his feedback "shared up the ladder." Even when this happens, the feedback can be important to improve the work life of the employees in that department or division. Managers must nurture the informal leader and make him/her a part of the process in managing and assessing the organization's culture.

The closed communication style is one-way, top-down, and filtered and controlled by organizational leadership. An uptight culture is often built around the closed style of communication. In the absence of accurate communication, employees will fill in the blanks. That generally produces negative results. A good example is how the closed organization communicates salary information. It is carefully guarded, with only a few individuals privy to how the compensation system works. While this may sound absolutely necessary to managers of the organization, a leader knows the value of sharing basic information about the compensation system. Once it is fully understood by employees, the compensation system can be seen as a valuable component of the employee's work life. Without this knowledge, employees may feel the system is inequitable and unfair.

Beliefs and Rituals

Beliefs and rituals can be defined or hidden within the culture. A service award program, which recognized employees with long-term service, is an example of defined beliefs and rituals. An example of a hidden belief or ritual is how employees are encouraged to interact with one another and with the organization's external customers. This hidden ritual can help create a caring and responsive culture. If employees are empowered to resolve customer issues on the spot, it can result in a positive impact on customer relations.

FIGURE 24.4 Open vs. closed communication.

COMPANY A: OPEN COMMUNICATION STYLE

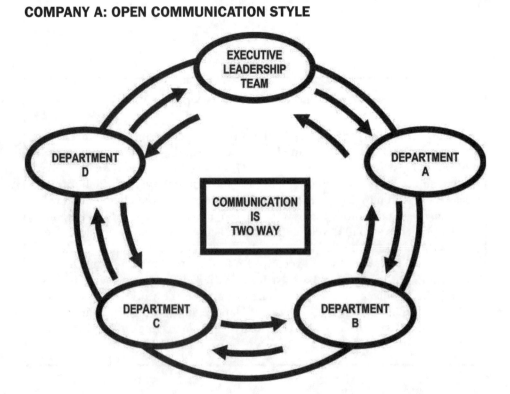

COMPANY B: CLOSED COMMUNICATION STYLE

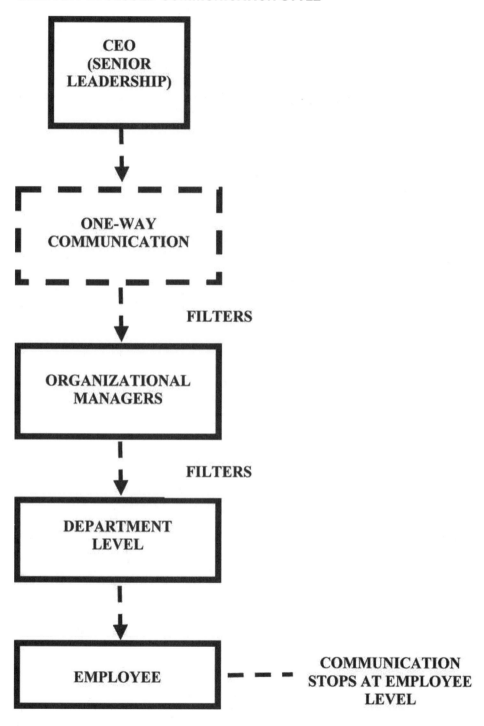

Reader Discussion Point

How do you survive in an organization that practices a closed communication style? Many organizations are "tight-lipped." To survive in this type of organization, managers must create "an alternate reality." This alternate reality focuses on the needs of the subculture and how to best communicate with the employees. This does not mean that the manager fabricates what should be but is not supported by top leadership. It does mean the manager must actively share information that he/she knows is accurate. It also means that the subculture must focus on open communication to be effective and productive. This is where the manager can be most valuable. The byline for this approach is: "Focus on what you have control over." Most managers have more control over the flow of communication within their subculture rather than the culture as a whole. Do not advocate being insubordinate or refusing to work within the boundaries established by the overall culture. Instead, utilize the informal leaders and employees within the subculture to create an open and positive communication approach. Start this by having frequent department/unit meetings where open communication is encouraged and practiced. If there is a geographic separation, open communication should be practiced virtually as well as in person. In a virtual setting, the use of "employee chat rooms" and "hotlines" should be encouraged. Keep in mind that this approach should not be subversive but should be used as an adjunct to the overall culture that unfortunately practices a closed approach to communication. It is useful to model an open approach to communication with employees and colleagues when working in a closed environment to set an inviting tone.

The espoused mission (i.e., the written mission hanging on the wall) needs to be absorbed into the culture if it is to have any meaning. Often, it is the enacted mission that drives the organization's culture. For example, if the mission states "we strive to deliver timely and courteous service to our customers" and the organization instead regularly mistreats its customers and rarely delivers anything on time, the organization is functioning at a different mindset than what it is actively communicating to its employees and customers. The mission can be a driving force for the culture or a useless statement that some "management geek" made up to appease the public.

Diversity

Cultural sensitivity and diversity have a behavioral impact on the organization's culture. If an organization is tuned in to how differences can work to the advantage of the organization, a richer and more representative culture can result. Organizations with very little commitment to "equal employment opportunity," or honoring the heritages and backgrounds of their employees, produce controlled cultures incapable of adapting to change or crisis. Trust also intertwines with diversity and cultural sensitivity. Employees will develop a high level of trust when the organization is committed to serving and stewarding them rather than controlling their work habits.

This concept is vital to how the culture leads or manages its employees. Figure 24.3 identified stewardship as an important leadership component. The servant or steward leader builds trust because she/he helps her/his followers succeed. A "trust gap" develops when the leader or the organization is not sensitive to the needs of his/her followers and employees. An organization that hides information or fails to provide appropriate resources, rewards, and compensation levels to its employees produces a trust gap that is difficult to overcome.

Formality and Innovation

The final two components of culture are greatly impacted by one another. Formality refers to how the organization is structured. For example, is the organization very formal, with well-defined policies and procedures along with a very definitive organization hierarchy? Or is the organization loosely organized with very little dependence on formal structure, policies, or practices?

Formality generally impacts how innovation is incorporated into its culture. A very formal structure may discourage innovation if it changes the "status quo." An informal organization may be more open to innovation and new ideas because it generally relies more on change since formal policies and practices are not well entrenched in the organization. Both formality and innovation define how the culture can adapt and adopt new ideas and changes. Formal organizations are generally slower to adapt than informal organizations. Organizations driven by innovation and creative ideas are more apt to provide total rewards programs that reinforce this commitment. If innovation is eschewed by the organization, the culture will be more controlled and stagnant.

Reader Discussion Point

The concept of "shared" and "closed" cultures is not meant to be a value judgment, but to point out the importance of having a shared culture. If the culture is not shared, it obviously will have less impact and importance. Many organizations have closed cultures with a "top down" approach to managing. This "top down" approach is a real concern for some managers and one they must try to reconcile with their own management beliefs. For others, the closed culture works and "fits" with the leadership styles of their organization. This style is not as effective as a shared culture because it relies more on control rather than active communication and proactive results. Both of these concepts are presented in the hopes the reader will carefully review those contained within a shared culture.

IMPORTANCE OF CULTURE

Culture provides direction to the organization and its members by influencing behavior so that organizational goals and strategies can be accomplished. The degree with which culture is shared will determine if it has a significant impact on the organization. Figure 24.5 identifies characteristics of shared and closed cultures. Notice that the most important element of a shared culture is the pervasiveness and degree it is accepted. According to Professor Richard Scholl of the University of Rhode Island, pervasiveness is an extremely important cultural attribute because it indicates that the culture has widespread acceptance and identity.

Shared cultures focus on strategic planning, people, and the future. Closed cultures pay more attention to protecting the status quo. The importance of culture is fairly obvious from reviewing these attributes. It is the foundation from which to build a successful organization. This foundation determines how to:

1. *Frame organizational strategy.* This is impacted by how open the culture is to adapting to change and new ideas. It is virtually impossible to implement strategy that focuses on growth if the culture is driven by daily operations.
2. *Build organizational success.* A strong culture is the driver for the organization's success. Strong cultures already have mechanisms in place to solidify financial and customer success. These mechanisms include a strong customer focus, cooperative and diverse teams, and the ability to adapt to new ideas and change.

FIGURE 24.5 Attributes of shared and closed cultures.

Shared Cultures Are:
- *Pervasive:* Culture is widely shared among the organization.
- *Accepted:* Culture is widely accepted and valued by organizational members.
- *Diverse:* Composition is representative of various cultures and beliefs.
- *Adaptable:* Has the ability to adapt to change and address crises.
- *Encouraging:* Encourages organizational members to do their best.
- *Driven by Outcomes:* Focus on goals and strategies.
- *Cooperative:* Organizational members work well together.
- *Strategic:* Focus on the future success of the organization.
- *Innovative:* Creativity and risk taking are valued.
- *Customer Focused:* Both internal and external customers are valued.
- *Identity Based:* Provides a positive identity to its members.

Closed Cultures Are:
- *Disjointed:* There is not a system of shared values and beliefs.
- *Controlled:* New ideas are not valued. Organizational make-up is not representative of the external environment.
- *Competitive:* Individual achievement displaces cooperation and team spirit.
- *Cost Focused:* The bottom line is more important than people.
- *Process Based:* Current processes are maintained at the expense of creativity and innovation.
- *Driven by Daily Routine:* There is very little attention given to strategic planning.
- *Ambiguous:* There are no goals or strategies to drive the organization.

3. *Grow adaptive organizational members.* Strong cultures focus on team spirit and cooperativeness. Strong cultures are also driven by creativity and innovation. This innovative spirit motivates employees to learn, contribute, and achieve. Employees who are encouraged to learn and contribute are more open to strategic change. Organizations are sometimes surprised that their employees are intimidated by change. A closer look generally reveals that the organization's culture does not encourage new ways of doing things. One example of a total rewards program that may help build a status quo culture is "automatic salary adjustments," which are not tied to performance or contribution.

Finally, culture has a dramatic impact on individual and group behavior. How organizational members embrace the culture will determine its impact. Shared cultures generally have highly visible leaders. Those leaders help mold the culture so it has a high level of support from its key stakeholders. The biggest impact that leaders have on culture is to provide a strong role model for its followers. If the leader can provide a cultural connection by being a positive role model, followers will be more committed to the culture and to the organization. For some leaders, like former General Electric chief executive officer Jack Welch, this identification with the culture can encompass the organization. Some leaders are so identified with the culture that it is hard for followers to separate the two. This is why it is important to "walk the talk" and provide a positive image for followers.

MATCHING CULTURE WITH STRATEGIC GOALS

Figure 24.6 provides a checklist that can be used to integrate culture with strategy. Not surprisingly, this checklist begins with leadership. The other five components in the checklist build on leadership and how the organization responds to each cultural area.

Leaders of an organization must keep well informed about the culture and how it impacts strategy. For example, how would culture impact the following strategy, which relates to organizational integration?

Strategy: Create a single operation and point of contact for key support functions to improve efficiency and reduce costs.

The leaders of this organization had better have a good idea of how the culture will support such a lofty goal. This strategy, in effect, changes the organization from a decentralized to a centralized operation. This strategy will change how decisions are made within the organization. Key questions for leadership in this example would include:

1. Can the culture support a change from a decentralized to a centralized organizational structure?
2. Will key stakeholders understand the need to make this change?
3. Why is this change needed in the first place?
4. How can this change be effectively communicated to key stakeholders?
5. Is the organizational climate willing to support this change?
6. Will other initiatives impact the success of this strategy?
7. Does this strategy fit with what the culture has traditionally deemed to be important?
8. What training and development will key stakeholders need before this strategy can be implemented?

FIGURE 24.6 Checklist for integrating culture with strategy.

_____1. **Leadership**

_____Must be team oriented, well informed, and knowledgeable of the culture.

_____Must be open to suggestions, concerns, and "insights" of how culture can impact organizational strategy.

_____2. **Strategy**

_____Must be clear and specific with few written goals.

_____Is relevant to cultural issues and capable of dealing with any problems as they arise.

_____Should reflect the impact of the organization's culture on the organization's success.

_____Integrates cultural preferences with the capabilities of the organization.

_____3. **Climate**

_____Must be open to new strategic approaches.

_____Must demonstrate a willingness to accept change.

_____Should align positively with the culture and the strategy.

_____4. **Communication**

_____Provides extensive feedback opportunities.

_____Sends positive and proactive messages to organizational members.

_____Feeds the grapevine with accurate information.

_____Enriches the cultural beliefs and values.

_____5. **Culture**

_____Determines if strategy is a "fit" for the organization.

_____Establishes prevailing attitudes regarding strategy.

_____Must be aligned with the strategy.

_____Encourages support and acceptance of the strategy.

_____6. **Training and Development**

_____Seeks to match culture with the strategy.

_____Enlightens stakeholders about the strategy.

_____Provides an unbiased source for learning about strategic planning process.

If the culture focused on empowering employees and allowing decision making at the department level, it will be difficult to implement this strategy. Strategy simply cannot be forced with any degree of great success when it contradicts tradition and culture. To be successful, organizations must ensure that the strategy is a good fit for the culture _before_ making dramatic shifts in strategic direction.

IMPACT OF CULTURE ON TOTAL REWARDS PROGRAMS

Figure 24.7 details how total rewards programs are culturally driven. The bottom half of the circle graph delineates programs aimed at "work-life strategies." These programs are driven by the intrinsic needs of the employee. All employees have personal needs, which are distinguished from their basic financial needs. To address

FIGURE 24.7 Culturally driven total rewards programs.

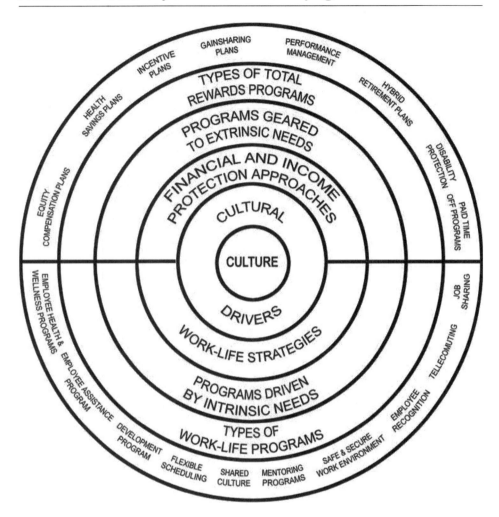

those needs, organizations must offer work-life programs that help employees cope with their personal lives and the daily grind of the workplace. Some of these programs include:

- *Shared culture.* Employees who work for an organization that has a shared culture have a distinct advantage over those individuals stuck in a closed one. Shared cultures are well defined and widely communicated, which positions the organization when developing strategy and making changes. Employees generally are more confident about their work experience when the culture is in sync with their personal values and beliefs.
- *Flexible scheduling.* These programs provide opportunities for employees to match their work schedules with their personal needs. *Job sharing* is a type of flexible scheduling arrangement where two or more employees share a full-time position. The individuals who share the position are empowered

to take responsibility for staffing it. Job sharing has produced outstanding results in the insurance, retail, and health care fields. *Telecommuting* provides another flexible approach that allows employees to work from home. This is accomplished with the aid of microcomputers and other technological devices. It has spawned the concept of "virtual teams." These teams are comprised of telecommuters and may include participants in remote or global locations. These teams provide unique work-life benefits. However, they offer some unique challenges to organizations in effectively managing them.

- *Employee recognition.* Recognizing employees for a job well done is an important component of the total rewards strategy. Employee recognition programs can range from formal, which provide monetary incentives, to very informal, which provide on-the-spot recognition. Employee recognition programs can also be used to focus the culture on a strategic goal. One such example is a recognition program that places a high value on providing excellent customer service. This program helps the employee focus on the customer, which ultimately can create a "customer-friendly culture."

- *Development programs.* These programs provide training to employees and other key stakeholders. Some organizations have created on-site, corporate universities for the convenience of their employees. Mentoring programs that place experienced employees with new employees have become widely accepted. Mentoring is more than on-the-job training. It allows the new employee to be indoctrinated into the organization's culture. The new employee has a seasoned resource at the ready to offer advice, training, and initial orientation. Some of these mentoring relationships become long lasting. Organizations with a high commitment to training and development can build a learning culture that values new ideas and creativity.

- *Employee health and wellness.* These programs focus on healthy lifestyles and disease prevention. Cultures placing a high value on health and wellness know the value of taking care of the total employee. Obviously, a healthy employee is generally more productive, happier, and more positive about their work experience. Some examples of health and wellness programs include on-site fitness centers and employee health functions, health counseling programs, employee health fairs, and weight loss programs. To address stress and other personal problems, some organizations offer employee assistance programs to provide counseling services to the employee and their family members. These services are generally provided off site and in a confidential setting. Finally, providing a safe and secure work environment free of workplace injuries and violence has become a major challenge to employers. According to the National Institute for Occupational Safety and Health (NIOSH), at least one million employees are victims of workplace violence annually, with at least 1,000 of these cases resulting in homicides. According to statistics maintained by the Occupational Safety and Health Administration (OSHA), workplace homicides are the leading cause of fatal occupational injuries for women and the second leading cause for men. This difficult problem has been exacerbated by the potential threat of terrorism since the September 11, 2001 attacks. Employee accidents represent another major risk factor for employers. Most organizations have a safety committee or safety officer who monitors unsafe work practices and develops in-house safety programs.

The aforementioned list of work-life programs is not exhaustive. Many organizations continue to devise unique ways to enhance the employee's work experience. For example, J. M. Smucker, *Fortune's* "Best Company to Work For" in 2004, serves complimentary bagels and muffins complete with their signature jams to their employees on a daily basis. Smucker's goal is to create a "family-oriented" culture. The financial and income-protection approaches identified in the top half of Figure 24.7 should complement the work-life strategies. Financial and income-protection approaches focus on the "extrinsic needs" of the employee. These programs "pay the bills." Figure 24.7 identified only a few, although countless compensation and employee benefits programs exist. Looking at this vast number is beyond the scope of this chapter. Instead, let's focus on the following three approaches:

1. *Performance management.* These programs provide monetary rewards for meeting certain defined performance criteria. A merit performance program is the most common approach. It rewards employees for achieving varying levels of work performance (e.g., Outstanding—7 percent, Very Effective—5 percent, and Effective—3 percent). The problem with this approach is that it generally fails to produce a positive impact on the culture. For a performance management program to be linked to the culture, it must reward those factors that are most significant to its success. For example, rewarding specific behaviors for customer service links it to the culture, as opposed to arbitrarily checking some vague measures on a fixed performance scale. A "culturally anchored evaluation" relies heavily on the leader's involvement in observing the employee performing certain highly valued behaviors. Figure 24.8 compares a traditional way of evaluating customer relations' skills to a culturally anchored approach.

   In Figure 24.8, the focus is on building positive work behaviors. The result is to reward and reinforce behavior that will lead to the development of a "customer-friendly" culture. Those individuals who do not embrace these behaviors will generally self-select out of the organization.

2. *Incentive plans.* The goal of an incentive plan is to provide a structured schedule for rewarding certain individual or group performance. From a cultural perspective, incentives should also reinforce behavior and performance that matches the organization's strategic direction. Some examples of culturally designed incentives include:
   - *Cultural sharing plans.* Incentive bonuses are paid based on the quality, service, and financial performance of the organization. Cultural sharing plans are similar to gainsharing plans that share some of the revenue gains with employees. The major difference between the two types of approaches is that cultural sharing plans seek to link strategy and culture with the incentive. Specific improvements in quality, service, and value are drivers for these culturally based incentives. If customer service, for example, improves, the other two elements are generally impacted, and vice versa. The cultural-sharing plan establishes specific trigger points (i.e., increased customer service scores, fewer product returns, community-based involvement) to reward employees. If these factors are effectively reinforced, the bottom line will be positively impacted and the image of the organization in the community will be enhanced.

FIGURE 24.8 Traditional vs. culturally anchored performance evaluation.

Example: Evaluating Customer Relations Skills

Traditional Evaluation Approach	Culturally Anchored Approach
(1) Evaluation Instructions:	**(1) Evaluation Instructions:**
Evaluate the employee on their customer relations skills using the following rating scale. Check only <u>one</u> rating level.	Evaluate the employee on the following cultural aspects regarding customer service. Check <u>all</u> that apply.
(2) Performance Rating Scale:	**(2) Cultural Contributions:**
___**OUTSTANDING:** Performs at the highest levels.	___Enhances and enriches the culture when delivering customer service.
___**VERY EFFECTIVE:** Performance is performed in a competent manner with few examples of errors.	**Provide examples:** _____ _____
___**EFFECTIVE:** Performance is adequate and acceptable.	___Has made one or more contributions to the success of the team in the past quarter.
___**MINIMALLY SATISFACTORY:** Performance is marginal and fails to meet standards.	**Identify contributions:** _____ _____
___**UNSATISFACTORY:** A deadline for improvement must be established or the employee will be terminated.	___Received one or more compliments from customers regarding service delivery.
	Provide examples: _____ _____
	___Successfully resolved at least one customer concern in the last three months.
	Detail problem(s) resolved: _____ _____ _____

- *Group cultural incentives.* These incentives are based on organizational units (e.g., marketing, financial services, sales, production, etc.) achieving certain culturally related goals. Some examples of these departmental contributions would include increasing customer relations scores; reducing departmental turnover rates; developing new work processes or improving existing ones; improving service turnaround times; or developing new quality and service initiatives.
- *Individual incentives.* These incentives are based on verifiable contributions of the individual employee to the organization. Some examples of contributions to the culture might include the enhancement of the individual employee's job skills: The employee successfully completes a critical competency-based training program; the employee takes the lead in developing new programs or approaches that will positively impact the organization's culture; and the employee suggests new ideas or processes that contribute to the financial success of the organization. The purpose of the individual incentive is to reward contributions that enhance the culture and the organization's strategy.

3. *Hybrid retirement plans.* Culturally driven rewards programs should adapt to the unique needs of its employees. Income-protection plans, which focus on such areas as retirement, health coverage, and disability protection, can be customized to meet these unique expectations of the culture. One such example is a cash balance retirement plan. This hybrid retirement approach bases benefits on the career average earnings of the employee. This type of retirement plan is perfect for those organizations that have a younger workforce. Cash balance plans are more portable than a traditional retirement plan and can be paid out in a lump sum when the employee leaves. This is extremely attractive to younger employees who want to build their career without staying in one place. Traditional defined benefit plans place more weight on the last 5 or 10 years of employment when paying out benefits. However, organizations that have a preponderance of long-term employees would *not* want to eliminate defined benefit plans in favor of a cash balance approach. Long-term employees are better off having a defined benefit plan because its value increases as the employee ages. Takeaway: Offer benefit plans geared to the employee's needs, age, service tenure, and income levels. A well-designed benefits program can enhance the culture by providing employees with a sense of security and belonging.

The total rewards programs offered by the organization can make or break its "cultural reputation." The Container Store, a previous "Best Company to Work For," provides health insurance coverage to everyone who works 18 hours or more a week. The Container Store understands the importance of providing health coverage to lower-paid retail employees. The result has been lower employee turnover and a dramatic commitment to the organization's culture and mission.

Notes

CHAPTER 12

1. Jerome A. Colletti and Stockton Colt, "Identifying a Complex Sales Environment: Results of a Special Member Survey," *workspan*, April 2004.

2. Paul W. Mulvey, Gerald E. Ledford, Jr., and Peter V. LeBlanc. "Rewards of Work: How They Drive Performance, Retention and Satisfaction." *WorldatWork Journal*, Third Quarter 2000.

CHAPTER 13

1. An alternative view is that executives, who possess inside information, introduce/revise these plans when they believe the corporation is undervalued. Thus, the increased price reaction is a response to the information released, rather than the initiation/revision of the plan itself.

2. While not a major risk, executive theft or malfeasance does happen, for example, Tyco International (see Maremont and Cohen [2002] for details). Another example is the currently unfolding scandal on the backdating of options.

3. For an example of these problems in less-developed nations, see Leggett (2000).

4. One reason the board cannot review every decision is the limited amount of time they have to spend on corporate matters, especially if the corporation is not their primary employer. For example, Silverman (2000b) reports that directors work an average of 173 hours annually.

5. The decrease in the use of stock options prior to the date for expensing mandated under SFAS 123(revised) can be explained by the fact that mandatory expensing was widely anticipated.

6. Bebchuk and Fried (2004b) refer to pensions as stealth compensation.

7. To elaborate, as risk-averse individuals, most executives prefer fixed to conditional compensation. Exacerbating the desire for fixed compensation, if the executive does take conditional compensation (e.g., stock options), and the share price goes up significantly, he or she will earn what appears to be a windfall profit and will be widely criticized for doing so—especially if he or she has the misfortune to exercise those options in a year where the share price did not do so well.

8. Benefit less related costs.

9. This has traditionally been the case, driven in part by the favorable accounting treatment allowed fixed options granted at or above the market price. For example, Matsunaga (1995, note 6) finds only 5 percent of his sample firms issued options with an exercise price below the fair market value at the grant date. Given that fixed stock options no longer have favorable accounting treatment, their use may wane relative to other forms of compensation.

10. When share prices fall after the date of grant, resulting in the exercise price of the option being greater than the share price, companies sometimes grant additional options at the lower price and/or reduce the exercise price on the existing option.

11. Exhibit 99.2 of Pepsico Form 8-K filed with the Securities and Exchange Commission February 2, 2006.

12. A Form 4 is a Statement of Changes in Beneficial Ownership.

13. John T. Cahill, Form 4 filed with Securities and Exchange Commission February 3, 2006.

14. In some cases, companies have set up programs with investment bankers that allow (for a commission) the executive to engage in a simultaneous exercise of their options and sale of the shares acquired upon exercise. This allows the executive to avoid having to pay the exercise price on the shares being acquired, and, as a result, lowers the costs of the two transactions.

15. To the executive, a stock appreciation right is preferred to a stock option, as it allows the executive to avoid transaction costs associated with the exercise of the option and the subsequent sale of the shares acquired upon exercise. The corporation, on the other hand, prefers stock options, which are a source, rather than a use, of cash. In addition, in the past, pre-SFAS 123(revised), the financial reporting treatment for stock options was more favorable than that for stock appreciation rights (see Balsam and Paek [2001] for a discussion of these issues).

16. These plans are known as defined benefit plans.

17. These plans are known as defined contribution plans, the most common of which would be 401(k)s.

18. There are costs to these supplemental plans that do not exist for tax-qualified plans. With a tax-qualified plan, the corporation funds the plan and takes an immediate deduction at the time of funding, whereas the employee does not recognize income until the time he or she receives the pension. In contrast, supplemental plans cannot be funded or the employee would have to immediately recognize taxable income. Consequently, as the plan is not funded, the corporation cannot take an immediate deduction.

19. The corporation need not disclose the value of the benefits if "the aggregate amount of such compensation is the lesser of either $50,000 or 10% of the total of annual salary and bonus reported for the named executive officer" (Securities and Exchange Commission regulation S-K 229.402 (b)(2)(iii)(C)1). (Note: A proposal to revise this regulation is under consideration.)

20. Some financial incentive does exist. If the corporation performs well as a result of his or her actions, the CEO could get a raise from his or her current employer, and/or increase his or her reputation/value in the managerial labor market.

21. As an example of the risk involved, Reingold (2000) reports that starting in 1997, the top five executives of the Borders Group elected to take options in lieu of salaries. Reingold states that, "With his options under water, Vice-Chairman Bruce A. Quinnell had to borrow to pay his living expenses."

22. Most CEOs are covered by two defined benefit pension plans. The basic plan is at least partially funded, governed by ERISA (Employee Retirement Income Security Act), and guaranteed somewhat by the PBGC (Pension Benefit Guaranty Corporation). However, limits imposed by ERISA and the Internal Revenue Code limit the payouts from these plans. Thus, most corporations have a supplemental plan for their top executives. Given that the supplemental plan is not tax-qualified, if it were funded, the executive would be taxed immediately. Thus, these plans are generally unfunded.

23. For example, assuming the requirements set by the Internal Revenue Code are met, payments for employee life insurance and health care benefits are deductible by the employer but not recognized as income by the employee. Thus, the employee is better off having the employer purchase these items on his or her behalf than if the employer would have paid those amounts as salary, with the employee purchasing those benefits with his or her after-tax salary.

24. Miller and Scholes (1982) show this occurs when the corporate tax rate is less than that of the individual.

25. A plethora of possible explanations exist. One is that under prior accounting standards, an expense would have to be recognized for market-adjusted options (whereas none is recognized for most options currently granted); hence, accounting treatment has kept corporations from granting these options. The other is that managers want the upside potential associated with unadjusted options, and may have other mechanisms, for example, repricing, to control downside risk.

26. Fairclough (2000).

27. Corporations are not always successful in this retention, and many acknowledge that when multiple candidates are competing for the same position, the losers in the competition are likely to depart. For example, when Jeffrey R. Immelt was named to be John F. Welch's successor as CEO of General Electric, it took the two other internal candidates, Robert L. Nardelli and W. James McNerney, only nine days to secure positions as CEOs of Home Depot and Minnesota Mining & Manufacturing, respectively, leaving positions to be filled at GE Power Systems and GE Aircraft Engines (Lublin, Murray, and Brooks 2000).

CHAPTER 18

1. Variable pay usually is stated as compensation in the form of bonus, profit sharing, or incentive pay. The payout of variable pay is dependent upon certain criteria being met. The criteria may be company-based—return on expense (ROE), return on investment (ROI), profit targets—or it may be based on meeting organizational, group/team, or individual performance criteria.

Profit sharing is a form of compensation typically provided to all employees based on the company's profits. Companies usually have predetermined goals and formulas for calculating the amount that will be allocated to employees. Profit-sharing plans are implemented most often to achieve employee participation and identification with the organization's success. Payouts may be given as cash, deferred cash in a qualified retirement plan, company stock, or a cash/stock combination.

Performance-sharing plans base rewards on the performance of a combination of quantitative and/or qualitative measures. The popular balanced scorecard describes groupings of a family of measures. The primary objectives of performance-sharing plans are to increase employee identification with the organization's success and to increase employee understanding of what is important to the organization. Typical performance factors are based on measures from financial, business process, customers, and work force development.

The purpose of this chapter is to discuss four types of cash bonuses—sign-on, referral, spot, and retention.

Total Rewards Glossary

WORLDATWORK COURSE NAMES

This glossary is essential for every HR practitioner's library. It contains more than 1,350 total rewards terms compiled from WorldatWork's CCP®, CBP, and GRP® professional certification programs. WorldatWork courses that are related to the terms in this glossary are noted under each term and definition [e.g., C6, T11]. WorldatWork courses are listed here.

C1: Regulatory Environments for Compensation Programs
C2: Job Analysis, Documentation and Evaluation
C4: Base Pay Management
C5: Elements of Sales Compensation
C6: Principles of Executive Rewards
C6A: Advanced Concepts in Executive Compensation
C11: Performance Management—Strategy, Design, and Implementation
C12: Variable Pay—Incentives, Recognition, and Bonuses
C15: Global Compensation—Strategy in Practice
C17: Market Pricing—Conducting a Competitive Pay Analysis

B1: Fundamentals of Employee Benefits Programs
B2: Retirement Plans—Design and Management
B3: Health Care and Insurance Plans—Design and Management
B3A: Health Care and Insurance Plans—Financial Management
B5: Managing Flexible Benefits

W1: Introduction to Work-Life Effectiveness—Successful Work-Life Programs to Attract, Retain, and Motivate Employees
W2: The Flexible Workplace—Strategies for Your Organization

W3: Health and Wellness Programs—Creating a Positive Business Impact
W4: Organizational Culture Change—A Work-Life Perspective

T1: Total Rewards Management
T2: Accounting and Finance for the Human Resources Professional
T3: Quantitative Methods
T4: Strategic Communication in Total Rewards
T6: Mergers and Acquisitions: Benefits, Compensation, and Other HR Issues
T9: International Remuneration: An Overview of Global Rewards
T11: Fundamentals of Equity-based Rewards
T12: Outsourcing and Managing HR Service Partners

GR1: Total Rewards Management
GR2: Quantitative Methods
GR3: Job Analysis, Documentation, and Evaluation
GR4: Base Pay Management
GR5: Performance Management—Strategy, Design, and Implementation
GR6: Variable Pay—Incentives, Recognition, and Bonuses
GR7: International Remuneration: An Overview of Global Rewards
GR9: Strategic Communication in Total Rewards

For complete descriptions of all WorldatWork courses and certification requirements, go to www.worldatwork.org, or call Customer Relations at (877) 951-9191 United States and Canada only, or +1 (480) 922-2020.

Term	Definition	Courses
360-degree feedback	Assesses employee performance from several sources (i.e., peers, subordinates, supervisors, customers).	[T1, GR1]
401(k)	A required annual SEC filing for a public company that provides certain financial and related business information.	[C6, C6A, T11]
401(k) plan	A defined contribution benefit plan established by an employer that enables employees to make pretax contributions through salary reduction agreements within the format of a cash or deferred arrangement (CODA).	[B1, B2, C6, C6A, T6, T11, T12]
403(b) plan	A tax-sheltered annuity plan for not-for-profit organizations. There are similarities between 401(k) and 403(b) plans.	[B1, B2, T11, T12]

Term	Definition	Courses
457 plan	A tax-deferred retirement plan available to government employees and tax exempt organizations. There are similarities between 401(k), 403(b) and 457 plans.	[B1, B2, T12]
Ability to pay	The ability of a firm to pay a given level of wages or to fund a wage increase while remaining profitable. A frequent issue in union contract negotiations.	[C4, GR4, GR5]
Absolute frequency distribution	A table indicating the number of observed data in defined categories. For example, one column could contain numeric categories (e.g., 1–10, 11–20, etc.) or nominal categories such as cities (e.g., Richardson, Dallas, etc.), and the second column could contain the number or quantity in each category.	[T3, GR2]
Accelerated death benefit rider	Rider added to a life insurance policy that provides for payments (lump sum or monthly) while still living upon the occurrence of certain events (e.g., terminal illness). Accelerated benefits paid out reduce the benefits payable to beneficiaries at the policyholder's death.	[B3]
Accidental death and dismemberment insurance (AD&D)	Insurance that provides benefits in the event of loss of life, limbs or eyesight as the result of an accident. It is a term insurance product sold on a cents-per-thousand basis.	[B1, B3, B3A, B5, T6]
Account manager	The primary client contact (within the service partner) that handles many aspects/services of the client's account.	[T12]
Accounting Principles Board (APB)	Source of authority regarding rules and conventions for accounting from 1959 to 1973, when it was replaced by the Financial Accounting Standards Board (FASB).	[C6, C6A, T2, T11]

Term	Definition	Courses
Accounting Research Bulletin (ARB)	From 1939 to 1959, published generally accepted accounting principles (GAAP).	[T2]
Accounts payable	Money owed by a company to vendors/suppliers for goods and services received. Accounts payable is a current liability on the balance sheet.	[T2]
Accounts receivable	Money due to a company by its customers for goods and services sold. Accounts receivable is a current asset on the balance sheet.	[T2]
Accrual accounting	Accounting method that records revenue and expenses when incurred, regardless of whether revenue actually was received or expenses actually were paid. As an example, a manufacturing company records a sale when a product is shipped to the customer even if the sale was on credit. It also records at that time all expenses associated with that sale, regardless of whether the actual cash has been transferred.	[C6, C6A, T2, T11]
Accrual basis	In accounting, the principle of crediting sales to the period in which earned and matching expenses; no consideration is given to when cash is actually received or disbursed. Hence, net income is the difference between sales earned and expenses incurred during the period when the sale is recognized, usually no longer than a year.	[B3A]
Accrual of benefits (pension plans)	For defined benefit (DB) plans, it is the process of accumulating pension credits for years of credited service, expressed as an annual benefit to begin payment at normal retirement age.	[B1, T6]

Term	Definition	Courses
	For defined contribution (DC) plans, it is the process of accumulating funds in the individual employee's plan account.	
Accumulated benefit obligation (ABO)	The actuarial present value of benefits (whether vested or nonvested) attributed by the pension benefit formula to employee service rendered before a specified date and based on employee service and compensation (if applicable) before that date. The accumulated benefit obligation differs from the projected benefit obligation in that it includes no assumption about future compensation levels. For plans with flat-benefit or no-pay-related or service-related pension benefit formulas, the accumulated benefit obligation and the projected benefit obligation are the same.	
Acid test	See quick ratio.	[T2]
Acquired rights	The legal notion in many countries that once an employer provides an employee with a benefit on a regular and repeated basis, there is a contractual agreement between the employer and the employee to continue to provide that benefit.	[C15, T6, T9, GR7]
Acquisition	A transaction in which one company purchases some or all of another company, and the resulting entity resembles the purchaser.	[C11, C15, T2, T6, T9, GR7]
Across-the-board increase	An identical pay raise—either in a flat rate such as cents per hour or as a percentage of salary—given to all eligible employees. Also known as a general increase.	[C4, T1, GR1, GR4]

Term	Definition	Courses
Actively-at-work provision	A provision in many insurance policies stipulating that, if an employee is not actively at work on the day the policy goes into effect, coverage will not begin. The Interim Final Rules for Nondiscrimination in Health Coverage in the Group Market published in the Federal Register on Jan. 8, 2001 prohibit such provisions, but do provide limited exceptions (e.g., an employee may be required to begin work before coverage becomes effective).	[B3]
Actual contribution percentage (ACP) test	A nondiscrimination test applied to employer matching contributions to a 401(k) plan to determine if those contributions discriminate in favor of highly compensated employees (HCEs).	[B2, T6]
Actual deferral percentage (ADP) test	A nondiscrimination test applied to employee contributions to a 401(k) plan to determine if those contributions discriminate in favor of highly compensated employees (HCEs).	[B2, T6]
Actual hours worked	The time worked in a pay period by an employee, as opposed to scheduled hours. Calculation of actual hours worked includes regular hours plus overtime hours, less absences.	[C1, C4, GR4]
Actuarial assumptions	Assumptions made by actuaries to determine certain benefits costs (e.g., investment yield, mortality rate, employee turnover, salary increases, etc.)	[B2, B3A, T6]
Actuarial equivalent	An alternative form of benefit that is expected to be equal in present value to the original benefit.	[B1, B2]

Term	Definition	Courses
Actuarial valuation	The process used to estimate the present value of benefits to be paid under a plan, to compute the amount of contributions required to cover the estimated future liability for benefits, and to determine the expense to be reported on the company's books.	[B2, B3A, C15, T6, T9, GR7]
Actuary	A person trained in mathematics, statistics and legal accounting methods, and in the principles of sound operation of insurance, annuities and pension plans, who employs life-expectancy, demographic and financial projections and related data in the funding and management of such plans.	[B1, B2, B3A, C15, T6, T9, GR7]
Administrative services only (ASO)	A claims services arrangement provided by insurance carriers or third-party administrators (TPAs) to employers with self-insured health and/or disability benefits plans.	[B3, B3A, T6]
Administrative Simplification Provisions of 2001	Guarantees patients' rights and protections against the misuse or disclosure of their health records. Covers all medical records and other individually identifiable health information used or disclosed by a covered entity in any form, whether electronically, on paper or orally. Also referred to as the Privacy Rules of 2001.	[B3]
Administrator	The person or organization (frequently the plan sponsor or employer) specifically designated, by the terms of the instrument under which a pension or welfare plan operates, to direct the plan.	[B1, B3, B3A, B5]

Term	Definition	Courses
Adverse impact	The result of a facially neutral (i.e., not obviously discriminatory) human resources management practice and/or policy that affects a protected group differently than the other employees (i.e., to the disadvantage of the protected group).	[C1]
Adverse selection (anti-selection)	The tendency of individuals with a higher probability of incurring claims (high risk) to select the maximum amount of insurance protection, while those with lower probability elect lower levels of, or defer, coverage.	[B3A, B5]
Affiliate (less than 50 percent ownership)	A company in which another company has enough of an interest that the two companies are closely aligned with each other.	[T2]
Affiliated director	A member of the Board of Directors of a company who although not a current employee of the organization is either a retired employee and/or does business with the company (such as a financial or legal consultant or advisor).	[C6, C6A, T11]
Affirmative Action (AA)	Specific actions in recruitment, hiring, upgrading and other areas designed and taken for the purpose of ensuring equal employment opportunity and eliminating the present effects of past discrimination. For federal contractors, it may include goals to correct underutilization, relief such as back pay or correction of problem areas.	[C11]
Age Discrimination in Employment Act of 1967 (ADEA)	Federal legislation that made employees between the ages of 40 and 65 a protected class. The 1978 amendments to this act raised the minimum age limit for mandatory retirement to 70	[B1, B3, B3A, C1, C11]

Term	Definition	Courses
	for most employees. Amendments in 1986 effectively ended mandatory retirement based solely on age and expanded benefits entitlement (in the Older Workers Protection Act) by restoring the "equal benefit or equal cost" requirement for age-based differences in employee benefits plans. A 1996 amendment allows an exemption based on public safety, allowing police and fire departments and airlines, for example, to establish maximum hiring and mandatory retirement ages.	
Agent/ broker	Member of an indirect sales channel who sells products but does not take ownership of goods.	[C5]
Aggregate stop-loss provision (health and disability plans)	A provision that caps the maximum amount of losses at a specific dollar amount for a specific period of time, regardless of the number of incidents.	[B3]
Aging survey data	The practice of increasing market survey data by an assumed percentage representative of wage movement to bring the data to a consistent point in time. This practice also is known as "advancing" or "trending" the data.	[C2, C17, T3, GR2, GR3]
Allowance	Supplemental payments made to an expatriate such as those for hardship, relocation or the education of dependent children. Often referred to as premiums.	[C15, T9, GR7]
All-salaried workforce	A pay policy that makes exempt/ nonexempt status "invisible" to workers. Under this policy, all employees are paid on a salaried basis, and all pay is defined in the same terms, such as	[C4]

Term	Definition	Courses
	a monthly or annual salary. Fair Labor Standards Act (FLSA) requirements for overtime and minimum wage still must be met.	
Alternative minimum tax (AMT)	Introduced in the tax act of 1969, the AMT requires that any person with "preference" income as defined in the Internal Revenue Code (IRC) must complete the AMT calculation and pay the larger of that or the regular income tax. Under the AMT calculation, unrealized gain on exercise of an incentive stock option is considered preference income and must be included in income for AMT calculations. In addition, several regular deductions, such as state income and real estate taxes, cannot be deducted in AMT calculations.	[C6, C6A, T11]
American Jobs Creation Act (AJCA) of 2004	A federal tax law that provides that all amounts deferred under nonqualified deferred compensation plans are currently includable in gross income to the extent that they are not subject to a substantial risk of forfeiture. A number of requirements must be met by deferred compensation arrangements in order to avoid immediate taxation and potential penalties. Because of the broad definition of "deferred compensation," the act has far-reaching implications potentially affecting a wide variety of compensation vehicles, including equity-based rewards, as well as annual bonus deferrals and executive retirement plans.	[C6, C6A, T11]

Term	Definition	Courses
American Stock Exchange (AMEX)	An organization that oversees the buying and selling of publicly owned shares of stock listed on the exchange.	[C6, C6A, T11]
Americans with Disabilities Act of 1990 (ADA)	A federal law that creates nondiscrimination protections for people with disabilities, similar to Title VII of the Civil Rights Act of 1964, which is extended to other minorities. Under the law, employers may not refuse to hire or promote a person because of a disability, and employers are required to make "reasonable accommodations" to allow people with disabilities to perform essential functions. Regulations are enforced by the Equal Employment Opportunity Commission (EEOC).	[B1, B3, C1, C2, C4, C11, T2, T6, W3]
Amortization	The allocation of the cost of an intangible asset on the income statement over the projected life of that asset (excluding goodwill).	[T2]
Anniversary date	(1) The date used by insurance companies for the purpose of determining the experience rating for the completed accounting period and establishing the premium rates for the next period. (2) The date used in some pay systems to trigger a review of the employee's salary and/or to trigger a potential salary increase. It may be the anniversary of hiring, last pay increase, promotion or some other reference point.	[B3A, C4, GR4]

Term	Definition	Courses
Annual benefits statements	Under the Employee Retirement Income Security Act of 1974 (ERISA), employers are required to provide participants in qualified plans specific information about the status of their projected pension income or account balances, if requested.	[B1]
Annual bonus	Usually a lump-sum payment (cash, shares, etc.) made once a year in addition to an employee's normal salary or wage for a fiscal or calendar year. Generally nondiscretionary and not based on predetermined performance criteria or standards.	[C4, C12, C15, C17, T1, T9, GR1, GR4, GR5, GR6, GR7]
Annual enrollment period	See open enrollment period.	[B1]
Annual incentive	See annual bonus.	[C6, C6A, C15, T1, T11, GR1]
Annual retainer	Annual amounts paid to members of the board of directors in recognition of their election/ service on the board.	[C6A]
Annual statement of total rewards	See total rewards statement.	[B1, T4, GR9]
Annualized increase percent (also, equivalent annual percent increase)	A salary increase expressed as an annual rate of increase. It is calculated by dividing the number of months since the last increase (denominator) into 12 (numerator) and multiplying the result by the actual percent increase: (12 / number of months since last increase) $\times$ (percent increase).	[C4, GR4]
Annuity	A series of regular periodic payments comprising principal and interest. In the case of retirement, an annuity usually is purchased from an insurance company that pays the	[B1, B2, C15, T6, T9, GR7]

Term	Definition	Courses
	purchaser a monthly amount while still alive. Annuities may have more complicated features such as indexing, guarantee periods and benefits payable to a spouse or other beneficiary after death. There are several types of annuities. See also life annuity, life annuity with years certain, joint and survivor annuity.	
Anti-cutback rules	Provisions in the Internal Revenue Code (IRC) that prohibits employers from reducing accrued benefits in a qualified retirement plan.	[T6]
APB 25	An accounting standard, interpreted by the Financial Accounting Standards Board (FASB), that requires employers to recognize compensation cost for stock-based employee compensation plans based on the difference between the fair market value of the stock and the amount an employee must pay to acquire the stock (the "spread") or, in the case of options, the spread at the time of option grant. See also FAS 123.	[C6, C6A, T11]
Area differential	(1) Allowance paid to compensate expatriate employees for medium-term cultural and hardship factors present in his or her country of assignment compared to the base country. (2) Allowance paid to domestic or expatriate employees in certain geographic areas based on different average pay levels and/or cost of living.	[C4, C15, C17, GR4]
Asian Economy 2005	Goal of Asia-Pacific Economic Cooperation (APEC) to remove all trade barriers by 2005.	[C15, T9, GR7]

Term	Definition	Courses
Asia-Pacific Economic Co-operation	Established in 1989 to promote open trade and economic cooperation between Asia-Pacific countries. Members include: Australia, Brunei Darussalam, Canada, Chile, People's Republic of China, Hong Kong, China, Indonesia, Japan, Korea, Malaysia, Mexico, New Zealand, Papua New Guinea, Peru, Philippines, Russia, Singapore, Chinese Taipei, Thailand, United States and Vietnam.	[C15, T9, GR7]
Asset investment performance review	Periodic review of the actions of the asset manager(s) who are investing qualified pension plan assets. The administrators of such plans have a fiduciary responsibility to conduct this review regularly.	[T6]
Asset sale	A type of acquisition in which the purchaser only acquires certain identified assets and/or liabilities of the seller, with no obligation for any nonidentified assets or liabilities of the seller (e.g., a buyer only acquires one line of product from a multiline manufacturer).	[T6]
Assets	What an organization owns as shown on the organization's balance sheet.	[T2, T3, T6, GR2]
Assignment location	The country in which an expatriate lives and works while on assignment.	[C15]
Association of Southeast	A political, economic and tourism alliance of 10 Southeast	

Term	Definition	Courses
Asian Nations (ASEAN)	Asian countries established in 1967. Members include: Indonesia, Malaysia, Philippines, Singapore, Thailand, Brunei Darussalam, Vietnam, Laos, Myanmar, and Cambodia.	[C15, T9, GR7]
Auditor	An independent reviewer who examines a company's financial statements or internal controls.	[T6]
Automatic enrollment	As used in connection with a 401(k) plan, automatic enrollment refers to the practice of enrolling all eligible employees in a 401(k) plan at a predetermined deferral percentage, without requiring them to submit a request to participate. Employees who do not want to participate must file a request to be excluded. Plan design specifies how automatic deferrals will be invested. Also known as passive enrollment or negative enrollment.	[B2]
Automatic wage progression	Automatically increasing wages after specified periods of service, until the employee reaches the top of his or her salary range. Automatic wage progression often is achieved through an automatic step-rate pay system. Also known as length-of-service increases.	[C4, C15, T9, GR4, GR7]
Average	The sum of all values of a data set divided by the number of values in that set. Equivalent to the mean.	[T3, GR2]

Term	Definition	Courses
Average frequency (of salary increases)	Used to determine how often a salary increase is granted. It is determined by summing the months between increases granted for the employee groups and dividing by the number of increases and employees. Normally calculated on a department-wide or company-wide basis.	[C4, GR4]
Averagehourly earnings	Used to determine the amount an employee has earned over a period of time. It is determined by dividing hours worked per period into the total wages earned for that period.	[C4, GR4]
Average per-cent increase	Used to determine the average salary increase given. It is calculated by dividing the sum of salary increase amounts for all eligible employees by the eligible payroll. Both the numerator and the denominator include those who were eligible and participated but received no increase.	[C4, GR4]
Award	An amount of cash, a prize, a symbol or an intangible reward given as a form of recognition. Awards can be in the form of money, prizes, plaques, travel and public commendations. The payouts of sales contests usually are called "awards."	[C5, C11, C12, T1, GR1, GR5, GR6]
Back pay	Amount of pay due a worker for work performed but not paid, or agreed to as part of a dispute resolution.	[C1]

Term	Definition	Courses
Bail out	An acquisition transaction in which the seller is in poor financial condition and another company purchases the financially troubled company and improves their financial condition. This is normally a seller-originated transaction.	[T6]
Balance sheet	A financial statement of a company or other entity, showing what it owns (assets), what it owes (liabilities), and the owner's investment (shareholders' equity) in the entity at a point in time, such as the end of the fiscal year. The balance sheet is required by generally accepted accounting principles (GAAP) and is one of the four principle statements required by the Securities and Exchange Commission (SEC) to be reported to shareholders for publicly traded companies.	[C6, C6A, T2, T11]
Balance sheet approach	An expatriate compensation methodology that protects or equalizes an expatriate's purchasing power while on assignment abroad. Its primary objectives are to ensure equity among expatriates and their home or base country peers and to facilitate global mobility. The balance sheet approach may be either headquarters-based (expatriate remuneration is tied to headquarter country's salary and benefits structure) or home-country based (expatriate remuneration is tied to the salary and benefits structure of the home country of each expatriate) or some variation of both.	[C15, T9, GR7]

Term	Definition	Courses
Balanced Scorecard appraisal	A performance appraisal approach that incorporates both operational/behavior-based measures and financial/results-based measures. For each scorecard item (e.g., customer success, business process success) goals, measures, targets and initiatives are quantified and qualified.	[C11]
Bar chart	A graphical tool that helps visualize a frequency distribution, used with discrete data.	[T3, GR2]
Base country	See home country.	[C15]
Base pay	The fixed compensation paid to an employee for performing specific job responsibilities. It is typically paid as a salary, hourly or piece rate.	[C1, C2, C4, C5, C11, C15, C17, T1, T6, T12, GR1, GR3]
Base pay structure	The hierarchy of job grades and pay ranges established within an organization. The salary structure may be expressed in terms of job grades, job-evaluation points or policy lines.	[C2, C17, T1, GR1, GR3]
Base payroll	The sum of annual salaries and/or wages (base rates) paid at the opening of business on the first day of the plan year or last day of prior year (e.g., Dec. 31) before any increase.	[C4, C17, GR4]
Base rate	The hourly or salary amount paid for a job performed (does include shift differentials and overtime).	[C1]
Basic earnings per share	The net earnings available to common shareholders of an organization divided by the weighted average of total shares outstanding. No consideration is given in this calculation for common stock equivalents such as stock options.	[C6, C6A, T2, T11]

Term	Definition	Courses
Basic plan with major medical	A medical insurance plan that provides for coverage of almost all hospital and surgical charges and some other medical expenses up to a specified amount, without a deductible under the basic plan. Thereafter, the major medical portion of the plan pays benefits, after a deductible and coinsurance requirements have been met, up to a maximum limit.	[B3, B3A]
Behavior-based appraisal	A performance assessment tool that focuses specifically on the behaviors of those being rated as opposed to results. In other words, appraisal is based on what individuals are doing to contribute to the organization—not what they produce.	[C11, GR5]
Benchmark job	A job that is commonly found and defined, used to make pay comparisons, either within the organization or to comparable jobs outside the organization. Pay data for these jobs are readily available in published surveys.	[C2, C17, T1, GR1, GR3, GR4]
Benchmark job data	Market and company data for surveyed jobs.	[T3, GR2]
Benchmark-ing	The process by which an organization seeks to identify top performing organizations and analyzes their strategies, policies and practices for the purpose of learning some or all of them.	[C12, C15, T9, GR5, GR6, GR7]
Beneficiary	The person designated to receive the benefits resulting from the death of an employee, such as the proceeds of a life or accident insurance policy or benefits from a pension plan.	[B2, B3, B3A]

Term	Definition	Courses
Benefit reductions	A cost-containment measure utilized by an organization to reduce its expenses through reduction in benefit coverage (e.g., increase in medical plan deductibles, increase in employee contributions, reduction in annual limits in dental plan, etc.).	[B3, B3A]
Benefits	Programs that an employer uses to supplement the cash compensation an employee receives. Benefits include income protection programs such as publicly mandated and voluntary private "income protection" programs that often are provided through insurance, pay for time not worked and other employee perquisites.	[B1, B3, C2, C5, C12, C15, C17, T1, T4, T11, T12, W1, GR1, GR3, GR6, GR9]
Bennett Amendment	An amendment to the Civil Rights Act of 1964 that states that it shall not be unlawful practice to differentiate compensation on the basis of sex if such differentiation is authorized by the Equal Pay Act.	[C1]
Bereavement leave	A paid absence that is the result of a family death. What constitutes a "family death" and the amount of time off allowed varies by organization.	[B1]
Beta	(1) A measure of volatility of a stock, normally ranging from 0.55 to 2.0, used in determining the cost of capital for a company. (2) In multiple regression, the weights of coefficients that apply to the model after all the variables (xs and ys) have been transformed to a common metric of z-scores. Beta weights	[C6, C6A, T3, T11]

Term	Definition	Courses
	indicate the strength of the relationship between an independent variable and the dependent variable. They also are known as standardized partial regression weights.	
Bi-modal	A distribution having two modes.	[T3, GR2]
Binomial option pricing model	A mathematical formula that determines a theoretical value for an option on stock subject to trade on an option exchange. May be used by a company that chooses to apply the FAS 123 rule to stock granted to employees. See also FAS 123.	[C6, C6A, T11]
Black-Scholes Model	A mathematical model originally developed by Fisher Black and Myron Scholes to value stock options traded on public markets. It estimates the theoretical price an individual would pay for a traded option and considers stock price on grant date, option exercise price, number of years till exercise, dividend yield, risk free rate of return and stock price volatility. See also FAS 123.	[C6, C6A, T11]
BlueBird	See windfall.	[C5]
Board of directors (BOD)	A group of individuals who are elected by the shareholders of a corporation to represent the shareholders' interests. The BOD make decisions on major company issues and monitor the managers of the corporation.	[C6, C6A]
Bona fide occupational qualification (BFOQ)	Typically refers to a valid job requirement. Origin of the term BFOQ is found in Title VII of the Civil Rights Act (1964), which prohibits employment discrimination on the basis of race, color, religion, sex or national origin. Under certain conditions, however, a requirement	[C1, C2, GR3]

Term	Definition	Courses
	for a specific gender or religious affiliation is allowed if the requirement is a BFOQ for a given job; for example, the requirement of Catholic affiliation for the job of Catholic priest.	
Bona fide wellness program	As provided by the Interim Final Rules for Nondiscrimination in Health Coverage in the Group Market (2000), a wellness program that provides a reward based on an individual's ability to meet a health-related standard related to health promotion or disease prevention. See also Notice of Proposed Rulemaking for Bona Fide Wellness Programs–2001.	[B3, W3]
Bond	A debt issued by a public (government) or private (corporate) organization that usually pays a fixed, guaranteed interest rate and repays the face or par value at maturity.	[B2, T2]
Bonus	An after-the-fact reward or payment (may be either discretionary or nondiscretionary) based on the performance of an individual, a group of workers operating as a unit, a division or business unit, or an entire workforce. Payments may be made in cash, shares, share options or other items of value. In the context of sales compensation, a defined, preestablished amount of money to be earned for achieving a specified performance goal. Planned bonus amounts commonly are expressed as a percent of the incumbent's base salary, salary range midpoint, percentage of target cash compensation or incentive compensation, or a defined dollar amount. See also discretionary and nondiscretionary bonus.	[C5, C11, C12, C15, T1, T2, T9, GR1, GR5, GR6, GR7]

Term	Definition	Courses
Bonus guarantee	A payment in addition to base salary that is made regardless of performance (e.g., an incentive award that is guaranteed, usually to a new hire or to a newly promoted person). It is usually non-recoverable by the company.	[C6, C6A, T11]
Bonus pay plans	Cash or other items of value, such as stock or stock options, based on accomplishments achieved.	[C17, T6]
Bonus progressivity	See incentive progessivity.	[C6, C6A, T11]
Bonus-eligible	A term referring to groups or classes of employees who are eligible to participate in a bonus program.	[C6, C6A, C12, T11, GR5, GR6]
Book unit award plan	A type of long-term incentive plan in which an employee is awarded stock units valued at the book value per share. In a book value appreciation plan an increase in the book value of the stock accrues to the benefit of the employee. In a full value book value plan the full value of the book value units accrues to the benefit of the employee, usually after fulfilling a vesting period.	[C6, C6A, T11]
Book value	Total assets minus total liabilities. Also known as shareholders' equity or net worth.	[T2]
Book value (BV) per share	Total shareholders' equity divided by the number of common shares outstanding. Book value sometimes is used in incentive plans in privately owned companies in which a fair market value of shares is not readily known.	[C6, C6A, T2, T11]
Book value purchase plans	An incentive program in which employees purchase shares of their organization at book value	[C6, C6A, T11]

Term	Definition	Courses
	per share. They subsequently can sell the shares back to the organization at the then book value.	
Bottom line	See net income after tax.	[C6, C6A, T11]
Break-in-service (BIS) year (ERISA pension plan standards)	An anniversary year during which a plan participant does not complete more than 500 hours of service and earns no pension benefits. If a nonvested employee incurs five or more consecutive break years, prior service may be disregarded in determining pension benefits.	[B1]
Broadband-ing	A pay structure that consolidates a large number of pay grades and salary ranges into much fewer broad bands with relatively wide salary ranges, typically with 100 percent or more difference between minimum and maximum.	[C2, C4, T1, GR1, GR3, GR4]
Broad-based stock option plan	A form of employee share ownership plan. Under a broad-based stock option plan, most (or all) employees are eligible to receive grants of options on company stock. A stock option gives an employee the right to purchase company shares at a specified price during a specified period of time.	
Broker	An individual or business that works on commission rather than consulting fees to assist with placing and managing employee benefits programs.	[T12]
Budget	A financial plan for the allocation of money to pay for wages and indirect compensation for a covered group of employees over a specified period.	[C4, GR4]

Term	Definition	Courses
Bureau of Labor Statistics (BLS)	The principle fact-finding agency for the federal government in the broad field of labor economics statistics. Useful statistics include: CPI, NCS data, labor statistics and other wage and benefits data.	[C1, C2, C4]
Business life cycle	Generally accepted as a four-stage cycle used to describe the life of a product or company: threshold (or start-up), growth, maturity and decline.	[C2, C4, C6, C6A, C17, T11]
Business plan	See business strategy.	[C6]
Business strategy	The broad principles and approaches that guide the day-to-day operations of the business, ensuring that the business supports the organization's mission, goals and objectives. The business strategy includes the advantage that the organization believes it has over its competition.	[C6, C11, C12, C15, T1, W1, W2, W3, W4, GR1, GR3, GR6]
Business travel accident (BTA) insurance	An insurance plan that provides benefits for an accident that occurs when an employee is traveling on company business.	[B1, B3, B3A, C6, C6A, C15, T11]
Buyers Health Care Action Group (BHCAG)	An employer health care purchasing coalition. Employers in the coalition combine their purchasing power to provide access to quality, cost-effective care for their employees. BHCAG also lobbies to stimulate health care reform.	[B3]
C corporation	An incorporated business that is a separate entity from its owners.	[T6]
Cafeteria approach	An expatriate compensation methodology in which, in addition to base pay, performance	[C15, T9, GR7]

Term	Definition	Courses
	incentives and normal domestic benefits, expatriates are offered a choice of some of a list of perquisites, some of which are cost-effective in various foreign countries.	
Cafeteria plan	As defined in the Internal Revenue Code (IRC) Section 125, a flexible benefits arrangement in which participants may choose between taxable and nontaxable compensation elements. Examples include premium conversion (pretax premium), flexible spending accounts and broad employee-choice programs that include certain tax-advantaged features.	[B1, B3, B3A, B5, T6]
Call-back pay	A guarantee of pay for a minimum number of hours when employees are called back to their work at times when they are not scheduled to work. They receive pay for at least the minimum number of hours established, even if they do not work that number of hours.	[C4]
Call-in pay	Guaranteed pay for a set minimum amount of time for employees who report to work at the usual time and for whom there is no work. The employees receive pay for at least the specified minimum number of hours, even if they did not work the minimum number of hours. Sometimes called report-time pay.	[C4]
Cap	The total incentive opportunity that can be earned in a given period. Cap may also refer to the maximum cash compensation an employee may earn in a given time period.	[C5, C12, GR6]

Term	Definition	Courses
Capital	Cash used/invested to generate future income.	[T2]
Capital assets	Long-term assets that cannot easily be converted into cash (e.g., property, equipment, furniture) and that are usually held for a long period, including real estate, equipment, and so on. Also called fixed assets, permanent assets or noncurrent assets.	[T2]
Capital budget	A plan to finance expenditures for capital assets over a specified period of time.	[T2]
Capital employed	A company's equity plus its long-term debt. Sometimes used as a performance measure for executive incentive plans. May also be referred to as permanent capital.	[C6, C6A, T11]
Capital gains taxation	The taxes applicable to gains realized on the sale of capital assets such as real estate or company shares. Tax laws specify time periods for holding assets to qualify for long term capital gains tax rates, which usually have been lower than ordinary tax rates or rates for short term capital gains. Congress periodically changes rates applicable to various types of income.	[C6, C6A, T11]
Capital lease	A method of financing operating equipment; a lease obligation that looks much like an installment purchase, as the lessee assumes nearly all of the risks and rewards that accompany ownership (e.g., lessee pays for the upkeep, maintenance and servicing of the equipment during the lease). A capital lease must be capitalized on the balance sheet	[T2]

Term	Definition	Courses
	(e.g., leased asset is recorded as a noncurrent asset, lease obligation is recorded as a noncurrent liability).	
Capitation	A fixed prepayment to a provider to deliver medical or dental services to a particular group of patients. The payment remains the same regardless of how many services each patient uses or the nature of the services used, so it is possible for the provider to lose money, break even or profit. Capitation is the characteristic payment method to providers in health maintenance organizations (HMOs).	[B1, B3]
Career average earnings (CAE)	See career average pay (CAP) pension plan.	[B1, B2]
Career average pay (CAP) pension plan	A type of defined benefit (DB) pension plan that bases retirement benefits on the average pay during an employee's career. Career average pay may also be defined as career average salary (CAS) or career average earnings (CAE).	[B1, B2]
Career average salary (CAS)	See career average pay (CAP) pension plan.	[B1, B2]
Career ladder	A series of defined levels within a job family where the nature of the work is similar (e.g., accounting, engineering) and the levels represent the organization's requirements for increased skill, knowledge and responsibility as the employee moves through a career. Parallel or overlapping, ladders called dual career ladders are sometimes created to allow for "cross-,	[C2, C4, GR3, GR4]

Term	Definition	Courses
	overs" into another ladder (e.g., from engineering into management). Also called career pathing.	
Career opportunities	A plan for employees to advance their own career goals and may include advancement into a more responsible position in an organization.	[T4, GR9]
Carve-out	Insurance that provides coverage for specific services (e.g., chiropractic treatments, behavioral health care) under a contract that is separate from the general health plan.	[B3]
Cash accounting	Accounting method that records income when received and expenses when paid.	[T2]
Cash balance pension plan	A defined benefit (DB) pension plan that blends the features of a traditional DB plan with the features of a defined contribution (DC) plan. In a cash balance plan, hypothetical individual accounts periodically receive a contribution credit and an interest credit. Contribution credits usually are a percent of pay and may vary with age and/or service. Cash balance plans are also referred to as hybrid pension plans.	[B1, B2]
Cash compensation	The sum of all cash payments made to an individual for services (i.e., employment) during a given year.	[C4, C17, GR4]
Cash flow	The amount paid out throughout the year coupled with the time of payment and all the attendant changes.	[C4, T3, GR2, GR4]

Term	Definition	Courses
Cash flow statement	A financial statement that outlines the amount of money actually received and paid out within a particular period, usually no longer than a year. It represents the change in the cash and cash equivalents account for the period involved.	[T2]
Cash option exercise	When an individual pays cash for the option exercise price of a number of shares exercised to purchase the shares.	[C6, C6A, T11]
Cash or deferred arrangement (CODA)	A qualified plan that gives an employee the option to contribute some of his/her salary to the plan on a pretax basis. One example is a 401(k) plan.	[B1]
Cash performance target plans	The right to receive a cash payment if company financial targets are achieved over a period of time (usually three to five years).	[C6]
Cash-based plans	Long-term incentive plans designed to motivate strategic performance with cash awards.	[C12, GR6]
Cashless option exercise	When an individual exercises an option through an outside broker or dealer with the broker in effect making simultaneous purchases and sales of the underlying option shares and delivering cash or stock to the individual for the option profit.	[C6, C6A, T11]
Cave-in	An incentive award that is lower than expected because of events outside the participants' control.	[C12, GR6]
Central tendency	In statistics, some clustering around a central value in a distribution of data usually determined by one of the measures of location; that is, mean, median or mode.	[C2, C17, T3, GR2, GR3]
Central tendency error	The result when some raters evaluate the individual	[C11, T3, GR2, GR5]

Term	Definition	Courses
	performance of subordinates toward the middle of a performance scale, reflecting the belief that everyone's performance is about average or that different performance levels are not discernible.	
Centraliz-ation	The extent to which pay policy determination and salary administration practices are controlled, usually by a central work group, across organizational units. The degree of depends on the culture and compensation strategy of an organization.	[C4, C6, C17, GR4]
Chance of loss	In insurance, the probability that an event (e.g., injury, death, etc.) will occur.	[B3A]
Change in control agreement/ provision	An agreement or provision related to a stated percentage change in ownership whereby provisions of an employment contract may cause an increase or an acceleration of specified payments or benefits.	[C6, C6A, T6, T11]
changes in methods in accounting	An election under Section 404(a) with respect to a qualified foreign plan constitutes the adoption of a method of accounting if the election is made in the taxable year in which the plan is adopted. Any election under Section 404(a) with respect to a preexisting plan, however, constitutes a change in method of accounting requiring the Commissioner's consent under Section 446(e) and an adjustment under Section 481(a). Additionally, any other change in the method used to determine the amount taken into account under	

Term	Definition	Courses
	Section 404(a), as well as the revocation of any election under Section 404(a), constitutes a change in accounting method subject to the consent and adjustment requirements of Sections 446(e) and 481(a). These sections provide procedures for obtaining the Commissioner's consent to make certain changes in methods of accounting under Section 404(a). Additionally, §1.404(a)-7 provides special procedural rules applicable (along with the rules under this section) for retroactive and transition-period elections under Section 404(a).	
Channel	Medium through which the message is transmitted between a sender and a receiver.	[T4, GR9]
Charge to earnings	When an organization recognizes an expense in the income statement. Generally accepted accounting principals (GAAP) accounting requires an organization to expense executive compensation programs over the time period when services are actually performed, not necessarily when the compensation is paid.	[C6, C6A, T11]
Circular models	Depict communication as a constantly revolving spiral of sending a message and receiving feedback about that message.	[T4, GR9]
Claims utilization report	Report summarizing the findings of an evaluation of employees' use of medical services under a health and welfare plan.	[T6, W3]
Classification method of job evaluation	A nonqualitative form of job content evaluation that compares jobs to predefined class descriptions established for each job grade. Jobs are placed in	[C2, C17, T1, GR1, GR3]

Term	Definition	Courses
	whichever classification best describes them.	
Cliff vesting	In executive compensation; 100 percent vested in three years after the grant.	[C6]
COBRA	See Consolidated Omnibus Budget Reconciliation Act of 1985.	[B1, B3, B3A, T6]
Coefficient of determination	The proportion of variation in the dependent variable that can be attributed to the relationship with another variable or combination of variables. It has values between 0.0 and 1.0. For simple linear regression, it has a value equal to the square of the correlation coefficient.	[T3, GR2]
Coinsurance	The percent of covered expense paid by the covered individual versus paid by the benefits plan (e.g., plan pays 80 percent coinsurance for hospital expenses, and the employee pays 20 percent coinsurance). See copayment.	[B1, B3, B3A]
COLA	See cost-of-living adjustment.	[C4, C15, T9, GR4, GR7]
Collateral	Assets pledged by a borrower as security for a loan or other credit.	[T2]
Collective bargaining agreements	Agreements between employee groups and employers detailing work conditions including working hours, vacation and holiday entitlements, termination of service provisions and sometimes benefit entitlements. These agreements may be specific to one company or industry or apply nationally.	[B1, B5, C4, C15, C17, T6, T9, GR4, GR7]
Collectivism	Degree to which a culture favors the needs of the broader society.	[C15, T9, GR7]

Term	Definition	Courses
Combination pay plan	A combination pay plan has two elements: a base salary and one or more cash incentive components, such as a bonus or a commission.	[C5]
Commercial paper	Short-term note issued by a company to finance short-term credit needs (e.g., accounts receivable, inventory).	[T2]
Commission	A payment based on a formula that is used to calculate the incentive compensation opportunity for salespeople. In this context, it provides a predetermined incentive amount for each discrete unit of sales made by the salesperson. Commissions commonly are expressed as a percent of each sales dollar (revenue), percent of gross margin (profit), or a dollar amount per unit sold. A commission-only compensation program is sometimes known as "full commission" or "straight commission."	[C5, C11, C12, C15, T1, T2, GR1, GR6]
Common review date	The date on which all (or a group of) employees receive pay increases. For example, a company may implement increases for all employees on April 1; employees hired off cycle usually receive prorated increases. Also known as focal point review date.	[C4, GR4]
Common shares	In corporate finance, the form in which an owner's interest is represented—distributed in units known as shares with voting rights and possibly dividends. Appreciation and dividends are not fixed or guaranteed.	[C6, C6A, T2, T11]
Common stock	See common shares.	[C6, C6A, T2, T11]

Term	Definition	Courses
Communication	Creating understanding and transferring meaning.	[T4, GR9]
Communication strategy	Utilizing effective communication to drive business performance, link business goals with personal outcomes for employees, lead to understanding and valuing, and defining employer/employee relationships.	[T4, GR9]
Community involvement	Corporate citizenship—not only external community outreach, such as company giving (foundations or direct), but also a renewed focus on building a strong internal sense of community. Formal ethics programs, shared (or catastrophic) leave banks, and disaster relief funds are some of the creative new ways of taking care of each other.	[W1]
Community-rated insurance	An insurance contract that allows for an increase in the insured benefit or premium rebate based on the overall experience of the insurance company's portfolio of business.	[B3, B3A]
Comparable worth	The doctrine that men and women who perform work of the same "inherent value" should receive similar levels of compensation. According to this doctrine, jobs have an inherent value that can be compared across jobs of quite different content. Those accepting this position maintain that women performing jobs of comparable worth to those performed by men should be paid the same as men, excepting allowable differences (for example, seniority plans, merit plans, production-based pay plans or different locations).	[C1, C2, C17, GR3]

Term	Definition	Courses
Compa-ratio	The ratio of an actual pay rate (numerator) to the midpoint or some other control point for the pay range (denominator). Compa-ratios are used to measure and monitor an individual's actual rate of pay to the midpoint or control point of their range. A compa-ratio can be calculated for a group, a department or an entire organization.	[C4, C17, T1, T3, GR1, GR2, GR4]
Compensable factor	Any factor used to provide a basis for judging job value to create a job worth hierarchy (job evaluation). The generic compensable factors established by the Equal Pay Act of 1963 are skill, effort, responsibility and working conditions.	[C2, C17, GR3]
Compensable factor degree	In quantitative job-evaluation plans, measurement scales or "yardsticks" that identify specific levels or amounts of a compensable factor. Usually, there are five to seven degrees for each factor.	[C2, C17, GR3]
Compensable factor weight	The percentage weight or "influence" a single compensable factor has in a quantitative job-evaluation plan.	[C2, C17, GR3]
Compensable factors	Any characteristic used to provide a basis for comparing job content in a job-evaluation scheme. The most commonly used factors include responsibility, skill required, effort and working conditions.	[T1, GR1]
Compensation	Cash provided by an employer to an employee for services rendered. Compensation comprises the elements of pay (e.g., base pay, variable pay, stock, etc.) that an employer offers an employee in return for his or her services.	[C2, C5, C11, C12, C15, C17, T1, T4, T9, T11, T12, W1, GR1, GR6, GR7, GR9]

Term	Definition	Courses
Compensation budget	See budget.	[C4]
Compensation committee	A subset of the board of directors that approves pay and incentive award programs involving senior management of the company.	[C4, C6, C6A, T11]
Compensation committee report	A narrative description of the policies, philosophies, considerations and events that influence the committee's pay decisions with respect to the chief executive officer and other senior managers in a company. The Securities and Exchange Commission (SEC) requires this report to be included in the company's proxy statement.	[C6, C6A, T11]
Compensation cost	The total cost to the organization, including the unrealized or unknown future cost effects of today's compensation decisions regarding the total compensation program. Included are base pay, incentive opportunities, benefits costs and liabilities, perquisite costs, time-off programs (vacations, sick pay, etc.).	[C4]
Compensation philosophy	Ensures that a compensation program supports an organization's culture.	[C1, C4, C11, C12, C17, T4, GR4, GR5, GR6, GR9]
Compensation policy	Ensures that a compensation program carries out the compensation strategy while supporting the compensation philosophy.	[C1, C4, C11, C12, C17, T4, GR4, GR5, GR6, GR9]

Term	Definition	Courses
Compensation strategy	The principles that guide design, implementation and administration of a compensation program at an organization. The strategy ensures that a compensation program, consisting of both pay and benefits, supports an organization's mission, goals and business objectives. It may also specify what programs will be used and how they will be administered.	[C1, C4, C12, C15, C17, T1, T4, T9, GR1, GR4, GR5, GR6, GR9]
Compensation tax axiom	A tax principle whereby the company only receives a tax deduction for compensation paid to an employee that results in ordinary income to the employee. The company's tax deduction is at the same time and in the same amount as an employee's ordinary income.	[C6, C6A]
Compensatory and punitive damages	Under the Civil Rights Act of 1991, plaintiffs (employees) may sue defendants (employers) for discrimination, and if they prevail, they may receive payment for suffering the violation and to penalize employers for such violation.	[C1]
Competency	A behavior, attribute or skill that is a predictor of personal success.	[C4, C11, C17, T1, GR1, GR3, GR4, GR5]
Competency-based appraisal	A performance assessment tool that focuses on the competencies of those being rated. Competencies may include traits, knowledge, skills, abilities or other personal attributes.	[C11]
Competency-based pay	A base pay delivery method that focuses on attributes, personality traits and behaviors of an employee. Competencies can be	[C11, T1, GR1]

Term	Definition	Courses
	defined for both behaviors and results.	
Competitive compa-ratio	The ratio of market pay to a company's midpoint.	[C17]
Competitive pay policy	The strategic decision an organization makes about which labor markets to use as comparison groups and how to set pay levels with respect to those groups. After choosing the comparison group, the organization must decide its market position with respect to the group.	[C4, C17, T1, GR1, GR4, GR5]
Completion bonus	A special, usually lump-sum, payment sometimes made upon the successful conclusion of an expatriate assignment. It is designed to encourage the expatriate to stay with the job until the task is completed.	[C15]
Complimentary and Alternative Medicine (CAM) therapies	A broad range of therapies not commonly used, studied, accepted, understood or prescribed by traditional U.S. physicians or hospitals. Examples include acupuncture, massage therapy, herbal therapies, biofeedback, naturopathy and homeopathy. Therapies may be used as an alternative to conventional treatment or in addition to conventional treatment ("complimentary"). In 1998, Congress established the National Center for Complimentary and Alternative Medicine (NCCAM) at the National Institutes of Health (NIH) to stimulate, develop and support research on CAM.	[B3]
Composite system	An expatriate compensation methodology in which different classes of expatriates are compensated under different	[C15, T9, GR7]

Term	Definition	Courses
	compensation programs. For example, senior expatriates may be paid under a balance sheet approach while management trainees are localized.	
Compound interest	The financial return that results when interest in succeeding periods is earned not only on the initial principal but also on the accumulated interest of prior periods. Also referred to as the value of money over time.	[T3, GR2]
Compound salary growth rate (CSGR)	The annualized percentage rate of growth in salary during a specified period of time. For example, an employee who was hired at $18,000 five years ago and earned $32,000 today has experienced a CSGR of 12.2 percent.	[T3, GR2]
Comprehensive flexible benefits plan	See full flex plans.	[B1, B5]
Comprehensive health plan	A medical insurance program that provides for coverage of almost all medical expenses under one plan or contract. Before benefits are payable, the plan usually requires an employee to pay an annual deductible and then coinsurance (usually 20 percent) thereafter until an annual out-of-pocket maximum is met. After the maximum is met, the plan provides 100 percent coinsurance for the rest of the year.	[B3, B3A]
Compressed work week	Work schedule that condenses a 40-hour week into fewer than 5 days or an 80-hour two-week period into fewer than 10 days.	[B1, B5, T1, GR1, W1, W2]

Term	Definition	Courses
Compression	Pay differentials too small to be considered equitable. The term may apply to differences between 1) the pay of supervisors and subordinates, 2) the pay of experienced and newly hired personnel of the same job, and 3) pay-range midpoints in successive job grades or related grades across pay structures.	[C4, GR4]
Consolidated Omnibus Budget Reconciliation Act of 1985 (COBRA)	A federal law that entitles employees and their covered dependents to elect to continue group health coverage after a qualifying event by paying the full cost of group coverage plus an administrative charge for a specified period of time, usually between 18 and 36 months. Qualifying events include termination of employment, reduced work hours, death, divorce and separation.	[B1, B3, B3A, B5, T6, T12]
Constructive receipt	The controlling tax principle for determining the timing of tax liability in case of a deferred payment. The law provides that when an individual can "reach out and take" compensation is the time when it is taxed, even if the employee chooses not to take it at that time. There are ways of legally deferring income without coming under the concept of constructive receipt.	[B5, C6, C6A, C15, T11]
Consumer Price Index (CPI)	An indicator of the cost of living published by the Bureau of Labor Statistics, U.S. Department of Labor. It is an indicator of the changing purchasing power of the dollar. Specifically, it measures price changes of items in a fixed "market basket" of goods and services purchased by a hypothetical average family.	[C4]

Term	Definition	Courses
Consumer-driven health plan (CDHP)	A plan that attempts to contain medical benefits costs by empowering consumers to make informed choices regarding the quality and efficiency of their health care. Consumer-driven health plans run on a continuum, with components that can stand alone or be coordinated with one another. CDHP today is often a plan including a personal health account, strategic deductibles and copayments. In future, plan design will likely include information on provider and hospital outcomes, along with incentives meant to steer consumers toward efficient providers.	[B1, B3, B5]
Continental pay	Increased labor mobility within regions may contribute to greater consistency in pay practices.	[C15, T9, GR7]
Contingency	A potential liability.	[T2]
Contingent compensation	Any potential pay or benefit that is dependent on employee behavior and/or performance.	[T1, GR1, GR5]
Contract	See service agreement.	[T12]
Contributory benefits plan	A program in which the employee contributes part (or all) of the cost, and any remainder is covered by the employer.	[B3A]
Control point	The point within a salary range representing the desired pay for a fully qualified, satisfactory performer in a job or group of jobs at a given time (usually the midpoint of the salary range).	[C4, C17, GR4]
Controlled foreign corporation	Controlled foreign corporation means any foreign corporation if more than 25 percent of (1) the total combined voting power of all classes of stock of	

Term	Definition	Courses
	such corporation entitled to vote, or (2) the total value of the stock of such corporation, is owned, or is considered by U.S. shareholders on any day during the taxable year of such foreign corporation.	
Convenience samples	Drawn from a population based on ease of the sampling set. Even though the goal is the same as in random sampling (i.e., to represent a population) most salary surveys are convenience samples.	[T3, GR2]
Convenience services	Save employees time and/or money by offering various products and services in the workplace. Examples include on-site services such as concierge, dry cleaning, day care, car wash, masseur/masseuse, take-home meals, as well as other services such as payroll deduction, purchase of home and automobile insurance, travel services and day care.	[B1, B5, C11, C15, T6, T9, T12, GR7]
Convertible bonds	See convertible debenture.	[T2]
Convertible debenture	A bond with privileges of being converted by the holder to ordinary common shares at specified times and prices.	[C6, C6A, T2, T11]
Convertible preferred stock	Preferred stock that offers the holder the option of converting to common stock at specified times and prices.	[C6, C6A, T11]
Convertible securities (such as debentures or preferred stock)	A bond or preferred stock offering the option of conversion to ordinary common stock.	[C6, C6A, T11]

Term	Definition	Courses
Coordination of benefits (COB)	A group health insurance policy provision designed to prevent an employee from collecting more than 100 percent of the charges for the same medical expense when the employee or one of their dependents are covered by two medical plans (i.e., as an insured under one plan and as a dependent under another). Also, referred to as standard or traditional COB. See also non-duplication of benefits.	[B1, B3, B3A, B5]
Copayment	A cost-sharing arrangement under a health plan in which the participant pays a specified charge for a specified service, usually at the time of service. Differs from coinsurance in that a copayment is expressed as a specific dollar amount, while co-insurance is a percentage of the cost of the service.	[B1, B3, T1, GR1]
Core hours	Specific range of hours when all employees must be at work (e.g., 9 A.M. to 1 P.M.)	[W1, W2]
Core-plus plans	Term used to describe a flexible benefits plan in which the employer mandates and pays for a defined base (core) of benefits and the employees are able to buy supplemental or additional benefits. May or may not involve credits.	[B5]
Corporate culture	The norms, beliefs and assumptions adopted by an organization to enable it to adapt to its external environment and integrate people and units internally. It is strongly influenced by the values and behavior of an organization's management. In turn, corporate culture influences both	[B1, B3, C1, C2, C11, C12, C15, C17, T1, T4, T6, T9, W3, W4, GR1, GR3, GR5, GR6, GR7, GR9]

Term	Definition	Courses
	the behavior of the members of the organization and the quality of the work experience.	
Corporate governance	Refers to a system or structure that clarifies how authority and responsibility are shared between the parties that have a vested interest in an organization's operations. Corporate governance establishes rights and relationships that are intended to provide oversight for financial and management decisions that affect the value the organization is delivering to its owners/shareholders.	[C6, C6A]
Corporate mission	What an organization needs to do to achieve its vision. The mission specifies an organization's goals and how to attain them.	[C11, C15, T1, T9, W1, W2, W3, GR1, GR7]
Corporate philosophy	A means of translating the present state of an organization into concrete policy action to achieve the long-range goals of that organization.	[C15, T3, T4, T9, W1, W2, W3, W4, GR7, GR9]
Corporate values	The beliefs of an organization.	[C11, W3, W4]
Corporate vision	What an organization wants to be.	[C11, C15, T4, T9, W3, W4, GR7, GR9]
Corporate-owned life insurance (COLI)	Life insurance product that insures the lives of selected employees, usually executives. The company, or a specially designed trust, is the owner and beneficiary. Companies typically purchase COLI products to help offset costs associated with deferred compensation plans, supplemental executive retirement plans and survivor income plans.	[B3A, C6, C6A, T6, T11]

Term	Definition	Courses
Correlation coefficient	A statistical index that measures the strength of linear association observed between two variables. This index sometimes is referred to as the correlation coefficient. Correlation will have a value from -1.0 (indicating a perfect negative relationship) to $+1.0$ (indicating a perfect positive relationship). A correlation coefficient of zero indicates no linear relationship at all between two variables.	[C2, C17, T3, GR2, GR3]
Cost containment	A strategy whereby an organization seeks to minimize the rising cost of certain health and welfare benefits by implementing selected programs that emphasize cost-effectiveness.	[B1, B3A]
Cost of capital	The cost of long term debt plus a cost attributable to common stock, taking into account the risk-free rate of return, a premium for risk and a factor related to the stock's volatility. Sometimes used as a measure in incentive plans.	[C6, C6A, T11]
Cost of goods available for sale	Calculated by adding net cost of purchases (purchases less discounts and returns and allowances) to beginning inventory. Also called goods available for sale (GAS).	[T2]
Cost of goods sold (COGS)	Calculated by subtracting ending inventory from goods available for sale (purchases and beginning inventory).	[T2]
Cost of labor	A measure of external pay practices where data on labor market costs (total compensation amounts) are obtained from labor market competitors and relied upon when establishing target cash compensation opportunity. It reflects a "cost to	[C5]

Term	Definition	Courses
	hire and retain" logic for setting target pay levels.	
Cost of sales	For sales compensation purposes, a relative measure of internal costs. It reflects an "ability to pay" logic for setting target pay levels. The cost of sales, expressed as a percent, is calculated by dividing the total sales dollar volume sold by the sales force into the total or aggregate cash compensation costs of the sales force.	[C5]
Cost shifting (health care)	A strategy in which the cost of providing employee health coverage is transferred from one party to another. It can refer to the case in which employers pass price increases along to employees, or when the government limits or reduces Medicare funding, leaving the private sector to bear a greater proportion of rising health costs.	[B1, B3, B3A, W3]
Cost spreading	Effort given to share costs through a merger, alliance, joint venture, and so on, for various capital-intensive investments.	[C15, T9, GR7]
Cost-of-living adjustment (COLA)	An across-the-board wage and salary increase or supplemental payment designed to bring pay in line with increases in the cost of living to maintain real purchasing power.	[B3, C4, C15, T1, T9, GR1, GR4, GR7]
Cost-of-living index	See Consumer Price Index.	[C4]
Covered compensation	Defined in Internal Revenue Service (IRS) regulations as the average of the 35 years of Social Security wage bases up to and including the year an employee reaches the age of eligibility for unreduced Social Security benefits. It is the basis for integrating	[B2]

Term	Definition	Courses
	pension plan benefits with Social Security.	
Covered wages	In benefits plans, the amount of employee wages or salaries used to determine corresponding benefit amounts (e.g., pension calculations usually are based on salary and normally do not include forms of variable compensation such as bonuses).	[B1]
Credential-ing process	A process that reviews a health care provider's credentials with the credentials required to participate in a managed care network or health plan.	[B3]
Creditable coverage	As defined by the Health Insurance Portability and Accountability Act (HIPAA), includes prior coverage under another group health plan, an individual health insurance policy, COBRA, Medicaid, Medicare, CHAMPUS, the Indian Health Service, a state health benefits risk pool, FEHBP, the Peace Corps Act or a public health plan.	[B3]
Credited service	The period of service recognized by a pension plan for eligibility, vesting and determining the participant's benefit amount. It is applicable to both defined benefit (DB) and defined contribution (DC) plans.	[B2]
Credits	The source of funds. A term used in accounting.	[T2]
Critical incident	A behavior-based approach to performance management that measures specific individual actions as either meeting (positive feedback) or not meeting (development opportunity) desired outcomes.	[C11, GR5]

Term	Definition	Courses
Culture	The holistic interrelationship of a group's identity, beliefs, values, activities, rules, customs, communication patterns and institutions.	[C15, T1, T6, T9, T12, W2, W3, W4, GR1, GR3, GR5, GR7]
Culture shock	Complete lack of understanding of cultural differences.	[C15, T9, GR7]
Cumulative performance period	For sales incentive calculation purposes, a type of performance period in which an incumbent's performance is accumulated and measured over time, and compared against goals that are also accumulated over various performance periods. For example, while incentive payouts might be made each month, actual performance for a salesperson might be accumulated in each successive month of a quarter and compared against accumulated goals. As an illustration, in the second month, the incumbent's performance is the sum of the performances of the first two months compared with the sum of the performance goals for the same two months.	[C5]
Currency exchange rate	The relationship of the currency of one country to the currency of another. Differential changes in currency rates, relative to the base country currency, cause the relative payroll costs of expatriates to fluctuate.	[C15, T9, GR7]
Current assets	A company's assets including cash and those items expected to be turned into cash within one year of the date of the balance sheet (includes accounts receivable, inventories and prepaid expenses).	[C6, C6A, T2, T11]

Term	Definition	Courses
Current liabilities	Debts of a company that are expected to be paid within one year of the date of the balance sheet.	[C6, C6A, T2, T11]
Current ratio	Current assets divided by current liabilities.	[T2]
Current taxes	Estimated current year tax liability.	[T2]
Cycling	A variation of performance above and below the baseline. Can result in no cumulative improvement over the course of the plan period because of performance during subsequent payout periods.	[C12, GR6]
Daily flex	Work hours differ from the workplace standard. For example, working 10:00 A.M. to 6:00 P.M. instead of a "traditional" nine to five.	[W1, W2]
Danger pay	A special payment for areas where violence, political or otherwise, is prevalent. It normally is paid in addition to a hardship allowance premium.	[C15, T9, GR7]
Day-at-a-time vacation	Mini-vacations instead of using one full week or more.	[W1, W2]
De minimis	Cash or noncash awards, property or services offered by an employer to an employee, the value of which is so small as to make accounting for such benefits unreasonable or administratively impracticable, taking into account the frequency with which they are provided by the employer to employees.	[B5]
Death benefit	Amount paid or payable to the beneficiary of a retirement plan or insurance policy, on the death of the employee or insured person.	[B1, B3A]
Debentures	Unsecured debt backed only by the creditworthiness of the borrower, not by collateral.	[T2]

Term	Definition	Courses
Debits	Use of funds. A term used in accounting.	[T2]
Debt	Amounts owed, usually called liabilities. Divided into current liabilities, due within one year of the date of the balance sheet, and noncurrent liabilities, due more than one year after the date of the balance sheet.	[T2]
Debt-to-equity ratio	Ratio of total liabilities to shareholders' equity.	[T2]
Decentralization	The extent to which pay policy determination is not housed within a single work group. Departments, units or teams have the ability to set pay policies.	[C6]
Deciles	A distribution divided into tenths.	[T3, GR2]
Decode	To translate the message into understandable language, often attaching meaning to the message.	[T4, GR9]
Deductible	An amount paid by an employee for covered expenses in a group medical or dental plan before the plan pays benefits. Normally, there is a deductible for the employee and for each dependent that must be met annually (plan year) up to a maximum amount—usually no more than the total deductible for three family members.	[B1, B3, B3A, T1, GR1]
Deductible carry over	The number of months that a member of a health or welfare plan can go into a new plan year and still apply the deductible from the previous plan year. Similar to a grace period whereby an employee who needs medical attention at the end of one year and the beginning of the next plan year isn't penalized by having to pay another deductible.	[B3]

Term	Definition	Courses
Deductible limit	Contributions made to a qualified funded plan under which the benefits are fixed or determinable are not taken into account under this section to the extent they exceed the amount that would be taken into account under Section 404(a), which are the same limitations that apply to U.S. qualified plans.	
Deferral option	An individual defers compensation and the amount deferred is used to reduce or "buy down" the option price of option shares by a specified amount, leaving the remainder to be paid when the option is exercised.	[C6, C6A, T11]
Deferred benefits	Refers to noncash compensation to which an employee may be entitled at a later date following employment, assuming he/she has enough credited years of service for vesting purposes (e.g., pension plans, 401(k) savings plans, stock options, etc.).	[B2, C6, C15]
Deferred compensation	Any of a number of compensation payments that are payable to an employee at some point in the future. These include voluntary deferral of earned incentives, mandatory deferrals of earned incentives as well as earnings and retirement plan vehicles.	[B5, C6, C6A, C12, C15, T6, T1, T11, GR1 GR5, GR6]
Deferred premium arrangement	A group insurance arrangement in which the insured is permitted to delay payment or premium for a specified period (i.e., 30, 60 or 90 days). The effect is to allow the insured to hold the IBNR (incurred but not reported) reserve, thereby reducing the current premiums	[B3A]

Term	Definition	Courses
	paid. At termination of the insurance contract, insured must pay a formula-based premium (i.e., the termination liability).	
Deferred profit-sharing plan	See profit-sharing plan.	[B1]
Deferred taxes	Tax obligation to be paid at a future date. Deferred taxes result when income or expenses are recorded on the company's income statement in a different time period than when they are reported on the company's tax return.	[T2]
Defined benefit (DB) pension plan	Defined by the Employee Retirement Income Security Act of 1974 (ERISA) and the Internal Revenue Code (IRC) as any retirement plan that provides for future income and is not an individual account plan. It is a pension plan that specifies the benefits, or the methods of determining the benefits, but not the level or rate of contribution. Contributions are determined actuarially on the basis of the benefits expected to become payable.	[B1, B2, C15, T1, T6, T9, T12, GR1, GR7]
Defined contribution (DC) pension plan	Defined by the Employee Retirement Income Security Act of 1974 (ERISA) and the Internal Revenue Code (IRC) as a plan that provides for future income from an individual account for each participant with benefits based solely on 1) the amount contributed to the participant's account plus 2) any income, expenses,	[B1, B2, C15, T1, T2, T6, T9, T11, T12, GR1, GR7]

Term	Definition	Courses
	gains and losses, and forfeitures of accounts of other participants that may be allocated to the participant's account. The benefit amount to be received by the participant at retirement is unknown until retirement.	
Defined contribution health plan	See consumer-driven health plan.	[B3]
Demotion	The (re)assignment of an employee to a job in a lower position in the organization's job worth hierarchy. Demotions may be the result of poor performance, a reorganization, re-engineering, or an employee request.	[C4, C11, GR4]
Denominator	The number below a fraction line, indicating the number of parts into which one whole is divided.	[T3, GR2]
Dental health maintenance organization (DHMO)	Provides a specified range of dental services for a set fee to participants. Participants must receive care from a participating provider; dentists receive a set fee each month per participant, regardless of the care received by the participant.	[B1, B3, B5]
Dental preferred provider organization (DPPO)	A fee-for-service program that allows a participant to choose any dentist but provides financial incentives to choose dentists who are part of the preferred provider organization network.	[B1]
Department compa-ratio	A tool that compares a department's total salary to its corresponding total midpoints in the pay ranges.	[T3, GR2]

Term	Definition	Courses
Department of Health and Human Services (DHHS)	The federal agency responsible for protecting the health of all Americans and providing essential human services to those in need. Responsibilities include public health, biomedical research, Medicare and Medicaid, welfare, social services and more.	[B3]
Department of Labor (DOL)	A regulatory agency that administers and enforces several federal laws including the Equal Pay Act of 1963, Fair Labor Standards Act of 1938 (FLSA), Employee Retirement Income Security Act of 1974 (ERISA) and Family and Medical Leave Act of 1993 (FMLA). Agencies under the DOL include the Bureau of Labor Statistics (BLS), Employment Standards Administration and the Pension and Welfare Benefits Administration (PWBA).	[B1, B2, B3, C2, C11, C17, T6]
Department of Treasury	Federal agency whose broad mission is to promote prosperous and stable national and world economies, manage the government's finances, safeguard the nation's financial systems, protect the nation's leaders and secure a safe and drug-free nation.	[B3]
Dependent care spending account	An arrangement whereby out-of-pocket expenses for care of dependent children or other wholly dependent individuals can be reimbursed through a pretax flexible spending account. Section 129 of the Internal Revenue Code (IRC) permits	[B1, B3A, B5, T6]

Term	Definition	Courses
	tax-free dependent care of up to a specified amount per year. This is in lieu of the dependent care tax credit, which may be better for some individuals. Also known as dependent care subsidy. See also flexible spending account and Section 129.	
Dependent care subsidy	See dependent care spending account.	[B5]
Dependent life insurance	Pays benefits upon the death of a covered dependent or in the event that the dependent sustains certain specified accidental injuries.	[B1, B3, T6]
Dependent variable	Denoted as the y-variable, it is the quantity, issue, problem or question that is to be explained, understood or predicted.	[T3, GR2, GR3]
Depreciation	The systematic and rational allocation of the cost of noncurrent tangible assets as an expense on the income statement over their useful lives. This excludes the cost of land.	[T2]
Derivative security	A security that may become a share of common stock. Included are stock options, warrants, and convertible securities among others.	[C6, C6A, T11]
Determination letter	Documentation provided by the Internal Revenue Service (IRS) that indicates full compliance of a welfare or pension plan with its rules and regulations to achieve qualified status.	[T6]
Development	Learning experiences designed to enhance employees' skills and competencies.	[T4, GR9]
Diagnostic related groups (DRGs) of service	A system of classification for inpatient hospital service based on primary diagnosis, secondary diagnosis, surgical procedures,	[B1]

Term	Definition	Courses
	age, sex, and the presence of complications. This system is used in determining reimbursement rates for these services.	
Differential	Compensation paid to accommodate certain working conditions. It is often part of the base pay component of compensation. An example is an expatriate differential that typically compensates for the difference in costs (e.g., housing, goods and services) between the home and assignment locations.	[C15, T1, T9, GR1, GR7]
Diluted earnings per share	A calculation that assumes conversion of all common stock equivalents to common shares and calculates earnings per share, using the treasury stock method. A publicly owned company must report diluted earnings per share even if it does not have common stock equivalents.	[C6, C6A, T2, T11]
Dilution (percent)	The decrease in ownership percentage of current owners when additional shares of stock are issued. Dilution of ownership decreases earnings per share because of the additional shares having been issued. Dilution occurs when a company issues additional shares either in a share offering or to settle stock option or other stock plan requirements.	[C6, C6A, T2, T11]
Direct channel	Manufacturers and service providers in a direct channel, service the end customers directly; they do not use external distribution channels.	[C5]
Direct observation	A job analysis technique that involves the direct observation of employee(s) actually performing work in order to understand job content. The method is	[C2, C17, GR3]

Term	Definition	Courses
	typically used for highly repetitive production jobs.	
Direct pay/cash compensation	Payments made to employees in exchange for their contributions to an organization.	[C17, GR5]
Direct seller	In sales compensation, one whose objective is to obtain an order from the end user.	[C5]
Director and officer (D&O) liability insurance	Insurance to protect members of boards of directors and key officers against law suits for various types of malpractice or oversight.	[C6, C6A, T11]
Disability	Under the Americans with Disabilities Act of 1990 (ADA), a disability is defined as a physical or mental impairment that substantially limits one or more of the major life activities of an individual. A disability is said to exist when record is made of such an impairment or the employer regards the employee as having such an impairment.	[B1, B2, B3, C1]
Disability benefits programs	Income replacement programs provided by employers or public agencies during the time an employee is unable to work because of a qualified disability.	[B3, T1, GR1]
Disability plans	See disability benefit programs.	[T1, GR1]
Disclaimer statement	A provision in a job description that states that job descriptions typically do not specify every duty or responsibility that an employee may be asked to perform; for example, "May perform other duties as required."	[C2, GR3]
Discount rate	The assumed rate of interest used in present value and future value calculations. Most often it is equal to the assumed rate of inflation plus opportunity cost.	[C15, T2]

Term	Definition	Courses
Discounted cash flow	Calculation of the future cash flows using an assumed interest rate to determine the current cash value of those future flows.	[C15, T2]
Discounted restricted stock purchase	Purchase of restricted stock by the employee, at a price below the current market price of the stock on date of purchase.	[C6, C6A, T11]
Discounted stock option	A stock option granted at an exercise price less than 100 percent of fair market value on date of grant.	[C6, C6A, T11]
Discrete data	In statistics, refers to variables that assume only specific, distinct values and are not continuous. For example, pay grades and performance categories are discrete variables while height and weight are continuous variables.	[T3, GR2]
Discrete performance period	Relative to employee performance, a type of performance period in which the performance of the incumbent is limited to a defined performance period without any connection to past or future performance periods. As an example: "Each month is discrete, because performance is measured for that month and payout is made for that month independent of past or future performance in other months."	[C5]
Discretionary bonus	A plan in which management determines the size of the bonus pool and the amounts to be allocated to specific individuals after a performance period. These have no predetermined formula or promises, and are not guaranteed.	[C12, GR5, GR6]

Term	Definition	Courses
Discrimination	Disparate treatment of employees based on factors not related to qualifications, skills or performance. (1) Under the terms of Title VII of the Civil Rights Act of 1964, the Age Discrimination and Employment Act of 1967 (ADEA) and the Equal Pay Act of 1963, discrimination occurs when any compensation decision is made on the basis of a person's age (over 40), race, color, national origin, religion or sex in a way that cannot be justified on the basis of job-relatedness and business necessity. (2) Under various sections of the Internal Revenue Code (IRC), certain benefits plans may be considered discriminatory if appropriate numbers of nonhighly compensated employees (NHCEs): (a) are not eligible to participate in the plan, (b) do not participate in the plan and (c) receive a disproportionate share of the benefits provided under a plan. The intent is to avoid giving tax-favored status to benefits plans that target only the highly paid employees in an organization.	[B3, C1, C15, T9, GR7]
Discrimination testing	A process that must be performed to determine if benefits within a plan are being provided to a broad range of employees on a fair and consistent basis.	[B3A, T6]
Disparate treatment	Any human resources management practice and/or policy that treats members of a protected class (under Title VII of the Civil Rights Act or the Equal Pay Act) differently from other employees. An example would be providing new fathers with a raise but not new mothers.	[C1]

Term	Definition	Courses
Disposition date	Refers to the date on which the optionee sells, exchanges or transfers the stock.	[C6, C6A]
Disqualifying disposition (of an ISO)	Sale of incentive stock option (ISO) shares before the completion of the required holding period: one year after exercise and two years after grant. A disqualifying disposition changes the tax treatment of the ISO so that it is taxed the same way as a nonqualified option.	[C6, C6A, T11]
Distribution	(1) Any payment to a participant from a defined benefit (DB) plan or defined contribution (DC) plan. (2) An ordered array of data.	[B1, B2, T3, GR2]
Distributor/ wholesaler	Selling member of an indirect channel who buys and resells another company's products.	[C5]
Divergent data	Measurements that vary by orders of magnitude or in which the bulk of cases tend to cluster at one extreme of a distribution.	[T3, GR2]
Divestiture	A transaction in which a company disposes of a part of its business (e.g., one division), usually through a sale to another entity or by setting up a new stand-alone company.	[T6]
Dividend	Payment to shareholders by a corporation that is paid from the company's retained earnings. Not all companies pay dividends. Dividends may be in cash or in shares of stock.	[C6, C6A, T2, T11]
Dividend equivalents	In some incentive plans, participants are paid an amount of money equal to the dividends that are paid per share of common stock.	[C6, C6A, T11]
Dividend for group insurance	The return to the policyholder (or the insured) of all or a portion of the excess premiums; that is, premiums not required	[B3A]

Term	Definition	Courses
	by an insurer to pay claims, establish reserves, meet expenses, and provide a profit (or, for mutual insurance companies, provide a contribution to surplus).	
Dividend tax	An individual's tax on dividends received that is at the same tax rates as long-term capital gains. Dividends must qualify to receive the favorable dividend tax rate (as compared to ordinary income tax). Dividends received from domestic corporations or qualified foreign corporations generally qualify.	[C6, C6A, T11]
Dollars for doers	A company contributes money to a nonprofit where an employee volunteers. Most have application processes. The contribution is based on a specific number of hours the employee volunteers.	[W1]
Domino effect	Success in a new territory makes it easier to enter another.	[C15, T9, GR7]
Double declining balance depreciation	A depreciation method whereby greater depreciation is recorded as an expense in the early years of a tangible, noncurrent asset's useful life.	[T2]
Double entry accounting	Accounting method that records every transaction as both a credit and a debit. Used in both accrual accounting and cash accounting.	[T2]
Dow Jones Industrial Average (DJIA)	The most widely quoted stock market index. It comprises 30 actively traded blue chip stocks, primarily industrial, listed on New York Stock Exchange. The index is calculated minute-by-minute and is published by Dow-Jones and Company. It is often considered a barometer of overall market activity.	[C6, C6A, T11]

Term	Definition	Courses
Downgrading	The movement of a job to a lower job grade and pay range within a pay structure.	[C4, GR4]
Downsizing	Reducing the size of the workforce.	[C11, C12, GR6]
Draw	A compensation payment that is paid in advance of performance. There are two types of draws: recoverable and nonrecoverable. In both cases, if performance produces incentive earnings in excess of the draw, then the sales representative receives the additional monies beyond the draw amount. If the sales representative's incentive earnings are less than a recoverable draw, then the sales representative must return the amount of the draw that was not earned, or the unearned amount is carried forward to the next performance period. However, with a nonrecoverable draw, if the incentive earnings do not exceed the draw, draw monies are not returned or carried forward—the sales representative gets to keep the draw.	[C5]
Due diligence process	Prior to completing an acquisition, the buying company thoroughly reviews all documents available, public and private, to ascertain the financial and operating stability of the seller.	[C15, T6, T9, GR7]
Early retirement age (pension plans)	The earliest age at which an employee is first permitted to retire and to elect either immediate or deferred receipt of income. If payments begin immediately, they generally are paid in a reduced amount.	[B2]
Earned time off	An incentive or reward that takes the form of pay for time not worked.	[C1, C12, GR5, GR6]

Term	Definition	Courses
Earnings	Total wages or cash received during a specified period of time (e.g., pay period, month, year) for time worked or service rendered, including all regular pay, overtime, premium pay, bonuses, and so on.	[C1, C12, C4, T1, GR1, GR4, GR5, GR6]
Earnings before interest and taxes (EBIT)	Income remaining after recognizing cost of goods sold (COGS) and selling, general and administrative expense (before other income and expenses and before provision for taxes).	[C6, T2]
Earnings before interest, taxes, depreciation and amortization (EBITDA)	Start-up or highly leveraged companies might use this as a performance measurement when cash flow is the focus and there is an incentive to generate cash.	[C6, T2]
Earnings per share (EPS)	The net earnings of an organization divided by total shares outstanding, with adjustments for common stock equivalents. Sometimes used as a criterion in executive incentive pay programs.	[C6, C6A, T11, GR2]
Earnings statement	See income statement.	[C6, C6A, T2, T11]
Economic benefit	A concept in the tax law whereby if there is a promise by the employer to pay some amount in the future that has been funded and thus there is no substantial risk of forfeiture, there will be a current tax liability.	[C6, C6A, T11]
Economic Growth and Tax Relief Reconciliation Act of 2001 (EGTRRA)	Enacted on June 7, 2001, includes numerous mandatory and optional modifications to the tax-qualified retirement plan rules. EGTRRA is designed to increase retirement savings for all Americans by making retirement plans more beneficial, portable and simpler to administer.	[B2, T11]

Term	Definition	Courses
	Barring future extensions, EGTRRA sunset provisions will return the Code to pre-EGTRRA status in 2011.	
Economic value added (EVA)	A concept related to measuring the economic profit of an organization by determining the excess or shortfall of the economic profit compared with the cost of capital. May be used in incentive programs. (Note: EVA is a trademark of Sterns Stewart.)	[C6, C6A, T2, T11]
Economies of scale	As an organization gets larger, the costs associated with operations will decrease because of increased knowledge and expertise within the organization.	[T12]
Educational assistance plan	Plan that provides employees with full or partial payment for tuition and/or books for training or educational courses. Plans may specify parameters for reimbursement (i.e., field of study of class or training, passing or specific grade, etc.).	[T6]
Effective date	(1) The date on which a benefits plan or insurance policy goes into effect, and from which time coverage is provided. (2) The date on which increases in salary or pay rate go into effect.	[C4, GR4]
Effective tax rate	The ratio of income tax actually paid divided by gross income, showing the percentage of income actually paid in taxes.	[C6, C6A, T11]
Eligibility date	The date an individual and/or dependents become eligible for benefits under an employee benefits plan.	[B1, B2, B3]
Eligibility for a plan	The basis for determining the individuals or classes of employees eligible to participate in a particular plan such as an incentive or a supplemental benefits	[B3, C5, C6, C6A, T6, T11, W3]

Term	Definition	Courses
	plan. This eligibility may be based on salary, job grade, organization unit or function or a number of other criteria.	
Eligible payroll	Determined by the sum of salaries and/or wages of those employees who are eligible to participate, including those who are eligible and receive no salary increase.	[C4, GR4]
Emergency flexibility	Fixed number of days off with pay for emergencies (allow time to be taken in hourly increments).	[W1, W2]
Emerging company	Company still growing to international maturity.	[C15, T9, GR7]
Emerging Issues Task Force (EITF)	A task force created by FASB that deals with issues not precisely covered by GAAP. Many questions about handling stock issued to employees have been decided by the EITF.	[C6, C6A, T11]
Employee assistance programs (EAPs)	Programs that provide counseling or referral services to employees. Services vary by employer, but may include assistance with chemical dependency, and psychological, financial, legal, family and career counseling. Services usually are provided by a third party to protect employee confidentiality, but may be provided internally by some employers. Typically, participation is voluntary unless a mandatory management referral is made.	[B1, B3, B3A, B5, T1, T6, T12, W1, W3, GR1]
Employee contribution	Payment made by an employee to fund a specific benefit, thereby defraying part or the entire employer's cost.	[B3, B5, C15, T1, GR1]
Employee participation	(1) The degree to which employees have a say in designing, implementing and administering pay and benefits, as well as	[C15, T1, GR1]

Term	Definition	Courses
	other organizational programs. (2) Actual voluntary participation in an employee benefits plan.	
Employee Retirement Income Security Act of 1974 (ERISA)	A federal act regulating private employer pension and welfare programs. Provisions cover eligibility for participation, reporting and disclosure requirements, fiduciary standards for the financial management of retirement funds, tax incentives for funding pension plans rather than maintaining them on a pay-as-you-go basis, and establishment of the Pension Benefit Guaranty Corporation (PBGC). ERISA is administered by the Department of Labor (DOL).	[B1, B2, B3, B3A, C1, C6, C6A, T6, T11, T12]
Employee stock option	See stock option.	[C6, C6A, T11]
Employee stock ownership plan (ESOP)	A qualified defined contribution (DC) plan that enables employees to receive company shares that they accrue as plan participants upon retirement or separation from the organization.	[B1, B2, C11, C12, C15, T1, T6, T9, T11, GR1, GR5, GR6, GR7]
Employee stock purchase plan (ESPP)	A benefits plan that allows employees to use payroll deductions to acquire company stock, usually at a discounted rate.	[C11, C12, C15, T6, T9, GR6, GR7]
Employment at will	Employment relationship where it is agreed that neither the employee nor the employer could sue upon termination of employment (firing or voluntary termination); subject to interpretation/requirements of individual state statutes.	[C11]
Employment contract	A contract that provides an incoming employee with a written guarantee of receiving certain rewards, regardless of the	[C6, C6A, C15, T11, GR6]

Term	Definition	Courses
	results produced on the job. The employee also may agree not to (1) compete with the present employer for the duration of employment and some reasonable time period thereafter, (2) disclose or discuss secret formulas, and so on, that are of value to the employer, and (3) hold another job.	
Encode	To express the ideas of the sender into some type of message.	[T4, GR9]
Entry-age normal actuarial cost method (also called entry-age actuarial cost method)	A technique for determining accrued liabilities in a defined benefit pension plan. The present value of projected benefits of the covered employee is allocated on a level basis, across the earnings or service period between age of entry to the plan and assumed retirement or exit date. The portion of the liability allocated to a valuation year is called the normal cost.	
Equal Employment Opportunity Commission (EEOC)	A commission of the federal government charged with enforcing the provisions of the Civil Rights Act of 1964, the Age Discrimination in Employment Act of 1967 (ADEA), the Equal Pay Act of 1963, the Americans with Disabilities Act of 1990 (ADA) and other fair employment practices legislation.	[B1, B3, C1, C11, T12]
Equal Pay Act of 1963	An amendment to the Fair Labor Standards Act of 1938 (FLSA) that prohibits gender-related pay differentials on jobs that are substantially equal in terms of skill, effort, responsibility and working conditions, and that are performed in the same location. Exceptions occur when such differentials are the result of bona fide seniority, merit- or	[B3, C1, C2, C17]

Term	Definition	Courses
	production-based pay systems, or any other job-related factor other than gender.	
Equal pay for comparable work	This doctrine is much broader than the U.S. Equal Pay Act of 1963. In effect, this doctrine moves beyond the four compensable factors embodied in the Equal Pay Act and specifies that so long as the work performed by women and men in question is comparable, charges of sex discrimination in pay can be brought under Title VII of the 1964 Civil Rights Act.	[C1]
Equal pay for equal work	This doctrine, embodied in the U.S. Equal Pay Act of 1963, is intended to protect women from sex discrimination in pay. It says that women may not be paid less than men on jobs that are substantially equal in terms of four compensable factors: effort, skill, responsibility and working conditions.	[C1]
Equity	Anything of value earned through the provision or investment of something of value. (1) In the case of compensation, an employee earns equity interest through the provision of labor on a job. Equity often is used as a fairness criterion (i.e., "equal treatment") in compensation. (2) On an organization's balance sheet, equity represents the book value of the owners' stake in the firm. See also shareholders' equity.	[C4, C15, C17, T1, T2, T6, T9, T11, GR1, GR4, GR7]
Equity investment	A financial investment that results in an ownership position and no fixed return or guarantee of the principal amount.	[B2, C6, C6A, T11]

Term	Definition	Courses
Equity theory	According to this principle, an individual perceives "fairness" by comparing his or her inputs and related outcomes with the inputs and outcomes achieved by others. If the comparison is equal, equity exists. If not, inequity is perceived and behavior may be modified to achieve equity (i.e., the individual might work harder or less hard). The inputs and outcomes compared while determining equity are unique to each individual. This theory is associated most frequently with the ideas of J. Stacy Adams.	[C11]
Equity-based plan	The use of company shares to create an equity interest in the company and foster identification with shareholder interests.	[C12, C15, T9, T11, GR6, GR7]
Equivalent annual percent increase (EAPI)	See annualized increase percent.	[C4, GR4]
Equivalent of a trust	Equivalent of a trust means a fund (1) The corpus and income of which is separately identifiable and segregated, through a separate legal entity, from the general assets of the employer; (2) The corpus and income of which is not subject, under the applicable foreign law, to the claims of the employer's creditors prior to the claims of employees and their beneficiaries under the plan; (3) The corpus and income of which, by law or by contract, cannot at any time prior to the satisfaction of all liabilities with respect to employees under the plan be used for, or diverted to, any purpose other than providing benefits under the plan; and (4) The corpus and income of which is held by a person who has a legally	

Term	Definition	Courses
	enforceable duty to operate the fund prudently.	
Ethnocentricity	The act of making assumptions about other societies/cultures that are based on the norms of one's own society. The features of one's own society/culture are defined as normal and those of others as abnormal.	[C15, T9, GR7]
European Community (EC)	See European Union.	[C15, T9, GR7]
European Union (EU)	A union of 15 independent states whose basic goal is economic and monetary union. Members include: Austria, Belgium, Denmark, Finland, France, Germany, Greece, Ireland, Italy, Luxembourg, the Netherlands, Portugal, Spain, Sweden and the United Kingdom. On January 1, 2002, a common currency, the euro, was introduced in 12 countries of the euro area (all countries listed above excluding Denmark, Sweden and the United Kingdom). EU was formerly known as European Community (EC) or European Economic Community (EEC).	[C15, T9, GR7]
Evergreen authorization	Shares made available for future grants under an option plan that represents a specified percentage of outstanding shares for each year of the plan. Unused shares from any year usually are carried forward for possible use in later years.	[C6, C6A, T11]
Evergreen plan	No termination date is specified after which grants can no longer be made. Normally such a plan would remain in effect until canceled by the board of directors.	[C6, C6A, T11]

Term	Definition	Courses
Excess formula	In a defined benefit (DB) plan, the method used to determine the excess portion of the benefit up to the Social Security integration level. Also known as step rate formula.	[B1, B2]
Excess plan	A nonqualified program for executives that generally is associated with welfare benefits (e.g., a $3,000 fund available for a CEO's medical claims not covered by the normal medical plan) or pension plans that provide benefits in excess of the ERISA limits.	[C6, C6A]
Exchange rate	(1) Economically defined as the intersect of the labor demand and the labor supply functions in an external market. It constitutes the wage rate that employers are willing to pay and labor is willing to accept. From an economic viewpoint, the exchange rate clears the market. From a compensation viewpoint, the exchange rate defines the criterion of external equity. (2) The value of the currency of one nation, stated in terms of the currency of another nation. Also known as rate of exchange (ROE).	[C15, T9, GR7]
Excise tax	A tax assessed upon the value of property or services, excluding real estate.	[T6]
Executive	While there is no absolute definition, an executive is considered to be anyone who has significant responsibility for the management of the organization, or sub unit of the organization.	[C6, C6A, T1, T11, GR1, GR6]
Executive benefits	Forms of noncash compensation provided to a small number of executives that are in excess of the benefits provided to all other employees (e.g., company	[C6, C6A, C15, T6]

Term	Definition	Courses
	car, supplemental insurance coverage, etc.).	
Executive compensation	Forms of cash compensation provided to executives.	[C6]
Executive officer	A person in charge of a principal company business unit or responsible for a major corporate policy function; depending on the circumstances, also may include a person performing a policy-making function at a company subsidiary. An executive officer may be designated as an "insider" by the Securities and Exchange Commission (SEC). See insider.	[C6, C6A, T11]
Executive Orders 11246 and 11375	Prohibits government contractors and subcontractors and federally assisted construction contractors and subcontractors from discriminating in employment and requires these contractors to take affirmative action to ensure that all employees and applicants are treated without regard to race, color, religion, sex or national origin.	[C11, T6]
Executive rewards	Forms of cash and noncash rewards provided to executives.	[C6]
Exempt employees	Employees who are exempt from the Fair Labor Standards Act of 1938 (FLSA) minimum wage and overtime provisions because of the type of duties performed. Include executives, administrative employees, professional employees and those engaged in outside sales as defined by the FLSA.	[C1, C2, C17, T1, T6, T11, W3, GR1]
Exercise (of a share option or other executive-plan feature)	The occasion when the holder takes possession of the shares, rights or proceeds determined by a plan's provisions (e.g., the actual purchase of stock under the terms of stock option grant).	[C6, C6A, T6, T11, GR6]

Term	Definition	Courses
Exercise cost	The cost to the employee to exercise an option.	[C6, C6A]
Exercise date	Refers to the actual date on which the optionee buys the stock from the company.	[C6, C6A]
Exercise period	The time frame during which the optionee is given the right to buy the stated shares at the predetermined price.	[C6, C6A, T11]
Expatriate	An employee who is assigned temporarily for usually one year or more outside his or her home or base country and expected to return there on completion of the assignment. Also referred to as foreign-service employee or international assignee.	[C15, T6, T9, GR7]
Expatriate premium	A generic term referring to one or more supplemental payments made to expatriates to compensate for hardship, the education of an expatriate's children in their native language or other assignment-location-specific conditions or costs.	[C15, T9, GR7]
Expectancy theory	According to this principle, people choose the behavior(s) that they expect will maximize their payoff. When this theory is applied to pay, an employee must believe that greater effort will increase performance, increased performance will lead to more pay and more pay is the reward that the employee wants most. This theory was first stated by V. H. Vroom.	[C11]
Expenses	Costs arising as a direct result of operating a business (e.g., rent, utilities, payroll).	[T2]
Experience rating	In group insurance, when premium rates are based on actual claims experience, usually the last three to five years, and expected claims to account for	[B3A]

Term	Definition	Courses
	changes in the insured group population.	
Experience-rated arrangement	An insurance arrangement in which premiums are based on the group's (or individual's) characteristics and prior incurred claims experience.	[B3A]
Expiration date	The last day of an option term at which point the option is cancelled if not exercised.	[C6, C6A, T11]
Export company	In a global economy, the first overseas operation(s) in place.	[C15, T9, GR7]
External equity	A measure of an organization's pay levels or bands or "going market rates" compared to that of its competitors. As a fairness criterion, external equity implies that the employer pays wages that correspond to prevailing, external market rates, as determined by market pricing.	[C2, C4, C17, T1, GR1, GR3, GR4]
External wage structure	The distribution of wage rates across external labor markets. The external wage structure defines the variety of different wage rates an employer faces across different occupations and different labor markets.	[C17]
Extraordinary items	A gain or a loss arising from an event that is unusual in nature and is nonrecurring. It is recorded net of tax separately by a company on its financial statements and fully described in the footnotes to the financial statements. An incentive plan related to net income may relate to income before or income after extraordinary items.	[C6, C6A, T2, T11]
Extrinsic rewards	Work-related rewards received for performance that have value measurable in monetary or financial terms.	[C4, C12, C15, C17, T9, GR4, GR5, GR6, GR7]

Term	Definition	Courses
Factor weight	In job evaluation, a weight assigned to each compensable factor to indicate relative importance.	[C2, C17, GR3]
Fair Labor Standards Act of 1938 (FLSA)	A federal law governing minimum wage, overtime pay, child labor and record-keeping requirements.	[B1, B5, C1, C2, C4, C12, C17, T6, T12, W2]
Fair market value (FMV)	Stock price, usually measured as the simple average of the high and low market prices of a share of a company's stock on a recognized stock exchange on a particular day.	[C6, C6A, T11, GR6]
Family and Medical Leave Act of 1993 (FMLA)	A federal law entitling eligible employees to take up to 12 weeks of unpaid, job-protected leave in a 12-month period for specified family and medical reasons. Specified family and medical reasons include: the birth and care of a newborn child of the employee; placement with the employee of a son or daughter for adoption or foster care; care of an immediate family member (spouse, child, or parent) with a serious health condition; or medical leave when the employee is unable to work because of a serious health condition. The FMLA is administered by the U.S. Department of Labor's Employment Standards Administration, Wage and Hour Division.	[B1, B3, C11, T6, T12, W1]
Family leave	Time off, either paid or unpaid, provided for an employee to care for their own serious medical condition or a seriously ill family member, a new baby or an adopted child. Family leave policies usually are broader than parental leave policies.	[T1, GR1]

Term	Definition	Courses
FAS 87	An accounting standard that applies to pension plans outside the United States. It requires that, for U.S. accounting purposes, information and required evaluation be provided for material foreign pension plans on an annual basis. It also specifies how to determine the set of assumptions, reporting format and measures that must be provided, such as the accumulated benefit obligation (ABO), projected benefit obligation (PBO) and the market value of assets for a funded plan.	[B3, C15, T9]
FAS 88	Addresses exceptions to FAS 87 in regards to pension settlements transactions, pension curtailments and special termination benefits. FAS 88 requires that companies accelerate the recognition of previously unrecognized gains and losses since the possibility of them being offset by future experience is eliminated.	[C15, T9]
FAS 106	See post-employment benefits.	[B3]
FAS 123	A statement issued by the Financial Accounting Standards Board in 1995. The statement permits a company to choose between using APB 25 or to use an option pricing model such as the Black-Scholes or the Binomial model to determine the accounting expense to be recorded with respect to stock issued to employees. If a company chooses APB 25 for its income statement, it must show the costs per the pricing model in the footnotes to the financial statements. All stock related plans for employees must be evaluated on the same approach. See also APB 25.	[C6, C6A, T11]

Term	Definition	Courses
FAS 123(R)	An accounting standard statement originally issued by the Financial Accounting Standards Board in 1995 and revised in 2004. The revised FAS 123(R) statement requires companies to recognize compensation expense for the fair value of employee share-based payment transactions on their income statement, eliminating the accounting choices previously available under APB 25 or the original FAS 123. For payment transactions with no observable market value (e.g., stock options), companies must use an option pricing valuation model (e.g., Black-Sholes, binomial) to determine the fair value.	[C6, C6A, T2, T11]
Federal Insurance Contributions Act (FICA)	The source of Social Security contribution/ withholding requirements, known commonly as the FICA deduction. This tax is paid by both the employee and the employer.	[B1, B2, C1]
Feedback	Information about the state or outcome of a system that can be used to modify or correct a system's operation. As the term usually is used with respect to compensation, it relates to the process in which supervisors give employees information about the status of their performance. Performance appraisals are an example of a feedback mechanism.	[C11, C12, C2, T1, T4, GR1, GR3, GR5, GR6, GR9]
Fee-for-service	The traditional method of payment for health care in which physicians and hospitals are paid for each service they provide. Fee-for-service is the system of payment used by conventional indemnity health plans.	[B1, B3]

Term	Definition	Courses
Femininity culture	Degree to which a culture is more concerned with people and the quality of life.	[C15, T9, GR7]
Fiduciary liability	A fiduciary is liable for a breach of fiduciary responsibility if he or she knowingly participates in or conceals a breach of responsibility, fails to comply with fiduciary responsibilities or has knowledge of a breach and makes no reasonable effort to correct it.	[B2]
Fiduciary/ fiduciary responsibility	The person or persons responsible for the oversight and compliance of a plan that is subject to the provisions of the Employee Retirement Income Security Act of 1974 (ERISA). The fiduciary exercises discretion or control over plan assets or administration, or provides investment advice for a fee. Fiduciaries are responsible for items such as: paying benefits to participants and beneficiaries, minimizing investment risk, complying with the plan document and acting with care, skill and prudence in all matters pertaining to the plan. Individuals who are not specifically named fiduciaries also may be considered fiduciaries as a result of their discretionary power over plan assets or administration.	[B1, B2, B3, B3A, B5, T6]
Field allowance	A special payment to compensate an expatriate for additional costs and difficulties of traveling and working in many different locations.	[C15, T9, GR7]
FIN 44	FASB Interpretation No. 44, Accounting for Certain Transactions Involving Stock Compensation, clarifies APB 25 when modifications are made to the	[C6, C6A, T11]

Term	Definition	Courses
	terms of previously fixed stock compensation awards, including the accounting treatment when awards are converted because of acquisition; clarifies the types of modifications to outstanding stock options or awards that can result in a new measurement date or variable accounting.	
Final average earnings (FAE)	See final average pay (FAP) pension plan.	[B1, B2, C15, T6, T9, GR7]
Final average pay (FAP) pension plan	A defined benefit (DB) pension plan that bases benefits on the final average salary of an employee at or during a selected number of years (typically three to five) immediately preceding retirement. Final average pay also may be defined as final average salary (FAS) or final average earnings (FAE).	[B1, B2, T6]
Final average salary (FAS)	See final average pay (FAP) pension plan.	[B1, B2, C15, T6, T9, GR7]
Final Privacy Rules of 2001	See Administrative Simplification Provisions of 2001.	[B3]
Financial Accounting Standards Board (FASB)	The organization that establishes the "generally accepted accounting principles" (GAAP) that govern accounting for publicly held U.S. companies. It is of particular importance in determining the rules connected with the accounting for stock and stock-related incentive programs, as well as accounting for pensions and other post-retirement programs. FASB is not a government agency.	[B3, B3A, C6, C6A, C15, T2, T6, T11]
Financial lease	See capital lease.	[T2]
Financial planning	A popular perquisite whereby a third party provides budgeting, estate planning, investments and	[C6, C6A, T11, W1]

Term	Definition	Courses
	tax planning and preparation to employees for a fee. Typically offered as a company-paid benefit to executives.	
Financial statements	Reports on the financial results for a fiscal period (income statement, statement of cash flows and statement of shareholders' equity) and the financial condition of the organization at the end of the fiscal period (balance sheet).	[B3A, C6, C6A, C15, T2, T11]
Financing activities	Methods of providing capital that include obtaining resources from owners and providing them with a return on (and return of) their investment, borrowing money and repaying amounts borrowed, and purchasing treasury stock.	[T2]
First in, first out (FIFO)	An approach to valuing inventory in accounting where it is assumed that the products obtained first are the ones that are sold first.	[T2]
Fixed accounting	Used to account for equity-based compensation when the number of shares and the amount the employee is required to pay are known at the grant date. Under APB 25 the measurement date determines whether fixed or variable accounting is to be used. Situations in which fixed accounting is used include traditional fair market value stock options and restricted stock.	[C6, C6A, T11]
Fixed budget	A budget that remains unchanged regardless of the number of units produced.	[T2]
Fixed pay	Nondiscretionary compensation that does not regularly vary according to performance or results achieved.	[C4, C12, C17, T1, T6, GR1, GR4, GR6]

Term	Definition	Courses
Fixed share authorization	Shares made available for grants as part of an option plan that represent a specified number of shares or a specified percentage of outstanding shares on a specified date over the life of the plan.	[C6, C6A, T11]
Fixed/flat benefit pension plan	A defined benefit (DB) pension plan that provides a specific benefit (e.g., a certain dollar amount or percentage of salary per month or per year of service).	[B1, B2]
Flat commission	Commission rate does not vary.	[C5]
Flex credits/ flex dollars	The unit of measure used by the employer to represent the amount the employer is allocating to each employee over and above any "core" benefits. The sum of the flex dollars allocated and employee contribution may or may not equal the true cost of benefits. Any difference would represent a hidden subsidy absorbed by the employer.	[B5]
Flexible approach	See cafeteria approach.	[C15, T9, GR7]
Flexible benefits	A plan under Internal Revenue Code (IRC) Section 125 that permits employees to select cash and/or benefits from a menu of choices provided by the employer. In some plans, employees receive subsidies (credits) from the employer to help pay for their choices. Plans commonly include tax-advantaged features and allow employees to select between taxable and nontaxable forms of compensation. Also known as cafeteria plans.	[B1, B3, B3A, B5, C11, T6]
Flexible budget	A budget that varies based on units produced.	[T2]

Term	Definition	Courses
Flexible spending account (FSA)	Under Internal Revenue Code (IRC) Sections 125 and 129, employees can set aside money on a pretax basis to pay for eligible unreimbursed medical and dependent care expenses. Accounts are subject to annual maximums and forfeiture rules.	[B1, B3, B3A, B5, T6]
Flexible work arrangements	Any one of a variety of alternatives that provide employees with options to meet work requirements through non-traditional scheduling (e.g., telecommuting, compressed workweek, job sharing, part-time, etc.).	[T1, T6, W2, GR1]
Flexible work schedule	Work schedule in which the workday is divided into core time and flexible time, and that permits employees to choose their arrival and departure times during the flexible time period. Also known as flextime.	[B1, B5, C11, T1, T6, W1, GR1]
Flextime	See flexible work schedules.	[B1, B5, T1, W1, GR1]
Focus groups	Generally consist of a small number of individuals (less than 12) with whom in-depth interactive interviews are conducted. Focus groups are an effective means of gathering employee opinions regarding total rewards programs. Also known as employee input.	[B5, C11]
Foreign service premium	A percentage increase in compensation used to encourage an employee to leave familiar working and living conditions to work overseas.	[C15]
Forfeiture	Loss of benefits or monetary entitlements not already received or vested.	[B2, B5, C6, C6A, T11]

Term	Definition	Courses
Form 8-K	A required Securities and Exchange Commission (SEC) form that companies use to file "current reports" soon after certain significant events that may affect company financial condition. Examples of significant events include a change in control, bankruptcy, changes in top management and/or directors, adoption of or amendments to employment agreements and other material executive compensation or benefits arrangements.	[C6, C6A]
Form 10-K	A required annual Securities and Exchange Commission (SEC) filing for a public company that provides certain financial and related business information.	[C6, C6A, T11]
Form 5300	A form filed with the Internal Revenue Service (IRS) to request a determination of a pension, profit-sharing or other deferred compensation plan's qualification status.	[T6]
Form 5310	A form filed with the Internal Revenue Service (IRS) to request a determination of a plan's qualification status when a pension, profit-sharing or other deferred compensation plan is terminated.	[T6]
Form 5310A	A form filed with the Internal Revenue Service (IRS) by the plan sponsor or administrator of a pension, profit-sharing or other deferred compensation plan that provides notice of a plan merger, consolidation, spin-off, or a transfer of plan assets or liabilities to another plan.	[T6]

Term	Definition	Courses
Form 5329	A form filed with the Internal Revenue Service (IRS) by persons who received an early distribution from a qualified retirement plan (other than a Roth IRA) during the previous calendar year.	[T6]
Form 5500	A form that must be filed annually with the Internal Revenue Service (IRS) for any retirement plan, welfare plan or fringe benefits plan.	[B2, B3, T6]
Form of payment (of an award or incentive)	The method used, which may be cash, stock, a combination, or some other valuable consideration.	[C6, C6A, T11]
Formulary	A preapproved list of drugs that are offered at a negotiated discount rate.	[B1, B3]
Free trade agreements	Agreements that seek to eliminate trade barriers and encourage investment and fair competition.	[C15, T9, GR7]
Frequency	The number of times (absolute frequency) or percentage of times (relative frequency) a value appears in a data set or in a category.	[T3, GR2]
Frequency distribution	A classification of data into mutually exclusive categories, with subsequent counting and percentage calculations.	[T3, GR2]
Fringe benefits	Refers to benefits such as vacation, holidays and pensions, which were once thought to be "on the fringe of wages."	[T1, GR1]

Term	Definition	Courses
	Given that employee benefits now increase direct wage costs by more than 40 percent, the term is widely considered to be obsolete.	
Front-end bonus	See signing bonus.	[C6, C6A, T11]
Frozen plan	Qualified plans in which future participation has been discontinued, but active participants as of the date of the plan continue to have full or partial participation rights.	[B2, T6]
Full choice plan	See full flex plans.	[B1, B5]
Full funding limitation	Notwithstanding any other provisions of §1.404(a)-1 through §1.404(a)-7, no amount may be taken into account under Section 404(a) if the amount causes the assets in the trust (in the case of a qualified funded plan) or if taking into account the amount causes the amount of the reserve (in the case of a qualified reserve plan) to exceed the amount described in section 412(c)(7)(a)(i). [Reg. §1.404(a)-5.]	
Full retirement age (FRA)	The age at which an individual becomes entitled to unreduced Social Security retirement benefits. Beginning with year 2000, FRA increases gradually from age 65 until it reaches 67 in 2022 for workers (or their spouses) born 1938 or later and for widows or widowers born 1940 or later. FRA affects the benefit amount received if an individual chooses to retire before FRA.	[B1, B2]

Term	Definition	Courses
Full value plan	Executive compensation plan under which a participant receives full value of the employer's capital share or equivalent; for example, restricted stock, phantom share without any investment or purchase required. Value may be based on market price, book value or determined by a formula.	[C6, C6A, GR6]
Fully pooled insurance	An insurance arrangement in which a fixed premium is created composed of all paid claims, all administrative fees and taxes, all insurers' profits, and an incurred but not reported (IBNR) claims reserve. Risk is transferred to the insurance carrier.	[B3, B3A]
Fund	Money in investments held in trust, or shares of an insurance company assets used for payment of pension benefits.	[B2]
Funded retirement plan	A defined benefit (DB) pension plan in which the company's past contributions are sufficient to cover current and future liabilities.	[T6]
Funding	The process of setting aside monies in a trust account or in the possession of an insurance company or another third party in advance of the date when benefits are payable.	[B1, B2, B3, B3A, T6]
Future value	The estimated value of a sum invested today at a specified rate of interest at some future point in time. For example, $1 invested for one year at an annual rate of five percent has a future value of $1.05.	[T2, T3, T11, GR2]
Gain multiple	See targeted gain.	[C6, C6A, T11]

Term	Definition	Courses
Gainsharing	Any one of a number of incentive programs (e.g., Rucker, Improshare, Scanlon) designed to share the results of productivity gains with employees as a group.	[C11, C12, GR5, GR6]
Gatekeeper	A primary care physician (i.e., family practice, pediatrician, gynecologist, internist) who is responsible for directing the medical care of an employee and covered dependents. To receive full benefits, employees and covered dependents must be referred to other medical specialists by their gatekeeper physician. This type of physician generally is found in health maintenance organizations (HMOs) and point-of-service (POS) health care networks.	[B3, B3A]
General increase	See across-the-board increase.	[C4, GR4]
Generally accepted accounting principles (GAAP)	The principles and rules of accounting applicable to U.S. companies, as prescribed by the Financial Accounting Standards Board (FASB) and its predecessors, and as deemed required to apply to all public companies by rules established and enforced by the Securities and Exchange Commission (SEC).	[C6, C6A, C15, T2, T11]
Geographic differentials	Pay differences established for the same job based on variations in costs of living or costs of labor among two or more geographical areas.	[C4, C17, T1, GR1, GR4]
Global company	An organization with worldwide operations, whose strategies, resources and technology are utilized globally, regardless of national or geographic boundaries.	[C15, T9, W3, GR7]

Term	Definition	Courses
Globalization	The expansion of trade and economic development that results from the movement of products, services, technology, capital and human resources throughout the world. Globalization often leads to local change as traditional economies and cultures evolve and transform to adapt to the influence of global market forces.	[C15, T9, GR7]
Goalsharing	A group incentive plan that is designed to measure performance against future-oriented business objectives or performance targets (i.e., not against history).	[C11, C12, GR5, GR6]
Going rate	Refers to the employer's best estimate of the wage rate that is prevailing in a labor market for a specific job. Also known as market rate.	[C2, C4, C12, C17, T1, GR1, GR4, GR6]
Golden handcuffs	Employee benefits and/or payments or incentives linked to an individual's continued employment with an organization. Leaving the organization results in forfeiting the value.	[C6, C6A, C15, T9, T11, GR7]
Golden parachute	A provision in an employment contract that provides for an increase or acceleration of certain benefit payments or vesting or other rights in the event the employee (usually an executive) loses his or her position because of a merger or takeover. Golden parachutes are sometimes a part of an anti-takeover strategy.	[C6, C6A, T6, T11]
Goods available for sale (GAS)	Beginning inventory plus additions to inventory. See also cost of goods available for sale.	[T2]

Term	Definition	Courses
Goods-and-services differential	The amount added to an expatriate's compensation to protect purchasing power for the higher cost of goods and services in an overseas assignment location compared to the base country. A minority of organizations will deduct an amount from an expatriate's pay if costs are lower abroad.	[C15, T9, GR7]
Goods-and-services index	A ratio used to compare the costs of goods and services in an assignment location with the base country. It is used in conjunction with goods-and-services spendable income to develop a goods and services differential.	[C15, T9, GR7]
Goods-and-services spendable income	The amount of money typically spent on goods and services in a base country by an expatriate's peer at the same salary and family size. This is often referred to as "host country spendable" in contrast to "home country spendable," which is the amount that an expatriate would spend in the assignment location for comparable goods and services.	[C15, T9, GR7]
Goodwill	The difference between the market value of assets and the higher price paid for those assets when a company is acquired or merged into another company. Goodwill appears on the acquiring company's balance sheet as an asset and is subject to impairment losses.	[T2, T6]
Grant date	See option grant date.	[C6, C6A, T11]
Grant multiple	In stock option plans, the number used at a given salary level to determine the grant size. This is done by	[C6, C6A, T11]

Term	Definition	Courses
	multiplying the number times the salary and dividing the product by the current stock price.	
Grant price	The price an employee will pay to exercise a market-based incentive device (typically stock options). The grant price for an incentive stock option is at least 100 percent, or the fair market value at the time of grant of the option.	[C6, C6A, T11]
Green circle rate	A rate paid to an employee that is below the established pay range minimum for a specific job.	[C4, GR4]
Gross domestic product (GDP)/ growth rate	The output of goods and services produced annually in a given country (gross and per capita) and the corresponding growth rate provide a reasonably clear picture of the business environment.	[C15, T9, GR7]
Gross margin	A profit measure: sale price minus the cost of goods before overhead, profits and taxes. Gross margin may be used as a performance measure in sales compensation plans.	[C5, T3, GR2]
Gross margin/gross margin ratio	Often used as a performance measure; it is calculated by subtracting the cost of goods sold from net sales. The gross margin ratio is obtained by dividing the gross margin by net sales.	[T2, GR2]
Gross sales	Total invoice value of sales prior to any discounts or allowances.	[T2]
Gross-up	The practice of increasing the amount of a cash payment to offset the tax impact on the individual resulting from the cash payment.	[C6, C6A, T11]

Term	Definition	Courses
Group insurance	The transfer of risk for more than one insured (i.e., group) where coverage for the group is provided under a single policy.	[B3, B3A]
Group permanent insurance	A benefits plan that usually combines life insurance with retirement benefits and uses the level premium method, under a group contract between the employer and the insurance company.	[B3]
Group practice association	An arrangement where physicians share facilities, equipment, records and personnel. The physicians may be salaried employees or compensated under a service contract.	[B1, B3A]
Group term life insurance	An annual renewable term insurance written on a group basis with the cost based on the currently expected or actual level of claims, expenses and a margin for the insurer's profit and contingencies.	[B1, B3, B3A, B5, T6]
Group universal life plan (GULP)	A form of group life insurance that combines term protection with an investment element for the policyholder. The accumulated assets can be used to create nontaxable permanent insurance or to accumulate tax-deferred capital. Participation is entirely voluntary and all premiums are paid by employees.	[B3, B3A, T6]
Guarantee	For sales compensation purposes, a compensation payment, possibly in addition to base salary, that is made regardless of performance. It is usually nonrecoverable. Guarantees may be temporary or permanent.	[C5, C6, C6A, T11]

Term	Definition	Courses
Guaranteed interest contract (GIC)	A pension plan funding vehicle that pays a fixed interest rate on a specific deposit for a defined period of time. At the end of the defined period, the deposited funds and the accumulated interest are returned to the plan sponsor. Also called a guaranteed income contract or a guaranteed investment contract.	[B2, T6]
Hardship allowance/ premium	An amount of compensation that bears no relation to the work to be done or to living costs, but is paid in recognition of extraordinarily difficult living conditions, harsh environment, isolation, political unrest or special health problems.	[C15, T9, GR7]
Hardship distribution	An in-service distribution from a retirement plan because of a participant's immediate and heavy financial need that cannot be satisfied from other resources. Internal Revenue Service (IRS) regulations contain examples of circumstances that constitute immediate and heavy financial need. These include expenses for medical care for the employee or their family, costs directly related to the purchase of a principal residence (excluding mortgage payments), tuition and related educational fees for the next 12 months of post-secondary education for the employee or their immediate family, and payments necessary to prevent foreclosure on the employee's principal residence.	[B2, T6]
Hazard	A condition that increases the chance of loss.	[B3A]

Term	Definition	Courses
Hazardous-duty pay	Similar to danger pay, except that it can also include physical as well as political dangers related to the job or assignment.	[C15, T9, GR7]
Headquarters country	The country in which the employer's corporate offices are located.	[C15, T9, GR7]
Headquarters expatriate (HQE)	National of the headquarters country who is expatriated. Also known as parent country national (PCN), expatriate.	[C15, T9, GR7]
Headquarters-based (balance sheet)	The compensation of international assignees are tied to the headquarter company's pay and benefits structure.	[C15, T9, GR7]
Health care flexible spending account	See flexible spending account. Also known as a medical reimbursement account.	[B1, B5, T6]
Health Insurance Portability and Accountability Act of 1996 (HIPAA)	A federal law, enforced by the Department of Labor (DOL), designed to protect individuals who move from one job to another, who have preexisting medical conditions or who are self-employed, by imposing a number of requirements on employer-sponsored health care plans. These requirements range from limiting preexisting condition exclusions to mandating that employers provide certificates of prior plan coverage. Acts and provisions under HIPAA include: Newborns' and Mothers' Health Protection Act of 1996, Mental Health Parity Act of 1996, Women's Health and Cancer Rights Act of 1998, Administrative Simplification Provisions (Privacy Rules)—2001 and Nondiscrimination Provisions—2001.	[B1, B3, B3A, T6, T12, W3]

Term	Definition	Courses
Health maintenance organization (HMO)	Prepaid group medical service organization that emphasizes preventive health care. An HMO is defined in the Public Health Service Act (Health Maintenance Organization Act) of 1973 as "an organized system for the delivery of comprehensive health maintenance and treatment services to voluntarily enrolled members for a prenegotiated, fixed, periodic payment."	[B1, B3, B3A, B5, T12]
Health reimbursement arrangement (HRA)	A tax-free health care reimbursement arrangement established and exclusively funded by employers. Employees use the funds in the account for general health care expenses prior to utilizing traditional health care coverage. These are theoretical accounts; money is not actually in an individual account into which the employee invests money. Benefit dollars remaining in the account at year-end can roll over and may be used to cover future medical costs.	[B1, B3, B5]
Health savings account (HSA)	A tax-advantaged trust or custodial account created for the benefit of an individual covered under a high-deductible health plan. Contributions can be made by the employer or the employee. Amounts not distributed are carried forward. Like an IRA, the HSA is owned by the individual who is the account beneficiary.	[B1, B3, B5]
Hierarchy of needs	According to this theory, a person's needs must be satisfied in a hierarchical order. Higher-level needs such as esteem and status cannot be satisfied until lower-level needs such as food and shelter are met. This theory was developed by A. H. Maslow.	

Term	Definition	Courses
Highest average pay plan	A defined benefit (DB) pension plan that bases benefits on the highest average salary of an employee for a selected number of years (typically three to five).	[B2]
Highly compensated employee (HCE)	Any employee who meets one or more of the following definitions: (1) owns 5 percent or more of the company in the current or prior year, (2) earned more than an annually indexed amount in the prior plan year, (3) at the employer's election, is in the top 20 percent of the organization's employees in terms of pay. The Internal Revenue Code (IRC) determines tax status of benefits programs based on how the plan treats highly compensated employees (HCEs), compared to other employees, and comparative eligibility and participation rates.	[B1, B2, B3, B5, C6, C6A, T6, T11]
Highly compensated individual (HCI)	Any individual who meets one or more of the following definitions: (1) one of 5 highest paid officers, (2) shareholder who holds more than 10 percent of stock in the company, (3) one of highest paid 25 percent of employees, disregarding nonparticipating excludable employees.	[B3]
Highly structured questionnaires	A job analysis technique that provides a written set of questions regarding job content that limits responses to a predetermined set of answers. Questionnaires are either behavior-based or task-based, require validation, and usually are analyzed using a computer program designed for that purpose. Also known as closed ended questionnaires.	[C2, GR3]

Term	Definition	Courses
Hiring bonus	A lump sum provided at time of hire, to provide extra enticement to accept a job offer or make up for compensation forfeited at the previous company. See signing bonus.	[C6, C6A, T11]
Hiring rate	As a matter of wage policy, the beginning rate at which people typically are hired into a job.	[C17]
Hold harmless agreement	An agreement in which one party to a contract makes a commitment not to hold the other party responsible for any damages or other liabilities arising out of the contract.	[T6, T12]
Hold harmless statement	See hold harmless agreement.	[T12]
Holidays	Specific days when most employees do not work but are paid as if they did. Employees who do work on such days typically receive premium pay or compensatory time off. The number of paid holidays granted by employers varies considerably by industry group and, to a lesser extent, by geographic region.	[B1, C1, C15, T1, W1, GR1]
Home country	The country designated as the expatriate's or third-country national's place of origin for employment and compensation purposes. Employers may define "home country" in several different ways (e.g., the country where an employee is hired or is a citizen, or the country of birth).	[C15, T6, T9, GR7]
Home country base salary	The expatriate's stated home country salary before any addition of differentials, allowances or incentives for foreign service or required contributions. Base pay is the salary that would be paid for the position on the basis of its level and salary range	[C15, T9, GR7]

Term	Definition	Courses
	in the home country. In some organizations, bonuses and similar payments typically paid in the home country are included.	
Home leave	A periodic (usually annual) leave that enables expatriates and their families to visit their home countries.	[C15]
Home-country based (balance sheet)	The compensation of international assignees is tied to the salary and benefits structure of the home country of each individual (HQ or third country).	[C15, T9, GR7]
Home-sale protection	A relocation benefit for expatriate employees that pays the costs (except for capital gains tax) associated with selling a house to take a foreign assignment. Because of increases in capital values of housing, most employees prefer not to sell, and many organizations now offer home rental protection that provides some property management services and reimburses expatriate employees for extraordinary expenses incurred because of the rental (e.g., credit checks on prospective tenants). Some organizations provide one or both benefits to domestic employees.	[C15, T9, GR7]
Host country	The country in which an expatriate or third-country national works.	[C15, T6, T9, GR7]
Host country pay	See localization approach.	[C15, T9, GR7]
Hourly	The rate of pay per hour for a job being performed. An "hourly" worker may be assigned to various rated jobs during any pay period and is paid the "rate" applicable to each job while working on it. The term hourly	[C1, C4, C17, T1, GR1, GR7]

Term	Definition	Courses
	also is used to distinguish between nonexempt and exempt employees.	
Hours of work	Under the Fair Labor Standards Act (FLSA), all time that the employer requires, suffers or permits the employee to be on duty at a prescribed workplace, including the employer's premises.	[C1, W2]
Housing allowance (differential)	A differential paid to compensate for differences between overseas local housing costs and the costs for similar housing in the base country. The allowance typically covers both rent and utilities.	[C15, T9, GR7]
Housing norm	The portion of base pay customarily paid for housing and utilities by an expatriate's home-country counterpart at equivalent salary level and family size.	[C15]
Human Resources (HR) Branding	Packaging of all human resources programs and initiatives under a specific, integrated set of symbols and key messages to communicate. HR branding establishes a consistent "image" the organization portrays to its employees and prospective employees.	[C11, T4, GR9]
Human Resources Information Systems (HRIS)	Computer system used within organizations that house human resources related data. The system can be as simple as containing employee addresses and position titles to calculating incentive and sales commissions.	[C2, C17, T1, T6, T12, GR1, GR3]
Human resources philosophy	Management's values and beliefs about its approach to the employee/employer relationship.	[W1, W2, W3, W4]

Term	Definition	Courses
Human resources strategy	The organization's overall plan for attraction, retention and motivation of employees.	[T1, W1, W2, W3, W4, GR1]
Hybrid pension plans	Retirement plans that exhibit characteristics of both defined benefit (DB) and defined contribution (DC) plans.	[B1, B2, T1, GR1]
Hybrid plan	See hybrid pension plans.	[T1, GR1]
Hypothetical tax	The amount retained from an expatriate's salary under "tax equalization" that is the equivalent of what an expatriate would pay for income tax if at home. The amounts deducted are used by employers to satisfy expatriate tax obligations worldwide.	[C15]
Immigration Reform and Control Act of 1986 (IRCA)	Requires employers to maintain certain records pertaining to citizenship of new employees.	[C11]
Impairment of goodwill	Under GAAP, goodwill is reviewed annually for impairment. Impairment losses may vary from year to year and reduce the goodwill balance on the balance sheet.	[T2]
Imputed income	Theoretical income that a company pays on behalf of an employee but the individual does not actually receive. This "theoretical income" must be added to the employee's gross wages. In general, imputed income refers to the value of excess group term life or dependent life coverage.	[B5, T6]
Incentive	Any form of variable payment tied to performance. The payment may be a monetary award, such as cash or equity, or a nonmonetary award, such as merchandise or travel. Incentives are contrasted with bonuses in that performance goals for incentives are predetermined.	[C5, C11, C12, C15, T9, GR5, GR6]

Term	Definition	Courses
Incentive compensation	Variable rewards for performance or achievement of short-term or long-term goals. Designed to stimulate employee performance.	[C6, C6A, C12, T11, GR6]
Incentive eligible	A term referring to groups or classes of employees who are eligible to participate in an incentive plan.	[C6, C6A, C12, T11, GR6]
Incentive pay plan	Formula-driven pay plan that is designed to reward the accomplishment of specific results. Rewards usually are tied to expected results identified at the beginning of the performance cycle. The plans can be individual, group, companywide or a combination or any. Incentive plans are forward-looking; in contrast to bonuses, they are not discretionary.	[C4, C12, C17, T1, GR1, GR4, GR6]
Incentive payments	Within the context of international compensation, any one of a variety of payments in excess of base pay made as an inducement either to accept, remain on or complete a foreign assignment.	[C12, C15, GR6]
Incentive plan	Plan that ties employees' earnings to their actual production on either an individual or group basis.	[C12, T2, T6]
Incentive progressivity	A concept whereby the percentage target potential of an incentive award is higher at higher income levels. May be applicable to either or both short term and long-term incentives.	[C6, C6A, T11]
Incentive stock option (ISO)	A stock option that qualifies for favorable tax treatment (no tax at exercise and long-term capital gains treatment if shares are held for one year after exercise and two years after grant before sale) and that meets other rules as specified by legislation. The	[C6, C6A, T11]

Term	Definition	Courses
	applicable section of the Internal Revenue Code (IRC) is Section 422.	
Income protection programs	Programs designed to protect the standard of living of the employee and his or her family.	[B1, B2, B3, B3A, B5, C15, T1, T2, T3, T6, T9, T11, GR1, GR2, GR7]
Income statement	One of the four principal financial statements of an organization. It includes the sales/revenues and expenses incurred applicable to a period in time, such as a quarter or year. Also called profit and loss statement on earnings statement.	[C6, C6A, T1, T2, T6, T11, GR1]
Incumbent	A person occupying and performing a job.	[C1, C2, C4, C17, GR3, GR4]
Incurred but not reported (IBNR) claims	Claims for losses that already have occurred but have not been presented for payment. A reserve for such liabilities, called the IBNR reserve, normally is created by insurance companies or companies' self-funded plans.	[B3, B3A, T6]
Indemnification agreement	An agreement between two parties in which one party agrees to reimburse the other up to a specific dollar amount for a specific loss/event.	[T6, T12]
Indemnify	To protect, financially or otherwise, against a loss.	[B3, B3A]
Indemnity plans	Medical plans that allow the participants the maximum amount of choice in selecting doctors, hospitals and other providers of benefits.	[T1, GR1]
Independent practice association (IPA)	A type of managed care organization in which physicians in private practice form an association	[B1, B3A]

Term	Definition	Courses
	and contract with one or more health maintenance organizations (HMOs) to provide medical services for a set fee. Physicians in an IPA also continue to provide medical services to nonmanaged care patients.	
Independent variable	Denoted as the x-variable, it is the quantity or item that is believed to have an impact on the dependent variable. It sometimes is referred to as the predictor variable. Often, more than one independent variable may impact the dependent variable.	[T3, GR2, GR3]
Indexed stock options	Stock options granted with an exercise price that is tied to a specified index or formula and not known on the grant date.	[C6, C6A, T11]
Indexing	An automatic adjustment of benefits in payment status to reflect changes in a consumer price, cost of living, or other index of inflation.	[C15]
Indirect channel	Manufacturers and service providers in an indirect channel use one or more levels of distribution (e.g., distributors, wholesalers, retail stores and agents) to reach customers.	[C5]
Individual equity	A criterion that provides a guideline for employers to establish wage rates for individual employees (people in the same job, in the simplest case) according to individual variation in merit.	[C4, C17, GR4]
Individual pay rate	The wage or salary level assigned to a given individual. Individual pay rates may vary for the same job or as a function of time and grade, performance, or some other basis for establishing	[C12, C17, GR5, GR6]

Term	Definition	Courses
	variation in the employee's value to the organization.	
Individual retirement account (IRA)	See traditional individual retirement account (IRA) and Roth individual retirement account (IRA).	[B1, B2, C1]
Individualism	Degree to which a culture favors the needs of the individual.	[C15, T9, GR7]
Inferential statistics	The set of scientific techniques for using statistics derived from a sample of data to estimate parameters of the subject population based on the mathematical theory of probability.	[T3, GR2]
Inflation	A term commonly used to refer to increases in prices for a constant "market basket" of goods/services. Inflation is caused by a general increase in the money supply, without a corresponding increase in the amount of goods and services available.	[C15, T1, T9, GR1, GR7]
Informal flexibility	Includes ways to reorganize the workday to allow employees more time to focus on critical tasks or have some "quiet time."	[W1, W2]
Initial public offering (IPO)	A company's initial sale of its shares to the investing public, or the re-entry into a public securities market of a company that was once public but subsequently was taken private.	[T11]
In-service distribution	A distribution of retirement benefits to a plan participant prior to retirement ("in-service"). Usually, in-service distributions received before age 59½ are subject to a 10 percent early withdrawal penalty.	[B2, T6]
Inside payroll costs	Employee benefits costs that are not segregated as such (e.g., paid rest periods and pay for time not worked, such as vacation, holidays, sick leave, etc.).	[B1]

Term	Definition	Courses
Insider	A shareholder who owns 10 percent or more of a company's stock, a member of the board of directors or an elected officer in a senior policy making role of a corporation, or anyone else who possesses information that is not publicly known about the company, but that is important in valuing its stock. Securities and Exchange Commission (SEC) regulations place restrictions on stock purchases and sales by insiders. Violations can result in fines or prison sentences. The SEC also imposes filing requirements on insiders with respect to their ownership and changes in ownership of company shares.	[C6, C6A]
Insource	A decision made by the organization to keep the administration of the plan (benefits, payroll, etc.) within the organization.	[T12]
Installment vesting	In executive compensation; vesting is staggered, with an equal percent vesting each year until 100 percent is achieved.	[C6]
Institutional investors	Organizations that invest in the financial markets on behalf of large groups of individual investors. Examples include pension funds, mutual funds, insurance companies and investment companies.	[C6A]
Insurance	The transfer of risk to a third party in exchange for a "consideration" or premium. The exchange creates an insurance contract in which the third party is a licensed (by a state insurance commission) insurer or insurance company, and the contract is subject to state insurance regulations.	[B3, B3A, C15]

Term	Definition	Courses
Insurance network	Either a multinational insurance company or a consortium of local companies that offers multinational pooling arrangements.	
Insured	The person, entity or property covered by an insurance policy.	[B3]
Insured plan	A pension plan funded with a life insurance company. The life insurance company guarantees the payment of annuities purchased.	
Intangible asset	Something of value that is of a nonphysical nature. Examples include brands, patents, goodwill and trademarks.	[T2]
Integrated pension plan	A retirement plan that is coordinated with Social Security. The plan pays a higher benefit as a percentage of salary for employees in higher salary ranges. The intent is to bring the total benefit (i.e., pension payments plus Social Security payments) as a percentage of salary close to the level of lower paid employees who receive a greater percentage of salary from Social Security.	[B1, B2]
Interactive voice response (IVR) system	Customized communications tool that gives employees access to information stored in a computer by calling a toll-free number.	[B1, T4, GR9]
Intercept	In a linear model $y = a + bx$, the intercept is denoted by the symbol a and is the value of y when x equals zero. Sometimes the intercept is also called the constant or the constant term. In a multiple linear model, the intercept is the value of y when all the x values are zero.	[T3, GR2]

Term	Definition	Courses
Interest rate	The percentage of return for money invested over a period of time.	[T3, GR2]
Interim Final Rules for Nondiscrimination in Health Coverage in the Group Market–2001	A set of rules that prohibit group health plans from establishing eligibility rules that would discriminate based on the following eight health factors: health status, medical condition (physical and mental), claims experience, receipt of health care, medical history, genetic information, evidence of insurability and disability. The rules also prohibit group health plans from charging an individual a different premium or contribution than a similarly situated individual based on those same eight health factors.	[B3, W3]
Internal equity	A fairness criterion that directs an employer to establish wage rates that correspond to each job's relative value to the organization.	[C1, C2, C4, C5, C6, C15, C17, T1, GR1, GR3, GR4]
Internal range	A salary range that is determined by using salary information within an organization. Many organizations have a range for a particular job rather than a single rate to allow for different levels of performance and experience.	[T3]
Internal Revenue Code (IRC)	All of the tax laws passed by Congress and administered by the Internal Revenue Service (IRS).	[B1, B2, B3, C6, C6A, T2, T6, T11]
Internal Revenue Service (IRS)	The agency of the federal government responsible for interpretation of tax laws, collection of income tax and enforcement of the Internal Revenue Code (IRC). Compliance with IRS rules often is an integral factor in the design of compensation and benefits programs.	[B1, B2, B3, C1, C6, C6A, T2, T6, T11]

Term	Definition	Courses
International Accounting Standards Board (IASB)	An independent, privately funded organization committed to developing a single set of global accounting standards. Board members are from nine countries and have a variety of backgrounds. The IASB's predecessor was the International Accounting Standards Committee (IASC), which ceased operations in March 2001.	[T2]
International division	Company that focuses mainly on the home market with some international business activity managed in an often independent manner.	[C15, T9, GR7]
International Financial Reporting Standard (IFRS) 2	"Share-based payment" is the international accounting standard for equity compensation issued by the International Accounting Standards Board (IASB).	[C6, C6A, T11]
International plan	A retirement plan for international transfers established in an offshore location and not in compliance with the benefits laws or regulations in any country.	[C15]
International remuneration	Pay practices covering employees who move across national borders, including headquarters expatriates and third-country nationals. The definition sometimes is extended to include domestic pay practices in foreign countries.	[T9, GR7]
Interquartile range	The difference between the 25th percentile (first quartile) and the 75th percentile (third quartile) in an ordered array of data. This range contains the middle 50 percent of the data.	[C4, C15, C17, T3, GR2, GR4]
Interval measurement	Measurement in which equal differences on the scale represent the same amount, no matter the location on the scale. No absolute zero exists.	[T3, GR2]

Term	**Definition**	**Courses**
Intrinsic motivation	Employee satisfaction contingent upon job content or job context, as opposed to job consequences. It is a result of factors such as the opportunity to perform meaningful work, experience complete cycles of work or finished products, experience variety, and receive feedback on successful work results.	[C12, GR5, GR6]
Intrinsic rewards	Rewards that are associated with the job itself, such as the opportunity to perform meaningful work, complete cycles of work, see finished products, experience variety, receive professional development training, enjoy good relations with coworkers and supervisors and receive feedback on work results.	[C4, C15, C17, T9, GR4, GR7]
Inventory	Finished and unfinished products that have not yet been sold and the raw materials needed to make them.	[T2]
Investing activities	Methods of contributing to net income that include the acquisition and disposal of property, plant and equipment.	[T2]
Investment management	The process of managing money.	[T6]
Job	The total collection of tasks, duties and responsibilities assigned to one or more individuals whose work has the same nature and level.	[C1, C2, C4, C17, GR3, GR4]
Job analysis	The systematic, formal study of the duties and responsibilities that constitute job content. The process seeks to obtain important and relevant information about the nature and level of the work performed and the specifications required for an incumbent to perform the job at a competent level.	[C1, C2, C4, C11, C17, T1, GR1, GR3, GR4]

Term	Definition	Courses
Job analysis interview	A method for gathering information about a job by conducting a question-and-answer session with a person who is knowledgeable about that job.	[C2, GR3]
Job cluster	A series of jobs, grouped together for job evaluation and wage-and-salary administration purposes on the basis of common skills, occupational qualifications, technology, licensing, working conditions, union jurisdictions, workplace, career paths, and organizational tradition.	[C2, GR3]
Job component method of job evaluation	A quantitative form of job content evaluation that uses multiple regression of market pay levels versus two or more independent variables to establish a job worth hierarchy.	[C2, C17, T1, GR1, GR3]
Job content evaluation method(s)	Methods that use job content as the primary determinant in developing a job worth hierarchy. With these methods, market pay levels typically are a secondary influence on the job worth hierarchy. Point factor is the most commonly used method.	[C2, C17, GR3]
Job description	A summary of the most important features of a job, including the general nature of the work performed (duties and responsibilities) and level (e.g., skill, effort, responsibility and working conditions) of the work performed. It typically includes job specifications that detail employee characteristics required for competent performance of the job. A job description should describe and focus on the job	[C1, C2, C4, C11, C17, GR3, GR4]

Term	Definition	Courses
	itself and not on any specific individual who might fill the job.	
Job doc-umentation	Written information about job content typically resulting from job analysis efforts. Documentation includes, but is not limited to, job descriptions, completed questionnaires, interview notes and efficiency study reports.	[C1, C2, C17, T1, GR1, GR3]
Job duties	A group of tasks that constitutes one of the distinct and major activities involved in the work performed.	[C2, C17, GR3]
Job enlargement	The practice of adding more tasks of a similar nature or a similar level of difficulty to a specific job (i.e., horizontal expansion of duties and/or responsibilities).	[T1, GR1, GR5]
Job enrichment	The practice of adding more responsibility and/or diversity to a specific job to make it more challenging for the incumbent (i.e., vertical expansion of duties and/or responsibilities).	[T1, GR1, GR5]
Job evaluation	A formal process used to create a job worth hierarchy within an organization. The two basic approaches are market data and the job content.	[C2, C4, C11, C15, C17, T1, T9, GR1, GR3, GR4, GR7]
Job evaluation committee	A committee whose membership is charged with the responsibility of (a) directing and/or conducting the process of job evaluation, and (b) assessing the success with which the job worth hierarchy has been developed.	[C2, GR3]

Term	Definition	Courses
Job family	A group of jobs having the same nature of work (e.g., engineering) but requiring different levels of skill, effort, responsibility or working conditions (e.g., entry-level vs. senior engineer).	[C2, T1, GR1, GR3]
Job grade	One of the classes, levels or groups into which jobs of the same or similar value are grouped for compensation purposes. Usually, all jobs in a grade have the same pay range: minimum, midpoint and maximum. However, sometimes different jobs in the same pay grade have different pay ranges because of market conditions for some of the jobs.	[C2, C17, GR3]
Job responsibility	One or a group of duties that identifies and describes the major purpose or reason for the existence of the job.	[C2, GR3]
Job satisfaction	An indication of how well a person "likes" his or her work, usually determined by a number of factors, including pay, promotional opportunities, supervision, coworkers, and the work itself. When there is a discrepancy between an individual's values and preferences and what the job provides, job satisfaction is reduced.	[T1, GR1, GR5]
Job scope	Magnitude of accountability for the job.	[C5, C6]
Job sharing	An arrangement that allows two or more employees, each working part-time, to share responsibility for a single job and arrange their vacations and days off so one is always at work during the normal work week.	[B1, B5, T1, T6, W1, W2, GR1]
Job specifications	A description of the worker characteristics (i.e., knowledge, skills, abilities and behaviors) required to competently perform	[C1, C2, GR3]

Term	Definition	Courses
	a given job. These characteristics must be bona fide occupational qualifications (BFOQs). Specifications, which commonly are referred to as "hiring" or "background" requirements, should be written before advertising or interviewing candidates for an open position. They should support the essential functions identified during job analysis to reduce potential liabilities under the Americans with Disabilities Act (ADA).	
Job title	The descriptive name for the total collection of tasks, duties and responsibilities assigned to one or more individuals whose positions have the same nature of work performed at the same level. Job titles should describe the nature and level of work performed. Titles often include the organizational function (e.g., Corporate Remuneration Analyst) or geographic responsibility (e.g., Eastern Region Sales Manager).	[C1, C2, C4, C17, GR3, GR4]
Job worth hierarchy	The perceived internal value of jobs in relationship to each other within an organization. The job worth hierarchy forms the basis for grouping similar jobs together and establishing salary ranges.	[C2, C4, C6, C15, C17, T1, T9, GR1, GR3, GR4, GR7]
Job-based pay	Compensation programs that base an employee's salary on the nature of a rigidly defined job instead of on individual's skills or knowledge.	[C4, GR4]
Joint and survivor annuity	A type of annuity that provides income for the lifetime of the primary beneficiary, and upon death a percentage of the pension continues to be paid to the spouse for the remainder of their lifetime. See also annuity.	[B1, B2, T6]

Term	Definition	Courses
Joint venture	A transaction in which two or more companies pool resources to achieve a goal that neither of them could as easily achieved on their own (e.g., developing new technology unique to a given industry). Often used in the context of two or more companies forming a separate company that they jointly own.	[C15, T6, T9, GR7]
Jumbo stock grant/option	When a company awards an executive a large number of restricted shares or option shares. The key issue is that size of the award compared with other normal awards is several times larger. When restricted stock is involved there may be a longer than usual vesting period. Often times the jumbo award is in lieu of awards that would otherwise be made in future years.	[C6, C6A]
Just in time (JIT) inventory ordering system	A strategy for inventory management designed to result in minimum inventory by coordinating the arrival of materials from the vendor or supplier just in time to be used, resulting in lower inventory costs.	[T2]
Keogh Plan	A program that enables a self-employed individual to establish a qualified tax-deductible pension or profit-sharing plan, subject to meeting Internal Revenue Service (IRS) requirements.	[C6, C6A]
Key employee	An officer of the employing organization who makes more than a specific dollar amount or who owns a certain percentage interest in the employing organization, as specified within the Internal Revenue Code (IRC).	[B3, B5]

Term	Definition	Courses
Key-contributor insurance	Insurance that is designed to protect the business against the possible death of an employee with unique, and largely irreplaceable, skills and knowledge. The business pays the premium and normally is the beneficiary.	[C6, C6A]
Kiosks	A computer-based interactive system installed in an area accessible by a majority of employees that allows employees to access general information about benefits, such as individual enrollment data.	[B1, T4, GR9]
Knowledge, skills and abilities (KSAs)	Common job specifications. Knowledge refers to acquired mental information necessary to do the job (e.g., principles of nuclear physics), skills refers to acquired manual measurable behaviors (e.g., lathe operation) and abilities, to natural talents or acquired dexterity (e.g., capacity to lift 200 pounds).	[C2, C17, GR3]
Knowledge-based pay	A system of salary differentiation based on the formal education, related experience or specialized training a professional employee has that qualifies the individual to deal with specific subject matter, or work effectively in a specific field. Salary level may not be dependent on whether the incumbent utilizes the knowledge.	[C11, C12, GR5, GR6]
Labor market	A location where labor is exchanged for wages. These locations are identified and defined by a combination of the following factors: (1) geography (i.e., local, regional, national, international); (2) industry;	[C1, C2, C4, C17, T1, T11, GR1, GR3, GR4]

Term	Definition	Courses
	(3) education, experience and licensing or certification required; and (4) function or occupation.	
Lag structure policy	This strategy dictates that the company will consciously set its pay equal to current market levels at the beginning of the year. The company will be "lagging" the market until the increase is implemented at the end of the year.	[C2, C4, C17, GR3, GR4]
Laissez-faire tax policy	Within the context of international compensation, a practice of noninvolvement of the organization in the income tax obligations of its expatriate employees.	[C15]
Last in, first out (LIFO)	An approach to valuing inventory in accounting where it is assumed that the products most recently obtained are the ones that are sold first.	[T2]
Lead structure policy	The company has decided to "outpace" the market. Pay is not set at current market levels, but at anticipated market levels.	[C2, C4, C17, GR3, GR4]
Lead-lag structure policy	A salary practice that is halfway between a lag and a lead policy. An organization's structure is set at the beginning of the plan year to its anticipation of the level the competition will reach by the middle of the plan year. It leads the market during the first six months, matches the competitive pay at the middle of the year and lags the market during the past six months.	[C2, C4, C17, GR3, GR4]
Least squares line	In regression analysis, the line fitted to the points that minimizes the sum of the squared deviations of the points (actual y-values).	[T3, GR2]

Term	Definition	Courses
Letter of intent	Formal document sent to potential service partners notifying them of the organization's intent to utilize the service provider's services.	[T12]
Level annual-premium funding method	A method of accumulating money for payment of future pensions, under which the level annual charge for a particular benefit is determined by the actuary for each age of entry and is payable each year until retirement, so that at that time the benefit is fully funded.	[T3]
Level cutters	Key words or phrases used in job descriptions with the same nature of work (e.g., accounting) to differentiate the level of the work performed (e.g., "complex" vs. "simple").	[C2, GR3]
Level of work	Critical data about job content that reflects the job's skill, effort, responsibility and working conditions.	[C2, C17, GR3]
Leverage	As used for sales compensation purposes, leverage is the amount of increased or "upside" incentive opportunity—in addition to target incentive pay—that management expects outstanding performers to earn.	[C5]
Leverage in financing	An indicator of the debt load a company is carrying. A highly leveraged company is carrying a greater percentage of total capital in the form of debt as opposed to equity. A debt-to-equity ratio is a measure of the entity's leverage.	[C6, C6A]
Leveraged buyout (LBO)	The purchase of a company using borrowed funds.	[T6]
Leveraged employee stock	A plan under which the company can borrow money using its stock as security or collateral for	[C6, C6A, C12, GR6]

Term	Definition	Courses
ownership plan (LESOP)	the loan and pay the principal back on a pretax basis. Under a LESOP, the organization borrows money from a financial institution, using its stock as security or collateral for the loan. During a prescribed period of time, the organization repays the loan, with principal and interest payments being tax-deductible. With each loan repayment, the lending institution releases a certain amount of stock held as security, which is placed into an employee stock ownership trust (ESOT) for distribution at no cost to qualified employees.	
Leveraged stock option	The company matches a multiple of stock options to the executive's purchase of fixed number of shares; for example, company provides four options for every one share purchased.	[C6, C6A]
Liabilities	What an organization or an individual owes and must be paid sometime in the future. Liabilities are shown on an organization's balance sheet.	[C6, C6A, T2, T6]
Life annuity	A type of annuity that provides income for life and ceases upon death. See also annuity.	[B1, B2, T6]
Life annuity with years certain	Provides income for life with a guarantee that the annuity will be paid for a certain number of years, regardless of whether the annuitant is alive. See also annuity.	[B1, B2, T6]
Life status changes	While enrollment is restricted to annual or periodic scheduled events, employees may be able to change their decisions in the event of certain life events, e.g., marriage, divorce, death of spouse, birth of a child.	[B3, B5]

Term	Definition	Courses
Lifetime retiree medical insurance	An insurance arrangement that provides lifetime medical benefits to retirees.	[T6]
Limitations and exclusions	Limitations are conditions or procedures covered under a health care policy at a reduced benefit level. Exclusions are conditions or procedures for which no coverage is provided. All health insurance policies specify limitations and exclusions.	[B3]
Limited liability company (LLC)	A legal entity that is taxed like a partnership, but shields personal assets from liability like a corporation.	[T6]
Line of sight	Employee's perception of the degree to which his or her contributions influence improvement.	[C12, GR6]
Linear regression	The statistical technique of fitting a straight line to a set of (x, y) data, using the method of least squares. Linear regression assumes that the basic relationship between the two variables is linear in nature.	[C2, C4, C17, T3, GR2, GR3, GR4]
Linear relationship	A situation in which the relationship between an x-variable and a y-variable can best be described by a straight line. The data points plotted on a graph of this relationship follow a straight line.	[T3, GR2]
Linear scales	Lines on which equal distances between increments represent equal intervals between increments.	[T3, GR2]

Term	Definition	Courses
Liquidity	An indicator of a company's ability to procure ready assets to meet short-term financial obligations. Cash is the most liquid asset.	[C6, C6A, T2, T11]
Living wage	A term that refers to a wage rate that allows an employee to maintain an acceptable standard of living.	[C1]
Local national	All personnel who are hired by a foreign-held company as regular employees in the country in which they reside. Usually they are citizens of that country. Within the context of international compensation, an employee who is paid as a national of the country in which he or she works.	[C15, T9, GR7]
Localization approach	An expatriate compensation methodology in which expatriates are paid the same compensation as local national peers and are usually supplemented by various permanent and/or temporary allowances for such factors as housing, transportation and children's education. Also known as host country pay.	[C15, T9, GR7]
Lock-in rules	To foster pricing stability, many flex plans feature restrictions on the highest level of medical and/or dental coverage available. Having chosen the highest level of coverage, the employee may be required to stay in that option for a two- or three-year period. Some degree of flexibility is sacrificed for the good of the overall plan.	[B5]
Logarithmic scales	Lines on which equal distances between increments represent equal ratios between increments.	[T3, GR2]

Term	Definition	Courses
Long-term bonus	Usually a form of deferred compensation that establishes an income stream in the form of a bonus over time, typically at a predetermined age or upon retirement.	[C11, C12, T1, GR1, GR5, GR6]
Long-term care (LTC) insurance	An insurance policy designed to provide a stream of benefits payments to provide assistance with daily living when a qualifying insurable event occurs. A qualifying, insurable event occurs when an individual cannot perform a given number (e.g., two of five) of daily living activities such as bathing, dressing, eating and moving from bed to chair.	[B1, B3, B3A, B5, T1, W1, GR1]
Long-Term Care Security Act of 2000	Federal law that made long-term care available to federal employees, members of the military or National Guard, and civilian and military retirees.	[B3]
Long-term disability (LTD) plan	A form of long-term income protection that provides for some continuation of income in the event of disability. Definitions of disability become increasingly narrow in LTD plans (e.g., disabled from engaging in one's own occupation or from any occupation.	[B1, B3, B3A, B5, T6]
Long-term incentive plan	Any incentive plan (usually limited to executives) that requires sustained performance of the firm for a period longer than one fiscal year for maximum benefit to the employee. Some plans are based on capital shares of the organization and may require investment by the employee, while others are based on financial performance.	[C6, C6A, C11, C12, GR5, GR6]

Term	Definition	Courses
Long-term transferee	See permanent transferee.	[C15, T9, GR7]
L-type agreements	Regardless of the host country location (as long as they are part of the agreement) or remuneration package covering the employee, the U.S. employer agrees to continue to make U.S. Social Security contributions (employer and employee portions) on the employee's behalf.	[C15, T9, GR7]
Lump sum (balance sheet)	The employer pays international assignees lump sums designed to cover all unusual costs associated with the assignment.	[C15, T9, GR7]
Lump-sum approach	An expatriate compensation methodology in which the employer pays expatriates lump sums designed to cover all unusual costs associated with the assignment in lieu of a series of allowances and differentials in addition to base pay.	[T9, GR7]
Lump-sum bonus	An award that is paid in a single cash payment.	[C11, C12, C15, GR5, GR6]
Lump-sum incentive award	An incentive award that is paid in a single cash payment.	[C6, C6A]
Lump-sum increase	Any increase in pay that is made in the form of a single cash payment. The most common form is the lump-sum merit increase.	[C4, C11, C17, T1, GR1, GR4]
Lump-sum merit payment	When merit pay is delivered in the form of a single cash payment separate from base pay (i.e., not folded in). It must be "re-earned" annually.	[C11, GR4, GR5]
Major medical insurance	Protection for large surgical, hospital or other medical expenses and services. Benefits are paid after a specified deductible is met and then generally are subject to coinsurance. Major medical usually is written in	[B3, B3A, C15]

Term	Definition	Courses
	conjunction with a basic medical plan and referred to as a supplementary plan. If written alone, it is referred to as a single-plan comprehensive medical program.	
Managed care network	An organized network of health care service providers that provide services to enrollees of a managed care plan.	[B3, T6]
Managed care plan	A health plan that attempts to control cost and quality of care by contracting with health care providers to deliver health care services on a capitated basis. Examples include health maintenance organizations (HMOs), preferred provider organizations (PPOs) and point of service (POS) plans.	[B1, B3, B3A, B5, C15, T6, T9]
Management by objectives (MBO)	An employee-development technique that consists of a process in which a superior and a subordinate, or group of subordinates, jointly identify and establish common performance goals as a basis for directing behavior and assessing performance. The unique feature of MBO is that the process requires involvement of subordinates in the setting of performance goals.	[C6, C6A, C11, C12, GR5, GR6]
Mandated benefits	Noncash total rewards elements that employers are required by law to provide to their employees (e.g., Social Security, unemployment, workers' compensation).	[B1, C1, T1, GR1]
Manual rates	In group insurance, the determination of premium payments based on the pool experience of the insurer and actuarial adjustments for future trends and not based on prior claims experience of the insured.	[B3A]

Term	Definition	Courses
Maquiladora	A maquiladora is a Mexican Corporation that operates under an in-bond (maquila) program approved for it by the Mexican Secretariat of Commerce and Industrial Development (SECOFI). A maquila program entitles the company, first, to foreign investment participation in capital; second, it entitles the company to special customers treatment, allowing duty free temporary import of machinery, equipment, parts and materials, and administrative equipment such as computers and communications devices, subject only to posting a bond guaranteeing that such goods will not remain in Mexico permanently.	[C15]
Margin	An insurer's "fudge" factor, error factor or margin of conservatism that is used when underwriting risk. Margin usually is expressed as a percentage of the premium.	[B3, B3A]
Marginal tax rate	The tax rate that applies to the next dollar of income generated.	[C6, C6A]
Market-adjustment	The percentage increase to organization, group or individual pay that is necessary to adjust it to the estimated market level.	[C2, C4, C17, GR3, GR4]
Market basket	The sample of representative items of goods and services that are priced in both the home and assignment locations to determine the difference in the costs of goods and services, and to compute the goods-and-services index. Typical categories include food at home, tobacco and alcohol, personal care, furnishings and household operation, clothing, medical care, recreation, transportation, domestic service and food away from home.	[C15, T9, GR7]

Term	Definition	Courses
Market capitalization	It is the result of multiplying the stock price times the number of shares outstanding. Thus if the stock price is $50 per share and the number of shares is 10 million, the market capitalization would be $500 million. Companies are often referred to as large cap, mid cap, small cap or micro cap depending on the size of their market capitalization.	[C6, C6A]
Market compa-ratio	The ratio of internal pay to competitive pay for a company, group or individual, calculated by dividing the internal weighted average pay by the related market weighted average pay.	[C4, C17, GR4]
Market cycle	See business life cycle.	[C2, C4, C6, C6A, GR3, GR4]
Market data	See market pricing.	[C6, C15]
Market index	An index computed by dividing the pay received by an individual by the market pay for that job. This figure can be computed for groups, departments and the entire organization. It is designed to provide a measure of how organizational pay compares to the market.	[C2, C4, C17, T3, GR2, GR3, GR4]
Market pricing	Relative to compensation, the technique of creating a job worth hierarchy based on the "going rate" for benchmark jobs in the labor market(s) relevant to the organization. Under this method, job content is considered secondarily to ensure internal equity after a preliminary hierarchy is established based on market pay levels for benchmark jobs. All other jobs are "slotted" into the hierarchy based on whole job comparison.	[C1, C2, C4, C5, C15, C17, T1, GR1, GR3, GR4]

Term	Definition	Courses
Market rate composite	The employer's best estimate of the wage rate that is prevailing in the external labor market for a given job or occupation. Also known as market rate.	[C1, C2, C4, C15, C17, T9, GR3, GR4, GR7]
Market value	(1) The price of an item or service as determined by willing buyers and sellers in a dynamic, open market. (2) The price or last reported price at which a security is trading and could presumably be purchased or sold. (3) What investors believe a company is worth; calculated by multiplying the number of shares outstanding by their current market price.	[C15, T2, T4, T9, GR7, GR9]
Marketable securities	Securities that are easily convertible to cash.	[T2]
Market-based salary increase budget	A salary increase budget based solely on what an organization's salary goals are with respect to the competition.	[T3, GR2]
Market-to-book ratio	The market price of a stock divided by its book value per share. In general a company with a high market to book ratio is perceived by the stock market to be a company with high growth potential.	[C6, C6A]
Masculinity culture	Degree to which a culture favors assertiveness and acquisition.	[C15, T9, GR7]
Matching contribution	A contribution made by an organization to the retirement account of the participant. Matching contributions usually are designed to equal the employee's contributions up to a certain amount or percentage of compensation.	[B1, B2]
Materiality	Accounting concept providing that important information about the financial transactions or condition of the company must be separately reported and explained.	[T2]

Term	Definition	Courses
Mature company	Company with heightened global cost consciousness.	[C15, T9, GR7]
Maturity curve	(1) A process of determining employees' salaries as a function of years from the time of the first degree earned. Maturity curves are most commonly used for pricing jobs in lieu of relying on job-evaluation techniques. The process assumes that years in the profession equates with more highly valued competencies. (2) A method of market survey data collection and reporting that expresses average/median pay as a function of years since bachelor's degree.	[C2, C17, GR3]
Maximum	Relative to sales compensation, the total incentive opportunity a sales representative can earn in a given time period. The term may also refer to the total cash compensation an employee may earn in a given time period. Sometimes a maximum is referred to as a "cap," "ceiling" or "lid."	[C5, C6, C15, T9, GR7]
Mealtime flex	Taking a longer meal break and making up time at the beginning or end of the day.	[W1, W2]
Mean	A simple arithmetic average obtained by adding a set of numbers and then dividing the sum by the number of items in the set.	[C2, C5, C17, T3, GR2, GR3]
Measurement date	Used to determine compensation expense in stock option(s) and award plans. It is the first date on which both the number of shares and the purchase price are known. This is defined in APB 25 issued by the Accounting Principles Board (APB).	[C6, C6A, T11]

Term	Definition	Courses
Measurement principle	Related to compensation for services that a corporation receives as consideration for stock issued through employee stock option, stock purchase and stock award plans. Compensation is measured by the quoted market price of the stock at the measurement date less the amount, if any, to be paid by the employee.	[C6, C6A, T11]
Median	The middle item in a set of ranked data points containing an odd number of items. When an even number of items are ranked, the average of the two middle items is the median.	[C2, C5, C17, T3, GR2, GR3]
Medicaid	A plan that provides health assistance to persons with low income in states that elect to participate; it is jointly financed by both state and federal governments. The plan reimburses health providers for specified services rendered to the elderly, the disabled and dependent children or others who meet the income tests.	[B1, B3, B3A]
Medical reimbursement account	See flexible spending account. Also known as health care spending account.	[B3, B5]
Medical savings (spending) account (MSA)	A savings account that can be used to pay medical expenses not covered by insurance. Contributions to the plan are deductible from an account holder's federal income tax and, where permitted, from state income tax. Self-employed individuals can accumulate funds in the account from year to year. Self-employed individuals with individual MSAs can make contributions themselves. Employers with small group MSAs may make contributions on behalf of employees, or employees may make the entire contribution.	[B1, B3, B3A, B5]

Term	Definition	Courses
Medicare	The federal health insurance program for people 65 years of age or older, certain younger people with disabilities, and people with end-stage renal disease. Unlike Medicaid, it is not based on financial-need; benefits are provided regardless of financial status.	[B1, B3]
Medicare risk HMO	A Medicare option under which the Medicare-eligible person has Medicare plans A and B coverage replaced by health maintenance organization (HMO) coverage that meets Medicare guidelines.	[B3, B3A]
Mental Health Parity Act of 1996 (MHPA)	A federal law prohibiting plans that provide mental health benefits from imposing aggregate lifetime or annual dollar limits for mental health benefits that are less than those imposed on medical/surgical benefits. The Act's sunset provision has been extended through Dec. 31, 2002.	[B3, B3A, T6]
Merco-sur Trade Agreement	Mercosur is a common market agreement between Argentina, Brazil, Paraguay and Uruguay, with Bolivia and Chile having observer status. Long-term goals include creating an integrated market across South America and, eventually, the full continental integration of North and South American markets.	[C15, T9, GR7]
Merger	A transaction in which two companies join to form a larger entity that usually will assume a new identity (i.e., different from either of the two previous companies).	[C11, C15, T6, T9, GR7]
Merit bonus	See lump-sum merit payment.	[C4, GR4]
Merit increase	An adjustment to an individual's base pay rate based on performance or some other individual measure.	[C11, C12, C4, T1, T6, GR1, GR4, GR5, GR6]

Term	Definition	Courses
Merit matrix	A methodology using an individual's performance level and placement within the salary range as a means of determining the amount of the pay increase, usually stated as a percentage of base salary.	[C4, C11, GR4, GR5]
Merit pay	A pay program in which pay is made contingent upon performance. Commonly called pay-for-performance.	[C11]
Merit pool	Total performance increase dollars available, expressed as a percentage of payroll at the end of the preceding period.	[GR5]
Merit progression	A formula for progressing an employee through a wage structure according to performance, or some other individual equity basis.	[C4, GR4]
Merit rating	A method for appraising the performance of an employee with respect to his or her job. It frequently serves as a basis for making pay adjustments, promotion decisions, or work reassignments.	[C4, GR4, GR5]
Message	Information being communicated.	[T4, GR9]
Metrics	A quantifiable means of monitoring and measuring key performance goals.	[W2]
Midpoint	The salary that represents the middle of a given salary range or pay grade.	[C4, C11, C15, C17, T1, T3, T9, GR1, GR2, GR4, GR7]
Midpoint differential	The difference in wage rates paid in the midpoints of two adjacent grades. A midpoint progression is calculated by taking the difference between two adjacent midpoints as a percentage of the lower of the midpoints. Also known as the midpoint differential.	[C2, C4, C17, T1, T3, T9, GR1, GR3, GR4]

Term	Definition	Courses
Midpoint progression	See midpoint differential.	[C2, C4, C15, T1, T3, T9, GR1, GR2, GR3, GR4, GR7]
Midpoint-to-midpoint differential	See midpoint differential.	[C4, T3, GR4]
Minimum premium insurance	A group insurance financing arrangement in which the employer is responsible for paying all claims up to an agreed-upon aggregate level, with the carrier responsible for the excess. The insurer usually processes all claims and provides other administrative services.	[B3, B3A]
Minimum wage	The lowest allowable hourly pay level for most Americans, established by Congress as part of the Fair Labor Standards Act (FLSA). Some states have laws that mandate higher minimum wages for some employees.	[C1, C15, T9, GR7]
Mission	A specific method outlining organizational goals and how to attain them.	[T4, GR9]
Mix	Relative to compensation, the relationship between the base salary and the planned (or target) incentive amounts in the total cash compensation package at planned or expected performance. The two portions of the mix, expressed as percentages, always add to 100 percent.	[C5, C12, GR5, GR6]
Mixed motive	Under Title VII of the Civil Rights Act, the result when a plaintiff demonstrates that an employer's decision was partially motivated by discrimination, but the employer demonstrates that it would have made the same decision regardless.	[C1]

Term	Definition	Courses
Mobility premium	A lump sum (usually two to three months' salary) paid at the time of expatriation, transfer from one expatriate assignment to another in a different country or repatriation. Its primary objective is to facilitate global mobility.	[C15]
Mode	The category or value that occurs most frequently in a set of observations. In a frequency distribution, it is the category with the highest frequency. Sometimes there is more than one mode.	[C2, C17, T3, GR2, GR3]
Model	A representation of reality that describes variables, the relationships among variables and the action of the system if changes are made in the variables or in the relationships. Models are major methods for examining alternative strategies and policies. They are used to solve problems and to understand relationships between data sets.	[T3, GR2]
Modified Accelerated Cost Recovery System (MACRS)	A system used in tax accounting that defines the rate and method under which a fixed asset will be depreciated. The Internal Revenue Code (IRC) has mandated the use of the MACRS.	[T2]
Modified home-country based (balance sheet)	Base pay is denominated in home-country currency and tied to home-country compensation levels of the peers of each assignee. However, payments for housing, goods and services in the host country are standardized for all nationalities at common job levels.	[C15, T9, GR7]
Modular plan	See simple choice plan.	[B5]

Term	Definition	Courses
Money market fund	A low-risk mutual fund that invests primarily in short-term securities.	[B2]
Money purchase plan	A type of defined contribution (DC) pension plan in which the employer contribution to the employee's account is based on a formula, regardless of profits.	[B1, B2, T11]
Morbidity table	A statistical table showing the incidence of illness for a large group of individuals.	[B3A]
Mortality experience	The rate at which participants in a plan have died. Also, the financial effect of deaths (that actually have occurred) on the operation of a plan.	[B2]
Mortality table	A listing of mortality experience according to age group. A mortality table permits the actuary to calculate, on the average, how long a male or female of a given age may be expected to live.	[B2]
Mortgages payable	Long-term debt secured by real property.	[T2]
Multicollinearity	In multiple linear regression, a situation where there is a high correlation between some of the x-variables, or where one x-variable is close to a linear combination of other x-variables. Multicollinearity occurs when one x-variable starts to become a surrogate for another x-variable or for a linear combination of other x-variables. When multicollinearity exists in a statistical inference situation, the model is not as stable as one would prefer.	[C15, T3, GR2]
Multi-employer pension plan	A pension plan that is contributed to by more than one employer and maintained according to collective bargaining agreements.	[B1, B2, T6]

Term	Definition	Courses
Multinational company	Company that conducts business in multiple countries, with each operation typically managed by local employees following a centrally coordinated strategy.	[C15, T9, GR7]
Multinational pooling	A method by which the insured benefits (i.e., typically risk benefits) of a multinational organization are linked by insuring the benefits locally with an insurance carrier belonging to a network of insurance companies. Organizations do this to reduce costs through economies of scale, gather better information, receive better underwriting terms and exert greater influence with local insurance carriers.	[C15, T6, T9, GR7]
Multiple coefficient of determination	In a multiple regression situation, the proportion of variation in the dependent variable that can be attributed to the relationship with the linear combination of the independent variables. It has values between 0.0 and 1.0.	[T3, GR2]
Multiple correlation coefficient	In a multiple regression situation, a measure of how well data points fall on a straight line in multidimensional space. It has a value equal to the square root of the multiple coefficient of determination.	[T3, GR2]
Multiple measure plan	Incentive plan designed to measure and reward performance using one or more goals. Plan may reflect several ways to measure performance against a single objective or several objectives.	[C12, GR6]
Multiple regression	The statistical technique of creating a model of a y-variable (dependent variable) as a function of more than one x-variable (independent variable) using the method of least squares. It	[C2, C17, T3, GR2, GR3]

Term	Definition	Courses
	allows an assessment of the joint impact of several x-variables on the y-variable.	
Multirater assessment	A performance assessment tool in which an employee is evaluated by more than one individual. An example of a multirater assessment approach is 360° feedback.	[C11]
Mutual fund	A pool of investment money that is managed by professionals and invested in a wide variety of securities, depending on the fund's objectives.	[B2]
Named individuals	Those persons who are named in a company's proxy statement and whose compensation is shown based on Securities and Exchange Commission (SEC) disclosure requirements.	[C6, C6A]
National Association of Securities Dealers Automated Quotation System (NASDAQ)	An organization that facilitates the trading of shares of stock in publicly traded companies.	[C6, C6A, T11]
National average earnings (NAE)	A measure of the average wage per person in an individual country as measured by a local government agency dealing in labor matters. In international applications, it is common to use twice this number as a broad measure of how multinational organizations pay an average employee.	[C15, T9, GR7]
National Committee for Quality Assurance (NCQA)	One of the most prominent accreditation organizations, it primarily accredits health maintenance organizations (HMOs). It has developed Health Plan Employer Data and Information Sets (HEDIS) that contain eight	[B3A]

Term	Definition	Courses
	broad criteria focused on outcomes and used as part of the accreditation process.	
National Institutes of Health (NIH)	One of eight health agencies of the Public Health Services that, in turn, is part of the Department of Health and Human Services. The NIH conducts and supports research with the goal of improving the prevention, detection, diagnosis and treatment of disease and disability.	[B3]
National Labor Relations Act of 1935 (Wagner Act)	A federal law that gives employees the right to organize unions, bargain collectively and engage in concerted actions for mutual protection. It also requires employers to recognize unions selected by employees and to bargain in good faith, and it prevents employers from conducting certain unfair labor practices.	[C1, C12, GR6]
National Labor Relations Board (NLRB)	The federal agency that enforces the National Labor Relations Act of 1935. Through secret-ballot elections, determines whether employees want union representation and investigates and remedies unfair labor practices by employers and unions.	[B3]
Natural logarithm	A logarithm that uses a base of e, a natural number approximately equal to 2.71828.	[T3, GR2]
Nature of work	Critical data about a job that reflect the job's duties and responsibilities.	[C2, C17, GR3]
Negative correlation	A relationship where higher values of y generally go with lower values of x, and lower values of y generally go with higher values of x.	[T3, GR2]
Negative differential	The result obtained when the costs of goods and services or housing are higher in the home	[C15]

Term	Definition	Courses
	country than at the assignment location. A majority of North American companies allow expatriates to receive a windfall when costs of either goods and services or housing are lower in the assignment location than in the base country.	
Negatively skewed	A distribution in which most of the scores cluster to the right of the mean and the "tail" of the distribution trails off to the left. The mean is smaller than the median, which in turn is typically smaller than the mode.	[T3, GR2]
Negotiation approach	An expatriate compensation methodology in which employers and their expatriates negotiate mutually acceptable compensation packages.	[C15, T9, GR7]
Net assets	Total assets less current liabilities. Used in calculating return on net assets (RONA), an important business measure, particularly in operating divisions of a company.	[T2]
Net income	Revenues less expenses. Also called net earnings or net profit.	[T2]
Net income after tax	A company's profit after accounting for all revenues and expenses applicable to the period including the taxes that will be due on that profit but before extraordinary items.	[C6, C6A, T2]
Net loss after tax	A company's loss after accounting for all revenues and expenses applicable to the period including any taxes due.	[T2]
Net present value (NPV)	The total of future net cash flows discounted to the present. See also present value.	[T2]
Net profit margin	See return on sales.	[T2]
Net revenues	See net sales.	[T2]

Term	Definition	Courses
Net sales	Gross sales minus returns, discounts and allowances.	[T2]
Net worth	Total assets minus total liabilities. In accounting, the equity section of the balance sheet represents net worth. Also often used to describe individual wealth. Also known as book value.	[T2]
New York Stock Exchange (NYSE)	The largest and most established stock trading organization. The NYSE is located on Wall Street in New York City. It is also referred to as the "Big Board."	[C6, C6A, T11]
Newborns' and Mothers' Health Protection Act of 1996 (NMHPA)	A federal law that affects the amount of time a woman and her newborn child are covered for a hospital stay following childbirth. Typically, plans and health insurance issuers that are subject to NMHPA may not restrict benefits for a hospital stay in connection with childbirth to less than 48 hours following a vaginal delivery or 96 hours following a delivery by cesarean section. Employers are required to notify plan participants of their rights under NMHPA.	[B1, B3, T6]
No correlation	A relationship in which no linear pattern is observed among variables.	[T3, GR2]
Noise	Anything that distorts the original message (can be physical or semantic noise).	[T4, GR9]
Nominal measurement	Measurement that uses numbers merely as labels or identifiers (e.g., numbering of companies or numbering of jobs in a salary survey).	[T3, GR2]
Noncash incentives/ recognition programs	Incentive payments that are not readily convertible to cash (e.g., extra time off, meal or merchandise awards, a reserved parking space, membership in a luncheon club).	[B5, C11, C12, T1, GR1, GR5, GR6]

Term	Definition	Courses
Noncompete agreement	A provision, or separate employment contract, that prohibits an employee from competing with the employer after termination of employment (or the contract) for a specified period of time. The agreement typically sets limitations regarding customers, products, services, or an industry (or a combination), after employment terminates.	[C6, C6A, C15, T9, T11, GR7]
Noncurrent assets	Assets of the company that are used in the production of the product or delivery of services and that have a useful life of more than one year. Shown on the balance sheet. Also occasionally referred to as long-term or fixed assets. Part of permanent capital.	[C6, C6A, T2, T11]
Noncurrent liabilities	Debts of a company that do not come due until after one year from the date of the balance sheet where they are reported.	[T2]
Nondiscretionary bonus	A plan in which management determines the size of the bonus pool and the amounts to be allocated to specific individuals after a performance period. These use a predetermined formula and promises.	[C11, C12, GR5, GR6]
Nondiscrimination provisions	Provisions in the Health Insurance Portability and Accountability Act of 1996 (HIPAA) that prohibit the establishment of eligibility rules or charging similarly situated individuals different premiums based on a health factor. The rules do not prohibit premium discounts or rebates given as a result of participation in a bona fide wellness program.	[B3]

Term	Definition	Courses
Nondiscrimination rules	Rules governed by the Internal Revenue Code (IRC) that require that a qualified pension plan or health and welfare benefits plan may not discriminate in favor of the group of employees consisting of officers, shareholders and other highly compensated individuals.	[B1, B2, B3]
Nonduplication of benefits	Similar to standard coordination of benefits (COB), but without allowance for higher benefits between plans. Secondary insurance plan pays up to promised coinsurance (i.e., 80 percent), but payments do not exceed promised coinsurance between primary and secondary plans.	[B1, B3, B3A]
Nonexempt employees	Employees who are not exempt from the minimum wage and overtime pay provisions of the Fair Labor Standards Act of 1938 (FLSA).	[C1, C2, C4, C17, T1, T6, GR1]
Nonfinancial reward	See nonmonetary awards.	[C11, C12, T1, GR1, GR5, GR6]
Nonformulary	An open or nonrestricted list of drugs that may be offered with no discount or special pricing.	[B1, B3]
Nonhighly compensated employee (NHCE)	An employee who does not meet the definition of a highly compensated employee. See also highly compensated employee (HCE).	[B1, B2, B3, T6]
Nonimmigrant visas	In the case of the United States, visas that permit non-U.S. citizens to work in the United States under special circumstances. The following are sample types, each with its own restrictions: B-1, temporary visitor on business; H-1B, alien employed in specialty occupation; H-2, temporary worker; H-3, temporary	[C15]

Term	Definition	Courses
	trainee; and L-1, intracompany transferee. Other countries also specify visas for U.S. or other citizens. Some visas entitle travelers just to visit the country, others to do some type of work, but not to earn money, and others to work and earn money just as locals of the country do.	
Nonlinear regression	A form of statistical analysis that develops a model based on nonlinear or curvilinear relationships between variables.	[C2, C17, T3, GR2, GR3]
Nonmandatory benefits	See voluntary benefits.	[T1, GR1]
Nonmonetary awards	Noncash compensation, such as travel and merchandise. It excludes other nontaxable items (not on W-2 form) such as gifts and plaques/pins.	[C5]
Nonparticipating insurance contract	An insurance contract that does not allow for participation in the profits of the insurance company by way of increased benefits or premium rebates.	
Nonqualified foreign plan	In the case of any plan that ceases to be a qualified foreign plan either by reason of the termination or revocation of a Section 404A election, the New Method Opening Amount is zero.	
Nonqualified plans	Plans that provide benefits in excess of those possible within qualified plans, or otherwise do not meet Internal Revenue Service (IRS) requirements, and therefore do not qualify for favorable tax treatment for the company.	[B1, B2, C6, C6A, T2, T11]
Nonqualified stock option (NQSO)	A stock option that does not qualify for special tax treatment under Section 422 of the Internal Revenue Code (IRC) or that is designated by the company as not being an incentive stock option (ISO). Also called a nonstatutory stock option.	[C6, C6A, T11]

Term	Definition	Courses
Nonquantitative job evaluation	A method that creates a job worth hierarchy based on the perceived value of the "whole job(s)" but does not employ quantitative methods (i.e., assigning evaluation "points"). Examples of nonquantitative methods are classification and ranking.	[C2, C17, GR3]
Nonrandom sampling	A process by which samples are drawn without using some form of randomized selection procedure. Findings are less statistically generalizable than those from random samplings.	[T3, GR2]
Nonstatutory stock option	See nonqualified stock option (NQSO).	[C6, C6A, T11]
Nonsymmetric distribution	A set of plotted data points in which one side is not the mirror image of the other. Graphed points tend to cluster more on one side than the other, leaving a "tail" on one side.	[T3, GR2]
Normal distribution	A particular bell-shaped distribution, used frequently as a basis for statistical inference. The fact that many naturally occurring phenomena are distributed normally (e.g., height) does not mean that organizational phenomena are. Many salary and performance distributions are non-normal.	[T3, GR2]
Normal retirement age (pension plans)	The earliest age at which eligible participants are permitted to retire with full pension benefits. Since unreduced Social Security retirement benefits are currently available at age 65, that is the most common normal retirement age. These retirement benefits are not available before age 65.	[B2]
Normal retirement date (NRD)	The date, defined by the terms of the pension plan, at which eligible	[B2]

Term	Definition	Courses
	participants will begin to receive benefits.	
Norms	Unwritten rules that establish expectations of behavior.	[C11]
North American Free Trade Agreement (NAFTA)	An agreement reached by the United States, Canada and Mexico that instituted a schedule for the phasing out of tariffs and eliminated a variety of other barriers to the flow of goods, services and investment between the three North American countries.	[C15, T9, GR7]
Notes payable	Unconditional written promise made by a company to pay a specific amount by a definite date.	[T2]
Notes receivable	Unconditional written promise by another party to make payment to a company by a specified date.	[T2]
Notice of Proposed Rulemaking for Bona Fide Wellness Programs–2001	Proposed rules within the Interim Final Rules for Nondiscrimination in Health Coverage in the Group Market (2000) that clarify the term bona fide wellness program. See also bona fide wellness program.	[B3, W3]
Numerator	The number above a fraction line, indicating the number of parts of the whole.	[T3, GR2]
O*NET	O*NET OnLine is an application that was created for the general public to provide broad access to the O*NET database of occupational information. The O*NET database includes information on skills, abilities, knowledges, work activities, and interests associated with occupations. This information can be used to facilitate career exploration, vocational counseling and a variety of human resources functions, such as developing job orders and position.	[C2]

Term	Definition	Courses
	descriptions, and aligning training with current work place needs.	
Objective-based plan	An incentive plan that links performance to a predetermined objective (e.g., a management by objectives plan).	[C11]
Occupation	A generalized job or family of jobs common to multiple organizations or industries.	[C2, GR3]
Occupational Safety and Health Administration (OSHA)	A federal government agency in the Department of Labor (DOL) with the primary goal of preventing work-related injuries, illnesses and deaths.	[T2]
Office of Federal Contract Compliance Programs (OFCCP)	The agency charged with enforcing affirmative action regulations for government contractors under the Vocational Rehabilitation Act of 1973.	[C1, C11]
Offset formula	In a defined benefit (DB) plan, the method used to determine the reduction portion of the benefit up to the Social Security integration level.	[B1, B2]
Offshore fund	A mutual fund headquartered outside the United States.	[T6]
Old Age, Survivors, Disability, and Health Insurance Program (OASDHI)	An omnibus federal social bill including retirement, survivors and disability insurance (Social Security), hospital and medical insurance for the aged and disabled (Medicare/Medicaid), black-lung benefits for miners, supplementary security income, unemployment insurance, and public assistance in welfare systems.	[B1, B2, B3, C1, T6]
Omnibus Budget Reconciliation Act of 1993 (OBRA)	A federal law that impacts many direct and indirect components of pay (such as qualified retirement plan limits), increases the Medicare tax base, eliminates	[B1, B5]

Term	Definition	Courses
	the deduction for executive pay in excess of $1 million under most circumstances, and extends the tuition reimbursement exclusion provided for Qualified Medical Child Support Order (QMCSO). It also requires the extension of medical coverage to adopted children and provides that Medicare is the primary insurance for disabled employees.	
Omnibus plan	A stock plan that allows administrators (usually the board compensation committee in a public company) to make various types of grants and to specify grant provisions without plan-related limitations except as specifically required for regulatory or shareholder approval purposes.	[C6, C6A, T11]
On-call pay	A nominal amount of compensation provided in return for an employee being available to report to work at employer's discretion. Because the employee is expected to be easily reachable and able to report to the work site on short notice, he or she is compensated for having restricted personal time.	[C1, C4, GR4]
Open enrollment period	The time period when an employee may sign up for or change elections of employer-sponsored benefit plans. Also known as annual enrollment period.	[B1]
Open pay system	A compensation program in which information about salary ranges—in some cases, even individual employee wage levels—is made public.	[C4, GR4]
Open-ended questionnaire	A job analysis technique that provides a written set of questions regarding job content, requiring a narrative response.	[C2, GR3]

Term	Definition	Courses
Operating activities	Methods of contributing to net income that include the cash effects of transactions.	[T2]
Operating cash	Cash generated by the sale of products or services or both.	[T2]
Operating expenses/ leases	Included are depreciation, amortization, selling, general, and administrative costs. Interest and tax costs are not included.	[C6, C6A, T2, T11]
Operating income	Income remaining after recognizing cost of goods sold (COGS) and selling, general and administrative expense (SG&A), before other income and expense and before provision for taxes.	[C6, C6A, T2, T11]
Opportunity cost	The cost of allocating available funds toward one investment opportunity versus another. As companies do not have truly unlimited access to investment funds, a company must evaluate various opportunities to make the most appropriate choices. Opportunity cost is a key to the time value of money principle used in net present value calculations.	[T2]
Option exercise price (or option price)	The stated price to be paid by an optionee to purchase shares covered by a stock option.	[C6, C6A, T11]
Option exercise proceeds	Cash, stock or other value received by a company as a result of stock option exercises including cash or stock paid by individuals to exercise and company cash savings on taxes because of deductibility of nonstatutory option profits at exercise.	[C6, C6A, T11]
Option grant date	The date the stock option becomes effective and the option term begins.	[C6, C6A, T11]
Option performance vesting	When an option becomes exercisable during its term based on	[C6, C6A, T11]

Term	Definition	Courses
	achieving predetermined performance objectives.	
Option profit	The excess of price at exercise of shares over the exercise price.	[C6, C6A, T11]
Option repricing	This occurs when the exercise price on outstanding options is changed other than by recapitalization type of adjustment. When done it is usually to reduce the price of underwater options.	[C6, C6A, T11]
Optional modes of settlement (insurance policies)	Types of payment available to an insured or beneficiary, in lieu of a lump-sum payment.	[B3A]
Opt-out	For some benefits, some plans allow the employee to waive, decline or opt-out of benefit coverage in favor of cash compensation.	[B5]
Opt-up/opt-down/add-on	Choices an employee has with his or her flex dollars or credits. The value of flex dollars or credits may be greater if an employee is opting-up to a higher benefit level than if he or she is opting-out and choosing cash compensation.	[B5]
Ordinal measurement	Measurement that indicates the order, or rank, of the items being measured.	[T3, GR2]
Ordinary income	Any income subject to ordinary tax treatment by the Internal Revenue Service (IRS). Wages, bonus payments, gains for exercise of time-qualified stock options, interest and tips are all ordinary income.	[C6, C6A, T11]
Ordinary income tax	An individual's tax on earnings from wages, tips and all other sources except capital gains. Includes option profits on exercise of nonstatutory options.	[C6, C6A, T11]

Term	Definition	Courses
Organization for Economic Cooperation and Development (OECD)	An association of 30 member countries who share a commitment to democratic government and a market economy. The OECD develops policy recommendations and guidelines, some of which are binding (e.g., anti-bribery convention) and assists governments ensure responsiveness by monitoring economic changes in member countries.	[C15]
Organizational culture	See corporate culture.	[C2, C11, C17, T6, GR3]
Organizational development (OD)	Systems and programs aimed at improving organizational and individual behavior and performance through training and development. Specific techniques may include group exercises, management by objectives (MBO), sensitivity training and group discussion.	[C12, GR5, GR6]
Organizational mission	See corporate mission.	[C11]
Organizational values	See corporate values.	[C11]
Organizational vision	See corporate vision.	[C11]
Out-of-pocket limit	The amount that an employee will pay for covered health care expenses during the covered period, usually a calendar year, before the plan pays 100 percent of the covered charges.	[B1, B3, B3A]
Outplacement assistance	A benefit often made available to employees who are dismissed because of downsizing, reduction in force or change in business strategy. It typically consists of employment counseling, résumé writing, temporary office space and secretarial assistance.	[B3A, C6, C6A]

Term	Definition	Courses
Output-based plans	Short-term cash incentive plans that use output as the basis for payouts.	[C12, GR6]
Outside director	Member of the board of directors of an organization who is not a current employee of the organization.	[C6, C6A, T11]
Outside payroll costs	Benefits costs that are incurred apart from the organization's direct payroll (i.e., legally required benefits such as Social Security and workers' compensation, and other benefits, such as pension, health and life insurance, etc.).	[B1]
Outsourcing	A business relationship wherein activities traditionally performed within a company are performed by people other than the company's full-time employees.	[B3, T12]
Over the counter	Securities in companies that are publicly traded, but not on one of the established stock exchanges such as the NYSE, AMEX, NASDAQ or one of the regional exchanges.	[C6, C6A, T11]
Overhang	A measure of potential dilution from stock compensation plans equal to: the number of shares in outstanding grants plus those remaining available for grants divided by common shares outstanding. Expressed as a percentage, overhang is often a measure considered by shareholders in assessing company requests for additional shares for stock plans.	[C6, C6A, T11]
Overlap	See pay-range overlap.	[C4, C17, GR4]
Overtime	Under the Fair Labor Standards Act of 1938 (FLSA), nonexempt employees must be paid one-and-a-half times their normal wage rates for all hours worked in excess of 40 in any work week.	[C1, C4, C17, T6, W2]

Term	Definition	Courses
	Some states require overtime be calculated by other than a 40-hour week or at greater than 1 1/2 times normal wage rate.	
Owners' equity	See shareholders' equity.	[T2]
Paid time off (PTO) bank	A design option for paid leave that combines sick, holiday, vacation and personal leave time into one category of available time off that the employee manages with certain employer guidelines.	[B1, B3, B5, T6, W1]
Paid-in capital	Capital received from investors for stock, equal to capital stock plus paid-in capital. Also called contributed capital.	[T2]
Paired comparison	A ranking technique that compares each job being evaluated individually to every other job in a pair-wise fashion to determine which job has a higher value. The final score for a job is the number of times it is considered the most valuable in the pair comparisons. Ranks then are created from these scores.	[C2, GR3]
Par value	For stocks, an arbitrary number assigned to a stock issued, required by the registration requirements in certain states. As some states do not impose this requirement, many companies do not have a par value for the shares. For bonds, the par value is the amount that will be paid to investors at the maturity of the bond issue.	[T2]
Partial plan termination	Under Internal Revenue Service (IRS) rules, if approximately 20 percent of the participants in a pension plan are terminated, the plan can be determined to be partially terminated. In this case, all of the divested	[T6]

Term	Definition	Courses
	participants become immediately vested, regardless of service credit.	
Participating insurance	An insurance arrangement in which premiums are based on the positive or negative experience (difference between the premium charged and actual experience) of the insured organization.	[B3, B3A]
Participation	The number of individuals granted pay increases, expressed as a percentage of all employees in the group. To calculate participation over a period of up to 12 months, the total number of employees in the group at the beginning of the period is used. For longer periods, averaging may be necessary. [A] Actual Participation = (Number of Employees Receiving Increases / Total Employees) × 100. [B] Planned Participation = (Number of Employees for Whom Increases are Planned / Total Employees) × 100.	[C4, GR4]
Partnership	An unincorporated business with two or more owners. A partnership is not subject to tax, and passes income and losses through to its partners, who are taxed individually.	[T6]
Part-time schedule	Working less than full-time hours with full or pro-rated benefits.	[W1, W2]
Patent	The exclusive right, granted by the government, to make, use or sell an invention or process for a specific period of time. Also includes the right to license others to make, use or sell an invention or process.	[T2]

Term	Definition	Courses
Pay adjustment	A general revision of pay raises. The adjustment may be either across-the-board, such as cost-of-living adjustments (COLA), or spot adjustments for increases in prevailing wage rates.	[C4, GR4]
Pay as you go	The most common method of financing social security; it means that today's contributions pay current benefits. In other words, active employees today pay for current retiree benefits. There is growing concern in some countries, particularly in Western Europe, as to whether this system will be viable given that the proportion of actively employed people vs. retirees is expected to decrease.	[C15, T9, GR7]
Pay at risk	A variable pay plan funded on the basis of a reduction in base pay that usually is offset by the possibility of a larger variable pay plan payout.	[C5, C11, C12, GR6]
Pay compression	See compression.	[C4, GR4]
Pay delivery matrix	See merit matrix.	[C11]
Pay for performance	Links pay (base and/or variable), in whole or in part, to individual, group, and/or organizational performance.	[C4, C11, C15, T9, GR4, GR6, GR7]
Pay for presence	Rarely utilized form of pay progression awards increases based primarily on continued employment.	[C15, T9, GR7]
Pay for time not worked	Refers to time off work with pay. Typically, it includes: holidays, vacations, personal days, jury duty, approved paid leaves, military duty, and so on.	[B1, B3, B3A, B5, C1, C12, T1, T11, GR1, GR5, GR6]

Term	Definition	Courses
Pay grade	The grade to which a given type of job is assigned.	[C2, C4, C17, GR3, GR4]
Pay in lieu of notice	This pay arrangement for terminated employees is a continuation of normal pay and benefits after the last day of work for a defined period of time. It differs from severance pay, which is a lump-sum payment on the last day of work and is based on a prescribed formula.	[C1]
Pay mix	The profile of various components of direct pay expressed as a percentage of the total (e.g., 50 percent base salary, 35 percent short-term incentives, 15 percent long-term incentives).	[C6, C6A]
Pay plan	A schedule of pay rates or ranges for each job in the classification plan. May include rules of administration and the benefits package.	[C4, GR4]
Pay policy	The desired position of an organization's pay with respect to competitive pay at a certain point in time.	[T3, GR2]
Pay policy line	The level at which the organization decides to set its pay against the external market; usually the midpoint of the salary structure is set as an estimate of the market going rate.	[C4, C17, GR4]
Pay progression	The position the employee is within the pay ranges, and the ability for pay movement based upon performance.	[C4, C11, GR4, GR5]
Pay range	The range of pay rates, from minimum to maximum, established for a pay grade or class. Typically used to set individual employee pay rates.	[C2, C4, C11, C15, C17, T1, T9, GR1, GR2, GR3, GR4, GR7]

Term	Definition	Courses
Pay satisfaction	The degree to which an employee perceives little difference in the pay he or she thinks is deserved and the pay actually received. When pay satisfaction is low, the potential for reduced productivity, strikes, turnover, grievances and absenteeism increases. Also referred to as pay equity.	[C4, GR4, GR5]
Pay steps	Specified levels within a pay range. Employees may progress from step to step on the basis of time-in-grade, performance, or the acquisition of new job skills.	[C4, GR4]
Pay survey	Gathering, summarizing and analyzing data on wages and salaries paid by other employers for selected key classes of jobs or benchmark jobs.	[C2, C5, C17, GR3]
Payout frequency	The timing of incentive payouts. Payouts commonly are made weekly, monthly, quarterly or annually.	[C5, C12, GR6]
Pay-range overlap	The degree to which the pay ranges assigned to adjacent grades in a structure overlap. Numerically, the percentage of overlap between two adjacent pay ranges.	[C4, C17, T3, GR2, GR4]
Pay-range width	The width or spread of a pay range, measured by the ratio: width = (maximum pay − minimum pay) / minimum pay.	[C4, C15, C17, T9, GR4, GR7]
Pay-trend line	A line fitted to a scatter plot that treats pay as a function of job values. The most common technique for fitting a pay-trend line is regression analysis.	[C4, C17, GR4]
Peer comparison	A concept used in some incentive plans where a company's results in specified financial measures are compared with those of a group of other companies determined to be peer	[C6, C6A]

Term	Definition	Courses
	companies. The comparative results can be used in incentive formulas.	
Pension	A fixed sum of money paid to an employee who has retired from a company and is eligible under a pension plan to receive such benefits. May be funded (paid from a trust) or unfunded (paid from the company assets).	[B1, T1, T2, GR1]
Pension and Welfare Benefits Administration (PWBA)	A division of the Department of Labor (DOL) responsible for administering and enforcing the fiduciary, reporting and disclosure provisions of Title I of the Employee Retirement Income Security Act of 1974 (ERISA).	[B1, B2, B3A, T6]
Pension Benefit Guaranty Corporation (PBGC)	A federal corporation within the Department of Labor (DOL), which guarantees vested pensions (defined benefits) up to a maximum dollar amount established annually. Insurance premiums are paid by employers with covered pension programs.	[B1, B2]
Pension equity plan (PEP)	A defined benefit (DB) plan with some characteristics of a defined contribution (DC) plan. Under a PEP, for each year worked, participants are credited with a percentage that will be applied to their final average earnings. The percentage increases with the age and/or length of service of the participant. Pension equity plans are a type of hybrid pension plan.	[B1, B2]
Pension plan	A plan that provides income benefits, after retirement, from a trust or other separately maintained fund, by the purchase of insurance, or from general assets (unfunded plan).	[B1, B2, T6]
Pension reform act	See Employee Retirement Income Savings Act (ERISA).	[B1]

Term	Definition	Courses
Percent	A ratio expressed in relation to 100 that is obtained by dividing one number into another and then multiplying by 100. The sum of all percents related to a total amount must equal 100 percent.	[T3, GR2]
Percent change	A difference in some variable over time expressed as a percentage of the value of that variable at the initial time. For example, the percent change in a wage rate that grows from $10 to $12 is 20 percent.	[T3, GR2]
Percent difference	The percent that the value of one item differs from a referenced item. In compensation decision-making, the data on which action will be taken should be the referenced item and, as such, should be in the denominator of the calculation. That way, the percent difference will be expressed in terms of the reference. For example, market adjustment is equal to 100 × (market data – company data) ÷ company data.	[C4, T3, GR2, GR4]
Percentile	A measure of location in a distribution of numbers that defines the value below which a given percentage of the data fall. For example, the 90th percentile is the point below which 90 percent of the data fall.	[C2, C17, T3, GR2, GR3]
Percentile bar	A graphic device used to summarize data that shows percentiles of common interest in the data graphically.	[T3, GR2]
Performance	The alignment and assessment of organizational, team and individual efforts toward the achievement of business goals.	[T4, GR9]

Term	Definition	Courses
Performance appraisal	Any system of determining how well an individual employee has performed during a period of time, frequently used as a basis for determining merit increases.	[C1, C12, T1, W2, GR1, GR5, GR6]
Performance culture	A set of shared norms and attitudes relating to performance in an organization. An organization with a performance culture based on teamwork, for example, is unlikely to be fertile ground for a reward system based on competitive performance among individuals. A merit pay system may reflect an individual ethic within an organization's performance culture.	[C12, GR5, GR6]
Performance cycle	When performance of the job incumbent (or group) is measured on a year-to-date basis (e.g., a third quarter incentive payment based on the cumulative results from the beginning of the year through the third quarter).	[GR5]
Performance dimensions	Aspects of performance, critical to a job, on which the incumbent will be rated. Dimensions can be related to outcomes or behavioral criteria pertinent to the job assignment.	[GR5]
Performance management	A systematic approach for managing individuals and/or groups that involves planning, monitoring, appraising, rewarding and improving performance in support of the business strategy.	[C11, C12, T1, GR1, GR5, GR6]
Performance measurement	Any technique employed to gather data that provides a basis for exercising performance appraisal judgment.	[C12, GR5, GR6]
Performance measures	The quantitative basis by which performance is evaluated against objectives.	[C11, W3]

Term	Definition	Courses
Performance period	A predetermined span of time during which individual (or group) performance is measured.	[C5, C6, C6A, C11, C12, T11, GR5, GR6]
Performance rating	See merit rating.	[C11, C12, GR5, GR6]
Performance review	A formal meeting between a manager and subordinate to discuss the subordinate's performance and development. Frequently involves written documentation in the form of a written performance appraisal.	[C11]
Performance share plan	A stock (or stock unit) grant/award plan in which the payout is contingent upon achievement of certain predetermined external or internal performance goals during a specified period (e.g., three to five years) before the recipient has rights to the stock. The employee receiving the shares pays ordinary income tax on the value of the award at the time of earning it. These grants are subject to the variable accounting provisions of APB 25 as the measurement date is the date on which the shares or cash is paid to the participant.	[C6, C6A, C12, C15, T6, T11]
Performance sharing	An incentive plan design in which performance is defined in terms of selected criteria (e.g., quality, customer satisfaction, responsiveness, profit, etc.), standards are established and incentive awards are made contingent upon meeting these standards, typically at the business-unit or organizational level.	[C11, C12, T6, GR5, GR6]
Performance standards	The defined performance levels, derived from organizational objectives, that an organization expects from individuals and/or groups with respect to specific objectives.	[C11, C12, T12, W2, W3, GR5, GR6]

Term	Definition	Courses
Performance targets	Tasks or behavioral goals established for an employee that provide the comparative basis for performance appraisal.	[C11, C12, W3, GR5, GR6]
Performance unit plan (PUP)	Similar to a performance share plan, except that unit value is not related to stock price. The actual award payment may be in cash, stock or a combination.	[C6, C6A, C12, T11, GR6]
Performance vesting	Vesting is based on achievement of certain performance criteria.	[C6, C6A, T11]
Performance-accelerated restricted-stock award plan (PAR-SAP) or performance-accelerated stock option plan (PASOP)	A restricted-stock award or grant that vests eventually in any event based on continued employment, but vesting can occur on an accelerated basis, if preset and stated objectives or performance levels are reached. Favorable grant date accounting treatment applies because of the vesting occurring with continued employment whether the performance objectives are met or not. Occasionally referred to as time-accelerated restricted stock award plan (TARSAP).	[C6, C6A, T11]
Performance-accelerated vesting	An established vesting schedule may be accelerated, that is, vesting may occur earlier, if certain performance criteria are met; vesting eventually occurs based on achievement of time commitment (e.g., continued employment, retirement) regardless of whether or not performance criteria are met.	[C6, C6A, T11]
Performance-based pay	The practice of using pay to manage and motivate performance.	[C11, C15]
Performance-based restricted stock	Restricted actual shares of stock awarded to an executive in which the shares are contingent on the achievement of either internal or external performance	[C6, C6A, T11]

Term	Definition	Courses
	measures or an increase in the company's stock price. Subject to the "variable" accounting provisions of APB 25 and FAS 28.	
Performance-based stock options	The future of the option price is known, typically increasing each year by a constant dollar or percentage.	[C6]
Peril	The ultimate cause of a loss (e.g., accident, illness, flood and fire).	[B3A]
Permanent capital	The capital of a company that is expected to be part of the balance sheet for more than one year. Includes equity and non-current liabilities.	[T2]
Permanent transferee	A relocated employee who is not expected to return to his home country or undergo any further transfers. Also known as a long-term transferee.	[C15, T9, GR7]
Permitted disparity	The allowable difference between benefit and contribution rates for highly compensated and nonhighly compensated participants in qualified pension plans that are integrated with Social Security benefits as permitted by Internal Revenue Service (IRS) regulations.	[B2, C1]
Perquisite	A benefit or "perk" tied to a specific key or management level job (e.g., a company car for personal use, free meals, financial counseling or use of company facilities). A perk's status value often exceeds its financial value.	[C6, C6A, C15, T1, T6, T9, T11, GR1, GR7]
Personal days	Days off with or without pay (usually a fixed number), to be used by employees for personal reasons.	[W1]
Person-based pay	Compensation programs that base an employee's salary on that individual's skills or knowledge rather than on the nature	[C4, C12, GR4, GR5, GR6]

Term	Definition	Courses
	of a rigidly defined job. Types include skill-, knowledge- and competency-based pay.	
Phantom options	Options on units equivalent to shares but not real shares, or rights to the appreciation on shares without related option rights.	[C6, C6A, T11]
Phantom stock (full value)	A long-term incentive plan in which the participant receives a payment in cash based on a formula. Under a full value plan the full value of the formula is paid. The formula may or may not involve the actual stock price.	[C6, C6A, C12, T11, GR6]
Phantom stock (incremental value)	Similar in concept to the full value phantom stock grant, except that the amount paid is the increase or appreciation in the value as calculated in the formula. The formula may or may not involve the actual stock price.	[C6, C6A, T11]
Pharmacy benefit manager (PBM)	An individual or a company that manages pharmacy benefits. A PBM typically establishes and maintains a formulary, negotiates prices with drug manufacturers and wholesalers, approves and processes claims, and provides health plans with periodic financial and utilization reports.	[B1]
Phase-back	Extended maternity leave with graduated return.	[B5]
Phase-out	Gradual retirement.	[B5]
Piece rate	A direct performance payment based on production by an individual worker. A payment is made for each piece or other quantity unit of work produced by an employee.	[C1, C4, C12, T1, GR1, GR4, GR5, GR6]
Piece work	Work for which an incentive payment is made. The payout depends on the number of	[C1, C4, C11, GR4, GR5]

Term	Definition	Courses
	pieces produced or operations completed.	
Plan administrator	As defined by the Employee Retirement Income Security Act of 1974 (ERISA), the person or organization (frequently the plan sponsor) designated to administer a pension or welfare plan by the terms of the instrument under which the plan operates.	[B2, T6]
Plan sponsor	The entity responsible for establishing and maintaining the plan.	[B2, T6]
Plan year	The calendar, policy or fiscal year for which plan records are maintained.	[B2, B3, T6]
Point factor method of job evaluation	A quantitative form of job content evaluation that uses defined factors and degree levels within each factor (usually five to seven levels, which are also defined). Each factor is weighted according to its importance (to the organization). Job content descriptions are compared to definitions of the degree levels and the corresponding points assigned to the appropriate level are then awarded to the job and added for all factors to determine the total job score. The total scores are used to create a job worth hierarchy.	[C2, C17, T1, GR1, GR3]
Point of service (POS)	A type of managed care medical plan, in which the level of benefits received depends on how an employee elects to receive care at the "point of service" that care begins. For example, if care begins with the gatekeeper physician in the network, benefits would be higher than if care was received outside the network.	[B1, B3, B3A, B5]

Term	Definition	Courses
Polynomial model	A model that can be expressed with powers of the x-variable. The order of the model is the value of the highest exponent of x. A straight line or linear model is a first-order polynomial: $y = a + bx$. A quadratic model is a second-order polynomial: $y = a + bx + cx^2$. A cubic model is a third-order polynomial: $y = a + bx + cx^2 + dx^3$. Polynomials of order higher than on are used to describe nonlinear relations.	[GR2]
Population	In statistics, the set of all elementary units of interest in a given situation.	[T3, GR2]
Portability	A pension plan feature that allows participants to change employers without changing the source from which benefits are to be paid for both past and future accruals.	[B1, B2]
Position	The total duties and responsibilities requiring the employment of a single employee. The total number of positions in an organization equals the number of employees plus vacancies.	[C2, C17, GR3]
Positive correlation	A relationship where higher values of y generally go with higher values of x, and lower values of y generally go with lower values of x.	[T3, GR2]
Positively skewed	A distribution in which most of the scores cluster to the left of the mean and the "tail" of the distribution trails off to the right. The mean is larger than the median, which in turn is larger than the mode.	[T3, GR2]
Post-employment benefits (FAS 106)	Financial Accounting Statement No. 106 (FAS 106) requires employers to account for future nonpension retirement benefits in current financial statements.	[B3, T2]

Term	Definition	Courses
Power distance	Degree to which a culture accepts that there will be inequality between individuals within organizations.	[C15, T9, GR7]
Preauthorization	An assessment of medical necessity introduced as a way to control the costs associated with unnecessary procedures and hospital stays.	[B3]
Preexisting condition limitation/ exclusion	Health insurance plan limitation or exclusion for a physical or mental condition of a newly insured individual that was present before joining the plan. Definitions of preexisting conditions vary by plan and the associated exclusions and limitations generally last from 6 to 12 months. Severe conditions may be defined as lifetime exclusions, depending on the plan.	[B3]
Preferred provider organization (PPO)	An entity representing a network of health care providers (e.g., hospitals, physicians, dentists, etc.) that offers volume discounts to employers sponsoring group health benefits plans. In turn, employers commonly extend financial incentives to employees to use participating providers.	[B1, B3, B3A, B5]
Preferred shares	Money provided to a company through the issuance of equity securities in which an owner's rate of return is fixed and receives a higher priority to be paid back in the event of liquidation or a bankruptcy than the common stockholders.	[C6, C6A, T2, T11]
Preferred stock	See preferred shares.	[C6, C6A, T2, T11]
Pregnancy Discrimination Act of 1978	An amendment to Title VII of the Civil Rights Act of 1964 that prohibits discrimination on the basis of pregnancy, childbirth or related medical conditions.	[C11]

Term	Definition	Courses
Premature distribution	In a defined contribution (DC) plan, certain emergency situations allow for payment of vested balances to be made to an active participant before age 59½. However, unless certain requirements are met, a 10 percent tax is imposed on such premature distributions and reported on Form 5329.	[T6]
Premium	(1) An amount added onto the base wage to pay extra for something such as weekend work, the graveyard shift, or being away from home. (2) In an international context, the term premium refers to an incentive paid to expatriates for undertaking a foreign assignment. It is typically 10 to 20 percent of base pay and continues month to month for as long as an employee is an expatriate.	[T1, C15, T9, GR1, GR7]
Premium conversion	Insurance plan feature that allows the employee to convert coverage from a group to an individual policy upon termination of employment. The former employee assumes responsibility for the entire premium.	[B3, B3A]
Premium conversion plan	A plan that allows employees to contribute on a pretax basis to any employer-sponsored health or welfare plan. Also known as premium-only plans.	[B1, B5, T6]
Premium for risk	The typical amount of (expected) additional return on investment required by investors for choosing a higher-risk investment.	[C6, C6A]
Premium pay	Extra pay, beyond the base wage rate, for work performed outside or beyond regularly scheduled work periods (e.g., Sundays, holidays, night shifts, etc.). Also may refer to extra pay for high-demand knowledge or skills.	[C4, C12]

Term	Definition	Courses
Premium stock option	An option whereby the exercise price is set above the fair market value (FMV) at the date of grant.	[C6, C6A, T11]
Premium-only plan	See premium conversion plan.	[B5, T6]
Prepaid expenses	An asset consisting of payments made in advance for items normally charged to expense, (e.g., prepaid insurance, prepaid rent and supplies on hand).	[T2]
Present value	The value of an amount of money at the present time or at the beginning of a specific period of time. The concept recognizes that receipt of a dollar in five years is less desirable than receipt of a dollar today. Present value formulas take into account assumptions about interest rates to produce an estimate of the current worth of the guaranteed delivery of a dollar at some specified point in the future. Present value formulas and variants are used in determining funding requirements for several compensation and benefits programs.	[C6, C6A, T2, T3, T6, T11, GR2]
Prevailing wage rate	The amount paid by other employers in the labor market for similar work. The Davis Bacon Act of 1931 requires most federal contractors (in construction and related areas) to pay the wage rates and fringe benefits prevailing in the area. The McNamara-O'Hara Service Contract Act of 1965 requires certain federal contractors who provide services to the federal government to pay area prevailing wage rates.	[C1]
Price at exercise	The stock price at the time an individual exercises an option. This determines the option price after the option exercise price is subtracted.	[C6, C6A, T11]

Term	Definition	Courses
Price-earnings ratio (P-E ratio)	The ratio of a stock's market price to its net earnings per share, sometimes used as an index of the financial performance of an organization.	[C6, C6A, T2]
Primary care physician (PCP)	An employee-selected physician that provides all routine medical care within a Health Maintenance Organization (HMO). The PCP also serves as a gatekeeper by controlling specialist referral, therefore curbing unnecessary medical expenses.	[B1]
Primary source of job information	In job analysis, the job incumbent or immediate supervisor.	[C2, GR3]
Prior service liability	The liability associated with service before a plan is implemented (retroactive) or attributable to a benefit increase for service prior to the date the plan is amended.	[T6]
Privacy Rules of 2001	See Administrative Simplification Provisions of 2001.	[B3]
Pro forma	Hypothetical accounting, financial or other statements or conclusions based on assumed or anticipated facts.	[T2]
Productivity	Any index measuring the efficiency of an operation, usually involving a ratio of outputs to inputs or costs. Rewards frequently are tied to productivity-related measures.	[C12, W3, GR5, GR6]
Profit and loss (P&L) statement	See income statement.	[C6, C6A, T2]
Profit-sharing pension plan	A defined contribution (DC) plan providing for employee participation in the profits of the organization. The plan normally includes a predetermined and defined formula for allocating profit shares among	[B1, B2, T6, GR5, GR6]

Term	Definition	Courses
	participants, and for the distribution of funds accumulated under the plan. Profit-sharing plans that are administered as retirement plans defer taxation of participants' accounts until distribution.	
Profit-sharing plan	A plan providing for employee participation in the profits of an organization. The plan normally includes a predetermined and defined formula for allocating profit shares among participants, and for distributing funds accumulated under the plan. However, some plans are discretionary. Funds may be distributed in cash, deferred as a qualified retirement program or distributed in a cash/deferred combination.	[C6, C6A, C11, C12, C15, T1, T2, T11, GR1]
Progressive incentive formula	A rewards program in which the incentive payout rate increases as performance exceeds predetermined levels (e.g., nonlinear sales commission formulas).	[C5, C12, GR6]
Progressivity of incentives	See incentive progressivity.	[C6, C6A]
Prohibited transaction (fiduciary)	Behavior or transaction that is not permitted for individuals who act in a fiduciary capacity (e.g., investing money or property for which the fiduciary is responsible in investments that are speculative or imprudent).	[T6]
Projected benefit obligation (PBO)	The portion of the present value of benefits that is attributed to service already rendered for employees who are both vested and nonvested, including the additional impact of future salary increases. This also is known as the accrued liability with salary increases or the ongoing liability.	

Term	Definition	Courses
Promotion	The (re)assignment of an employee to a job in a higher grade or range in the organization's job worth hierarchy.	[C4, C11, C15, T9, GR4, GR7]
Promotional increase	An increase in a salary or wage rate that accrues to a person because of a promotion to a higher-level job.	[C4, C11, GR4]
Prospective Normal Retirement Pension (PNRP)	The expected pension payable at normal retirement age for an employee assuming that they remain in service to that date and their pensionable salary remains unchanged. Also referred to as projected benefit.	
Prospectus (1)	A required Securities and Exchange Commission (SEC) filing to register shares authorized for grants under a stock option plan, which must be filed before the options become exercisable. Prospectuses are also required for other reasons by SEC.	[C6, C6A, T11]
Provision for taxes	Reported on a company's income statement as the amount that is estimated to be due in taxes on reported income. This usually is different from a company's actual tax obligation for the year because of the differences in tax accounting and generally accepted accounting principles (GAAP).	[C6, C6A, T2, T11]
Proxy statement	A document required by the Securities and Exchange Commission (SEC) for a publicly owned company that notifies shareholders of the company's annual (or any special) meeting, and that transmits information relevant to matters that will be voted upon by shareholders including election of officers. Also included is information about compensation of the company's highest paid executive officers.	[C6, C6A, T11]

Term	Definition	Courses
Proxy voting services	Organizations that provide research, ratings and other resources, in support of stronger governance and corporate responsibility. Examples include Institutional Shareholder Services (ISS) and the Investor Responsibility Research Center (IRRC).	[C6A]
Prudent person standard	Standard that requires an individual to exercise the care that a "prudent person" normally would exercise when handling the property of others.	[B3]
Purchasing power	In cost-of-living agreements, any index that measures the power of a dollar to purchase goods. The Consumer Price Index (CPI) is a measure of the purchasing power of a current dollar in terms of a 1967 base year.	[C4]
Purchasing power parity (PPP)	The rate of currency conversion that equalizes the purchasing power of different currencies by eliminating the differences in price levels. When a given sum of money is converted into different currencies at PPP rates, you can buy the same goods and services in all countries.	[C15, T9, GR7]
Pyramiding	The process whereby an individual owner of one share of stock can use a simultaneous stock-swap technique to exercise a stock option of any size without using cash. The Financial Accounting Standards Board (FASB) requires shares to have been held for at least six months before they can be used to exercise an option, to avoid an earnings charge; this requirement has effectively eliminated the practice.	[C6, C6A, T11]

Term	Definition	Courses
Qualified beneficiary	An individual covered by a plan on the day before a qualifying event who is either the employee, the employee's spouse or dependent child. In some cases, a retired employee, their spouse and dependent children may be qualified beneficiaries.	[B3, B3A]
Qualified business unit	Any separate and clearly identified unit of a trade or business of a taxpayer that maintains separate books and records.	[C6, C6A, T2]
Qualified domestic relations order (QDRO)	A court judgment, decree or order that specifies the portion of an employee's defined benefit (DB) plan account or defined contribution (DC) plan that must be allocated to an alternate payee (e.g., a former spouse).	[B2, T6]
Qualified foreign plan	In general, Section 404(a) provides the exclusive means by which an employer may take a deduction or reduce earnings and profits for deferred compensation in situations other than those in which a deduction or reduction of earnings and profits is permitted under Section 404(a). A deduction or reduction of earnings and profits is permitted under Section 404(a) for amounts paid or accrued by an employer under a foreign deferred compensation plan, in the taxable year in which the amounts are properly taken into account under §§1.404(a)-1 through 1.404(a)-7, if each of the following requirements is satisfied: (1) The plan is a written plan maintained by the employer that provides deferred compensation. (2) The plan is maintained for the exclusive benefit of the employer's employees or their beneficiaries.	[C15, T9, GR7]

Term	Definition	Courses
	(3) Ninety percent or more of the amounts taken into account under the plan are attributable to services performed by non-resident aliens, the compensation for which is not subject to U.S. federal income tax. (4) An election under §1.404(a)-6 or 1.404(a)-7 is made to treat the plan as either a qualified funded plan or a qualified reserve plan and to select a plan year.	
Qualified funded plan	A qualified foreign plan for which an election has been made under §1.404(a)-6 or 1.404(a)-7 by the taxpayer to treat the plan as a qualified funded plan.	[C15, T9, GR7]
Qualified matching contributions (QMACS)	Nonforfeitable matching contributions made by an employer to a retirement plan. QMACs are normally made when a plan fails the actual contribution percentage (ACP) test.	[B2]
Qualified medical child support order (QMCSO)	A judgment, decree or order by a court that requires a group health plan to provide coverage to the children ("alternate recipients") of a plan participant, pursuant to state domestic relations law.	[B3, B3A, T6]
Qualified nonelective contributions (QNECS)	Nonelective, nonforfeitable contributions made to non-highly compensated employees (NHCEs) whether or not they participate in a plan. QNECs are normally made when a plan fails the actual deferral percentage (ADP) test.	[B2]
Qualified plan (pension or profit sharing)	A pension or profit-sharing plan that qualifies under certain Internal Revenue Service (IRS) statutory requirements, consequently having certain tax advantages for employer and/or employee. (Namely, deferral of	[B1, B2, C6, C6A, T6, T11]

Term	Definition	Courses
	employee tax to a future date while still allowing for a current tax deduction for the employer.) To qualify, a plan must not discriminate in favor of highly compensated employees (HCEs). It may be either a defined benefit (DB) or a defined contribution (DC) plan.	
Qualified reserve plan	A qualified foreign plan for which an election has been made by the taxpayer under §1.404(a)-6 or 1.404(a)-7 to treat the plan as a qualified reserve plan.	[C15, T9, GR7]
Qualified stock option	A type of stock option specifically authorized by tax legislation. This type of option no longer exists under this name. Currently the form of option that may have favorable tax treatment is the "incentive stock option." It can be stated that it is a "qualified" form of option because it does qualify for long-term capital gains tax treatment if all legal requirements are followed.	[C6, C6A, T11]
Qualifying event	Certain specified events whose occurrence would cause an individual to lose insurance coverage (e.g., termination of employment, divorce, death of an employee, reduction in hours, loss of coverage because of the end of student status or attainment of maximum age).	[B3, B3A]
Qualitative measures	Measures that allow for a greater degree of judgment. Typically used for behaviors and assessments that are based on observation and perception.	[T4, W2, W3, GR9]
Quantitative job evaluation	A method that creates a job worth hierarchy by analyzing jobs in terms of specific factors and numerical indices. Examples	[C2, C17, GR3]

Term	Definition	Courses
	of quantitative methods are job component and point factor.	
Quantitative measures	Measures that lend themselves to precise definition and assessment, with very little room for variability of data. Typically "number" based.	[T4, W2, W3, GR9]
Quartile	A distribution divided into fourths. The first quartile corresponds to the 25th percentile, the second to the 50th percentile, the third to the 75th percentile and the fourth to the 100th percentile.	[C11, T3, GR2]
Quick ratio	Short-term liquid assets (cash, marketable securities and receivables) divided by current liabilities. Excludes inventories and prepaid expenses. Also known as the acid test.	[T2]
Quintiles	A distribution divided into fifths.	[T3, GR2]
Quota	A predetermined performance goal. Quotas can be expressed as absolute numbers, a percent (100 percent), percent change or units sold. Also referred to as goal, objective and performance target.	[C5, C12, GR6]
Quota setting	The process of setting quotas. Quotas can be established by senior management ("top down"), by the field sales force ("bottom up") or through a negotiated process involving both headquarters and the field sales force ("combination").	[C5]
Rabbi trust	A trust established to protect nonqualified and/or deferred compensation benefits against various risks such as a change in control of the company or a management change of heart. The trust is irrevocable and inaccessible to present or future	[C6, C6A, T6, T11]

Term	Definition	Courses
	management, and it may be currently funded. A rabbi trust does not protect benefits in the event of bankruptcy. The funds belong to the corporation and, in the event of bankruptcy, they are specifically within the reach of the organization's creditors. The first such trust approved by the Internal Revenue Service (IRS) was established by a synagogue protecting the benefits of its rabbi.	
Raise	An increase in salary or wages.	[C4, C17, GR4]
Ramped commission	Commission rate changes after an objective has been met. The rate may either increase (progressive) or decrease (regressive).	[C5]
Random samples	Drawn from a population in which every possible sample of that size has an equal chance of being selected.	[T3, GR2]
Random sampling	A process by which subsets of a population are drawn using a selection procedure in which every member of the population has an equal chance of being chosen. Common procedures to obtain random samples include using a table or random-number generator, or drawing numbers from a hat.	[T3, GR2]
Range	(1) For a set of data, the difference between the maximum value and the minimum value. (2) For a pay grade, the percentage by which the maximum pay exceeds the minimum.	[C4, C17, T3, GR2, GR4]
Range of earnings	The amount of total cash compensation opportunity available for minimum to excellence performance.	[C5]

Term	Definition	Courses
Range penetration	The level of an individual's pay compared to the total pay range (rather than compared with midpoint, as in compa-ratio). Range penetration is calculated as: RP = (Pay − Range Minimum) / (Range Maximum − Range Minimum).	[C4, C17, GR4]
Range spread	See pay-range width.	[C4, C17, GR4]
Ranking method of job evaluation	The simplest form of job evaluation. A whole-job, job-to-job comparison, resulting in an ordering of jobs into a job worth hierarchy from highest to lowest.	[C2, T1, GR1, GR3]
Rate	See wage rate.	[C4, GR4]
Rate of exchange	See exchange rate.	[C15, T9, GR7]
Rate range	See pay range.	[C4, GR4]
Rating bias	Any of a number of common nonperformance-related errors made by raters because of poor information-processing capabilities rather than ethnic or sexual prejudice. The use of explicit performance standards and the training of raters has been shown to reduce much rating bias.	[GR5]
Ratio	With ratio scales a true zero point exists; measurements are meaningful and indicate how much of the quantity is being measured.	[T3, GR2]
Ratio measurement	Measurement that indicates how much, or the quantity, of the item or attribute being measured. There is a true zero, where zero indicates nothing of what is being measured. Examples include number of employees, salaries, sales volume and production rates. Also known as cardinal measurements.	[T3, GR2]

Term	Definition	Courses
Real wages	Wage earnings, deflated by a price index such as the consumer price index (CPI). Used as an index of the purchasing power of the money received in the form of wages.	[C4]
Reasonable and customary (R&C) charges	The charges that an insurance carrier determines are normal for a particular medical or dental procedure within a specific geographic area. If charges are higher than what the insurance carrier considers normal, the carrier only will pay up to the determined reasonable and customary amount; the balance is the responsibility of the insured.	[B1, B3]
Receiver	The person or group of persons that the communication or information reaches.	[T4, GR9]
Reclassification	The (re)assignment of a job to a higher or lower grade or range in the organization's job worth hierarchy because of a job content (re)evaluation and/or significant change in the going rate for comparable jobs in the external labor market.	[C2, C4, GR3, GR4]
Recognition	Give special attention to employee actions, efforts, behavior or performance.	[T4, GR9]
Recognition program	A policy of acknowledging employee contributions after the fact, possibly without predetermined goals or performance levels that the employee is expected to achieve. Examples include giving employees clocks or other gifts on milestone anniversaries, granting an extra personal day for perfect attendance or paying a one-time cash bonus for making a cost-saving suggestion.	[C5, C11, C12, T1, GR1, GR5, GR6]

Term	Definition	Courses
Red circle rate	An individual pay rate that is above the established range maximum assigned to the job grade. The employee is usually not eligible for further base pay increases until the range maximum surpasses the individual pay rate.	[C4, GR4]
Reengineering	Analysis and revision of current business practices, approaches and processes with the objective of improving organizational performance through improvements in the organization's existing performance measures.	[C11]
Re-enlistment bonus	A payment to encourage expatriates to remain in an assignment beyond the originally agreed-upon duration. This type of bonus is paid in the U.S. military services and is now particularly common in the Middle East, where many former military personnel are employed by U.S. multinationals.	[C15]
Regional systems	An expatriate compensation methodology in which different (less generous) compensation packages are developed for employees who are mobile within regions compared to those who are globally mobile.	[C15, T9, GR7]
Regression analysis	The statistical technique of creating a model of a y (dependent) variable as a function of one or more x (independent) variables using the method of least squares.	[C2, C4, C17, T3, GR2, GR3, GR4]
Regressive incentive	In a regressive incentive formula, the incentive rate declines as performance exceeds preestablished levels.	[C5]

Term	Definition	Courses
Regular rate of pay	Under the Fair Labor Standards Act of 1938 (FLSA), the amount of compensation that is used to calculate overtime rates. The regular rate of pay includes the base rate, shift premium, piece rate, pay allowances and bonuses.	[C1, C12]
Reinforcement theory	As applied to the workplace, this principle maintains that employees will tend to behave in ways that get rewarded and avoid behaviors that are not rewarded or that are punished.	[C11, GR5]
Reinsurance	The acceptance by one or more insurers, called reinsurers or assuming companies, or a portion of the risk underwritten by another insurer that has contracted for the entire coverage.	[B3A]
Relationship manager	Internal contact, within the organization, who handles many aspects of the relationship between the service partner and the client.	[T12]
Relative frequency distribution	A table indicating the relative amounts of data in defined categories. One column contains the categories (numeric such as 1-10, 11-20, etc., or nominal such as Richardson, Dallas, etc.), and the second column contains the percent or proportion in each category.	[T3, GR2]
Reliability	The quality of a measuring device, including human raters and evaluators, that determines how free the device is from common measurement errors, operationalized by correlating measures from two or more separate observations using the same measures on the same subjects.	[C2, C11, C12, C17, GR3, GR5, GR6]

Term	Definition	Courses
Reload options	When a company provides an employee additional stock options equal to the number of shares that the executive delivers to a company upon a stock-for-stock exercise of an option, with the term of exercisability of the reload option limited to the remaining term of the original option grant and the option price equal to the fair market value (FMV) at the time of exercise that triggered the reload option.	[C6, C6A, T11]
Relocation premium	In expatriate compensation, a lump-sum amount to assist with extraordinary relocation expenses (e.g., luggage; conversion of old, or purchase of new, appliances; auto licenses and registration fees).	[C15]
Remote-site allowance	A special payment sometimes made if the work location is isolated or difficult to reach.	[C15]
Remuneration	The sum of the financial and nonfinancial value to the employee of all the elements in the employment package (i.e., salary, incentives, benefits, perquisites, job satisfaction, organizational affiliation, status, etc.) and any other intrinsic or extrinsic rewards of the employment exchange that the employee values.	[C15, T9]
Reportable event	Any occurrence that results in a material change to either a defined benefit (DB) or defined contribution (DC) plan (e.g., acquisition, divestiture, change of formula, etc.).	[T6]
Representations and warranties	Statements of fact and assurances of truth made by one party to a potential contract to another.	[T6]

Term	Definition	Courses
Request for information (RFI)	One of the first steps in the service provider selection process, designed to eliminate those service providers that would absolutely not fit within the scope of the project to be outsourced. The RFI cannot be used as a basis for a competitive award.	[B3, T12]
Request for proposal (RFP)	An invitation to a service provider to provide a company with a bid or proposal. A lengthy document used to gauge or grade potential service providers as the selections are narrowed.	[B3, T12]
Reserve	Those elements of income other than goods and services, housing or taxes. Common forms of reserve are savings, insurance, social security payments and investment portfolios.	[C15]
Residual employees	See rightsizing.	[T6]
Responsibility	A duty or group of duties that describes the major purpose or reasons for the existence of a job.	[C2, C17, GR3]
Restricted stock	Stock that is given (or sold at a discount) to an employee, who is restricted from selling or transferring it for a specified time period (usually three to five years). The executive receives dividends, but must forfeit the stock if he/she terminates employment before the restriction period ends. If the employee remains in the employ of the company through the restricted period, the shares vest, irrespective of employee or company performance.	[C6, C6A, C12, C15, T6, T11, GR6]

Term	Definition	Courses
Restructuring	A reorganization of a corporation to make the structure more congruent with organizational strategies.	[C6, C6A, C11, T1, T11, GR1]
Results-oriented appraisal	A performance assessment tool that focuses on outcomes. Examples of a results-oriented approach include work planning and review (WPR) and management by objectives (MBO).	[C11]
Retained earnings	An account on the balance sheet that represents net profits less dividends paid to shareholders.	[T2]
Retention	The portion of the premium retained by an insurer to cover risk, expense charges, profit or contribution to surplus.	[B3A]
Retirement plan	Any plan that provides retirement income to employees and results in deferral of income until termination of employment or retirement from the workforce. The two primary types of retirement plans are pension plans and capital accumulation/savings plans.	[B2, C15, T6, T9, GR7]
Retirement Security Advice Act of 2001	Permits life insurers and other financial-services companies that provide retirement plans and educational materials to provide investment advice, with certain limitations, to plan sponsors and participants.	[B2]
Retrospective premium arrangement	A group insurance arrangement in which insurer's margin is eliminated from the current premium, but insurer retains the right to require additional payments (i.e., to "call" the margin) up to a specific amount based on the insured's claims.	[B3A]

Term	Definition	Courses
Return on assets (ROA)	The ratio of net income to the total assets of an organization. A key financial measure, sometimes used as a criterion in incentive plans.	[C6, C6A, C11, C12, T2, T11, GR2, GR6]
Return on capital employed (ROC, ROTC, ROCE)	The ratio of net income, plus after-tax interest on long-term debt, to shareholders' equity with the long-term debt. A key financial measure, sometimes used as a criterion in incentive plans. Sometimes referred to as return on total capital (ROTC).	[C6, C6A, T2, T11]
Return on equity (ROE), return on shareholder equity (ROSE)	The ratio of the net income attributable to common shares to shareholders' equity. Often used as a measurement in incentive plans.	[C6, C6A, C11, T2, T11, GR2, GR5, GR6]
Return on investment (ROI)	In financial analysis, any of the "return" measures including return on assets, return on equity, return on net assets and return on total capital.	[B1, B5, C6, C6A, C11, C12, T1, T2, T4, T11, GR1, GR6, GR9]
Return on net assets (RONA)	The ratio of net income to net assets (total assets less current liabilities). A financial measure, sometimes used as a criterion in executive incentive plans, especially at the business unit level.	[C6, C6A, T2, GR6]
Return on sales (ROS)	The ratio of net income to net sales. A key financial measure, sometimes used as a criterion in incentive plans.	[C6, C6A, C12, T2, GR2, GR6]
Return on shareholders' equity (ROSE)	See return on equity.	[C6, C6A, T2]
Returns allowances	An offset to sales revenue that estimates the dollar amount of possible returns of a company's products by its customers.	[T2]

Term	Definition	Courses
Revenue	The money generated by a company from sale of goods or services including rental income. Often referred to as sales in manufacturing and merchandising companies.	[C5, C6, C12, T2, GR6]
Rewards system	An organization's choice of cash and noncash motivational elements and the mix of its total rewards program that is used to support its business strategy.	[C11, GR7]
Rightsizing	The practice of eliminating nonessential and/or redundant positions to reduce the workforce to the smallest possible size without adversely affecting normal operations. Residual employees are those who remain after this process and whose duties may change and/or increase significantly.	[C11, T6, T12]
Ripple effect	The decision by a supplier on whether to follow a customer abroad or risk losing a domestic contract.	[C15, T9, GR7]
Risk	In insurance, it is the uncertainty regarding the occurrence of loss.	[B3A]
Risk premium	The amount of expected additional return on investment required by investors for choosing an investment with greater risk than U.S. Treasury securities.	[C6, C6A]
Risk-free rate of return	The yield on U.S. Treasury securities, which represents assured payment of interest and repayment of capital. Often used in determining the cost of capital.	[C6, C6A, T11]
Rollover	The process of taking a distribution from a qualified plan of a former employer and investing that amount in a qualified plan with another employer or in an individual retirement account (IRA).	[B1, B2, T6]

Term	Definition	Courses
Roth individual retirement account (IRA)	A type of IRA established in the Taxpayer Relief Act of 1997. It differs from a traditional IRA in that taxes are paid on contributions to a Roth IRA, but withdrawals, subject to certain rules, are not taxed at all.	[B1, B2]
Rucker Share of Production Plan	A gainsharing cost-reduction program in which specific cost savings that result from an employee effort are shared with employees.	[C11, C12, GR6]
Rule of three	Rule that states "three companies will always garner the lion's share of the market, while those that arrive late receive only crumbs."	[C15, T9, GR7]
Run rate	Provides a measure or snapshot of the relative use of shares within the greater scope of shares outstanding. It is calculated by dividing annual shares granted (net of cancellations) by the total number of shares outstanding.	[C6, C6A, T11]
S corporation	A corporation with 75 or fewer shareholders whose shareholders have elected to be taxed like a partnership.	[T6]
Sabbatical	A perquisite that provides a leave of absence for a specific period of time (e.g., six months) to allow for pursuit of some outside endeavor (e.g., a civic or charitable project, or completion of an advanced degree).	[B1, B5, C6, C6A, W2]
Salaried	Refers to compensation paid by the week, month or year rather than by the hour. Generally applies to higher-level, nonrepetitive or supervisory jobs that are exempt from the provisions of the Fair Labor Standards Act of 1938 (FLSA). In some cases, nonexempt jobs can be salaried.	[C1, T1, GR1]

Term	Definition	Courses
Salary	Compensation paid by the week, month or year (rather than per hour). Generally applies to jobs that are exempt from the provisions of the Fair Labor Standards Act of 1938 (FLSA), but in some cases, nonexempt jobs can be salaried as well.	[C4, C15, C17, T9, GR7]
Salary budget	An amount or pool of money allocated for payment of salaries and wages during a specified period. Salary budgets must be taken into account when planning structure adjustments or individual employee adjustments.	[C4, C15, GR4]
Salary grade	A group of jobs of the same or similar value, used for compensation purposes. All jobs in a salary grade have the same salary range: minimum, midpoint and maximum.	[C4, C17, T6, T9, GR7]
Salary increase budget	The difference between the values of an organization's current pay and its pay goals.	[T3, GR2]
Salary increase cost	(1) The cost of the increase in the current (i.e., first) year is determined by multiplying the eligible payroll by the average increase percent and the participant rate, adjusted for the percent of the year the increase is in effect. (2) The annualized cost of the increase (future year cost) is determined by multiplying the eligible payroll by the average increase percent and the participant rate.	[C4, GR4]
Salary index	See compa-ratio.	[C4, GR4]
Salary range	See pay range.	[C2, C11, C17, GR2, GR3]
Salary structure	The hierarchy of job grades and pay ranges established within an organization. The salary structure may be expressed in terms	[C2, C4, C11, C15, C17, T6, T9, GR3, GR4, GR7]

Term	Definition	Courses
	of job grades, job-evaluation points or policy lines.	
Salary structure change	An adjustment in salary structure expressed as the percentage by which the sum of all midpoints of the new structure exceed (or lag) the corresponding sum of the midpoints of the old structure.	[C17]
Sale and purchase agreement	The written contractual representation of the transaction framework and details.	[T6]
Sale of stock	The disposition, exchange or transfer of shares for a cash equivalent consideration.	[C6, C6A, T11]
Sales	See revenue.	[T2]
Sales channel	The means a manufacturer or service-providing company might employ to interact with and manage relationships among its final, end-user customers. Such channels might be direct, in which the manufacturer uses a sales force to sell to its end-use customers, or they might be indirect, such that the manufacturer employs a third-party company to represent its products to the marketplace of customers.	[C5]
Sales compensation	Monetary amounts paid to sales representatives or sales management that vary in accordance with accomplishment of sales goals. Sales compensation formulas usually attempt to establish direct incentives for sales.	[C5, C12, GR6]
Sales contest	An event entailing a short-term sales effort to maximize results for a nonrecurring purpose in an effort to win a prize. Usually short in duration, such contests are designed to be supplemental to the regular sales compensation program, not to replace it.	[C5]

Term	Definition	Courses
Sales cycle	The time, starting with identifying the customer (prospect), it normally takes to close the sale.	[C5, GR6]
Sales event	An occurrence when a sale may be counted for compensation purposes.	[C5]
Salvage value	The expected value obtainable for a noncurrent asset after the end of its useful life. Used in certain calculations of depreciation.	[T2]
Same desk rule	Effective January 1, 2002, the same desk rule was repealed under the Economic Growth and Tax Relief Reconciliation Act of 2001 (EGTRRA). Previously, under this rule, certain distributions of qualified plans were prohibited to be made to employees if the employee remained in a similar job for a successor employer.	[T6]
Sample	In statistics, a subset of the elementary units of the (subject) population.	[T3]
Sampling errors	In statistics, a subset of the elementary units of the (subject) population.	[C2, C17, GR3]
Sarbanes-Oxley Act of 2002	A federal law regulating accounting oversight, corporate responsibility (to include certified financial statements), documentation and reporting. The law also requires that written notification be provided for periods where employees cannot trade company stock [for 401(k) and other deferred compensation plans] and limits insider trading during such periods, prohibits the extension of credits/personal loans to directors and officers and limits auditing firms' ability to provide additional services to their client.	[C6, C6A, T6, T11]

Term	Definition	Courses
Savings (thrift) plan	A defined contribution (DC) plan that allows employees to make contributions on a discretionary basis with limits. Employee contributions may be matched by the employer. Contributions commonly are made with after-tax earnings.	[B1, B2, T6]
Scanlon Plan	A gainsharing program in which employees share in specific cost savings that are the result of employee effort. The Scanlon Plan involves formal employee participation, a predetermined incentive formula and periodic progress reporting.	[C11, C12, GR6]
Scattergram	A mathematical technique of displaying a "picture" of a relationship between two variables by plotting (x, y) points. Also called a scatterplot.	[T3, GR2]
Scope	A set of quantifiable job characteristics that ascribe value to a job. Typical measures include sales volume, asset size of the organization, number of subordinates and size of budget managed.	[C2, C6, C6A, C12, C17, GR3, GR6]
Scope measurements	In many wage surveys, specific job characteristics such as sales volume or budget are provided to help ensure an appropriate job match. On wage survey questionnaires, there is sometimes an opportunity for respondents to indicate degree of job match, resulting in a general measure of comparative job scope.	[C2, C6, C6A, C12, C17, GR6]
SEC Rule 10b(5)	An SEC rule that prohibits anyone, inside or outside the company, who has inside information to take advantage of the insider information to profit from sale or purchase of company shares.	[C6, C6A]

Term	Definition	Courses
Secondary source of job information	See scope.	[C2, GR3]
Section 16	A section of the SEC regulations that identifies "insiders," that precludes insiders from unfairly profiting from the purchase and sale of company stock, and that provides certain exceptions related to transactions involving stock for insiders.	[C6, C6A, T11]
Section 79	Section of the Internal Revenue Code (IRC) that addresses the taxability of group term life insurance purchased for employees. Section 79 specifies that the cost of group term life insurance must be included in the gross income of an employee when the cost exceeds the sum of (1) the cost of $50,000 of such insurance, and (2) the amount (if any) paid by the employee toward the purchase of such insurance.	[B3, B5, T6]
Section 105	Section of the Internal Revenue Code (IRC) that excludes from an employee's gross income any amounts received under an employer-provided medical plan. Subject to nondiscrimination rules.	[B3]
Section 125	Section of the Internal Revenue Code (IRC) that addresses cafeteria plans. Section 125 specifies that, in general, benefits and monies in a cafeteria plan shall not be included in the gross income of an employee. The section also addresses the exceptions pertaining to highly compensated employees and key employees.	[B3, B5]
Section 129	Section of the Internal Revenue Code (IRC) that specifies that, in general, amounts paid (up to a specified amount) by an em	[B3]

Term	Definition	Courses
	ployer for dependent care assistance provided to employees' dependents shall not be included in the gross income of employees.	
Section 162(m)	Section of the Internal Revenue Code (IRC) that generally disallows a tax deduction to public companies for compensation of more than $1 million paid to the company's chief executive officer or any of the four most highly compensated executive officers (other than the chief executive officer). Section 162(m) provides that qualifying performance-based compensation will not be subject to the tax deduction limit if certain requirements are met.	[C6, C6A, T6, T11]
Section 404(a)	See qualified foreign plan, qualified funded plan and qualified reserve plan.	[C15, T9, GR7]
Section 409A	A section of the Internal Revenue Code created by the American Jobs Creation Act (AJCA) that defines nonqualified deferred compensation arrangements and the tax liability associated with such plans.	[C6, C6A, T11]
Section 415	Section of the Internal Revenue Code (IRC) that contains the benefits limits and contributions limits applicable to individual plan participants in a tax-qualified pension and profit-sharing plans. Commonly referred to as the 415 limits.	[B1, B2, C6, C6A, T6, T11]
Secular trust	An irrevocable trust established to protect nonqualified and/or deferred compensation benefits. It is similar to a rabbi trust, except that funds in a secular trust are not subject to the claims of general creditors in the event	[C6, C6A, T6, T11]

Term	Definition	Courses
	of bankruptcy. Participants are taxed and the company receives a deduction at the time money is put into the trust.	
Securities and Exchange Commission (SEC)	The federal agency that enforces the Securities and Exchange Act of 1934 and other securities acts and issues rules and regulations on related matters, such as insider trading and required disclosures on executive compensation. The SEC establishes rules for companies reporting to shareholders about the financial and business results of the enterprise for publicly owned companies.	[B1, C6, C6A, C15, T2, T6, T9, T11, GR7]
Self-administered	Refers to a defined benefit (DB) or welfare benefit plan in which the company assumes responsibility for full administration of the plan, including asset investment and claims administration.	[B3A]
Self-administered trusteed plan	A retirement plan under which contributions to purchase pension benefits are paid to a trustee (generally a bank) that invests the money, accumulates the earnings and interest, and pays benefits to eligible employees under the terms of the retirement plan and trust agreement. This plan is administered by the employer, or by a committee appointed by the plan sponsor under the terms of the plan and the trust agreement.	[B1, C6, C6A, C15, T2, T6, T9, T11]
Self-funding (self-insurance)	A benefits plan funding method in which the employer carries the risk for any claims. The employer may contract with a third-party administrator (TPA) to pay claims in its behalf, or may develop its own department to administer the program. Self-funded plans are regulated	[B1, B3, B3A, T6]

Term	Definition	Courses
	by the Employee Retirement Income Security Act of 1974 (ERISA) rather than state insurance regulations, and are not required to pay state insurance premium taxes.	
Selling, general and administrative (SG&A)	Part of the income statement where employee compensation is typically found.	[C6, T2, T6]
Sender	Person or group of persons with a given purpose for engaging in communication; the sender is often the source of information.	[T4, GR9]
Seniority	Status determined by the length of time an employee has worked for a given employer, often as the basis for rights, privileges and benefits. The term also may be used to reflect time worked for a division, group or specific occupation. Union contracts often provide for multiple seniority calculations.	[C1, C4, T1, GR1, GR4]
Separate health benefit account [401(h)]	A funding arrangement for health benefits for retirees that is part of either a defined benefit (DB) or defined contribution (DC) pension plan, segregates assets for health benefits into a separate account, and is subject to Internal Revenue Code (IRC) limitations.	[B3A]
Sequential exercise	The exercise of stock options in the order in which they were granted. Formerly, a legal requirement for incentive stock options.	[C1]
Service agreement	A legally binding document that details the relationship between the client and the service partner. Typically, the service agreement will contain information regarding the service provided,	[T12]

Term	Definition	Courses
	length of time the service will be provided, the cost of the service provided, and so on.	
Service partner	An organization that provides an outsourcing service to a client for a fee.	[T12]
Service team	The internal group within a service partner that is dedicated to work with the client concerning the client's account.	[T12]
Severance/ benefits continuation	Continuation of an employee's salary after termination that is paid either in a lump sum or on a continuation basis. The amount usually is based on the employee's length of service. Benefits continuation may be a part of a severance package to provide continued coverage under the medical or other benefits plans for the employee and/or dependents for a period after termination.	[B1, B3, B3A, T2, T6]
Shadow stock plans	See phantom stock plans.	[C6]
Shapes of distribution	The appearance of the placement of data values when graphed.	[T3, GR2]
Shared leave program	Donating personal/vacation time to others facing emergency situations.	[W1]
Shareholder	Individuals that have a vested interest in the organization through stock ownership in the company.	[C6, C6A]
Shareholder protection formula	A formula related to a company's bonus plan that sets aside a specified portion of profit for shareholders before any portion of the excess is made available for bonus awards.	[B1, B3, B3A, T2, T6]
Shareholder value	See total shareholder return.	[C6, C6A, T11]

Term	Definition	Courses
Shareholders' equity	Money provided to the company by the owners through the issuance of equity securities and/or through retained earnings. This also represents the book value of the company.	[C6, C6A, T2, GR6]
Sherman anti-trust act (1890)	A federal law passed to protect the public from abuses of corporate monopolies; however, in 1908, the Supreme Court ruled that it applied to unions as well. In terms of compensation, the exchange of wage information can be seen as "price fixing" wages.	[C1, C2, C17]
Shift differential	Extra pay allowance made to employees who work on a shift other than a regular day shift (e.g., 9 A.M. to 5 P.M., Monday through Friday) if the shift is thought to represent a hardship, or if competitive organizations provide a similar premium. Shift differentials usually are expressed as a percentage or in cents per hour.	[C1, C4, T1, GR1, GR4, GR5]
Shift flexibility	Options for employees to trade, pick-up or drop work shifts with other employees.	[W1, W2]
Shortfalls	A sales result significantly below expectations that is not influenced by the sales representative.	[C5]
Short-term assignment	A federal law passed to protect the public from abuses of corporate monopolies; however, in 1908, the Supreme Court ruled that it applied to unions as well. In terms of compensation, the exchange of wage information can be seen as "price fixing" wages.	[C15, T9, GR7]
Short-term debt	See current liabilities.	[T2]

Term	Definition	Courses
Short-term disability (STD) plan	A benefits plan designed to provide income during absences because of nonoccupational-related illness or injury, when the employee is expected to return to work within a specified time, usually within six months. Usually coordinated or integrated with sick leave at the beginning and with long-term disability (LTD) at the end of STD.	[B1, B3, B3A, B5, T1, T6, GR1]
Short-term incentives	Rewards that are based on the attainment of short-term results of 12 months or less (e.g., net income). See also annual incentive.	[C6, C6A, C11, C12, C15, T1, T11, GR1, GR5, GR6]
Sick leave	Paid time off provided to employees suffering from nonoccupational illness or injury. Usually coordinated or integrated with short-term disability (STD) plans.	[B1, B3, B3A, B5, T1, T6, W1, GR1]
Signing bonus	A specific bonus given at the beginning of a service period, usually for accepting an employment offer. It could also be used at the beginning of a new reward program. Typically, it is used to offset forfeited benefits left behind.	[C6, C6A, T11, C12, GR6]
Similarly situated individuals	As clarified by the Interim Final Rules for Nondiscrimination in Health Coverage in the Group Market (2001), in determining a premium or contribution, plan participants are similarly situated individuals if they are in a similar "bona fide employment-based classification." Under the rules, similarly situated individuals must be uniformly provided with the same benefits and uniformly subject to the same restrictions of a health policy.	[B3]

Term	Definition	Courses
Simple choice plan	A retirement plan that allows employees to choose from a limited number of benefits packages (as opposed to benefits options) typically designed to accommodate the needs of varying demographic groups. Employee contributions may be required for one or more of the packages offered. Also known as a modular plan.	[B1, B5]
SIMPLE plan (savings incentive match plan for employees)	A type of qualified retirement plan [either IRA or 401(k)] designated for employers with up to 100 employees. No top-heavy or nondiscrimination tests must be passed, but fixed or matching company contributions must be made.	[B2]
Single measure plans	Incentive plans based on a single measure (financial or productivity) of performance.	[C12, GR6]
Single-rate system	A compensation policy under which all employees in a given job are paid at the same rate instead of being placed in a pay range. Generally applies in situations where there is little room for variation in job performance or skill level.	[C4, GR4]
Skewed distribution	A set of plotted data that is non-symmetric, with a tail of extreme values in one direction.	[T3, GR2]
Skill-based pay	A person-based compensation system based on the repertoire of skills an employee can perform, rather than the specific skill that the employee may be doing at a particular time. Pay increases generally are associated with the addition and/or improvement of the skills of an individual employee, as opposed to better performance or seniority within the system. Pay	[C2, C4, C11, C12, T1, GR1, GR3, GR4, GR5, GR6]

Term	Definition	Courses
	level generally is not dependent on whether any of the skills are utilized.	
Skills inventory	A planning tool that specifies all people currently employed by the organization and classifies them according to their skills, job assignments, age, sex and other factors relevant to human resource planning. The device is employed primarily as a way of classifying internal labor supplies for human resource planning.	[C4, GR4]
Slope	In a simple linear model, $y = a + bx$, the coefficient b is the change in the value of y, the dependent variable, for each unit change in the value of x, the independent variable. Graphically, slope represents the "rise" over the "run" of a given line and directly determines a line's steepness. In a multiple linear model, $y = a + b1x1 + b2x2 + \ldots + bkxk$, each xi has a slope bi, which is sometimes called a b-weight, partial regression weight or regression coefficient. Each bi is the change in y for each unit change in the corresponding xi when all the other xs are held constant.	[C2, C4, C11, C12, C17, T3, GR2, GR6]
Slotting	The act of placing a job into a job worth hierarchy established by some other job-evaluation method. The method involves comparing the job to one or more jobs in an already established hierarchy; consequently, it cannot be used as a stand-alone method.	[C2, C17, GR3]
Small-group incentive	Any incentive program that focuses on the performance of a small group, usually a work team. These incentive programs are most useful when	[C11, C12, GR5, GR6]

Term	Definition	Courses
	measurable output is the result of group effort and individual contributions are difficult to separate from the group effort.	
Social Security	The program of federal government-provided old age, survivors, disability and health insurance benefits provided under the Social Security Act of 1935. Beneficiaries are workers who participate in the Social Security program, their spouses, dependent parents and dependent children. Benefits vary according to (1) earnings of the worker, (2) length of time in the program, (3) age at which benefits start, (4) age and number of beneficiaries other than the worker, and (5) state of health of recipients other than the worker. See also Old Age, Survivors, Disability and Health Insurance Program (OASDHI).	[B1, B2, B3, C15, T6, T9, GR7]
Sole proprietorship	An unincorporated business owned by one person who is personally liable for all business debts.	[T6]
Spendable income	The amount of money needed for goods and services in the assignment location to equal the purchasing power of the expatriate's counterparts in the home country. Under the balance sheet approach, assignment location spendable income equals the sum of home country goods-and-services spendable income and foreign goods-and-services differential. Assignment location spendable income usually is denominated in assignment location currency.	[B1, B2, B3, C15, T6, T9]

Term	Definition	Courses
Sphere of experience	The perceptions, attitudes and prior knowledge each sender and receiver has that shapes both the transmission and the reception of the message	[T4, GR9]
Spin-off	A divestiture where a division or subsidiary becomes its own company.	[T6]
Split credit	The division and assignment of sales credit to more than one salesperson.	[C5]
Split-dollar insurance	Not a type of policy, but a method of paying for a policy in which the premium and death benefits associated with a life insurance policy are split between the employer and the insured employee. It may be used to secure executive benefits for nonqualified arrangements; this form of split-dollar insurance is known as corporate-owned life insurance (COLI).	[C6, C6A, T6, T11]
Split-pay system	A portion of salary is paid in hard currency outside the country; pay package is divided into home- and host-country portions each denominated in its own currency. These two amounts are then separate payrolls, one in the home country and one in the host.	[C15, T9, GR7]
Spot award	A type of informal recognition that is delivered spontaneously or "on the spot."	[C12, T1, T6, GR6]
Springing rabbi trust	A rabbi trust that receives only minimal assets at the time of establishment. Full funding is only required when a specifically defined contingency occurs, such as an actual or impending change of control.	[T6]
Stakeholder	A person or organization that has a financial interest in a	[C6, C6A, T11]

Term	Definition	Courses
	company. This may include management, other employees, customers, suppliers, members of the community and shareholders.	
Standard & Poors (S&P) 500	A market-value weighted index that measures the movement of the 500 largest publicly traded U.S. corporations. Similar to the Dow Jones Industrial Average, except that not all of the stocks are listed on the New York Stock Exchange.	[C6, C6A, T2, T11]
Standard deviation	The square root of the average squared difference between data points and the mean. Standard deviation is a measure of variability that indicates an average relative distance between each data point and the mean. The larger the standard deviation, the more the data is spread out from the mean. Mathematically, it is the square root of the variance.	[T3, GR2]
Standard error of estimate	A measure of the variability of data points about the regression line or model. It can be used to construct a set of confidence limits for estimates of the y-variable based on the regression model.	[T3]
Standard rate	The rate established for a job, based on job evaluations and/or job pricing.	[C4, C17, GR4]
Standstill agreement	A commitment by an acquiring company not to purchase a target company's stock for a specific time period without the target company's permission.	[T6]
Starting rate	See hiring rate.	[C4, C17, GR4]
State disability insurance program	Five states (New York, New Jersey, Rhode Island, California and Hawaii) and Puerto Rico	[B3]

Term	Definition	Courses
	have state disability insurance programs that provide temporary, nonwork-related disability benefits for a limited period of time (e.g., 6 to 12 months).	
Statement of cash flows	See cash flow statement.	[T2]
Statement of retained earnings	A financial statement that explains the changes in retained earnings over a specified period of time.	[T2]
Statement of shareholders' equity	Financial statement that shows the same basic information as the statement of retained earnings, but also shows the changes in all shareholders' equity accounts.	[T2]
Statutory stock options	See incentive stock options.	[C6, C6A, T11]
Step rate formula	See excess formula.	[B1, B2]
Step rates	Standard progression pay rates that are established within a pay range. Step rates usually are a function of time in grade and often are referred to as automatic. However, they also can be variable or can be used in conjunction with merit programs.	[C4, C11, T1, GR1, GR4]
Step rules	Rules in a flexible benefits plan that allow the employee to change coverage at every enrollment, but only allow the employee to change, up or down, one level of coverage each year.	[B5]
Stock alternatives	Plans that do not involve the actual ownership of shares or rights to shares, but whose potential value to participants is based on a financial measurement.	[C6]
Stock awards	Plans that provide stock to employees without a cost to them.	[C6]

Term	Definition	Courses
Stock for stock exercise	An arrangement in which a holder of a stock option uses the fair market value (FMV) of stock already owned to finance the exercise of a stock option. A widely used technique. It is sometimes referred to as a stock-swap.	[C6, C6A, T11]
Stock for tax withholding	When shares delivered to an individual upon settlement of an option exercise are reduced for the individual's withholding taxes.	[C6, C6A, T11]
Stock grant plan	Plan that provides stock to employees without any cost to them. Stock grants take two basic forms: (1) stock-appreciation grants and (2) full-value grants. Stock-appreciation grants entitle the employee to the appreciated value of a share of stock (or number of shares or units) over a designated period of time. These grants may be qualified or nonqualified under Internal Revenue Service (IRS) regulations. A full-value grant entitles the employee to a total value of the worth of the share of stock (or number of shares or units) over a predetermined period of time.	[C6, C6A, C11, C12, T6, T11, GR5, GR6]
Stock option	A right to purchase company shares at a specified price during a specified period of time. This is sometimes referred to as share options in countries outside the United States.	[C6, C6A, C11, C12, C15, T1, T2, T6, T9, T11, GR1, GR6, GR7]
Stock ownership guidelines	Written directive that establishes parameters about the levels of stock that executives/officers and directors must own, how long they have to acquire this level of stock ownership and if/when they can sell the stock.	[C6A]

Term	Definition	Courses
Stock purchase plan	Any program under which employees buy shares in the company's stock. A qualified plan is a program that meets the Internal Revenue Service (IRS) statutory requirements and results in more favorable benefits and tax treatment for the employee and company. Stock may be offered at a fixed price (usually below market) and paid for in full by employees. A nonqualified plan does not qualify for favorable tax treatment and may include any terms (e.g., discounts below statutory IRS limits).	[C6, C12, T11, GR5]
Stock purchase plan (nonqualified)	A plan that is, in effect, a management stock purchase plan. It allows senior management or other key personnel to purchase stock in the business. There are, however, certain restrictions: (1) the stockholder must be employed for a certain period of time, (2) the business has the right to buy back the stock, (3) stockholders cannot sell the stock for a defined period of time.	[C6, C6A, T11, GR6]
Stock sale	A type of acquisition in which the buyer takes full ownership of the entire company being purchased.	[T6]
Stock split	An increase in the number of shares issued by a company through grants of additional shares to existing shareholders. A 2 for 1 stock split will double the number of shares held by each shareholder, but reduce the par value per share by half, and will tend to reduce the market value of a single share by approximately 50 percent. A reverse 1 for 2 split will halve the number of shares of each shareholder, but double the par value	[T11]

Term	Definition	Courses
	per share and approximately double the market value per share.	
Stock swap	See stock for stock exercise.	[C6, C6A, T11]
Stock-appreciation rights (sars)	An executive incentive plan in which the corporation grants an executive the right to receive a dollar amount of value equal to the future appreciation of its shares, often in lieu of the executive exercising a share option. Typically is granted as a companion (in tandem) to a share option, and the executive must surrender a matched number of option shares to "cash-in" the SAR. Usually are not used except by U.S. companies operating in some foreign countries where tax and other laws preclude the use of stock options.	[C6, C6A, C12, T6, T11, GR6]
Stop loss policy	A provision in an insurance policy that caps covered losses at a specific dollar amount.	[T6]
Stop-loss provision (health and disability plans)	A provision in a self-funded plan that is designed to limit the risk of employer losses to a specific amount. If claim costs (for a month, year or per claim) exceed a predetermined level, an insurance carrier will cover the excess amount. Alternatively, this term may refer to the annual "out-of-pocket maximum" feature in a group medical plan. The out-of-pocket maximum, or employee stop-loss limit, is the most an individual or family must pay in covered expenses, after meeting appropriate deductibles each year.	[B1, B3, B3A]
Straight-line depreciation	An accounting method whereby equal amounts of depreciation are recorded each year during	[T2]

Term	Definition	Courses
	the useful life of a tangible non-current asset.	
Strategic alliance	No transfer of assets or change of ownership. The two parties are sharing resources for a temporary period to accomplish specified tasks.	[C15, T6, T9, GR7]
Strategic business unit (SBU)	A subunit of a larger organizational structure (e.g., division or subsidiary) that is viewed as a contributor to the overall success of the enterprise. Many incentive plans are designed around the accomplishment of SBU financial results.	[C6, C6A, C11, C12, GR5, GR6]
Strategic planning	The process of establishing or developing organizational objectives, environmental constraints and opportunities, competitive strengths and weaknesses, and organizational structure and culture, and using this analysis to develop policies and programs that are most conducive to achievement of key organizational objectives.	[T2, W2, W3]
Strategy	The science or art of employing a careful plan to achieve a specified goal.	[B3, C11, T6, T12, W2, W3]
Subrogation/ right of reimbursement	The right of one who has paid an obligation owed by another to collect from the party originally owing the obligation. For example, an insurance company has the right to recover from a third party the amount it paid to its insured for a loss.	[B3]
Subsidiary (more than 50 percent ownership)	A company that is wholly or partially owned/controlled by another company.	[T2]
Succession planning	A process that involves identifying potential replacements for key employees who are known to be leaving an organization or	[C11, T6]

Term	Definition	Courses
	whose sudden departure would pose a risk to the operation of the organization.	
Summary annual report (SAR)	Under the Employee Retirement Security Act of 1974 (ERISA), employers are required to disclose certain financial information related to benefits programs, which is reported on an annual Form 5500 tax return.	[B1, B3, T6]
Summary of material modifications (smms)	Under the Employee Retirement Security Act of 1974 (ERISA), employers are required to provide employees with a summary of significant changes in the provisions of a plan or in the administration of the plan. A material modification exists when there is a change to any of the required information disclosed in a summary plan description.	[B1, B3, T6]
Summary plan description (SPD)	Under the Employee Retirement Security Act of 1974 (ERISA) employers are required to provide employees with an explanation of certain benefits programs in language that can be easily understood by an average employee.	[B1, B2, B3, T6]
Summer hours	An arrangement whereby employees have reduced working hours during the summer months (e.g., half day on Fridays).	[B5, W2]
Summer time flex	Work hours differ during the summer months. For example, starting work at 7:00 A.M. instead of 8:30 A.M.	[W1, W2]
Sum-of-the-years'-digits (SOYD) method	A method of calculating depreciation of an asset that assumes higher depreciation charges and greater tax benefits in the early years of an asset's life.	[T2]

Term	Definition	Courses
Superannua-tion	A common reference to the Australian retirement benefits environment, it essentially means putting money aside during the individual's working life for use in retirement. Superannuation can refer to private company plans as well as industry or union funds.	[C15]
Superannua-tion Industry (Supervision) Act ("SIS") Section 404A	A series of standards and rules legislated in Australia effective with the fund's 1994–95 year covering the government's constitutional powers, responsibilities of Trustees, member representation on Trust bodies, dispute resolutions, and so on.	
Superinten-dent of Pension Fund ("SAFP")	In Chile, the individual who authorizes the existence of the Administradoras De Fondos De Pensiones (A.F.P.'s) and supervises the operation of the A.F.P.'s with respect to legal, administrative and financial respects.	
Supplemen-tal death benefits (supplemental life insurance)	An executive perquisite that provides payment to beneficiaries, on the death of the executive, over and above normal life insurance policies.	[B3A, C6, C6A]
Supplemen-tal disability benefits	An executive perquisite that provides benefits in addition to those normally provided by the company's short and long-term disability plans.	[B3A, C6, C6A]
Supplemen-tal executive benefits	Forms of compensation provided to a small number of executives that are in excess of the benefits provided to all other executives. Because of the higher income levels, tax burdens and statutory limitations for executives, their unique circumstances often require companies to use "nonqualified" pay delivery for	[C6, C6A]

Term	Definition	Courses
	attraction, retention and motivation.	
Supplemental executive retirement plan (SERP)	A form of nonqualified pension plan that need not be funded and can be lost if the corporation goes bankrupt. It offers the organization the ability to grant more liberal benefits and to ensure that retirement amounts beyond those authorized under the Employee Retirement Income Security Act of 1974 (ERISA) can be provided to the highly paid employee. SERPs that restore benefits lost under ERISA are called 415 plans, as that is the section in the Internal Revenue Code (IRC) describing limits as qualified plans. Other SERPs are structured to provide benefits (typically for short service) beyond that provided by the basic pension plan.	[B1, B2, C6, C6A, T6]
Supplemental medical	Annual physicals and additional replacement income disability protection plans that are offered to executive employees, recognizing different compensation levels, tax burdens and/or other circumstances in recruiting executives.	[C6, C6A]
Supplemental unemployment benefits (SUB)	An employer-funded plan that supplements state unemployment insurance payments to workers during temporary periods of layoff. SUB plans are largely concentrated in the automobile, steel and related industries, and usually are part of a negotiated labor contract.	[B1, B3A]
Survey	The gathering of information about a situation. Often, surveys consist of sampling data from a population. Examples include a benchmark salary survey that	[C2, C4, C15, C17, T3, T9, GR2, GR4, GR7]

Term	Definition	Courses
	collects pay data for benchmark jobs from a defined labor market, a maturity salary survey that collects both pay and experience data from a defined labor market for benchmark jobs or jobs in a given discipline at a given degree level, and a benefits survey that collects benefits data from a defined labor market.	
Survivor benefits	Payments a spouse or dependent would receive under an insurance policy if the insured died.	[B3, T1, GR1]
Survivor income benefit (SIB) insurance	A type of group life insurance that provides income benefits if a "qualified survivor" survives the insured. Usually the qualified survivor category includes only the insured's spouse and children. Benefits are calculated based on the age and gender of the spouse, and the number of dependent children and their ages. Payments are on an annuitized (i.e., monthly) basis.	[B1, B5]
Symmetric distribution	A plotting of data in which one half is the mirror image of the other half. The point of symmetry is the median.	[T3, GR2]
Take-home pay	An employee's earnings less taxes, Social Security and other deductions (both voluntary and involuntary) made by the employer.	[C4]
Target benefit (pension) plan	A hybrid pension plan that blends features of a defined benefit (DB) plan within a defined contribution (DC) plan. In a target benefit plan, individual employee accounts are credited with percentages that are individually calculated at the time of plan inception. The goal is to provide each participant with a targeted amount of pension at	[B2]

Term	Definition	Courses
	normal retirement (usually age 65).	
Target cash compensation (TCC)	As it relates to sales compensation, the total cash compensation (including base salary and incentive compensation) available for achieving expected results.	[C5]
Target compa-ratio	The organization's planned average salary for the organization, group or individual divided by the corresponding average (or total) midpoint. Can also be calculated on total salaries and total midpoints.	[C4, GR4]
Target compensation	The expected pay for a position, including both base pay and at-risk pay. The variable portion of target compensation is based on what the employee ought to earn on average, given satisfactory performance. High performers will exceed target earnings and poor performers will fall short of the target. Initially used primarily in sales compensation, but as at-risk pay becomes more widely used, so does the term.	[C17, GR4]
Target performance	The expected and/or planned level of sales results. It is often called the "quota" or "goal."	[C5, C6, C12, GR6]
Targeted gain	A future value method that can be used to determine the appropriate size of a stock option grant based on assumptions of increases in the stock price over a prescribed period. The projected increase in the value of a share is then divided into the total targeted gain to determine	[C6, C6A, T11]

Term	Definition	Courses
	the number of shares to be awarded.	
Tariff countries	Countries where the insurance market is regulated by the government by establishing a mandatory basis for determining the premium rates for insurance.	[T9, GR7]
Task	One or more task elements making up a distinct activity that constitute logical and necessary steps in the performance of work by an employee.	[C2, C15, C17, GR3]
Task element	The smallest step into which it is practical to subdivide any work activity without analyzing separate motions, movements or mental processes.	[C2, C17, GR3]
Tax equalization	A method whereby an expatriate pays neither more nor less tax than the assumed home-country tax on base remuneration. The employer usually deducts the assumed home-country tax from monthly salary and reimburses the employee for all taxes paid in the country of assignment and for any actual home-country tax on company remuneration only. It differs from tax protection in that, if the expatriate employee is in a low-tax country, he or she may obtain a "windfall" under tax protection, but not under tax equalization.	[C15, T9, GR7]
Tax Equity and Fiscal Responsibility Act of 1982 (TEFRA)	A federal law that limited the contributions and benefits that can be provided through qualified retirement plans.	[B1]
Tax preference income (TPI)	Includes adjusted gross income plus nontaxed gains on exercise of incentive stock option plan and nontaxed income from tax shelters.	[C6, C6A]

Term	Definition	Courses
Tax Reform Act of 1986	A federal law that changed the ground rules for much of compensation planning. Termination of favored tax treatment for capital gains, for example, has made many former executive compensation techniques less attractive. Change of treatment of benefits has altered the relative attractiveness and feasibility of benefit types.	[B1, C6]
Team	A small number of people with complementary skills who are committed to a common purpose, set of performance goals and approach for which they hold themselves mutually accountable.	[C12, GR6]
Team incentive	Any incentive that focuses on work teams or larger sets of workers operating as a unit. It is based on predetermined objectives being met to qualify for a payout.	[GR5, GR6]
Team pay	A bonus payment based on the performance of a group of workers operating as a unit, often allocated in equal amounts to all eligible employees. Also called group bonus.	[GR5, GR6]
Telecommuting	See telecommuting/telework	[B1, B5, C11, T1, T6, W1, W2, GR1]
Telecommuting/telework	The process of allowing employees to work from an independent location (most typically from home) anywhere from one day a week to working at home full-time. Technology connects an employee to office and/or business.	[B1, B5, C11, T1, T6, W1, W2, GR1, GR5]
Temporary disability insurance	See state disability insurance program.	[B3]

Term	Definition	Courses
Term life insurance	A renewable life insurance contract that specifies beginning and ending dates for coverage and that has no cash value at termination.	[B1, B3, B3A, B5]
Termination indemnity	Legally required payments due to employees upon dismissal or retirement. These payments can be extremely high in certain countries and at times may be payable under any termination circumstances, including voluntary resignation by the employee.	[C15, T6, T9, GR7]
Third-country national (TCN)	An employee from one country working temporarily in a second country for an employer with headquarters in a third country.	[C15, T6, T9, GR7]
Third-party administrator (TPA)	In a defined benefit (DB) or welfare benefit plan, the person or organization with responsibility for plan administration, including claims payment, asset investment and fund management.	[B3, B3A, B5, T6, T12]
Threshold	The minimum level of performance that must be achieved before an incentive can be earned.	[C5, C6, C12, GR6]
Tiered pay plan	A compensation system that differentiates salary based on time of hire (i.e., new employees are paid less than current employees for performing the same or similar jobs) as well as on nature of work performed.	[C4, GR4]
Time off with pay	An employee benefits category that includes vacation, holidays, sick leave, lunch periods, and other miscellaneous leave for which the employee is compensated. Also known as pay for time not worked.	[B1, B3, B3A, B5, C1, C12, T1, GR1, GR5, GR6]
Time-accelerated restricted stock award plan (TARSAP)	See performance-accelerated restricted-stock award plan (PARSAP).	[C6, C6A, T11]

Term	Definition	Courses
Timing of payment	Payment may either be current or deferred to some future date or a combination of current and deferred.	[C6, C6A, T11]
Tin parachute	A severance pay contract for all employees, not just high-ranking officers, that is triggered by a change in control.	[T6]
Title VII of the Civil Rights Act of 1964	Prohibits discrimination in all aspects of employment when that discrimination is based on race, color, religion, sex or national origin. It is unlawful for employers to segregate or classify employees based on the above so that they are adversely impacted. The act was amended in 1991 to clarify prior legislation and authorize compensatory and punitive damages and jury trials in Title VII cases in which plaintiffs allege and prove intentional illegal discrimination.	[B1, B3, C1, C11]
Top hat plan	In executive compensation programs, the supplemental benefits or perquisites provided to senior executives in excess of those provided to lower paid executives or employees.	[C6, C6A, T6]
Top pay approach	In executive compensation; executive pay will be set as the "top pay" for executives, instead of "pay for position." For this approach, organizations can either utilize executive compensation surveys or proxy statements.	[C6]
Total cash compensation	Total annual cash compensation (base salary and annual incentives/bonuses).	[C6, C6A, C17, T6, GR4, GR7]
Total direct compensation	In executive compensation, total annual cash compensation plus the annualized value of long-term incentives.	[C6, C6A]

Term	Definition	Courses
Total payroll	The sum of salaries and/or wages paid at the opening of business on the first day of the plan year or the close of business on the last day of the prior year.	[C4, C17, T3, GR4]
Total quality management (TQM)	A managerial approach that stresses process improvement and, in turn, product quality. Concepts include "continuous improvement" and a "get it right the first time" philosophy.	[C11]
Total remuneration	The sum of the financial and nonfinancial value to the employee of all the elements in the employment package (i.e., salary, incentives, benefits, perquisites, job satisfaction, organizational affiliation, status, etc.) and any other intrinsic or extrinsic rewards of the employment exchange that the employee values.	[C15, T9, GR4, GR5, GR7]
Total returns	Interest on debt and profit for shareholders.	[T2]
Total rewards	The monetary and nonmonetary returns provided to employees in exchange for their time, talents, efforts and results. Total rewards involve the deliberate integration of five key elements that effectively attract, motivate and retain the talent required to achieve desired business results.	[B1, B2, B3, B3A, B5, C1, C2, C3, C4, C5, C6, C6A, C11, C12, C15, C17, T1, T2, T3, T4, T6, T9, T11, T12, W1, W2, W3, W4, GR1, GR2, GR3, GR4, GR5, GR6, GR7, GR9]
Total rewards statement	An annual statement issued individually to each employee of an organization that quantifies the total value of his or her rewards received in the previous calendar year. Statement includes income from all compensation sources as well	[B1, T4, GR9]

Term	Definition	Courses
	as the cash value of all benefits and work experience elements received. The objective of the statement is to communicate the value of employer expenditures on behalf of each employee.	
Total share-holder return (TSR)	The return to shareholders over a period of time taking into account both share price movement and dividends.	[C6, C6A, T2, T11]
Totalization agreements	Intercountry social security arrangements that are intended to 1) protect the social security benefits of employees who move between countries, and 2) ensure single country social security coverages for employees on assignment.	[C15, T9, GR7]
Traditional individual retirement account (IRA)	A tax-deferred retirement account that allows individuals to set aside a specified amount of money annually, with earnings tax-deferred until withdrawals begin at age 59½ or later (or earlier, with a 10 percent penalty). Only individuals who do not participate in a pension plan at work or who do participate and meet certain income guidelines can make deductible contributions to an IRA. Interest accumulates tax-deferred until the funds are withdrawn. The Internal Revenue Code (IRC) specifies the annual maximum deductible contribution and applicable income guidelines.	[B1, B2]
Trailblazing	The process of seeking new markets and leading the pack into those markets.	[C15, T9, GR7]
Treasury shares/ treasury stock	Shares of a company's stock that have been purchased by the company for later re-issuance. Sometimes used in employee stock plans.	[C6, C6A, T2, T11]

Term	Definition	Courses
Treasury stock method	The method used in calculating diluted earnings per share whereby common stock equivalents such as unexercised stock options exist. Generally accepted accounting principles (GAAP) require that this method be used in calculating and reporting to shareholders whenever common stock equivalents exist.	[C6, C6A, T11]
Trimmed mean	A process used to eliminate outliers to determine the true mean of a data set.	[T3, GR2]
Tri-modal	A distribution having three modes.	[T3, GR2]
True insurance	The spreading of losses incurred by the few over the many through premiums such that average loss is substituted for actual loss.	[B3A]
True zero	Where the value of zero indicates an absence of what is being measured.	[T3, GR2]
Trust agreement	The contract between a pension plan sponsor and the trustee that details the trustee's authority and responsibilities for investing and administering plan assets.	[T6]
Trust fund	A common method of financing benefits obligations used by organizations. Essentially, the vehicle involves establishment of a legal trust for purposes of covering the obligations specified under a benefits plan (typically, a retirement plan). A trust usually requires the appointment of trustees whose primary obligations are prudent management and investment of the fund for the benefit of plan members. Organizations establish trusts for a variety of reasons, usually	[B3A, T6, T11]

Term	Definition	Courses
	for the security of plan members (real assets back the obligations) and for legal and tax benefits. This is a complex issue that requires legal, tax and actuarial review.	
Trustee	The person appointed, or required by law, to hold legal title to assets held "in trust" for the benefit of another person (the beneficiary) and who must carry out specific duties with regard to those assets.	[B2, C15, T6]
Turnover effect (wash-out, slippage)	The difference between actual year-end average pay and expected average pay. This difference is caused by a variety of changes in employee status, including promotions within the organization, departures from the organization, and new people joining the organization. The turnover effect can be plus or minus, but typically is the latter, since higher-paid people generally are replaced by lower-paid, shorter-service employees.	[C4, GR4]
Turnover ratio	Inventory turnover is a measure of the time from receipt of inventory to its sale. Its turnover ratio is calculated by dividing cost of goods sold by average inventory. Receivables turnover measures the time it takes to collect receivables. Its turnover ratio is calculated by dividing net credit sales by average net receivables.	[T2]
Two-tier pay plan	A dual pay structure that attempts to control labor costs by grandfathering the current structure for existing employees, but starting new employees under a second, lower-level pay structure.	[C4, GR4]

Term	Definition	Courses
U.S. permanent resident alien status	A permanent resident alien, often called a green card holder, who is entitled to all the rights, privileges and obligations of an American citizen except the right to vote.	
Uncertainty avoidance	Degree to which a culture accepts ambiguity and deviation from the norm.	[C15, T9, GR7]
Underfunded pension plan	A defined benefit (DB) pension plan in which the company's past contributions are insufficient to cover current and future liabilities.	[T6]
Underwater options	An outstanding option where the option price is above the stock's current market price.	[C6, C6A, T11]
Underwriting	(1) Assuming financial responsibility for an insurable event; (2) assuming the risk or loss for a particular event and to create an economically feasible premium by evaluating the potential degree of risk.	[B3A]
Unemployment insurance (unemployment compensation, unemployment benefits)	State-administered programs that provide financial protection for workers during periods of joblessness. These plans are wholly financed by employers except in Alabama, Alaska, New Jersey and Pennsylvania, where there are provisions for relatively small employee contributions.	[B1, B3, B3A, B5, C1, C15]
Unexercised options/SARS	The rights that have not yet been exercised. They may consist of both exercisable (vested) and nonexercisable (nonvested) rights.	[C6, C6A, T11]
Uniform distribution	A symmetrical distribution in which the frequency in each interval is about the same; it looks "flat" when graphed.	[T3, GR2]
Uniform Employee	Guidelines that establish a uniform set of principles governing	[C11]

Term	Definition	Courses
Selection Guidelines	the use of employee selection and testing procedures.	
Uniformed Services Employment and Reemployment Rights Act of 1994 (USERRA)	A federal law that requires employers to honor reemployment rights for employees that fulfill military service and reserve responsibilities while employed as a civilian. USERRA is administered by the Department of Labor (DOL).	[B1, T6]
Uni-modal	A distribution having only one mode.	[T3, GR2]
Units-of-production method	A method of calculating depreciation that assigns an equal amount of depreciation to each unit of product manufactured or used. Unlike straight-line depreciation and sum-of-the-years'-digits (SOYD) depreciation, this method of depreciation disregards the passage of time.	[T2]
Unreasonable (or excessive) compensation	A potential tax issue in privately held or closely held companies is executive compensation. The Internal Revenue Service (IRS) may challenge executive compensation in such organizations as excessive or unreasonable, and as a distribution of corporate profits rather than salary (IRS Sec. 162). If the IRS is sustained, the payment is a dividend and subject to double taxation as corporate income and as individual income.	[C6, C6A]
Unweighted (simple) average	See unweighted mean.	[C2, C17, GR3]
Unweighted mean	A simple arithmetic average of individual means.	[C2, C17, T3, GR2, GR3]
Upgrading	The advancement of a job to a higher grade or salary range.	[C4, GR4]
Upside potential	See leverage.	[C5]

Term	Definition	Courses
Usual, customary and reasonable charges (UCR)	The charges that an insurance carrier determines are normal for a particular medical procedure within a specific geographical area.	[B3]
Utilization management (UM)	A systematic review and appraisal of medical program requirements to achieve quality and cost containment goals. As contrasted with utilization review (UR), UM addresses the wider program requirements, whereas UR is more limited in scope, addressing the physician's diagnosis, treatment and billing amounts.	[B3]
Utilization review (UR)	A health-care cost management program in which a medical plan contracts with an organization to assess the medical necessity, appropriateness and charges associated with proposed treatment plans. The goal is to assure appropriate treatment at reasonable cost, and avoid unnecessary treatment. Sometimes the UR is conducted by the insurance company providing the coverage. See also utilization management.	[B1, B3, B3A]
Vacation	The amount of time off from work with pay given to employees by an organization. The amount of time off given for vacation is usually based on an employee's length of service.	[B1, W1]
Vacation borrowing	Employees may borrow up to one week (typical) of vacation from the following year.	[W1]
Vacation buying	Employees pay for a specified number of additional vacation days each year.	[W1]
Vacation sharing	Employees donate their vacation to another employee who needs additional paid time off because	[W1]

Term	Definition	Courses
	of an illness or other personal situation.	
Validity	The quality of a measuring device that refers to its relevance (i.e., is the device actually measuring what it is intended to measure?). This quality is extremely important for job analysis and job evaluation measures as well as for performance appraisal devices.	[C2, C11, C17, T3, GR2, GR3, GR5]
Valuation date	The designated time of closing (monthly, quarterly, etc.) for determination of account balances in a defined contribution (DC) or defined benefit (DB) plan. It also can refer to the date when pension assets and liabilities are valued when a merger or acquisition occurs.	[T6]
Variable	A measured characteristic of an entity that can have a number of different values. Two aspects of variables are important: 1) the measured characteristic is of interest and 2) the measured characteristic varies.	[T3, GR2]
Variable accounting	Used to account for equity-based compensation when the number of shares and/or the amount the employee is required to pay are not known at the grant date. Under APB 25 the measurement date determines whether fixed or variable accounting is to be used. Situations in which variable accounting is used include indexed options, SARs, performance shares and phantom stock plans.	[C6, C6A, T11]
Variable commission	Commission rates in a particular incentive plan are not constant and may vary depending on the salesperson's performance or on the particular measurement used.	[C5]

Term	Definition	Courses
Variable pay	Compensation that is contingent on discretion, performance or results achieved. It may be referred to as pay at risk.	[C4, C6, C6A, C11, C12, C15, C17, T1, T6, T9, T11, T12, GR1, GR4, GR5, GR6]
Variance	A measure of dispersion (in interval or ratio data) that is defined as an average of the squared deviation of each data point from the mean. It is used to calculate the standard deviation.	[T3, GR2]
Variation ratio	A measurement used in statistics to represent how dispersed the data is. Refers to the percent of items that are not included in the mode.	[T3, GR2]
Vendor	See service partner.	[T12]
Vested benefit obligation (VBO)	The present value of benefits entitlements that have accrued to date for employees who are vested.	[C15]
Vesting	(1) A term typically used in conjunction with a pension or stock plan. Under a pension plan, vesting assures that a participant will, after meeting certain requirements, retain a right to their accrued benefits (or some portion of them), even if employment under the plan terminates before retirement. Nonvested benefits are forfeited by the participant upon leaving the plan. Employee contributions are always fully vested. (2) For a stock option, vesting refers to the point in time when stock options or stock appreciation rights become exercisable, or when other executive compensation becomes nonforfeitable.	[B1, B2, C6, C6A, C15, T6, T9, T11, GR7]

Term	Definition	Courses
Viatical settlement	Enables an insured to sell their life insurance policy to a third party in exchange for a reduced amount of the face value. Restrictions may include age, health status, death benefit and number of years policy has been in force. Some people with terminal illnesses use a viatical settlement to get cash for living expenses or medical bills. Viatical companies are not necessarily insurance companies, therefore, are not subject to the regulatory standards of the insurance industry.	[B3]
Vietnam Era Veterans' Readjustment and Assistance Act of 1974 (VEVRAA)	Requires that employers with federal contracts or subcontracts of more than a specified dollar amount provide equal opportunity and affirmative action for Vietnam era veterans.	[C11]
Vocational Rehabilitation Act of 1973	Section 503 of this act is intended to promote job access for qualified individuals with disabilities. All employers with contracts or grants from the federal government in excess of $10,000 must take affirmative action or positive measures to employ qualified individuals with disabilities. Those employers with contracts of $50,000 or more who employ 50 or more people must take affirmative action as well. Any pay differentials between disabled employees and other employees with similar jobs are subject to Office of Federal Contract Compliance Programs scrutiny, and they must be justified on the basis of differential output or seniority.	[C1, C11]

Term	Definition	Courses
Voluntary (employee-pay-all) benefits	Supplemental benefits plans provided by employers on a voluntary, employee-paid basis. Typical coverages include life insurance (term or permanent), disability income supplements and vision. Group auto and homeowners insurance also may be offered. Depending on type of coverage, rates may be relatively low because of group-scale economies.	[B3, B3A]
Voluntary Employees' Beneficiary Association (VEBA)	As defined in Section 501(c)(9) of the Internal Revenue Code (IRC), a tax-exempt trust or nonprofit corporation providing benefits to members of an association, their dependents or beneficiaries. No part of net earnings accrues to the benefit of any private shareholder or individual other than the payment of benefits.	[B3A, T6]
W-2 form	The form a company gives an individual at the end of the year that reflects total earnings reported to the government along with the total of all items withheld for various purposes, including federal, state, local and FICA taxes.	[B2]
W-4 form	The form a company gives an individual at time of initial employment that is used to estimate probable tax liabilities (given number of dependents, outside income expected, etc.) and to authorize federal income tax withholding amounts. Any change in status (e.g., marriage, divorce) may justify revising the W-4.	[C1]
Wage and price controls	A program under which wages and prices are frozen or limited to some low percentage of growth through government	[C1]

Term	Definition	Courses
	regulation until they are deemed to be under control.	
Wage contour	A way of considering an external wage structure, developed by labor economist John Dunlop. He defines a wage contour as a stable group of wage-determining units (for example, bargaining units, plants or firms) that have common wage-making characteristics because they are so linked together by (a) similarity of product markets, (b) similar sources for labor, or (c) common market organization or custom.	[C4, GR4]
Wage differential	Differences in wage rates (for similar jobs) that can occur because of location of company, hours of work, working conditions, type of product manufactured, or a variety of other circumstances.	[C4, C15, T9, GR4, GR7]
Wage level	The average of all salaries paid to workers in an occupation, an industry or group of industries.	[C4, GR4]
Wage movement	An increase or decrease in the wage level for a particular job or occupation in a wage market.	[C4, GR4]
Wage rate	The money rate, expressed in dollars and cents, paid to an employee per hour.	[C4, R4]
Wage structure	See salary structure.	[C4, GR4]
Wage survey	A survey of a labor market to determine the going rates for benchmark jobs.	[C2, C4, C17, GR3, GR4]
Waiver of premium	Provision in an insurance policy that continues the policy without payment of premiums by the employee under certain specified conditions, most frequently, in the case of total or permanent disability.	[B3]

Term	Definition	Courses
Walsh-Healey Public Contracts Act of 1936	A federal law requiring certain employers holding federal contracts for the manufacture or provision of materials, supplies and equipment to pay at least the federal minimum wage. There is little difference between this act and the Fair Labor Standards Act of 1938 (FLSA).	[C1]
Warrant	A security entitling the holder to buy a specific amount of securities at a specified future date at a specified price, usually above the market price at the time the warrant is issued.	[T2]
Weighted average	See weighted mean.	[C2, C17, GR3]
Weighted mean	An average of means calculated by weighting each individual mean according to the number of data points that made up that individual mean.	[C17, T3, GR2, GR3]
Weighted-average method	A method of costing ending inventory calculated by dividing the total units purchased plus those in beginning inventory into cost of goods available for sale.	[T2]
Welfare plan	Plan that provides dental, vision, disability, life insurance, medical, surgical or hospital care, or benefits in the case of sickness, accident, death or unemployment. Under the Employee Retirement Income Security Act of 1974 (ERISA), plans also may include other benefits, such as vacation or scholarship plans.	[B1, B3, B3A, T6]
Windfall	A sales result that was realized outside the normal influencing role of the sales representative. Because the sales person had low or no involvement in creating the sale, a windfall is sometimes excluded from normal incentive compensation treatment.	[C5, C12, GR6]

Term	Definition	Courses
Window period	The 10-day period, from the third to twelfth day after public release of a company's quarterly financial statements, when insiders may exercise their stock-appreciation rights for cash without violating Securities and Exchange Commission (SEC) rules for short-term trading.	[C6, C6A, T11]
Women's Health and Cancer Rights Act of 1998 (WHCRA)	A federal law that provides protections to patients who choose to have breast reconstruction in connection with a mastectomy. WHCRA does not require health plans or issuers to pay for mastectomies. However, if a group health plan or health insurance issuer chooses to cover mastectomies, then the plan or issuer is usually subject to WHCRA requirements.	[B1, B3, T6]
Work redesign	A method of assessing how work is designed and structured, determining what tasks are essential, creating an efficient work flow, and eliminating unnecessary work and inefficiencies.	[W1, W2]
Worker Adjustment and Retraining Notification (WARN) Act	Protects workers, their families and communities by requiring employers to provide notification 60 calendar days in advance of plant closings and mass layoffs. The WARN Act is enforced by the Department of Labor (DOL).	[T6]
Workers' compensation insurance	State laws that have the goals of providing: (1) medical care or cash payment to cover health services for workers who are injured on the job or who suffer a job-related illness, (2) partial wage-replacement benefits and (3) rehabilitation services to restore workers to their fullest economic capacity. All benefits are totally employer-financed.	[B1, B3, B3A, B5, C1, T6]

Term	Definition	Courses
Working capital	Current assets minus current liabilities.	[T2]
Work-life	See work-life effectiveness.	[T4, GR9]
Work-life effectiveness	A specific set of organizational practices, policies and programs, as well as a philosophy that actively supports efforts to help employees achieve success within and outside of the workplace.	[T4, W1, W4, GR9]
Workplace flexibility	A variety of flexible work options that enable greater customization over when, where and how work gets done. The three most common full-time options are flex time, telecommuting and compressed workweek. The three most common part-time options include job sharing, phased return from leave and regular part-time work.	[W1, W2]
Works council	A body of elected worker/employee representatives who have a right to be informed about company decisions affecting employment conditions. They are particularly strong in Western European countries such as Germany.	[C15, T9, GR7]
Written plan	A plan that is defined by plan instruments or required under the law of a foreign country, or both. An insurance contract can constitute a written plan.	
Year before the year principle	For constructive receipt; the election is made before the year during which it will be earned has even started.	[C6]
Yield	The rate of return on an investment. A yield on a bond (yield to maturity) will be determined by considering the market value of the bond, the stated rate of interest and the par value of the bond. The yield of a stock	[C6, C6A, T11]

Term	Definition	Courses
	(dividend yield) is equal to the dividends paid divided by the market value of the stock.	
Zero coupon bond	A bond that is sold below redemption value. At a specified date the redemption value is paid to the holder.	[T2]
Zero-based budget	Requires that budget data be estimated and justified starting from zero and not based on historical activity.	[T2]
Z-score	The number of standard deviations an item is above or below the mean of the set of data to which it belongs. It is calculated by subtracting the mean from the item and then dividing the difference by the standard deviation.	[T3, GR2]

Handbook References

Editor's note: WorldatWork developed the content for this handbook by assembling, deriving, updating, editing, and reprinting work from the following WorldatWork publications. All of these resources, including complete books and articles, are composed from the WorldatWork body of knowledge and can be accessed and/or purchased by association members and nonmembers through WorldatWork certification courses as well as the WorldatWork bookstore, library, and other educational offerings (www.worldatwork.org).

CHAPTERS 1 TO 5 (TOTAL REWARDS)

2000. *Total Rewards: From Strategy to Implementation.*

2002. *The Best of Communicating Total Rewards: A Collection of Articles from WorldatWork.*

Kantor, Richard, and Tina Kao. 2004. "Total Rewards: Clarity from the Confusion and Chaos." *WorldatWork Journal,* Third Quarter: 7–15.

Kantor, Richard, and Tina Kao. 2004. "Total Rewards: From Clarity to Action." *WorldatWork Journal,* Fourth Quarter: 32–40.

O'Neal, Sandra. 2005. "Total Rewards and the Future of Work." *workspan,* January: 19–26.

Rogers, Susan, Karl W. Lohwater, and Holly Hager. 2006. *Communicating Total Rewards: How-to Series for the HR Professional.*

Stoskopf, Gregory A. 2004. "Using Total Rewards to Attract and Retain Health Care Employees." *WorldatWork Journal,* Third Quarter: 16–25.

CHAPTERS 6 TO 16 (COMPENSATION/PERFORMANCE MANAGEMENT)

2002. *Market Pricing: Methods to the Madness.*

2004. *FLSA Compliance: An Overview for the HR Professional.*

2006. *Cash Bonuses: Four Ways to Attract, Retain and Motivate Employees, Second Edition.*

2006. *Job Evaluation: Methods to the Process.*

2006. *Survey Handbook & Directory: A Guide to Finding and Using Salary Surveys.*

2006. WorldatWork Course T11: Fundamentals of Equity-Based Rewards

Balsam, Steven. 2007. *An Introduction to Executive Compensation, Second Edition.*

Barton, G. Michael. 2006. *Recognition at Work: Crafting a Value-Added Rewards Program.*

Colletti, Jerome A., Mary S. Fiss, Ted Briggs, and S. Scott Sands. 2006. *Sales Compensation Essentials: A Field Guide for the HR Professional.*

Davis, John H., and Janet F. Koechel. 2006. "Fundamentals of Salary Surveys." *Survey Handbook & Directory: A Guide to Finding and Using Salary Surveys.*

Delves, Donald P. 2006. *Stock Options and the New Rules of Corporate Accountability: Measuring, Managing and Rewarding Executive Performance. Second Edition.*

Engelmann, Curtis H., and Robert C. Roesch. 2001. *Managing Individual Performance: An Approach to Designing an Effective Performance Management System.*

Evans, Elaine M. 2006. *Compensation Basics for HR Generalists: How-to Series for the HR Professional.*

Hillgren, James, S., and David W. Cheatham. 2006. *Understanding Performance Measures: How-to Series for the HR Professional.*

Kovac, Jason, and L. Kate Beatty, Executive Editors. 2006. *Elements of Base Pay Administration.*

Longnecker, Brent M. 2006. *Stock Option Alternatives, Second Edition–FASB and AJCA Update.*

Overton, Bruce B., and Mary T. Steele. 2004. *Designing Management Incentive Plans: How-to Series for the HR Professional.*

Purushotham, Daniel P., and Stephanie Y. Wilson. 2004. *Building Pay Structures: How-to Series for the HR Professional.*

Seltz, Steven P., and Robert L. Heneman. 2004. *Linking Pay to Performance: How-to Series for the HR Professional.*

CHAPTERS 17 TO 21 (BENEFITS)

2006. WorldatWork Course B1: Fundamentals of Employee Benefits Programs.

Barocas, Victor S. *Planning Benefits Strategically: How-to Series for the HR Professional.* [out of print]

Bianchi, Alden J. 2003. *Benefits Compliance: An Overview for the HR Professional.*

Markowich, M. Michael. 2005. *Employee Benefits Basics: How-to Series for the HR Professional.*

Sanes, Richard, and Joseph L. Lineberry Jr. *Implementing Flexible Benefits: How-to Series for the HR Professional.* [out of print]

CHAPTERS 22 TO 24 (WORK-LIFE)

Barton, G. Michael. 2006. *Culture at Work: Building a Robust Work Environment to Help Drive Your Total Rewards Strategy.*

Rose, Karol M. 2006. *Work-Life Effectiveness: Bottom-Line Strategies for Today's Workplace.*

WorldatWork Bibliography

PUBLISHER: WORLDATWORK, SCOTTSDALE, ARIZONA

2001. *Before the Ink is Dry: Negotiating a Sound Contract* (Selecting & Managing Service Providers).

2002. *The Best of Attraction & Retention: A Collection of Articles from WorldatWork.*

2002. *The Best of Broadbanding: A Collection of Articles from WorldatWork.*

2002. *The Best of Communicating Total Rewards: A Collection of Articles from Worldat-Work.*

2002. *The Best of Global HR: Five Years of International Articles by WorldatWork.*

2003. *The Best of Performance Management: A Collection of Articles from WorldatWork.*

2001. *The Best of Retirement Benefits: A Collection of Articles from WorldatWork.*

2002. *The Best of Sales Compensation: A Collection of Articles from WorldatWork.*

2001. *The Best of Variable Pay: Incentives, Recognition and Rewards.*

1999. *Calculate This: Formula Book.*

2006. *Cash Bonuses: Four Ways to Attract, Retain and Motivate Employees, Second Edition.*

2000. *Domestic Partner Programs.*

2001. *Equity at Work: Constructing a Broad-based Stock Option Plan.*

2001. *Financial Education.*

2004. *FLSA Compliance: An Overview for the HR Professional.*

2001. *Getting It Right From the Start* (Selecting & Managing Service Providers).

2005. *Global Rewards: A Collection of Articles from WorldatWork.*

2006. *Job Evaluation: Methods to the Process.*

2001. *Life at Work: Beyond Compensation and Benefits.*

2002. *Market Pricing: Methods to the Madness.*

2001. *Mergers & Acquisitions: A Checklist for Total Rewards Professionals.*

2000. *Out of the Vortex: Finding Order in Merger and Acquisition Chaos, A Guide for Compensation and Benefits Professionals.*

2006–07. *Salary Budget Survey* (published annually).

2006. *Survey Handbook & Directory: A Guide to Finding and Using Salary Surveys.*

2006. *Total Rewards Glossary.*

2000. *Total Rewards: From Strategy to Implementation.*

Balsam, Steven. 2007. *An Introduction to Executive Compensation, Second Edition.*

Barton, G. Michael. 2006. *Culture at Work: Building a Robust Work Environment to Drive Your Total Rewards Strategy.*

Barton, G. Michael. 2006. *Recognition at Work: Crafting a Value-Added Rewards Program, Second Edition.*

Beatty, Kate, and Jason Kovac, Executive Editors, 2006. *Elements of Base Pay Administration.*

Bianchi, Alden J. 2003. *Benefits Compliance: An Overview for the HR Professional.*

Colletti, Jerome A., Mary S. Fiss, Ted Briggs, and S. Scott Sands. 2006. *Sales Compensation Essentials: A Field Guide for the HR Professional.*

Davis, John H. 2003. *Salary Surveys and Antitrust: An Overview for the HR Professional.*

Delves, Donald P. 2006. *Stock Options and the New Rules of Corporate Accountability: Measuring, Managing and Rewarding Executive Performance, Second Edition.*

Ericson, Richard. 2004. *Pay to Prosper: Using Value Rules to Reinvent Executive Incentives.*

Klein, James A. 1998. *Understanding & Influencing the Federal Legislative & Regulatory Process.*

Ledford, Gerry, Paul Mulvey, and Peter LeBlanc. 2000. *The Rewards of Work: What Employees Value.*

Longnecker, Brent M. 2006. *Stock Option Alternatives, Second Edition—FASB and AJCA Update.*

Longnecker, Brent M. with Christopher S. Crawford. 2006. *The Power of Restricted Stock, Second Edition–FASB and AJCA Update.*

Markowich, M. Michael. 2004. *Becoming a Champion of Change: How to Build Support for HR Initiatives and New Programs.*

Markowich, M. Michael. 2007. *Paid Time Off Banks: Program Design and Implementation.*

Markowich, M. Michael, and Dwight Benecke. 2004. *Employee Guide to Becoming a Smart Benefits Shopper: Shopping for Medical & Retirement Benefits in a Consumer-Driven Era.*

Masternak, Robert. 2003. *Gainsharing: A Team-Based Approach to Driving Organizational Change.*

McSweeney, Mary Helen. 2002. *Long-Term Care: An Emerging Employer Benefit.*

Mulvey, Paul W., Peter V. LeBlanc, Robert L. Heneman, and Michael McInerney. 2002. *The Knowledge of Pay Study: E-mails from the Frontline.*

Rose, Karol. 2006. *Work-Life Effectiveness: Bottom-Line Strategies for Today's Workplace.*

Sotherlund, Jude. 2003. *When Pay Plans Go Wrong: Managing Compliance Issues Before the Audit.*

Zingheim, Patricia K., and Jay R. Schuster. 2007. *High-Performance Pay: Fast Forward to Business Success.*

WORLDATWORK HOW-TO SERIES FOR THE HR PROFESSIONAL

Altmansberger, Harold N., and Marc J. Wallace Jr. 1998. *Designing a Goalsharing Program: An Approach to Rewarding Employees for Achieving Business Goals.*

Barocas, Victor S. 2007. *Planning Benefits Strategically.*

Bjorndal McAdams, Jane, A., and Linda K. Ison. 2006. *Mastering Market Data.*

Clampitt, William H. 2005. *Employee Compensation Basics.*

Colletti, Jerome A., and David J. Cichelli. 2005. *Designing Sales Compensation Plans.*

Craggs, Andrew R. 2002. *Entering Global Markets: An Approach to Designing HR Programs and Policies.*

Engelmann, Curtis H., and Robert C. Roesch. 2001. *Managing Individual Performance: An Approach to Designing an Effective Performance Management System.*

Evans, Elaine M. 2006. *Compensation Basics for HR Generalists.*

Fried, Elizabeth N., and John H. Davis. 2004. *Developing Statistical Job-Evaluation Models.*

Hackett, Thomas J., and Valerie C. Williams. 2004. *Documenting Job Content.*

Hay, Donald. 2004. *Maximizing the Impact of Recognition.*

Heller, Gretchen. 2001. *Unveiling Your Total Rewards Perspective: An Approach to Effective Web Design.*

Hillgren, James S., and David W. Cheatham. 2006. *Understanding Performance Measures.*

Kardas, Carol L. 2002. *A Business Primer for HR Professionals.*

Lister, Brenda J. 2006. *Evaluating Job Content.*

Longnecker, Brent M. 2005. *Administering Stock Option Plans.*

Markowich, M. Michael. 2005. *Employee Benefits Basics.*

Markowich, M. Michael. 2006. *Paying & Managing Absences.*

Matson, Gary, and Larry R. Heckathorn. 2007. *Strategic Outsourcing of Benefits Administration.*

McMahon, James R. and Janice S. Hand. 2006. *Designing & Conducting a Salary Survey.*

Meehan, Robert H., and G. Victor "Gus" Lemesis. 2006. *Determining Compensation Costs.*

Overton, Bruce B., and Mary T. Steele. 2004. *Designing Management Incentive Plans.*

Purushotham, Daniel P., and Stephanie Y. Wilson. 2004. *Building Pay Structures.*

Reynolds, Calvin. 2006. *Compensating North American Expatriates.*

Rogers, Susan, Karl W. Lohwater, and Holly Hager. 2006. *Communicating Total Rewards.*

Rubino, John A. 2004. *Communicating Compensation Programs.*

Sanes, Richard, and Joseph L. Lineberry Jr. 2007. *Implementing Flexible Benefits.*

Schlachtmeyer, Albert S., and Nancy L. Winfield. 2000. *Communicating Benefits Programs: An Approach to Providing Information to Employees.*

Seltz, Steven P., and Robert L. Heneman. 2004. *Linking Pay to Performance.*

Shaw, Douglas G., and Craig E. Schneier. 2002. *Benchmarking Rewards Systems: An Approach to Identifying and Applying Best Practices to Facilitate Organization Change.*

Shea, Dennis F. 2000. *Mergers & Acquisitions: A Guide to Understanding the Employee Benefits Basics.*

Simmons, Patrick I. Jr. 2000. *ERISA Basics: Complying with the Rules for Fiduciary Responsibility.*

Wilson, Thomas B., and Susan Malanowski. 2004. *Rewarding Group Performance.*

Index